1960

1960

LBJ vs. JFK vs. NIXON

The Epic Campaign That
Forged Three Presidencies

David Pietrusza

UNION SQUARE PRESS

An imprint of Sterling Publishing Co., Inc.

New York / London
www.sterlingpublishing.com

STERLING and the distinctive Sterling logo are
registered trademarks of Sterling Publishing Co., Inc.

Library of Congress Cataloging-in-Publication Data Available

10   9   8   7   6   5   4   3   2   1

Published by Sterling Publishing Co., Inc.
387 Park Avenue South, New York, NY 10016
© 2008 by David Pietrusza
Distributed in Canada by Sterling Publishing
c/o Canadian Manda Group, 165 Dufferin Street
Toronto, Ontario, Canada M6K 3H6
Distributed in the United Kingdom by GMC Distribution Services
Castle Place, 166 High Street, Lewes, East Sussex, England BN7 1XU
Distributed in Australia by Capricorn Link (Australia) Pty. Ltd.
P.O. Box 704, Windsor, NSW 2756, Australia

Book design and layout by T. Reitzle/Oxygen Design

Manufactured in the United States of America.
All rights reserved

Sterling ISBN 978-1-4027-6114-0 (Hardcover)
              978-1-4027-7746-2 (Paperback)

For information about custom editions, special sales, premium and
corporate purchases, please contact Sterling Special Sales
Department at 800-805-5489 or specialsales@sterlingpublishing.com.

To
Harry Price and Catherine Newbold,
two of my finest teachers of the art of history

———————————

Requiescant in pacem et lux perpetua luceat eis.

Contents

Cast of Characters x

ONE
January 1

TWO
"My son will be President in 1960" 2

THREE
"Independent as a hog on ice" 19

FOUR
"You're my boy" 33

FIVE
"Kicked in the head by a horse" 53

SIX
"When Bobby hates you, you stay hated" 61

SEVEN
"I am not a candidate for the vice presidency
of anything" 66

EIGHT
"An independent merchant competing
against a chain store" 77

NINE
"The rich man's Harold Stassen" 95

TEN
"Committing a sin against God" 109

ELEVEN
"A little black bag and a checkbook" 121

TWELVE
"All the eggheads are for Stevenson" 131

THIRTEEN
"They were a dime a dozen" 145

FOURTEEN
"A clean bill of health" 157

FIFTEEN
"First blood for Kennedy" 170

SIXTEEN
"We had to win on the first ballot" 177

SEVENTEEN
"Too shallow a puddle" 190

EIGHTEEN
"I'm not going to die in office" 194

NINETEEN
"He is not a big man" 207

TWENTY
"A two-fisted, four square liar" 213

TWENTY-ONE
"The man who will succeed Dwight D. Eisenhower . . .
Richard E. Nixon" 221

TWENTY-TWO
"Why do you think they did that, Sammy?" 233

TWENTY-THREE
"Nothing takes precedence over his oath
to uphold the Constitution" 245

TWENTY-FOUR
"Matt Dillon ain't popular for nothing" 259

TWENTY-FIVE
"Nixon did everything but sweep out the plane" 268

TWENTY-SIX
"I seen him, I seen him" 282

TWENTY-SEVEN
"You bombthrowers probably lost the election" 291

TWENTY-EIGHT
"The most dangerous man in America" 299

TWENTY-NINE
"No one could tell him anything" 307

THIRTY
"He felt cool, calm, and very alert" 320

THIRTY-ONE
"They've embalmed him before he even died" 335

THIRTY-TWO
"The bones of a single American soldier" 349

THIRTY-THREE
"Senator Kennedy is in clear violation of
the spirit of the law" 366

THIRTY-FOUR
"They know not what they do" 381

THIRTY-FIVE
"I'm just out for a little ride" 391

THIRTY-SIX
"The help of a few close friends" 400

THIRTY-SEVEN
"Dies irae" 411

Notes 419

Bibliography 494

Acknowledgments 509

Index 510

About the Author 523

Cast of Characters

JOSEPH ALSOP—Fifty-year-old syndicated columnist. Brother of Stewart Alsop. Blue-blooded establishment Republican. JFK's neighbor and enthusiastic supporter.

BOBBY BAKER—"Little Lyndon." Secretary of the U.S. Senate. Lyndon Johnson's thirty-two-year-old South Carolina–born right-hand man.

CHESTER BOWLES—Fifty-nine-year-old liberal Connecticut congressman. JFK's naively idealistic foreign adviser.

BEN BRADLEE—Boston Brahmin. Salty thirty-nine-year-old Harvard-educated *Newsweek* correspondent. JFK's Georgetown neighbor, companion, and confidant. "Little by little," Bradlee would say, "it was accepted by the rest of *Newsweek* . . . that Kennedy was mine."

EDMUND G. "PAT" BROWN—California's Democratic governor. JFK's erstwhile but unreliable ally in his quest for the nomination. In Bobby Kennedy's judgment the fifty-five-year-old Brown remains "a leaning tower of putty."

MURRAY M. CHOTINER—Veteran Nixon campaign hatchet man. Skewered by RFK in congressional hearings, Chotiner is now shunted aside by the "new" Nixon.

CLARK CLIFFORD—Fifty-five-year-old former Truman White House counsel and campaign aide. Washington power broker. Symington campaign adviser. Kennedy family lawyer.

JOHN B. CONNALLY—LBJ's tough, charismatic, and capable forty-three-year-old campaign manager. "Big Jawn," observes LBJ, could "leave more dead bodies in the field with less remorse than any politician I ever knew."

PROFESSOR ARCHIBALD COX—Thirty-eight-year-old Harvard law professor. Head of JFK's academic speechwriting team. Cox crafts late-campaign statements regarding Cuba that will infuriate Nixon.

RICHARD CARDINAL CUSHING—Boston's very political, very pro-Kennedy sixty-five-year-old Roman Catholic archbishop of Boston. "I'll tell you who elected John Kennedy," Cushing boasts. "It was his father, Joe, and me, *right here in this room* . . ."

MAYOR RICHARD J. DALEY—JFK's faithful—and invaluable—Chicago ally. "With a little bit of luck and the help of a few close friends," the fifty-eight-year-old Daley assures JFK on election night, "you're going to carry Illinois."

SAMMY DAVIS JR.—Frank Sinatra's black Rat Pack buddy. "I . . . would do all in my power to help [JFK]," says the thirty-four-year-old Davis, "even if I were called upon to make a great personal sacrifice." Even if it means deferring his marriage to a white woman until *after* JFK's election.

DWIGHT D. EISENHOWER—Supreme commander of Allied troops at Normandy. Liberator of Europe. Two-term, two-heart-attack, seventy-year-old president of the United States—and exceedingly reluctant supporter of Richard Nixon to succeed him. "Goddammit," Ike finally explodes, "he looks like a loser to me!"

JOHN D. EHRLICHMAN—Thirty-five-year-old Seattle attorney. Recruited by his UCLA classmate and fellow Christian Scientist Bob Haldeman to work as a Nixon advance man—with a specialty of spying on the Rockefeller and Kennedy camps. "Campaigning," Ehrlichman gleefully explains, "was like running away to the circus."

JUDITH CAMPBELL (EXNER)—Ravishing twenty-six-year-old Hollywood divorcée and—thanks to Frank Sinatra—JFK's latest mistress. "Do you think you could love me?" JFK coos. "I'm afraid I could," she whispers back.

ROBERT H. FINCH—Thirty-five-year-old California attorney. Nixon's ablest campaign aide.

JOHN KENNETH GALBRAITH—Fifty-two-year-old best-selling Harvard economist. Erstwhile Stevensonian. JFK speechwriter and convention floor manager.

SAM "MOMO" GIANCANA—An unusually thuggish Chicago mobster, even by Chicago standards. In RFK's words the fifty-two-year-old "chief gunman for the group that succeeded the Capone mob." Judith Exner is Momo's mistress. Jack Kennedy is Momo's candidate.

BARRY M. GOLDWATER—Fifty-one-year-old U.S. senator from Arizona. Tough-talking right-wing GOP standard-bearer. Author of 1960's best-selling *The Conscience of a Conservative*. Increasingly frustrated with the Eisenhower-Nixon brand of "me-too" Republicanism, Goldwater nonetheless lectures conservatives to "grow up" and support Nixon.

PHILIP GRAHAM—Forty-five-year-old *Washington Post* publisher. Influential LBJ backer.

H. R. "BOB" HALDEMAN—Rising star in the Nixon campaign apparatus. Brutally tough thirty-six-year-old brush-cut J. Walter Thompson advertising executive. Richard Nixon's chief advance man. The Haldeman-Nixon relationship, says one observer, is "darkness reaching for darkness."

LEONARD W. HALL—Former Republican national chairman and Richard Nixon's longtime champion and advocate. Perhaps the GOP's savviest political operative. In 1960, Nixon repays the sixty-year-old Hall by largely ignoring his counsel.

LOU HARRIS—JFK's thirty-nine-year-old house campaign pollster. His off-kilter predictions in Wisconsin and West Virginia jeopardize the Kennedy effort.

DON HEWITT—Thirty-seven-year-old CBS News producer—in charge of the crucial first installment of 1960's "great debates."

JIMMY HOFFA—Forty-seven-year-old corrupt Teamsters union boss. Sworn enemy of the Kennedy brothers—particularly Bobby. "As Mr. Hoffa operates [the Teamsters]," RFK writes, "this is a conspiracy of evil."

J. EDGAR HOOVER—Longtime FBI director. Keeper of the secrets. The sixty-five-year-old Hoover knows all about JFK's fling with a suspected Nazi spy—and JFK knows he knows.

HOWARD HUGHES—America's singularly most bizarre and reclusive billionaire. Kennedy operatives will expose the fifty-four-year-old Hughes's suspicious loan to Richard Nixon's older brother Donald—in an "October surprise" designed to derail Nixon's chances.

HUBERT H. HUMPHREY—Fifty-one-year-old U.S. senator from Minnesota. Passionately ebullient liberal. Pioneer civil rights advocate. JFK's financially outgunned opponent in the Wisconsin and West Virginia primaries. "I feel," Humphrey complains, "like an independent merchant competing against a chain store."

DR. ARNOLD A. HUTSCHNECKER—Sixty-two-year-old German-born Park Avenue psychotherapist, and Vice President Richard Nixon's secret shrink. "Fear," Hutschnecker reveals, "was a virus that infected Nixon's life."

MAX "DR. FEELGOOD" JACOBSON—JFK's sixty-year-old, German-born, celebrity-treating, amphetamine-injecting physician. He was, notes his own nurse, a "quack," a "butcher."

LADY BIRD JOHNSON—Lyndon Johnson's forty-nine-year-old wife. The key to his Texas broadcasting fortune. A woman strangely tolerant of her husband's indiscretions. "Lyndon loved *people*," Lady Bird explains. "It would be unnatural for him to withhold love from half the people."

LYNDON BAINES JOHNSON—The ultimate politico, Lyndon seldom thinks of politics "more than 18 hours a day." "Master of the Senate" as its fifty-two-year-old majority leader—but suspected by the nation's liberals. Mercurially tempered and maddeningly indecisive as a presidential candidate. "We ran a halfhearted campaign . . . ," said John Connally, "because we had a halfhearted candidate." Halfhearted as a presidential candidate—and brokenhearted as JFK's vice-presidential candidate.

EDWARD M. "TEDDY" KENNEDY—Youngest—just twenty-eight—of the Kennedy clan and JFK's hardworking Western states organizer. In awe of brother Jack, Frank Sinatra is not impressed by Teddy's choice of women.

JACQUELINE BOUVIER KENNEDY—Jack Kennedy's beautiful thirty-one-year-old blue-blooded wife. Very pregnant during the 1960 campaign, very cheated upon, and very uncomfortable in the public eye. "I feel as though I had just turned into a piece of public property," she says. "It's really frightening to lose your anonymity at thirty-one."

JOHN FITZGERALD KENNEDY—Forty-three-year-old Harvard-educated scion of a nouveau riche Boston Irish family. Hero of PT-109. Pulitzer Prize–winning author. Democratic U.S. senator from Massachusetts with an undistinguished record (save for absenteeism) and suspect liberal credentials. Photogenic, charismatic, charming, bright, and Catholic—but also seriously, and recklessly, adulterous. JFK's older brother Joe Jr. was supposed to be the presidential candidate. But Joe is dead, and now JFK carries the family banner into the 1960 campaign.

JOSEPH PATRICK KENNEDY SR.—JFK's sociopathically ambitious and grasping seventy-two-year-old arch-capitalist father. Boston banker, movie mogul, bootlegger, anti-Semite, isolationist, "crude, blatant and ignorant in everything he did or said." Joe will do—and spend—anything to capture the White House for his family.

ROBERT F. KENNEDY—JFK's ruthless, fanatically loyal, and often quite unpleasant thirty-four-year-old younger brother. Racket-busting Senate investigator, former aide to Red-hunting Senator Joe McCarthy. "Bobby's my boy," Joe Kennedy boasts. "When Bobby hates you, you stay hated."

ROSE FITZGERALD KENNEDY—JFK's seventy-year-old mother. Daughter of Boston's legendary mayor John F. "Honey Fitz" Fitzgerald, and wife of Joseph P. Kennedy. Fanatically religious. Strangely distant from her large family. Still socially insecure. "Tell me," she demands, "when are the nice people of Boston going to accept us?"

MARTIN LUTHER KING JR.—Charismatic, eloquent thirty-one-year-old leader of the Southern civil rights movement. King's Atlanta sit-in arrest—and JFK's and Nixon's antipodal responses to it—dramatically shift 1960's black vote. Nixon, King observes, "has a genius for convincing you he is sincere . . . if Richard Nixon is not sincere, he is the most dangerous man in America."

HERBERT G. KLEIN—Forty-two-year-old former San Diego newspaper editor and Nixon's low-key but increasingly frustrated press secretary—both at the press and at his own candidate.

PATRICIA KENNEDY LAWFORD—JFK's thirty-six-year-old sister. Married to Hollywood's Peter Lawford.

PETER LAWFORD—Fading thirty-seven-year-old English-born movie star and husband of JFK's sister Patricia—"the brother-in-Lawford." Sinatra Rat Pack member.

HENRY CABOT LODGE JR.—Fifty-eight-year-old Boston Brahmin. JFK's vanquished opponent in Massachusetts's 1952 senatorial campaign. Ike's ambassador to the United Nations. Dick Nixon's patrician, liberal, but ill-considered choice for the vice-presidential nomination.

EUGENE J. MCCARTHY—Forty-four-year-old liberal U.S. senator from Minnesota. His eloquent nominating speech for Adlai Stevenson ignites the 1960 Democratic Convention—though McCarthy is really fronting for LBJ. "I should be the candidate for President," the ambitious McCarthy boasts. "I'm twice as liberal as Humphrey, twice as smart as Symington, and twice as Catholic as Kennedy."

SENATOR WAYNE MORSE—Sixty-year-old maverick Oregon Democratic U.S. senator. JFK's weak competition in the Maryland and Oregon primaries.

SENATOR THRUSTON MORTON—Fifty-two-year-old Republican national chairman. The Kentucky moderate covets the GOP vice-presidential nod.

BILL MOYERS—Lyndon Johnson's marvelously talented and doggedly loyal twenty-six-year-old boy-wonder personal assistant. LBJ's liaison to the Kennedy campaign.

F. DONALD NIXON—Richard Nixon's ne'er-do-well younger brother. Originator of the "Nixonburger." Recipient of a controversial loan that helps sink his brother's chances for the White House.

PATRICIA RYAN NIXON—Richard Nixon's forty-eight-year-old "Republican cloth coat" wife. A potential First Lady frustrated by the political life.

RICHARD MILHOUS NIXON—"Tricky Dick." Forty-seven-year-old former California congressman and senator. Hero of the Alger Hiss espionage case. Ruthless campaigner. Tearful survivor of the Checkers incident. Dwight Eisenhower's Uriah Heep–like vice president. The 1960 Republican nominee. Hampered by a bad knee and worse makeup and strategy, he spectacularly loses the first debate to JFK. Jack Kennedy, says John Kenneth Galbraith, "felt sorry for Nixon because he does not know who he is, and at each stop he has to decide which Nixon he is at the moment—which must be very exhausting."

LAWRENCE F. O'BRIEN—Veteran JFK campaign aide. "Tough but amiable." Master of volunteer efforts. Director of Kennedy's 1960 national campaign.

KENNETH P. O'DONNELL—RFK's Harvard classmate and JFK's campaign scheduler. He looked, muses Arthur Schlesinger, "like one of the young IRA men in trenchcoats in . . . *The Informer*."

THOMAS P. "TIP" O'NEILL—Boston Irish congressman. Skeptical observer of JFK's rise to power. "I've never," Tip will say, "seen a congressman get so much press while doing so little work."

DR. NORMAN VINCENT PEALE—One of America's most popular—and powerful—Protestant clergymen. The sixty-two-year-old Peale's anti-JFK, anti-Catholic campaign statement ignites a firestorm. "I find Paul appealing," quips Adlai Stevenson, "and Peale appalling."

DAVID F. POWERS—Longtime JFK crony; a campaign aide with no real role beyond traveling companion and raconteur.

SAM RAYBURN—Seventy-eight-year-old Speaker of the House of Representatives. LBJ's chief booster for the White House, the Texas-born "Mr. Sam" doubts a Catholic can be elected president. "If we have to have a Catholic [for vice president]," Rayburn says in 1956, "I hope we don't have to take that little pissant Kennedy."

GEORGE REEDY—LBJ's forty-three-year-old long-suffering press secretary.

WALTER P. REUTHER—President of the United Auto Workers. Wary of JFK in 1956 (when Kennedy asks how to garner UAW backing, Reuther snaps, "Improve your voting record"). More wary of LBJ in 1960.

JACKIE ROBINSON—First black to play in modern Major League Baseball. Aggressive on the diamond and for civil rights. Not impressed by JFK. For Hubert Humphrey in the primaries and Richard Nixon in November. Publicly, the forty-one-year-old Robinson says, "Kennedy is not fit to be president." Privately, he fumes: "Nixon doesn't deserve to win."

NELSON ALDRICH ROCKEFELLER—Fifty-two-year-old heir to the Rockefeller billions. Maverick liberal Republican New York governor. "I hate the thought," Rocky says, "of Dick Nixon being president." Rockefeller's machinations threaten to disrupt 1960's Republican National Convention.

ELEANOR ROOSEVELT—FDR's still passionately activist widow. The keeper of the flame for New Deal Democrats—and for Adlai Stevenson. Seventy-six-year-old Eleanor cannot forgive JFK's friendship with Senator Joe McCarthy. She has no respect for "someone who understands what courage is and admires it but has not quite the independence to have it."

FRANKLIN D. ROOSEVELT JR.—FDR's forty-six-year-old son. Former Manhattan congressman. JFK's bought-and-paid-for hatchet man against Hubert Humphrey ("I don't know where he was in World War II") in the West Virginia primary.

JAMES M. ROWE—Fifty-one-year-old former New and Fair Dealer. Longtime LBJ ally. In 1960, a staffer first for Humphrey, then for Johnson.

PIERRE SALINGER—Plucky Pierre, JFK's thirty-five-year-old rotund, self-confident, thrice-married, sophisticated—but chronically unorganized and often temperamental—San Francisco–born press secretary.

ARTHUR M. SCHLESINGER JR.—Forty-three-year-old Pulitzer Prize–winning, politically ambitious Harvard historian. Schlesinger leads the "egghead" switch from Adlai to JFK. "Arthur's attitude toward Stevenson," observed an old friend, "seemed to be similar to that of a man who has left his wife and run off with a new woman."

EUNICE KENNEDY SHRIVER—JFK's tough-minded thirty-nine-year-old sister. Wife of R. Sargent Shriver. "If she'd been a little older," recalled a family friend, "and if it had been like today . . . I suspect the history of the Kennedy clan would have been quite different."

R. SARGENT "SARGE" SHRIVER—Forty-five-year old Yale-educated husband of JFK's sister Eunice. Manager of the family's Chicago Merchandise Mart property. Head of JFK's civil rights campaign section.

FRANK SINATRA—The Chairman of the Board. Swinging, swaggering, forty-four-year-old leader of Hollywood's Rat Pack. For Jack Kennedy all the way. The attraction is mutual. "Let's just say the Kennedys are interested in the lively arts," observes Peter Lawford, "and that Sinatra is the liveliest art of all."

STEPHEN E. SMITH—Thirty-three-year-old husband of JFK's sister Jean. Scion of a wealthy New York City maritime family—upper-class but hard-boiled. Brilliant, ruthless finance chairman of JFK's 1960 campaign.

THEODORE C. SORENSEN—Jack Kennedy's thirty-two-year-old eloquent, brilliant, and loyal Nebraska-born speechwriter and special assistant. Ask not who provides JFK's finest rhetoric—it's usually Ted Sorensen.

ADLAI E. STEVENSON—Sixty-year-old, twice-failed Democratic presidential nominee. Beloved for his wit and erudition. In 1960, still the favored candidate of Eleanor Roosevelt, the party's liberal "egghead" wing—and Nikita Khrushchev. The Hamlet of American politics, more coy now than ever: "If I said I'd accept a draft, I'd be courting it; if I said I would not, I'd be a 'draft evader.'"

SENATOR STUART SYMINGTON—Moderate fifty-nine-year-old Democratic U.S. senator from Missouri. Like JFK, a critic of Ike's alleged "missile gap." Halfhearted, lackluster candidate for president—and then vice president.

DR. JANET G. TRAVELL—JFK's physician. An expert on skeletal muscle pain. During the campaign, the fifty-eight-year-old Travell declares, "John F. Kennedy has not, nor has he ever had . . . Addison's disease." It's a lie.

HARRY S. TRUMAN—The salty seventy-six-year-old former "buck stops here" president. Harry likes Stu Symington, has contempt for Adlai Stevenson and Jack Kennedy, and loathes Joe Kennedy—but, ever the partisan, his flames of pure hatred for Ike and Dick burn brighter still.

HARRIS WOFFORD—Forty-four-year-old Yale-educated Notre Dame law professor. Kennedy civil rights adviser. When Martin Luther King is jailed in Georgia, Wofford convinces Sargent Shriver that JFK must phone Coretta Scott King in sympathy. "You dumb ——," Bobby Kennedy storms at Shriver, "you've blown the election."

January

THE DATE: SATURDAY, January 2, 1960, as slow a news day as ever there was.

The time: 12:30 p.m.

The location: the crowded parameters of the U.S. Senate office building's historic red-carpeted, elaborately chandeliered, Corinthian-pilastered, third-floor Caucus Room, witness to investigations into everything from the sinking of the *Titanic* to Warren Harding's Teapot Dome scandal to Senator Joe McCarthy's televised anti-communist crusades—and, just recently, to equally dramatic probes into the often violent and corrupt world of organized labor.

The speaker: John Fitzgerald Kennedy, a veteran (along with his younger brother Bobby) of those most recent investigations, tanned from a recent Jamaica vacation, junior U.S. senator from the Commonwealth of Massachusetts, his voice strong, his mien serious and somber (though a tad too somber and leaden—he had yet to perfect his stride), his tousled forelock fastidiously trimmed to add an air of maturity to his forty-two-year-old countenance, standing before his thirty-year-old wife, Jacqueline, and nearly three hundred friends, supporters, and reporters to formally announce to them and to the world his candidacy for president of the United States of America.

It was all very dramatic, yet all very anticlimactic. For John F. Kennedy had, in fact, been running—whether he announced it or not, knew it or not, or wanted it or not—for fifteen years, four months, and twenty-one days—since August 12, 1944.

The day his older brother Joe was blown to bits.

"My son will be President in 1960"

IN 1960, AMERICA was ready for someone new, someone glamorous and young and witty and smart—an American Cary Grant, who knew not only how to stir a martini and woo a damsel but how to stir voters and woo delegates. A change was overdue on Pennsylvania Avenue. It had been a *very* long time since a TR had stormed San Juan Hill and America's hearts. John F. Kennedy—the Pulitzer Prize–winning former PT-109 commander with his custom-made Brooks Brothers suits, his glamorous bride, his vigorous younger siblings, and more bushy hair and gleaming teeth than any president had enjoyed or employed in a long time—was moving toward his moment in history. And America, or at least enough of it, was moving with him.

* * *

It all seems so natural now, so inevitable—John F. Kennedy, thirty-fifth president of the United States of America. But Jack Kennedy had not been born to be president, had not originally coveted the office, or any political office at all. Neither Camelot nor even the U.S. Congress had been in his original plans—but, then, legends are not always born from plans.

At least not at first.

* * *

He was born at the family home—a comfortable, but hardly opulent, two-story, six-room abode in suburban Brookline, Massachusetts—at around 3 p.m. on Tuesday, May 29, 1917, the second child and, more importantly, the second *son*, of Joseph Patrick and Rose Elizabeth Fitzgerald Kennedy.

What Joseph P. Kennedy Sr. then foresaw for his offspring remains impossible to say. More than likely, Joe Kennedy was still concentrating upon his own ascending destiny—building East Boston's small Columbia

Trust Company bank, of which he was then president (America's youngest bank president when he took it over from his own father in 1913). In any case, for two decades young Jack Kennedy would be too sickly and too much the family dreamer to pin many—if any—dynastic hopes upon.

Their family was Irish and Catholic—Jack was an altar boy at Brookline's St. Aidan's—and highly political. Rose Kennedy's father, John "Honey Fitz" Fitzgerald, had been a boss of Boston's North End and, ultimately, a spectacularly colorful and corrupt mayor whose career was extinguished when it became a tad too spectacular even for normally forgiving Irish Democratic voters—particularly the part about a twenty-three-year-old lady friend named "Toodles" Ryan ("Great Lovers in History: From Cleopatra to Toodles" was the title of a speech threatened by Fitzgerald's adversary James Michael Curley). Joe Kennedy's father, the saloon keeper, banker, liquor importer, and coal dealer Patrick J. Kennedy, had served in the state house and senate, dominated Boston's Ward Two, and helped rule all of Boston's dominant Democratic Party.

Joe Kennedy had graduated from both Boston Latin School (though he stayed behind his junior year) and Harvard, where he learned firsthand of anti-Catholic, anti-Irish prejudice, and where, despite all the favors and honors tendered him as an influential politician's son, he honed the nouveau riche arts of resentment and bitterness to razorlike sharpness.

Jack Kennedy survived childhood illnesses. Joe Kennedy grew richer still. His family just grew: from Joe Jr. and Jack and Rosemary to Kathleen ("Kick") and Eunice and Patricia to Robert and Jean and Edward ("Teddy"). "The measure of a man's success in life," Joe Kennedy would contend, "is not the money he made. It's the kind of family he has raised."

In 1927, the family, enriched by Joe's stock market speculations (and rum-running), shook the dust of Brahmin Boston from its brogans, relocating first to New York and then (for tax purposes) to Palm Beach. All the while, Jack attended the best of private schools, culminating in his entrance into elite Choate School (already graced by brother Joe Jr.), where despite two serious hospitalizations (at one point he weighed only 125 pounds) and mediocre grades (sixty-fourth out of a class of 112), he was still voted "Most likely to become president."

He intended to study at the London School of Economics (again following in Joe Jr.'s footsteps), traveled to England, was hospitalized once more, and sailed for home. He enrolled in college—not at Harvard, but, several weeks late in the 1935 academic year, at Princeton (Joe Sr. pulled strings), and was hospitalized for two months for possible leukemia. He was, his mother sadly wrote, a boy "whose body could not keep pace with his dreams."

JFK enrolled at Harvard in September 1936 (following both his father and brother—and at his father's insistence), but when Joseph P. Kennedy, a key FDR backer in 1932, won appointment as ambassador to Britain in 1938, Jack followed. Assisting in his father's work, he toured a continent galloping toward war, while compiling his senior honors thesis and cementing his lifelong fascination with England and all things upper-class English: manners, morals, attitudes, and history. For while the Kennedys appealed to the Irish for their votes, little about the lower-class Irish particularly appealed to them. So much about the English, especially their upper classes, did. Of Joe Kennedy's six progeny who married, not one married Irish.

Kennedy père, long rich and recently famous, harbored presidential ambitions, but thanks to his now-unfashionable isolationist sentiments (and oft-voiced anti-Semitism) he had by 1940 become politically radioactive. His fallback plan: Son Joe Jr., immensely talented, charming, intelligent, and ambitious (although considered arrogant by many), would someday become America's first Catholic president. It is impossible now, decades later, to properly gauge Joe Jr.'s potential. To us, there is no reason why his promise glistened so strongly, so inevitably. He held no public offices save for delegate to the 1940 Democratic convention, built no industries, wrote no books—yet all around him saw it, and if all around him saw him as brighter, harder, more driven, more eloquent, and more charming than his sickly brother Jack, we must honor their judgment.

Few possessed, recalled Harold Laski of the London School of Economics, "either [Joe Jr.'s] eager zest for life or his gift of winning's one's affection. . . . He has often sat in my study and submitted with that smile that was pure magic to relentless teasing about his determination to be nothing less than President of the United States."

If Joe Jr. was to be president, what might Jack (graduated cum laude from Harvard in June 1940) become? A businessman perhaps (he briefly audited courses at the Stanford Graduate School of Business)? Perhaps, but not likely. A writer? Yes, Jack Kennedy, fascinated by current events and by history, particularly English history, showed real interest in that. When he completed his senior thesis, "Appeasement in Munich," his father, masterly intuitive at sensing opportunities, corporate or political, recognized the possibilities inherent in the document's wider circulation—both to boost his second son's career track ("You would be surprised how a book that really makes the grade with high-class people stands you in good stead for years to come") and, perhaps more so, as an apologia for his own notable failures in opposing Nazi aggression. The result was *Why England Slept*, published in July 1940 with an introduction by *Time*'s Henry Luce. Assisted by the author's father's considerable connections, it became a national best seller—a remarkable eighty thousand copies.

It was, for all the fortuity of its timing and the charm of its youthful author, an unlikely best seller. The senior thesis it was based upon was frankly not all that good—the faculty awarded it Harvard's lowest honor grade. Accordingly, *Why England Slept* required substantial reworking by *New York Times* columnist Arthur Krock, a longtime Joe Kennedy ally, and originator of the tome's title; by Joe's speechwriter and publicist Harvey Klemmer; and even by JFK's classmate Blair Clark —although JFK remained forever sensitive to charges of ghostwriting. Years later, when Clark reminded JFK of his help, Kennedy angrily shot back, "What do you mean? You never did a goddamn thing on it. You never saw it!"

When war came, both Joe Jr. and Jack enlisted in the Navy (his father pulling strings to get his sickly son in), Joe piloting PB-4Ys in anti-submarine missions and Jack eventually sent to serve on PT boats in the Solomon Islands. His volunteering for service was all the more remarkable, patriotic, and, yes, heroic, considering his precarious constitution.

In April 1943 the Navy assigned Jack Kennedy to command the eighty-foot, forty-ton PT-109. In the very early morning hours of August 2, 1943, his ship lay in Blackett Strait between Kolombangara and Arundel islands, one of fifteen American PT boats stalking a Japanese convoy. Suddenly, the Japanese destroyer *Amagiri* smashed into the PT-109, slashing it asunder, leaving two crew members dead and the remainder clinging to shattered wreckage. It was, all in all, an inexcusable disaster. "It was a big strait," observed one squadron skipper.

"Kennedy had the most maneuverable vessel in the world. All that power and yet this knight in white armor managed to have his PT boat rammed by a destroyer. Everybody in the fleet laughed about that."

There was no laughing about what to do next. Kennedy and ten surviving crewmen made for land, which was infested by armed Japanese. Beyond that, machinist's mate Patrick "Pappy" McMahon had been badly burned about the face, neck, and arms when the PT-109's high-octane fuel tanks exploded. The twenty-six-year-old JFK towed the thirty-nine-year-old McMahon three and a half miles to minuscule Plum Island, but Plum Island provided little safety, so Kennedy returned to the water, swimming first to Naru Island, then to Olasana Island, and finally back to Plum Island before leading his men again to Olasana, where they were rescued six days later by a search party of Solomon Islanders.

Kennedy won the Navy and Marine Corps Medal for his actions following the PT-109's sinking. He was lucky not to have been court-martialed for losing it. "The medal," JFK's squadron commander officer Lieutenant Alvin Peyton Cluster, a close Kennedy friend, said later, "was for the survival phase. Not the preceding battle." Even JFK would admit, "It was a question of whether they were going to give [me] a medal or throw [me] out."

JFK survived. Joe Jr. did not. On August 12, 1944, Joe Jr., perhaps jealously attempting to match his kid brother's well-publicized exploits, lifted off from Fersfield Airdome in East Anglia on a crucial—a risky, some said foolhardy—volunteer mission to destroy Nazi V-1 launching sites in France. His PB4Y Liberator bomber, overloaded with 22,000 pounds of TNT—an incredible amount of explosives—never made it. It exploded—vaporized—off the coast of France. One witness called it "[t]he biggest explosion I ever saw until the pictures of the atom bomb." The blast took Lieutenant Joseph P. Kennedy Jr. and the hopes and dreams of the Kennedy family with it.

"Joe's worldly success was so assured and inevitable," eulogized JFK in his privately printed volume, *As We Remember Joe*, "that his death seems to have cut into the natural order of things."

"You know how much I had tied my whole life up to his," mourned Joe Sr., devastated by his son's loss. "And what great things I saw in the future for him."

Now, with both a period of mourning and a world war ended, Joe Jr.'s future would be transferred to brother Jack. "I can feel Pappy's eyes on the back of my neck," JFK confided to his old Solomon Islands Navy buddy Paul "Red" Fay at Christmas 1944. "When the war is over and you are back there in sunny California . . . I'll be back here [in Massachusetts] with Dad trying to parlay a lost PT boat and a bad back into political advantage. I tell you, Dad is ready right now and can't understand why Johnny boy isn't 'all engines full ahead.'"

Jack seemed ready to drift into journalism, turning out assignments for the Hearst chain (another position secured through paternal influence), but Joe Kennedy would never tolerate journalistic scribbling as anything more than a temporary avocation. Jack moved back to Massachusetts, with his father's initial political designs centering upon the lieutenant governorship. But when seventy-one-year-old congressman James Michael Curley, who had recaptured Boston's City Hall in November 1945, was convicted of federal mail fraud charges in January 1946, his safely Democratic, dirt-poor Eleventh District seat opened up—and JFK's fate was sealed.

Joe Kennedy and all his minions and relations went to work, but for all their resources and talent and instinct, their task was not necessarily an easy one. Their candidate, so long absent from Massachusetts (save for his four years at Harvard he had not lived there since he was six), was looked upon as the "Miami candidate." He spoke poorly, was stiff in meeting voters, and faced a host of better known opponents, primarily Cambridge mayor Mike Neville, a one-time speaker of the Massachusetts House. And above all, John Kennedy simply looked like hell, all sickly and scrawny, more a candidate for a VA hospital than for Congress—and far too young and inexperienced for the job.

The answer was hard work—by the candidate, by his staff, and particularly by his numerous relatives who flooded the district, hosting rallies and teas from the North and West Ends to East Boston to Cambridge to Charleston. But the real answer to what was needed came from JFK's harelipped sixty-six-year-old cousin Joe "Pickles" Kane, a one-termer in the city council: "The first is money and the second is money and the third is money."

"We're going to sell Jack," Jack's father/campaign chief boasted, "like soap flakes."

"Joe Kennedy," recalled Thomas P. "Tip" O'Neill, who would succeed JFK in that same congressional seat, "spent $300,000 on that race which was six times what I spent in a very tough congressional campaign . . . six years later." A frustrated Mike Neville pinned a ten-dollar bill to his shirt pocket and dubbed it his Kennedy campaign button.

Nine men and one woman (a thirty-five-year-old former WAC major, campaigning occasionally in her old gleaming dress whites) competed. Because the district, particularly in the North End, East Boston, Somerville, and even Cambridge, had over the years become noticeably Italian, veteran Boston Third Ward councilman Joseph Russo also had to be reckoned with. The Kennedys ran another "Joseph Russo," a mere janitor, to confuse voters and split the "real" Russo's vote.

And, yes, the Kennedys possessed another advantage: Jack Kennedy himself. For as spindly and awkward as he still was, he nonetheless radiated the charm he always had possessed, and always would. "Your Jack is worth a king's ransom," Pickles Kane informed Joe. "He has poise, a fine Celtic map. A most engaging smile."

And his war record. In fact, looking stiff and malaria ridden only made JFK seem more like a man who had sacrificed his health for his country's freedom in the South Pacific. That he pretty much looked like that *before* he entered the service—that his bad back dated from the elite Harvard gridiron and not Blackett Strait—was not considered worthy of mention.

Facilitating matters was an admiring account of JFK's PT-109 adventures—"Survival"—that John Hersey had published in the *New Yorker*. Joe Kennedy arranged to have it republished in the mass-circulation *Reader's Digest*, and then had 100,000 copies reprinted and circulated throughout the Eleventh District.

And so, while Jack Kennedy knew too much about his wartime exploits to trumpet them himself (he forever retained a charmingly ironic detachment regarding his own accomplishments and limitations), the legend of PT-109 nonetheless grew all the grander about him, even then accreting plot points for dramatic—and political—ends. "My story about the collision is getting better all the time," he said with some humor and some annoyance. "Now I've got a Jew and a Nigger in the boat, and with me being a Catholic, that's great."

Few real issues intruded upon the campaign's hoopla and hand-shaking. Everyone was sufficiently anti-communist. *Look* even praised JFK as a "fighting conservative." The issue ultimately was young Jack Kennedy and his real ambitions, for warming a backwater congressional seat could not possibly be a Kennedy goal. "Why, you fellows are crazy," Joe Kennedy matter-of-factly informed a Neville supporter. "My son will be President in 1960."

Jack Kennedy trounced Neville 22,183 to 11,341, with Charleston judge John Cotter receiving 6,671 votes, the "real" Joe Russo 5,661, and the half dozen also-rans splitting 8,000 votes. He had received just 40.5 percent of the vote in a primary in which just 30 percent of district Democrats voted—a mere 12 percent of total party voters. But he had won, and that was enough. In November, in an otherwise historic Republican year, JFK demolished his GOP opponent by 69,093 votes to 26,007.

Entering Congress in January 1947, JFK looked and dressed like a skinny, sloppy kid, half man and half adolescent (he was sometimes mistaken at the Capitol for an elevator operator). "If you had to pick a member of that freshman class who would probably wind up as president," recalled JFK's closest congressional friend, Florida's George "Gorgeous George" Smathers, then a fellow congressman and later JFK's Senate colleague, "Kennedy was probably the *least* likely. He was so shy he could hardly tell you his name. One of the shyest fellows I'd ever seen."

And yet Kennedy had something neither Smathers nor four hundred other congressmen possessed: a real chance for the brass ring. It was fueled not only by Joe Kennedy's fortune (Kennedy Sr. was by now among the nation's wealthiest individuals; he would eventually be worth $400 million, his banking, liquor, and Wall Street fortunes augmented by tens of millions accumulated in Hollywood and in prime Manhattan and Chicago real estate), but also by his and his son's willingness, even eagerness, to create an image that would sell.

Jack Kennedy's friend and Harvard classmate Charles F. "Chuck" Spalding recalled that JFK "began at that time, and girls were a part of it, to consider this business of image":

It wasn't even called image then but the very first person to understand about public relations was Mr. [Joseph] Kennedy . . . the first person I ever knew who really understood that what you did was to merchandise a conception and he had enough experience in radio and motion pictures to grope around in that whole thing. . . . Jack would go out to California and notice the parallels between people out there—like personalities drawing crowds. Why did [Gary] Cooper draw a crowd? We'd spend hours talking about it. His magnetism, did he have it or didn't he? And the whole thing. And other people he met out there, Spencer Tracy and Gable . . . So that self conscious as he was in this way, he was always interested in seeing whether he had it or didn't have it.

And he was not dumb, no mere pretty face. Though he then only rarely chose to apply his brains, he possessed a facility not only for current affairs and history, but also for economics. He romped to re-election in 1948 and 1950, and could have retained his House seat forever without breaking a sweat. But that was not the plan. Although 1952 looked like a Republican year, a chancy opportunity for Democratic advancement either to the governorship or to the U.S. Senate, JFK had to act before his fragile body betrayed him. In that year he would challenge Massachusetts's Henry Cabot Lodge for Lodge's seemingly safe U.S. Senate seat.

"I will work out the plans to elect you President," Joe informed his son. "It will not be more difficult for you to be elected President than it will to win the Lodge fight. . . . You will need to get about twenty key men in the country to get the nomination, for it is these men who will control the convention."

On a superficial level, Lodge and John Kennedy were stark opposites. One was Boston Brahmin, one Boston Irish. One was Protestant, one Catholic. One Republican, one Democrat. But beyond the surface their careers revealed eerie similarities. Both were young, strikingly handsome men. Both had grandfathers of some political repute—JFK had Honey Fitz and Lodge had Henry Cabot Lodge Sr., U.S. senator from Massachusetts. Lodge Sr. and Honey Fitz had indeed battled head-to-head for the Senate in 1916. Both Lodge and Kennedy were children of wealth, graduates of exclusive private schools and of Harvard. Both had first practiced the journalistic art before entering the political lists. Both, while still very young, had authored books critiquing U.S. foreign policy. Both sprang from isolationist families but had fought in World War II. Both were moderates, earning the suspicions of ideologues within their respective parties.

The difference was in degrees. Lodge was handsomer, with more distinguished careers both in journalism and in government, and he had sacrificed far more to enter military service (having resigned his Senate seat in 1944 to serve on active duty, but regaining it in 1946). But Kennedy, by 1952, was already more at ease with average voters, more energetic, more focused on the Senate race, and, above all, possessed of more intense ambition.

Moreover, Lodge had become dangerously distracted by presidential politics, not by his own candidacy, though he had been mentioned as presidential timber as early as 1938, but as an advocate for General Dwight Eisenhower. Though Eisenhower enjoyed widespread popularity with the general populace, Lodge's course contained perils, specifically that of alienating the old-guard Robert Taft wing of the GOP.

Lodge had also displeased Wisconsin senator Joseph R. McCarthy by displaying insufficient enthusiasm for McCarthy's communists-in-government issue. Beyond that, the social-climbing Kennedys and the ostentatiously rough-hewn McCarthy manifested an odd but real affinity for each other. McCarthy vacationed with the Kennedy family, played softball and boated with them. Joe professed that McCarthy would "be a sensation." The Wisconsin senator dated Jack's sisters Pat and Eunice and was a guest at Eunice's wedding to R. Sargent Shriver. Jack Kennedy attended McCarthy's wedding at St. Matthew's Cathedral in Washington, D.C. In 1951 Joe served as godfather to Bobby's first child, Kathleen.

Massachusetts, with 750,000 Irish Catholics, was McCarthy country. Had McCarthy stumped for fellow Republican Lodge, he might have dealt a substantial, perhaps even fatal, blow to Jack Kennedy's challenge. He would not. First, McCarthy was not that enamored of Lodge. But more importantly, Joe Kennedy lobbied hard for McCarthy's neutrality. Some say his entreaties were sweetened with a three-thousand-dollar contribution to McCarthy's own re-election campaign. Jack ("I wouldn't doubt it for a minute") never denied it.

Three thousand dollars was chump change for Joe Kennedy. A much higher amount secured the support of the *Boston Post*, owned by financially troubled Taft Republican John Fox. Joe Kennedy extended Fox $500,000 in loans. The *Post* abruptly endorsed Jack Kennedy.

With Lodge's moderate record, the Kennedys had trouble attacking him on the issues, but they took their opportunities as they found them. Above all, Kennedy outworked Lodge, and when Lodge did campaign it was often out of state, for Eisenhower. "He was . . . ," Robert Kennedy said of Lodge, "a very, very lazy man as a campaigner." JFK was everywhere, and had *been* everywhere since he had won election to Congress. And where he could not be, his family was, smiling the Kennedy smile, giving speeches, shaking hands, holding teas, winning votes.

On Election Day 1952, while Eisenhower carried Massachusetts by 208,800 votes and Republican gubernatorial candidate Christian Herter won by 14,456 votes, Kennedy beat Lodge 1,211,984 to 1,141,247.

Jack Kennedy could now begin his entrance to the national center stage.

He still eschewed membership in his party's liberal wing. "I never joined the Americans for Democratic Action or the American Veterans Committee," he informed a *Saturday Evening Post* reporter in 1953. "I'm not comfortable with those people." And he remained tacitly allied with Joe McCarthy. In 1953, Joe Kennedy secured son Bobby the position of assistant counsel and deputy staff director with McCarthy's headline-generating Permanent Subcommittee on Investigations. Bobby, finding himself enmeshed in a rivalry with equally talented, equally youthful, equally brash subcommittee chief counsel Roy Cohn, soon departed, joining Democrats on the subcommittee—again with his father's assistance. But McCarthy and the Kennedys remained close, and JFK feared a backlash from pro-McCarthy constituents. "Joe McCarthy," observed former Democratic governor Paul Dever, "is the only man I know who could beat Archbishop Cushing in a two-man race in South Boston."

Accordingly, JFK "made no speeches against [McCarthy]," as chief JFK speechwriter Ted Sorensen noted in rare disapproval.

Eventually, McCarthy's luck played out. Having made too many enemies in both parties, he was censured by the Senate in December 1954. Only one senator refused to record a vote for or against McCarthy—Jack Kennedy, hospitalized since October for a truly serious, three-hour lumbar operation, but not so serious that he could not record his opinion one way or the other.

The operation *was* serious. Kennedy's health had not grown better. On a September 1947 visit to London he became so ill he received the last rites of the Roman Catholic Church. A physician diagnosed him with Addison's disease—a rare and, until very recently, invariably fatal endocrine disorder. The doctor placed Jack on a strict daily regimen of oral cortisone. Joe Kennedy feared his son was dying and, in Arthur Krock's presence, he wept openly. But once composed, he also stashed doses of cortisone about the country so his son would not be caught short. On a 1951 trip to Korea, however, JFK grew lax about medicating himself, and his Addison's disease flared up once more. Running a 106-degree fever, he came dangerously near death. Cortisone, moreover, weakened his already severely bad back. Walking from his Senate office to the Capitol grew daunting. Finally, he was reduced to crutches. His October 1954 spinal operation was as much an act of desperation as of hope—so risky, particularly in terms of postoperative infection, that it bore recording (with the famous patient's name discretely excised) in the American Medical Association journal *AMA Archives of Surgery*.

"Jack was determined to have the operation," his mother recalled. "He told his father that even if the risks were fifty-fifty, he would rather be dead than spend the rest of his life hobbling on crutches and paralyzed by pain."

That his pain had grown so horrendous as to be no longer disguisable played a part in his decision, for he could not abide displaying weakness. "Jack had an actor's control," Chuck Spalding recalled. "It was like the kind of control that Joe Montana had playing for the Forty-Niners. Montana said, 'It's the damnedest thing. The game's pretty rough and you're fighting for your life out there, but you're always watching yourself.' That's the way I always felt about Jack, as if he was always watching the scene."

It took him months to mend, to walk once more free from crutches. Not until February 1955 did he return to the Senate, his recovery remaining slow, unsteady, and emotionally and physically draining. In 1955 he consulted Manhattan physician Dr. Janet Travell, a grandmotherly specialist in matters orthopedic, particularly musculoskeletal pain. Her new patient was a wreck, but under her care—an all-inclusive program of "local procaine or novocaine" injections at "trigger points," increased vitamin-B dosages, prosthetic shoes, a firmer mattress, and even the iconic JFK rocking chair—he became, at least by his standards, relatively pain free. He could now envision moving on to other things and other attitudes. The physical barriers, and the accompanying mental ones, to fulfilling his father's grand obsession were falling by the wayside.

"There wasn't so much talk about death," his old Choate roommate and Princeton classmate Kirk LeMoyne "Lem" Billings said about JFK's postoperative attitudes. "Jack had grown up thinking he was doomed. Now he had a different view. Instead of thinking he was doomed, he thought he was lucky."

In early 1956, JFK phoned Ted Sorensen, informing him that he was thinking of running as a "New England favorite son in the New Hampshire Presidential primary." He never did, but Kennedy maneuvering accelerated during that year's Democratic convention. First, he delivered Stevenson's nominating speech (written by Sorensen with the proper soupçons of Adlai Stevenson–like wit and urbanity, though even pro-Kennedy historian James McGregor Burns termed it "fulsome"). Then, as a bonus, Hollywood producer Dore Schary selected JFK to narrate the party's campaign film, *The Pursuit of Happiness*. And while he may have been too young and inexperienced for a favorite-son presidential bid, neither attribute disqualified him from pondering a vice-presidential nomination. When Stevenson tossed that selection to convention delegates ("the goddamned stupidest move a politician could make," snapped Senate majority leader Lyndon Johnson), Kennedy, for once ignoring his father's wishes, went for it. Not everyone favored him ("If we have to have a Catholic," groused House Speaker Sam Rayburn, "I hope we don't have to take that little pissant Kennedy"), but many did, and he nearly defeated Tennessee senator Estes Kefauver for the honor. But then again, perhaps delegates didn't yet like JFK at all, since so many roundly despised Kefauver (often called "the most hated man in the Senate").

Much of Kennedy's support came from Kefauver's fellow Southerners, who saw the crime-busting Tennessean as a turncoat on racial matters. Northern liberals still viewed Kennedy with often undisguised suspicion. At one point JFK found himself sharing an elevator with United Auto Workers (UAW) president Walter Reuther, a Kefauver supporter. Kennedy inquired what he might do to garner UAW backing. "Improve your voting record," Reuther snarled.

Failure only emboldened Kennedy's ambitions. "With only about four hours of work . . . ," he confided to his close aide Dave Powers, "I came within thirty-three-and-a-half votes of winning the Vice-Presidential nomination. . . . If I work hard for four years, I ought to be able to pick up all the marbles."

Assisting his chances was another literary effort. During his prolonged convalescence he had authored another little book, this time chronicling examples of senatorial political fortitude. Titled *Profiles in Courage*, it won Kennedy the Pulitzer Prize in May 1957—though, once again, charges of ghostwriting materialized, with his principle speechwriter Ted Sorensen (paid six thousand dollars by Kennedy's publisher) usually rumored as the project's suspected spectral influence.

In December 1957 syndicated columnist Drew Pearson appeared on ABC-TV's *The Mike Wallace Interview* charging that Kennedy had not written the book. Joe Kennedy ordered high-powered Washington attorney Clark Clifford to sue for $50 million. Neither Wallace nor Pearson showed any interest in an apology, but ABC itself caved, issuing a retraction—ghostwritten by Ted Sorensen.

With a Pulitzer Prize under his belt, JFK moved on to finally begin fashioning at least the semblance of a legislative profile—for, in truth, he had yet to accomplish much of anything in Washington, D.C., not in the House (Tip O'Neill: "I've never seen a congressman get so much press while doing so little work") or in the Senate (Ted Sorensen: "John Kennedy was not one of the Senate's great leaders").

He now began his move. In a July 1957 Senate speech, he alienated the foreign policy establishment but improved his still-meager standing with party liberals by lambasting French colonialism in war-torn Algeria. On the domestic front, in tandem with brother Bobby, he helped conduct a series of investigations into Dave Beck and Jimmy Hoffa's notoriously corrupt Teamsters union. The Kennedys' anti-Teamster crusade not only ingratiated them with anti-union conservatives (most helpfully Southern Democrats), but also with anti-Teamster unionists such as the UAW's Reuther. Cementing himself further with Reuther, whenever Senate Republicans probed UAW violence during the then-notorious four-year-long Kohler strike, JFK rode to the rescue. "Every time we were getting into trouble," UAW chief legal counsel Joseph L. Rauh Jr. recalled, "Jack would enter the hearings room . . . and help us out. It got to be a joke inside our crowd."

Beyond that, congressional hearings had made the reputations of such Democratic stalwarts as Harry Truman and Estes Kefauver. Jousting with an obvious hoodlum like Jimmy Hoffa couldn't hurt.

But, first, re-election beckoned. JFK desired no mere return to office in 1958, but a landslide. Massachusetts Republicans, seeing little chance of vanquishing JFK, nominated a threadbare East Boston attorney, Vincent J. Celeste, whom Kennedy had thrashed for Congress back in 1950. Now Kennedy smashed this gnat Celeste with a sledgehammer. Hoping for a half-million-vote margin, he succeeded beyond his wildest dreams, capturing 73.6 percent of the vote and crushing his hapless opponent by a record 874,608 votes (1,362,926 to 488,318).

There was no thought of turning back. Just a week later, a goodly portion of the Kennedy circle, JFK excepted, gathered for dinner at Manhattan's exclusive Le Pavillon. When Lem Billings dared crack wise regarding his absent friend, Joe Kennedy just glared—then lacerated him with an explanation: "LeMoyne, you are one of the people who must understand this. You can never know who might be listening. From here on, you must think of Jack less as a friend and more as a potential candidate for President of the United States. I will tell you right now that the day is going to come when you will not call Jack 'Jack.' You will call him 'Mr. President.'"

Joe meant it; he would countenance nothing that would harm the image of this future president, instinctively realizing that so much of what would make his son the next president *was* image. "Jack is the greatest attraction in the country today," Joe Sr. boasted. "I'll tell you how to sell more copies of a book: Put his picture on the cover. Why is it that when his picture is on the cover of *Life* or *Redbook* that they sell a record number of copies? . . . He can draw more people to a fund-raising dinner than Cary Grant or Jimmy Stewart. Why is that? He has more universal appeal. That is why the Democratic Party is going to nominate him. The party leaders around the country realize that to win they have to nominate him."

It was all true. "In my life," concluded the hitherto unimpressed Tip O'Neill, "I never saw anybody grow the way Jack did; he turned into a great personality and a beautiful talker." The Kennedy candidacy would be based on newness, freshness, boldness, vigor, a determined look toward the future, almost contempt for what was past and even what was present. His career had been built on impatience, an impatience built partially on Kennedy family hubris and partially on the unpleasant but very real fact that he had to achieve so much so fast before his imperfect body inevitably betrayed him one piece at time—or, more horribly, but not impossibly, all at once. In *Life* magazine in 1957 JFK staked out his program: "With a new breed of respected, dynamic professional politicians coming into prominence, we can no longer afford to continue in official party positions tired or tarnished holdovers from another era—men who keep busily attending meetings, filing gloomy forecasts, and complaints, and fighting zealously to hold on to their positions."

It was his friend the columnist Joseph Alsop who provided the best thumbnail sketch of the JFK persona:

> He is, in reality, a deeply serious man, reflective in his mental habits, historically minded, and given to seeing men and nations and events in the sobering context that history provides.
>
> As a human being, he is also humorous, easily bored by dull routine but open to all fresh experience, careless of the superficialities of life, warmly loyal to his friends, and oddly detached about himself. His most curious trait, in fact, is his way of discussing his most vital affairs with the dry humor and cool analytical remoteness that most people reserve for the affairs of others.

JFK proposed to be no timeserver, no mere Eisenhower caretaker or Stevenson pontificator. He would be the action hero of politics, the embodiment of an up-and-coming generation, too impatient for power and, yes, glory, to wait any longer in line. In the process, he would transform the nation's politics. "America's politics," Norman Mailer would write in an article for *Esquire* in 1960, "would now be America's favorite movie."

Yet issues dogged Kennedy. Liberals remained unconvinced that Joe Kennedy's son, Joe McCarthy's pal, was one of them—or ready even for the Senate, let alone the presidency. I "would hesitate," Eleanor Roosevelt jeered on ABC TV, "to place the difficult decisions that the next President will have to make with someone who understands what courage is and admires it but has not quite the independence to have it."

And while Jack Kennedy certainly possessed charisma, it was charisma of an unusual sort—not the hail-fellow gab of the normal Irish pol (JFK was never the normal Irish pol) but the remote, almost-shy charm of a male Garbo. "I know some people do think of me as a cold fish," Jack Kennedy would explain in the quiet privacy of his campaign plane. "As far as backslapping with the politicians, I think I'd rather go somewhere with my familiars or sit alone somewhere and read a book. I think it's more a matter of personal reserve than a coldness, although it may seem like a coldness to some people."

Problems of chronology compounded those of personality and ideology. If elected, he would be forty-three on assuming office, far too young for the White House by historical standards. There were few comparisons that worked for him. Theodore Roosevelt was forty-two when he became president in 1901, but he hadn't been elected. If an assassin had not murdered William McKinley, most likely TR would never have become chief executive. Unfortunately, the closest comparison proved to be the perennially unsuccessful Thomas E. Dewey. Dewey was thirty-nine when he was the front-runner in 1940 and lost the nomination to Willkie; he was forty-three when he first won the nomination in 1944; and he was forty-seven when he blew everything sky-high in 1948. The average age at inauguration was fifty-four years, six months. Back in 1955 pollster George Gallup had asked respondents: How old should a president be? The answer: fifty-one. That's precisely how old FDR was when he took office in 1933. JFK, the man who couldn't wait, might just have to.

He refused. His Georgetown neighbor and friend, *Washington Post* correspondent Ben Bradlee, gingerly asked if he was afraid of assuming the White House. "Yes," JFK responded, "until I stop and look around at the other people who are running for the job. And then I think I'm just as qualified as they are."

Lyndon Baines Johnson would have disagreed.

THREE

"Independent as a hog on ice"

BY ROUGHEST COUNT, the bumptious Senate majority leader—LBJ—and the cool junior senator from Massachusetts—JFK—shared four common attributes. They were Democrats. They were U.S. senators. They suffered from worse health than they normally cared to admit. And they both wanted to be president.

Their differences were legion—of religion, region, experience, senatorial clout, temperament . . . and, most starkly and unalterably, of background.

Lyndon Baines Johnson was born, most appropriately, on a storm-tossed Texas Sunday morning, August 27, 1908. His family, not nearly as distinguished as it pretended to be ("the Johnsons could strut sitting down"), had nonetheless long before enjoyed its slaveholding and cattle-driving moments, and though the infant's grandfather soon predicted that this newborn would one day become a U.S. senator, there was little in the Johnson family background to indicate that his prediction might ultimately prove true.

As Lyndon grew older, his family grew poorer. His state legislator father ("nothing but a drunkard") invested poorly in land. Losing elective office, he survived on the most menial forms of patronage, a risky livelihood in the shifting sands of Texas politics. Friends and neighbors who once cheered Sam Johnson now jeered the impoverished, debt-ridden former lawmaker—and his family.

Poverty and ignominy aside, young Lyndon proved aggressive, precocious, and jocular. But, following high school, he seemed at loose ends. More rebellious than smart, the lanky six-foot fifteen-year-old snuck away with four friends to Southern California, where he toiled at odd jobs and pursued an ill-fated scheme to study law with a ne'er-do-well relative. Eventually he returned home with his tail firmly between his legs, to live once more with his parents. He supported himself through such menial jobs as elevator boy and, like his once prestigious father, on backbreaking road construction for two to three dollars per day.

In 1926, he enrolled in Southwest Texas State Teachers College at San Marcos, taking leave in September 1928 to instruct fifth- , sixth- , and seventh-grade Mexican children in the frontierlike south Texas town of Cotulla. He took his assignment seriously, working tirelessly to educate these previously neglected students. "When he saw those hungry children digging into garbage," observed his HEW secretary Wilbur Cohen, "it was the first time he had really seen grinding poverty."

Graduating from San Marcos State in August 1930 with a B average and a BS in education and history, LBJ briefly taught high school—first at tiny Pearsall, Texas, then in Houston. Already, he had developed an insatiable taste for politics—for winning votes, for currying attention and favor from those around him, even for stealing elections. "Everyone knew that something wasn't straight," recalled one San Marcos classmate regarding Johnson's early electoral exploits. "And everyone knew that if something wasn't straight, it was Lyndon Johnson who had done it."

Along the way Lyndon sank to courting the shy daughter of the former mayor and richest man in San Marcos—strictly for pecuniary reasons, which he bragged about. Then when the affair unraveled, Johnson concocted a fanciful tale that he had been rejected only because the girl's father was a Klansman (the man, in fact, opposed the KKK).

In 1931, Richard M. "Mr. Dick" Kleberg, a part owner of the vast King Ranch and a former rodeo cowboy, won a special election for Texas's vacant congressional seat representing the Fourteenth District, in which the Johnson family home was located. Kleberg, uninterested in hands-on politics, needed an administrative assistant with drive. Hiring Johnson for $267 a month, he obtained the busiest, most political twenty-three-year-old on the Potomac.

To Johnson, everything was politics. "He had the most narrow vision," his Washington roommate recalled. "Sports, entertainment, movies—he couldn't have cared less." As at San Marcos, Johnson now cheated in Washington, stuffing ballots to win election as president of the congressional staff organization known as "The Little Congress."

In August 1935, Kleberg's wife, "Miz Mamie," uneasy with Johnson's already unbridled ambition, forced him out. By now, however, Lyndon had accumulated sufficient political clout to rebound rapidly upward. Assisted by such allies as liberal San Antonio–area congressman Maury

Maverick and the already powerful Dallas-area representative Sam "Mr. Sam" Rayburn (who had served with Johnson's father in the Texas legislature), LBJ secured a plum appointment as Texas director of FDR's National Youth Administration. A mere twenty-six, Lyndon now commanded a major regional New Deal patronage operation, and he was ready to dispense that patronage to good use.

In 1937 death opened up Texas's Tenth District congressional seat. Against seven other candidates, Johnson campaigned as the most ardent New Dealer, and from a hospital bed (he was stricken with appendicitis, which many suspected he exploited for sympathy) Lyndon won the February 1937 special primary. At twenty-nine he was going back to where the action was—Washington, D.C.

As many Southern Democrats were galloping away from the Roosevelt administration, LBJ quickly established himself as a solid FDR ally. Far more liberal than his Dixie colleagues, he quickly filled a congressional void, establishing himself as a young man with solid White House connections.

Solid in Washington, that is . . . but not so back in Texas. There he muted his FDR adulation and trimmed his liberal legislative sails, the better to avoid starboard Texas gusts. "Don't forget our friend Maury [Maverick] . . . ," LBJ warned New Deal insider James H. Rowe Jr., referencing his old patron, who, having proved too progressive for Texas mores, involuntarily departed Congress after just two terms. "There's nothing more useless than a dead liberal."

Above all, Johnson honed his already substantial sycophantic skills. In high school and in college he had shamelessly ingratiated himself with whatever teachers might assist him, mastering the practice in Austin and Washington. Now he fastened himself to a trio of powerful mentors: Franklin Roosevelt (who proceeded to offer him the national directorship of the Rural Electrification Administration); Carl "The Georgia Swamp Fox" Vinson, the brazenly autocratic House Naval Affairs Committee chairman; and, most particularly, future House Speaker Sam Rayburn.

"Lyndon Johnson is one of the finest young men I have seen come to Congress," Rayburn wrote an associate in 1938. "If the District will exercise the good judgment to keep him here, he will grow in wisdom and influence as the years come and go."

Yet, Johnson could also exercise independence. As he chose his mentors for how they could advance him, he chose new ones for the same reasons. If old and new "daddies" clashed, Johnson was not so beholden to them, or to any position, that he might not jettison men or ideals appropriately. Or, as Mr. Sam would soon complain (though he would never break with Johnson), Lyndon was "a damn independent boy; independent as a hog on ice."

There was, perhaps, a deep-seated psychological need to be so independent, so ambitious, so grasping, and so transparently ruthless. Lyndon's father (whom the boy himself had once adulated) had been idealistic, never accepting a dime or a favor, and had concluded his career as a town laughingstock with few dimes for himself *or* his family. Lyndon, so embarrassed by his family's precipitous political, economic, and social downturn, vowed never to repeat Sam Johnson's mistakes—a pledge beyond Scarlett O'Hara's vowing to "never go hungry again." It was a promise not merely to *be* devious, but to publicly *glory* in that deviousness.

In April 1941, death's bony hand opened yet another door for Lyndon Johnson, but this time he would not storm through it. Texas's veteran U.S. senator Morris Sheppard died of a brain hemorrhage, and Johnson, Governor W. Lee "Pappy" O'Daniel, and ten others battled to succeed him. On primary night, LBJ—again running as FDR's man in Texas—enjoyed a 5,112-vote lead. It didn't hold. In the runoff, O'Daniel triumphed by 1,311 votes (of 600,000 cast). LBJ believed—probably quite rightly—that victory had been stolen from him.

Hard-driving and ambitious, Lyndon Johnson nevertheless accepted defeat. But he was not about to accept it *again*.

As war brewed in both Europe and Asia, LBJ held a widely coveted slot on Carl Vinson's Naval Affairs Committee. Overcoming the pacifist leanings of his family's Christadelphian beliefs, he quickly emerged as an aggressive proponent of increased military spending. His efforts meshed neatly and profitably with his burgeoning relationship with the Texas engineering and construction firm of Brown & Root. Starting with Johnson's assistance in completing Brown & Root's work on the Austin-area Mansfield Dam project (which had been hamstrung by the small detail that the federal government did not actually own the land on which the federally funded project was built), he would proceed to assist the growing company in securing any number of lucrative federal projects, including a $100 million cost-plus contract at Corpus Christi Naval Station. He also lobbied FDR to slash Brown & Root's back taxes from $1.6 million to a more manageable $372,000. In return, the firm provided generous support to Johnson's political campaigns, particularly his 1941 (a reported $150,000 in laundered contributions) and 1948 Senate races.

That 1941 run had been conducted within the context of a raging debate regarding American war preparedness, and LBJ vowed, with more vehemence than sincerity, that he would not vote to send any mothers' sons off to war without joining them "in the front lines, in the mud and blood"—an amusing promise to those remembering young Lyndon as perhaps the least combative Texan in recent memory, and that was phrasing it with considered charity. "[H]e wouldn't fight," bluntly recalled one classmate. "He was an absolute physical coward."

Nonetheless, on December 8, 1941, Lyndon Johnson became the first member of Congress to enter the service after Pearl Harbor—though not in the trenches. He would become a naval lieutenant commander con-ducting bloodless, mudless Texas and West Coast inspection tours while still running his congressional operation, vainly plotting a rematch against O'Daniel, and hoping to inveigle a major Pentagon assignment back in Washington—perhaps even as secretary of the Navy. Texans, however, began noticing Johnson's notable lack of derring-do. The generally friendly *Houston Post* wrote: "If Mr. Johnson should merely be getting himself a safe, warm naval berth . . . the voters would be certain to react accordingly." LBJ reacted with a twofold strategy: To provide Lyndon with a graceful exit from military life, Mr. Sam Rayburn would lobby FDR to order congressmen home from the war—but before that hap-pened, Johnson would quickly go to the South Pacific for a brief, but politically essential, taste of "combat" experience.

Scheduled to observe a truly dangerous mission over a Japanese base on the north shore of New Guinea, Johnson was supposed to fly aboard the *Wabash Cannonball*, a B-26 Marauder medium bomber. But he was bumped from that plane (it was shot down) to another, the *Heckling Hare*. By all accounts, Johnson flew into combat with (for him) remarkable calm, almost a sense of detachment. Nonetheless, he remained essentially a glorified passenger aboard the *Heckling Hare*, which never even reached its target, having jettisoned its payload elsewhere. When LBJ returned to base in Australia and reported to General Douglas MacArthur, MacArthur spontaneously awarded spectator—virtually tourist—Johnson the Silver Star. Lyndon wore the egregiously undeserved decoration, the third highest for valor in the face of the enemy, for the rest of his life.

On July 9, 1942, FDR ordered all members of Congress in the military to return home or to resign their seats. Four stayed in service (one was killed in action). Four others, including Lyndon Johnson, returned stateside.

Johnson's homecoming proved melancholy. His dreams of a Senate career seemed extinguished. The best he might hope for was plodding advancement in the House (and at worst, timeserving stagnation), trapped in a seniority-driven system that awarded power to balding old men such as Rayburn and Vinson, who had arrived in town before the First World War.

His consolation: growing wealth. In 1943, his wife Claudia Alta Taylor "Lady Bird" Johnson, flush with a recent $36,000 inheritance, purchased Austin's run-down, debt-ridden 250-watt radio station KTBC for $17,500. Her diligence and business acumen turned the moribund enterprise around, but without her husband's Washington connections KTBC would have remained of little note—or profit. The FCC approved increased wattage and evening broadcasts. From CBS—ever mindful of federal regulation of broadcasting—came a lucrative network hookup.

When FDR died in April 1945, LBJ was distraught. "He was just like a daddy to me always," he said, weeping. But as wildly and overtly emotional as LBJ invariably was, emotion never completely overshadowed cold political calculation, and he continued speaking in a strangely clinical and ambivalent fashion, considering that it was the hour of deepest mourning for a beloved, just-deceased "daddy": "They called the President a dictator and some of us they called 'yes' men. Sure, I yessed him plenty of times—because I thought he was right—and I'm not sorry for a single 'yes' I ever gave. I have seen the President in all kinds of moods . . . and never once . . . did he ever ask me to vote a certain way, or even suggest it. And when I voted against him—as I have plenty of times—he never said a word." Johnson biographers Rowland Evans and

Robert Novak accordingly noted, "Johnson's overt move to the right may be said to have started in earnest the day of Roosevelt's death."

FDR was gone. Texas's oil barons and rock-ribbed conservatives remained. Lyndon Johnson, while never really the conservative that Northern liberals feared he was, now embarked on a measured quadrille twixt left and right—particularly regarding two of the most controversial issues dividing white Southern Democrats from Northern liberals: civil rights and labor reform. "I never claimed to be a liberal," he coldly informed one disappointed friend as early as 1943.

Even his closest associates could not divine the real Lyndon. "On many important votes it was impossible to know why he had voted a certain way," puzzled Southern California congresswoman Helen Gahagan Douglas, "whether it was from conviction or political considerations. He was willing to make the compromises necessary . . . to guarantee that he stayed in the Congress. In fact, he made fun of those who refused to bend . . . And he wanted to play an active role at the head of the majority, not at the head of the minority."

Aggravating Johnson's fears was his relatively close call in his 1946 primary against Austin attorney Hardy Hollers. The underfinanced, undersupported Hollers significantly cut into Johnson's vote totals. Linking LBJ to Brown & Root, Hollers charged that his opponent was "an errand boy for war-rich contractors."

"If the United States Attorney was on the job," Hollers charged, "Lyndon Johnson would be in the federal penitentiary instead of in Congress. Will Lyndon Johnson explain how the charter for KTBC, owned by Mrs. Johnson, was obtained? Will Lyndon Johnson explain . . . his mushrooming personal fortune?"

Such talk was enough to sour a public servant's taste for office.

In 1948, Pappy O'Daniel was ready to retire from the Senate (most likely to be thrown out if he didn't), leaving Lyndon Johnson with a difficult decision. In 1941, he had contested for the Senate in a special election, at no real risk to his House seat. But running in 1948 meant risking all. With only painful memories to guide him, indecision gripped Johnson. He delayed his decision, and even considered running in his stead his thirty-one-year-old protégé John Connally (of whom LBJ would later say, presumably approvingly, Connally could "leave more dead bodies in the field with less remorse than any politician I ever knew").

In the end LBJ ran, his only significant opposition being Texas's sixty-one-year-old governor, the laconic conservative Coke "Calculating Coke" Stevenson. The time had long since passed when Lyndon Johnson would run as a New Deal liberal. Now LBJ bragged of voting for Taft-Hartley labor reform ("Labor's not much stronger in Texas than a popcorn fart") and informed voters: "The civil rights program is a farce and a sham—an effort to set up a police state in the guise of liberty. I am opposed to that program. I have voted AGAINST the so-called poll tax repeal bill; the poll tax should be repealed by those states which enacted them. I have voted AGAINST the FEPC [the Fair Employment Practices Commission]; if a man can tell you whom you must hire; he can tell you who you can't hire." Campaigning furiously, he flayed Stevenson from the left and from the right (often simultaneously), delivering 350 speeches in sixty days—and amazing rural audiences by crisscrossing the state in a Bell helicopter, blaring his message to waiting crowds via loudspeaker.

LBJ ("old enough to know how and young enough to get the job done") would not capitulate, as he had surrendered on primary night 1941. Stevenson's gang might be as proficient at stuffing ballot boxes as Pappy O'Daniel's, but Johnson's gang—primarily George B. Parr, the dapper "Duke of Duval," who delivered the sizable Mexican American votes of Duval, Jim Wells, and Zapata counties by the sombreroful—simply outstole them. Lyndon Johnson—now forever to be derided as "Landslide Lyndon"—defeated Coke Stevenson by eighty-seven highly suspect votes.

A new job, a new House of Congress, a new mentor. FDR remained dead. Sam Rayburn and Carl Vinson remained behind in the House. Now numbered among the most junior members of the U.S. Senate, Lyndon, more resigned than ever to downplaying his populist inclinations ("My state is much more conservative than the national Democratic party. I got elected by eighty-seven votes and I ran against a caveman"), turned his attentions to the dean of Southern Democrats, Georgia's skilled, highly diligent, brilliant—and profoundly conservative—Richard B. Russell.

The brash LBJ bonded with the shy, actually quite lonely, Russell, the result being that Johnson's influence grew among Senate

Democrats—so much so that in 1952 Lyndon considered seeking his party's vice-presidential nomination, hoping perhaps to build momentum for larger stakes in 1956.

In 1952, however, Democrats lost not only the White House, but the Congress, including the seat of Senate Democratic leader Ernest McFarland of Arizona (in an upset to Phoenix department store magnate Barry M. Goldwater). In this situation, Richard Russell might well have stepped in as minority leader—as might more moderate Southerners Russell Long or Lister Hill. Instead, Johnson, with Russell's tacit backing, quickly moved to lasso support for himself—including a subtle overture to Massachusetts's newly elected Jack Kennedy. Early the morning following the election, two hours behind Boston time, Johnson phoned JFK to congratulate him on his narrow victory over Henry Cabot Lodge. With a puzzled look on his face, Kennedy turned to aide Kenny O'Donnell: "That was Lyndon Johnson in Texas. He said he just wanted to congratulate me. The guy must never sleep."

Not when the minority leader's position was on the line.

Commanding an awkward coalition of Southern conservatives and Northern liberals, and fearful of confronting the still immensely popular Eisenhower (even Ike was a bit of a "daddy" to Lyndon), minority leader Johnson steered a measured course. The country was now ragingly moderate. By mid-decade Harry Truman, Robert Taft, and Joe McCarthy would all vacate center stage. When even Eleanor Roosevelt chose to write to Adlai Stevenson in the course of the 1956 campaign that "I think understanding and sympathy for the white people of the South is as important as understanding and sympathy for the colored people," one did not have to be a Walter Lippmann to discern that moderation was in vogue.

And so, when Senate Democrats gained a slim majority in January 1955, minority leader Johnson became majority leader Johnson. The sky seemed the limit—until the late afternoon of Saturday, July 1, 1955. At Brown & Root partner George R. Brown's palatial Middleburg, Virginia, estate, the increasingly worn-out Lyndon Johnson suffered a massive heart attack. Initially in critical condition, he remained in Bethesda Naval Hospital for six weeks. For four months after that, he convalesced at his Texas ranch.

The heart attack plunged him into depression. He had survived—but barely. His life, his political career, might yet still vanish. His flickering presidential hopes seemed crushed.

But he soon recovered his health. At a time when a heart-attack victim might ordinarily have suffered a disqualifying stigma, Johnson was lucky that Dwight Eisenhower had also suffered one, in September 1955. If Ike might be re-elected president following a heart attack, surely Lyndon Johnson could continue as majority leader—and, perhaps, even someday revive his own grander dreams.

LBJ was, from the very beginning, ambitious, a tough man to work for—mercurial, insulting, vain yet insecure, always driving, driving, driving. He seldom thought of politics, he said by his own admission, "more than 18 hours a day." Politics meant legislating to Lyndon Johnson and legislating meant not speeches from the Senate floor but work in committee rooms and back rooms, conniving and bargaining and, above all, arm-twisting. It meant "The Treatment," described by his press secretary George Reedy as "an incredibly potent blend of badgering, cajolery, promises of favors, implied threats." It meant, Reedy continued, leaving Johnson's victims "absolutely helpless. . . . [I]t would be like standing under Niagara Falls. . . . It was just unbelievably potent. Sometimes I think he did it just for practice."

And while Jack Kennedy gathered ever more people toward him, like a rolling snowball, Lyndon Johnson had difficulty retaining any but his closest staff. "I've talked to a lot of . . . ex-Johnson people," recalled columnist Stewart Alsop (Joe Alsop's younger brother). "I found none that I can remember who really detested him, who considered themselves enemies. They all spoke with a curious mixture of admiration and exasperation about Lyndon Johnson. . . . But after awhile they just couldn't work for him anymore. . . . It was more than human flesh could bear!"

"Why members of his staff stuck with him—including me—," Reedy pondered, "is a question I cannot answer to this day. It had something to do with a feeling that he was a truly great man and that we owed it to the country to put up with his rampages so he would be there when he was needed."

Maddening, too, was LBJ's indecision regarding his very identity. Not only did he change his ideology with the season; he also physically aped those he admired—an FDR or a Winston Churchill—even when the pose seemed laughable. His diet, his wardrobe, his hair, his eyewear (horn-rimmed versus rimless versus contacts), all underwent constant metamorphosis.

Yet constants existed—not just a drive for power, but also a genuine concern for the underprivileged. He possessed no great empathy for the middle class, and they, in turn, cared little for him. Virtually his entire political program involved assisting the underdog, particularly if they were Southern underdogs, whether poor whites or poor blacks. He was, as biographer Robert Dallek so wonderfully observed, "a magnificent scoundrel, a self-serving altruist, a man of high ideals and no principle, a chameleon on plaid."

The year 1956 witnessed another stillborn LBJ attempt at storming the national ticket, this time as a possible favorite-son candidate. Through an LBJ ally, former FDR adviser "Tommy the Cork" Corcoran, Joe Kennedy promised support—with a condition: "My son Jack as your running mate." LBJ refused—and refused again when Joe phoned him directly with it.

"Young Bobby was infuriated," Corcoran recalled. "He believed it was unforgivably discourteous to turn down his father's generous offer." JFK himself sounded out Corcoran regarding Lyndon's ultimate intentions. "Listen, Tommy . . . ," he demanded, "Is Lyndon Johnson running without us?. . . Is he running?"

"Of course he is," Corcoran responded. "He may not think he is. And certainly he's saying he isn't. But I . . . know he is. I'm sorry that he doesn't know it."

LBJ dispatched word ("Tell him I want it") to Adlai Stevenson regarding his availability for the second slot. A full hour passed without Stevenson's response. LBJ dispatched another message to Adlai: he didn't want it at all.

Such fantasies adjourned, when Adlai threw the vice-presidential selection to the delegates, Johnson supported JFK's erstwhile bid—more from dislike of Estes Kefauver than anything else—switching Texas's second-ballot votes from Tennessee senator Albert Gore Sr. to Kennedy. "Texas," Lyndon trumpeted, "proudly casts its 56 votes for the fighting sailor [JFK] who wears the scars of battle."

Nineteen-fifty-eight's off-year election solidly increased Johnson's Democratic majority, but also significantly shifted power within the Democratic caucus from Southern conservatives to Northern liberals. Though Johnson was by now widely heralded as the "Master of the Senate," liberals grumbled that his mastery was essentially hollow—that LBJ feared to confront the popular Eisenhower, the country's growing anti–big labor sentiment, or Johnson's own entrenched Southern colleagues such as Richard Russell or Mississippi's James Eastland and John Stennis.

Civil rights issues proved particularly vexing. *Brown v. Board of Education* and the resulting September 1957 Little Rock school integration crisis slid black expectations and white Southern fears dangerously near to collision. Lyndon Johnson, from Jim Crow Texas, relying on support from party liberals and party conservatives, had to tread a particularly fine line. When, in March 1956, South Carolina's Strom Thurmond and Virginia's Harry Flood Byrd drafted the "Southern Manifesto" justifying segregation, only three of twenty-two Southern senators—Tennessee's Kefauver and Gore, and Texas's Johnson ("I am not a civil rights advocate")—refused to sign. Southern signatories calculated, however, that having Johnson as their protector as majority leader counted for far more than having another name on a document.

Southern colleagues also forgave his leadership regarding 1957's Civil Rights Bill, submitted originally by Dwight Eisenhower. It was not a strong bill, particularly when the Senate got through with it (some said fewer Southern blacks voted in 1960 than in 1956), and Johnson convinced recalcitrant, filibustering Southerners that this tepid measure was far preferable to what might follow if it failed. "The Negroes," he argued to Richard Russell, "they're getting pretty uppity these days. . . . Now we've got to do something about this, . . . just enough to quiet them down, not enough to make a difference. For if we don't move at all, . . . we'll lose the filibuster and there'll be no way of putting a brake on all sorts of wild legislation. It'll be Reconstruction all over again." It passed— the first civil rights act since 1875. Nobody got exactly what they wanted, but nobody seemed particularly angry either. Lyndon Johnson's presidential chances remained intact.

Yet, his maddening indecision remained, compounded by unresolved issues concerning his health. "Bobby," he said to his key assistant Bobby

"Little Lyndon" Baker, "you never had a heart attack. Every night I go to bed, and I never know if I'm going to wake up alive the next morning. I'm just not physically capable of running for the presidency."

In 1957 he went still further, informing Harvard historian (and liberal Democratic activist) Arthur M. Schlesinger Jr. that he would not even seek re-election to the Senate.

And then, of course, there was the issue of why he *should* run. What sort of president would Lyndon Johnson make? In 1957 JFK confided to MIT economics professor Walt Whitman Rostow, "The Democratic Party owes Johnson the nomination. He's earned it. He wants the same things for the country that I do. But it's too close to Appomattox for Johnson to be nominated and elected. So, therefore, I feel free to run." Two years later JFK told the National Press Club, "Lyndon would make the ablest president of any of us running, but he can't be elected."

Politics and ambition, however, seem to have been Kennedy's true perspective. To *Look* in August 1959, he sputtered, Lyndon "fluctuates and is not a heavyweight thinker."

Eisenhower's vice president thought better of LBJ—sort of. "He is the ablest [Democrat]. He would be a successful President," Richard Nixon informed reporters one night in the late 1950s at the Denver airport. "If he had only one strike against him, he might make it, but I don't think he can with two [health and region]."

LBJ may have worshipped FDR but, as Lyndon's presidential ambitions advanced, Franklin's widow clearly failed to worship him. In February 1960, when Eleanor's friend Mary Lasker, a New York philanthropist and the widow of Warren Harding's 1920 campaign advertising director, tried convincing her that Johnson was a "secret liberal," Mrs. Roosevelt responded in no uncertain terms: "You're crazy."

Months passed. While JFK's determination solidified, Johnson's indecision grew mushier than grits. In January 1959 Lyndon's longtime ally Jim Rowe, his frustration at the breaking point, gave up—he enlisted in Senator Hubert Humphrey's hardly promising campaign.

Yet there existed signs of movement. In the spring of 1959 Texas changed its laws to allow a candidate to run for two offices simultaneously—a prerequisite for a Johnson run. In 1948 he had not been comfortable risking everything, when "everything" meant a lackluster

House seat. Jeopardizing his Senate majority leadership in 1960 was a non-starter. Now, in October 1959, House Speaker Sam Rayburn unveiled a "Johnson for President Committee." Still, nothing much happened. John Connally and Johnson's top aide Walter Jenkins opened a campaign head-quarters at Washington's Ambassador Hotel. Nothing much happened there, either.

Johnson fretted. "All this talk about my candidacy is destroying my leadership," he moaned to Rayburn. "I'm trying to build a legislative record over there. The Senate is already full of presidential candidates. If I really get into this thing, they'll gang up on me as leader so that I'll be disqualified for nomination."

The Lyndon Johnson of 1960, exalted majority leader of the U.S. Senate, gritty master of the back room, would not stoop to that. Jack Kennedy, the pampered multimillionaire's son, would. "Johnson," JFK would later say, "had to prove that a Southerner could win in the North, just as I had to prove a Catholic could win in heavily Protestant states. Could you imagine me, having entered no primaries, trying to tell the leaders that being a Catholic was no handicap? When Lyndon said he could win in the North, but could offer no concrete evidence, his claims couldn't be taken seriously."

Bad judgment regarding his erratic stop-and-mostly-stop presidential campaign paralleled increasingly poor, even reckless, management and personal style. "Before the heart attack," wrote George Reedy, "his darkest side was kept under a modicum of control. After the heart attack, he stopped short only of supreme disaster—and not very short of that. Sometimes it seemed as though he really wanted to get caught doing something outrageous so he would no longer have to make decisions or accept responsibilities."

"I've already done everything but hold a gun to Lyndon's head," a frustrated Mr. Sam confided to Bobby Baker. "We've had more trouble between us about this damn campaign than anything within my memory. Lyndon's using his friends to raise money and court delegates and he's making them as well as himself look silly by declaring himself a non-candidate. He ought to shit or get off the pot."

FOUR

"You're my boy"

IT WAS, INDEED, a sad little job, the Constitution defining it thusly:

> The Vice President of the United States shall be President of the Senate, but shall have no vote, unless they be equally divided.

The office's first occupant summed it up as "the most insignificant . . . that ever the invention of man contrived or his imagination conceived."

A dead end.

Thus it was all the more remarkable that, as 1960 opened, the vice president of the United States, forty-six-year-old Richard Milhous Nixon, was the putative Republican nominee for president.

Nixon had transformed the vice presidency—and himself—into a national force and presence, traveling and campaigning and speaking out on the issues. Sometimes he did it all a tad too roughly or artificially, but he had answered his party's call when it needed him, and in the 1950s, when the GOP boasted little talent beside Dwight Eisenhower and John Foster Dulles, it needed Richard Nixon with regularity. He seemed a comer, a man not biding his time or satisfied with capping his career with a grandiloquent title before trundling off to take his partnership in a law firm, pen his memoirs, or sonorously bask in gentlemanly retirement.

But Nixon also had luck. He had ascended because he was so young while Eisenhower was so old, and so partisan while Eisenhower was so nonpartisan. For much of his life, Ike had not only been removed from partisan maneuvering; he was not even stateside. A stranger even now to the stalwarts of the Republican Party, Eisenhower displayed scant interest—or respect—for them. On the other hand, for the past fourteen years Richard Nixon had immersed himself in politics, in his party, in collecting favors—in making, if not friends, at least acquaintances and allies. Yes, Richard Nixon was a comer. The GOP would turn to him.

It had to.

★ ★ ★

Richard Milhous Nixon was born on the evening of January 9, 1913, in the small white frame farmhouse in Yorba Linda, California, that his father, Francis Anthony "Frank" Nixon, had built just a year previously for eight hundred dollars' worth of materials.

The Kennedys were a family (a privately held corporation, really—Joseph P. Kennedy Sr., sole proprietor) on the way up. The Johnsons were a family lurching precariously downward. The Nixons were just an American family, neither noteworthy nor notorious, remarkably unremarkable. "Preachers, ministers, shopkeepers, school principals, yes," Richard Nixon's mother, Hannah Milhous Nixon, once mused, "but I can't think of a Nixon or a Milhous holding an office higher than sheriff."

Sixth-grade dropout Frank Nixon had been a Columbus, Ohio, streetcar motorman, but after suffering frostbitten feet, and battling management to improve working conditions, he relocated in 1908 to warmer Southern California. There, he moved from Pacific Electric motorman (fired after his train hit an automobile) to oilfield roustabout to borrowing five thousand dollars to start an Atlantic Richfield gas station. Soon he had added to his enterprise a general store, the Nixon Market, and a modest lunch counter.

Hannah Nixon was quiet, private, college educated—two years at local Quaker-operated Whittier College—and intensely, yet still privately, religious. It was through her that Richard inherited his Quaker roots.

From his father, mercurial in both politics and temperament, Richard Nixon took his drive. Frank Nixon was a domestic tyrant, a "stern disciplinarian" according to Nixon, who bullied not only his family, but even his customers. "I tried," Nixon would write, "to follow my mother's example of not crossing him." It is not hard to read between the lines.

Nixon's Park Avenue psychotherapist, Dr. Arnold Hutschnecker, first consulted by Nixon in the 1950s, certainly did some reading. "Nixon's father was brutal and cruel," Hutschnecker observed. "[He] brutalized the mother, and this is of enormous importance."

"My mother was a saint," Richard wept as he was being driven from the White House in 1974, and perhaps she was, but some saints may produce as much anxiety as inspiration. "Fear was a virus that infected Nixon's life," Dr. Hutschnecker posited, "that he never recovered from—the fear that he would be regarded as weak. What would Mama think?

What would Daddy say? . . . I believe that the image of the saintly but stern face of his mother defeated him more than any other factor. . . . His mother was really his downfall."

Dick Nixon's salvation was his intelligence. He was bright—he could play the piano, violin, and clarinet—and he could talk, winning numerous oratorical prizes, first in his class at Whittier High School. He had hopes of a full scholarship to Yale, but with his family impoverished by the fatal illnesses of his brothers Harold and Arthur, he could not avail himself of it. Enrolling at modest Whittier College, he continued debating, acted ("usually . . . the character parts"), was elected student body president, finished second in his class, and won a full scholarship to Duke University Law School, where he finished third in his class.

"I came out of college more liberal than I am today," he recalled in 1958, "more liberal in the sense that I thought it was possible for government to do more than I later found it was practical to do." He sought a job in government with J. Edgar Hoover's still highly admired FBI and came very near to being hired, but in the end saw his application rejected. Returning home in 1937, he entered private practice, dabbling in Citra-Frost, a frozen orange juice company that failed, but, more importantly, in politics, as Whittier deputy city attorney. When a state assembly seat fell vacant, Nixon dared ask for the nomination. Local GOP chieftains curtly informed him that he was too young for the job.

Though no one remembered him dating at Duke, he now seriously courted Thelma Catherine "Pat" Ryan, so named because she was born late on St. Patrick's Day Eve 1912 to a fallen-away Catholic father. A $190-a-month Whittier High School business teacher, of far meaner and much more Democratic origins than his own, she was a very attractive young woman in her own tall (5 feet 5½ inches), high-cheekboned, dignified way. She had even worked as an extra in a handful of Hollywood films.

He loved her, pursued her, but courted her in very Nixonian ways—at one point writing to her:

From the first days I knew you, you were destined to be a great lady—You have always had that extra something which takes people out of the mediocre class. And now, dear heart, I want to work with you toward the destiny you are bound to fulfill.

As I have told you many times—living together will make us both grow—and by reason of it we shall realize our dreams. You are a great inspiration to me, and though you don't believe it yet, I someday shall return some of the benefit you have conferred on me.

It is our job to go forth together and accomplish great ends and we shall do it too.

On June 21, 1940, she married him anyway.

In December 1941, just days before Pearl Harbor, Richard Nixon received a $3,200-a-year offer to join the federal Office of Price Administration. Looking forward to working in Washington, he took it. But feeling the pull of patriotism, and the weight of eight months in the federal tire-rationing bureaucracy, Nixon soon applied for a naval commission. He was assigned to a naval air station—at Ottumwa, Iowa. It was not his, nor anyone's, idea of sea duty.

He transferred to the North Solomons, serving at Bougainville and on the Green Islands, but only in a support capacity. His combat experience, despite later hints to the contrary, may have been infinitesimal at best and nonexistent at worst. Known to his comrades as "Nick" Nixon, he earned popularity by wheeling and dealing to liberate rations of fresh meat and booze for his men. Ordered stateside in July 1944, he remained in the Navy back East when the war ended, working on naval contract terminations. Then, in September 1945, a letter arrived from Whittier asking whether he was interested in contesting the 1946 Twelfth District congressional race against the five-term Yale-educated former Socialist, Jerry Voorhis.

He certainly was.

The year 1946 looked like a Republican year, but the race would not be easy. Nixon, an unknown with little record of achievement in the community, possessed no great personal fortune to finance his effort. He did, however, possess an increasingly Republican tilt in the largely anti-union district. This included an active and enthusiastic cadre of Republican businessmen and party faithful working on his behalf, as well as support from conservative Republican Norman Chandler's powerful *Los Angeles Times*. Finally, of course, he had his own substantial native drive and intelligence.

Nixon's campaign focused on an anti–big labor theme, tying Voorhis's voting record to the left-leaning Congress of Industrial Organizations

(CIO) and its recently organized political arm, the Political Action Committee (PAC). Nixon's pamphlets screamed that "A vote for Nixon is a vote against Socialization of free American institutions, . . . the PAC . . . and its communist principles." Excoriating PAC's "gigantic slush fund," they pointed out that "43 [of 46] times Voorhis voted the PAC Line!"

Nixon's debating skills tipped the scales. In five encounters, Nixon lacerated Voorhis's record, exposing his incompetence on the platform. This caused voters to ask how five-termer Voorhis could effectively represent his district in Washington, D.C., if he could not hold his own against this baby-faced unknown. Nixon also mercilessly linked Voorhis to PAC. "Jerry," said Los Angeles Democratic congressman Chet Holifield to Voorhis after one debate, "he murdered you."

Richard Nixon trounced Voorhis by 65,586 votes to 49,994. In Congress, Nixon might have easily become lost among a welter of Republican freshmen, but for his assignment to the controversial House Committee on Un-American Activities. In August 1948, *Time* magazine editor and confessed Soviet espionage agent Whitaker Chambers testified before the committee, identifying Carnegie Endowment for World Peace president Alger Hiss as a communist agent. The virtual embodiment of the Ivy League–educated foreign-policy establishment, Hiss had graduated from Johns Hopkins and Harvard Law, become a high State Department official, and performed crucial roles at such key international conferences as Dumbarton Oaks, Yalta, and San Francisco.

Hiss haughtily derided Chambers's charges. When Chambers repeated them on NBC's *Meet the Press*, Hiss sued for libel. Washington's elite rallied round Hiss ("I know Alger Hiss," snapped columnist Walter Lippmann. "He couldn't be guilty of treason"), and all seemed ready to abandon Chambers—save for Nixon. Chambers produced dramatic documentary evidence (the "Pumpkin Papers") of Hiss's perfidy, Hiss went to Lewisburg federal penitentiary for perjury, and freshman congressman Richard Nixon emerged as the unlikely star of America's war on domestic communism. Those who had crawled out on a limb for Alger Hiss, those who would forever believe in his innocence, and those who viewed the entire anti-communist security effort as a mere Republican plot to embarrass FDR's New Deal—those people would never forgive Richard Nixon.

He continued dabbling in anti-communism. An internationalist abroad, he was cosponsor of the Nixon-Mundt Act, requiring registration of American communists, and he won both the Republican *and Democratic* nominations for Congress in 1948.

By 1950, Nixon was ready to move up. Two-term U.S. senator Sheridan Downey, a moderate-to-conservative Democrat, declined to seek re-election, and left-wing Beverly Hills congresswoman Helen Gahagan Douglas, a one-time Broadway actress as well as the wife of film actor Melvyn Douglas, emerged as the Democratic nominee. Nixon's campaign against Douglas, largely engineered by veteran Southern California political operative Murray Chotiner ("the only man Dick ever really listened to"), proved to be very much a rerun of the anti-PAC brickbats he had launched against Voorhis. Nixon likened Douglas's voting record to that of ultra-left-wing (many said communist) East Harlem congressman Vito Marcantonio ("Let's Look at the Record! You pick the Congressman the Kremlin Loves!") and derided her as the "Pink Lady." In return, Mrs. Douglas borrowed the phrase "Tricky Dick" from a *Los Angeles Independent Review* editorial writer and pinned it on Nixon—for life.

Numerous former Downey loyalists supported Nixon, as did that family of Eastern anti-communist Democrats, the Kennedys. One day Jack Kennedy strolled into Nixon's Washington office with an odd message: "Dick," he said, "I know you're in a pretty rough campaign, and my father wanted to help out. . . . I obviously can't endorse you, but it isn't going to break my heart if you can turn the Senate's loss into Hollywood's gain." Kennedy handed over a $1,000 contribution from his father. Tip O'Neill claimed that Joe Kennedy told him he had given Nixon $150,000.

Richard Nixon swamped Helen Gahagan Douglas for the Senate with a massive 59 percent of the vote—2,183,454 to 1,502,507.

"I was glad," JFK wrote to "Red" Fay, "to . . . see Nixon win by a big vote."

The year 1952 promised to be as great a Republican year as had 1946—particularly if General Dwight David Eisenhower led the party's ticket. Richard Nixon had always been anti-liberal, but never hardline conservative. His voting record had been moderate, anti-communist yet internationalist. Nominating Ohio senator Robert A. Taft, a colorless conservative isolationist, held no appeal for Richard Nixon. Neither did liberal California governor Earl Warren's favorite-son candidacy. Warren had, after all, refused to endorse Nixon over Voorhis, and Nixon repaid the favor, cagily undermining Warren by supporting Eisenhower's nomination. Before long, New York governor Thomas E. Dewey (still the moving force in the party's Eastern liberal wing—and now supporting Ike) had sounded out Nixon regarding the vice presidency. Nixon's success in the Hiss case, his cosponsorship of anti-communist legislation, and his tireless bashing of the faltering Truman administration, made him attractive—or, at least, acceptable—to conservatives. His youth and Washington experience balanced Eisenhower's age and absence of hands-on political experience (Ike had never even voted). His California roots (unpredictable Golden State voters had sunk Republican "sure things" in both 1916 and 1948; Tom Dewey was painfully aware of the latter circumstance) only added to the package. In the end, however, Ike did not choose Nixon. Party leaders convening in a suite at Chicago's Conrad Hilton Hotel did—with Tom Dewey first suggesting Nixon to them. And it was Robert Taft who first opposed him ("a little man in a big hurry . . . [with] a mean and vindictive streak in him which came to the surface when he couldn't get his way"). Taft's counsel carried little effect.

"That's fine by me," Ike replied blandly when informed of Nixon's selection—and Nixon it would be.

JFK, his own vice-presidential dreams yet to be dashed, differed—or at least *said* he differed—with Taft, dispatching this handwritten note:

> Dear Dick:
>   I was tremendously pleased that the convention selected you for V.P. I was always convinced that you would move ahead to the top—but I never thought it would come this quickly. You were an ideal selection and will bring to the ticket a great deal of strength.
>   Please give my best to your wife and all kinds of good luck to you.
> Cordially,
> Jack Kennedy

Besides youth and geographical balance, Richard Nixon brought something far more visceral to the campaign. "Eisenhower," Nixon would write, "also knew that to maintain his above-the-battle position he needed a running mate who was willing to engage in all-out combat, and who was good at it. In a sense, the hero needed a point man."

Or hatchet man.

Nixon eagerly battered the Truman record of "Communism, Corruption, and Korea." In Bangor, Maine, in early September 1952, he sounded his call: "If the dry rot of corruption and communism, which has eaten deep into our body politic during the past seven years, can only be chopped out with a hatchet, then let's call for a hatchet!"

It was Nixon, however, who soon found himself on the chopping block. Reports from California—amplified by sensational headlines ("Secret Rich Men's Trust Fund Keeps Nixon in Style Far Beyond His Salary") in the left-leaning *New York Post*—essentially accused him of being on the take, the pampered errand boy of special interests. In actuality, there was nothing to the story. The $18,235 fund described by the *Post* merely assisted in defraying Nixon's substantial campaign, office, and travel expenses between elections. Nonetheless, the tale quickly assumed a life of its own, moving from paper to paper and state to state, rattling Republicans still jittery over Dewey's 1948 debacle. If an opportunity existed to spectacularly blow an election, Republicans feared they would inevitably unearth it—and that they had in Richard Milhous Nixon.

Jittery or not, the GOP might normally have shrugged off such gossamer charges against its vice-presidential candidate, but neither the party's inner circle (Eisenhower campaign manager Sherman Adams, in particular, had little use for Nixon) nor Eisenhower himself possessed any substantial emotional attachment to Ike's yet-untested running mate—and the general never would develop any. Accordingly, a callous disregard for Nixon accompanied suspicion and panic in Republican leadership ranks, augmented by negative editorials in such influential papers as the *New York Herald Tribune* (the flagship paper for the Eastern GOP establishment) and the Democratic-leaning *Washington Post*. Nixon's fate hung by the thinnest of threads.

Tom Dewey, unsure of which way the political winds would ultimately blow, nonetheless phoned Nixon with sage advice: "I think you ought to go on television. I don't think Eisenhower *should* make this decision. Make the American people do it. At the conclusion of the program, ask people to wire their verdict in to you. You will probably get a million replies, and that will give you three or four days to think it over. At the end of that time, if it is 60 percent for you and 40 percent against . . . that is not enough of a majority. If it is 90 to 10, stay on. If you stay on, it isn't blamed on Ike, and if you get off it isn't blamed on Ike. All the fellows here in New York agree with me."

Republicans scraped together $75,000 for thirty minutes on sixty-four NBC television stations, 194 CBS radio outlets, and virtually all of the Mutual Broadcasting System's 560 radio stations. On Tuesday evening, September 23, 1952, Richard Nixon would issue his apologia to the American people. All the while, Eisenhower provided no support whatsoever for his young running mate. Just before midnight on September 21, they spoke by phone. Ike still failed to indicate what Nixon should do—or even what he, Ike, would do after Nixon's televised talk. "If my staying on the ticket would be harmful I will get off and take the heat," Nixon exploded, "but there comes a time to stop dawdling; once I have done this television program you ought to decide. There comes a time in matters like this when you've either got to shit or get off the pot."

Ike remained porcelain bound. Nixon remained angry and resentful. When Dewey asked Nixon what to tell party insiders regarding the content of Nixon's upcoming address, Nixon spat back, "Just tell them that I haven't the slightest idea as to what I am going to do and if they want to find out they'd better listen to the broadcast. And tell them I know something about politics too!" For good measure, he slammed the phone down on Dewey.

What the GOP leadership—along with fifty-eight million other Americans, the largest TV audience ever—saw broadcast from Hollywood's 750-seat El Capitan Theater was history's famous "Checkers Speech," an address as controversial decades later as it was in 1952. Nixon's critics deride it as bathetic, shameless, and manipulative. Nixon's defenders term it a dramatically gutsy tour de force by an innocent man fighting for survival. Whatever it was—and, perhaps, it was everything both critics and supporters said it was—it saved Dick Nixon's career.

In thirty minutes he laid bare his entire financial structure—his assets, his debts, his GI term life insurance policy, his 1950 Oldsmobile. It was not an impressive or lucrative balance sheet. He had certainly not enriched himself at the public trough, and he had not—"not one cent"—used the fund for personal expenses.

And with a dig at the Truman administration's mink coat–driven scandals, he added, "Pat and I have the satisfaction that every dime that we've got is honestly ours. I should say this—that Pat doesn't have a mink coat. But she does have a respectable Republican cloth coat. And I always tell her that she'd look good in anything."

Nixon revealed one gift his family *had* received: "It was a little cocker spaniel dog in a crate that he sent all the way from Texas. Black and white spotted. And our little girl—Trisha, the 6-year-old—named it Checkers. And you know they, like all kids, love the dog and I just want to say this right now, that regardless of what they say about it, we're gonna keep it."

He slogged forward, pointing to his humble origins, slapping back at Democratic national chairman Stephen A. Mitchell, who had stupidly jibed that anyone who could not afford it should not go into politics, and chided Adlai Stevenson (who clearly could afford to go into politics) on his own similar, but substantially larger, private expense fund. Finally, he concluded with a plea to voters for support, coupled with an obsequious plug for the man who had tortured him for the preceding five hellish days, far worse than Chairman Mitchell ever could—General of the Army Dwight David Eisenhower:

> I don't believe that I ought to quit, because I am not a quitter. . . . But the decision, my friends, is not mine. . . . Wire and write the Republican National Committee whether you think I should stay on or whether I should get off. And whatever their decision is, I will abide by it.
>
> But just let me say this last word: Regardless of what happens, I'm going to continue this fight. I'm going to campaign up and down in America until we drive the crooks and the Communists and those that defend them out of Washington. And remember folks, Eisenhower is a great man, believe me. He's a great man. And a vote for Eisenhower is a vote for what's good for America.

Nixon believed he had failed, sobbing when he had finished, but sobbing sympathetically with him was the TV crew around him—and the nation. "The telephone," Nixon television adviser Ted Rogers shouted to Nixon as he left the stage, "is lit up like a Christmas tree."

Mamie Eisenhower wept, too. Ike did not. "He was tapping the pad with his pencil," recalled one observer. "Twice he jabbed the pencil right into the pad, the second time so hard the lead broke. Before that, I'd always liked and admired Ike, of course, but I'd often wondered how smart he really was. After that, I knew—Ike got what Dick did was getting at right away, while the others were weeping and carrying on."

Dick Nixon had put Ike on the spot—and Ike didn't like it one bit.

At 9:57 the following evening, Nixon's DC-6B landed at Wheeling, West Virginia's Stifel Field. The general, who had waited an hour for his arrival, keenly aware that the public had rallied overwhelmingly to Nixon's defense, fairly ran to his now-vindicated running mate, reaching him before he even reached the tarmac. Nixon protested that that was not necessary. "Why not?" Eisenhower grinned, placing his arm about the running mate he had until now cruelly stiff-armed, as photographers' flashbulbs popped all about them. "You're my boy." He announced that Dick was staying on the ticket. Nixon gave a speech of his own, and when California senator William Knowland said simply, "That was a great speech, Dick," Nixon, emotionally drained and worn from stress, collapsed and burst into tears. Knowland put his arm around him, and Dick Nixon publicly wept on Big Bill Knowland's shoulder.

Funds and cocker spaniels behind them, the Eisenhower-Nixon ticket swept to victory, carrying virtually every state outside the old Confederacy (and Texas, Florida, Tennessee, and Virginia within the South), boosting the GOP to majority status in both the House and Senate.

Nixon continued as Ike's loyal battering ram. When the administration split with Joe McCarthy—and determined to break him—Nixon proved invaluable in isolating his fellow Red hunter from McCarthy's GOP natural allies. "When they finally decided to do McCarthy in," his former aide Roy Cohn bitterly recalled, "Nixon was the fellow they selected, and he was perfectly willing to turn on his conservative friends and cut their throats—one, two, three. . . . Nixon was a superb hatchet man."

Yet, despite Nixon's best, almost frantic, efforts (as when, in March 1954, he infuriated Democrats by asking, "And incidentally, in mentioning Secretary [John Foster] Dulles, isn't it wonderful finally to have a Secretary of State who isn't taken in by the Communists?"), the social and emotional gaps between president and vice president never diminished.

The Eisenhower-Nixon relationship was indeed a father-son rela-tionship, but hardly cheerful or sentimental. This son too eagerly coveted the family business, was too eager to prove his salt, too eager to imple-ment all manner of modern ideas. This father feared the son would only run everything into the ground. This son was an unloved or adopted stepson, deprived of praise, handed only the father's dirtiest, most unwanted jobs: "Take out the garbage, Dick! Sweep up the floor!"

"Eisenhower," revealed Dr. Hutschnecker, "was always telling Nixon to straighten his tie or pull back his shoulders, or speak up or shut up."

As 1956 approached, Eisenhower remained wary of retaining Nixon on the ticket, and was frantically seeking alternatives. Usually, his mind—and heart—settled on deputy secretary of defense (later his treasury sec-retary) Robert B. Anderson, a Texan and former Democrat. At one point Ike personally offered the job to Anderson, who refused, saying he was too recent a convert to sell to the Republican base. But there remained no shortage of other possibilities—or, at least, of *bad* possibilities, a crazy quilt of personalities, résumés, and ideologies revealing most of all Eisenhower's eagerness to dump his running mate.

Complicating everything, of course, was Ike's September 1955 heart attack. The fears it generated were only compounded by his June 1956 emergency operation for ileitis, a blockage in his lower intestine. Now, the vice presidency became ever more important. On December 26, 1955, Ike tendered Nixon a deal: If Dick abandoned the vice presidency, he could have any cabinet post he wanted save for treasury (being saved for Anderson) or state (Dulles's bailiwick). Although Ike argued that the move would ease a 1960 Nixon presidential run, Nixon wasn't buying it. He was no less gullible a few weeks later when Ike pitched his scheme again. Nixon's answer remained no. The story leaked to *Newsweek*, and Nixon could not rule out Ike himself as its source.

Dumping Nixon did possess some logic. He simply wasn't all *that* popular. In a February 1956 hypothetical Gallup poll Nixon-Stevenson match-up, Stevenson, hardly wildly popular himself, swamped Nixon by 59 percent to 41 percent.

As 1956's national convention approached, Eisenhower's special assis-tant for disarmament, Harold Stassen, organized a dump-Nixon move-ment. Ike again let Dick twist in the wind, and many suspected him of not merely tolerating Stassen's ploy but fomenting it. Nixon's torment was made all the worse by news from home in Southern California: Seventy-seven-year-old Frank Nixon, beset by severe abdominal disease, lay dying. Nixon, however, retained remarkably broad intra-party support, and remained on the ticket. That fall, Democratic nominee Adlai Stevenson bluntly warned that a GOP victory would "probably" make Richard Nixon "president of this country within the next four years." Voters ignored Stevenson's self-serving medical prognosis, re-electing the Eisenhower-Nixon ticket in a 57.4 percent to 42 percent landslide.

Richard Nixon—not Dwight Eisenhower—was now the presumptive GOP front-runner for 1960. Yet, there remained a hollowness in the man, in both policy and personality. You could expect to see Nixon earnestly advocating for one official position, then earnestly for its 180-degree reversal. He might argue for intervention in Indochina, and then, if Eisenhower failed to act, he would appear again, praising Ike's calm restraint. This Nixon, free from any great attachment to any issue (*National Review* publisher William A. Rusher once complained, "I do not doubt Nixon's anti-communism. I object to its shallowness"), was not a *leader of* the Republican Party, identified with any body of thought like Taft or McCarthy or Goldwater or Dewey or Warren, but rather the premier *lawyer for* Republican Party, Inc.

And, yet, how many of the premier politicians of that era proved much better, more principled? Perhaps a Taft or a Humphrey. Certainly not an LBJ careening from left to right to left again with each change of his constituencies. And certainly not JFK, who remarked, quite frankly and quite obviously, "We were interested not so much in the ideas of politics as in the mechanics of the whole thing." No, it wasn't Dick Nixon's ideological "flexibility" that separated him from his peers—it was his pronounced lack of charm in displaying that flexibility.

Conversely, it was not Jack Kennedy's ideological flexibility that separated him from the pack, but his uncanny, almost hypnotic magnetism in transcending issues, in propelling charisma to the fore. "Isn't it possible," marveled JFK's official 1952 campaign manager Mark Dalton, "that there is something in Jack's chemistry or personality that makes people transfer their own views to him?" Yes, there was—and Richard Nixon admired JFK for it. Conversely, JFK recognized reflections of his own opportunism—

stripped of its glamour and naked in its artlessless—the longer he observed Richard Nixon.

When Richard Nixon looked at Jack Kennedy he saw what he never could be—and envied JFK. When Jack Kennedy looked at Richard Nixon he saw what he had become—and loathed Dick Nixon for it.

"I think Nixon had a greater admiration for Kennedy than Kennedy had for Nixon," recalled George Smathers, who served with both men in Congress. "Nixon told me several times he admired Jack, and I happen to know the feeling was not particularly mutual. I don't think Jack ever thought too highly of Nixon, either of his ability or of him as a man of great strength of character. . . . He felt that Nixon was a total opportunist."

Personally, Richard Nixon seemed an unsettling unknown—a riddle wrapped in a mystery, inside a good Republican cloth coat. "The Vice-President," noted Ike's puzzled personal secretary Ann Whitman, "sometimes seems like a man who is acting like a nice man, rather than being one."

Even those most favorably disposed to him possessed their doubts. Journalist Ralph de Toledano had been a Nixon ally since the Hiss case. Yet when author Theodore H. White issued this hardly complimentary— indeed, disturbing—description of Richard Nixon, de Toledano praised it as "the most serious evaluation" of his man:

> Having made it on his own, he has had to learn to court people whom he has necessarily disliked. He has had to realize how vulnerable a naked man, without money or family prestige, can be in a hostile world that over and over savages him for no reason he can define. . . . A brooding, moody man, given to long stretches of introspection, he trusts only himself and his wife—and after that his confidence, in any given situation, is yielded only to the smallest possible number of people. . . . No other candidate [operated] with fewer personnel or kept more of the critical decisions in his own hands. Richard Nixon is a man of major talent—but a man of solitary, uncertain impulse.

Nixon had his weaknesses, but as the late 1950s ended, compared to Republican Party, Inc., he remained a tower of strength. By 1958 the GOP had plunged into a miasma of serious trouble. Recession, right-to-work controversies (most notably in California and Ohio), and Secretary of

Agriculture Ezra Taft Benson's farm policies all spelled hard times for the party—as did scandals surrounding Nixon nemesis and White House chief of staff Sherman Adams. Displaying his hands-off style, by now honed to perfection, Ike dawdled. Refusing to play the bad guy and boot out the now morally suspect Adams, Ike merely prolonged a public relations nightmare, gutting the GOP's already slim off-year chances.

With Eisenhower not willing (and physically hardly able) to stump for candidates, the job, as ever, fell to Nixon. "I was deluged by appeals . . . ," he recalled. "In the end, I took on the task because it had to be done, and there wasn't anyone else to do it."

The year 1958 proved a GOP disaster, among its worst ever. Republicans won only eight of twenty-one gubernatorial races. They lost forty-seven House and thirteen Senate seats. The House now featured a lopsided margin of 282 Democrats to 153 Republicans (the GOP vote total in House races had plummeted from 28,697,321 to 19,943,882). The formerly nearly evenly divided Senate now stood at 62 to 34 in favor of the Democrats.

As his party's most visible campaigner, Nixon received some of the blame. A June 1957 Gallup matchup found him just three points behind Jack Kennedy, 51 percent to 48 percent. A year later, he trailed JFK by 59 percent to 41 percent.

Republican national chairman Leonard W. Hall bluntly informed Nixon that if he were at all interested in the presidency, he had to decide immediately. Nixon asked about his chances. Hall, blunter still, rated newly elected New York governor Nelson Rockefeller ahead of Nixon, but projected that Rocky's advantage would soon evaporate once the realities of governing set in. Far more worrisome, warned the savvy Hall, were Nixon's general election chances—five to one against—but he still might persevere with hard work and a few breaks. Nixon's race would be a closely run thing at best, *but it could be won.*

Yes, it could, thought Nixon—but only if he could "persuade five to six million Democrats to . . . vote Republican." It was this audacious goal that would transform the newest New Nixon into something even more moderate in thought, word, and ideology than had ever existed previously. The tattered banner Richard Nixon retrieved from the field of battle was not that of Taft or McCarthy, but rather that of Eisenhower and Dewey and Lodge.

Ike, however, retained his normal skepticism, considering Nixon better than JFK, LBJ, or even Rockefeller, but worse than virtually anyone else in his governing circle. Ike still preferred Robert Anderson. "Boy, I'd like to fight for him in 1960!" he was quoted as saying, and he told Anderson point blank: "I'll quit what I'm doing, Bob. I'll raise money. I'll make speeches. I'll do *anything* to help."

In truth, Dwight Eisenhower hated politics—but loved power. His real preference was not Robert Anderson or anyone else in his inner circle; it was Dwight Eisenhower himself. "Those closest to him," Sherman Adams—and he was among those closest—would write, "believed Eisenhower might have even considered running for a third term if there had been no Constitutional prohibition against it."

Riding to the embattled Nixon's rescue were his own enemies. Previously, they had been domestic—whether the cocksure Alger Hiss or the headline writers at the *New York Post* or Harold Stassen—but in the late 1950s they stood on foreign soil, and they made Richard Nixon a star in his own right. In Caracas, Venezuela, in May 1958, an angry anti-American mob nearly tore the visiting Nixon's limousine apart. Nixon remained cool, unflappable, tough—a symbol of the American nation buffeted worldwide by hostile forces. At Moscow's Sokolniki Park in July 1959 he engaged in a forceful, finger-jabbing "kitchen debate" with bumptious Soviet dictator Nikita Khrushchev. From Hollywood, actor Ronald Reagan spoke for many, approvingly writing to Nixon that while in Moscow the vice president had conveyed to the Soviets "truths seldom if ever uttered in diplomatic exchanges."

Richard Nixon—the ultimate Lazarus of American politics—rose yet again from his sepulcher. Against both Democratic front-runners—Kennedy and Stevenson—he suddenly displayed remarkable resilience, as witnessed in the following Gallup poll numbers:

	NIXON	KENNEDY
May 1959	43%	57%
June 1959 (pre-Moscow)	39%	61%
August 1959 (post-Moscow)	48%	52%
September 1959	51%	49%
November 1959	53%	47%

	NIXON	STEVENSON
July 1959	44%	56%
August 1959 (pre-Moscow)	51%	49%
September 1959 (post-Moscow)	54%	46%
November 1959	56%	44%

It now appeared increasingly likely that 1960 would witness a clash between two men in their forties, both former congressmen and senators—Richard M. Nixon and John F. Kennedy.

★ ★ ★

Kennedy was a comet, blazing across our sky, his presidency flickering a mere thousand days, a career so fleeting that Adlai Stevenson bested him in the polls a mere eleven months before his election and Lee Harvey Oswald would best him a mere thirty months afterward.

John Kennedy was a comet, blazing across our sky.

Richard Nixon *was our sky* for five decades—a clouded, storm-tossed, often lighting-scarred firmament, but one that nonetheless endured beyond all frailties and against all odds.

Kennedy and Nixon had arrived in Congress together, so different in so many ways, but, at least at first, sharing a strange affinity for each other. They had already debated—in McKeesport, Pennsylvania, in 1947, a friendly little joust on labor relations with barely a hundred people present, and the two men flipping a coin for the upper berth on the ride back. It was Nixon who sponsored JFK's membership at the exclusive Burning Tree golf club in Bethesda, Maryland—and following JFK's dicey 1954 back surgery, he dissolved into tears upon learning that Kennedy might not survive. After JFK's May 1955 operation, Nixon dispatched an overflowing fruit basket.

Kennedy initially reciprocated Nixon's goodwill. "Nixon is a nice fellow in private, and a very able man," commented JFK privately. "I worked with him on the Hill for a long time, but it seems he has a split personality, and he is very bad in public, and nobody likes him."

And to a woman at a Washington dinner party who had bashed Nixon, thinking JFK would respond in kind, he instead retorted: "You have no idea what he has been through. Dick Nixon is the victim of the worst press that ever hit a politician in this country. What they did to him in the Helen Gahagan Douglas race was disgusting."

"Jack told me something I'll never forget," recalled *Chattanooga Times* Washington correspondent Charles Bartlett, a family friend. "Jack told me [at dinner on a New Year's eve as the election neared] that if the Democrats didn't give him the nomination, then he was going to vote for Nixon."

Politics being politics, however, JFK possessed no compunction against bashing Nixon publicly. In October 1958 he informed the Richmond Junior Chamber of Commerce, "When Mr. Eisenhower talks about the party of the future, he is talking about the party of Richard Nixon. And I cannot believe that the majority of American voters would want to entrust the future to Mr. Nixon."

★ ★ ★

In the end, Richard Nixon outraged liberals and left conservatives disappointed. The Right should have listened better. Nixon never really painted himself as a conservative, consistently describing himself as a Wilsonian—in other words, as a progressive. He cited as his idols not such chief executives as his friend and ally Herbert Hoover, or even the middle-ground Dwight Eisenhower, but progressives such as Woodrow Wilson and Theodore Roosevelt. As early as 1950 he had proposed a national federal pension. For the 1950s, he was surprisingly liberal on racial issues (an honorary NAACP member). As vice president he worked on establishing medical care for those over sixty-two, and on increasing federal aid to education. "The Vice President," noted blue-blooded estab-lishment Republican columnist Joseph Alsop approvingly, "is in fact a much less conservative man, or at least a much more pragmatic man, than the President."

Conservative unease festered. Meanwhile, liberal animus not only held steady; it expanded exponentially, frustrated by repeated failures to destroy liberalism's most hated enemy. "It seems to me unthinkable," Stevenson wrote to a friend, "that a man with his background of slander, abuse, innuendo, expediency and resort to all the most devious political devices should ever occupy an office which we have tried for generations to exalt in the esteem of young people and the world."

To Stevenson and Harry Truman and hosts of Nixon haters, Nixon really was that Herblock cartoon of him: slouched, squinting, and beetle browed, five o'clock shadowed, ski nosed like some malevolent Bob Hope, puffy jowled like some sinister chipmunk, clutching his dripping, rhetorical tar bucket, ever ready to smear those innocent liberals who dwelt in the Herblock universe—earnest, decent, upstanding men dumbstruck by calumny—and, despite their status and influence, the good families they sprang from, the better schools they attended, and the powerful institutions that employed them, all of whom were mysteriously incapable of defending themselves and mankind from the former assistant city attorney of Whittier, California.

Richard Nixon had his own discontents, of course. He would never have recognized it, but he was Eisenhower's Roy Cohn—dark featured, hard-hitting, smart as a whip, overwhelmingly ambitious, brilliantly cunning. And though he affected an air so mature, he was guilty of the offense calculated to raise more jealousy than any other.

He was so very young.

But he was also less than Cohn. For while Roy Marcus Cohn enjoyed Joe McCarthy's trust and respect, Richard Nixon could not claim Ike's. It grieved McCarthy greatly to finally toss Cohn overboard. Eisenhower would have shed no tears to jettison Nixon. Eisenhower would have golfed.

Nixon's critics' animosity never diminished. In fact, it grew and solidified. And his antipathy toward them burned molten red, glistened bright, and hardened solid and impenetrable like finished steel. His insecurities solidified as well. It was not just the Democrats and the Herblock cartoons, or Eisenhower and the men around him who could be thanked in part for that.

Buffeted by hostility, Nixon could have given up. Pat Nixon, increasingly unhappy in Washington (CBS News correspondent Robert Pierpont, who knew her from high school, was shocked by the change in her—"her tension, nervousness, and drawn appearance . . . she seemed so totally remote") certainly wanted him to. In 1952, as Nixon stood on the verge of his first national nomination, she compelled her husband to sign an agreement to leave politics in 1956, to return to Whittier and the law and a normal life. He signed it, but significantly he did not entrust it to her. Instead he folded it and stuck it in his wallet, and, until a helicopter swept them both off the South Lawn of the White House in 1974, he never honored it.

He did not give up because despite all the slights he knew he was good, knew he was smart and tough—just what the Republican Party, the nation, and indeed the world needed. He may not have received validation from Ike or the Eastern press, but he heard the cheers and the applause when he went out on the stump for the GOP. He knew what the party faithful wanted to hear, and he knew how to say it. They gave him the support he needed, and he stayed on.

Calvin Coolidge summed it up best. "The political mind," he once explained, "is the product of men in public life who have been twice spoiled. They have been spoiled with praise and they have been spoiled with abuse."

No political mind was ever spoiled worse than that of Richard Nixon.

FIVE

"Kicked in the head by a horse"

IN EVERY PRESIDENTIAL ELECTION, only one president is elected. In each party only a single nominee emerges—though innumerably more hopefuls fancy themselves both nominee *and* chief executive. The Democratic Party of 1960 contained any number of such grand men possessing such grand illusions.

There was, of course, the party's perennial reluctant warrior, the mid-century Hamlet of American politics, Adlai Stevenson. Would he run yet once again? And would the party's convention again stampede lemminglike behind his unique, but electorally poisonous, blend of erudition and indecision?

There were favorite sons, each dreaming gossamer dreams that lightning might strike and deliver unto them an unlikely nomination—if not for president, then, with cards played right, at least for the vice presidency, or a cabinet post. This favorite-son role was usually played by governors, and as 1960 approached, possible dusky equines in this category included Ohio's Mike DiSalle, California's Pat Brown, and New Jersey's Robert B. Meyner—not a likely (or even unlikely) president in the bunch. Both DiSalle and Brown suffered from the same handicap plaguing JFK—Catholicism—but without benefit of Kennedy cash, connections, and charisma. Meyner's handicap may have been even more damaging—*ex*-Catholicism.

Normally, however, at least one governor would be in *actual* play—often indeed capturing the big prize, or at least the nomination—a Stevenson, a Dewey, a Landon, a Roosevelt, a Dewey, a Wilson, a Smith. In 1958, however, two liberal gubernatorial favorites—New York's richer-than-Croesus W. Averell Harriman and Michigan's almost-as-rich G. Mennen "Soapy" Williams—had fallen by the wayside: Harriman in a landslide defeat to fellow multimillionaire Nelson Rockefeller, and the invariably green-bowtie-clad Williams barely surviving to win a sixth two-year term.

A goodly portion of Democratic leadership remained Southern white, too conservative and segregationist for national tastes. Like nineteen-century Boston Irish, "no Southerners need apply" for the top slot of the national ticket. The rule might yet prove flexible for individuals from the fringes of the old Confederacy (Tennessee's Estes Kefauver and Albert Gore Sr., or Texan LBJ—now conveniently posing as a cowboy-hat-wearing, ranch-owning Westerner, not a Southerner), but that was yet to be proven.

Chances were only marginally better for many senatorial liberals—such as Wisconsin's William Proxmire, Minnesota's Eugene McCarthy, Maine's Ed Muskie, Indiana's Vance Hartke, or Wyoming's Gale McGee. Most were too recently arrived in Washington and often too fractious to be considered for the brass ring. In any case, senators rarely made the jump from upper house to White House, the ill-remembered Ohio Republican Warren Harding being history's singular exception.

Such precedents, however, deterred neither Jack Kennedy nor Lyndon Johnson, nor a trio of their senatorial rivals—Minnesota's fifty-one-year-old Hubert Humphrey, Missouri's fifty-nine-year-old Stuart Symington, and Oregon's sixty-year-old Wayne Morse.

Morse's effort was clearly the most quixotic—but, then, everything about Morse seemed the most quixotic. Wispy mustached and bushy eye-browed, the mercurial left-winger possessed a face constructed by committee—the result resembling Walter Cronkite wearing the upper half of a Groucho mask. In 1944 Morse won election as a Republican to the U.S. Senate, and soon established a solid progressive—though often vituperative—record. "Mr. Morse could be a fiery, though prolix speaker," the *New York Times* would eventually note. "His long-windedness did not sting nearly so much as his epithets; but he considered his outspo-kenness a virtue."

He supported Dwight Eisenhower for the presidency, but when Ike selected Dick Nixon as his running mate, Morse, coveting the job for himself, snapped—announcing in October 1952 his support for Stevenson and his abandonment of the GOP to become a political inde-pendent. In January 1953 he arrived ostentatiously in the Senate chamber carrying a folding chair so he might easily relocate from the Republican to the Democratic side of the aisle. Majority Republicans kept Morse seated on their side of the chamber—but stripped him of all committee assignments. Re-elected in 1956, he formally switched to Democrat. His vitriol merely increased. In 1959, when Morse opposed Clare Boothe

Luce's nomination as ambassador to Brazil, the equally brash Luce, wife of *Time* publisher Henry Luce, retorted that her difficulties with her critic dated "back some years when Morse was kicked in the head by a horse."

September 1959 also saw Morse (acting largely from personal pique) tangling with JFK over Kennedy's efforts at comprehensive labor legislation. Morse, one of only two senators voting against JFK's final bill, filmed a twenty-eight-minute diatribe against Kennedy to be aired on Oregon television stations. Anti-Kennedy unions, primarily Jimmy Hoffa's Teamsters, ordered dozens of copies for nationwide broadcast.

Beyond excoriating JFK's labor record, Morse faulted what he termed his colleague's "highly reactionary voting record in the fields of agriculture, military and taxes." For good measure, he also lambasted other Democrats who dared to support Kennedy, calling them "phraseological liberals" and "gutless wonders."

His ambitions festered. In July 1959 Morse submitted an affidavit stating "I am not now and do not intend to become a candidate for the . . . nomination." A scant month later he was a favorite-son candidate, and before long was competing in other states.

"Half the time, Wayne claps me on the shoulder and congratulates me," a puzzled and somewhat bemused Jack Kennedy informed colleagues. "The other half, he denounces me as a traitor to liberalism and an enemy of the working class. It all reminds me of *City Lights* and the millionaire who, when he is drunk, loads Charlie Chaplin with gifts and insists that he spend the night, but, when he is sober, can't recognize him and throws him out of the house."

While the Democratic Party might relish Morse pillorying Richard Nixon or Clare Booth Luce, it had little stomach for his sabotage of its own most promising presidential hopefuls. Accordingly, when on January 23, 1960, the Democratic National Committee hosted a hundred-dollar-a-plate "presidential campaign kick-off dinner," it invited virtually every potential candidate it might imagine—JFK; LBJ; Senators Humphrey and Symington; Governors Williams, Brown, and Meyner; and even the famously reluctant Stevenson.

But it did not bother to invite Wayne Morse.

★ ★ ★

Missouri's Stuart Symington (Jack Kennedy's Georgetown neighbor—he lived just down N Street) certainly possessed less flair than Wayne Morse—but, then again, he possessed less flair than just about any other serious, or semiserious, candidate for the presidency.

Unlike 1960's other Democratic hopefuls, Yale graduate William Stuart Symington III had distinguished himself in the business world before entering the political sphere—as president of the Rustless Iron and Steel Corporation, manufacturers of stainless steel, and later as head of the St. Louis–based Emerson Electric Company, World War II's largest manufacturer of aircraft gun turrets.

In Harry Truman's administration, Symington served as the nation's first secretary of the air force and as head of the Reconstruction Finance Corporation. Elected to the Senate in 1952, he won notice battling Joe McCarthy on McCarthy's Investigations Subcommittee, earning McCarthy's opprobrium as "Sanctimonious Stu." Acquiring a national reputation as a forceful defense advocate and a critic of the nation's alleged "missile gap" ("He never talks about people—just people in rela-tion to missiles," jibed comic Mort Sahl), Symington won re-election in 1958 with 66.4 percent of the vote.

Symington was, like Warren Harding in 1920, the "available man"— presidential in mien, ready to serve if all other candidates failed, vaguely acceptable to all factions. As William S. White wrote in the July 1959 *Harper's*, Symington was "the most possible of all" nominees, but he was also a man lacking "any deep and abiding political philosophy, of the kind which at some point or another is found in most top politicians."

Jack Kennedy noted much the same thing. "[Symington]," he reflected, "comes from the right state, the right background, the right religion [Episcopalian], age and appearance, with a noncontroversial voting record and speaking largely on matters of defense which offend no one. His appeal is largely to the older-line professional politicians . . . and their hope is that the convention will find objections with each of the other candidates and agree on Symington."

As *Newsweek*'s Ben Bradlee recalled, JFK "liked Stuart Symington as a human being, and felt the . . . convention would most likely turn to Symington if they stopped him, but he stood in less than awe of his intel-lectual ability and said so often and bluntly to reporters."

Adlai Stevenson was the candidate of the old FDR crowd, Stuart Symington that of the remnants of Harry Truman's administration, starting with fellow Missourian Truman himself—with Truman fancying himself filling Symington's Senate term if he were elected.

Also on board for Symington were Truman's secretary of state, fellow Yale man Dean Acheson (he had originally preferred Johnson), former New York governor W. Averell Harriman, and key Truman adviser Clark Clifford. Clifford and Truman would prove more hindrance than help to their old associate, for, while Symington's sons, James and Stuart Jr., urged their father to enter the upcoming primaries, particularly those in the Midwest, both Truman and the supposedly brilliant campaign tactician Clifford (who largely took credit for Truman's 1948 whistle-stop strategy, though it appeared to be Jim Rowe's brainchild) counseled paralyzing caution. "Your strength is to be everybody's second choice," Clifford reassured Symington. "By not entering the primaries, you will be fresh and untouched."

While Symington dithered, his opponents boxed him in. Symington and Lyndon Johnson, two relative moderates, had been close until the late 1950s, when Johnson, cognizant of the Missourian's burgeoning ambitions, began sabotaging his Senate movements, most notably blocking Symington—a logical choice for the job—from chairing high-profile hearings into the space and air programs. "What Johnson did," Symington would recall, "was to bottle me up and to hamper me in the Senate every possible way he could."

Moreover, delegates Clifford and Symington—fancied as "available" at state conventions and in back rooms—were being rapidly scooped up by the Kennedys, as Symington aides discovered when they traveled to Wyoming in search of support and found that Teddy Kennedy had preceded them, charming natives with talk of buying a ranch there.

"Funny thing," the locals added, "he doesn't want any cows."

★ ★ ★

As 1960 approached, few observers extended Minnesota senator Hubert Humphrey's presidential ambitions much of a chance. He was too liberal, too voluble, and too deficient in funds to make much of a splash.

He would make a *great* splash.

The young Hubert Humphrey shared something with the young Lyndon Johnson—a family that had seen better days. Born on the South Dakota plains, Hubert Horatio Humphrey had witnessed his druggist father's business quite literally reduced to barter during the Great Depression, and the family home put up for sale to pay bills. "Childhood came to an end on the day that we sold that beautiful house," Hubert would recall.

A magna cum laude graduate of the University of Minnesota (supporting himself and wife Muriel by managing the apartment building in which they lived), he earned his master's degree at Louisiana State University, taught at the University of Minnesota and Macalester College, and served in FDR's Works Projects Administration's Workers Education Service and War Manpower Commission. In 1943, challenging Minneapolis's incumbent mayor, Humphrey lost by just 5,750 votes. The following year he managed FDR's Minnesota re-election effort (Roosevelt won the state), helped merge the state's rival Democratic and Farmer-Labor parties, and in 1945 did win for mayor—by 31,114 votes. Energetic, enthusiastic, and corruption busting, he established himself as an Upper Midwest edition of Fiorello LaGuardia. In 1947, Humphrey was re-elected by a record margin of 102,696 votes to 52,338.

At 1948's Democratic National Convention, Humphrey—who in Minneapolis had implemented the nation's first municipal fair employment practices commission—strenuously pushed for an unprecedentedly strong civil rights plank. So forcefully and so successfully did he campaign for civil rights that Southern delegates stormed out of the convention, sparking that year's Dixiecrat revolt, and further jeopardizing Harry Truman's already dubious election chances. Humphrey, however, did not endanger his own chances. That year he challenged the anti-union incumbent, U.S. senator Joseph Ball. Humphrey, just thirty-seven, swamped Ball by 729,494 votes to 485,801, capturing eighty-five of eighty-seven counties and becoming the first Democratic U.S. senator in Minnesota history.

After a rough start in the Senate—even some Northern liberals walked out during Humphrey's emotional February 1950 attack on Virginia's venerable conservative Democrat Harry Flood Byrd—the generally likable Humphrey settled into a working relationship with the rest of the Senate. Colleagues might disagree with Humphrey, but they respected his work ethic, his encyclopedic knowledge of the issues, and, yes, even his growing tact. "Be civilized," he learned to say. "Grudges are for Neanderthals."

In 1956, Humphrey dared launch his own vice-presidential bid (some said he was Stevenson's own preference), and by late 1958 Eleanor Roosevelt was on TV praising Humphrey as coming closest to possessing "the spark of greatness" that the next chief executive would require.

In an era increasingly devoid of oratory—and of passion—Humphrey exhibited both, often spectacularly. When Humphrey addressed University of Virginia law school students in 1959, JFK asked for a report from brother Teddy, then a UV student. Teddy remembered telling older brother Jack that he "had never heard anyone speak like Hubert Humphrey. He had a packed student audience, they were crawling all over the roof, and he just got standing ovation after standing ovation. That wasn't quite the answer [Jack] wanted to hear."

Yes, HHH could talk. When JFK and Humphrey had both addressed the UAW that October, JFK received mere polite response—the impassioned Humphrey, a twelve-minute ovation.

Humphrey, unlike Symington, exhibited little compunction about entering the primaries, threatening from the start to compete in the District of Columbia, Oregon, and Wisconsin, and possibly even in Nebraska and West Virginia.

But there was far more to the Humphrey campaign than met the eye—far more than merely an idealistic yet ambitious progressive grabbing for the brass ring. In 1960, though, Hubert Humphrey could have won every primary he entered and *still* not captured the nomination. Though he denied antipathy toward the South, white Southerners had not forgiven his adventures in 1948; they would not vote for him in the convention or in the general election. If Hubert Humphrey headed the ticket, the substantial swatches of Dixie that Eisenhower had captured in 1956 would remain Republican, while other states, such as the Carolinas, might easily tumble into the GOP column.

Beyond that, Humphrey lacked the sense *not* to talk about certain things in an election year. Perhaps it was his loquacity, perhaps something more. But, initiating his run, he spoke of raising taxes to correct "a series of problems that have been swept under the rug" during the Eisenhower administrations. That the top marginal tax rate already ran to 91 percent did not seem to faze him.

Hubert Humphrey could not win. In an October 1959 *Congressional Quarterly* poll he registered just 1 percent, down from a heady 2 percent that April. "I don't have to worry with Humphrey . . . ," JFK remarked to reporter Peter Lisagor. "[He] is dead."

Yet Humphrey ran, and otherwise levelheaded, hardheaded people supported him—including Washington types ordinarily having better use for their productive hours. But for them, it was not about Hubert Humphrey—it was all about stopping Jack Kennedy

"There were two Humphrey camps," recalled Joseph L. Rauh, the longtime liberal activist who had drafted Humphrey's 1948 civil rights plank. "One Humphrey camp was for Johnson and was 'Stop Kennedy,' and the other Humphrey camp was for Humphrey and against Johnson. We who were all for Humphrey a hundred percent . . . The others were really for Johnson with Humphrey taking the vice-presidency or whatever crumbs he could get. So the Humphrey camp was not one camp but two, and quite bitter and unpleasant. It wasn't a very happy time."

Prominent among those Johnson people composing the Humphrey camp was Jim Rowe, frustrated at LBJ's inability to flat-out declare for the presidency, but still hoping that Lyndon—if Hubert Humphrey held the fort for him long enough—might yet, by early July, fashion a majority at Los Angeles's upcoming national convention.

Morse, Symington, Humphrey, Johnson. It all added up to a surprisingly fractured, disorganized, and in many ways unappetizing menu of alternatives to Jack Kennedy's otherwise fatally damaging combination of inexperience, suspect liberalism, lack of proven convictions and accomplishments—and, of course, Catholicism.

Charm could carry one only so far—but against this quartet, it might yet carry one all the way.

SIX

"When Bobby hates you, you stay hated"

THE MORSES, Symingtons, Humphreys, and Johnsons faced tough opposition.

"What's $100 million," Joe Kennedy once confided, "if it will help Jack?" After all, as Joe Kennedy would say on numerous other occasions, "For the Kennedys, it is the castle or the outhouse—nothing in between."

If any Kennedy felt quite the same way as Joe Sr., it was the hard-bitten, demanding, often rude, but sometimes surprisingly sensitive Bobby.

Ten years Jack's junior, Robert Francis Kennedy trod much the same early path: elite private boarding schools; Harvard; a brief, albeit totally undistinguished, stint in the wartime Navy; and even a fleeting stab at journalism—he covered the 1948 Palestinian war and the 1951 San Francisco peace conference with Japan for John Fox's *Boston Post*. November 1951 saw RFK join the Justice Department, initially investigating internal security matters in Washington and later prosecuting fraud in Brooklyn—hardly qualifications to allow him to run his brother's uphill 1952 run against Henry Cabot Lodge. But Bobby had his brother's trust, a superhuman capacity for work, and a steely facility for playing bad cop to his elder brother's charming good-cop persona. JFK campaign aide Kenny O'Donnell had thought the 1952 campaign was headed toward an "absolute catastrophic disaster," until Bobby arrived. "Those politicians," RFK would recall, "just wanted to sit around and talk about it and have their pictures taken at the rallies. That's all they did." He went around the politicians, found workers, not talkers, and turned it around.

Jack's victory won, Bobby then found employment with the U.S. Senate, first for Joe McCarthy and soon afterward (some said aided by Joe's greasing Arkansas senator John McClellan's palm) for McCarthy's Democratic opponents on the Permanent Subcommittee on Investigations. RFK proved to be a tirelessly—and mercilessly—effective investigator. In 1956 RFK helped nail air force secretary Harold Talbott

61

on conflict-of-interest charges. He also made the case against Murray Chotiner, Richard Nixon's most effective (and abrasive) campaign operative, for his ethically suspect White House lobbying efforts—thus destroying Chotiner's viability within the Nixon camp.

In 1957 Bobby's main chance finally beckoned: the formation of John McClellan's Senate Select Committee on Improper Activities in the Labor or Management Field and its high-profile probe into the seamy, brutal realm of labor racketeering. It was not an easy assignment. Many northern Democrats were all too willing to turn a blind eye to big labor's often violent and corrupt shortcomings. Joe Kennedy fumed and shouted in opposition. Brother Jack expressed discomfort—but joined McClellan's committee when Washington State senator Henry "Scoop" Jackson (fearful of labor's wrath) resigned from the panel. Bobby oversaw a staff of more than a hundred, taking testimony from 1,525 sworn witnesses—of whom 343 hid behind the Fifth Amendment.

The resultant hearings—particularly Bobby's dramatic televised jousting with Teamster bosses Dave Beck and Jimmy Hoffa—helped make JFK's reputation, but more so cemented Bobby's growing public persona as an intractably fearless crusader for the public good. No shades of gray existed in the RFK palette where Jimmy Hoffa was concerned. "As Mr. Hoffa operates [the Teamsters]," RFK would write, "this is a conspiracy of evil."

To the rough-hewn Hoffa, the contest revolved as much around social class as around morality or legalities. "Here's a fella," Hoffa groused about his inquisitor's Palm Beach manner, "[who] thinks he's doing me a favor by talking to me. . . . It was as though he was asking, with my limited education, what right did I have to run a union like this?"

Bobby, being a Kennedy, capitalized on his experiences by issuing a critically acclaimed best seller on the topic, *The Enemy Within.* With a foreword by the ever helpful Arthur Krock, the book was strategically published in February 1960—and even more strategically issued in paperback that June.

Fame aside, Bobby still carried significant liabilities. First, he remained very much the little rich boy, careless concerning money and so pampered that each day his butler transported a wicker basket of food from Hickory Hill—RFK's six-acre, thirteen-bedroom, thirteen-bathroom estate in McLean, Virginia—to please his master's finicky palate.

And, of course, there was his temperament.

Once asked to reply to a British journalist's comment that her surly husband appeared "like a Sioux brave about to take a scalp," RFK's wife (and mother of his eleven children) Ethel responded with a touch of humor—and truth: "Why should I, since he generally is about to be?"

In 1956 Congressman Tip O'Neill, never an enthusiastic Robert Kennedy fan ("To me, he was simply a self-important-upstart and a know-it-all. To him, I was simply a street-corner pol"), stepped aside so Bobby might serve as a delegate to that year's Democratic National Convention. RFK exhibited no gratitude whatsoever. "Tip, let me tell you something," Joe Kennedy said to O'Neill. "Never expect any appreciation from my boys. These kids have had so much done for them by other people that they assume it's coming to them."

"That young man," Adlai Stevenson similarly complained, "never says please. He never says thank you, he never asks for things, he demands them."

"The first time I remember meeting Bob, in 1953," Ted Sorenson would note with nuanced understatement, "he had not yet developed the degree of patience and perspective which would later make him so valuable as a member of the Cabinet."

And RFK remained very much a fanatically loyal McCarthyite—if not to the crusade, at least to the crusader. When Joe McCarthy died in May 1957, a distraught Bobby shuttered his Senate office for an hour. "I want to do this," he wept. "It was the only time I had ever seen tears in his eyes," recalled Bobby's personal secretary. He attended McCarthy's funeral services, and not only in Washington—he also flew to remote Appleton, Wisconsin, to accompany the casket to the grave. He was enough in control of his emotions, however, to ask friendly reporters to omit reporting his presence. They did.

Where Bobby Kennedy traveled, his terrible temper and reputation for ruthlessness accompanied him. "I was at a fund-raiser for John Kennedy's campaign in Rhode Island," recalled JFK supporter Perry Gildes. "Bobby Kennedy was there, but he didn't so much as say thank you for the hundred thousand dollars we raised. His sole interest that night was trying to meet all the blondes he could find at the private beach club. Toward the end of the evening somebody called his father a Nazi and Bobby spat in the guy's face. Some diplomat!"

"You can trample all over [Jack] and the next day he's there for you with loving arms. But Bobby's my boy," boasted Joe to Tip O'Neill. "When Bobby hates you, you stay hated."

"Robert Kennedy," worried J. Edgar Hoover, "has got to be watched. He is a dangerous fellow."

It was inevitable that RFK would manage his brother's presidential efforts—would serve as Jack's hatchet man as Dick Nixon had served as Ike's—though Bobby enjoyed immensely more trust and authority. "Inside the campaign," wrote historian Arthur Schlesinger, a key member of the 1960 Kennedy team, "he was the tireless invigorator and goad, responsible for everything except the speeches. Outside, he became the man to do the harsh jobs, saying no, telling people off, whipping the reluctant and the recalcitrant into line."

Yet for all Bobby's bile there remained in him a strong, contradictory streak of gentleness, solicitude, even softness. "He was never unkind or inconsiderate of anybody who was down in the lower echelon," remembered JFK staffer (and later U.S. senator) Joseph Tydings.

RFK, added JFK campaign staffer Joan Braden, was "the most terrific man to work for that I've ever known. His decisions were made [clap] like that. You went in and you said, 'I would like to do boom, boom, boom, boom.' And he'd say, 'Do this, do this. Don't do this. And do this.' If he said 'No' and you wanted to do it, he would listen; and he might change, but he didn't want you to stay in there an hour and go over and over it."

"Bob could be tough and he was not the most gregarious man in politics," concluded key JFK campaign operative Larry O'Brien, "but he was unfailingly loyal to those who had been loyal to him—or to his brother."

"Jack was the tough one. Not Bobby," Kenny O'Donnell confided in 1964. "Jack would cut you off at the knees. Bobby would say, 'Why are we doing that to the guy?'"

RFK's occasional solicitude never, however, seemed to extend to Lyndon Johnson. They were so different, and they had never gotten along, dating from the days when Bobby would lunch at Joe McCarthy's table in the Senate cafeteria. LBJ would walk by and say hello, and RFK would just glare in response.

In the late fall of 1959, JFK dispatched Bobby to LBJ's Texas ranch to sound him out on a number of issues regarding the upcoming presidential election. Why JFK—a U.S. senator—did not directly approach his colleague (indeed, his superior), Johnson, is a question easily asked—and answered. Doing so would place the patrician John F. Kennedy and the cornpone Lyndon Johnson on an equal footing, and that would never do. JFK dispatched RFK, and Lyndon assured Bobby he would not be a presidential candidate, nor would he endorse a candidate, in 1960. Business adjourned, LBJ took RFK deer hunting—from the ease and safety of an elevated concrete platform. "This isn't hunting," chided RFK, "it's slaughter." RFK fired. The recoil sent him to the ground.

"Son," LBJ taunted, as he helped Bobby up, "you've got to learn to handle a gun like a man."

SEVEN

"I am not a candidate for the vice presidency of anything"

EVEN A FORCE AS PRIMAL as Robert F. Kennedy operated within the framework of the traditional electoral political system.

Not so Nelson Aldrich Rockefeller.

For while Dick Nixon had the Republican nomination all but locked up, Nelson Rockefeller—possessing a personal fortune and a personal ambition that made the Kennedys look modest in both regards—would still battle Nixon, and on his own terms. Though Rocky couldn't win, he could create havoc. Like some rogue nation or organization, oil rich and possessing a nuclear weapon or two, he couldn't triumph in a traditional armed conflict—but he did retain the capacity to detonate enough of your world to make life very uncomfortable.

And that was a big problem for Richard Nixon.

★ ★ ★

Nelson Rockefeller was, of course, most basically a Rockefeller—a name beside which *Kennedy* and even *Ford* and *Hearst* paled in comparison. Nelson's wizened paternal grandfather, John Davison Rockefeller—"John D." himself—had fashioned the grandest of the great monopolies. From humble beginnings, that sixteen-year-old Cleveland bookkeeper had created Standard Oil, which at one time sold 90 percent of the kerosene used in the United States, and, as late as 1911, 64 percent of its petroleum. John D.'s fortune—not including his personal properties and possessions—peaked in 1912 at $815,647,796.89.

Notwithstanding his donating hundreds of millions of dollars to charity ("Make all you can and give all you can"), America despised Rockefeller Sr. as a monopolist and robber baron. Worsening his reputation was the 1914 Ludlow Massacre of Standard Oil coal-mining employees (at least two women, twelve children, six miners and union officials, and one National Guardsman died—though many sources place the total far higher), although the tragedy accelerated the journey of his only son, John D. Rockefeller Jr., to political and social liberalism and to further increasing family philanthropy—all the while still amassing gargantuan sums from traditional family sources as well as from new ones, such as midtown Manhattan's twenty-two-acre, seventeen-million-square-foot Rockefeller Center.

John D. Jr.'s second son, Nelson, was also an Aldrich—his maternal grandfather being Rhode Island U.S. senator Nelson Wilmarth Aldrich. The Aldriches were certainly not poor, but Senator Aldrich's forte was great power, not immense wealth. A senator for thirty years, this longtime chair of the Senate Finance Committee and de facto leader of all Senate Republicans virtually dictated national tariff and economic policy. When Nelson Aldrich decided things should happen, they happened—the Payne-Aldrich Tariff of 1909, the federal income tax, the Federal Reserve System. It was from him, as much as from Standard Oil billions, that Nelson Aldrich Rockefeller impatiently assumed that his family—and more specifically *he*—was born to rule.

Nevertheless, Rockefeller's path to power initially seemed downright leisurely. A 1930 graduate of Dartmouth (dyslexia ruled out Harvard or Yale), he initially occupied himself in the family business, particularly at Rockefeller Center and in Venezuelan oil, and, less profitably, in founding and operating the Museum of Modern Art. His initial forays into government, while hardly entry-level civil service positions, were nonetheless hardly calculated to quickly springboard him to levels of power to which a Rockefeller might normally aspire: coordinator of inter-American affairs and assistant secretary of state for Latin American affairs under FDR; chairman of the Advisory Board on International Development (the Point Four Program) under Truman; and, finally, health, education, and welfare assistant secretary (at $17,500 a year) and special assistant for foreign affairs to Dwight Eisenhower. He enjoyed his successes—combating Axis influence in Latin America and planting the idea for Eisenhower's 1955 Open Skies program—but with his ego straining from a decade of playing second, or even third, fiddle in the Potomac symphony, he departed Washington in 1955, his eye on higher stakes and, ultimately, a properly grand return.

He focused first on the formulation of national policy debates. In the 1950s, Democrats and liberals, now removed from power, asked why. Finding themselves blameless and Republicans too pathetic to have much influence, the liberals identified a culprit in the nation itself. To 1950s intellectuals and academics, America had settled into a morass of dull list-lessness. The idealism of the New Deal had been elbowed aside by consumerism, and a plethora of books, articles, and, even movies obses-sively scrutinized the nation's supposedly advertising-driven economy. America, its social commentators diagnosed, required real goals and visions—to "get moving again" as Jack Kennedy would later phrase it. Nelson Rockefeller would help shape those goals, his Rockefeller Brothers Fund initiating, in 1955, a Special Studies Project to inform an America that was too preoccupied with tract housing, Zenith television sets, Swanson TV dinners, Chevys with fins, drip-dry suits, and room air-conditioning—when what it *should* be thinking about was the *big* issues.

The Special Studies Project was spearheaded by a blue-ribbon panel (*Time*'s Henry Luce, Notre Dame's Theodore Hesburgh, General Lucius Clay, Bell & Howell's young executive Charles Percy, NBC's Robert Sarnoff, the Rockefeller Foundation's Dean Rusk, Connecticut con-gressman Chester Bowles) handpicked by Rockefeller to imprint the proper gravitas upon the project. To do the actual work he hired dozens of staffers to research and actually compile its final product. Rocky's choice to act as honcho to this now largely forgotten effort was the German-born Harvard professor Henry Kissinger. Kissinger proved frac-tious regarding Rockefeller's tight oversight ("Why don't you tell Nelson," Kissinger snarled to a colleague, "that he's wasting his money buying Picassos? Why doesn't he get somebody to draw pictures and then get a bunch of housepainters, let them pick the colors and throw them at the board?") and quit five times. Rockefeller lured him back each time.

"He has a second-rate mind," Kissinger later observed, "but a first-rate intuition about people. I have a first-rate mind but a third-rate intu-ition about people."

"Because Nelson's never had to worry about money," recalled one associate on the eve of the 1960 race, "he has no real idea of its value. And he's just as extravagant with people as he is with money. He had some-thing like eighty people working for him in that [Truman administration] cold-war adviser's job . . . [but] there wasn't enough work for half a dozen. The budget and the bureaucracy would both get out of hand if he ever became President."

Thinking about big issues was all well and good if all one cared about was big issues, but Nelson Rockefeller also cared about returning to Washington to command all those other Ivy League–bred assistant secretaries and special presidential assistants. To accomplish that, he would have to detour north from Manhattan—to Albany.

New York's then-governor (elected by a scant margin of 11,125 votes in 1954) was fellow multimillionaire W. Averell Harriman, not the worst governor the Empire State had yet known, but politically simply abysmal. "He was a very fine gentleman," Nassau County Republican assemblyman Joseph Carlino would observe about the Democrat Harriman, "well bred with a tremendous background, but he didn't know shit from shinola about politics."

Proving Carlino correct, in July 1956 Harriman appointed Nelson Rockefeller to chair a temporary commission on a state constitutional convention. "Don't worry, Averell," Rocky assured Harriman, "I'll never run against you." Before long he had proceeded to replicate his Special Studies Project on the state level, furiously barnstorm New York, and host high-profile hearings highlighting the work of the temporary commission—and, of course, its selfless, public-spirited chairman.

Rockefeller had rebuffed entreaties to run for mayor in both 1953 and 1957, for governor in 1954, and for senator in 1956, but now his constitutional convention efforts caused observers to ponder whether Nelson Rockefeller might indeed compete for governor. For his part, Rockefeller approached former governor Tom Dewey regarding the possibility. "I think that's a poor idea, Nelson," Dewey demurred. "You're not well known enough." Then he added, somewhat enthusiastically, but oddly, "You know I think I could arrange to have you appointed postmaster of New York City!"

Rockefeller suspected he might do better, and an opportunity even presented itself for him to return to Washington—as undersecretary of defense, a position he might truly relish. But secretary of defense George Humphreys wanted no part of an ambitious spender such as Rockefeller, and vetoed the idea. Rocky's fight would have to be in New York.

A race for the governor's mansion held promise. The Empire State's manufacturing-based economy, reflective of the entire Northeast, had already begun its slide into oblivion; its cities, from New York City to Buffalo, displayed undeniable decay. Moreover, Harriman lacked charisma and eloquence—"A wooden speaker," as authors Walter Isaacson and Evan Thomas described him (and few thought otherwise), "graceless at small talk, and about as far removed from the common man as it is possible to be in a modern democracy."

"The deciding factor," noted an early Rockefeller biographer, "was [Rocky's] realization that probably never again would he have the opportunity of running against a man—Averell Harriman—whom the public thought as rich as Nelson Rockefeller."

To obtain the governorship, Harriman had aligned himself with Carmine De Sapio's resurgent but still corrupt Tammany Hall, even appointing the sinisterly sunglass-clad De Sapio (his eyesight made such eyewear necessary) as his secretary of state. Rockefeller would run primarily against this Tammany connection (and against Harriman's acquiescence in nominating Tammany's Frank Hogan for the U.S. Senate), rallying not only Republicans, but also reform-minded Democrats and independents.

First, however, Rockefeller needed to slide past whatever opposition resided within New York's Grand Old Party, primarily former national chairman Leonard Wood Hall. In 1957, as the glad-handing, balding, 225-pound Hall departed the RNC, President Dwight Eisenhower cooed, "If Len Hall is going to run for governor of New York, he is going to have one booster in me." But when Rocky entered the scene, Ike's backing for Hall evaporated. It proved the same in New York State itself. Rockefeller money, influence, organization, and drive carried the day—and the nomination.

But Rockefeller faced two great problems: Nineteen-fifty-eight looked to be a Democratic year—De Sapio predicted that Harriman would win by five hundred thousand votes—and Rockefeller seemed too wealthy a Republican ever to attain office. While New Yorkers didn't seem to mind millionaires in the governor's mansion—FDR, Herbert H. Lehman (of Wall Street's Lehman Brothers investment firm), and Harriman—they had all been Democrats. Republican officeholders—

even Grandpa Aldrich—tended to originate from more modest means. "Nelson Rockefeller!" said the experts, as one reform Manhattan Democratic leader recalled it. "Who's gonna vote for this rich guy? Most hated family name—most hated family in America."

Some suggested that Rockefeller—quite liberal in his own right, surrounded by Democratic advisers, a veteran of the New Deal and the Fair Deal—might find more comfort in a different party. "Nelson," advised former NBC president Sylvester "Pat" Weaver, a Dartmouth classmate, "there's one thing you should face right away. You should do exactly what all the other guys in your position have always done—Lehman, Franklin Roosevelt, Harriman. You should turn your back on your people, become a Democrat, and embrace the masses."

"I used to play tennis [in Washington] with [New Dealers Henry] Wallace and [Rexford] Tugwell," Rockefeller responded, "and I was also uncomfortable with their very leftish views. The way I saw it, if I became a Democrat, I'd always be in the position of holding the party back, whereas if I stayed a Republican, I'd be pushing the party forward."

He pushed forward in 1958 in a whirlwind campaign that was as energetic as Harriman's effort was sluggish. Rocky waded into crowds, waving wildly, calling out to strangers (a raspy "Hiya! Fella!" virtually became his trademark), riding subways, devouring knishes and pizza, traversing the upstate county fair circuit, speaking Spanish to East Harlem voters—all as if to his manner born. "He made crowds quiver," noted one eyewitness. "He demonstrated that vaunted, celebrated, feared Rockefeller personality which, like beauty in women, was both given and self-conceived."

Specters, however, haunted the Rockefeller campaign. The first was Nelson's wife, Mary Todhunter Clark Rockefeller, called "Tod," whose hatred and fear of campaigning made shy Jackie Kennedy seem like Eleanor Roosevelt, and whose personality had grown increasingly more brittle and her tongue more caustic over the years—a situation scarcely improved by her husband's numerous affairs. The second specter was Rockefeller's ties both to Dwight Eisenhower's administration— particularly onerous in the midst of a national recession—and to that bête noire of Manhattan liberalism, Richard Milhous Nixon. In Washington, Dick Nixon had been as close an ally as Nelson Rockefeller possessed, but

Rocky now pointedly avoided (at least for as long as he respectfully could) Nixon when, in late October 1958, the vice president campaigned upstate and on Long Island for GOP Senate aspirant Congressman Kenneth B. Keating.

But beyond pure campaign strategy, other feelings stirred in Nelson Rockefeller regarding Richard Nixon. If Rocky captured the governorship, he would then set sights on a higher goal in 1960, necessarily trampling Nixon to arrive there. "Honestly and truly," Nelson nevertheless declared, "all that I am interested in is becoming Governor."

Helping Rocky become governor was a bizarre incident late in the campaign's waning days. Averell Harriman, appearing on New York City radio station WMCA, intimated that Rockefeller and Standard Oil had somehow influenced the Eisenhower administration's policy during the 1956 Suez Crisis—and, by extension, policy toward the embattled state of Israel. *New York Post* publisher Dorothy Schiff had just endorsed Harriman, but, suddenly offended by Harriman's "vile demagoguery . . . such libels," she ensured that her tabloid's front page now frantically urged readers, "[D]o not vote for Averell Harriman."

Rockefeller won by 573,034 votes—and several dozen knishes.

★ ★ ★

Taking office, Rockefeller, one of only fourteen GOP governors nationwide, did two things: One, he raised taxes ($277 million worth), making skeptical national Republicans still warier of him. And, two, he started running for president anyway. He was not, he pronounced, sure he would indeed "spend the next four winters in Albany."

Rockefeller's shadow had already fallen across Nixon's path for many months. As Harold Stassen's 1956 machinations progressed, some people speculated that it might be Rockefeller—not Massachusetts's Christian Herter—who ultimately emerged as Nixon's replacement, perhaps even with Eisenhower's blessing. But such rumblings merely cemented the moderate Nixon's backing from the party's faltering conservative wing.

The pattern for a Rockefeller campaign had already revealed itself—massive publicity followed by an energetic flurry of appearances, all backed by the best (or, at least, the biggest and the most expensive) team money could buy.

A November 1958 Gallup poll showed Rocky, if not neck and neck with Nixon, at least displaying remarkable strength for someone who had not yet assumed any office: Nixon led by 51 percent to Rockefeller's 31 percent, with both at 29 percent among independents. Gallup also revealed Rockefeller rolling over Stevenson by 51 percent to 45 percent, winning independents by 58 percent to 27 percent, with Nixon losing 47 percent to 46 percent. Such numbers merely fueled Rockefeller's now-consuming ambitions ("I hate the thought of Dick Nixon being president of the United States") and also illustrated Nixon's weakness from being tarred with his party's massive debacle. "Most of us are not for Rockefeller," one Southern Republican confessed, "but we are getting skeptical of Nixon too."

And so Nelson Rockefeller began running for president—furiously but gingerly, making all the moves of a candidate: issuing policy statements, viewing with alarm, pointing with pride, traveling about the nation, tête-à-têteing with party chieftains and the rank and file—and yet, all the while, denying furiously that he coveted what he so obviously coveted.

Richard Nixon studiously remained aligned with Dwight Eisenhower's policies, whether agreeing with them or not. But Nelson Rockefeller, busy defining new national goals, exhibited no such compulsion, particularly concerning national defense. He sounded hawkishly more like free-spending Democrats Kennedy and Symington than Eisenhower or Nixon—or, at least, the private Nixon, for Nixon, too, possessed reservations about Ike's relatively parsimonious Pentagon spending. During a June 1960 session with GOP congressional leaders, Eisenhower suddenly departed to meet with the Peruvian prime minister. Nixon, temporarily free to speak his mind, advised, "What Rocky is saying about defense can have a big impact. We cannot allow this charge of weakness to stand. Not that the President's judgment is bad, but we just can't ignore Rocky's 'sitting duck' charge."

In August 1959 Rocky announced he *might* indeed run, soon pronouncing that he might compete "under certain circumstances"—pointedly adding "I am not a candidate for the vice presidency of anything." That fall he blitzed the West Coast. In November he embarked on a 5,636-mile trek through Indiana, Missouri, Minnesota, Wisconsin, Oklahoma, Texas, and Florida.

Time drew near for announcing—observers had long since concluded that a decision already *had* been reached—but the more Rockefeller traveled, and the more pollsters polled, the conclusions became inescapable. Shabby little Dick Nixon was not only holding his own against glamorous, exciting Nelson Rockefeller—with each day, he was *pulling away*.

The erosion started early and never quite reversed itself. By late 1959, even New Jersey, next door to Rocky's New York, favored Nixon by a lopsided 76 percent to 20 percent margin. Rockefeller publicly admitted that in the midst of his tours "perhaps 70 per cent" of the GOP workers supported Richard Nixon.

One powerful wild card remained: the nation's first real test of popular strength, the March 8, 1960, New Hampshire primary. In a small state, early in the process, Dartmouth graduate Rockefeller could deluge any opponent with stacks of cash and human waves of campaign professionals.

"Nixon spent a lot of time worrying about Rockefeller's challenge in the fall of 1959," recalled Nixon campaign aide Robert H. Finch ("the ablest man Nixon was to recruit for his labors," thought Teddy White), "and he got us to focus early on New Hampshire. By the time the Rockefeller people started . . . we had the delegates, we had a statewide organization headed by the Governor, we had the halls booked, we practically had the votes counted."

Rocky's failure was not by accident. One never stops a Rockefeller by pure chance or by allowing nature to simply run its course. His old adversary, the wily and indefatigable Leonard Hall, knew not only Rockefeller's foibles; he knew every Republican leader in the country worth a phone call. Most owed him favors and might require future favors from him. The result was that every door Nelson Rockefeller knocked on in 1959 remained shut in his face—barred with a smile and a pleasant tone, but shuttered nonetheless.

By October 1959 Rocky's poll numbers were abysmal, and, try as he might, he could not raise them:

GALLUP POLL—REPUBLICAN VOTERS' PREFERENCE

	Oct. 1959	Nov. 1959	Dec. 1959
Nixon	68%	67%	66%
Rockefeller	18%	19%	19%

To outside observers, however, the Rockefeller presidential machine seemed to crank sanguinely along. On Christmas Eve 1959, the Associated Press reported on its scope—seventy employees, comprising six divisions, filling two West Fifty-fourth Street townhouses, comparable "in size and scope with those formed on a national scale by the major parties after their nominating conventions." It certainly appeared—whatever the polls said—that Rocky was going all the way.

He wasn't.

As AP teletypes clattered, Rocky conferred at his private East Fifty-fifth Street offices with his closest political advisers. His latest tour had indeed proven so dismal that even while still embarked upon it he ordered staff to draft his withdrawal statement.

The only decision that remained was how it should read. Cheerily sportsmanlike? Blunt and bitter? In the end his principle speechwriter—Ike's old speechwriter, the liberal, former *Time* magazine writer Emmet John Hughes—trod a sullen middle ground. From New York's state capital on Saturday, December 26, Nelson Rockefeller jolted everyone by announcing: "The great majority of those who will control the Republican Convention stand opposed to any contest for the nomination. . . . [M]y conclusion, therefore, is that I am not and shall not be a candidate for nomination for the presidency. This decision is definite and final."

Democrats were gleeful, twitting the GOP, relieved they would not face Rockefeller's millions in the election to come. Generally, when a candidate withdraws and only one other contender remains viable, he endorses that candidate. Rocky didn't. No praise of Richard Nixon escaped his lips. Nor did any interest in the number two slot—"I shall not at any time entertain any thought of accepting nomination to the vice-presidency."

Nor, even more tellingly, did Rocky utter any refusal to accept a draft at June's Republican National Convention.

"The tone of [Rockefeller's] statement," noted *Time*, "was as eyebrow raising as his decision to back down. He skirted any pledge of support for . . . Nixon. . . . Rocky's statement indicated that he was ready to serve as a witness for the prosecution of the Eisenhower Administration. . . . As far as the Democrats were concerned, nothing became Rocky's candidacy like his leaving of it."

More than they even knew. His departure did little to cement party unity—but his absence from spring primaries and state conventions would shift the focus away from Richard Nixon and onto his Democratic rivals, depriving Nixon of badly needed publicity, sucking the air out of his campaign for the first half of the calendar year.

"The more I campaign," Rocky had smirked privately, "the more I put Nixon on the front pages and the better I make the party look in general."

Nixon's people phrased it less delicately. "We've just been kicked," one admitted, "in the groin."

EIGHT

"An independent merchant competing against a chain store"

NELSON ROCKEFELLER wasn't entering any primaries. Jack Kennedy was not about to enter them all.

JFK recognized that primaries were important—in fact crucial ("For fifty years no Republican or Democrat has reached the White House without entering and winning at least one contested primary")—but he knew they weren't the only game in town. Much remained to be said for state party conventions and, of course, the always remarkably efficacious backroom deal. Nevertheless, success in the primaries was critical to creating a popular bandwagon effect and to overcoming the nagging questions still surrounding JFK—his youth, his religion, his spotty legislative record, and his fuzziness on the issues.

Entering all sixteen primaries was mere foolishness, though. Challenging favorite sons might only alienate local Democrats, losing one delegates. Entering too many contests might spread one's resources too thin. Few states featured primaries worth even exploring, boiling down to New Hampshire (March 8), Wisconsin (April 5), Illinois (April 12), Pennsylvania (April 26), Ohio (May 3), Indiana (May 3), the District of Columbia (May 3), West Virginia (May 10), Nebraska (May 10), Maryland (May 17), Oregon (May 20), and California (July 1).

Symington and Johnson pursued their waiting game, entering none ("My chief competitors . . . remain safely on the sidelines, hoping to gain the nomination through manipulation"). Hubert Humphrey entered Wisconsin, the District of Columbia, South Dakota (unopposed), and West Virginia; Wayne Morse, the District of Columbia, Maryland, and his home state of Oregon. Meanwhile, John F. Kennedy cannily weighed his options. The big delegate prizes—Pennsylvania, Illinois, Ohio, and California—were not the big *primary* prizes. Pennsylvania's and Illinois's primaries were merely advisory. One might easily win headlines but alienate delegates in the process, for old-line bosses—such as Illinois's

Colonel Jacob M. Arvey and Chicago mayor Richard J. Daley, Pennsylvania governor David Lawrence (still pining for Stevenson), Philadelphia congressman Bill Green, and Pittsburgh mayor Joseph Barr (a Johnson man)—did not particularly relish being forcefully advised. They would take their time, weigh their options—and make their deals. And besides, as Jack Kennedy had "joked" to his dad, Pennsylvania and Illinois were *his* states. Joe Kennedy would know, in his own mysterious way, how to secure them.

Ohio and California were altogether different matters, both ruled by Democratic governors who under different circumstances might themselves contend. Ohio, after all, had been the "mother of presidents." California increasingly produced those who fancied themselves presidential timber—from Hiram Johnson to Earl Warren to Bill Knowland to Richard Nixon. Yet, neither Ohio's Michael V. DiSalle nor California's Edmund "Pat" Brown rose even to dark-horse level. Both were Catholic—and, if there were to be any Catholic nominee in 1960, it would be Jack Kennedy. Neither had held his office very long—both had been elected just two years previously. Neither the fifty-four-year-old, graying, bespectacled Brown nor the fifty-two-year-old, pudgy, five-foot-five DiSalle ("a man constructed like a mature pear," noted the *New York Times*) possessed anything even tangentially resembling the Kennedy glamour.

Nonetheless, frontal assaults on either state contained peril. California remained a Stevenson stronghold. In Ohio, DiSalle faced heavy pressure from his old mentor Harry Truman (HST had appointed him director of the Office of Price Stabilization) to support Stuart Symington.

Left to his own devices, DiSalle would have remained placidly aboard the Truman-Symington train, tying up his state's sixty-four delegates, the convention's fourth-largest total, via his own favorite-son candidacy. The Kennedys might have left DiSalle's Ohio alone, as they had Illinois and Pennsylvania, but, since Ohio might jump-start Symington's potentially dangerous campaign, they had to dynamite its delegates loose.

JFK could have directly confronted DiSalle in Ohio's May 3 primary, but that presented certain logistical problems. Mulling whether to enter Wisconsin's April 5 contest (highly Catholic Wisconsin allowed crossover voting; i.e., Catholic Republicans could jump party lines to vote for JFK),

Kennedy's forces would simply be spread far too thin if contesting Ohio and Wisconsin simultaneously. "It had to be one . . . or the other," Kenny O'Donnell would later confess. "[JFK] did not have the resources to run in both of them."

Mike DiSalle did not know that.

He knew, however, that the Kennedys were threatening to pour five million dollars into Ohio to seize the state's delegation by force, humiliate him in the process (they produced a Harris poll showing 63 percent of Ohio Jewish Democrats, 66 percent of Catholic Democrats, and 73 percent of Protestant Democrats for Kennedy), and ally themselves with DiSalle's Cuyahoga County–based rivals to kneecap his career. Elected largely by fluke in 1958's Democratic landslide, DiSalle recognized all too well that fortune might yet again turn its back upon him.

Just prior to JFK's January 2, 1960, formal announcement, DiSalle and JFK (registered under the aliases of Smith and Brown) along with RFK and Connecticut Democratic chair John M. Bailey, an early Kennedy loyalist, huddled secretly at a motel just beyond the Pittsburgh airport. Bobby was at his threatening best—or worst. "Bailey," Kenny O'Donnell would recall, "subsequently told me that Bobby was all over DiSalle, 'like a fly on shit.' He gave him a real tongue-lashing, and in the end DiSalle capitulated."

DiSalle endorsed JFK on Tuesday, January 5. He would remain on Ohio's ballot as a favorite son but dutifully surrender all delegates to JFK. As Wayne Morse indelicately, though not inaccurately, phrased it, Mike DiSalle had progressed from "favorite son to favorite stooge."

His eastern Midwestern flank secured, Kennedy now took his fight to Wisconsin. The decision remained difficult. Bobby Kennedy had argued long and hard against entering Wisconsin. Campaign aides Kenneth O'Donnell and Larry O'Brien, integral members of Kennedy's famed "Irish Mafia," shared RFK's concern, and even key JFK Wisconsin backer Mayor Ivan Nestigen of Madison calculated that Kennedy would fare better in Ohio. Nonetheless, JFK required primary victories—real victories in real contests—and with Kennedy private pollster Lou Harris giving JFK a healthy 63 percent of Wisconsin's vote, and slight leads in a minimum of eight of its ten congressional districts, JFK moved forward. "You've got to do it, Jack," his father had warned. "You've got no choice."

On Thursday, January 21, JFK announced he would compete for that state's twenty delegates, but before he faced Hubert Humphrey in Wisconsin, major news arrived from California.

The Brown-Kennedy relationship had hardly begun smoothly. In the spring of 1959, JFK had traveled to California and met privately with Brown. "Here's a fellow I never met before in my whole life," JFK fumed to aides Kenny O'Donnell and Dave Powers, "and I am sitting down to have breakfast with him, just the two of us in the room, and he looks at me and the first thing that comes out of his mouth is, 'I understand you've got Addison's Disease.'"

Brown had his own problems as 1960 opened, increasingly embattled as he was by controversy surrounding the long-delayed execution of convicted "Red Light Bandit" Caryl Chessman, and the larger issue of the death penalty. Brown was only too happy to avoid further controversy.

On Tuesday, January 19, Brown announced his own presidential candidacy, dodging whether he was a favorite son—and not endorsing Jack Kennedy. He also did not divulge his complicated agreement with JFK: If Kennedy arrived at July's Democratic National Convention having won New Hampshire, Wisconsin, and West Virginia, and finishing a respectable second to Wayne Morse in Oregon—*and* holding the delegate lead, Brown would throw his votes, presumably all of the Golden State's eighty-one delegates, to Kennedy.

This, of course, meant trusting Pat Brown to deliver. Trust isn't always the most solid commodity in politics, and Joe Kennedy urged his son to contest California anyway. JFK, with polls showing him trailing Brown in a direct confrontation, refused.

Brown's ability to deliver was hardly unproblematic. California's party faithful were among the most liberal nationwide. At February 13's convention of the California Democratic Council, Brown announced the names of the year's potential standard-bearers. LBJ was actually booed. JFK, the only candidate actually present, managed to receive more applause than Governors Soapy Williams and Robert Meyner, but that was about it, Kennedy being easily outdone by both Humphrey and Symington. However, applause and foot stomping for liberal icons Adlai Stevenson and Congressman Chester Bowles all but rocked the auditorium. Recruiting California's vociferous eggheads would not prove easy.

Meanwhile, Joe Kennedy continued to work his magic, despite his troubles in New Jersey, where his overtures to local bosses merely infuriated Bob Meyner, a remote in-law to Adlai Stevenson. Meyner's favorite-son bid—unlike DiSalle or Brown's—remained crankily independent, New Jersey's forty-three votes solidly outside the Kennedy column. New York went better for Kennedy. In New York, Joe not only ignored the party's reform wing; he conducted an additional end run against the supposed organization powers—state chairman Mike Prendergast and Tammany's Carmine De Sapio—concentrating his efforts on such old-time, old-line local bosses as Bronx congressman Charles A. Buckley, Brooklyn's Gene Keogh, Buffalo's Peter J. Crotty, and Albany's veteran party chieftain Daniel P. "Uncle Dan" O'Connell.

Negotiations were hands-on, practical, purely face-to-face—no Ivy League theorizing or posturing. The seventy-four-year-old O'Connell knew enough about Joe to regard him as "a bootlegger and a pimp," and, beyond that, he thought Joe Kennedy was kidding him about a forty-two-year-old becoming president. "I don't think this is the time for your boy to run . . . ," "Uncle Dan" informed JPK. "My advice to your boy, Jack, would be to wait until 1964."

"He is young," Joe countered, "but I'm seventy-two and I want to be around to enjoy it."

Joe Kennedy departed Albany with two and a half O'Connell delegates. Uncle Dan received a downtown Albany office building owned by Joe Kennedy to use—at a bargain rate—as his "new" county office building.

Preceding Wisconsin was the New Hampshire primary, but the Kennedys didn't see it as much of a contest. Nobody serious was reckless enough to challenge the "Senator from New England" in New England, though evidently it had crossed some minds. "Joe Kennedy has apparently sewed these up [votes] for Jack and there would be no point of coming in second-best," *Manchester Union-Leader's* publisher William Loeb, a Republican, told Stuart Symington, advising him to avoid the New Hampshire primary. "Especially when you can probably pick up these delegates after Jack fails to make it."

Only the non-serious dared face JFK in New Hampshire. These included the forty-seven-year-old TV cowboy singer Elton "The World's Highest Yodeler" Britt; the forty-six-year-old Chicago ballpoint pen manufacturer Paul C. Fisher, advocate of abolishing taxes on incomes under ten thousand dollars; and the forty-six-year-old perennial crackpot candidate Lar "America First" Daly, a Chicago bar-stool manufacturer who campaigned while wearing an Uncle Sam suit. On January 30, New Hampshire's secretary of state Harry E. Jackson ruled that Britt and Daly had too many dead and unregistered voters on their petitions to qualify. Kennedy's camp suspected Fisher of being yet another anti-JFK stalking horse (it seemed that everyone, save Lyndon Johnson, *had* to be). But, as it turned out, Fisher was merely a Chicago ballpoint pen manufacturer.

Any real excitement originated outside the party, when New Hampshire Republican governor Wesley Powell, Richard Nixon's state chairman, dared to allege that JFK was soft on communism. The charge fell flat. JFK, not particularly agitated by it, expressed hope that Nixon would repudiate Powell's charge. Nixon—the "New Nixon"—did.

New Hampshire's results surprised only by their magnitude. It was JFK's margin that astonished, vanquishing the unknown Fisher with 85 percent of the vote, 42,986 to 6,784, with a mere 375 write-ins for Stuart Symington. The New Hampshire Democratic primary's highest previous vote total was Estes Kefauver's 21,701 in 1956. No one had dared project JFK with more than 38,000 votes. He had exceeded all expectations.

Wisconsin was yet another matter. Hubert Humphrey was no Paul Fisher, and while Jack Kennedy was "New England's Senator," Hubert Humphrey's backers touted him as "Wisconsin's Third Senator." HHH did not have anywhere near the money, organization, or charisma Jack Kennedy possessed, but boasted a far more attractive farm record than JFK (Kennedy's lack of interest, even hostility, to Midwestern agriculture interests helped sink his 1956 vice-presidential bid). Humphrey's Minnesota home base was near enough to Wisconsin to enable his volunteers to don their overcoats, scrape off their windshields, and make it a fight.

And Kennedy badly needed a fight. Vanquishing ballpoint pen manufacturers proved nothing, and with Stuart Symington and Lyndon Johnson playing possum and Wayne Morse quite the joke, JFK, like a prizefighter aiming to transform himself from a club fighter to a contender, required a decent match. As his speechwriter Richard Goodwin would note:

[B]y taking on Kennedy, [Humphrey] transformed the primaries. . . . [W]ithout significant opposition, [Kennedy's] victories would have been meaningless. Against the formidable Humphrey, they were to be decisive.

One should not wonder that some candidates ignored the primaries of 1960 in the expectation that the convention would ultimately turn to them. Until 1960 no Democrat had ever won the nomination because of the primaries, although a few had been driven from the field by defeat. . . . The primaries were largely symbolic exercises, interesting but inconclusive tests of a candidate's skill and appeal. But that was just what John Kennedy needed: a symbol.

Though Kennedy would soon tout Wisconsin as a tough fight, a historic test of whether Americans might lay aside bigotry to elect—or at least again nominate—a Catholic for the presidency, his Wisconsin chances were, from the start, quite excellent. That meant it would not do to enter the first—and, quite possibly, the only—real contest of the primary season in "excellent" fashion and depart displaying mere mediocrity. Politics was a game, a game as much of expectations as of votes. So JFK, commencing Wisconsin's game with a projected 63 percent of the vote, now began playing the underdog.

While it was not the most genuine role to assume in Wisconsin, it was nevertheless far easier there than nationwide. In February 1960 a Gallup poll revealed not just that JFK was pulling away from the pack, but that each of his senatorial colleagues barely registered any support at all:

Kennedy	35%
Stevenson	23%
Johnson	13%
Humphrey	6%
Kefauver	6%
Symington	5%
Others	5%
None, No opinion	7%

There were, as there had been for a century, two Democratic parties—one Northern, one Southern. In the North, JFK commanded a hefty lead, followed by Adlai Stevenson:

Kennedy	37%
Stevenson	30%
Kefauver	6%
Symington	6%
Humphrey	5%
Johnson	5%
Brown	2%
Williams	2%
Meyner	2%
Others	1%
None, No opinion	4%

Adlai retained surprising Northern strength, but also a fatal flaw. For November, as ever, he looked like a bad bet—one that Democrats need not gamble on. Jack Kennedy exactly tied Richard Nixon, each with 50 percent. But Nixon walloped Stevenson 55 percent to 45 percent.

In the South, Lyndon Johnson held sway—more from geography and the unacceptable liberalism of his competition than anything else:

Johnson	35%
Kennedy	20%
Stevenson	18%
Kefauver	6%
Symington	4%
Humphrey	4%
Others	3%
None, No opinion	10%

Such overall data spelled significant trouble for Lyndon Johnson. His 5 percent showing outside the South was abysmal, behind even the lackluster Symington and dead even with the ultra-liberal, ultra-unfunded, unelectable Humphrey. Within LBJ's Southern stronghold, he gathered just 35 percent, equal to Kennedy's Northern total. But with JFK posting a solid 20 percent in Dixie, fate favored JFK over LBJ. One-on-one, the polls showed Kennedy defeating Adlai by 50 percent to 43 percent, and Lyndon by 48 percent to 32 percent.

JFK hoped to also demolish Humphrey, in part by flooding Wisconsin with Kennedy siblings, Kennedy spouses, and one (but definitely not both) Kennedy parents. "Bobby didn't want me to come," mother Rose would explain to clearly charmed Wisconsin audiences, "but here I am. Jack said I could." Nobody *ever* said Joe could come.

Twenty-eight-year-old Teddy Kennedy (barely out of law school, but already a veteran of Jack's 1958 re-election) came, too, appearing at Madison's Black Hawk Ski Club, cajoled by the locals into attempting his first ski jump—and it was no small one. "I went to the top of the 180-foot jump," Teddy, a veteran downhill and cross-country skier, would recall, "and watched the first three jumps. Then I heard the announcer say, 'And now at the top of the jump is Ted Kennedy, brother of Senator John F. Kennedy. Maybe if we give him a round of applause, he will make his first jump.' I wanted to get off the jump, take off my skis and go down the side, but if I did, I was afraid my brother would hear of it. And if he heard of it, I knew I would be back in Washington licking stamps and addressing envelopes for the rest of the campaign."

He was terrified. But he jumped.

Teddy was brave. Bobby was braver. Having left Eau Claire bound for some small town beyond nowhere, he and Chuck Spalding found their train snowbound. RFK plowed on on foot, through the drifts and gales, to a meeting hall where he would meet . . . practically no one. "I don't think that I could say enough to emphasize that aspect of Bobby," Spalding remembered, "Like somebody with a coat turned up, bareheaded . . . just driving from place to place. . . . You can't paint that picture too vividly. I haven't seen it matched by anybody in anything, in any other field. . . . He was searching this thing out for his brother, and he literally couldn't rest."

"They're all over the state, and they all look alike and sound alike," a frustrated Humphrey complained. "Teddy or Eunice talks to a crowd, wearing a raccoon coat and a stocking cap, and people think they're listening to Jack. I get reports that Jack is appearing in three or four different places at the same time."

Humphrey, hopeful of local labor support, found it sadly lacking, as JFK pointedly warned Wisconsin union leaders of the pitfalls of crossing a Kennedy. "I don't expect an endorsement from labor," he curtly informed the Milwaukee County Labor Council. "Neither do I expect them to endorse Humphrey. I sit on the Senate Labor Committee, and whether I win or lose, I will be in a position to work with you people." Labor got the message.

Further assisting Kennedy was logistical superiority. In September 1959 Joe Kennedy had purchased a $385,000 twin-engine Convair turbo-prop from his former mistress, Janet Des Rosiers (then a Convair employee). The *Caroline*, as the plane was renamed, would be leased to JFK's campaign at a bargain-basement $1.75 per mile. With Des Rosiers remaining on as flight attendant, the *Caroline* provided JFK with a virtually immeasurable advantage over opponents, saving not only time and money, but also a commodity as valuable as any in the campaign—the candidate's energy.

Such disadvantages unnerved Humphrey. Trying to get some sleep one night aboard his humble, uncomfortable campaign bus, he heard a plane flying overhead. Assuming the worst, he shouted, "Come down here, Jack, and play fair."

"I cannot win by competing in glamour or in public relations," he would complain. "The Kennedy forces are waging a psychological blitz that I cannot match. I'm not the candidate of the fat cats. . . . I feel like an independent merchant competing against a chain store."

But chain stores have problems, and so did Jack Kennedy. In unfamiliar Midwestern territory, he was shaking hands with farmers and small-town folks who often returned greetings with silent, cold stares. "So many people talk about the well-oiled Kennedy machine," reflected JFK associate Bill Walton, a former *Time* correspondent. "[Kennedy brother-in-law R. Sargent] Shriver gave me three counties to take care of and all he told me was, 'We'll send you plenty of material later on after you get started.' And the only other thing he gave me was the telephone number of a woman in Chicago who knew the area. That was it, the sum total of my political instructions. The well-oiled political machine!"

For Jack Kennedy, who only made campaigning *look* easy, it was, in fact, often anything but. An old woman approached him on a Wisconsin street. "You're too soon, my boy," she scolded, "too soon." Jack Kennedy, his mind never distant from Addison's disease and mortality, took her hand, smiled, and said quite earnestly and quite truthfully, "No, this is my time. My time is now."

Strange things might happen on Wisconsin thoroughfares. On St. Patrick's Day a drunk offered JFK a snort out of his bottle. "That might play well in certain parts of Boston," Kennedy confided to JFK press secretary Pierre Salinger, "but the *New York Times* wouldn't like it."

No, JFK did not enjoy physical contact with strangers, or with crowds, and when *Chicago Sun-Times* reporter Peter Lisagor asked if he liked "this sort of thing," he responded, "I hate it"—then he went out and did it again.

And he could be tough on himself. "My speech was dead," he complained up in Superior.

> I should have lifted it somehow. I think I'm primarily rational rather than emotional. I need more emotion in my speeches. But at least I've got a control over the subject matter and a confidence so that I can speak more and more off the cuff, and I know how much better that is than the prepared speech. Maybe when I get enough control and even more confidence, then I'll be able to make my speeches less declamatory and more emotional. We need more jokes, too, I know, and I'm always looking for them. Since we've broken up our ideas into sections, I now know these sections pretty well and so I can pretty easily piece them together into a speech aimed at the problems of a specific area. . . .
>
> Of course, when the campaign really starts, we'll have to get a lot more fresh material so the news guys can have fresh story leads to file. And I'll have to be more careful about the off-the-cuff stuff so that I get the essence of the press release in the speech, so that reporters don't get crossed up on filing stories about speeches that aren't said. I guess we keep learning all the time.

It had yet to be verified whether the younger Mrs. Kennedy, noted for reading General De Gaulle's memoirs in the original French during one Milwaukee motorcade, might prove an adept campaigner. *The Reporter*, while conceding her attractiveness, found her "looking slightly bewildered," and one could never predict when Jacqueline Bouvier Kennedy might answer a question as she did to one member of the press, regarding her preference for where 1960's Democratic National Convention might convene:

"Acapulco!"

Such humor, after all, might not resonate with a significant percentage of Eau Claire or Kenosha voters.

One evening the Kennedys were due at a Polish social hall outside Milwaukee, and, as was so often the case, the vaunted Kennedy juggernaut ran late. The PT-109 crew—Paul Fay and company—went into a stall. So, did Baltimore Colts fullback Alan "The Horse" Ameche (a Kenosha boy) and local congressman Clement J. Zablocki. The Kennedys arrived fifty minutes late, Jackie taking the stage first, apologizing in her breathy shyness. "We're terribly sorry to have kept you waiting so long when you've been so nice to come," she said. "With so much to do in a campaign, it's a wonder that more mistakes aren't made which inconvenience people who are so kind and thoughtful as to encourage the candidate."

Her words disarmed the impatient crowd.

"I have a great respect and affection for the Polish people," she continued, "besides my sister is married to a Pole"—and with that she concluded with "Poland will live forever"—*in Polish*—igniting frenzies of cheers and, yes, tears, for Poland had not enjoyed much life or freedom in the past quarter century and not much more in the century and a half before that.

"How would you like to try and follow that?" Jack Kennedy marveled to Paul Fay.

Jackie charmed the great bulk of Wisconsin Democrats. Her foray into the state, however, proved to be her undoing regarding further campaigning, for it was in Wisconsin, sometime in February, that she—for the fourth time in five years—conceived a child. At least temporarily, Jack's thoughts turned from polling demographics to those of a highly personal nature.

In Ashland, Wisconsin, Jack and Jackie had been awakened by JFK's brother-in-law Stephen Smith (husband of sister Jean). "While [Smith and JFK] were talking about the news stories and things like that," Jackie would recall, "I packed my bag and got dressed. Neither of us is very talkative so early in the morning, especially me, but I remember something in the car going to the airport in Ashland. I saw a crow and I told Jack we must see another crow, and I told him the jingle I learned as a little girl: 'One crow sorrow, two crows joy, three crows a girl, four a boy.' And you should have seen Jack looking to find four crows. I guess every man wants a boy. But that was a tender thing, I thought."

In the background—save, of course, when it assumed the foreground—was the religious issue. Wisconsin was 32 percent Catholic, the highest percentage in the Midwest, and the Kennedys often warned audiences, particularly in Catholic areas, of the dangers of bigotry. It was an issue Hubert Humphrey could not win and tried avoiding—though it exploded in his face when a "Square Deal for Humphrey Committee," under the chairmanship of state AFL-CIO political affairs director Charles M. Schultz, placed an ad in some 250 rural, weekly papers (total circulation: five hundred thousand) in the state, warning:

> Protestants: a leading pollster reports five out of six Catholics interviewed favor Kennedy over Humphrey, many of them normally Republican voters who say they would back Nixon against any Democrat but Kennedy. Should these Republican voters determine who the Democratic nominee should be? Let's give Humphrey a square deal.

Humphrey promptly repudiated the ad. The AFL-CIO censured Schultz.

The "Square Deal for Humphrey Committee" was sure providence for JFK. Sometimes, however, the Kennedys provided providence a hand. Such was the case when massive amounts of anti-Catholic, anti-Kennedy literature, postmarked Minnesota, started arriving in Wisconsin mailboxes. Such an event might normally be regarded as confirming JFK's oft-repeated warnings of anti-Catholic bigotry, save for one curious fact: The majority of said screeds were delivered to *Catholic* homes, in many cases even in care of the local Knights of Columbus hall. The culprit? Not Hubert Humphrey, but Bobby Kennedy's favorite, though least savory, operative—the ex-leftist, ex-McCarthyite Paul Corbin.

This was only the forty-six-year-old Corbin's most spectacular Wisconsin misdeed. Usually he confined himself to more mundane activities such as passing off veteran JFK loyalist Helen Keyes as a Protestant whenever voters questioned Jack Kennedy's religious qualifications to be president. "Well, this lady's a Baptist from Boston," Corbin would boom, "and she's for Kennedy."

"I kept expecting to be struck down by lightning," Keyes remembered, "for denying my faith."

Hubert Humphrey meanwhile was blundering into the religious issue himself—though not into its usual Catholic-Protestant parameters. On Tuesday, April 3, he spoke at Milwaukee's Jewish Community Center, and he was ranting: "They say the Humphrey campaign is disorganized—but I want you to know that the most organized thing that ever happened almost destroyed civilization." He was talking about the Holocaust. It was a clear swipe at old Joe Kennedy's isolationism and his anti-Semitism.

Humphrey spent only $116,500 in Wisconsin, while Joe Kennedy had already spent $1 million on JFK's campaign as far back as July 1959. But beyond the financial inequities, HHH's Wisconsin effort was marked by inefficiencies, confusion, and botched event planning. "Humphrey's [staffs]," a friend would recall, "were filled with starry-eyed idealists who were ready to change the world but who couldn't type more than forty words a minute or con a precinct boss."

Tempers frayed on both sides. As JFK returned to Washington for a key Senate vote, he erupted to staffers, "It's just one ——ing lie after another. First I'm some kind of a witch-hunter because I was in the hospital when that censure vote on McCarthy was taken. Then it's the money Dad gave to Nixon ten years ago. Hell, he's a businessman. He gave to everybody. Then it's Bobby out buying votes. Do you know how many voters there are in Wisconsin? I know we're rich, but not that rich. He talks about me, about my family, about my friends, the only thing he won't discuss are the issues. Son-of-a-bitch."

"We've got some pretty good stuff on Humphrey," a staffer interjected, "we could put it out. . . ." Suddenly, Kennedy's anger dissipated. He calculated the dangers such an approach might inflict. Annoying as they were, Humphrey's charges had so far failed to inflict any real damage, but JFK knew there were other charges one might level that could. It was no use declaring any wars that nobody—save for Lyndon Johnson or Adlai Stevenson or Richard Nixon—might win.

"I don't think so," JFK responded. "I'm winning this thing on my own terms, and if we start exchanging smears the whole campaign will become an issue of credibility. Whose lies do you believe? I'd rather have people make a judgment about who can lead the country, and who can win." He thought once more: "And if I'm wrong, there'll be other primaries. You better hold on to that stuff, just in case."

There were, however, few if any real issues in the Kennedy-Humphrey race. It was personality driven. Hubert Humphrey knew it—and knew it would be his downfall. Jack Kennedy knew it, too. Even Rose Kennedy knew it. "There weren't any essential points of disagreement between them . . . ," she would write, "except one: Who was going to be the Democratic nominee?"

In October 1959 Connecticut congressman Chester Bowles had signed on as JFK's foreign policy adviser, hoping to eventually emerge as JFK's secretary of state. Bowles had issued a caveat, however: He would not turn his back on either of his old liberal allies, Adlai Stevenson or Hubert Humphrey. But in Wisconsin (as everywhere), in the heat of the campaign every JFK man was expected to do his duty, and, in Bowles's case, that was to denigrate Hubert Humphrey. Bowles refused.

The Kennedy forces suspected not only that the congressman might be keeping options open if JFK crashed and burned, but also that he was holding yet another door ajar if a "draft Bowles" somehow erupted at the convention. None of these scenarios particularly ingratiated Bowles to the Kennedy team, particularly to Sargent Shriver, who was responsible for corralling votes in the liberal (and largely Protestant) Madison-centered Second Congressional District, or to Bobby Kennedy, who was occasionally known to forgive slights to himself—but never to brother Jack. Chester Bliss Bowles ("I was not really close to Kennedy") would never be secretary of state.

As primary day approached, Kennedy confidence grew. Governor Gaylord Nelson's press secretary Edwin Bayley (a JFK partisan) routinely and publicly predicted that JFK would carry all ten districts. JFK and Ben Bradlee recorded their predictions and placed them in an envelope. Bradlee guessed seven to three, Kennedy nine to one. Bobby Kennedy, publicly maintaining properly low-key expectations, nonetheless was overheard to crow, "It's in the bag." A CBS correspondent reported RFK's comment, infuriating Bobby, who accused the newsman of being a "Stevenson Jew." The latter remark, witnessed by the *New York Times*'s W. H. "Bill" Lawrence, was potentially damaging enough—and doubly so, considering Joe's anti-Semitic reputation—to sink the whole campaign. Jack made Bobby apologize. The incident was not reported.

JFK, meanwhile, was himself hardly the model of restraint. Supremely confident not just of defeating but of *crushing* his Minnesota colleague, he issued a pledge he assumed contained no actual peril, no chance of having to be redeemed. "If I am beaten," JFK assured reporters, "I am out." Humphrey, harboring no false illusions of victory, conversely assured reporters that he would slog on even in defeat. It was not a pledge he necessarily meant to keep.

On primary day, April 5, light snow and strong winds buffeted Milwaukee, though the rest of the state enjoyed relatively warm weather. Of Wisconsin's 2.3 million eligible voters residing in its ten congressional districts and 3,440 precincts, 1 million were expected to vote in either the Democratic or Republican primary, and with little action on the uncontested GOP side, that meant increased turnout on the Democratic front. In one ward, for example, in Wauwatosa, just northwest of Milwaukee, ninety Democrats voted in the primary's first hour compared to just fifteen in a local primary a month previously.

That evening, Kennedy received returns in his third-floor suite at Milwaukee's Hotel Phister, sipping chicken soup as the precinct returns came in. For a solid hour, Hubert Humphrey maintained a shaky, yet nonetheless real, lead. Eventually, JFK moved comfortably ahead, but considering his expectations—and everyone else's—his performance disappointed. He had carried but six of the state's ten congressional districts—the barest majority. He had marshaled thirty thousand volunteers in Milwaukee alone, but the 63 percent Lou Harris had posted for him in January had shrunk to just 56 percent—defeating HHH by 476,024 votes to 366,753. Kennedy's total was, indeed, the highest for any candidate in a Wisconsin primary in fifty-seven years, but it wasn't enough.

He had won Wisconsin's First District (a Catholic district assigned to

Sarge Shriver), the Fourth and Fifth (in Milwaukee and heavily Catholic), the Sixth and Eighth (Joe McCarthy's old stomping grounds and again heavily Catholic), and the Seventh (just barely). He lost the Second (Shriver's Madison-area district), and Third, Ninth, and Tenth Districts (the last three rural, and all four quite Protestant).

JFK had placed the religious issue at campaign center stage. He hoped winning Wisconsin (not particularly Protestant, not particularly anti-Catholic—after all, it had twice elected Joe McCarthy) would refute any innuendos that a Catholic could not be elected president. But these results—particularly with so many Catholic Republicans crossing over to vote for him—proved nothing.

Wisconsin, though JFK valiantly contended otherwise, was conclusively inconclusive.

"We carried Janesville, for instance, which is only 12 per cent Catholic," JFK argued to skeptical reporters. "I also believe the people had pretty much made up their minds before the religious issue came up." Lou Harris had caused much of the problem. His last poll had Kennedy within striking distance within the far-northern, Protestant Ninth and Tenth districts, but hopelessly trailing in the Second. Accordingly, Kennedy concentrated on the Superior area, wasting critical time. He lost both the Ninth and Tenth handily. Had he campaigned in Madison he might have recouped the Second District and carried the state's districts by seven to three. Had JFK captured seven districts, the underfunded Humphrey would have surrendered then and there.

Having failed to meet his—and their—expectations, Jack Kennedy now tried convincing the press that he was satisfied to win six districts, adding, "Anything else would be gravy."

They didn't buy it. "There was," the Associated Press jibed, "no gravy."

To a man on starvation rations, however, a Wisconsin bratwurst looks and tastes like filet mignon, and that is how 44 percent seemed to Hubert Humphrey. "I suppose numerically I'm the defeated candidate," he chirped, "but if I'm defeated I certainly don't hurt. In light of the predictions made, we have every reason to believe we did well."

"In the meeting in Humphrey's suite that night there was a question of whether to go on," Joe Rauh would recall. "We didn't have much money and so forth. But I guess everybody in the end was for going on figuring we'd recoup in West Virginia."

"What does it all mean, Johnny?" Eunice Kennedy Shriver asked her brother.

"It means," JFK answered, "that we have to do it all over again. We have to go through every one and win every one of them—West Virginia and Maryland and Indiana and Oregon, all the way to the convention."

NINE

"The rich man's Harold Stassen"

IF JACK KENNEDY now grasped exactly what he had to accomplish, Richard Nixon was no longer quite so sure.

Far from simplifying Dick Nixon's life, rival Nelson Rockefeller's impetuous exit merely compounded his ever-present uncertainties. Previously, Nixon had not known the identity of his ultimate Democratic opponent (although he hoped it would not be JFK), whether or when or how Dwight Eisenhower might ultimately deign to endorse him, and how closely he might safely hew to Ike's increasingly shaky record. Now, Nixon knew less than ever regarding what havoc Rocky might wreak upon him and the national party.

Shaky as well was Nixon's formal announcement, as he flung away any chance to proclaim any bold—or even merely safe and steady—vision. On Tuesday, January 9, 1960, Nixon's forty-seventh birthday, Nixon press chief Herb Klein merely informed reporters, while the vice president was en route to New York, that Richard Nixon had consented to having his name entered in the New Hampshire, Ohio, and Oregon primaries and, specifically, had telegraphed New Hampshire secretary of state Harry Jackson of his assent.

"This will be," pronounced Klein, "as formal an announcement as there will be."

Reporters demanded details. Klein offered none save that while Richard Nixon was no "reluctant" candidate, he possessed "no plans to be in any of these primary states—not even once—as a campaigning candidate."

Klein, his thankless task complete, concluded, "I see no necessity to make a formal announcement."

Others might have recognized some necessity—after all, Nelson Rockefeller retained his billions, his ambitions, and his antipathy toward the party's seemingly inevitable nominee. Arizona's Barry Goldwater certainly recognized the necessity of taking Rocky seriously. Just the previous day, as Goldwater had addressed the Manhattan Young Republicans, he dismissed

Rockefeller's withdrawal as more strategic than final. "Anyone who says he wouldn't run if it was offered is a darned liar," snorted the Arizonan.

At Washington's Sheraton-Park Hotel in late January, Rocky addressed a "Dinner with Ike" audience of 2,500, launching none-too-veiled shots at his party's chances for 1960, bolting from the dais and working the tables like a candidate—and pointedly omitting any reference to putative nominee Richard Nixon.

Such energy failed to impress New Hampshire voters, however. True to his word, Richard Nixon did not appear once in the state, but obtained a record 65,077 votes in the March 8 primary, surpassing Ike's 56,464-vote record set in 1956. Rockefeller's 2,890 write-ins barely exceeded Democratic ballpoint pen manufacturer Paul Fisher's 2,087-vote total.

Meanwhile, Ike continued to blunder toward finally endorsing his vice president. Having had many chances, he had walked away from each opportunity. He declined to endorse Nixon at a January 13 press conference. From Palm Springs (where he busied himself at golf) on January 31, reports circulated that no endorsement would materialize until summer. At a February 3 press conference, he not only refused to endorse Nixon ("There are a number of Republicans, eminent men, big men, that could fulfill the requirements of the position"); he promised nothing until the July convention, although—and here he held out a rare bone—he would be "not dissatisfied" if Nixon were nominated as expected.

Not until March 12—at Washington's exclusive Gridiron Club dinner—did Ike finally more or less endorse Nixon. His remarks, like all comments at each year's Gridiron affair, were to be off the record, but British reporters, not feeling bound by their American counterparts' ground rules, reported them anyway, generating banner headlines in two British dailies. Stateside, columnist Doris Fleeson (unhappily absent from the dinner, as the Gridiron barred women until 1974), published another report.

The cat was not about to be put back in the bag.

Four days later at a White House press conference, Ike responded to veteran Associated Press correspondent Merriman Smith's guarded inquiry with, "If anyone is wondering whether I have any personal preference or even bias with respect to the upcoming Presidential race, the answer is yes, very definitely"—*still not naming Nixon.*

Ike being Ike, there remained no actual mention of Nixon's name until the morning's fourth question, and no actual clarification of who Ike preferred until question six, when *Baltimore Sun* reporter William H. Y. Knight dared ask: "Mr. President, in answer to Mr. Smith's question, you used the word 'bias.' Were you also speaking there of Mr. Nixon?"

"Was there any doubt in your mind?" Ike laughed.

"No, sir," Knight responded.

"Alright," said Ike, and, that is how presidential endorsements found themselves extended in 1960. Only later did Eisenhower think to phone Nixon (in New York City for, among other matters, a charity event with fellow Republican Ethel Merman) to inform him of the backing that had been so long in coming.

Eisenhower was not the only veteran Nixon associate harboring doubts. Something about Richard Nixon just did not quite add up. He possessed intelligence, drive, and experience, but while virtually any politician's motives might be questioned, Nixon's seemed altogether too flexible. Observers wondered not whether he strayed too far from core principles, but if he had any at all.

Early in 1960, after Whitaker Chambers paid a rare visit to his old anti-communist ally, he found himself fearing that not only did Richard Nixon lack any compelling reason to seek the presidency—even his ambition seemed wearier, less intelligent and less visceral than it should have been—but Nixon's chances might prove as halting as the crusade itself. The depressed Chambers revealed his thoughts in this March 16, 1960, letter to *National Review* editor William F. Buckley Jr.:

I came away with a most unhappy feeling. . . . I suppose the sum of it was: we have really nothing to say to each other. While we talked, I felt crushed by the sense of the awful burden he was inviting in the office he wants. I felt dismay and a gnawing pity, which is pointless and presumptuous, since he seeks the office. He is asking to assume the first post of danger at the moment of the most fearful and (at least) semifinal stages of the transition from the older age to the new. If he were a great, vital man, bursting with energy, ideas (however malapropos), sweeping grasp of the crisis, and (even) intolerant convictions, I think I should have felt: Yes, he must have it, he must enact his fate, and ours. I did not have this feeling (I believe Ralph [de Toledano] has it). So I came away with unhappiness for him, for all. . . . Mr. Nixon may do wonders; he may astonish us (and himself), a new *stupor mundi* ["wonder of the world"]. Then I shall have proved the man who, privileged to see the future close up, was purblind. I hope so. I hope, too, that he gets his chance, since that is his wish. But I could not help wondering too: Suppose he misses it? I cannot imagine what such a defeat will do to him. Yet I cannot bring myself to believe that his victory is in the bag. In short: I believe he is the best there is; I am not sure that is enough, the odds being so great.

Stupor mundi or not, absent or not, in primary after primary, Nixon rolled along, gathering momentum as he went. Wisconsin proved less auspicious, however, than New Hampshire. With Catholic Republicans crossing over to support JFK, Nixon secured 339,383 votes—a total below Ike's in 1956 and far below the combined 577,000 votes won by Robert Taft and Earl Warren in 1952. In Massachusetts on April 26, with no names on the ballot and no one campaigning, he defeated Rockefeller by 86 percent to 7 percent. On the same day in Pennsylvania, with his the only name from either party on the ballot, he garnered 98 percent of the vote. His 954,205 votes exceeded Ike's 1956 total of 951,932.

On May 3 he demolished the Rockefeller stalking-horse former congressman and U.S. senator George H. Bender in the Ohio primary. Next door in Indiana he outpolled JFK 402,000 to 352,000. He rolled through Illinois on April 12 with 782,849 votes, besting Ike's 781,710 four years previously; Nebraska on May 10, defeating Rockefeller 74,000 to 2,000 in write-in efforts; Oregon on May 20, besting Rocky 162,547 to 2,176; and California, where he received 1,475,000 votes to Pat Brown's 1,327,000 in the Democratic contest. Nixon's home state totals had been augmented in part by design. The Los Angeles County Republican Committee, for example, warned Republicans that if Brown's totals exceeded Nixon's, "Khrushchev will interpret the vote as an indication that the administration's tough attitude toward Communism is not supported by the American people. And Chou En-lai will take it as the first step by the United States in the admission of Red China to the U.N."

But in a campaign season in which Republicans found no firm reason to leave home (even in Los Angeles), Richard Nixon had nonetheless scored remarkable, though completely ignored, totals. Not only had he soundly humiliated Nelson Rockefeller 4,360,000 to 26,000 and accumulated more votes than John F. Kennedy (1,850,000), he had won more primary votes than JFK, Brown, Humphrey (533,000), Morse (139,000), Stevenson (48,000), Symington (20,000), and LBJ (15,000) *put together* (3,932,000). And in his never-ending competition against his reluctant patron, Nixon had—last but not least—also exceeded Ike's 1956 total of 4,306,000 Republican primary voters.

It was, all in all, a good spring's work—and, had anyone noticed, compelling evidence that no matter what odds might be arrayed against him, nor how many wounds (self-inflicted and otherwise) he might endure, it remained pure wishful thinking ever to count Richard Nixon out.

Nelson Rockefeller remained imperiously oblivious of such overwhelming numbers. Ignoring four million Republicans not only failing to vote for him, but daring to vote for his clearly inferior competition, he also ignored poll numbers that were nearly as abysmal. He even ignored Dwight Eisenhower's tortured, halting endorsement of his rival.

All of which should have proven only mildly surprising, since Nelson Rockefeller tended to ignore even his own withdrawal. From the beginning, he had been unwilling to utter a single positive word regarding his party's odds-on nominee. Quite often he had revealed an inability to even utter Richard Nixon's *name*, as though by not deigning to mention his rival he could somehow deny his rival's legitimacy.

But providing a slight ruffle to Rocky's feathers were the recurring suggestions that he now settle for second place. They came from all sides—from GOP national chairman Senator Thruston B. Morton, from Tom Dewey, and from just about everywhere within GOP non-conservative factions. Each time, Rockefeller rebuffed them—as he did Morton's prognostication that Rockefeller would eventually campaign for Nixon. "When I have anything to say about my position . . . ," Rocky sniffed, "I shall say it myself."

By April, Rockefeller's angry silence ended. On April 13, a *Denver Post* editorial observed not only that "to win, Republicans must launch a draft for Nelson Rockefeller," but that Richard Nixon "simply does not impress people as being of presidential caliber." The latter, the *Post* charged, was something many Republicans were saying "in whispers."

The next day Rockefeller announced that, in the coming weeks, he would embark upon four out-of-state trips, including campaigning in two special congressional elections (a Pennsylvania House seat and a North Dakota Senate race) and major policy addresses at the University of Chicago and to Philadelphia's World Affairs Council.

Nixon fretted about such Rockefeller moves—and a sluggish economy. In March Dr. Arthur Burns, former chairman of Eisenhower's Council of Economic Advisers, warned the administration that the nation tottered upon the verge of yet another recession, its nadir due that October—just before Americans went to the polls. Recessions had hamstrung Republican chances in both 1954 and 1958, and Nixon begged for action. Eisenhower ignored him.

Rocky remained much on Nixon's mind as well. Able to deliver much-needed moderate or even liberal votes to the ticket, he might swing New York's shaky but critical forty-five electoral votes (by far the contest's biggest haul) into the GOP column. And while Rockefeller infuriated party right-wingers, few national figures expressed much concern regarding their displeasure. As Atlanta-based syndicated columnist Ralph McGill sneered, "Mr. Nixon does not really need them. They have no place to go."

And so Richard Nixon gingerly courted Nelson Rockefeller. On Wednesday, May 4, he arrived in New York to inspect preparations for that city's 1964–65 world's fair. "It is premature to talk of running mates," Nixon danced, "but I will say this: a number of party leaders, Republican leaders, believe that Governor Rockefeller has a very strong pull among voters generally and would add strength to the ticket." Rocky, Nixon continued, "certainly has all the qualities of national leadership."

The Republican National Committee offered Rockefeller another proposition—his choice of chairing or keynoting the upcoming convention. But Rocky wasn't interested in being keynoter or convention chairman—or vice president. His gruff response: He would not even attend.

But while Nixon straight-armed the Republican Right, Nelson Rockefeller gingerly courted it—or at least he courted the Eisenhower cabinet's most conservative member, agriculture secretary Ezra Taft

Benson. As Nixon's presidential ambitions grew more pronounced, his enthusiasm for the controversial free-market Benson slackened. Benson noticed, and when the liberal Rockefeller seemed more amenable to Benson, Benson proved more amenable than he logically should have been to Rockefeller. In late February 1960, this Republican odd couple, the Manhattan billionaire and the Utah proto-Bircher Mormon, secretly conferred at Rocky's West Fifty-fifth Street offices. While both conceded Rockefeller's chances for the nomination were slim, "both agreed, however," as Benson noted, "that the Vice President would have great difficulty . . . unless something occurred which would make it possible for him to pull out all the conservatives or else [draw] heavily from the independent and Democratic sectors of the electorate."

March saw Rockefeller continue courting the disaffected Benson. Benson (in contact with Goldwater and angling for a Rockefeller-Goldwater ticket—Goldwater never responded) urged the hardly shy Rocky to speak out on the issues. "Much as I like Barry," Rockefeller responded, "I would rather have Ezra Taft Benson as my running mate."

But whether Rockefeller displayed brashness or coyness, no matter how he maneuvered or how pundits speculated upon his possibilities, his actual popularity with the Republican rank and file refused to budge. A May 1960 Gallup poll showed him trailing Nixon 75 percent to 13 percent, and, worse yet, later that month Gallup gave the lie to Rocky's "Nixon can't win" argument, revealing Nixon with a competitive 51 percent to 49 percent versus JFK, but Rockefeller with a pathetic 57 percent to 43 percent.

Fate, however, soon handed Rocky the opportunity to position himself as an energetic, visionary champion riding to rescue the GOP from Ike and Dick's enervated clutches. On May 1, 1960, an American U-2 spy plane, piloted by CIA agent Francis Gary Powers, was brought down near Svedlovsk in the Soviet Union. A world-class liar himself, Soviet premier Nikita Khrushchev expected Ike to lie about the U-2 mission. Instead, a painfully embarrassed Eisenhower ("I would like to resign," he had confessed at one point to his secretary Ann Whitman) told the truth, infuriating Khrushchev even further.

Eisenhower refused Khrushchev's May 16 demand for an apology, and the upcoming Paris Summit, which included Ike, Khrushchev, France's Charles De Gaulle and Britain's Harold Macmillan, promptly collapsed. Neither Eisenhower nor Richard Nixon needed such embarrassment. Foreign policy seemed out of control, beyond American grasp, whether on the riot-torn streets of Caracas and Tokyo, in Fidel Castro's Cuba, amid the collapse of Syngman Rhee's South Korean government, or in the decline of American prestige and the concomitant growing Soviet influence in the emerging Third World.

Sensing opportunity, Nelson Rockefeller attacked on May 23, calling for a debate within the GOP. "It would be false and frivolous—and ultimately damaging to both nation and party—to dismiss criticism of specific American conduct as a peril to our national unity," he charged.

Two days later, Harold Stassen materialized to predict that Richard Nixon would, if nominated, carry but five states (Maine, Vermont, New Hampshire, Indiana, and Arizona) and to suggest nominating either Rockefeller, or Henry Cabot Lodge, or Robert Anderson instead. The same day, Rocky ("these are very fast-changing times") declared that not only would he now attend the GOP National Convention, but more significantly that he would accept a draft. But even he conceded that his chances seemed slim. Asked by reporters a day later if he considered Nixon "well trained" for the White House, he barked he didn't "know what you mean by qualified."

Dwight Eisenhower pondered multiple scenarios—on one level positing how to jump-start Nixon's invisible non-campaign, and on another speculating that leaking vice-presidential possibilities might divert attention from the far more compelling competition in the other party. In March, Ike wrote to broadcaster "Tex" McCrary, a longtime backer, suggesting a huge list of potential running mates for Nixon: Rockefeller, of course, but also Cabot Lodge (since 1953 Ike's ambassador to the United Nations); a quintet of cabinet members (attorney general William Rogers—perhaps Nixon's closest Washington associate—along with Treasury's Robert Anderson, Labor's Jim Mitchell, HEW's Arthur Flemming, and Interior's Fred Seaton); three moderate-to-liberal U.S. senators (Thruston Morton, Connecticut's Prescott Bush, and Pennsylvania's Hugh Scott); Bell & Howell's Chuck Percy; House minority leader Charles Halleck; Michigan congressman Gerald R. Ford; General Alfred Gruenther; and even former defense secretary (and former head of Proctor & Gamble) Neil McElroy.

On a more calculating plane, Ike wrote to former HEW secretary Oveta Culp Hobby in May, suggesting that she promote Bob Anderson as Texas's favorite son—and then he raised the notion of Hobby herself joining the fray. "How about a lady 'favorite son'?" Eisenhower asked, his mind churning with possibilities. "At least it will remind people that there are ladies who believe in moderate government, fiscal responsibility, and official and personal integrity." Hobby was not about to make history.

Nixon, meanwhile, kept his silence and monitored Rockefeller's activities. As Rocky stumped North Dakota for two days, Bob Finch dispatched an operative—thirty-five-year-old Seattle attorney John Ehrlichman—to track his every move. Ehrlichman's political experience was negligible. His connection to the campaign originated with his ties to Nixon's chief advance man, H. R. "Bob" Haldeman, Ehrlichman's UCLA classmate and fellow Christian Scientist.

To Ehrlichman, the thrill had vanished from practicing law in Seattle. Enlisting in Nixon's effort reminded him of a story his father had told him—of a stockbroker periodically joining the Ringling Bros. circus to work as a clown and escape his profession's pressures. "I was more and more the creature of my growing clientele, working long hours, evenings and weekends to represent their interests," recalled Ehrlichman. "I handled their problems well enough, and my income was substantial, but I was bored. . . . Bob Haldeman was suggesting that I run away to the circus for a little while, and it was irresistible."

Ehrlichman's mission proved largely superfluous. The Rockefeller welcoming committee was already honeycombed with Nixon supporters, all of whom might easily supply Finch with information. Nonetheless, Ehrlichman embarked for Fargo, eventually finding himself in a pompous local banker's living room, attending a Nelson Rockefeller reception with a very weary, very unenthusiastic Tod Rockefeller. "She stood alone in a corner," Ehrlichman recalled:

holding a drink, watching her husband with undisguised disapproval. He was grabbing shoulders, shaking hands and slapping backs, grinning broadly, thoroughly enjoying himself.

Mrs. Rockefeller and I turned away from him at the same time and looked at each other. She shook her head.

"Isn't this awful?" she asked.

The following morning Ehrlichman chauffeured in Rocky's Fargo-to-Bismark motorcade: "Oh, it was wonderful. The Rockefeller people thought I was from North Dakota, and the North Dakota people thought I was with Rockefeller. . . . I had decided before arriving in Fargo that I would not lie to anyone about my identity or what I was doing there, if I was directly asked. But no one asked."

On Wednesday, June 8, Rocky invited himself to breakfast at the White House. Six hours later he unleashed a two-thousand-word bombshell, a "call for plain talk" slamming GOP leadership in general and Richard Nixon more specifically:

> [T]hose now assuming control of the Republican Party have failed to make clear where this party is heading and where it proposes to lead the nation. . . .
>
> I know it is unconventional—on the political scene—to mention lack or lapses in one's own party. But the times we live in are not conventional. . . .
>
> In this spirit, I am compelled to say two things bluntly. One: I find it unreasonable—in these times—that the leading Republican candidate for the Presidential nomination has firmly insisted upon making known his program and his policies, not before, but only after nomination by his party. Two: I find it reasonable—and urgently necessary—that the new spokesmen of the Republican Party declare now, and not at some later date, precisely what they believe and what they propose, to meet the great matters before the nation. . . .
>
> I can no longer be silent on the fact. We cannot, as a nation or as a party, proceed—nor should anyone presume to ask us to proceed—to march to meet the future with a banner aloft whose only emblem is a question mark.

Dwight Eisenhower might not have greatly minded any barbs launched at his vice president, but he took powerful offense at those aimed at his defense policies. Rockefeller's call for an astronomical $3.5 billion hike—from $1.5 to $5 billion—in defense spending reminded Ike of constant Democratic harping on the subject, particularly for air force spending. At a January 1960 press conference, the *Manchester Union-*

Leader's Sarah McLendon asked if he was "kissing off" Democratic defense criticism. Ike visibly reddened. "I've spent my life on this," he shot back, "and I know more about it than almost anybody."

Privately, Ike displayed his own bluntness. "By getting into this numbers racket," he informed Republican leaders, "and by scaring people, they [Democrats like Symington and Kennedy] are getting away with murder. . . . [H]ow much deterrent could possibly be wanted by the critics? Did they just want to build more and more [Atlas missiles] for storage in warehouses? It was unconscionable."

"I suspect," he fumed, "that Nelson has been listening too closely to half-baked advisers." He also suspected, and quite rightly, that Rocky's broadside had originated from Ike's own former speechwriter, thirty-nine-year-old Emmet John Hughes, crafter of Eisenhower's "I shall go to Korea" speech. "I see," Ike remarked, "the fine hand of Emmet in this."

If Rockefeller had previously possessed any hopes of securing Eisenhower's pre-convention blessings, this stunt terminated them with extreme prejudice. "The tenor and substance of the statement deeply offended Eisenhower," admitted former Rockefeller speechwriter Joseph Persico. "Thus Nelson had turned a popular and beloved leader into a tacit but unforgiving opponent of his own presidential ambitions."

Nixon's response was to *invite* Rockefeller (challenge would be too strong a word—sons of gas station owners do not publicly challenge sons of Standard Oil's owner) to a televised joint discussion of the issues. Rockefeller refused, jibing that Nixon "does not need me to interrogate him on television. Once the vice president has made his position clear on the specific issues I have raised, I shall be glad to debate these issues with him."

There seemed no end to Rockefeller's nerve. The day after meeting—and later sandbagging—Ike, Rocky dared telephone the president to angle for at least a tacit endorsement, and to ask "whether or not he should be an avowed candidate." Two days later, Eisenhower, with Ann Whitman off to the side taking notes, phoned back and warned Rocky that if he ran he'd be termed an "off again, on again, gone again, Finnegan," a "lone wolfer—a [Robert] LaFollette." Ike also chided Rockefeller for his recent warnings on defense spending. Whitman recalled Ike saying that "he did not believe it was right to alarm people unnecessarily."

"He suggested," Whitman also recalled, "Nelson take his [New York] delegation to Chicago, if someone wants to propose his name on the floor fine—Nelson would have the opportunity to put facts before the convention. He was sure everybody would welcome that. The President said he thought Nelson's chances were very remote."

And, finally, while urging Rockefeller to support whoever secured the nomination, he reminded Rocky of something he very well knew—that if nominee Richard Nixon fell by the wayside in 1960, Nelson Rockefeller would occupy a strong position for 1964. It was hardly something Rockefeller needed reminding of—and nothing that might logically cause him to provide Richard Nixon with any aid.

From Texas that very day, Oveta Culp Hobby, Nelson's former boss at HEW, phoned Ike to commiserate regarding Rockefeller's blast, but also ominously added, "[T]he other one [Nixon] is not easy." Eisenhower, his normal ambivalence toward Nixon tempered by Rockefeller's antics, protested. "Dick is growing in stature daily," he said. Mrs. Hobby nonetheless warned that Nixon's partisanship was scaring the Lone Star State's numerous Democrats and independents. She wanted Ike to ask Nixon to refrain from constantly playing Mr. Republican. Ike passed on Hobby's comments, adding, "[P]ersonally I concur."

Rockefeller now released polls aimed at confirming his supposition that "Nixon can't win." Most specifically, he pointed out that in crucial New York, JFK would wallop Nixon 49 percent to 28 percent—and that a full 30 percent of 1956 New York Eisenhower voters would switch to JFK. It was all very self-serving stuff, and because Rockefeller had paid for the poll, no one, not even pundits who might normally extend him credence, or at least sympathy, bought into it.

Republicans were starting to lose patience. "I don't think these statements qualify him to be such a hot campaigner," pronounced the normally unflappable Thruston Morton. And Barry Goldwater jeered that Rockefeller is "the rich man's Harold Stassen."

But Republicans everywhere—not just Rocky—seemed ready to abandon the Eisenhower record. That June when Ike vetoed a federal pay hike, few Senate Republicans voted to sustain his action. "The President . . . ," noted White House assistant Bryce Harlow, "is at a loss . . . as to what Republicans really stand for. Fiscal integrity is the keystone to which all Republicans have adhered, [Ike] said, and he could hardly see how he could contend vigorously . . . that the Republican Party is the party of responsibility when the majority of the Republicans vote exactly the opposite."

Eisenhower said, sadly, that he had "the feeling [I] was being 'read out of the party.'"

Personally, Ike retained immense popular appeal. Politically, he *was* out of step. Fiscal conservatism appeared merely gauche among Republicans desperate to retain power in 1960. To his cabinet that month, Ike declaimed for a full half hour regarding the old virtues—fiscal restraint and self-reliance—that he thought lay at the heart of the Republican Party. When he concluded, Ezra Taft Benson exclaimed, "That's exactly the way I feel. Mr. President, that is exactly the way I feel also."

But even in a city crammed with yes men and sycophants, no one else— neither cabinet members nor vice president—extended a word of support.

Support was hard for everyone to come by. In late June, when the fifty-second annual Governors' Conference convened at Glacier Falls, Montana, eleven Republican governors signed a pledge supporting Richard Nixon. Nelson Rockefeller pointedly refused.

And when Nixon entreated Ike to cajole his former subordinate Rockefeller to deign to join a Nixon ticket, Ike demurred. "I don't see very well how I can get down on my knees to him." Eisenhower feared another Rockefeller sandbagging, suspecting that if he did ask, "Nelson would go out and tell it to the world."

"Nelson," he concluded, "has a terrible amount of personal ambition."

Still, the lure of a Nixon-Rockefeller dream ticket would not fade, and on Sunday, July 10, Ike phoned Republican National Committee executive secretary Dr. Gabriel Hague, the quintessential "modern Republican," and discussed the issue. Again Ike begged off approaching Rockefeller, though he offered a novel twist on the whole concept: "I told [Hague] that Nixon was the only man who might persuade Nelson to accept the nomination as Vice President. Dick could succeed by promising to take himself out of the political picture in 1964 and leave the field to Rockefeller should they be successful in 1960, I suggested, only half-seriously. Nelson might accept such a proposal, but of course I could not imagine anyone of Nixon's relative youth ever making it."

As Richard Nixon would say after the election, Ike "was far more complex and devious than most people realized."

Nor could an astute observer conceive of Nelson Rockefeller playing second fiddle to Richard Nixon, even for four years, even for a clear field to the nomination. Matters had simply progressed beyond rational calculation. Rockefeller, as Henry Kissinger would soon reveal to Arthur Schlesinger, simply "loathes Nixon."

And, even in politics, loathing sometimes trumps calculation.

JFK aboard the fabled, but ill-fated, PT-109. "[I]t was," his friends remember him confessing, "a question of whether they were going to give him a medal or throw him out." (JOHN F. KENNEDY LIBRARY)

JFK and Harry Truman in 1959. "I never liked Kennedy," Truman would fume in 1960. "I hate his father. Kennedy wasn't so great a Senator. . . . However, that no good son-of-a-bitch Dick Nixon called me a Communist and I'll do anything to beat him." (LBJ LIBRARY PHOTO BY FRANK MUTO)

The very pregnant Jackie Kennedy stood at her
husband's side on the day following his victory.
(COLLECTION OF THE AUTHOR)

Newsweek's Ben Bradlee (left),
his wife Antoinette "Tony"
(next to JFK), and the
Kennedys. Bradlee had gingerly asked JFK if he was afraid
of assuming the White House.
"Yes," Kennedy responded,
he was, "until I stop and look
around at the other people
who are running for the job.
And then I think I'm just as
qualified as they are."
(JOHN F. KENNEDY LIBRARY)

Rebel with a cause: Robert F. Kennedy. "Bob could be tough and he was not the most gregarious man in politics," concluded Larry O'Brien, "but he was unfailingly loyal to those who had been loyal to him—or to his brother." (COLLECTION OF THE AUTHOR)

top left:
JFK's sister Kathleen "Kick" Kennedy in 1943. The second of four Kennedy siblings to die young. (JOHN F. KENNEDY LIBRARY)

top right:
JFK's sister Patricia Lawford (circa 1948). She met her future husband, actor Peter Lawford, at the 1952 Republican convention. (JOHN F. KENNEDY LIBRARY)

left:
Rose Fitzgerald Kennedy in 1939.
"Tell me," she once mourned, "when are the nice people of Boston going to accept us?" (JOHN F. KENNEDY LIBRARY)

bottom:
The Kennedy family in Hyannis Port in 1948: Jack (looking not particularly congressional), Jean, Rose, Joseph, Patricia, Bobby, Eunice, and Ted (kneeling). Joe Jr. and Kathleen were already dead. Rosemary had been lobotomized. (JOHN F. KENNEDY LIBRARY)

Joseph Patrick Kennedy at work in his Boston bank in 1914. "The 1960 campaign was Joe's show entirely," said George Smathers, "yet he managed to organize it from behind the scenes. Because of his past record, he was forced to stay out of the limelight. But he called the shots, and you could sense his influence and imprint on many of Jack's ideas." (JOHN F. KENNEDY LIBRARY)

Lyndon Baines Johnson. He was, observed historian Robert Dallek, "a magnificent scoundrel, a self-serving altruist, a man of high ideals and no principle, a chameleon on plaid." (COLLECTION OF THE AUTHOR)

top:
Lady Bird Johnson at the U.S.
Capitol. (LBJ LIBRARY PHOTO
BY FRANK MUTO)

left:
LBJ and Lady Bird Johnson
at the Johnson ranch in 1959.
"Lyndon loved *people*,"
Lady Bird once explained.
"It would be unnatural for
him to withhold love from
half the people." (LBJ LIBRARY
PHOTO BY FRANK MUTO)

above:
Richard Nixon campaigning in 1960.
"Nixon is a nice fellow in private, and
a very able man," said JFK privately.
"I worked with him on the Hill for
a long time, but it seems he has a split
personality, and he is very bad in public,
and nobody likes him."
(COLLECTION OF THE AUTHOR)

left:
LBJ addresses the 1960 Democratic
National Convention. "I'm forty-three
years old," JFK had argued to Kenny
O'Donnell. "I'm not going to die in
office. So the vice presidency doesn't
mean anything." (LBJ LIBRARY)

left:
The Nixons—Pat, Tricia, Julie, and Richard. Asked what she most wished to see during the Republican convention, Tricia, parked alongside her sister in a Santa Barbara summer camp for a month, responded, "My parents." (COLLECTION OF THE AUTHOR)

below:
Richard Nixon and Dwight Eisenhower. "Goddammit," Ike would exclaim at the close of the 1960 campaign, "he looks like a loser to me!" (COLLECTION OF THE AUTHOR)

GOP literature from the 1952 Eisenhower-Nixon campaign. (COLLECTION OF THE AUTHOR)

THEY'RE SCRAPPERS

A **vote** for Ike and Dick is a vote **against** **Communism**

and besides—

THEY'RE REGULAR GUYS

A **vote** for Ike and Dick is a vote **for your own peace of mind**

What Senator Kennedy <u>really</u> thinks of Hubert Humphrey.

"The time has come to face the facts frankly about... Hubert Humphrey.

"First in Wisconsin, now in West Virginia, he has distorted my record, attacked my integrity and played fast and loose with smears and innuendos...

"He cannot win the nomination—he cannot win the election—he cannot be President of the United States. So why, you might ask, is he conducting a gutter campaign against me here in West Virginia? Why is he letting himself be used as a tool by the strangest collection of political bedfellows that has ever joined to gang-up on one candidate? And why should he ask West Virginians to waste their vote on him?"—*The White Sulphur Sentinel, (W. Virginia) May 4, 1960.*

POL. ADV.—Inserted by Committee for Political Consistency. Kermit Thiesse, Chairman, at regular advertising rates.

A GOP-sponsored ad in a Minnesota newspaper. The bitterness of the primaries came back to haunt Hubert Humphrey in the 1960 general election. (COLLECTION OF THE AUTHOR)

Hubert Humphrey—JFK's outgunned opponent in the key Wisconsin and West Virginia primaries. "I feel," Humphrey mourned, "like an independent merchant competing against a chain store." (COLLECTION OF THE AUTHOR)

U.S. senator Stuart Symington of Missouri, JFK's rival for the nomination. "You know damn well," Joe Alsop bluntly informed JFK, "that Stu Symington is too shallow a puddle for the United States to have to dive into." (COLLECTION OF THE AUTHOR)

New York governor Nelson A. Rockefeller. "I hate the thought," Rocky admitted, "of Dick Nixon being president." (COLLECTION OF THE AUTHOR)

Stuart Symington with Harry Truman. (COLLECTION OF THE AUTHOR)

Arizona senator Barry Goldwater. "When you compare Nixon and Goldwater," JFK confided, "Goldwater seems like Abraham Lincoln." (COLLECTION OF THE AUTHOR)

United Auto Workers counsel Arthur J. Goldberg. He helped smooth labor's ruffled feathers after LBJ's selection as VP. (JOHN F. KENNEDY LIBRARY)

Treasury secretary Robert B. Anderson (seen in 1953) was Dwight Eisenhower's first choice to succeed him. (COURTESY: U.S. NAVY DEPARTMENT)

Georgia conservative U.S. senator Richard Russell served as mentor to LBJ. (COLLECTION OF THE AUTHOR)

Oregon senator Wayne Morse. "Half the time, Wayne claps me on the shoulder and congratulates me," a puzzled, and somewhat bemused, Jack Kennedy informed colleagues; "the other half, he denounces me as a traitor to liberalism and an enemy of the working class." (COLLECTION OF THE AUTHOR)

California favorite-son governor Edmund G. "Pat" Brown. Brown, fumed RFK, was a "leaning tower of putty." (COLLECTION OF THE AUTHOR)

Heavily pressured Ohio favorite-son governor Mike DiSalle threw his delegates to JFK. DiSalle, sneered Wayne Morse, had progressed from "favorite son to favorite stooge." (COLLECTION OF THE AUTHOR)

W. Averell Harriman. "The deciding factor," noted an early Rockefeller biographer regarding Nelson Rockefeller's run against Harriman, "was [Rocky's] realization that probably never again would he have the opportunity of running against a man— Averell Harriman—whom the public thought as rich as Nelson Rockefeller." (COLLECTION OF THE AUTHOR)

West Virginia senator Robert Byrd, a former Klansman, opposed JFK in the West Virginia primary. "*Byrd*," fretted JFK, "is getting *meaner*." (COLLECTION OF THE AUTHOR)

Washington State's senator Henry "Scoop" Jackson was on JFK's vice-presidential short list, before ending up as Democratic national chairman. (COLLECTION OF THE AUTHOR)

JFK deputized Connecticut governor Abraham Ribicoff to make peace with fractious Harry Truman.
(COLLECTION OF THE AUTHOR)

"I've come to believe," Eleanor Roosevelt would finally admit, "Governor Stevenson may not have some of the characteristics I thought he had."
(COLLECTION OF THE AUTHOR)

The Kennedy family—Jack, Jackie, and Caroline—was not what it seemed. "If I don't get the nomination," JFK had informed Judith Campbell in his Georgetown bedroom after making love, "Jackie and I have arranged we will separate."
(COLLECTION OF THE AUTHOR)

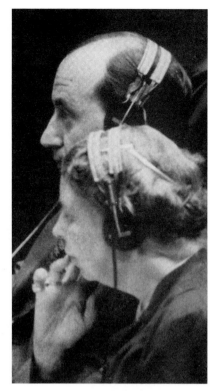

Special telecast today
3:00-3:30 PM on the CBS-TV Network
Mrs. John F. Kennedy *talks to*
Senator Kennedy *about the*
issues women want him to discuss
and **Henry Fonda** *joins Mrs. Kennedy to show*
us family snapshots, photos and home movies
featuring Caroline Kennedy
Today WHTN-TV—3:00-3:30 PM
Channel 13—Wed.-Nov. 2
Sponsored by Citizens for Kennedy-Johnson

An ad for a late campaign television appearance by Jackie and Caroline Kennedy and actor Henry Fonda. (COLLECTION OF THE AUTHOR)

Adlai Stevenson and Eleanor Roosevelt at the United Nations. (COLLECTION OF THE AUTHOR)

Joseph P. Kennedy and Herbert Hoover in 1949. (JOHN F. KENNEDY LIBRARY)

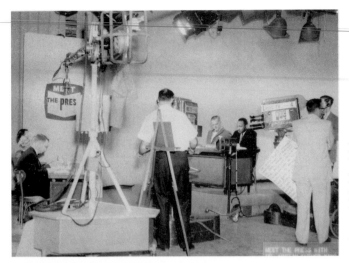

Martin Luther King on NBC's *Meet the Press*, April 1960. "If Richard Nixon is not sincere," King had once observed, "he is the most dangerous man in America."
(COLLECTION OF THE AUTHOR)

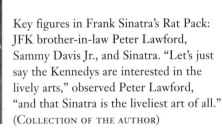

Key figures in Frank Sinatra's Rat Pack: JFK brother-in-law Peter Lawford, Sammy Davis Jr., and Sinatra. "Let's just say the Kennedys are interested in the lively arts," observed Peter Lawford, "and that Sinatra is the liveliest art of all."
(COLLECTION OF THE AUTHOR)

Key Nixon supporter Jackie Robinson (with the author). "Kennedy is not fit to be President . . . ," Robinson fumed. "Nixon doesn't deserve to win."
(COLLECTION OF THE AUTHOR)

"Committing a sin against God"

NELSON ROCKEFELLER'S POLLS—at least, those he paid for—
were quite positive.

And so were Jack Kennedy's in West Virginia.

JFK's decision to compete in the Mountain State was hardly hasty. Lou
Harris had polled the state nearly two years previously, in June 1958, even
prior to JFK's Senate re-election. By December 1959, Harris's data revealed
Jack Kennedy winning West Virginia 70 percent to 30 percent—stronger
numbers than JFK simultaneously displayed in Wisconsin (63 percent).

The evening of JFK's Wisconsin "victory," the *Caroline* whisked RFK,
Larry O'Brien, and Kenny O'Donnell (all quite hung over) to Charleston,
West Virginia, in anticipation of meeting local volunteers the following
morning at the city's rather faded Kanahwa Hotel. "What I would like,"
Bobby Kennedy bluntly began, "is to have a cold-blooded appraisal from
each one of you on whether we can win the State of West Virginia,
whether . . . these ministers will start telling people that they can't vote for
a Catholic because the Pope is coming over. . . . I want to go over,
county by county, as to what chances we have."

A man stood up. "There's only one problem," he blared. "He's a
Catholic. That's our God-damned problem!"

A torrent of shouts enveloped the room. Its message: Within the
week, the state's voting public—now suddenly aware of John Kennedy's
religion—had turned upon him with a fury.

"I looked at Bobby," O'Donnell recalled. "He seemed to be in a state
of shock. His face was as pale as ashes." RFK headed for the nearest pay
phone, to call Jack in Washington. Bobby begged JFK: Negotiate with the
threadbare, battle-weary Humphrey to secure his withdrawal. "It can't be
that bad," JFK pooh-poohed, reminding Bobby of his 70 percent Harris
rating. "The people who voted for you in that poll have just found out
that you're a Catholic," RFK retorted.

"Come back to Washington," JFK ordered, "and we'll see what we can do with Hubert."

Kenny O'Donnell phoned UAW chief Walter Reuther's assistant Jack Conway. Conway phoned Reuther. Reuther phoned Humphrey. So did Jim Rowe, Minnesota governor Orville Freeman (a year behind Hubert at the University of Minnesota), and New York State Liberal Party leader Alex Rose. But Humphrey, pressured by numerous Adlai Stevenson supporters—and most prominently by Lyndon Baines Johnson—hung tough.

Humphrey had not always been so determined. In January 1960 he had confided to British Labor Party chieftain Hugh Gaitskell that he harbored no actual hope of nomination and little hope beyond securing more than a couple hundred delegates and emerging as a "factor at the Democratic convention." Even then, HHH posited, his delegates would "probably" end up in Kennedy's grasp.

But that was before the charges started flying, before Humphrey's respectable Wisconsin showing, and before West Virginia Democrats remembered that they were Protestant and Jack Kennedy was Catholic. Lou Harris now called the Mountain State 60 percent to 40 percent for Humphrey.

Nationwide, however, Minnesota's "Happy Warrior" remained mired in single digits. But while JFK still led the pack, he was far from attaining majority Democrat support. March's Gallup poll revealed:

Kennedy	34%
Stevenson	23%
Johnson	15%
Symington	6%
Humphrey	5%

Such numbers encouraged Humphrey, Johnson, and Symington—and, yes, even non-candidate Stevenson. The numbers told them to hold firm, to wait for the Kennedy cavalcade to hit the wall of Catholicism, youth, or immaturity—and, hopefully, the wall of insufficient first-ballot delegates.

But between Wisconsin on April 5 and West Virginia on May 10, JFK faced a string of lackluster but largely uncontested, lower-tier primaries—

Illinois (April 12), New Jersey (April 19), Pennsylvania and Massachusetts (April 26), Indiana and the District of Columbia (May 3), and Nebraska (May 10). And while few observers paid much attention to the results of these contests, they demonstrated two salient points: one, the difficulty of defeating John F. Kennedy without your name on the ballot against him; and, two, the difficulty of defeating him even if *his name* wasn't on the ballot.

Many of these contests were write-in or purely advisory (as was West Virginia, for that matter). In April 12's Illinois vote, Kennedy, with 34,332 write-ins (65 percent) defeated Illinois's own Adlai Stevenson (15 percent), Symington (11 percent), Humphrey (8 percent), and Johnson (less than 1 percent—an infinitesimal 442 votes).

New Jersey's contest proved nearly devoid of any interest, save that the state's forty-one votes would—at least through the first ballot—remain in the iron grasp of favorite-son governor Robert Meyner.

The two primaries on April 26 proved remarkably dissimilar. Massachusetts could not even be classified as JFK's to lose—it was just his, period. With no names on the ballot and no candidates campaigning, he walked away with 92 percent of the vote.

Pennsylvania proved very different. The state's longtime Democratic state chairman, seventy-year-old governor David L. Lawrence, was both Catholic and a staunch Stevenson man. He was also, unlike Mike DiSalle and Pat Brown, a man *not* to be trifled with. Accordingly, *no* Democrat was about to enter the state's primaries. Keystone State delegates would have to be negotiated for, not won. To complicate matters, Lawrence—the state's first Catholic chief executive—was wary both of any Catholic presidential bid and of JFK's "personal problems." Nevertheless, a JFK write-in campaign—neither encouraged nor aided by the skittish Kennedy camp—emerged. "We wanted no pro-Kennedy write-in movement that could be interpreted as an effort by us to put pressure on Lawrence and [Philadelphia congressman Bill] Green," noted Larry O'Brien. "All of Kennedy's political operatives were given strict orders not to set foot in Pennsylvania."

Even so, Pennsylvania's Kennedy boomlet proved unstoppable. On primary day, 183,073 voters wrote in Jack Kennedy, giving him 71 percent of the vote. Adlai Stevenson finished far back, with just 12 percent.

"I called [JFK]," O'Brien recalled, "and woke him up to give him the first returns and we were both surprised and thrilled. . . . The write-in vote in Pennsylvania was ideal so far as Kennedy and I were concerned. The record was clear that we had not sought it, yet Lawrence and Green had to be impressed."

Not so impressed, however, as to board the Kennedy bandwagon. Nor to refrain from firing a Philadelphia precinct captain who dared abet JFK's write-in effort.

Less pleasing to Kennedy was Indiana. If any Northern state might derail a Catholic candidate, it would be Indiana, the epicenter—not just in the Midwest, but nationwide—of the 1920s Ku Klux Klan.

Freshman Democratic senator Vance Hartke urged Lyndon Johnson to enter Indiana's fray, but, as usual, LBJ drew back. LBJ didn't particularly worry JFK. Lou Harris revealed that fewer than 40 percent of Hoosiers possessed *any* opinion of Johnson. Most who did were hardly complimentary, often dismissing him as a "politician's politician . . . cunning and clever."

James and Stuart Symington Jr. strongly urged their father to enter Indiana, but Symington père, heeding the counsel of his moribund brain trust—Harry Truman and Clark Clifford—remained placidly inactive. Not until Thursday, March 24—a full two weeks and two days after JFK won the New Hampshire primary—would Symington even formally announce his candidacy. His listless Washington ceremony featured a vague prepared statement, 149 St. Louis high school students who had "just happened" to wander into town of their own accord, no endorsement from Harry Truman, and the hangdog admission from the announcing candidate that he had fallen quite far behind John F. Kennedy.

With Symington absent from Indiana, JFK faced merely ludicrous opposition—the inevitable crackpot Lar Daly and a sixty-four-year-old retired Rockville, Indiana, pipe fitter named John Hugh Latham, who was running to abolish party conventions. Still, after Wisconsin's inclusive result, JFK required a strong Midwestern showing, and Indiana found itself host to the usual quota of Kennedy kin—and money.

For whatever reason—anti-Catholicism, a simple preference for Symington or Johnson, mere suspicion of JFK—a remarkable 19 percent of Indiana Democrats voted for either "America First" Daly (40,482 votes) or pipe fitter Latham (43,285), hardly the result JFK's team needed heading into West Virginia.

May 3 witnessed another odd pairing of contests: Ohio and the District of Columbia, with JFK directly competing in neither. Ohio was, of course, locked up for Kennedy, with all prospective delegates—in both the DiSalle and the anti-DiSalle camps—pledging JFK at least grudging loyalty.

No Kennedy slate competed in the District of Columbia's primary, which became a Humphrey-Morse shoot-out, with Adlai Stevenson supporters vainly mounting their own unauthorized effort. The Humphrey and Morse camps traded charges regarding which candidate was more favorable toward integration, and Wayne Morse spoke from black church pulpits—convincing hardly anyone. In an extremely low turnout, Humphrey trounced Morse 57 percent to 43 percent (7,831 votes to 5,866).

Race, however, proved no such factor in West Virginia, its great majority being white, and, with the decline of its coal-mining industry, too often extremely *poor* white. West Virginia's coal industry was not in recession. It was in *depression*. In 1950, 117,000 men worked the mines; in 1960, only 40,000. In twenty of the state's fifty-five counties, at least 15 percent of families received federal surplus food allotments. In McDowell County, 32 percent received such allotments; in Mingo, on the Kentucky border, the number was 41 percent.

It was a rough place, far more hardscrabble and distant from Cambridge and Palm Beach than Eau Claire and Kenosha could ever dream of being (or would ever want to). "I remember I was standing in front of a coal mine," Sargent Shriver recalled. "One of the guys came out and I handed him a pamphlet. He looked at the picture of Kennedy and then he looked at me and spit right in my face."

"My first night in West Virginia, I was taken to a minstrel show," Shriver continued. "White guys got dressed up in black face and mimicked black people. There was lots of fanfare and revelry to accompany it. That gave me an idea of how backwards parts of the state were."

Neither Sargent Shriver nor Jack Kennedy had ever witnessed such pervasive poverty, nor conceived that it might exist in such a large area of the United States. Seeing it astonished JFK. "Imagine," he said, "just imagine kids who never drink milk."

"Until [JFK] saw firsthand the way so many people in West Virginia were forced to live, he'd thought of poverty as an abstract issue," said Kennedy's chief advance man Jerry Bruno, no stranger himself to hard times. "Now . . . he began speaking emotionally about the outrage of children going without milk or protein or anything decent to eat, about not having enough clothes to go to school, about how there were no jobs."

And, as John Kennedy's unlikely West Virginia voyage progressed, a strange empathy began unfolding. No, not his growing feelings for the poor and the downtrodden—that might easily be expected. The surprise was how the unemployed coal miners and minimum-wage mill workers and dirt farmers began to take to *him*.

A miner, perhaps even kin to the one who spat in Sarge Shriver's face, fixed JFK with a stare and dared to ask, "Is it true you're the son of one of our wealthiest men?"

Kennedy conceded that was probably so.

"Is it true that you've never wanted for anything and had everything you wanted?"

Again, Kennedy couldn't argue.

"Is it true you've never done a day's work with your hands all your life?"

The same went for that.

"Well, let me tell you this," Kennedy's interrogator concluded; "you haven't missed a thing."

And that was it. Kennedy glamour was taking hold, the same hold that made shopgirls identify with Marilyn Monroe and filling-station attendants with James Dean. There was nothing special, they knew, in being a coal miner or a filling-station attendant—or a South Dakota pharmacist's son. But there *was* something special about being Jack or Jackie Kennedy—or even in just seeing them walk down your ramshackle main street or stride onto your high school auditorium stage.

"There was no question," remembered JFK's West Virginia campaign aide Charles Peters, "that instead of identifying with the woman who was like them—Muriel Humphrey—they identified with the Princess. You could tell they wanted Jackie. They had a wondrous look in their eyes when they saw her."

"The staff was always grumbling that [Jackie] wasn't interested in campaigning," recalled Nuala Pell, wife of future Rhode Island senator Claiborne Pell, "but I must say, the times she came out and talked to those coal miners or whatever, she was fabulous and they all sort of oohed and aahed at her."

Wit and charm comprised as much of her appeal as youth and fashion, as she joked that daughter Caroline's first words were "West Virginia," adding, "I am so sorry so few states have primaries or we would have a daughter with the greatest vocabulary of any two-year-old in the country."

Economic issues should have reigned supreme in West Virginia, but with both JFK and HHH displaying the appropriate passion for such panaceas as job-training programs, a minimum-wage hike, government-sponsored health care, and the like, West Virginia Democrats, like Democrats nationwide, now found little to differentiate between the always-liberal Humphrey from the now increasingly liberal Kennedy

What did still separate the two contenders was, of course, their respective faiths. West Virginia was among the nation's least Catholic states—95 percent Protestant, less than 5 percent Catholic. This imbalance had caused Joe Kennedy, always sensitive to slights to a faith he only sporadically practiced, to advise skipping West Virginia entirely. "It's a nothing state," he warned, "and they'll kill [Jack] over the Catholic thing."

The issue was certainly dangerous. While Hubert Humphrey's West Virginia theme song was sung to "Give Me That Old-Time Religion," Kennedy staffers maintained sectarian silence. "We were instructed," JFK speechwriter Richard Goodwin recalled, "never to mention, even by implication, the question of religion."

As the campaign progressed, however, strategy changed. It may have been JFK's growing ease with his audiences—and their growing comfort with him. It may have simply been the millionaire Kennedy's compulsion to reach for outsider and underdog status on the basis of his minority religion. On Tuesday, April 19, Kennedy campaigned at Bethany College, a Disciples of Christ school, a half hour from fairly Catholic Wheeling. A heckler—who had stalked him through Wisconsin and northern West Virginia—demanded to know how JFK might reconcile being president and Catholic.

"I don't take orders from above," Kennedy shot back. "I am going to go to church where I want, regardless of whether I'm elected president or not." When Bethany's students responded with applause, Kennedy felt emboldened to confront the issue elsewhere.

But it was not so much a reaffirmation of his Catholicism as it was a gentle distancing of JFK from his church's hierarchy, its magisterium, its doctrines and disciplines. What Kennedy was doing was eroding the old notion of what it meant to be Catholic *and* a politician, and at the same time creating a new concept—of the politician who defined himself as one *born* Catholic, but who now relegated Mother Church to second place behind Motherland.

In Morgantown, he grew bolder. "I refuse to believe," he challenged his audience, "that I was denied the right to be president on the day I was baptized. Nobody asked me if I was a Catholic when I joined the United States Navy. . . . Nobody asked my brother if he was a Catholic or a Protestant before he climbed into an American bomber plane on his last mission."

"How did it go?" he asked Larry O'Brien in the car. O'Brien, seeing how his chief's new attitude had resonated with the crowd, nonetheless had never witnessed Kennedy raise his Catholicism to a Protestant audience. Unsure, O'Brien still muttered, "Very good. Keep it up."

JFK did.

And at 10:30 p.m. on the Saturday before primary day, on live West Virginia television, answering questions on the religious issue put to him by Franklin Roosevelt Jr., Jack Kennedy looked the camera in the eye to reassure voters: "[W]hen any man stands on the steps of the Capitol and takes the oath of office of President, he is swearing to support the separation of church and state; he puts one hand on the Bible and raises the other hand to God as he takes the oath. And if he breaks his oath, he is not only committing a crime against the Constitution, for which the Congress can impeach him and should impeach him but he is committing a sin against God."

With one final flourish, he repeated ever so gently, "a sin against God"—and with a bow toward the fealty Protestants felt toward Holy Scripture, he elevated his hand, as if from the Good Book and toward the Almighty, and added, "for he has sworn on the Bible."

Bigotry was, in truth, no longer what it had been, and voting *for*

Kennedy would now become a means of proving that downtrodden West Virginians were *not* bigots, *not* inbred, Bible-thumping, snake-handling Fundamentalist hicks. West Virginians might not have had much beyond memories of lost jobs in the mines, thirty-five-dollar-a-week unemployment checks, and federal surplus food, but they had their pride. As the *Charleston Gazette* editorialized:

> Joseph Alsop, who rarely supports Democrats, appears to be determined to prove West Virginia is peopled by slack-jawed oafs sworn to overthrow the Papacy by fair means or foul. . . .
>
> With motives outrageously transparent, Alsop attributes all Humphrey votes to a dark anti-Catholic conspiracy and lets it go at that. . . .
>
> Those who vote for Kennedy are always alert, intelligent and unprejudiced. Humphrey supporters are rubes, slatterns and intractable Pope-haters.

"Let me put it this way," recalled West Virginia Associated Press statehouse correspondent Herbert C. Little:

> [T]he Kennedy people seemed determined to make a bigger thing out of the religious issue than it really was. They tried to convey the idea that JFK was an underdog fighting against great odds. It was the rare case among political campaigns where a candidate's handlers would take offense if you wrote something suggesting that he might be the favorite. . . . JFK would . . . often solicit questions at the end of his speech. And after a while, nobody was bringing up the matter of his Catholicism. So, about midway through the campaign, he changed his tactic: he began bringing up the issue himself. The Kennedys played the underdog role to the hilt.

And though it garnered little notice, another bigotry issue took shape—race. In mid-April, Humphrey, appearing at Washington's black Capital Press Club, responded positively to a query: If elected, would he consider appointing a qualified Negro to his cabinet? *Newsweek* reported the exchange, and before long West Virginia papers were running

Humphrey's answer on their front pages. West Virginia bigots now had to prioritize their prejudices.

The Kennedys, as usual, took no chances regarding Hubert Humphrey. Without money, Humphrey was a problem, a danger. *With* money, he might prove fatal. Accordingly, word went out: Anyone funding Humphrey—up to and including former Connecticut U.S. senator William Benton (a five-thousand-dollar donor)—would never again receive a political appointment or nomination.

On May 7, LBJ startled observers with a sudden visit to West Virginia, and though he failed to endorse either Kennedy or Humphrey, he did appear at one dinner in Clarksburg with Humphrey (JFK was away, shoring up his base in Nebraska). Coyly, Johnson teased his audience and eagerly listening reporters, ever-so-slowly drawling, "I have been considering this announcement for a long time, and I believe I'll make it tonight, if you'll bear with me. I'm going on the record and tell you that I'm going to support"—long pause—"these men for any office the Democratic convention chooses to nominate them."

In Wisconsin Kennedy had refused a Humphrey challenge to debate, averring there was nothing to debate. Issues, however, are never the real reason why one debates. If behind, one throws the dice, issues the challenge. If safely ahead, one invariably refuses or tries to limit the damage. In Wisconsin, Kennedy, ahead and knowing it, refused Humphrey's challenge.

Humphrey now led—in votes—but JFK led in money and TV time. Increasingly enraged at Kennedy family tactics, Humphrey re-issued his challenge. Now trailing, JFK accepted.

Ted Sorensen carefully coached JFK to play the victim (of "unfair attacks," a "gang-up," and "bigotry"); to employ the passive tense ("I have been called . . . it has been suggested that . . . people are being asked to vote against me because") in order to avoid accusing Humphrey of anything that might shift sympathy to him; and, above all, to focus on the very human needs of West Virginia's poor.

"Simple words, short sentences and calm dignity," Sorensen summarized, "are essential."

On Wednesday night, May 4, they debated from ABC affiliate WCHS's Charleston studios. JFK produced a visual aid, a sample of the federal surplus food package—powdered milk, rice, peanut butter, flour, and so on—distributed to so many of the state's poorest residents. No one seemed pleased with the show. One observer spoke of how this "rambling program oozed to its conclusion." The debate's sponsor, the *Charleston Gazette*, damned its own creation as a "boring gabfest."

And while the debate may not have had a winner, it produced a loser: Hubert Humphrey, and he knew it. Following the event, both camps found themselves together. Humphrey, not normally a drinker, had a few, and committed yet another blunder, approaching volatile Bobby Kennedy. "Bobby," HHH admitted, "I made your brother look good tonight. I'll be the first to admit he won. . . . But I've still got to campaign against you in Wheeling tomorrow morning, and I've spent so much time, I've missed the plane to Wheeling. How about letting me have the *Caroline* to whistle me over to Wheeling?"

RFK's profane answer shocked and disgusted even his fellow Kennedy men.

It was perhaps the low point in a campaign that for weeks had grown uglier, meaner in spirit, and baser in style. By comparison, Wisconsin seemed focused on issues—a latter-day Lincoln-Douglas debate by contrast. Kennedy—outspending Humphrey by a minimum of four to one, and a maximum of sixty-five to one—constantly carped that he was being "ganged up" on. Humphrey "cannot win the election," Kennedy had told the people of West Virginia; he "cannot be President of the United States. So why, you might ask, is he conducting a gutter campaign against me here in West Virginia? Why is he letting himself be used as a tool by the strangest collection of political bedfellows that has ever joined to gang up on one candidate? And why should he ask West Virginians to waste their votes on him?"

Kennedy also took a shot at the other "contenders": "If Johnson and the other candidates want your vote in the November elections, why don't they have enough respect for you to come over here and ask for your vote in the primary?"

"It has always seemed rather amusing to me," Humphrey countered, "to see Jack publicly challenge other candidates to enter the primaries and then when someone does enter he complains that there is a conspiracy to stop him and deny him the nomination."

"Poor little Jack," Humphrey scoffed. "I wish he would grow up and stop acting like a boy. . . . [W]hat does he want, all the votes?"

"Gutter politics," JFK retorted. "In 14 years of public life . . . I have never been subjected to such personal abuse. I am puzzled that a candidate . . . should indulge in such tactics. I am saddened that he has chosen this course for his campaign."

The tone grew so vituperative that in late April former Senator Joe McCarthy counsel Robert Kennedy dared compare HHH's tactics to those of his late boss. "I'd suggest that brother Bobby examine his own conscience about innuendoes and smears," Humphrey roared. "If he has trouble knowing what I mean, I can refresh his memory very easily. It is a subject he should not want opened."

Few local politicians dared inject themselves into this sulfurous fray, but forty-two-year-old West Virginia freshman U.S. senator Robert Byrd was not among them. "Johnson is my first choice for the presidency," Byrd boldly informed constituents. "Stuart Symington is my second choice. And Senator Humphrey is my choice for vice president . . . If you are for Adlai Stevenson, Senator Stuart Symington, Senator Johnson or John Doe, this primary may be your last chance."

Byrd's actions infuriated Jack Kennedy ("If they want to stop me, why don't they run themselves?"), and, even more so, RFK, who exploded at staffer Charlie Peters when Peters conveyed the news. "He just got angry at me and started berating me," Peters remembered. "And that made an impression on me—I disliked him. I admired Jack but I did not admire Bobby. I respected him; he was a hardworking political manager who, when the right things were pointed out to him, usually did them. But as a guy you like—no, I just disliked him."

Byrd, a Baptist, protested that opposition to Kennedy need not be based upon religious issues. "The effort is being made to put Senator Humphrey in the role of the anti-Catholic candidate," Byrd contended. "It is regrettable that anyone who happens to be for someone other than Senator Kennedy is immediately attacked as being anti-Catholic. . . . I am finding that there are a few persons who, while they abhor religious bigotry, prove themselves to be very intolerant of those of us who just happen to favor someone other than their candidate."

But then again—unlike Robert Carlyle Byrd—most people who opposed Jack Kennedy were *not* former members of the Ku Klux Klan.

ELEVEN

"A little black bag and a checkbook"

LYNDON JOHNSON had Robert Byrd. Jack Kennedy had Franklin Delano Roosevelt Jr.

FDR Jr., neither a U.S. senator nor a West Virginian, was in 1960 merely a divorced, heavy-drinking, former three-term East Side Manhattan congressman, an unsuccessful aspirant for New York governor (Tammany had given Averell Harriman the nod), a failed candidate for New York attorney general, a lobbyist for Dominican dictator Rafael Trujillo, and, now, an importer of Fiats and Jaguars.

He was, however, named *Franklin Delano Roosevelt* Jr.

West Virginians loved—almost worshipped—FDR Sr. "There were more monuments to Roosevelt in West Virginia than perhaps anywhere else," observed reporter Peter Lisagor. "By monuments I mean bridges, structures that were built in Roosevelt's time."

Somehow or other, empirically or instinctively, Joe Kennedy knew this. He had employed FDR Jr. to campaign for Jack in the 1952 Connecticut race against Lodge, and now he thought of using FDR Jr. similarly in the Mountain State.

"You know, Franklin," Joe flattered his prey, "if it hadn't been for that guinea [Carmine De Sapio, who had swung the 1954 gubernatorial nomination to Harriman], you would have been elected governor, and now we would all be working for you."

Such tactics may or may not have impressed Roosevelt ("I think Jack's father was one of the most evil, disgusting men I have ever known"), but he needed a means to resuscitate his now-defunct political career.

Not that he was particularly impressed with JFK either, for that matter. In 1959 Roosevelt had been invited to dine at JFK's Georgetown home, Jack's agenda being how they might bring Franklin's mother, Eleanor, aboard the Kennedy bandwagon. "I came away," Roosevelt noted, "with a real dual impression of him. I said to my wife, 'How can a guy this politically immature seriously expect to be president?' The only thing Jack could talk about at that dinner was himself and his political problems. I'd never met somebody so completely obsessed in himself as Jack is now. And the trouble with Jack is that he's always had it smooth, he's never been clobbered. . . . He needs something to flatten out that overaggressive ego, and maybe this campaign will do it."

Sincere or not, car salesman FDR Jr. proved to be everything Joe Kennedy had hoped for. "While Kennedy went up through the valley," said Lisagor, "Roosevelt was with us. He would make remarks on the back of a truck. You could see in the people when he started hammering away that they were quite fascinated and intrigued, that this was the son of their great idol."

"Sure am glad to meet you, Mr. Roosevelt," a miner might say. "My daddy was a mine worker all his life before me. Still has your daddy's picture in his bedroom."

It was, marveled one West Virginia journalist, akin to "God's son coming down and saying it was all right to vote for this Catholic, it was permissible, it wasn't something terrible to do."

Moreover, FDR Jr., speaking in Groton accents uncannily like his father, could lay it on thick, even daring to inform audiences of JFK: "His father and mine were this close." His gesture illustrating this affinity was, shall we say, exaggerated.

And he served another, nastier, function.

In Wisconsin, Chester Bowles had refused to assume the role of anti-Humphrey hatchet man. In West Virginia, with Humphrey increasingly under JFK's skin ("Tell Hubert to lay off in West Virginia or we will unload on him," JFK had warned Gene McCarthy), the need had only increased for someone willing to perform the campaign dirty work. It could not be Chester Bowles or Ivy League supporters such as Harvard's Arthur Schlesinger or John Kenneth Galbraith—all too intellectual and grand for West Virginia. Nor could it be a Kennedy—they being too Catholic for the job.

The job was this: Jack Kennedy, as voters had been reminded in each election, was a World War II veteran. Hubert Humphrey, married with a small son and 4-F with a hernia during the war, was not, and anonymous Minnesota sources had supplied JFK's operatives with alleged correspondence between Humphrey and his draft board. The contrast might easily resonate in West Virginia, which had sent more men per capita into the service after Pearl Harbor than any other state—and a similar percentage to Korea.

The Kennedy campaign desired to have Humphrey's patriotism and courage assailed, and divined that FDR Jr., himself a decorated World War II Navy combat veteran, was the man for the job. "Nightly," Roosevelt would recall, "I received calls from Bobby asking me, 'When will you lower the boom.' Then, Larry O'Brien and others all put pressure on me to attack."

"Hubert Humphrey has always been a loyal Democrat," Franklin finally declared on Wednesday, April 27, "but I don't know where he was in World War II. . . ." Then he proceeded to question Humphrey's deferments as a schoolteacher during the war (actually they were for physical disabilities), and may or may not have literally branded him a "draft dodger."

"It is a sorry spectacle for . . . New Dealers," Humphrey fired back, "to see the proud and illustrious name of his father being so degraded by Junior when he performs as the 'hatchet man' for the Kennedy forces."

JFK conveniently denied culpability. "Any discussion of the war record of Senator Humphrey was done without my knowledge and consent," he piously contended, "as I strongly disagree with the injection of this issue into the campaign."

"Of course, Jack knew," Roosevelt admitted years later. "But I always regretted my role in the affair. Humphrey, an old ally, never forgave me for it. I did it because of Bobby. . . . RFK was already a full-blown tyrant. You did what he told you to do, and you did it with a smile."

Kennedy forces also exploited the Hoffa angle, since Humphrey was now formally endorsed by West Virginia's 6,730-member Brotherhood of Teamsters. "Jimmy Hoffa," JFK would charge, "gave the orders to join the gang-up [on me] . . . because he knows that if I am successful here I will win the Democratic nomination."

Such accusations had already triggered a Humphrey explosion. On his campaign bus, he fumed to reporters:

I can't afford to run through this state with a little black bag and a checkbook. . . . I can't buy an election. . . . Kennedy is the spoiled candidate and he and that young, emotional, juvenile Bobby are spending with wild abandon. . . . Anyone who gets in the way of teacher's pet—I should change that to Papa's pet—is to be destroyed. Bobby said that if they had to spend half a million to win here, they would do it. I don't have any daddy who can pay the bills for me. . . .

If I criticize anything he's doing, I'm supposed to be a bigot. But he accused me of stealing votes, taking money from Symington, Johnson, and Jimmy Hoffa, and I'm just supposed to sit around and take it.

The Teamsters was virtually the only union daring to cross the front-running Kennedy. Despite antipathy to the Kennedys and sympathy for Humphrey, John L. Lewis's United Mine Workers, crucial in any West Virginia race, remained officially neutral. Walter Reuther's UAW, having gained nothing from its 1952 and 1956 endorsements, decided in early 1959 to rule out any until after the convention. Beyond that, Reuther now proved unimpressed with Hubert Humphrey. After Wisconsin, Jack Conway recalled, "Walter's attitude toward Jack Kennedy changed in the sense that he saw for the first time a guy who did have the potential to get nominated. . . . Hubert ran like he was running for sheriff."

Reuther, Joe Rauh added, "didn't go for Hubert, because . . . that's [what] you let idealists do. . . . You don't go for a guy who is not going to win."

Humphrey's whining about "black bags" and "checkbooks" was, of course, mere understatement. Officially, JFK outspent Humphrey in West Virginia by more than four to one—$100,000 to $23,000 ($34,000 on television alone). Unofficial estimates of Kennedy spending ran as high as $1.5 to $2 million.

West Virginia saw its opportunities—and took them. Under the best of circumstances, its politics were notoriously corrupt. "Most of these coal field counties are for sale," one politico bluntly wrote to FDR Jr. "It is a matter of who gets there first with the most money."

Such competition favored the rich, and rumors flew of Kennedy largesse. Congressman Tip O'Neill would regale listeners with the tale of Boston real estate man Eddie Ford, an elderly bachelor who had been dispatched southward with "a pocket full of money," instructed to deposit it in useful, friendly hands. "Sheriff," Ford would inform the locals, "I'm a businessman from Chicago, and I'm on my way to Miami. I think this young man would be great for the country, and I'd like to give you three thousand dollars to see if you could help him. I'll be coming back this way, and I'll be happy to give you a bonus if you're able to carry the town."

"They passed money around like it was never seen," O'Neill added.

"Votes were being bought and sold openly in the streets of [Charleston] today," wrote *Baltimore Sun* correspondent Howard Norton. He was re-assigned.

Rumors swirled that JFK brother-in-law Stephen Smith had withdrawn all the one-dollar bills from Charleston's banks. Their purpose: for primary-day payoffs.

"Every time I'd walk into a town," JFK advance man Jerry Bruno admitted years later, "they thought I was a bagman."

Who authorized what remains a mystery, though history provides some clues. "I keep reading these books by the young men around Jack Kennedy and how they claim credit for electing him," Boston's Richard Cardinal Cushing informed Hubert Humphrey in 1966. "I'll tell you who elected John Kennedy. It was his father, Joe, and me, right here in this room. . . . We decided which church and preacher would get two hundred dollars or one hundred dollars or five hundred dollars. . . . It's good for the church. It's good for the preacher, and it's good for the candidate."

Larry O'Brien defended all disbursements to local politicians as "legitimate Election Day expenses," but also spoke of thousands in cash kept in a "suitcase under [a] bed." O'Brien: "I negotiated our payments for campaign expenses. Neither Jack nor Bob Kennedy knew what agreements were made—that was my responsibility." Considering Bobby Kennedy's penchant (or, rather, obsession) with knowing every detail of the campaign, this assertion rings true only if the expenditures in question were indeed *not* "legitimate."

On at least one occasion, RFK did directly involve himself in such negotiations. Decades later, Clarksburg Democrat Victor Gabriel revealed that he personally conferred with RFK and Chuck Spalding to determine the amount necessary to deliver Harrison County. Gabriel said five thousand dollars should suffice, and Spalding shot back, "You don't know what you're talking about." His tone strongly implied that the Kennedys had grown used to dealing in far larger sums.

That was certainly true in Logan County, where, after local boss Raymond Chafin met with JFK, Kennedy's minions bluntly asked Chafin: How much? "Thirty-five," Chafin answered, meaning thirty-five hundred dollars. Later, at Logan's modest Taplan Airport, two JFK operatives handed over two briefcases containing thirty-five *thousand* dollars in cash.

How effective was Kennedy's largesse? In supposedly virulent anti-Catholic southern West Virginia, JFK garnered 84 percent of the vote (13,896 to 2,720) in McDowell County, 78 percent in Wyoming County, and 56 percent in both Logan and Mingo counties. The *Logan Banner* alleged "flagrant vote-buying, whiskey flowing like water, and coercion of voters. . . . You name it and we just about had it." Votes, charged *Banner* editor Charles D. Hylton, went for "two dollars and a drink of whiskey to six dollars and two pints of beer for a single vote."

"I know," Kennedy's exceedingly loyal secretary Evelyn Lincoln conceded in a 1994 interview, "they bought the election."

Worse still were the rumors of mob connections.

Various versions exist of how it all came about and how it all went down. Judith Campbell (Exner) claimed that JFK met personally with vicious Chicago mob boss Sam "Momo" Giancana at Miami Beach's Fontainebleau Hotel to arrange the deal: mob cash in West Virginia for an easy-on-organized-crime policy in any forthcoming Kennedy administration. Exner was mistress to both men.

Another version holds that former rum-runner Joe Kennedy ("We need help in West Virginia. We've got to get the labor vote because it's going to Hubert Humphrey"), either through connections in Chicago or through JFK brother-in-law Peter Lawford's Rat Pack pal Frank Sinatra, contacted Giancana—who desired a reversal of New Jersey mob leader Joey Adonis's January 1956 deportation to Milan.

Most versions hold that Giancana's money and influence ("We even had to muscle the taverns to convince them to play Frank Sinatra's song 'High Hopes' on the jukeboxes. Those hillbillies hate the idea of an East Coast Irish Catholic President") were disbursed through mob-connected Atlantic City nightclub owner Paul "Skinny" D'Amato, whose "500 Club" regularly hosted numerous West Virginia sheriffs. The dollar amount allegedly involved, however—fifty thousand dollars—barely seemed worth either the mob's or the Kennedys' efforts, though it wasn't so small that D'Amato didn't brag about it on FBI wiretaps.

It may, however, have been much more. Sam and Chuck Giancana, Momo Giancana's godson and brother, respectively, contended that Giancana "put in a half million of his own money." At least two witnesses have testified to seeing huge stacks of mob-supplied cash funneled through Frank Sinatra. In Las Vegas, as Sinatra's Rat Pack campaigned for JFK (and with JFK in town), Peter Lawford summoned fellow Rat Packer Sammy Davis Jr. with an odd request. "If you want to see what a million dollars in cash looks like, go into the next room," Lawford advised. "There's a brown leather satchel in the closet; open it. It's a gift from the hotel owners for Jack's campaign." Sammy demurred. There are, he confessed, "some things you don't want to know."

On another occasion actor Brad Dexter (the least magnificent of *The Magnificent Seven*) partied with Sinatra. "We got back," Dexter recalled, "and he [Sinatra] said there was a valise in his car, and to go get it for him. I brought it in, and he said, 'Open it.' The goddamn valise was chock-full of hundred-dollar bills, wrapped in packages. There had to have been a hundred, two hundred thousand dollars in there."

"Don't worry about it," Sinatra advised. "There's more where that came from," explaining that the cash came from "the boys"—the mob—for JFK.

Meanwhile, Hubert Humphrey struggled for funds. Very late in the campaign as he breakfasted in Charleston, an aide approached. If Humphrey did not produce enough cash in advance, the aide said, his election eve telethon would be canceled. Humphrey looked to Jim Rowe for help. Tapped out from helping the cause, Rowe responded with the blankest of looks. "All right, I'll pay it myself," Humphrey snarled, and he wrote out a personal check for $750, dipping into funds reserved for his twenty-one-year-old daughter Nancy's wedding in Minneapolis the following Saturday.

While a father struggled to pay for a daughter's wedding, favored son Jack Kennedy had everything bought for him. "I got a wire from my father:" he informed audiences. "'Dear Jack: Don't buy another vote, I'll be damned if I'll pay for a landslide.'"

Hubert Humphrey wasn't laughing.

Having failed once already on television, Humphrey now failed yet again. On election eve, the upbeat Humphrey-style telethon that he had planned was a bit more kinetic than he had hoped for. Facing a barrage of unscreened calls ("You git out of West Virginia, Mr. Humphrey! You git out, do you hear?"), Humphrey looked more disorganized and less competent and presidential than ever. It was a disaster.

There began to be stirrings that a Humphrey victory was just not foreordained. An increasing number of polls now pointed to a Kennedy victory—in some cases, a substantial triumph. In early May the *Wall Street Journal*'s Al Otten twice surveyed opinion in not particularly Catholic Charleston. JFK scored 55 percent, then 57.5 percent. In April, Wesleyan University queried students in grades six through twelve nationwide on their presidential preferences. West Virginia students voted massively for Kennedy: JFK, 5,309; Stevenson, 943, Humphrey, 943; LBJ, 776; Symington, 594.

Kennedy's own man, Lou Harris, and columnist Joe Alsop polled voters in the southern West Virginia coal-mining community of Slab Fork, where, as Alsop noted, nearly all whites were FDR Democrats, the few blacks Republican, and only two Catholics resided within the town's environs. Even there, with a fair amount of anti-Catholic sentiment rearing its head ("Our people built this country. If they had wanted a Catholic to be president, they would have said so in the Constitution"), JFK edged Humphrey 30 to 27 (with ten respondents undecided).

Yet, JFK's own men remained only marginally more optimistic than the hugely negative prognoses they leaked to newsmen. Pierre Salinger privately placed his candidate's chances at 51 percent to 49 percent. Local JFK operative Bob McDonough called the race fifty-fifty. Unstated was a great, uneasy fact of political life: Politicians who predict slender victories rarely win.

Burned by high expectations in Wisconsin, the Kennedy camp furiously lowered them in West Virginia, and Joe Kennedy pondered how to spin defeat, to keep a Humphrey win from writing finis to all his hopes and plans. At a properly expensive Manhattan restaurant, he gathered his key New York allies—Bronx boss Charles Buckley and Tammany's Carmine De Sapio among them. "Now," he asked, "my boy is going into the West Virginia primary within a few days. All the experts say that if he wins thirty-five percent of the vote because of the religious problem, it will be considered a victory, even in defeat. . . . Will you gentlemen issue a statement calling it such if he polls that percent of the vote?"

They had all been in politics a long time. Never had they heard of 35 percent being considered a victory. Even a Republican running in the Bronx might choke on that claim. Only Buckley chirped up that he would do JPK's bidding. The rest refused. "All right then," Joe responded with barely controlled hatred, "you can go to blazes."

In southern West Virginia on May 5, JFK predicted he would be lucky to secure 40 percent, a prognosis so low, the *New York Times* dismissed it as JFK's "poor mouth" position. Such pessimism flew in the face of a Fayette County telephone poll released that very day, revealing a massive switch from an April 29 40 percent–to–60 percent deficit into a 61 percent–to–39 percent lead, Humphrey losing nearly a third of his supporters directly to JFK—and *nobody* deserting JFK for HHH. While a huge number (39 percent) of respondents remained undecided, such trends could only auger well for Kennedy.

Aboard the *Caroline*, JFK, his voice too raw to use, had scrawled his thoughts upon a yellow pad: "My poll . . . in W.V. showed me *41*%[,] HH . . . 43%–44%—rest undecided—but the rest are Protestants. The reason I think we should do well if we get over 40% is *UMW* [United Mine Workers] will get the word out[.] *Byrd* is getting *meaner*. The fundamentalists are getting active. To drag out 50% under these conditions seems optimistic."

Lou Harris's April 30 survey showed JFK gaining but still behind. By now Harris's results were so volatile, and Harris so nervous, that few of Kennedy's advisers heeded his results—even when, after the JFK-Humphrey debate, his data indicated a slight lead.

Reporters, meanwhile, puzzled over the immense, enthusiastic crowds cheering JFK at nearly every stop. Why, they asked, were so many pulling for Jack Kennedy if so few would vote for him? The paradox reminded them of a previous disconnect betwixt poll and reality: the throngs greeting supposedly doomed, but ultimately victorious, Harry Truman and his frantic 1948 whistle-stop tour.

Kenny O'Donnell predicted a 51 percent–to–49 percent squeaker—but didn't believe it. RFK and Larry O'Brien huddled. If they lost by no worse than 53 percent to 47 percent, they would bravely boast of "a moral victory, as Humphrey had done in Wisconsin."

Tuesday, May 10, 1960—a dreary, rainy primary day. From 6:30 a.m. to 8:30 p.m., in 2,750 precincts, 670,000 registered Democrats were eligible to cast ballots. Bobby Kennedy ("If we lose here today, we might as well stay home and watch the convention on television. Damn that Hubert Humphrey!") remained in Charleston. Jack Kennedy fled the state. For a month he had jeered those lacking the courage to face West Virginia's voters. Tonight, he too was afraid—and absent—having flown home to Georgetown. After dinner, he and Jackie, along with Ben and Tony Bradlee, strolled down from N Street to take in a movie—Elizabeth Taylor and Montgomery Clift in Tennessee Williams's *Suddenly Last Summer* at the Trans-Lux. Theater management, however, barred latecomers (even presidential aspirants), and the two couples drifted into the nearby Plaza Theater ("which then as now," as Bradlee later wrote, "specialized in porn") to watch a low-budget, new-wave, soft-core film named *Private Property*.

Upon his return home, Kennedy's phone rang. Bradlee saw JFK's hands shake as he received the news from Bobby: Victory! JFK whooped. A champagne cork popped. But there was no time for celebrating. JFK called Steve Smith. Get the *Caroline* ready, he ordered; we're flying to Charleston. Another call, this time to Joe Kennedy. Joe had already talked with Bobby and, though he didn't acknowledge it, knew the score. Joe Kennedy always knew the score.

It was more than a win. It was a 61 percent–to–39 percent landslide, thumping Humphrey 236,510 to 152,187, sweeping forty-eight of West Virginia's fifty-five counties, even carrying Robert Byrd's hometown.

"How the hell can they stop me now?" Kennedy crowed to Bradlee aboard the *Caroline*. Landing at 3 a.m., he addressed the voters he had fled only hours before.

"I had no doubt," he blandly dissembled, "that you would cast your vote on the basis of the issues and not on any religious prejudice."

TWELVE

"All the eggheads are for Stevenson"

HUBERT HUMPHREY knew he had failed.

Wisconsin lay just next door to Minnesota. But he lost Wisconsin in a landslide.

West Virginia was 95 percent Protestant. His early poll ratings projected 60 percent of the vote—but he lost West Virginia in a bigger landslide. Rationalizations no longer worked. His campaign was broke. If HHH personally propped it up, even momentarily, he'd be broke, too. The "Stop-JFK" crowd within his entourage cared but marginally for his needs. Committed more to LBJ or Stevenson, they urged him onward, to continue bloodying Jack Kennedy. But Hubert Humphrey would only ever be able to nick JFK—and slash his own wrists in the bargain.

Time to give up.

His concession statement terminated his campaign. His run for glory concluded, Humphrey now switched gears, to live to fight another day, to concentrate on re-election to the Senate that fall.

The news elated the Kennedy camp. Five minutes after HHH spoke, a hotel clerk appeared at Humphrey's suite, bearing word that Mr. Kennedy would soon arrive. The Humphreys hoped to be treated like equals in defeat—to be tendered some respect by a former adversary who now needed support and would certainly require it in November.

Bobby Kennedy showed up.

No one was pleased. "The door opened. Bobby walks in," recalled Joe Rauh. "It was like the Red Sea opening for Moses. Everybody walked backwards, and there was a path from the door to the other side of the room where Hubert and Muriel were standing. I'll never forget that walk if I live to be a hundred. Bobby walks slowly, deliberately, over to the Humphreys. He leaned in and kissed Muriel.

"Muriel stiffened, stared, and turned in silent hostility, walking away from him, fighting tears."

She would not speak to him. Bobby hauled Hubert downstairs, past the country guitarist still twanging and singing "I'm for Hubert Humphrey, he's for you and me," and into JFK headquarters, where the unhappy Happy Warrior delivered as gracious a second concession as he could.

And, in one final ignominy, when it was all over, the Humphrey campaign bus—the one that had carried him into the hallows, along precipitous mountains, through West Virginia towns and cities—this bus that had been parked illegally outside Humphrey's Charleston hotel for the last three weeks . . . finally got a ticket.

★ ★ ★

Jack Kennedy had succeeded in eliminating liberal icon Hubert Humphrey, but he had hardly vanquished the strongest opposition liberal Democrats might offer. Humphrey's national ratings had, in fact, remained pathetic, mired in single digits—and rarely even high single digits. In his entire *career*, despite ultimately winning the 1968 Democratic presidential nomination, he would triumph in but a single contested primary—the May 1960 District of Columbia contest against Wayne Morse.

Yes, West Virginia had done wonders for Jack Kennedy's campaign, but it had been an accomplishment worked against a man few yet took seriously as presidential timber. As the *Wall Street Journal* jibed, in defeating jabbering little Hubert Humphrey, JFK had merely established himself as "Jack the Dwarf Killer."

JFK had not faced the real giant, and the sentimental favorite, of American liberalism—Governor Adlai Ewing Stevenson II.

JFK would never have crushed Adlai as he had obliterated Hubert. Money, brains, and enthusiasm would have fallen in behind Stevenson as they never had for Humphrey. So would votes. Straws, great and small, blew in the wind. A fall 1959 *Congressional Quarterly* survey revealed not only how strongly Stevenson would fare against JFK, but also that his strength was, in fact, growing:

	April 1959	October 1959
Stevenson	35%	44%
Johnson	17%	20%
Kennedy	25%	17%
Symington	17%	14%
Humphrey	2%	1%

December 1959's Gallup poll showed Adlai topping JFK 26 percent to 24 percent. Then in February 1960 freshman Democratic congressman Robert W. Kastenmeier polled his Madison, Wisconsin–area Second District constituents—34 percent wanted Stevenson, 29 percent Humphrey, and just a paltry 26 percent Kennedy.

To oppose such a potential behemoth, however, JFK's forces possessed a potent, almost invaluable weapon: Adlai Stevenson himself.

★ ★ ★

Jack Kennedy's family money was newly minted, his national political power still to be wielded. Adlai Stevenson's familial resources were more venerable. His grandfather, the first Adlai Ewing Stevenson, had helped arrange the original Lincoln-Douglas debates, had been elected to Congress, and had occupied the office of vice president of the United States. Adlai II's aunt had helped found the Daughters of the American Revolution. His father had served as Illinois secretary of state and had been considered for the 1928 vice-presidential nomination.

Adlai II graduated from Choate and Princeton, attended (and dropped out of) Harvard Law, clerked for Supreme Court justice Oliver Wendell Holmes, married a Gold Coast Chicago socialite, and literally had a sister nicknamed "Buffie." If Chicago had Brahmins, Adlai Stevenson might well have been one.

A practicing lawyer, he served the New Deal in the Navy and State departments, and under Harry Truman became a delegate to the newly formed United Nations. In 1948, Illinois Democrats seeking to defeat two-term Republican governor Dwight Green drafted Stevenson as their candidate (Adlai would have preferred the Senate nomination). In an unexpected banner year for state Democrats, Stevenson triumphed by 572,067 votes, the largest gubernatorial margin in state history. The race, however, taught Stevenson a seductive lesson, one difficult to unlearn: that power would seek him, and that he need not soil his hands or even expend much effort in reaching out to grasp its levers.

Stevenson cracked down hard on gambling and oversaw a competent, honest, progressive administration. Re-election seemed assured in 1952, and as late as that April only 2 percent of Democrats preferred him for the presidency. But fate—in the form of his welcoming address to that year's

133

Democratic National Convention—intervened. His stirring words and erudite bearing resonated with Democrats. With Harry Truman not running (and in fact backing the reluctant Stevenson), with vice president Alben W. Barkley too old at seventy-four, and with no compelling alternative offering itself, delegates nominated Adlai Stevenson on the third ballot—by one and a half votes.

His campaign combined healthy doses of wit ("[M]y opponent is worrying about my funnybone. I'm worrying about his backbone"), slashing attacks on Republicans (particularly on Joe McCarthy and Richard Nixon), and, of course, a very famous, much-photographed hole in his right shoe. "He has," gushed CBS's Eric Sevareid, "revealed an integrity rare in American politics, a luminosity of intelligence. . . . [H]e has excited the passions of the mind."

His sense of integrity inspired a generation of liberal Democrats, and even some who were not so liberal. "One reason I admire him is that he is not a political whore like most of the others," Jack Kennedy would say. "Too many politicians will say anything when they think it will bring them votes or money. If he had said the things [in 1956, after Suez, that his supporters] wanted, he could have had a lot of money out of that room; but he refused. I admired that. You have to stick to what you believe."

Not particularly helpful, however, was the crushing weight of Stevenson's erudition, crammed with literary and historical references that sailed over the heads of most of the populace. Nor could Adlai's oratory, heavy with such phrases as "like a new fog bank rising from a troubled sea," or "we shall survive with sacrifice or perish cheap," compete with a simple, direct, declaratory Eisenhower sentence like, "I shall go to Korea."

Yet as Stevenson failed to convince the general public, his appeal to intellectuals (and those who merely fancied themselves cerebral) continued to grow. "Sure," quipped John Alsop, Joe and Stewart's Connecticut Republican brother, "[a]ll the eggheads are for Stevenson, but how many eggheads are there?"

Not enough, it turned out. Stevenson predicted privately that he would capture 381 of 531 electoral votes, a landslide. In the end he garnered only 89, carrying but nine Southern and border states, defeated in a rout.

The experience failed to humble him, however, as he blamed the greatest Democratic Party debacle in a quarter century not on himself, but on outside forces—on Harry Truman's unpopularity and, above all, on the difficulties of competing against a wildly popular national hero with no record of his own to defend, save that of a world war (Ike, 1; Hitler, 0).

Stevenson harbored thoughts of another run, and, once again, he saw it not really as a run, or even a gentle lope. In his mind's eye he visualized himself being hoisted upon an adoring party's shoulders and carried across the finish line—in other words, another draft. "If the party wants me, I'll run again," he confided in 1955, with an attitude unique for someone who had just carried a mere nine states. "But I'm not going to run like I did before and run to all those shopping centers like I'm running for sheriff."

Estes Kefauver's strong 1956 start (crushing Adlai in New Hampshire and Minnesota) caused Stevenson to finally bestir himself and enter the primary field with a bit of energy. Once he had captured the nomination, however, his normal indecision returned—reflected not only in his tossing the vice-presidential decision to convention delegates, but also in the for-lorn campaign that followed. Aboard this undisciplined effort was young Robert Kennedy, to gain campaign seasoning. Having embarked for duty with a negative attitude (Arthur Schlesinger remembered Bobby as "an alien presence, sullen and rather ominous, saying little, looking grim, and exuding an atmosphere of bleak disapproval"), RFK found the campaign's incompetence and the candidate's own lofty dithering disgusting.

"Nobody asked me anything," Bobby groused, "nobody wanted me to do anything, nobody consulted me. So I had time to watch everything—I filled complete notebooks with notes on how a Presidential campaign should be run." Or not. Thoroughly put off by Stevenson's indecisiveness and laziness, RFK voted for Ike in 1956.

And though memories of Harry Truman had grown blurry and Ike now had his own record to defend (a recession, Suez, Hungary, plus a heart attack and ileitis), the incumbent's Election Day voting percentage only increased—to a landslide 57 percent, prevented from rising even higher only by the white South's residual Democratic loyalties.

Stevenson appeared humbled—though only briefly. In December 1956, he spoke of not running. But after that it was all winks and nods, all clever and coy hints for his egghead constituencies to rise from their ivory towers and library stacks to once more storm party battlements on his behalf.

But while Adlai nodded, Jack worked.

"I don't think [JFK]'d be a good president," Stevenson now advised one confidant. "I think he's too young; I don't think he fully understands the dimensions of the foreign affairs dilemmas that are coming up."

And when a law partner gingerly informed Adlai that he was now in the Kennedy camp, Stevenson could only blandly respond, "The Catholic issue is going to be badly against him, and, after all, Nixon must be beaten." The partner translated that as, "I want to be urged to run, and I want to be nominated."

"He wanted it," acidly noted Agnes Meyer, wife of *Washington Post* publisher Eugene Meyer, "but didn't have the stomach to fight for it."

In January 1960, Stevenson received an odd and distinctly unwelcome offer of support. It came during an equally unusual secret visit to the Soviet Union's Washington embassy. Following caviar, wine, and assurances that the room was not bugged, Ambassador Mikhail A. Menshikov removed a carefully folded document from his suit pocket. Inside, the ambassador told Stevenson, was a message from Nikita Khrushchev. "He wishes me to convey the following: When you met in Moscow in August, 1958, he said to you that he had voted for you in his heart in 1956. He says now that he will vote for you in his heart again in 1960. . . . We are concerned with the future, and that America has the right President. . . ." With that pre-amble, the ambassador handed Stevenson the Soviet premier's letter:

When we compare all the possible candidates . . . we feel that Mr. Stevenson is best for mutual understanding and progress toward peace. These are the views not only of myself—Khrushchev—but of the Presidium. We believe that Mr. Stevenson is more of a realist than others and is likely to understand Soviet anxieties and purposes. . . .

Because we know the ideas of Mr. Stevenson, we in our hearts all favor him. And you [Ambassador Menshikov] must ask him which way we could be of assistance to those forces . . . which favor friendly relations. We don't know how we can help to make relations better and help those to succeed in political life who wish for better relations and more confidence. Could the Soviet press assist Mr.

Stevenson's personal success? How? Should the press praise him, and, if so, for what? Should it criticize him, and, if so, for what? (We can always find many things to criticize Mr. Stevenson [for] because he has said many harsh and critical things about the Soviet Union and Communism!) Mr. Stevenson will know best what would help him.

The idea of Premier Khrushchev's backing—and his interference in the American political process—shocked and angered Stevenson. "I get more and more indignant about being 'propositioned' that way," Adlai confided to a friend, "and at the same time, more and more perplexed, if that's the word, by the *confidence* they have in me. I shall do one thing only *now*: politely and decisively reject the proposal—and pray that it will never leak, lest I lose that potentially valuable confidence."

Fear now entered Adlai Stevenson's heart, a raging terror that word of Khrushchev's unwanted affection might be revealed. Of the relatively few confidants he told, among them was the *New York Times*' Scotty Reston. "I've got enough troubles," Stevenson complained to Reston, "without help from them." Reston kept Stevenson's secret.

But more respectable company also backed Stevenson. In December 1959 an informal "Draft Stevenson" committee formed. What it boasted in enthusiasm, it lacked in humility (it wasn't Stevenson, but *America*, that deserved "another chance in 1960"). It also lacked an actual candidate. Not deigning to formally run for office, Stevenson ran instead for the border, embarking on a two-month, ten-nation Latin American tour. On February 9, flying out of Chicago in a snowstorm, Stevenson demonstrated his maddening dithering to the reporters gathered to see him off. "I have never said I wouldn't accept," Adlai informed them. "I hope I shall always do my duty by my party and my country. But I don't think a nomination will be offered." Once abroad, he continued the same theme. Meanwhile, he held communists (though not an "extremely guilty" Castro) blameless for deteriorating Cuban-U.S. relations. Most notably, from Costa Rica in February Stevenson decried that "the amount of money being spent [on campaigning] is phenomenal, probably the highest amount spent on a campaign in history." It was a remark that, not surprisingly, nettled Kennedy partisans.

His April homecoming was greeted by the formation of a more structured Stevenson for President Committee. "If I said I'd accept a draft I'd be courting it," said Adlai at a Manhattan press conference. "If I said I would not, I'd be a 'draft evader.'" But with the New Hampshire and Wisconsin primaries already concluded, the jokes were wearing thin.

Hubert Humphrey's disappearance after West Virginia focused attention on Stevenson's reappearance. Neither Lyndon Johnson nor Stuart Symington inflamed liberal ardor, and only a small segment of Stevenson's "egghead" base had embraced Jack Kennedy. That, as ever, left Adlai. And when, on May 19, at a Democratic fund-raiser in Chicago, Stevenson laid into Dwight Eisenhower for his U-2 fiascos, especially the derailed Paris conference, he seemed very presidential indeed:

> Premier Khrushchev wrecked this conference. Let there be no mistake about that. When he demanded that President Eisenhower apologize and punish those responsible for the spy plane flight, he was in effect asking the President to punish himself. This was an impossible request, and he knew it. But we handed Khrushchev the crowbar and the sledgehammer to wreck the meeting. Without our series of blunders, Mr. Khrushchev would not have had a pretext for making his impossible demand and wild charges. Let there be no mistake about that either.

He went on to seemingly excuse Khrushchev's angry response, terming it "predictable, if not his violence."

"How would we feel," he asked, "if Soviet spy planes based in Cuba were flying over Cape Canaveral and Oak Ridge?

"We resent deeply and bitterly the gross affront to the President and his office," the non-candidate continued. "There is no question about national unity in a time of crisis. But . . . it is the duty of responsible opposition in a democracy to expose and criticize carelessness and mistakes, especially in a case of such national and world importance as this. . . . We cannot sweep this whole sorry mess under the rug in the name of national unity."

By June 1 he was sounding yet more like a candidate, proposing a five-point "grand strategy for peace," among whose features was the necessity to "talk and bargain with the Communist countries for many years to come." In this proposal, Stevenson's old eloquence did not fail him: "Our approach to disarmament has been: 'Yes but,'" he said. "It ought to be: 'Why not?'"

Some thought Stevenson might have won the Oregon primary had he entered it, an event that could have altered the entire nominating process. But he didn't. "That was the way he ran for the presidency," James Reston would conclude. "As a spectator, as if someone else was doing it."

Viewed from history's rearview mirror, Stevenson's indecisive hold on 1950s liberalism is not easy to comprehend. A comparison—not logical on its face but still valid—is in order: Adlai Stevenson was to liberal Democrats what the Old South—the Lost Cause—was to several generations of Southerners. To 1950s liberals, Stevenson was Robert E. Lee, Ashley Wilkes, and D. W. Griffith's Little Colonel rolled into one erudite persona—the refined, gentlemanly upholder, the very embodiment, of an old regime's lost virtues in a depressing dark era of Republican occupation.

Eventually, however, a key coterie of liberals saw him as more Ashley Wilkes and less Robert E. Lee, concluding that he would never rise again but that if he did the result would only be Appomattox III. Chester Bowles had leaped off the bandwagon early. So had Pulitzer Prize winner Arthur Schlesinger Jr. On June 17, 1960, sixteen prominent left-of-center intellectuals, functionaries, and office holders jumped en masse to Kennedy. Among them were Schlesinger and Joe Rauh; fifty-two-year-old best-selling Harvard economist John Kenneth Galbraith; historians James McGregor Burns and Allen Nevins; United Steel Workers counsel Arthur M. Goldberg; Washington congresswoman Edith Green; and Wisconsin lieutenant governor Phileo Nash. "Now that Senator Humphrey has withdrawn from the race and Mr. Stevenson continues to stand aside," they averred, "the liberals of America turn to Senator Kennedy for President. . . . We are convinced that Senator Kennedy's adherence to the progressive principles which we hold is strong and irrevocable. He has demonstrated the kind of firmness of purpose and toughness of mind that will make him a great world leader."

It was not an easy choice. Sentiments die hard—love is blind, and friendship tries not to see—but many of Stevenson's former acolytes were tired of averting their gaze and losing elections, as Arthur Schlesinger confided to his journal:

> S[tevenson] is a much richer, more thoughtful, more creative person; but he has been away from power too long; he gives me an odd sense of unreality. . . . I find it hard to define this feeling—a certain frivolity, distractedness, over-interest in words and phrases? I don't know; but in contrast K[ennedy] gives a sense of cool, measured, intelligent concern with action and power. I feel that his administration would be less encumbered than S's with commitments to past ideas or sentimentalities; that he would be more radical; and, though he is less creative personally, he might be more so politically. But I cannot mention this feeling to anyone.

While Arthur Schlesinger abandoned his idol, Eleanor Roosevelt remained steadfast. For her it was not merely a question of "loving Adlai madly," as his old campaign slogan went. It was a matter of intensely disliking John F. Kennedy, and not just his waffling on McCarthyism, nor his suspect liberalism as a whole, nor his paternal ancestry. It was something more insidious than that. Eleanor Roosevelt—like so many of the barefoot, coalfield folks her cousin Joe Alsop had interviewed in West Virginia—possessed profound anti-Catholic tendencies.

"Jack invited me to dinner at his house the other night [the same occasion at which he had been so bored by JFK]," Franklin D. Roosevelt Jr. noted in 1959. "I know why. [Joe Kennedy associate] Jim Landis had already had lunch with me, to ask if I could and would talk to Mother about somehow changing her attitude on Jack.

"You remember that Mother was asked if she thought that any Catholic was qualified to be president, and she said, 'No.' Now you know Mother, she's stubborn."

On June 10, just a day short of a month before her party's convention opened, her stubbornness manifested itself by her endorsement of stubbornly non-candidate Stevenson in her newspaper column:

> So far he has been unwilling to become a candidate and I can well understand how a proud and sensitive man would be unwilling to offer himself as a candidate for a third time when he has been twice

defeated.

[T]he leading candidate for the nomination is Senator Kennedy. . . . Up to the time of the Summit conference my political mail hardly mentioned any of the other candidates. I was either being berated for not coming out for Kennedy or I was being berated for fear I would come out for Kennedy. . . . Since the Summit conference, however, I have not had a letter in my political mail mentioning anybody but Governor Stevenson. . . . [T]he world now requires maturity, it requires experience, and that the only man meeting these requirements since the failure of the summit is Adlai E. Stevenson.

Soon, she declared—on her own—that Stevenson was now a candidate. He still wasn't. "My message to Mrs. Roosevelt speaks for itself," Adlai responded to her and to the nation. "I reiterated the position I have taken for several years that I will not seek the nomination for President at the Democratic convention. Therefore I am not a candidate."

"Oh, dear," he then thought, "I suppose this will get me into it with Eleanor, won't it?"

Not really. She got the news from a member of the press at Hyde Park while she was hosting a visit from her son Franklin, Walter Reuther, and author and playwright Gore Vidal, a Hudson Valley neighbor who was mulling a long-shot congressional run. Following a curt "no comment" to the reporter, Eleanor turned to her guests, informing them, "Adlai has said—they say—that he will not be a candidate."

"Ma, give him up," protested an exasperated FDR Jr.

"There's still a chance, once we're at the convention."

Her son could barely contain himself: "This Hamlet routine of his!"

"Well, dear," argued Eleanor, gently but firmly, displaying boundless patience for a candidate and a man she had grown to so fondly admire, "you must take people as they are. He is what he is—"

"And that," interrupted Walter Reuther, who no longer loved him so, "is why we don't want him as the candidate."

The continuing, seemingly indestructible affection that those such as Eleanor Roosevelt held for Adlai provided a continuing source of fear for Jack Kennedy. He knew he was ahead. He knew the nomination was now his to lose. But he knew he *could* lose it, and, if he did, it might be to two-time loser Stevenson. If there was one egghead who had to be wooed, it was Stevenson himself.

A week after his West Virginia win, JFK phoned Arthur Schlesinger from the campaign trail in Maryland: "[Stevenson] is the essential ingredient in my combination," Kennedy informed Schlesinger. "I don't want to go hat in hand to all those southerners. But I'll have to do that if I can't get votes from the north."

Tempering JFK's intuitive knowledge of Stevenson's utility was a growing sense of Stevenson's personal futility. The longer Jack Kennedy campaigned and saw what presidential campaigns required, the more he realized what Stevenson lacked—and the less he respected him. As Ted Sorensen noted, "Their relationship had deteriorated . . . partly because they were political rivals and partly because JFK regarded Stevenson as weak and indecisive in the convention and pre-convention maneuvering. Ironically, had Stevenson been tougher and more determined in battling it out with him for the nomination, JFK would have respected him more."

To some it seemed that JFK could not respect Stevenson less. When the *Chicago Sun-Times'* Peter Lisagor had dared to suggest that Stevenson would emerge as the eventual nominee, JFK's response was immediate. Lisagor recalled that he "leaned forward—I remember this so vividly— almost the only time I saw him angry . . . and he said, 'Why, that's simply impossible. Adlai Stevenson is a bitter man. He's a bitter, deeply disillusioned, deeply hurt man.'"

Indeed, most of the Kennedys now displayed, let alone felt, little sympathy for their party's former standard-bearer. When Stevenson speechwriter William Attwood queried Jack regarding his willingness to accept second place on a third Stevenson ticket, the normally apolitical Jackie exploded, "Let Adlai get beaten alone! If you don't believe Jack, I'll cut my wrists and write an oath in blood that he'll refuse to run with Stevenson!"

And when JFK became president his opinion would not improve. Feeling frustration with the inefficiency displayed by his State Department, he once fumed, "They're not queer, but well, they're sort of like Adlai."

Following Oregon's primary, Larry O'Brien (some say it was RFK) cajoled JFK ("against his better judgment") into stopping by Adlai's Libertyville, Illinois, home to mend fences and secure support. But as this was a visit without any coherent strategy, possessing nothing but hope (and not much of that), the meeting was star-crossed from the beginning.

For once, LBJ had beaten JFK to the campaign punch, preceding him to Libertyville just days before in order to try to nudge Adlai into the race (or at least keep him neutral, flattering him: "If I don't get it, it will be you"). Beyond that, JFK's mission was further cursed by a conversation he held just before meeting Stevenson—with Adlai's law partners Newton Minow and William McCormick Blair Jr. Minow, displaying proper Stevensonian rectitude, gently, hesitantly, cautioned JFK (who had asked, "Do you think I ought to offer him the State Department?") against doing anything so crass as offering Adlai Foggy Bottom: "No, It would be a great mistake. For one thing, he would resent it. For another, you don't want to tie your own hands."

Absent that card to play, the game went nowhere. Informed of Johnson's visit, JFK exploded. "I told him," Kennedy later informed Arthur Schlesinger, "that Lyndon was a chronic liar; that he had been making all sorts of assurances to me for years and has lived up to none of them."

"It was downhill from there," Stevenson would later reveal to Chicago attorney George Ball, formerly his director of volunteers, now a JFK partisan. "Kennedy behaved just like his old man."

"I have the votes for the nomination," JFK supposedly threatened Adlai, much as RFK had demolished the hapless Mike DiSalle, "and if you don't give me your support, I'll have to shit all over you. I don't want to do that but I can, and I will if I have to."

"I should have told the son of a bitch off," Stevenson told Ball, "but, frankly, I was shocked and confused by that Irish gutter talk."

It was one of the lesser forty-five minutes of the JFK campaign. Riding back to the airport with Blair and Minow, Jack Kennedy could not believe his charm—and his inevitability—had failed him. "Why doesn't [Stevenson] come out for me?" JFK demanded, and when Adlai's men protested that he had merely meant to preserve his neutrality, JFK shot back, "Don't kid me. That means he wants to get it himself."

Blair asked if Kennedy had offered Stevenson the State Department, a query that certainly puzzled JFK ("No, certainly not. [Minow] told me not to bring it up"), and Blair now wondered if his counsel might have done more harm than good.

On reaching the airport, JFK posed one final query. "Guess who the next person I see will be—the person who will say about Adlai, 'I told you that son-of-a-bitch has been running for President every moment since 1956'?"

"Daddy," Bill Blair answered.

Correct.

THIRTEEN

"They were a dime a dozen"

VOTERS, IT SEEMED, were not always John Fitzgerald Kennedy's highest priority.

That distinction belonged to women—to such an extent that the sheer scope and recklessness of his lust threatened not merely his marriage but, concurrently, his political career.

He had come by his failings almost by inheritance. Joe Kennedy's adulteries were not merely numerous; they were flagrantly, boorishly, crudely ostentatious. Whether his assignation was with Hollywood silent star Gloria Swanson or his green-eyed twentysomething of the 1950s, Janet Des Rosiers—or with any number of women in between—JPK took little care to disguise his activities or desires.

Neither did his sons.

"I was at some posh restaurant in Washington," recalled Washington socialite and old family friend Kay Halle, "and the waiter brought me a note inviting me to join friends at another table. It was Joe and his two sons, Jack and Bobby. Jack was a congressman then. When I joined them the gist of the conversation from the boys was the fact that their father was going to be in Washington for a few days and needed female companionship. They wondered whom I could suggest, and they were absolutely serious."

Things might have proved different for JFK had it not been for Dad, and for the fact that his first sexual experience, at seventeen, involved not love but cash—three dollars for a white Harlem prostitute. At Harvard, his conquests—and carelessness—continued. He contracted gonorrhea and, later, chlamydia, for which he had to ingest massive doses of antibiotics. He also had to confess the embarrassing fact to Jackie.

An early conquest, accomplished while on Navy duty in Washington, attracted the notice of Walter Winchell's newspaper gossip column—and J. Edgar Hoover's FBI files. Four years older than Jack, former Danish beauty queen and a competitor for the title of Miss Europe Inga Arvad—"Inga Binga," as JFK dubbed her—had married and divorced an Egyptian diplomat, dabbled in journalism, attended Nazi deputy führer Hermann

Goering's wedding (Adolf Hitler was best man and she had enjoyed exclusive interviews with him), been asked to spy by German foreign minister Joachim von Ribbentrop, acted in a Danish movie, married Hungarian film director Paul Fejös, emigrated to America, and attended the Columbia School of Journalism. Arthur Krock helped Inga find employment with the *Washington Times-Herald*. In Washington, she roomed with fellow *Times-Herald* reporter (and JFK's sister) Kathleen "Kick" Kennedy.

In his own way, Jack Kennedy loved Inga; as her son Ronald McCoy would later tell interviewers, "There was a certain amount of insensitiveness, an awful lot of self-centeredness." JFK wanted to marry her, but she was still married.

The liaison made the papers on January 12, 1942, when Broadway columnist Winchell (who was, perhaps coincidentally, a great admirer of—and mouthpiece for—FDR) revealed:

One of Ex-Ambassador Kennedy's eligible sons is the target of a Washington gal columnist's affections. So much she has consulted her barrister about divorcing her exploring groom. Pa Kennedy no like.

No, Pa Kennedy ("Damn it, Jack! She's already married") did *not* like, and neither did J. Edgar Hoover, with Inga under surveillance as a possible Nazi agent (she wasn't, but with Jack then assigned to naval intelligence, the FBI wasn't taking chances). Between Winchell and Hoover, not to mention JPK, the days of the Kennedy-Arvad romance were numbered. The navy transferred Lieutenant Kennedy to South Carolina—and eventually to the Pacific. Returning stateside in 1945, JFK resumed his high-profile affairs. There was a fling with Hollywood's Gene Tierney, then in the process of divorcing fashion designer Oleg Cassini. Between her marital status, Jack's religion, and Tierney's retarded child, the affair never stood a chance, and JFK quickly bid adieu.

Reports circulated of JFK's impregnating a staffer during his 1946 campaign, and even of marriage ("a high school prank, a bit of daring that went too far") to Palm Beach socialite Durie Malcolm. Most denied the marriage's existence. Chuck Spalding contended it was all true.

Being an elected official might cause some men to consider their reputations. Congressman Jack Kennedy was not among them. "I went to his house in Georgetown for dinner," recalled JFK's old Choate and Princeton classman Ralph "Rip" Horton. "A lovely looking blonde from West Palm Beach joined us to go to a movie. After the movie we went back to the house, and I remember Jack saying something like, 'Well, I want to shake this one. She had ideas.' Shortly thereafter, another girl walked in. . . . I went to bed figuring this was the girl for the night. The next morning, a completely different girl came wandering down for breakfast. They were a dime a dozen."

Such behavior was hardly appropriate for those coveting the presidency, a fact recognized by America's foremost sexual hypocrite, Joseph P. Kennedy, who, through Washington attorney Nick Chase, employed the Williams J. Burns detective agency to shadow his own son. "He wanted private detectives to keep a watch on Jack in Georgetown," recalled Chase. "He used a private eye or two to check Jack's conduct. The old man wanted to know what he was doing and who he was horsing around with because he figured it would affect him politically. He made him, and he felt he owned him."

JFK clearly needed settling down, at least in his public image, and that is exactly what his very public September 1953 marriage to twenty-four-year-old socialite Jacqueline Lee Bouvier was designed to accomplish ("There was no love there," thought Evelyn Lincoln. "That I'm sure"). Nonetheless, old vices failed to expire. His philandering continued apace, and husbandly neglect stemming from adultery combined with husbandly neglect stemming from politics caused his bride's nerves—and patience—to fray. Rumors of imminent divorce regularly filled the capital. Gossip swirled that Joe Kennedy, fearing that a nasty scandal might doom Jack's presidential dreams, had offered the former Miss Bouvier a million dollars to remain Mrs. John F. Kennedy—plus a bonus if Jack brought home a disease.

At one Washington luncheon, Jackie complained to Knight-Ridder newspaper chain founder Walter Ridder of her absent husband. "He's gone," she said. "He's somewhere and I haven't heard from him. He's campaigning, but I bet he's off with some dame. I've got to divorce him." When Ridder responded, "I can understand this, but do you want to really ruin his chance of being president?" Jackie responded, "No."

Even during 1960's primary season, Red Fay heard rumors that Jackie would stay with Jack "only until [he] was nominated or the election is over." Jack denied all.

Uglier than rumors was blackmail. On April 8, Lyndon Johnson's man Bobby Baker, his eye more on shifting political winds than on loyalty to his chief (and never informing LBJ of the incident), contacted JFK with an unusual message and a warning of the utmost peril. In response, JFK scrawled out a memo to his files, had Pierre Salinger also sign it, and three days later ordered Salinger to seal it in an envelope and deposit it with his secretary Evelyn Lincoln for safekeeping. It read:

> I talked today with bobby baker. He informed me that three weeks ago an attorney he knew named Mickey Wiener from Newark (?) Hudson Co. called him. Wiener stated that if Sen. Johnson would give $150,000 to the wife of "a well known movie actor" (baker did not know her name or who the actor was) she would file an affidavit that she had had an affair with me. Baker said he thought it was blackmail, and did not inform Johnson of the matter. He did tell Joe Alsop that he was concerned about an attempt at blackmail of me and did not go with the details.

In all likelihood, the woman in question was a thirty-one-year-old blonde, Alicia Darr (born Barbara Maria Kopczynska), married since April 1957 to British-born film star Edmund Purdom. Revelations of any of JFK's affairs would be unpleasant and dangerous for Kennedy at this juncture, but reports of one with a woman such as Darr would prove especially embarrassing.

According to FBI reports, the Polish-Jewish immigrant Darr had operated brothels in both Boston (where she first met Kennedy) and later New York. Darr contended that she had once been engaged to JFK, but Joe Kennedy, displeased not so much that a future daughter-in-law might be a prostitute but that she was a Polish Jew, intervened and bought her off. Now, in 1960, her marriage to Purdom in tatters and her financial situation dire, Alicia Darr turned, according to some sources, to blackmail.

The Kennedys, as in the Drew Pearson *Profiles in Courage* imbroglio, sought Clark Clifford's counsel. Though Clifford now masterminded JFK rival Stuart Symington's mindless campaign, he agreed to take on the case. Clifford would eventually acknowledge that he had received an incredibly sensitive assignment from the Kennedys in early 1960, though never divulging its nature beyond that its "public knowledge could have blown the Kennedy nomination out of the water."

"I had a conversation," he did say, "with Jack Kennedy that was so dramatic that if I could live to be a million years old, I could never forget it."

Clifford finally, however, begged off—"I told Jack that I was not the right fellow to handle it. And they turned it over to [James] McInerney."

The Kennedys were no strangers to McInerney, who had supervised the FBI investigation of Inga Arvad. When McInerney entered private legal practice in 1953, the Kennedys were among his first clients, and among his duties for them was damage control in a case uncomfortably similar to Darr's—that of Georgetown debutante and JFK staff member Pamela Turnure and her curious Washington landlady, Mrs. Florence M. Kater.

Late one evening in 1958—too late for any conventional social visit—Florence Kater and her husband, Leonard, observed JFK departing the brunette twentysomething Turnure's apartment. Subsequently—on July 11, 1958, at approximately 1 a.m.—Leonard Kater photographed Jack Kennedy again leaving Turnure's abode. The Katers' original motivations appear less than simon-pure, at one point attempting to shake down the family for a Modigliani painting. McInerney was brought in to negotiate, and, with the Kennedys inclined to play hardball (McInerney repeatedly threatened Leonard's job), no painting was exchanged, no silence bought. Instead, Florence Kater, either from genuine disgust over JFK's moral failings or from the rage of a blackmailer scorned, initiated an extended, if spectacularly unsuccessful, campaign to expose Jack Kennedy. In May 1959, she mailed her allegations—plus copies of her husband's photograph of JFK—to fifty prominent editors, reporters, and politicians. Not one responded. During the 1960 campaign, she picketed JFK—during the Democratic convention, at the University of Maryland, and even in front of Harry Truman's Independence, Missouri, home. Save for a brief, almost innocuous mention in the *Washington Star*, no paper dared touch her story.

Editors had their reasons. Many, of course, simply liked and admired JFK. But there also existed an unwritten journalistic rule: Unless a sexual peccadillo went to court or entered the justice system, respectable media ignored it.

Beyond that, unmasking JFK might create a dangerous precedent, with numerous and sundry other politicians' infidelities now becoming fair game, most notably that of JFK's wiliest opponent, Lyndon Baines Johnson. LBJ's affairs, though nowhere near at JFK's prodigious levels, were, nonetheless, both long-standing and numerous. As Lady Bird Johnson herself once tolerantly pronounced, "Lyndon loved *people*. It would be unnatural for him to withhold love from half the people." Many said that Richard Nixon's old nemesis, Helen Gahagan Douglas, and the statuesque mistress and later wife of Texas newspaper baron Charles Marsh, Alice Glass, were numbered among Lyndon's conquests, but as 1960 commenced, LBJ had also become involved with one of his own staffers. The relationship was not merely carnal but also intensely emotional, and Johnson, contends JFK biographer Herbert Parmet, was "sufficiently enchanted to consider leaving Lady Bird."

Beyond all this, an editor might simply think several times before trusting the Katers' tale. Their famous photo merely revealed a hand shielding a man's face. Was that face really that of a U.S. senator? Where was the picture snapped? And when? At 1 a.m.? Or at a more innocent, explainable hour?

Still, Florence Kater's story might yet have gone further. *Washington Star* reporter Bob Clark interviewed the Katers and found them credible, particularly when they claimed to possess more substantial evidence: two tape recordings of JFK within the Turnure apartment. Clark approached *Star* editor Charles Seib with the news. Seib ordered Clark off the story.

Which brings us back to James McInerney and Alicia Darr. The Katers were amateur blackmailers; Alicia Darr evidently was not. In 1952, according to FBI reports, she had been involved in a New York society blackmailing ring, and the photos she possessed may not have been as innocuous and ambiguous as the one the Katers produced.

The Darr case went away in 1960. Why? How? The answers may never be definitely revealed, but the answer to those questions may very well resolve certain glaring ambiguities relating to JFK, the mob, and the West Virginia primary. Rumors have long circulated of mobster Sam "Momo" Giancana's funding of Jack Kennedy's West Virginia primary victory, reports too persistent to easily be dismissed—yet containing so many serious inconsistencies or incongruities as to render their entire proposition dubious.

Why would the Kennedy family, sitting atop a four-hundred-million-dollar fortune, have to beg mobsters—or anyone, for that matter—for cash? Hubert Humphrey might need a financial boost. The Kennedys did not.

Why the great discrepancies regarding the amount of mob cash involved? Sam Giancana's family placed the number at $500,000. Wiretaps of supposed mob agent Skinny D'Amato revealed the number to actually be a mere $50,000. Again, why would the Kennedys soil themselves for a mere $50,000?

And, if only a mere $50,000 was involved, why was Frank Sinatra seen at least twice with suitcases full of mob cash—hundreds of thousands of dollars' worth—to be delivered to the Kennedys?

Why would JFK—as his mistress Judith Campbell (Exner) claimed—meet personally with Giancana to arrange the deal? Such hands-on activity stood completely outside JFK's normal modes of operations.

The answer may finally be found by connecting the dots to the generally little-known Darr case.

On June 4, 1961, J. Edgar Hoover dispatched a memo to now attorney general Robert Kennedy, informing RFK that in recent New York State court proceedings two former attorneys for Alicia Darr had alleged that prior to the 1960 election he—Robert Kennedy—"went to New York and arranged a settlement of the case [between JFK and Darr] for $500,000." There was, in actuality, no "case" in any court. "Case" may simply have been a euphemism for their shakedown operation, or, as another court would characterize matters, "the commission of a contemplated crime."

The $500,000 figure neatly matches the $500,000 sum that the Giancana family alleged the Kennedys received. It coincides very roughly with the stacks of cash seen being funneled in suitcases and satchels from the mob to Frank Sinatra and then to the Kennedys. Although the Kennedys had no need of cash to fuel their West Virginia effort, they may have required *huge* amounts of untraceable cash in a *very short period of time* to prevent Darr's going public.

But what about the $150,000 figure Bobby Baker quoted to JFK? That may have been the figure for LBJ, but when the game shifted suddenly toward a transaction with the far wealthier Kennedys, the stakes may have risen quite substantially.

And what of Skinny D'Amato and his $50,000 West Virginia effort? D'Amato biographer Jonathan Van Meter makes the point that D'Amato, though he knew all the best (and worst) mobsters, was never one himself. Van Meter theorizes that D'Amato's West Virginia junket may not have been at Giancana's behest, but rather on behalf of D'Amato pal Frank Sinatra.

And the so-out-of-character JFK-Giancana Fontainebleau Hotel tête-à-tête? Extraordinary circumstances breed extraordinary behavior, and JFK's panic may have triggered such a meeting. Consider this sequence of events: At very nearly the exact time Bobby Baker informed JFK of the shakedown attempt, JFK coincidentally contacted Judith Campbell to arrange a meeting with Sam Giancana. JFK delivered his memo detailing the blackmail attempt to Evelyn Lincoln on April 11, 1960. He met with Giancana *the following day.*

Judith Immoor Campbell, a statuesque, raven-haired, stunningly beautiful twenty-six-year-old Southern California divorcée, was JFK's newest fling—and Sam Giancana's main squeeze. Sometime around 1959 she had drifted into Frank Sinatra's libidinous circle of friends, and on Sunday evening, February 7, 1960, she moved into the Kennedy orbit when, at Las Vegas's Sands Hotel, Sinatra introduced both Jack and Teddy Kennedy to her. "She was," recalled Sinatra's thirty-three-year-old black valet George Jacobs, "the perfect Eisenhower era pinup of the girl next door. That she charged for her wholesomeness was beside the point."

"I hitched a ride on the Kennedy campaign plane going from Texas to Oregon," CBS reporter (and Kennedy classmate) Blair Clark recalled. "The plane stopped at Las Vegas at noon, and there was no goddamn reason for stopping there except fun and games. I remember Jack took two of us to Frank Sinatra's suite at the Sands. We had a couple of drinks and the two of us left because we sensed that Jack and Frank and a couple of the girls were going to have a party. One of the girls was Judith Campbell, although I have absolutely no memory of that charmer. The plane didn't leave until the next morning."

"I was at a table at the Sands with Peter and Pat and Jack," recalled Peter Lawford's agent Milt Ebbins. "The lights were low but I sensed a lady come sit down beside me—maybe it was her perfume. And she said, 'I'm Judith Campbell. I'm a guest of Mr. Sinatra's. He's asked me to sit at this table.'"

When JFK ("So handsome," she thought, "in his pin-striped suit. Those strong white teeth and smiling Irish eyes") and Judith left—to go upstairs—Ebbins further remembered that he "went to Peter later and said, 'Who is this girl?' And Peter said, 'She's a hooker. Frank gave her $200 to stop at our table . . . to go to bed with Jack.'"

Campbell remembered it in more romantic terms, recalling that she found Kennedy to be attractive and, better still, "the world's greatest listener," possessing "an almost insatiable interest in what and who I was." They rendezvoused on March 7, 1960, in Room 1651 of New York's Plaza Hotel, and there—at least in Campbell's version—consummated their relationship. Later that month, Sinatra provided Mrs. Campbell with yet another introduction, this time to "Sam Flood," in reality, Sam Giancana. Unlike Sinatra, Giancana could not readily be identified as a Kennedy "fan." Bobby Kennedy had publicly identified him as the "chief gunman for the group that succeeded the Capone mob," and, during July 1959 Senate hearings, had publicly ridiculed the Chicago tough guy. "I thought only little girls giggled, Mr. Giancana," Bobby taunted Sam. Mr. Giancana did not suffer slights lightly.

All of which meant that Mrs. Campbell's introduction to Jack Kennedy may have represented more than just simple friendliness on Sinatra's part, for Judith Campbell had another link to Sam Giancana besides Frank Sinatra: She had also been keeping company with Hollywood and Las Vegas mob boss Johnny Roselli, and some have claimed that it was Roselli who had arranged the initial JFK-Campbell introduction.

The JFK-Campbell assignation was soon news within—and beyond—the mob. "With the old-style PBX system we had," recalled Sands Hotel pit boss Ed Walters, "the phone operators knew who was calling who and heard things. Kennedy's family back east worried about him, about it getting out that he was being seduced by Sinatra and the girls, and about his medical problems—he had a doctor with him when he came. We wondered, if he was running for president, about how close he was getting to Sinatra."

On March 23, 1960, FBI chief J. Edgar Hoover received a memo detailing a mob-connected informant's claims that JFK had recently, while in Miami, bedded a stewardess, and, more interestingly, that:

> in Miami he [the informant overheard] a conversation which indicated that Senator Kennedy had been *compromised* [emphasis added] in Las Vegas, Nevada. . . . Senator Kennedy was staying in the Sands Hotel in Las Vegas about 6 or 8 weeks ago during the filming of a movie entitled "Oceans 11," starring [Frank Sinatra and] Dean Martin. He stated that he observed Senator Kennedy in the nightclub of the Sands Hotel, during this period, but has no idea as to the identity of any possible female companion.

Or, as Sam's younger brother Chuck Giancana claimed to have been told beforehand, "Frank's got it all handled with the broads for Kennedy . . . one Frank says is a dead ringer for Jack's wife. . . . Frank's gonna introduce them."

According to Chuck Giancana, however, the Campbell ploy was mere insurance for a grander Sam Giancana arrangement involving both Jack and Joe Kennedy, one already in place. Many of Chuck Giancana's revelations read like mere fantasy. But one that's all too possible concerns Sam informing his brother: "I've already got enough dirt on Jack Kennedy and his lousy old man to ruin ten politicians' careers. I've got pictures, tape recordings, film, you name it, all safe and sound in a safe-deposit box."

As Los Angeles–based (but Chicago-connected) mobster Mickey Cohen observed, "I know that certain people in the Chicago organization knew that they had to get John Kennedy in. There was no thought that they were going to get the best of it with John Kennedy. . . . The choice becomes the best of what you've got going. John Kennedy was the best selection. But nobody in my line of work had an idea that he was going to name Bobby Kennedy attorney general. That was the last thing anyone thought."

So it was that Sam Giancana's name surfaced between Jack Kennedy and Judith Campbell, first in a phone call, and then on the evening of April 6, 1960, as the two, with Jackie absent, trysted at JFK's Georgetown home. It was all so very dangerous, much more so than dallying with a high-priced Boston madam or a Georgetown staffer—or even a suspected Nazi agent. Jack Kennedy had come too near forces that no one should approach at all.

Which brings us back to . . . Alicia Darr. Sam Giancana, confident that he now "owned" the next president of the United States, did not relish seeing his wonderful opportunity jeopardized by such unpleasantries. If anyone was going to blackmail JFK, it would be him, and if Sam Giancana could assist his new associate in silencing a rival blackmailer when so much more than mere cash was at stake, well, then . . . what indeed *was* a half million between friends?

As congressional investigators G. Robert Blakey and Richard Billings would later write of history's strange trio of Jack and Judith and Sam:

> You are all right, it is said, just so long as you do not "sleep with them," that is, you do not take favors, either money or sex.
>
> From the mob's point of view, Kennedy had been compromised. He had crossed the line. In the Greek sense, the liaison with Judith Campbell was, we came to believe, Kennedy's fatal flaw.

It may not have been as literally fatal as Blakey and Billings meant to suggest, but it remained dangerous and stupid and beneath a man who held himself out to be the next leader of the Free World.

Bedding gangsters' molls within the boundaries of the family home was also not the sort of activity designed to solidify an already-shaky marriage. Even if Jackie Kennedy did not know the details, the astounding *immensity* of it all, she knew enough. When she could not be in West Virginia, she dispatched Teddy's wife, Joan, as a surrogate, informing Joan that voters would love meeting her because her "name was Kennedy" (as opposed to a Jean Smith or a Eunice Shriver). But that was not the real reason. Jackie was using Joan, in a very subtle way, to keep JFK from roaming.

"If I don't get the nomination," JFK had informed Judith Campbell in his Georgetown bedroom after making love, "Jackie and I have arranged we will separate. We will part. I want you to know that this has nothing to do with you."

Fast-forward to Wednesday, September 12, 1960: Jack Kennedy, on the road in Texas, fresh from a triumphant, even pivotal, address to the

Greater Houston Ministerial Association, phones home. Jacqueline Kennedy should be pleased by the news and by the enthusiastic reception he had received that day in Houston, El Paso, Lubbock, and San Antonio. She is not.

She cradles the receiver. "Today's our wedding anniversary," she informs everyone in the room, "and Jack never mentions it."

FOURTEEN

"A clean bill of health"

WEST VIRGINIA HAD for all intents and purposes concluded the primary season. But it hadn't concluded the great delegate hunt leading up to the convention.

In the three lackluster primaries that followed West Virginia, Kennedy forces had elbowed out the unexciting first-term Maryland governor J. Millard Tawes from his state's May 17 contest, and, left with only token opposition from Wayne Morse (some said aided by Jimmy Hoffa money), rolled to a 70 percent to 17 percent victory. Kennedy's next stop was more difficult, on Morse's Oregon home turf. Lyndon Johnson, still not an official candidate, was also on the ballot. Oregon law provided that the only way a widely rumored candidate might remove himself from the process was to file a disclaimer reading, "I am not now and do not intend to become a candidate for President." Johnson would not take that step. On May 20, JFK easily slipped past the irascible Morse (50 percent to 32 percent), even defeating him three to two in his home county. Humphrey (6 percent), Symington (4 percent), Johnson (4 percent), and Stevenson (3 percent) garnered mere negligible support.

Morse withdrew the next morning, vowing to "of course, discontinue any further efforts in other states to obtain delegates to the convention," and grudgingly vowing to support Kennedy if he were the nominee as "he would be ten times better than Nixon." But as Kennedy vanquished Morse, the Gallup organization revealed that JFK's lead over Nixon had eroded to 51 percent to 49 percent, down from 54 percent to 46 percent just a few weeks previously. The Catholic-Protestant divide was stark: Even matching Nixon against the Unitarian Stevenson, Nixon captured 60 percent of the Protestant vote, while Stevenson captured 58 percent of Catholics. JFK captured 79 percent of his co-religionists (down from 81 percent), while 64 percent of Protestants went for Nixon (up from 61 percent).

"Well, the seven primaries are over," Joe Kennedy wrote to his friend British press magnate Lord Beaverbrook on May 27, "and we won an overwhelming victory. If we get a break at all in Pennsylvania and a reasonable break in California, we're home. . . . The only thing that will make it possible for Nixon to win is if they steal the nomination from Jack."

The nation's final contested primary—California's—arrived on July 1, and Kennedy (31 percent) defeated Pat Brown (23 percent), local pension reformer George H. McLain (11 percent), Hubert Humphrey (10 percent), George Smathers (5 percent), and Mike DiSalle (5 percent). Between his relatively strong popular showing and his agreement with Brown, JFK thought he had the Golden State delegation secured. Beneath the surface, however, strong Stevenson support (as well as lesser support for Symington and LBJ) festered. State Democratic Committee executive director Joe Cerrell bragged, "California Democrats are something like a girl who has just got rid of her teeth brace[s] and thrown away her glasses; she doesn't say yes to the first suitor"—a quote broadcast nationwide by twenty-nine-year-old *Wall Street Journal* reporter Robert Novak. "Bob, you really got this one wrong," JFK called Novak to say. "We have California all wrapped up. If we don't, I'll eat your story."

Primaries, no matter how dull or preordained, generate headlines. Back rooms do not—though it was in the back rooms that the bulk of the heavy lifting remained. Teddy Kennedy, for example, found that his chief assignment lay not in Wisconsin or West Virginia, but in scouring the far West for delegates. "When we divided up the country at Bobby's house, my job was to cover the Western states," he recalled. "They gave me a two-page memorandum with about ten different names on it, plus a speech my brother made in Montana in 1957. The rest was up to me. Lucky I learned how to fly a plane when I went to law school." For the campaign, Teddy relocated to San Francisco, seeing his twenty-three-year-old wife, Joan, only thirteen nights in one three-and-a-half month period.

It was in the big states, such as California, Pennsylvania, New York, and Illinois, that the nomination hung in the balance. Chicago mayor Richard J. Daley had long been receptive to JFK, had enthusiastically supported him at the 1956 convention, and had required virtually no courting from the Kennedy camp. He had been informally on board by early 1959 at the latest, and in many ways the Kennedys had taken him for granted. In September 1959, Daley and Kennedy operative Pat Lynch happened to be attending a testimonial dinner in New York State. The next morning they attended 5 a.m. Mass together, and Lynch gingerly inquired, "How is our boy doing out there in Chicago?"

"Who's our boy?"

"Jack Kennedy. Who else?"

"I don't know how he's doing," Daley responded. "I haven't heard from him in six months."

Lynch, nearly panic-stricken, phoned Kenny O'Donnell. "I know he wasn't lying, because I met him at the five o'clock Mass. We don't tell lies to each other at a five o'clock Mass. Maybe at an eleven o'clock Mass or a twelve o'clock Mass, but not at a five o'clock Mass. It sounds to me like we might no longer have Dick Daley."

O'Donnell passed Lynch's warning on to Jack. JFK didn't seem particularly nervous, but his staff arranged for Kennedy and Hizzoner to rendezvous at Chicago's Comiskey Park for that fall's White Sox–Dodgers World Series. They sat together. They watched the game. That was it. "He doesn't talk much, does he?" Daley asked afterward.

Kennedy had much the same reaction. "All he did was watch the game," JFK told his men. "Dick didn't mention politics. He was too busy watching the game."

New York, torn between old-line bosses including Carmine De Sapio, Dan O'Connell, and Charlie Buckley, and the reform wing led by Eleanor Roosevelt and Herbert Lehman, saw the Kennedys again align with the bosses. In fact, JFK's people exhibited little respect for party liberals. "I'm here to elect a President of the United States," RFK once yelled at New York reformers (including Lehman and Eleanor). "I don't give a damn what happens to your people afterward."

Muttered the eighty-two-year-old Lehman: "He's a nasty little man."

In Pennsylvania, Governor Lawrence and Philadelphia's Mayor Green ruled, and, though Catholic themselves, they remained stubbornly suspicious of a Catholic presidential candidacy. Jack Kennedy phoned Congressman Tip O'Neill for advice. O'Neill picked the brain of Pittsburgh Steelers owner Art Rooney, whose Plymouth, Massachusetts, summer cottage adjoined O'Neill's. The Republican Rooney suggested approaching Pennsylvania state treasurer Joe Clark (not to be confused with Democratic Pennsylvania U.S. senator Joe Clark, a Nelson Rockefeller in-law). "Joe Clark," advised Rooney, "is the one who made David Lawrence governor and Green the boss, and they'll do anything he says. He's the man you want."

JFK had never heard of *this* Joe Clark, but forwarded his number to his father anyway. Two days later, Jack Kennedy advised Tip, "Tonight Joe Clark and his wife are staying with my parents in their Fifth Avenue apartment in New York. I guess you had the right guy."

It was coming together. By Saturday, June 11, NBC News estimated that, with 761 votes needed to nominate, Jack Kennedy was closing in:

Kennedy	698 ?
Johnson	449
Symington	119
Humphrey	68 ?
Stevenson	58

By late June the Kennedys believed their Pennsylvania efforts had borne fruit. "Well, that's it," Joe Kennedy crowed in Lake Tahoe. "We've got a majority."

In actuality, the Kennedys had neither Pennsylvania nor a majority. Soon both Lyndon Johnson and former president Harry Truman were roaring at them full throttle. Johnson was now on the march, fulminating against recent JFK comments that Dwight Eisenhower might apologize to Nikita Khrushchev for the U-2 affair. On a belated six-state Western tour, LBJ contrasted himself with JFK, particularly on the experience issue, literally shouting to a Washington State Democratic Convention at Spokane on May 30, 1960: "I am not prepared to apologize to Mr. Khrushchev—are you? I am not prepared to send regrets to Mr. Khrushchev—are you?" On the same day, in Bismark, North Dakota, Lyndon's Senate ally, Washington State's Warren Magnuson, sniped, "The summit collapse has slowed the Kennedy parade. It may have stopped it."

"The most impressive thing to me in this tour," LBJ observed, "is the determination of the Democratic delegates to make up their own mind. They are not about to be stampeded by propaganda or power plays. . . . Anyone who thinks the nomination is going to be settled before the delegates actually vote is going to be a very surprised man."

On June 2 Sam Rayburn unveiled a Citizens Committee for Lyndon

Johnson, predicting five hundred votes on arrival in Los Angeles. Truman's interior secretary, the left-wing Oscar Chapman, would serve as Johnson's campaign chairman—an ironic appointment, noted the *Chicago Tribune*, for a candidate running, however haltingly, "as a conservative." Mrs. India Edwards, former *Chicago Tribune* society editor and vice chairman of the DNC, would co-chair. John Connally would be executive director. Asked if LBJ had okayed his move, Mr. Sam could merely respond, "I told him what we were going to do."

It was all, of course, too little and too late. An April 1960 Gallup poll revealed Kennedy gaining, Johnson deteriorating:

	March 1960	April 1960
Kennedy	34%	39%
Stevenson	23%	21%
Johnson	15%	11%
Humphrey	5%	7%
Symington	6%	6%
Brown	2%	3%
Others	6%	5%
None, No opinion	8%	8%

Johnson's situation was even more dire in the South, with Bostonian JFK now nearly on a par with Austinian LBJ:

	December 1959	March 1960	April 1960
Johnson	31%	35%	30%
Kennedy	16%	20%	27%
Stevenson	20%	18%	13%
Humphrey	3%	4%	6%
Symington	3%	4%	5%
Others	14%	9%	8%
None, No opinion	13%	10%	11%

Johnson's delegate hunt suffered special disappointment in the next-door Southwest. In New Mexico, LBJ enjoyed support from Senators Dennis Chavez and Clinton Anderson and expected all seventeen state delegates, but JFK picked off four. The situation had proved even more depressing in Arizona in early May. LBJ enjoyed backing from octogenarian senator Carl Hayden and from former governor and senator Ernest McFarland, but Tucson's forty-year-old pro-JFK congressman Stewart Udall out-organized his party's elders, sweeping the entire delegation for Kennedy. "There I was," LBJ mourned, "looking for the burglar coming in the front door, and little did I know that the fox was coming through the fence in back. When I woke up, the chickens were gone."

Lyndon Johnson had now approached Chicago's Richard Daley for support. "Lyndon," said Daley, "all of us out here like you. We think you've done a great job as our majority leader in the senate, and you would make a fine President. But Jack Kennedy will get more votes for us in Illinois than you can get, so we've got to be for Kennedy."

Minnesota Democrats literally laughed at India Edwards when she tried convincing them LBJ was a liberal. Beyond that, Johnson's delegate hunters were rank amateurs, good old boys lost in concrete canyons. "The Kennedys just got out first," recalled LBJ operative Lloyd Hand, "and they had more muscle, they had more money, and they were more sophisticated. Most of the people in the Johnson organization hadn't been involved in national delegate hunts before. Good men—able men— I loved them dearly, but getting a fellow from south Texas to go into Manhattan to talk to delegates . . . you know. A lot of people . . . they just hear some South in your mouth, and they automatically think you're dumb. They think if you talk funny, you are funny."

"Mr. Johnson," Evelyn Lincoln later noted, "was getting reports on his delegate strength that bore as much relation to realism as the fellow who planted toads and expected to grow toadstools."

The Kennedy people displayed decreasing respect for Lyndon Johnson. Ben Bradlee, after covering one of Johnson's speeches, had told JFK back in 1959 that LBJ lacked "the requisite dignity. . . . He's somebody's gabby cousin from Fort Worth. . . . He's to be feared not as a potential winner but as a game-player who might try to maneuver you right out of the contest in Los Angeles."

By July 1960, open warfare loomed. When Bobby Kennedy and Bobby Baker happened upon each other at a Washington movie theater, RFK contemptuously introduced Secretary of the Senate Baker to his group as "Little Lyndon Johnson—and you should ask him why Big Lyndon won't risk running in the primaries against my brother." RFK's crude hostility shocked Baker. He tried defusing the situation, but Kennedy bore on. "They're supposed to make 'em tough in Texas, but Big Lyndon doesn't look tough to me."

But even RFK wouldn't have tried that with Harry Truman. In Independence, Missouri, HST fumed. He despised the Kennedys, hated settled conventions, and, if truth be told, hated, most of all, being ignored in the whole process.

There was a reason for his being ignored, of course. In 1960 Harry Truman remained the Herbert Hoover of the Democratic Party, an inconvenient ghost, a best-forgotten memento of a failed administration. And he was a nasty, ill-tempered Herbert Hoover to boot.

On Saturday, July 2, Truman called a press conference at his Independence presidential library and museum, an event broadcast nationally on radio and on the CBS and NBC television networks. Dean Acheson tried to warn him to choose not only his words but his fights carefully:

Clark Clifford told me this was not going to be good at all—he was going to be very extreme in his opposition to Kennedy. So I called Mr. Truman on the telephone and we had a long conversation in which I pointed out that this was not going to do any good at all. He would not defeat the nomination and that, if he thought that, he was exaggerating his own power. But he could hurt the situation, as there were a lot of people who had a great respect for Mr. Truman's judgment, and it would be a mistake to say something which later on he would regret. . . . I finally got him to promise that he would not say certain things which he had in mind to say. He kept his word on this and did not do that. I urged him not to say anything at all and he promised me that he would take that under consideration, which was his usual phrase. . . . And of course, as you know, he did.

Considering what Mr. Truman eventually said, it is intriguing to speculate on what Acheson dissuaded him from articulating. Truman dropped a bombshell, resigning as a delegate to the Democratic National Convention that was scheduled to open in Los Angeles in just nine days.

He charged the deck was stacked, the process sabotaged, the convention rigged. And by whom? He left that unstated, but obviously he was referring to the unseasoned, inexperienced, unworthy Jack Kennedy and his family and supporters.

"Senator," Truman asked, addressing the candidate directly, "are you certain you are quite ready for the country, or that the country is ready for you in the role of President in January 1961?

"May I suggest you be patient."

Accordingly, Harry Truman enumerated a raft of "good men," candidates acceptable to him: Senators Symington, Johnson, Joe Clark of Pennsylvania, Eugene McCarthy of Minnesota, Henry Jackson of Washington, and Albert Gore of Tennessee. He also mentioned Governors Meyner of New Jersey, Orville Freeman of Minnesota, and T. Leroy Collins of Florida, plus Kennedy's own foreign policy adviser, Congressman Chester Bowles.

But no Kennedy.

Truman's testy blast shook the Kennedy camp. Not yet holding a majority of delegates, they were wary of what might stampede a jittery party. Ted Sorensen, who viewed Truman's performance from JFK's Los Angeles headquarters, hurriedly caught a plane for Hyannis. Meanwhile, in Washington, John Kennedy's Senate aides switched on their television. It didn't work. Herb Klein let them watch on Nixon's. They didn't like what they saw.

JFK was in Hyannis, resting. The primaries had worn him out, so he had headed home for ten days of pre-convention R & R. But his TV set worked just fine. It just didn't provide a restful experience.

Two days later, at midtown Manhattan's Hotel Roosevelt, JFK delivered his response before a hundred newspeople. Sorensen flew down with him, and so did pregnant Jackie. A hundred and fifty supporters packed the room and cheered him. NBC and CBS broadcast his rebuttal live on both radio and TV.

"If we are to establish a test for the Presidency whereby fourteen years in major elective office is insufficient experience . . . ," JFK responded, "all but a handful of our Presidents since the very founding of this nation should be ruled out, and every President elevated to that office in the twentieth century should have been ruled out, including the three great Democratic Presidents, Woodrow Wilson, Franklin Roosevelt and Harry Truman himself.

"To exclude from positions of trust and command all those below the age of 44 would have kept Jefferson from writing the Declaration of Independence, Washington from commanding the Continental Army, Madison from fathering the Constitution, Hamilton from serving as Secretary of the Treasury, [Henry] Clay from being elected Speaker of the House and Christopher Columbus from even discovering America."

It was a skilled, cool, controlled, even masterful performance. Reporters and supporters laughed at JFK's jibe that Truman's idea of an open convention was one that "studies all the candidates—reviews their records—and then takes his advice."

Truman claimed he didn't even bother to watch JFK's response. Eleanor Roosevelt did, writing to friends:

We all listened to Truman's press conference in which he charged the convention was rigged for Kennedy & resigned as a delegate. I got a feeling he wouldn't mind having it rigged for Lyndon Johnson & he listed 10 possible candidates & never mentioned Adlai! Yesterday Kennedy answered in a press conference. He did very well. Firm about not giving up but most courteous to Pres. T. I have a feeling he did himself good but H. S. T. did himself harm.

JFK now advanced on all fronts. On Friday, July 1, 1960, the day preceding Truman's blast, he had conferred with Stuart Symington and importuned the Missouri senator to drop out, hinting rather broadly that second place might be his if he did. Kennedy's position had been strengthened by June's Gallup poll, which revealed a substantially increased lead:

	May 1960	June 1960
Kennedy	34%	42%
Stevenson	21%	24%
Johnson	11%	14%
Symington	7%	8%
Others	16%	5%
None, No opinion	4%	7%

Symington, however, wasn't buying Kennedy's offer. Calculating that his longshot odds increased immeasurably if a deadlock resulted, he was unwilling to trade his chance at the brass ring for a vague promise of a vague office.

As Democrats feuded, Republicans surged. Nixon now edged Kennedy 51 percent to 49 percent. A Nixon-Rockefeller ticket defeated a Stevenson-Kennedy combination by the same margin. On Tuesday, July 5, just six days before the convention, LBJ finally leaped—officially—into the fray. Holding forth at a Senate office building news conference, natty in custom-tailored blue suit, a three-point white handkerchief peeking from his breast pocket, Johnson formally announced his candidacy for the presidency of the United States of America. It was, as was so much of any LBJ operation, barely controlled chaos, with LBJ losing a contact lens beforehand and *Washington Post* editor Phil Graham (a key—though very emotional—Johnson friend and ally) on hands and knees looking for it. "I am a candidate for President," Lyndon told the packed room, his voice reaching a higher pitch than normal, "and I expect to be nominated for President." Sam Rayburn, he announced, would place his name in nomination. He scorned Americans for Democratic Action (ADA) backing, accusing the liberal organization of not wanting "any Catholic Americans or Baptist Americans" to become president.

Johnson was obsessed by Kennedy, who roiled him more than any Republican did. "I am not going to go elbowing through 179 million Americans," he fumed, "pushing aside other Senators and Governors and Congressmen to shout 'Look at me—and nobody else. . . . Those who have engaged in active campaigns since January have missed hundreds of . . . votes. This I could not do—for my country or my party. Someone has to tend the store." The message was, while Kennedy had been out tooting his own horn, Johnson had stayed home and placed himself second to the business of Congress. Johnson had taken the high road.

But on the very day previous, Johnson's representatives India Edwards and John Connally had done anything but. Instead, they had revealed to the nation—a populace that didn't particularly want to hear it—the truth regarding John F. Kennedy's precarious personal health. Kennedy himself had provided the Johnson camp the proverbial last straw on that subject during his rebuttal to Harry Truman, when he posited that the presidency demanded "the strength and health and vigor of young men." To Johnson's people, that was a slap at their heart-attack-victim candidate.

Ominous rumors concerning Kennedy's own health had circulated for years. In early 1960, Richard Rovere prepared a piece on JFK for *Esquire* bearing the disturbing title "Kennedy's Last Chance to Be President" and providing the reason why: Addison's disease. Before the article ran, however, Rovere phoned Gore Vidal (a tenuous in-law of Jackie Kennedy), warning, "Your friend isn't going to be—can't be—nominated."

Rovere went on to explain: "The wife of a friend of mine has Addison's disease," he said. "They sent her to the Leahey Clinic in Boston, to the doctor who looked after Kennedy when he was close to dying from Addison's. Apparently, the doctor had invented a new treatment for Kennedy, some kind of pellet under the skin that creates adrenalin, but only for so long, which means he is not apt to live through the next four years."

Vidal conveyed Rovere's warning to JFK, a few days later receiving the only phone call he would ever receive from Kennedy. No hello, no introduction, merely a curt, "Tell your friend Rovere that I don't have Addison's disease. How could I and keep the schedule I do? I did have malaria and was treated for it in Boston." JFK then rambled, dissembling with all sorts of false and misleading information to disprove Rovere's thesis. Vidal, with no great reason to doubt JFK, conveyed it all to Rovere, adding dollops of if-not-JFK-then-Nixon caveats. Rovere's damaging information never ran.

LBJ's people proved less easily gulled. Johnson operatives Walter Jenkins and Don Cook conducted the research. India Edwards delivered the message. "Let me do it," she warned John Connally, "because I have no career ahead of me, and you have. You're a young man. It will make a terrible stink. It won't matter to me."

"Doctors have told [JFK he] would not be alive if it were not for cortisone," Mrs. Edwards charged in a press conference, positing that it was "no disgrace" to have Addison's and no "serious defect so long as it can be kept under control," but she "objected to his muscle flexing in boasting about his youth."

Connally, however, couldn't keep silent. He questioned JFK's prolonged health-related absences in 1954, and offered to release LBJ's medical records—by implication, challenging JFK to do likewise. Predicting more than five hundred first-ballot votes for Johnson, "Big Jawn" unrealistically estimated that Kennedy would have fewer than five hundred. Conceding that Kennedy had won seven primaries, Connally reminded voters that Kefauver had won seventeen in 1956 and failed to capture the nomination.

Johnson feigned innocence. "So far as I am aware," said LBJ, "all the candidates are in good health. Senator Kennedy had some difficulty in 1954 that kept him out of the Senate for months. I had some difficulty in 1955 which kept me out for weeks—and I am very glad that both of us were tough enough not to let it get us down."

Lyndon Johnson bitterly resented mention of his "difficulties"—his heart attack. Nor did he savor rumors—false rumors, as they turned out to be—of a new heart attack. Since these rumors conveniently surfaced on the eve of Texas's recent Democratic State Convention, Johnson immediately suspected the Kennedys. "It's that little bastard, Bobby," he fumed, though when Bobby Baker confronted RFK regarding LBJ's suspicions, Bobby Kennedy feigned pure innocence. "You don't mean to say you think we would do a thing like that?" he said.

Baker shot back: "When that story crops out in the three biggest cities of Texas on exactly the same day, one day before the Texas convention and your brother Teddy is in Texas. What do you expect us to think?"

The Kennedys denied responsibility for false rumors about LBJ and denied true rumors about JFK. "John F. Kennedy does not now have nor has he ever had an ailment described classically as Addison's disease, which is a tuberculose destruction of the adrenal gland," RFK lied in a prepared statement: "Any statement to the contrary is malicious and false. . . . In the postwar period [he had] some mild adrenal insufficiency. This is not in any way a dangerous condition. . . . Doctors have stated that this condition he has might have arisen out of his wartime experiences of shock and continued malaria."

"It is a sure sign of the desperateness of the opposition," argued Pierre Salinger, "that they should resort to such desperate tactics just before the convention."

It was an ugly time. Two burglaries occurred in Manhattan—into the offices of JFK physicians Dr. Janet Travell and Dr. Eugene J. Cohen. Intruders couldn't penetrate the steel door to Travell's inner office but did ransack Dr. Cohen's files. "All the K's were spread around the floor but nothing was missing," revealed Cohen, adding that Kennedy's folder had been secreted in "another letter from K."

"It didn't take [the police] long to put two and two together," Cohen revealed. "They asked who our patients were and when both of us came up with Kennedy, it was obvious what it was all about."

Burglars were one thing—pressure from Bobby Kennedy was quite another. In the end, RFK produced a letter from Travell and Cohen skirting everything they knew to be true about their distinguished patient and his disease. "I sat down at the typewriter and we went over it," recalled Travell. "We fought over every word of it. We spent three or four hours on it. I typed it out. Gene Cohen said he would sign it provided that it should not be released with his name, with our names on it. I said, 'All right.'"

The resulting June 11 letter was bland at best, disingenuous at worst:

Your fine record of accomplishment during the primary campaigns for the presidential nomination speaks for itself. . . . Your superb physical condition under severe stress indicates that you are able to hold any office to which you aspire. . . .

With respect to your old problem of adrenal insufficiency as late as December 1958 when you had a general checkup with a specific test of adrenal function, the result shows that your adrenal glands do function.

"Did you hear the news?" a mocking LBJ inquired of Minnesota Republican congressman Walter Judd, himself a medical doctor.

"What news?"

"Jack's pediatricians have just given him a clean bill of health!"

FIFTEEN

"First blood for Kennedy"

SHOWTIME DREW NEAR. Actors assumed their places onstage. One by one, contenders and pretenders arrived in Los Angeles, opening headquarters, staging rallies, gulling the press, and, above all else, feverishly courting wavering delegates.

The last would now be first. Laggard in joining the race, Lyndon Johnson arrived early, touching down in a private plane on the Friday before the convention convened. Sporting a cowboy hat and ebulliently flashing the Churchill V sign, LBJ—accompanied by Lady Bird and their daughters, sixteen-year-old Lynda Bird and thirteen-year-old Luci Baines—was met by "Mr. Sam" Rayburn fronting a ten-piece band playing "Everything's Coming Up Roses." Behind Rayburn were hundreds of supporters (Kennedy forces charged that they were supplied courtesy of Jimmy Hoffa). Queried on the tarmac if he might accept the vice-presidential nod, LBJ sarcastically suggested he might offer it to Kennedy. "The vice-presidency is a good place for a young man who needs experience. It is a good place for a young man who needs training."

Johnson's ill-disguised contempt for Kennedy only heightened as the voting neared and LBJ bounded from one delegation to another. Before Washington State's contingent, he ripped into Joe Kennedy's isolationism. "I was never any Chamberlain umbrella policy man," he fumed. "I never thought Hitler was right."

He also criticized JFK's life of easy privilege. "I haven't had anything given to me," LBJ said. "Whatever I have and whatever I hope to get, will be because of whatever energy and talents I have."

Behind-the-scenes infighting took even uglier turns. An LBJ friend offered Theodore White "pictures of Jack and Bobby Kennedy in drag at a gay party in Los Angeles if I would promise to publish them." White said no thanks.

LBJ knew very well what JFK's real preferences were. "Probably got himself a half dozen starlets," he groused to Rayburn.

"Now, now, don't be jealous, Lyndon," Mr. Sam responded.

"Jealous?" LBJ spat back. "Chickenshit. I'm not jealous, I'm just pissed off that I'm working my ass off and he's playing tiddly-winks."

JFK had the girls, and, worse, the delegates. Beyond Dixie, Lyndon Johnson remained a hard, nearly impossible, sell. "I was trying to work the New York delegation," Texas advertising executive Jack Valenti recalled. "I got the impression that I was a leper."

Such events compounded the chronically insecure Johnson's already unhealthy quotients of anxiety and self-doubt. Sometimes he believed he just might pull everything off; other times pessimism and depression ruled. "It's all over with," he brooded at one point to his inner circle. "It's going to be Kennedy by a landslide."

One by one, his rivals arrived in Los Angeles, their own bands playing and their own supporters cheering as frantically as their respective candidacies might warrant. Adlai Stevenson still refused to say yes, but couldn't bear to say no. As comedian Mort Sahl told it, "Jack Kennedy got off the plane and said, 'I came here to accept the nomination.' Lyndon Johnson got off the plane and said, 'I'm sorry I'm late, but I've been busy running the country,' and Adlai Stevenson said, 'I don't want the nomination and I'm not here.'"

Equally significant as the candidates' own grand arrivals were those of the key delegations—Illinois, California, Minnesota, and Pennsylvania— but also the uncommitted smaller states, primarily Kansas, Iowa, and Wyoming. Chicago's Mayor Richard J. Daley arrived on Sunday morning, July 10, at Union Railroad Station. Dodging hundreds of waiting Illinois Democrats, he shepherded his wife, sons, and daughters to 9 a.m. Mass at the nearby Old Mission Church. If it was a hint that he leaned toward the Catholic hopeful, it was also, in Daley's case, simply standard operating procedure.

Some went to Mass that Sunday, some to television studios. JFK, LBJ, and Stu Symington all appeared on a special ninety-minute edition of NBC's *Meet the Press*, with Kennedy displaying properly guarded optimism: "I think we are going to win the nomination. But I don't think it is wrapped up. . . . No convention is."

Within Iowa's delegation, Johnson operative Sherwin J. Markman, ostensibly for Stevenson, vainly fought to prevent a JFK endorsement.

Learning that Governor Herschel C. Loveless, Iowa's favorite son, would release his state's twenty-eight votes to Kennedy—in return for promises of a Loveless vice presidency ("It has to be a Midwesterner, Herschel")—Markman begged Loveless to confer with Minnesota governor Orville Freeman, contending that Freeman had received similar assurances. Outraged, Loveless reported Markman's warnings to Ted Kennedy. Teddy had to be physically restrained from attacking Markman.

Kansas supported Symington—by one vote. It switched. When James Symington inquired why, the defector burst into tears, fleeing from the convention floor, begging, "Don't ask me, I can't tell you."

JFK dangled the number two slot not only to Loveless and Freeman, but also to Kansas governor George R. Docking. John Kenneth Galbraith, suspicious of either Loveless's or Docking's chances—or qualifications—asked Kennedy why. "They would rather be mentioned and passed over," JFK, a cynical, but astute, judge of human nature, responded, "than not be mentioned at all."

Flattery, promises—and threats. At midnight Teddy Kennedy worked the Alaska delegation. Again, rumors of promises filled the air. "The Kennedys knew much more about all the delegates than we did," added James Symington. "They knew all about their families, knew all the pressure points—and used them. They were fighting and they were honed. I guess we were just country boys in that department."

"I particularly saw Robert Kennedy on the floor," recalled New and Fair Deal veteran David Lilienthal. "He didn't make a very favorable impression on me. The word was spread . . . that Robert Kennedy was bearing down on people, meaning something a little more than just persuasion."

Iowa (twenty-eight votes), Kansas (twenty-one), and Alaska (nine)—even the convention's black contingent (just eighty-nine individuals out 4,509 delegates and alternates)—were but small potatoes in the big picture. The real game remained, as ever, with Pennsylvania, Illinois, and California.

On Sunday, July 10, Illinois caucused at the Hotel Hayward. Everything depended on Richard Daley's wishes, and when Daley turned to freshman congressman Dan Rostenkowski to ask, "Why don't you nominate Kennedy?" just about everyone made up his mind.

"I was for Kennedy," Rostenkowski recalled, "and most of my friends were for Kennedy. But if the mayor asks me to nominate somebody else, I would have to nominate somebody else."

The results: fifty-nine and a half votes for JFK, six and a half for Symington and, just two for Adlai Stevenson.

"First blood for Kennedy," as Teddy White would crow.

On Monday morning, July 11, after Symington, Johnson, Kennedy, and Oklahoma senator A. S. "Mike" Monroney—a Stevenson surrogate—addressed Pennsylvania's delegates, Governor David Lawrence called the caucus to order. Announcing without explanation that he was for Kennedy, Lawrence watched as his state awarded JFK sixty-four and a half of its eighty-one first-ballot votes. Lawrence, a Stevenson man *almost* to the end, wept as he did it.

The news hit LBJ hard. "I am not a naive person," he confessed, "and no one ever said I didn't know where the ball was. I know that a preponderance of the cards are stacked against me here." His campaign bitterly attacked the Kennedy "mob psychology." Symington reacted a tad better, merely saying he felt like he had just called up a girl for date to be informed, "Sorry, I'm going steady."

Everybody now seemed to be going steady except Stu. Harry Truman had informally switched to LBJ. Averell Harriman, once a Symington man, now enlisted to second JFK's nomination.

JFK retained hopes of corralling Minnesota's thirty-one votes—until Hubert Humphrey suddenly switched, out of "concern for my country," from Kennedy to Adlai. RFK didn't give up. "Hubert," he ordered, "we want your announcement and the pledge of the Minnesota delegation today or else."

"Go to hell," said Hubert.

"I'm going to get you," RFK responded.

"You know," pondered JFK, more philosophical than his younger brother, "you can never count on Hubert."

Minnesota was now completely fractured. Humphrey and Eugene McCarthy officially supported Stevenson. In actuality, both favored LBJ. McCarthy, either from principle or from mere jealousy (the latter seemed more likely), simply abominated the Kennedys. "I should be the candidate for President," he had famously bragged (then spent much time denying the quote). "I'm twice as liberal as Humphrey, twice as smart as Symington, and twice as Catholic as Kennedy."

Gene McCarthy was, indeed, twice as Catholic as Jack. He had attended seminary, still attended daily Mass, and was far more familiar with Catholic theology and thought than Jack Kennedy would ever pretend to be. Sometimes, however, McCarthy's Catholicism, like his politics, manifested itself in outré ways. Joe Alsop once told JFK about seeing McCarthy aboard a flight, head down inside a huge missal, all the way to Milwaukee. "Well, Joe," Kennedy responded, "there's this old saying in Boston politics, never trust a Catholic politician who reads his missal in the trolley car." But if John Kennedy or Adlai Stevenson were not available for vice president (and it was hard to see how they would be), Gene McCarthy—Northern, liberal, Catholic, and nearly as erudite as Adlai Stevenson—would have been a fully acceptable choice to balance a Lyndon Johnson ticket.

Mike Monroney asked Hubert Humphrey to nominate Stevenson. HHH responded that if he did, that would free his Minnesota delegates, and Governor Orville Freeman would cast them for JFK. He recommended McCarthy. Meanwhile, erstwhile Humphrey supporter Freeman, the vice presidency dangling before him (Hubert warned old friend Freeman to get it in writing), had accepted Jack Kennedy's offer to formally nominate the Massachusetts legislator.

Compared to California, however, Minnesota seemed as solid as Gibraltar. Ignoring Pat Brown's promises, state Democrats weren't about to toss away eight years of near-rabid loyalty to Adlai Stevenson. As delegates caucused at NBC's local studios, state Democratic chairman, Assemblyman Bill Munnell, plotted to hijack the delegation—and, indeed, on one roll call, Stevenson even held the lead. The unreliable Brown, fumed RFK, was a "leaning tower of putty."

Almost a delegation unto herself was Eleanor Roosevelt. The seventy-five-year-old former First Lady arrived on Sunday night, ignoring the four hundred Stevenson supporters awaiting her ("I wired them I didn't want any of this. Why didn't they believe me?") and announcing that she was walking to her hotel ("It's only a half-mile") and would carry her own cloth suitcase ("I want to keep it near me").

"Wasn't that Eleanor Roosevelt that just went by?" asked a startled airport mechanic.

Eleanor hit the ground running figuratively as well as literally. That evening she personally lobbied Pat Brown to return California to the Stevenson fold. On Monday she raised the stakes, suggesting that JFK's "unselfishness and courage" would soon cause him to take the vice presidency, where he might "grow and learn"—pointedly adding that she "did not believe Senator Kennedy could win the election, nor could he win the Negro vote."

LBJ stormed about the convention like a Texas bull running wild. At the Biltmore, Bobby Kennedy again verbally manhandled Bobby Baker. "You've got your nerve," RFK sputtered. "Lyndon Johnson has compared my father to the Nazis, and John Connally. . . . [He] lied by saying my brother was dying of Addison's disease. You Johnson people are running a stinking damned campaign and you'll get yours when the time comes. We'll ——ing kill you."

As late as Sunday, July 10, however, even Ben Bradlee feared LBJ might yet pull it off, and if LBJ didn't, he might engender sufficient chaos to force a perilous second ballot. That could possibly stampede enough delegates to resuscitate Adlai Stevenson—or if the deadlock went on long enough, even to transform "available man" Stuart Symington into 1960's version of Warren G. Harding.

Then came LBJ's challenge—publicly daring JFK to debate before a joint session of the Texas and Massachusetts delegations at the Biltmore Hotel ballroom. JFK's decision was not easily made. Joe Kennedy wanted no part of it. "But, Daddy, how can Jack say no?" Jean Kennedy Smith asked. "The man challenged us."

JFK dawdled. Even with the confrontation broadcast live on national television, he almost didn't show. "If you don't," warned South Carolina's thirty-eight year-old governor Ernest "Fritz" Hollings, "Johnson's really going to give it to you."

Johnson, meanwhile, was exhausted. "A Negro couple from the Ranch were in the room throughout our lunch," the *Washington Post*'s Phil Graham remembered, "and the three of us converged upon him, disrobed him, pajamaed him, and got him to bed." Refreshed after a thirty-minute nap, Lyndon was ready to go.

Jack Kennedy finally acquiesced, but without any clear plan at all. "What shall I say?" he asked Bobby. He shook—visibly. "I remember seeing that pant-leg fluttering there, as he waited for Johnson," recalled *Time*'s Hugh Sidey. "I thought he was shaking. I reported it to my office that way, but I guess it was a nervous twitch."

The tension was palpable, between the debaters and between their seconds. Johnson staffer Booth Mooney (now an aide to Texas oil billionaire H. L. Hunt) remembered that "When Jake Jacobsen, a Johnson campaign aide, passed glasses of water along to the men on the platform, Robert Kennedy unsmilingly tasted the water before handing a glass on to his brother. He found it safe."

LBJ's attack was all blunt force, chopping away at JFK's agriculture policy and his votes against flood control, and boasting how he, LBJ, had answered all fifty quorum calls on that year's civil rights bill "but some senators" had missed as many as thirty-four roll calls.

Johnson had used an axe. Kennedy wielded a rapier, leaving LBJ in shreds. "I assume," JFK replied with cool wit, "he was talking about some other candidate, not me." With tongue firmly in cheek, he praised his opponent's "wonderful record in answering those quorum calls."

"So I come here today," Kennedy concluded, "full of admiration for Senator Johnson, full of affection for him, strongly in support of him—for majority leader of the United States Senate."

"I yield to no man in my love and affection for Johnson," recalled Jack Valenti, "but he was handled with such skill by Kennedy[,] who was like some great toreador handling one of the great Andalusian bulls. Kennedy just massacred him."

"That," admitted John Connally, "was our last gasp. It was the end of the road."

"When [JFK] sat down," Hugh Sidey observed, "his leg no longer twitched."

SIXTEEN

"We had to win on
the first ballot"

HAD ARTHUR SCHLESINGER been present, he would have enjoyed the great LBJ-JFK debate. As it was, he wasn't enjoying the convention at all. With Stevenson fever boiling, emotion in that camp rose against deserters. Toward the turncoat Schlesinger, hostility increased exponentially.

Compounding events was Schlesinger's obvious angst—some might, and did, call it guilt. "Arthur's attitude toward Stevenson," observed one old friend, "seemed to be similar to that of a man who has left his wife and run off with a new woman; later he encounters his wife and is suddenly afflicted with all sorts of memories and doubts. There was no mistaking Arthur's inner turmoil."

John Kenneth Galbraith fared better emotionally, though he also sensed that he was now regarded by more fanatical Stevenson partisans as "an ingrate, a turncoat, a Kennedy opportunist and also morally and ethically leprous."

Leprous or not ("The worst personal betrayal in American history," Galbraith recalled being among the milder insults hurled at him), in other quarters Galbraith retained a certain utility based on what he was *not*. "On arriving in Los Angeles," Galbraith would note, "the Kennedys had discovered that there was no one in the entourage, apart from Theodore Sorensen, who was indispensable as an assistant and speech writer, who was not Jewish, Catholic, or Irish." Galbraith (not even planning to attend the convention until hearing an erroneous radio report that he had already arrived at Los Angeles) unexpectedly now found himself overseeing all delegations north of the Southwest and west of the Mississippi.

Those bitter, betrayed Stevensonians were, however, proving more persistent—and more dangerous—than anyone might have imagined a few short weeks before. A surprisingly noisy element of the Democratic Party was rising up and demanding a return to old principles—and old faces.

The eggheads were about to storm the joint.

Southern California was Stevenson country, at least among Democrats. This was particularly true among the film industry. JFK had his Rat Pack, but Adlai's prominent Hollywood admirers—including Dore Schary, Vincent Price, Lee Remick, Clifford Odets, Jan Sterling, and Mercedes McCambridge—still battled forcefully those in the Kennedy camp. As the convention began, an odd phenomenon evinced itself. Beginning on Monday, July 10, the Los Angeles Sports Arena found itself ringed by a constantly circling cordon of sign-bearing Stevenson partisans. The following day, their numbers only increased, swirling and shouting and chanting. "Catching contagion from one another, feeling strong in numbers," recorded Theodore White, "they made the throb of their voices heard clearly inside the Convention hall itself." And the power of their voices scared those halfheartedly pledged to any of the other hopefuls.

Nevertheless, the demonstrators were only moderately successful in energizing the object of their ardor, the still exceedingly coy Governor Stevenson. As Adlai's plane landed in Los Angeles, between five and ten thousand people—a huge crowd, the biggest in Los Angeles International Airport history—were on hand to meet him. Another impressive demonstration cheered him on a Monday visit to the Biltmore. In St. Louis, the *Post-Dispatch* endorsed Stevenson as "the ablest and best-fitted candidate." Yet, he continued to exhibit a painful inability to capitalize on such support.

On Tuesday morning, July 12, Adlai addressed the still-up-for-grabs Minnesota delegation. A ringing declaration, a call to arms, the declaration of a candidacy, or even a decent *hint* toward a candidacy would have galvanized his audience—perhaps even stampeding a handful of other wavering caucuses toward the Stevenson camp and a first-ballot deadlock.

He could not do it. Nothing of the sort issued from his lips. Arthur Schlesinger, watching with tears in his eyes and mixed emotions in his heart, could barely believe Adlai's failure of resolve. "There was less applause at the end," he recorded, "than at the start."

On Tuesday afternoon, Stevenson, officially an Illinois delegate, visited the convention floor. Custom dictated that candidates never made such appearances, but, then again, Adlai was never ever quite a candidate. Whatever his status truly was, his appearance ignited yet another wildly enthusiastic Bonaparte-home-from-Elba response. It required twelve minutes for Stevenson (quite petrified of large crowds—"he acted as if he was surrounded by monsters," noted one journalist) to progress through the chaos his appearance generated. In mere seconds he destroyed everything the demonstration had accomplished. Allowed to address the convention, he responded with even less than what he had provided Minnesota delegates—no call to action, only a lame joke: "I won't attempt to tell you how grateful I am for this tumultuous welcome to the 1960 convention. I have, however, one observation—after going back and forth through the Biltmore today, I know who's going to be the nominee of this convention—the last man to survive."

"More, more," some diehards cried, but few now followed their call. Within thirty seconds the convention had descended into an eerie near silence. Adlai Stevenson had not only lost his nerve; he had lost his wit.

"Mrs. Roosevelt and I sat there," recalled Agnes Meyer. "We and [former air force secretary Thomas K.] Finletter had worked hard for the demonstration—we had the applause there—but then he went up on that platform and throws it out the window. He could have swept that Convention. I could have murdered him."

Stevenson blundered on. At 1 a.m. he addressed 250 delegates and alternates, again not yet a candidate, and concluding not with a declaration of candidacy but merely with a selection from the collected works of Robert Frost:

The woods are lovely, dark and deep,
But I have promises to keep.
And miles to go before I sleep,
And miles to go before I sleep.

It transpired, however, that that *was* his declaration. Adlai Stevenson *was* a candidate. He awoke the following day to finally realize that he should contact his home-state delegation (publicly committed since Sunday to JFK) for its support. Richard Daley's patience was long gone. For months he had solicited Stevenson's intentions, receiving nothing in return, before formally jumping aboard the Kennedy train. Now he laid into Adlai, as bluntly as he could to his former governor and patron: "Governor, you're going to look foolish running for this nomination, because you'll get no support from Illinois. These delegates weren't for you in '56, but I made them vote for you then. I can't do it again." For good measure, Daley added, "You're lucky you got the two votes you've got."

Adlai Stevenson had dithered. Robert Kennedy and his staff had toiled. Failure in 1956 had proven instructive for Jack and Robert Kennedy. They had gone off half-cocked in seeking that year's vice-presidential nomination, and they learned from it. Chastened, they realized they had to deal with the Catholic and youth issues, and to improve communications with the nation's old-line Democratic bosses (increased sensitivity to what *they* wanted helped). And then there was the simple matter of logistics.

In 1956 Kennedy internal communications on the convention floor broke down. That would not happen in 1960. Connecticut governor Abe Ribicoff oversaw a staff of eight JFK floor managers, each armed not only with the highest-powered walkie-talkie (some said so high-powered they eavesdropped on Stevenson conversations) but also with a rather newfangled device then employed only by telephone company employees—"beepers." A beeper would beep, and a Kennedy man would rush to a phone to retrieve a crucial message. In 1960, that gave the Kennedys a cutting edge.

Beepers were high-tech. Four-by-six-inch blue file cards were not, and that is what Bobby Kennedy and a staff of forty, ensconced in a four-room Biltmore Hotel suite (officially Room 8314), maintained in a file known either simply or ominously, depending on how one looked at it, as "the box." Each card tracked where each targeted vote, or fraction thereof, stood politically, ideologically, economically, and personally—down to the target's hobbies and number of children. Whether the nomination would be won playing hardball or making small talk, the Kennedys were determined to win it.

As Larry O'Brien recalled, "[W]e developed a system of checking and rechecking every delegate. . . . [E]very state delegation was assigned to a Kennedy person, . . . and there were a large number of them then . . . [T]hey would literally live in the hotel where the delegation was located that they were assigned to monitor."

And everyone had to *work*, if not as hard as a Kennedy, then harder than they had ever worked before. Having learned that some coordinators had adjourned to Disneyland the previous day, RFK mounted a foot-stool, lashing out: "If any of you think it's more important to go to Disneyland than nominate the next President of the United States you ought to quit right now."

When he announced that on Tuesday morning they would convene promptly at 8 a.m., one volunteer mildly suggested a later start. "I didn't get back to my hotel until five, and it's the third night in a row," RFK said, glaring. "Look, nobody asked you here. You're not getting paid anything. If this is too tough for you, let us know and we'll get somebody else."

RFK demanded dedication and accuracy. By and large, he got both, his delegate counts retaining remarkable accuracy throughout the week. "I want the cold facts," Bobby curtly ordered. "There's no point in fooling ourselves. I want to hear the votes we are guaranteed to get on the first ballot."

Marveled Illinois's Colonel Jake Arvey, "Kennedy's got this country laid out like a switchboard."

While RFK courted votes one by one, Pierre Salinger employed mass persuasion, both to working media and to the delegates themselves. For reporters he developed elaborate press kits. And Salinger was also the publisher of a daily convention newspaper. Put out by Ron Linton (a labor reporter on leave from the *Louisville Courier-Journal*), two former newspaper editors (including Salinger's own brother Herbert), and two Baltimore college students, the paper was quite naturally adorned with flattering and self-serving news of JFK, but also enough general news (including items on the other hopefuls) to render it sufficiently credible. Salinger's paper emanated from a veritable "city room," containing not only its own AP ticker but its own darkroom. Additional staffers and vol-unteers delivered copies to the far-flung doors of every delegation by 6 a.m. With the paper's total circulation at twelve thousand (three thou-sand copies delivered to the newsstand near the Biltmore alone), JFK fretted over costs. Salinger reassured him that all seven editions had cost just six thousand dollars.

Even floor demonstrations required a certain amount of planning—and, of course, élan. It did no good for your troops to comport themselves without proper spirit, and even a soupçon of choreography. Kennedy aide Robert B. Trautman from Atlanta proved particularly ingenious in

181

securing advice from veteran Hollywood song-and-dance man George Murphy, soon to be a Republican U.S. senator. Not surprisingly, Murphy desired his involvement with Democrat Kennedy be kept under wraps.

All the while, Joe Kennedy remained an invisible, though significant, presence, tying up loose ends, providing sage advice and appropriate encouragement, and discretely cajoling delegates. En route to the convention, he deplaned in Las Vegas, partially for pleasure, partially to lay down some bets on his son. It was not a sporting or even pecuniary gesture, but a tactical one. He did not wish to read in the papers—and certainly did not wish for wavering delegates to read—that the Vegas odds, the smart money, on his son had dipped. That would not happen, not with his outlays propping them up.

Arriving in Beverly Hills, Joe settled into magnificent quarters, a whitewashed stucco, red-tile-roofed villa on seven acres at 1017 North Beverly Drive, rented from former screen star Marion Davies (Davies's aged lover, William Randolph Hearst, had died there). Just around a great bend from Valentino's and Chaplin's and John Gilbert's and Pickford and Fairbanks's former stomping grounds, it was also just down the block from JPK's ex-lover Gloria Swanson's old estate.

From poolside, Joe worked the phones, promising who knew what, securing who knew whom—and not going within sight of a reporter or photographer. Occasionally, selected guests might be invited. When Steelworkers president David MacDonald visited, JPK supplied a special bartender—Frank Sinatra.

No Kennedy person was to even discuss their controversial family enterprise's paterfamilias. When Jack Kennedy overheard Red Fay conversing with *Time*'s Hugh Sidey regarding Joe's influence ("the most vital force") on his offspring, JFK laid into him: "God, if I hadn't cut you off Sidey would have headed his article 'A Vote for Jack Is A Vote for Father Joe.' This is just the material *Time* magazine would like to have—that I'm a pawn in Dad's hands. That it's really not Jack himself who is seeking the presidency but his father. That Joe Kennedy now has the vehicle to capture the only segment of power that has eluded him."

Jack retained a ninth-floor Biltmore suite (officially Apartment Q), but also his own hideaway—an eight-room penthouse at 522 North Rossmore Avenue. Ostensibly for mere relaxation, in reality, with Jackie at home in Hyannis Port, this apartment was for decidedly more private purposes. Rented from actor Jack Haley—*The Wizard of Oz*'s Tin Man—JFK's sleek art deco suite boasted four unlisted phone numbers and a private elevator. Reporters soon discovered the hideout, and Walter Winchell even later claimed to have discovered a tryst.

JFK's life had progressed beyond mere trysts into sexual chaos. Contacting Judith Campbell, he invited her out to dinner. When she demurred ("It stunned me. I couldn't believe that a man in his position would take such a foolish chance"), he invited her to join him afterward at the Beverly Hilton. Arriving in Room 724 (Peter and Pat Lawford's suite), she found JFK in the company of six or seven men and one woman—"a tall, thin, secretarial type," as Campbell carefully noted, "in her late twenties, with brownish hair and rather sharp features. She kept circling the room like a bird of prey." The Lawfords soon entered, startled to see Campbell there. Jack ignored them, and they promptly exited, allowing JFK ("I know you'll enjoy it") to propose to Judith Campbell that she participate in a ménage à trois with the tall, thin secretarial type. Outraged, crying, Campbell refused.

Finally calmed, she prepared to depart. JFK asked a favor: Drop off Kenny O'Donnell at JFK's penthouse. O'Donnell hit on her ("All I could see were those lips coming at me"). She refused his advances. He seemed shocked, particularly when she ordered him out of the car and sped away by herself.

* * *

John Ehrlichman had been dispatched to Los Angeles by Bob Finch to gather information on the rival Democrats. Supplied with a variety of convention passes by Los Angeles's Republican mayor, Norris Poulson (Finch had once worked for Poulson), Ehrlichman navigated through the enemy's camp with remarkable ease, into six or seven caucuses, even through Kennedy headquarters. "The Kennedy operation was slick," Ehrlichman would note, "well financed and ruthless in its treatment of Lyndon Johnson's Southerners and the uncredentialed mob . . . trying to stampede the convention for Stevenson. . . . I . . . came away with tremendous respect for the Kennedy organization."

Liberals, fractured regarding a candidate, remained united regarding platform and convention staffing issues (securing the platform chairmanship for Chester Bowles, the keynoter's slot for thirty-six-year-old Idaho U.S. senator Frank Church, and, in a calculated nod to the South, the convention chairmanship for Florida governor "Liberal Leroy" Collins).

JFK, his eye on the big prize and wary of unnecessarily alienating fractious progressives, did not stand in the way of the magic that party liberals were working upon the platform—in fact, he supported their every move, most notably a civil rights plank unprecedented in its strength. In 1948, Southerners had stormed out in protest against the party's stand. In 1952 and 1956, liberals accordingly drew back. In 1960, the national Democratic Party was once more the civil rights party, and its Southern wing, secure in its congressional seniority and trusting Jack Kennedy to exhibit the prudence they had grown to admire him for, made some noise . . . and meekly gave up.

Time neared for real business. Frank Church delivered a cliché-filled keynote address on Monday night. Richard Nixon, watching on TV, thought it "inept." For once, he was in agreement with the mass of Democratic loyalists.

Bobby Kennedy continued to count votes. His brother had needed 600 votes on arrival in Los Angeles. He had secured them. He required 700 as the balloting neared. Thanks largely to Pennsylvania and Illinois and (somewhat) to California, he had secured them. He still needed 761 votes to win it all, and he needed them on the first ballot, or his only marginally loyal delegates might jump ship on the second.

On Wednesday, on the eve of balloting, RFK calculated that they remained twenty-one votes shy of victory. "We can't miss a trick in the next twelve hours," he warned his staff. "If we don't win tonight, we're dead."

It was not hyperbole. "We had to win on the first ballot," RFK explained to Arthur Schlesinger in 1965. "North Dakota, they had the unit system . . . we won it by half a vote. California was falling apart. . . . Carmine [De Sapio] came to me and said what we'd like to do is make a deal—30 [New York] votes will go to Lyndon Johnson and then you'll get them all back on the second ballot. I said to hell with that; we're going to win it on the first ballot. So, you know, it was all that kind of business. There wasn't any place that was stable."

It was not stable because while JFK had made the sale on a political level, he had not yet completed it on an emotional one. He was a new thing, and new things were scary. Perhaps that is why such powerful nostalgia bubbled for old thing Adlai Stevenson.

"And suddenly I saw the convention," Norman Mailer would write. "It came into focus for me, and I understood the mood of depression which had lain over the convention, because finally it was simple: the Democrats were going to nominate a man who, no matter how serious his political dedication might be, was indisputably and willy-nilly going to be seen as a great box-office actor, and the consequences of that were staggering and not at all easy to calculate."

The nominations occurred on Tuesday night: Sam Rayburn for LBJ, Orville Freeman for JFK (a "devoted liberal"), Missouri governor James T. Blair Jr. for Symington, Eugene McCarthy for Stevenson.

McCarthy set the hall ablaze, unleashing oratory many judged without convention peer. Having had but a few hours to compose his presentation, McCarthy started his address slowly, ignoring Stevenson at first, declaiming at length on the need for a second ballot—a ballot where delegates might freely vote their consciences. Sixteen long paragraphs into his speech, he finally turned attention to his ostensible candidate, beginning with a spirited apologetic for Adlai's often perplexing attitudes toward politics and nominations:

> I say to you the political prophets have prophesied falsely in these eight years. And the high priests of Government have ruled by that false prophecy. And the people seemed to have loved it so.
>
> But there was one man—there was one man who did not prophesy falsely. . . .
>
> History does not prove that power is always well used by those who seek it. On the contrary, the whole history of Democratic politics is to this end, that power is best exercised by those who are sought out by the people.

"And so I say to you Democrats here assembled," McCarthy concluded, tapping into their affections perfectly, his timing and inflections flawless, "do not turn away from this man. Do not reject this man. . . .

Do not reject this man who has made us all proud to be called Democrats. . . . Do not leave this prophet without honor in his own party. Do not reject this man."

The galleries erupted into an absolute frenzy. CBS's Mike Wallace, interviewing Larry O'Brien, paused to query him for his reaction. "Mike," O'Brien calmly responded, "why don't you look at the floor? The delegates are all in their seats. The people in the aisles, the demonstrators with the balloons and the horns and everything, all came from the balconies."

Stevenson's people had packed the galleries, securing tickets from various sources and even flooding the convention floor with demonstrators. Stevenson booster Mike Monroney pondered, "I've always had this feeling—I couldn't prove it—that Dore Schary, who had been a great movie producer, had counterfeited the Pinkerton uniforms and put them on his own men and removed the guards from the door by order so these Stevenson people were allowed to come in."

The tumult persisted for twenty-five minutes, egregiously over-staying its welcome. Eleanor Roosevelt and Eugene McCarthy, recognizing that its continuance only alienated impatient delegates, worked to end the frenzy their cohorts had worked so hard to create. Because in the end, it had all turned out to be sound and fury signifying . . . nothing.

Nominations on Tuesday. Voting on Wednesday. RFK's calculated margins remained razor thin. The Kennedy camp remained tense, unsure of what might transpire. "I rode out to the Sports Arena with Sargent Shriver and other members of the family," John Kenneth Galbraith recalled. "All were silent; it was as to a funeral."

Lyndon Johnson's edginess was Texas sized, not improved by his underdog status or liquid refreshments. Newspeople saw him drunk and angrily yelling about JFK. Lady Bird pulled him back into their suite, where he might still rail at his fates yet preserve dignity and reputation.

The roll call, so long awaited, arrived at 10:07 p.m. The machinations only accelerated. Kennedy's forces, fearful of being tarred too stickily with the segregationist brush, and hoping to provide some badly needed oomph for any second ballot, requested Alabama governor John Patterson to withhold some first-ballot votes. Florida favorite son George Smathers, JFK's longtime personal friend, would swing second-ballot votes to Johnson.

"It's your last chance!" Sargent Shriver shouted to James Symington. The implication: If Missouri pushes JFK over the top, a Kennedy-Symington ticket could be theirs.

"Go tell Bob Meyner that we're going to win this thing on the first ballot," barked JFK over the phone, "and this is his last chance. He either switches his [New Jersey] delegation to us or he's going to be rolled over." Meyner held firm.

★ ★ ★

At 522 North Rossmore, Jack Kennedy, sipping a Coke, settled down to watch the show.

"Alabama?"

"Alabama casts twenty votes for Johnson; Kennedy, three and a half; Symington, three and a half."

Everything went black—lights, TV, everything. "God Almighty!" JFK exploded. "I slave and knock my brains out for four years to get this nomination and now I can't sit here and watch it." A detective located a fuse box in the kitchen. The lights and the TV went back on, and JFK settled in to watch Arizona cast seventeen votes for . . . Bam! The fuse blew again—as did Kennedy. He ran downstairs to actor William Gargan's apartment, begging, "Do you mind, Bill? Both of our sets upstairs blew out."

"Please don't worry about your pajamas," JFK assured Bill and Mary Elizabeth Gargan, assuming the role of host in their home. "Sit down and be comfortable."

By California, JFK's power was back on—his bedroom air conditioner had been the culprit—and JFK now returned upstairs.

"Bill," JFK called as he left, "leave the door open. We might be back."

Upward his total spiraled. By Iowa he was at 200, by New York, 500, and by Pennsylvania, 650.

All heading toward Wyoming.

"My brother Bobby had it down in terms of numbers so accurately that he knew Wyoming was going to be the final key," recalled Teddy Kennedy. "We had ten and a half of Wyoming's fifteen votes. Bobby told me to make a deal with the delegation chairman to give us the full fifteen if it would make the margin of difference in getting the nomination."

"We're just starting this vote now," Wyoming's puzzled chairman Tracy McCraken told Teddy. "More than fifteen hundred delegates! And you're saying that those few votes are going to make the difference?"

"All we're saying is that if it comes to that, will you agree to give us the votes?"

"Sure," the white-haired McCracken agreed, "I'll make that deal."

RFK's numbers were holding extraordinarily well. "Tell them if we have all fifteen," Bobby told Ted over the phone, "Wyoming will cinch the nomination of the next President." Teddy forced his way back through the crowd, shouting at McCracken, "You have in your grasp the opportunity to nominate the next President of the United States. Such support can never be forgotten by a President."

Even in Wyoming they knew what that meant.

"Wyoming," McCracken boomed, "casts all fifteen votes for the next President of the United States."

And all who wished to come aboard came aboard, with the official final roll providing Kennedy with a more comfortable margin than had ever existed in actuality:

John F. Kennedy	**806**
Lyndon Johnson	**409**
Stuart Symington	**86**
Adlai Stevenson	**79.5**
Robert B. Meyner	**43**
Hubert Humphrey	**41**
George A. Smathers	**30**
Ross Barnett	**23**
Herschel Loveless	**1.5**
Orval E. Faubus	**.5**
Edmund "Pat" Brown	**.5**
Albert D. Rosellini	**.5**

It was, as ever for the Kennedys, a family moment. Rose Kennedy descended from her box to ascend the podium. Jack Kennedy left his apartment and conferred with Bobby outside the convention hall. And Jackie? "When the Wyoming vote was announced," Evelyn Lincoln recorded in her memoirs, "we knew, and the announcer knew, that the balloting was all over. John Kennedy had won. His immediate concern was to share the good news with Jackie. So he called her at Hyannis Port, Massachusetts."

Except . . .

Except . . .

Except, it was all a great lie.

Lincoln later contradicted her own testimony, "Some people say that Jack called Jackie . . . , but he didn't."

No, Jack Kennedy, who that very day sent Judith Campbell a dozen red roses, never phoned his wife.

"While he talked to his Dad," Evelyn Lincoln continued, "I was calling Jackie."

"There will be," Jack Kennedy had told Judith Campbell, "some changes in my life if I don't get the nomination."

SEVENTEEN

"Too shallow a puddle"

FATE NOT ONLY CAME very near to favoring Stuart Symington. For a few hours, it did.

As Jack Kennedy's march to the nomination progressed, rumors of a running mate galloped steadily along, gaining ground with every hope of the hopefuls themselves, and every vague (and not so vague) promise tendered by the front-runner. After all, Ted Sorensen had at one point compiled a list of twenty-two possible JFK running mates. "If they called a meeting of all the people to whom they've promised the Vice-Presidency," snarled Mike Monroney, "they couldn't find a room in Los Angeles large enough to hold it in."

There had been Adlai himself, of course, and then the purely hopeless cases—Kansas's George Docking and Iowa's Herschel Loveless, barely appropriate for sub-cabinet posts, let alone the vice presidency. There had been Hubert Humphrey. Arthur Schlesinger thought Kennedy was, for some time, "inclined" toward his beaten foe, JFK having revealed to Schlesinger that UAW counsel Arthur Goldberg had informed him of HHH's acceptability to labor. Humphrey, thought JFK (in Schlesinger's words), would "add more to the ticket than anyone else." In fact, Kennedy remained displeased by Humphrey's frenetic West Virginia campaign and feared what damage his verbal pyrotechnics might inflict in the run-up to November.

Humphrey harbored his doubts, the first being the traditional reluctance of any person of substance to accept the office. The second being the diciness of the entire proposition: Humphrey's Senate term expired in 1960. He could win re-election easily. The national ticket's chances hovered around fifty-fifty. A man of modest means such as Hubert Humphrey simply needed a job—and knew what it was like to be without one.

The third reason may have been the most powerful—the visceral antipathy the Humphrey family now harbored toward the Kennedys. "[Muriel] hated [Bobby]," Joe Rauh recalled. "It's one of the reasons

Hubert wasn't president after John Kennedy died, because the family hated the Kennedys so they tried to persuade Hubert not to run for the vice president with Jack Kennedy."

And so Humphrey withdrew his support from JFK, endorsed Adlai—and tossed away his chance for the second slot. With Humphrey persona non grata, serious vice-presidential consideration now centered upon just three names—Symington, Orville Freeman, and Washington State's Henry "Scoop" Jackson—Robert Kennedy confidentially sharing that list with *Wall Street Journal* correspondents Al Otten and Robert Novak. To Washington's delegation RFK averred that Jackson was his personal favorite. Joseph Alsop reported that Jackson was JFK's personal choice as well.

Some, however, believed Freeman the favorite. "Stuart Symington and Henry Jackson were mentioned importantly," noted Evelyn Lincoln, "but, it seemed to me, Orville Freeman was the front-runner in conversations as to who would be the best candidate if Mr. Kennedy got the nomination."

"I came to believe Freeman already had been chosen," theorized Robert Novak, "and Bobby put up the two senators as decoys."

Freeman progressed. Freeman receded—his utility perhaps being merely to entice Minnesota's wavering thirty-one votes. Whatever the case, once Kennedy secured the nomination, he quickly seized upon the idea of Cold War hawk Symington—Episcopalian, Midwestern, *and* border stater, a longtime Truman man, a prominent anti-McCarthyite, liberal but not *too* liberal—as his running mate.

As Symington was a logical choice, Clark Clifford—Symington strategist *and* Kennedy attorney—was the logical go-between. Before Wednesday night's roll call, JFK summoned Clifford to a hideaway in the Biltmore, away from reporters' prying eyes, informing him, "We are thinking seriously about Senator Symington on the ticket. Do you think you might persuade him to throw his strength to us? As we analyze it, he can't win."

Symington once again thought he'd take his chances upon the long-shot worth winning rather than on a consolation prize that might yield only regret. Beyond that, he thought he owed something to those few who had made the fight with him so far. Symington said no.

Once nominated, JFK phoned Clifford yet again, tendering the Missourian the second spot without reservations. "I took that back to Senator Symington," Clifford recalled.

Over dinner Symington conferred with his family. His wife and sons James and Stuart Jr. all argued that the Senate was preferable to the vice presidency's frustrating doldrums ("You didn't come here to hold someone's coat for four or eight years"). Clifford disagreed. "I don't see how [Symington] can refuse," he argued. "He'd like to be president. This has been said many times before: the vice president is just one heartbeat away. He must not turn this down."

Symington relented. His family remained skeptical. "We went to bed in a troubled state of mind," recalled James Symington, "fully expecting to wake up and find ourselves Little Goody Shoes in the trail of the Kennedy crowd, number two, and all being patted on the head."

And, in a far different way, Stu Symington also remained dubious. "I will bet you a hundred dollars," he challenged Clifford, "that no matter what he says, Jack will not make me his running mate. He will have to pick Lyndon."

Clifford conveyed Symington's assent to JFK, went to bed, and assumed all was well.

Meanwhile, advice was flooding in to JFK. Chester Bowles urged Hubert Humphrey. Hubert supported Adlai. Montana senator Mike Mansfield lobbied for Jackson. Walter Reuther, Mike DiSalle, Soapy Williams, and Dick Daley urged Symington. At JFK's Biltmore Hotel suite, Daley, hopeful of increasing the Democratic vote in Southern Illinois and of capturing the governor's and state attorney's offices, reminded JFK of how he had eased his nomination. "Not you or anybody else nominated us," Jack icily responded, infuriating Daley. "We did it ourselves."

At political and social antipodes from the plebian Daley stood Jack's Georgetown comrade Joe Alsop. "You know damn well that Stu Symington is too shallow a puddle for the United States to have to dive into," Alsop, along with the *Washington Post*'s Philip Graham, warned JFK. "Furthermore, what are you going to do about Lyndon Johnson? He's too big a man to leave up in the Senate." JFK merely smiled. Alsop, wise in divining the ways of Official Washington, concluded that Symington was already sunk.

He soon would be.

Kennedy summoned Clifford to his Biltmore suite the next morning. Clifford so hurried that he forgot to shave. "I must do something now that I have never done before in my life," JFK advised. "I am going back on my solemn commitment. I acknowledge that I made it [and] I meant it at the time. I have been persuaded that I made a mistake, and I must rectify it. I am withdrawing the offer I made to Senator Symington and I would appreciate it if you would take that message to him."

Symington proved remarkably sanguine ("He seemed very relaxed about it. He didn't seem to be hankering for it anyway," Clifford would report) regarding so callous a jettisoning—and then he reminded Clark Clifford that he owed him a hundred dollars.

Not long afterward, reporters, not yet cognizant of how near Stuart Symington had come to the second slot—that he had held it in his grasp for a few hours (mostly spent asleep)—inquired if he would have liked to have been the vice presidential nominee.

"I would have liked," he responded with more than the hint of a smile, "to have been the Presidential nominee."

EIGHTEEN

"I'm not going to die in office"

LYNDON JOHNSON had wanted to be president, too.

But it wasn't looking very likely.

When Wyoming had voted, the paisley-pajama-clad LBJ snapped off his television set. "Well, that's that," he exhaled. "Tomorrow we can do something we really want to do—go to Disneyland, maybe."

What Jack Kennedy planned for the next day remains a mystery, the mystery of the entire campaign, for his actions regarding the vice presidency do not smoothly fit together. There was certainly calculation in his actions, but no consistency. In his first great decision as presidential nominee there was not one decision but several—all very contradictory, panicky, and amateurish.

And yet, in the final analysis, it turned out to be the best decision of his campaign.

Few believed JFK would consider, let alone select, Lyndon as his running mate. Yet, while JFK might increasingly question LBJ's leadership qualities, he had none regarding his value to a prospective Kennedy ticket. To Chester Bowles, JFK mused that Johnson was (in Bowles's words) the "wisest choice," shocking Bowles, who considered Johnson little more than a legislative tactician. "But he'll never accept," JFK added, a hint of a smile upon his face. "The implication," thought Bowles, "was that by offering the second spot to Johnson he could gain credit with the South and that Johnson could be counted on to refuse."

And while hardcore liberals might not relish a JFK-LBJ ticket—nor even imagine it save as a charade—more pragmatic minds would.

On Monday, when Phil Graham (a solid Johnson man) and Joe Alsop (equally firm for JFK) conferred with JFK, their primary purpose was not to sink Stu ("too shallow a puddle") but rather to pitch LBJ ("much too big a man to leave up in the Senate"). The bespectacled Graham touted what LBJ might add to the slate—and JFK so readily assented that Graham doubted Kennedy's seriousness. "I restated the matter," Graham recalled, "urging him not to count on Johnson turning it down but to offer the VPship so persuasively as to win Johnson over."

Seventy-one-year-old ultra-conservative anti-Catholic Texas oil billionaire H. L. Hunt had supported Johnson through the spring—but now, seeking the best deal available, Hunt also angled for a Kennedy-Johnson slate. As the voting neared, Kennedy had reached out to Hunt. After all, it was advisable to have a man even richer than Joe Kennedy on your side, particularly in a state as crucial as Texas. But Hunt's strategy was to temporarily avoid contact with JFK. On Tuesday morning, July 12, Hunt and his assistant Booth Mooney were drafting a memo to Johnson urging him to consider the second slot. As they worked, Chicago oil man Robert W. O'Meara and Sargent Shriver arrived. Shriver and Hunt huddled for a while, and when they returned, Hunt ordered Mooney to revise their memo accordingly:

> Since writing the above Mr. Sargent Shriver arrived at Mr. Hunt's room unannounced, and in the course of their conversation wondered if there was any possibility that you would accept the vice-presidential nomination in case Senator Kennedy is nominated for president. Mr. Hunt told him he had no idea but suggested that lines of communication be kept open.

The same day, four senior House Democrats—two from Texas, two from Massachusetts—conferred. Tip O'Neill reported that Kennedy just about had it all wrapped up. When House majority leader John W. McCormack (never a great admirer of JFK) confirmed O'Neill's opinion, Texans Sam Rayburn and Wright Patman took notice. "Let me tell you something, Sam," Patman warned, knowing Rayburn opposed LBJ taking second place. "If Kennedy wants Lyndon for the vice presidency, Lyndon can't turn it down. Never in the history of this country has the mantle of the vice presidency been put on a man's shoulders and he has refused it. [Supreme Court] Justice William Douglas claimed that he had said no to Roosevelt, but there was no truth to that."

Rayburn must have already reconsidered. "John," he said to McCormack, "if Kennedy wants Lyndon as his running mate, Lyndon has an obligation to this convention to accept it. You tell Kennedy that if he wants me to talk to Lyndon, I'll be happy to do it. Here's my private telephone number, which you can give to Jack Kennedy." McCormack delegated the errand to O'Neill.

Meanwhile, Phil Graham prepared to lunch privately with Lyndon Johnson. Beforehand, he conversed with JFK, assuring him he would raise the vice-presidential issue with Lyndon. Graham never got a word in edgewise.

In an elevator that evening, "Tommy the Cork" Corcoran also propositioned Kennedy regarding the second slot. "We've got to patch up this split between you and Lyndon," Corcoran said. "I don't blame you for hating him tonight, but I'm talking politics."

"Stop kidding, Tommy," JFK said. "Johnson will turn me down." But Corcoran persisted—apparently gaining ground with Kennedy. "Tommy," he said, "you have peculiar abilities."

Later that evening, at Chasen's Restaurant, Tip O'Neill popped the question: "Jack, are you interested in Lyndon Johnson for the Vice Presidency?"

"Of course I want Lyndon Johnson," JFK answered. "The only thing is, I would never want to offer it and have him turn me down. . . . I would be terrifically embarrassed. He's a natural. If I could ever get him on the ticket, no way could we lose. We'd carry Texas."

Phil Graham's wheels churned wildly. At 10:45 the next morning he pitched a wild idea to Jack Kennedy—of cajoling Adlai Stevenson into addressing the convention on behalf of Lyndon for vice president. But JFK remained more worried about his own nomination than about who he might nominate twenty-four hours later. He asked whether an offer to Johnson could help push him over. Graham responded that naming LBJ might attract George Smathers's first-ballot Florida votes. Forget that, countered Kennedy—Smathers coveted the vice-presidential slot for himself.

On Thursday, July 14—with Kennedy's nomination won and vice presidential balloting scheduled for that evening—Joe Alsop published a column, woven largely from hopeful whole cloth, claiming that Kennedy was "pretty certain" to offer LBJ second place—and that it was "an absolute certainty" that Johnson would refuse. Alsop revealed that Kennedy polling had discerned that only two prospective running mates made any appreciable difference regarding the general election. Outspoken liberal Humphrey would damage the ticket not merely in the South, but in both the West and Midwest. LBJ, though costing Northern Negro votes, would more than recoup them in the increasingly volatile South.

If Stuart Symington and Hubert Humphrey viewed the vice presidency as a step down, a Senate majority leader might consider it equivalent to tumbling headfirst down three flights of stairs. To surrender the unprecedented power LBJ had built up in the leader's office for the sinecure widely compared to a "bucket of warm spit"—well, it seemed incomprehensible, or as a Capitol Hill gag had one reporter asking an unidentified senator: "Do you think Lyndon Johnson would settle for vice president?"

Answer: "I can't even understand why he's willing to settle for president."

Less apocryphally, on Tuesday, July 12, Bobby Baker caught wind of a Texas delegate maneuvering to place LBJ in the vice-presidential slot. "I want you to stop," Baker ordered. "We will not trade a vote for a gavel."

Or would they?

No matter what public office LBJ assumed—Texas National Youth Administration director, congressman, Senate majority leader, leadership of the "Little Congress," even teaching at Cotulla—he left it greater than when he found it. LBJ might think to do the same with the ultimate in cynosures, the vice presidency, his personality and will transforming even *it* into a fulcrum for leveraging real power.

But this time Lyndon Johnson would face one immeasurable obstacle: no mentor to flatter, no Mr. Sam or FDR or Carl Vinson or Dick Russell. Those days were gone, and, besides, he was too old for that game—and Jack and Bobby Kennedy were too young, too attached to real family to transfer affection and loyalty to those not of their blood or region or upbringing.

Lyndon Johnson was now an orphan—one too old and not cute enough to be adopted.

Yet he may have had no choice. He may, for all his current power and fame, have been cornered—compelled to fashion an ungainly jump into the victorious JFK's arms because no other alternative seemed viable, much less palatable.

Consider his choices.

If LBJ refused JFK's offer and Jack Kennedy lost, Johnson would be blamed for his defeat—and he would no longer be Senate leader in opposition to the phlegmatic Eisenhower but to the more energetic and vastly more calculating Nixon.

If LBJ refused and JFK won, he would be persona non grata with the new administration, his position jeopardized and perhaps even endangered. If Kennedy won and LBJ survived as majority leader, he would instantly be transformed from the nation's most powerful Democrat into a mere errand boy, compelled to implement the new Democratic chief executive's wishes—desires unlikely to be conveyed personally but rather by some underling like Larry O'Brien, or, even more cruelly, by "that little bastard" Bobby Kennedy.

Having enjoyed immense power, Johnson was now fretting mightily about what such vexatious futures might inflict upon his fragile health and psyche. None of those scenarios seemed more than grand dead ends and U-turns on the path to power that Lyndon Johnson had begun treading so many years before. Perhaps, then, LBJ calculated that he might transform the vice presidency into something far grander than anyone had ever thought it to be. After all, as he had often rationalized to startled allies, "Power is where power goes."

Meanwhile, JFK, for whatever reason, ignored every warning signal he had received that LBJ might accept the VP slot. Accordingly, Jack Kennedy now played the conciliation card, extending a grand but hopefully meaningless gesture, bereft of sincerity's slightest hint, to his defeated rival.

"The idea that he'd go down to offer him the nomination in hopes that he'd take the nomination is not true," RFK informed Arthur Schlesinger in 1965. "He thought that he should offer him the nomination; because there were enough indications from others that he wanted to be offered the nomination, . . . *but he never dreamt that there was a chance in the world that he would accept it*" (italics in the original).

As JFK had confided to John Kenneth Galbraith not thirty-six hours previously regarding the hapless governors of Kansas and Iowa and his dangling of national office before them, "They would rather be mentioned and passed over, than not be mentioned at all."

What Kennedy had forgotten, of course, was this: how, just four years previously, he himself had lusted over this supposedly worthless office—

and how, in the frenzy of a national convention, others—Lyndon Johnson included—might prove similarly enraptured.

JFK grew anxious to contact LBJ. The sooner the farce began, the sooner it would end, and he might then progress to more substantive matters. Before retiring, he asked Evelyn Lincoln if Lyndon Johnson would be present at his first meeting of the next morning, with the Southern governors. He would. Before she arrived back at her hotel room, however, the jittery JFK had phoned her room, dictating a memo to her husband, to be hand carried to Johnson:

Dear Lyndon: If it is agreeable with you, I would like to talk to you in your room tomorrow morning at 10:00 [signed] Jack.

Kennedy phoned her again, demanding to know if his note had indeed been delivered. Assured that it had, he demanded that its contents be read back to him.

Perhaps the key to the entire chain of events is its least noticed incident. Having discussed with RFK the possibility of insincerely offering Johnson the number two slot, JFK dispatched an emissary to Sam Rayburn's suite at 3 a.m. with the offer itself.

It was a move calculated to fail, on any number of levels.

First, awakening a seventy-eight-year-old man, in obviously declining health, indicated remarkable disrespect for the Johnson forces. Beyond that, Kennedy himself should ideally have tendered the offer. Failing that, any surrogate chosen should have been identified with, or at least friendly to, the Johnson camp. Any number of acceptable emissaries existed: Phil Graham and Tommy Corcoran spring instantly to mind. Even with Stuart Symington, far below Lyndon Johnson's status and immeasurably less prickly, JFK had carefully selected an envoy Symington would trust: Clark Clifford.

But to Sam Rayburn at three o'clock in the morning, he sent Robert Francis Kennedy.

True to form, RFK tendered Mr. Sam not so much an offer as a demand: "We want Lyndon to run for Vice President and we want you to persuade him to accept." True to form (and very possibly true to Jack Kennedy's plans), Bobby's visit infuriated Rayburn.

That night Sam Rayburn advised Lyndon Johnson to reject JFK's offer: "Don't get caught in that trap. Don't accept."

RFK, no doubt, returned bearing what JFK wanted to hear: no word of assent from the man most influential with LBJ. It would be safe to proceed. That morning, Dave Powers overheard RFK tell Jack, "If you are sure it's what you want to do, go ahead and see him."

Sargent Shriver arrived. Sometime during the night he'd been awakened by a close Johnson partisan with an assurance that Lyndon would accept. Shriver conveyed the news to JFK. JFK ignored it.

"I am going down now," Jack Kennedy informed Evelyn Lincoln, as he left for Lyndon Johnson's seventh-floor suite.

"Do you think he will accept?"

"No," JFK responded, "I don't."

At eight o'clock that morning, the phone had rung in the still-darkened Johnson suite, awakening Lyndon ("my first good night's sleep in several weeks") and Lady Bird. "Just a minute," Lady Bird responded, before turning to her husband. "It's Senator Kennedy, and he wants to talk to you."

"Yes, yes, yes, yes sure," LBJ muttered into the receiver, "come down about ten thirty."

"I wonder," Lady Bird asked, "what he wants."

LBJ knew exactly what JFK wanted. Shortly thereafter, Austin congressman Homer Thornberry, one of Johnson's most trusted allies, phoned to cheer his defeated friend. "Kennedy's coming to see me in a little while," Lyndon confided. "He may be wanting to talk to me about the vice presidency. What do you think?" Thornberry advised against it, then changed his mind, calling again, counseling Johnson to accept. "Well," Lyndon asked, "what do we do about Mr. Rayburn?" Thornberry replied that it was Kennedy's problem—not Johnson's—to convince Rayburn.

So assured, LBJ, as mercurial as ever, now met Kennedy—and accepted.

"I was up in his room when [JFK] came back," RFK later informed Arthur Schlesinger, "and he said, 'You just won't believe it.' I said, 'What?' and he said, 'He wants it,' and I said, 'Oh, my God!' He said, 'Now what do we do?' . . . We both promised each other that we'd never tell what happened—but we spent the rest of the day alternating between thinking it was good and thinking that it wasn't good that he'd offered him the Vice Presidency, and how could he get out of it."

It was already too late for escape. Too many wheels had been set in motion, all grinding toward a JFK-LBJ ticket. At 8 a.m. Thursday, Tommy Corcoran phoned Truman administration undersecretary of the Treasury Edward H. Foley regarding JFK's vice-presidential nod. Both were of the same mind: It must be Johnson—or the ticket was sunk. Corcoran informed Foley that he had already conveyed his opinion to LBJ, who responded with no more resolve than he had displayed at any other milestone on his halting and fumbling road to the White House. The Master of the Senate punted, saying he could not even consider the proposition without Sam Rayburn's approval.

Corcoran and Foley raced to Mr. Sam's Biltmore suite. En route, they shared an elevator with the moderate segregationist Virginia governor J. Lindsay Almond. Almond confided that without LBJ, the ticket could not hope to carry the Old Dominion.

In Sam's suite, Corcoran got nowhere. Foley cooled his heels outside. Louisiana congressman Hale Boggs (summoned by Corcoran) and Rayburn staffer D. B. Hardeman arrived, informing Foley that unless LBJ shared the slate, Richard Nixon would carry *his* state.

Corcoran, with Foley, Boggs, and Hardeman in tow, returned for one last try with Rayburn, who now argued, "I saw another Texan, Jack Garner, agree to run twice with Roosevelt, of whose political philosophy he disapproved intensely, and go back to Texas embittered for life." Yet, there was a bit of hesitation in Rayburn's bluster.

"What do you think about this?" he asked Boggs.

"Well," Boggs responded, knowing that Mr. Sam hated Richard Nixon even more than he disliked John F. Kennedy and all the archbishops from Boston to Los Angeles, "do you want Richard Nixon to be president of the United States?"

"You know I don't want that to happen."

"Well, unless you approve of Lyndon taking the nomination that's exactly what's going to happen. How can any man turn down being vice-president? You wouldn't turn it down."

Sam Rayburn had not become Speaker Rayburn by accident. He knew how to process information, to shift positions and loyalties as circumstances arose, and to shift them quickly—before the ground had given way beneath him.

"Well, that's right," Sam Rayburn said to Boggs, as if it were the most natural answer in the world, "he's got to do it."

"Get Senator Kennedy down here so we can decide immediately," he ordered, and Boggs scampered up to Jack Kennedy's suite, quickly returning with JFK and Kenny O'Donnell. Boggs and O'Donnell waited outside.

Kennedy had arrived praying that Mr. Sam's intransigence might yet save him from himself—and from Lyndon Johnson. He found instead a willing "ally."

"Up until thirty minutes ago," Rayburn informed JFK, "I was against it, and I have withheld a final decision until I could really find out what was in your heart. You know, Jack, I am a very old man and sometimes given to being a little selfish, I am sure. I am in the twilight of my life, walking down into the valley. My career is behind me, but Lyndon is only approaching the summit of his. I am afraid I was trying to keep him in the legislative end where he could help me. Now the way you explain it I can see that you need him more. You are looking at the whole [picture]."

Secrets survive in politics as long as it takes each recipient to reveal them—invariably not only to prove to the next recipient that the first has the clout to have received the embargoed information in the first place, but also to place the second recipient in his debt. Accordingly, word of this unlikely bombshell radiated across Los Angeles like shock waves emanating from a nuclear detonation.

Both the right and left wings of the party—and the Kennedy inner circle itself—reacted with barely controlled rage. "This is the worst mistake you ever made," Kenny O'Donnell railed at JFK. "You came out here to this convention like a knight on a white charger, the clean-cut young Ivy League college guy who's promising to get rid of the old hack politicians. And now, in your first move after you get the nomination, you go against all the people who supported you. Are we going to spend the campaign apologizing for Lyndon Johnson and trying to explain why he voted against everything you ever stood for?"

"I'm forty-three years old," Kennedy argued. "I'm not going to die in office. So the vice presidency doesn't mean anything. If we win, it will be by a small margin and I won't be able to live with Lyndon Johnson as the leader of a small majority in the Senate. Did it occur to you that if Lyndon Johnson becomes vice-president, I'll have Mike Mansfield as the leader of the Senate, somebody I can trust and depend on?"

Unaware that JFK had arrived at any decision, and secure in inaccurate knowledge that LBJ was off-limits, organized labor had dispatched a delegation to Kennedy, including Walter Reuther, Arthur Goldberg, and Alex Rose of New York's Liberal Party, to indicate that Humphrey, Symington, and Jackson were acceptable alternatives, and that, thanks to LBJ's maneuvering on 1959's Landrum-Griffin labor act, Lyndon was not. RFK had already assured Stevenson's people that LBJ would not be on the ticket. Goldberg, unusually quiet at the meeting, had somehow surmised that JFK had already decided on Johnson and remained behind. JFK subsequently persuaded Goldberg to support LBJ. Goldberg, along with Rose, approached the AFL-CIO's George Meany, quickly securing his pledge not to oppose Johnson.

It was a day of unusual dirty work for Robert Kennedy, for where JFK feared to tread he dispatched RFK. Bobby (with Kenny O'Donnell in tow; O'Donnell had refused to go alone) now went to the Statler Hotel to see the same labor group that had just met his brother. Despite all recent assurances to the contrary, Bobby told them, it *would* be Lyndon. Anger and gloom choked the room. "I don't think Robert Kennedy ever was so savagely attacked in his life," said O'Donnell. "They were just jumping out of ——ing windows," recalled one key Kennedy labor organizer.

Goldberg phoned International Ladies' Garment Workers' Union (ILGWU) president David Dubinsky at his Long Island summer home. The Russian-born, sixty-eight-year-old Dubinsky, almost alone among his colleagues, thought LBJ a "terrific" political choice. Dubinsky phoned Rose. Walter Reuther expected Dubinsky to react with rage. When he did not (Rose: "Dave Dubinsky thinks that this is the smartest thing that could have ever happened. It's wonderful! It's great!"), the mood in the room changed—if not to elation, at least to some semblance of resigned acceptance.

"Well, it may be all right with him," Reuther observed, still unswayed, "but it's not all right with us."

In other liberal precincts—the Michigan delegation, in particular—tempers flared like sunspots, and JFK pondered withdrawing his offer to LBJ. Once again, the messenger would be Bobby Kennedy.

Around 1:45 p.m. RFK arrived at Lyndon Johnson's suite, met by none other than Sam Rayburn, who reported Bobby's arrival to LBJ, Lady Bird, and Phil Graham. All three refused to deal with Bobby. "No," Graham ordered LBJ, "you shouldn't see him. You don't want it, you won't negotiate for it, you'll only take it if Jack drafts you, and you won't discuss it with anyone else."

To keep the lines of communication open—yet RFK free—LBJ dispatched Graham to phone JFK. During their conversation Kennedy complained of intense liberal reaction to LBJ—a sure prelude to a withdrawn offer à la Symington. Graham shot back, "Do you want to be another Stevenson?" virtually ordering Jack to call Lyndon.

The wait for JFK's call was excruciating. "Do you really want me?" LBJ plaintively asked JFK. Kennedy answered affirmatively, and Lyndon Johnson's tragicomic ordeal seemed finally over.

Meanwhile, LBJ had summoned leaders of the party's Southern and Western wings. Inside Johnson's suite assembled Rayburn, Baker, and Connally; Senators John Stennis of Mississippi, Clinton Anderson of New Mexico, and Robert Kerr of Oklahoma; former Kentucky senator Earle Clements; and Texas governor Price Daniel. "You're young," Anderson advised; "you'll be elected some day yourself. Don't take a chance on getting messed up now."

"I know what's up," stormed Kerr, "and I'll get my long rifle. It ain't going to happen."

With such vitriol in the air, "Yankee faces" Rowe and Graham ("We're not Southerners, Rowe, we better get out of here") beat a hasty retreat. Rayburn ("I'm a damn sight smarter than I was last night") led Kerr into the bathroom. When they emerged, Kerr informed Johnson, "Lyndon, if Jack Kennedy asked you to be his running mate, and if you don't take it, I'll shoot you right between the eyes."

Then, like an actor bounding onto the stage in the wrong scene (almost in the wrong play), Robert Kennedy entered.

His appearance triggered alarm in Johnson aide Bill Moyers. "Graham," Moyers fairly screamed, "my God, Bobby is in the room." LBJ fearing the worst, was, if anything, in worse emotional shape. "I've never seen him," recalled Jim Rowe, "in such a state of—not panic—confusion."

He was in such a state of panic that this time, he *did* allow RFK access. RFK repeated the usual word of overwhelming liberal opposition to LBJ, tendering Johnson a rather unappetizing offer—the chairmanship of the Democratic National Committee in lieu of the vice presidency. That was too much. "Piss off!" snarled Sam Rayburn. "Who's the goddamn candidate," John Connally demanded, "you or your big brother?"

Though no one else remembered it, Bobby recollected this scene: "I thought he'd burst into tears. He just shook, and tears came to his eyes, and he said, 'I want to be vice-president, and if the president will have me, I'll join him in making a fight for it.'"

"Well, then, that's fine," RFK claimed to tell Johnson. "He wants you as vice-president if you want to be vice-president, we want you to know. I've already announced that Johnson is the candidate."

Others recalled it far differently, noting that Phil Graham had once again gotten through to JFK. "Jack," Graham informed JFK, "Bobby's down here and he's saying that there is opposition and that Lyndon should withdraw."

"Oh, that's all right," JFK replied, as blandly as if the discussion concerned which soup to serve at lunch. "Bobby's been out of touch and doesn't know what's happening."

"All right," muttered a bruised LBJ, "all right, let me go out and accept."

Jack asked to speak with Bobby. "Well, all right," RFK said to his brother, and the issue, chaotic and tortured for the very worst part of a day, was now settled.

Obviously, something had occurred *very* recently, something between RFK's last communication with his brother and JFK's first call to Lyndon. What was it?

We will never definitely know, but it may very well have involved an OK from the man behind the scenes. "There is enough reason," notes Herbert Parmet, among the most dispassionate of JFK biographers, "to suggest that encouragement from Joe Kennedy may have clinched the issue. . . . That Joe Kennedy was close to the situation and backed Johnson has already been well established."

Prior to the convention's opening, Joe had been testing the waters for what then seemed to be an unlikely LBJ-JFK alliance, keeping open channels with his son's supposed adversaries. "[Tommy] Corcoran tells me," Dean Acheson then wrote to Harry Truman, "that the only person with whom, according to Joe Kennedy, John would run under the circumstances mentioned, is Lyndon. If, therefore, Kennedy threw his strength to Johnson, Adlai might be stopped, and the Johnson-Kennedy ticket might be nominated."

Thus, support from Kennedy Sr. remains as reasonable a rationale of the inexplicable as any: the man in the shadows as the explanation for the campaign's most shadowy event. If Joe Kennedy had not initiated JFK's great gambit, he had, at least, signaled his approval—and his opinion that this dangerous, sloppy game had gone on long enough, and that his sons should end it.

"Well, all right," RFK answered and trudged out to the corridor, now as disoriented as anyone in the Johnson entourage. "Jim," he asked Jim Rowe, "don't you think it's a terrible mistake? It should have been Symington or Jackson."

"You can't win with either Symington or Jackson," Rowe responded. "The only two fellows that can help you are either Johnson or Humphrey."

"If we weren't so tired," Bobby added, not really listening to anything Rowe might say, "this wouldn't have happened."

Back in his suite, LBJ remained unsure of what to do next—or perhaps of what might *happen* to him next. Phil Graham virtually shoved him out into the corridor. Standing upon a chair, his public persona now restored to properly bluff working condition, Johnson proclaimed to reporters, "When Senator Kennedy walked down three [*sic*; it was two] flights of stairs to ask me to be his running mate, I could not say no."

"Yesterday was the best day of my life," Bobby confessed to friends later and elsewhere, "and today is the worst day of my life."

NINETEEN

"He is not a big man"

RFK DID NOT EXAGGERATE. Wednesday's glory had become Thursday's ashes.

The Democratic Party—necessary to carry his brother to victory—seemed perilously fractured. Each faction seemed angry, dissatisfied—if not ready to bolt, then ready at best to sulk, and at worst to raise embarrassing hell.

One needed not even be present to be angry. At Independence, reporters solicited Harry Truman's views. "I have no comment," he snapped. "I can't talk to you this morning."

As quickly as JFK had cinched it, Eleanor Roosevelt called her friend Mayris "Tiny" Martin (wife of bandleader Hershey Martin), with whom she stayed while in Los Angeles. ER said but little: Get my bags, bring them to the airport; I'm leaving.

Eleanor was indeed angry. Incensed at Kennedy for winning—angrier still at her friend Stevenson for not having made a better fight of it.

But the issue of Truman's and Eleanor's angst paled next to the Lyndon problem. JFK's settling with Lyndon Johnson did not settle well with those who had problems with a *Vice President* Lyndon Johnson.

The liberals remained angry. Joe Rauh, having been personally assured by JFK that LBJ would not be a part of the ticket, felt particularly "double-crossed" and disgusted. Michigan governor "Soapy" Williams, among the earliest and most prominent liberal officeholders to endorse Kennedy, similarly felt he had played the fool. "This is preposterous," Williams fumed to his delegation. "After our remarkable achievement in obtaining the civil rights plank in the platform, it is like stepping down from the clouds. For some of us, the suggestion was catastrophic and we have made it known in no uncertain terms." His wife, Nancy, tossed away her Kennedy buttons in disgust.

Southerners, too, felt betrayed, calculating not that they might gain a vice president, but that they might forfeit a Senate majority leader. And Texans felt sandbagged most of all. "It is hard to imagine the depth of the emotion among the Texas delegates," noted John Connally. "Many of the delegates literally left and checked out of the hotel and went home. [My wife] Nellie and I saw friends who had been Johnson supporters forever but were now livid with rage, and cursed him as a double-dealer, a liar, and a hypocrite."

A floor fight not only loomed, but if tempers continued inflaming, Johnson's nomination might suffer outright rejection by outraged delegates.

Among the unimpressed was Luci Baines Johnson. As if Lyndon Johnson did not have enough on his mind that frantic Thursday, daughter Luci had gone missing. The Secret Service finally located her, and as she rode up the Biltmore elevator her outraged father demanded, "Where in the hell were you?"

"I went to Disneyland."

"We didn't come to California for you to go to Disneyland."

"Yeah?" she shot back. "We didn't come to California for you to be vice president either."

Joe Kennedy was on the move. That evening, Chuck Spalding visited Marion Davies's Beverly Hills villa and was surprised to find Joe packing. "You can't leave now," he protested. "Why don't you stick around for the speech. That means more to you than to anybody."

"No," JPK responded, "there's work to be done and I've got to get out of here."

Joseph P. Kennedy could do his work anywhere there was a phone line, and there were precious few places on earth where he could not afford one. No, Joe was leaving not to work, but to avoid being a distraction and an embarrassment to Jack in Jack's moment of triumph. And, yet, despite all that, he might have remained.

"If *asked*," he would later sadly state, "I would have stayed."

"Soapy" Williams, growing more instead of less disgusted, earnestly plotted a floor fight on the Johnson nomination. Joe Rauh schemed to nominate Orville Freeman. Working now at cross-purposes to his normal liberal allies, however, was the UAW's Walter Reuther, still unimpressed with JFK's choice but realistic enough to grasp that a fractured convention—and party—possessed little chance against Richard Nixon. "It is the power equation in politics that is decisive," Reuther argued. "In politics you arrive at that point you arrive at in collective bargaining. You exert all your influence, fight as hard as you can, and then you have to make a decision. . . . You wind up doing something short of perfect and that is where we are in the political struggle."

To Adlai Stevenson, JFK conveyed the obvious: "I want to win," and Williams and Rauh were ultimately dissuaded from doing anything overtly inflammatory, but balloting remained tense. Anything might happen at any time. As the roll reached Massachusetts (just before the fractious, 152-member, fifty-one-vote Michigan delegation), John McCormack moved to nominate Johnson by acclamation. Chairman LeRoy Collins placed McCormack's motion before the floor—and was greeted by a noisy, confusing welter of "ayes," "nays"—and boos. The convention's eighty-one-year-old parliamentarian, Missouri congressman Clarence Cannon, ruled that two-thirds had voted to acclaim—and Lyndon Johnson was the nominee. The arena erupted yet again in protest. But it mattered not. The deal was done, the ticket Kennedy-Johnson.

Democrats seemed largely startled by the combination. Republicans were not. Dick Nixon and Thruston Morton had consistently predicted such a development. In Newport, Rhode Island, vacationing Dwight Eisenhower and his aide Bill Robinson took everything in. "How could Lyndon Johnson—having said all the things he did about Kennedy, having said over and over again that he wouldn't be a vice-presidential candidate—even consider it?" Robinson demanded to know.

Ike, that most political of non-politicians, provided a ready answer. It was not flattering. "Of course, that's very sound thinking and fairly good deduction," he responded, "unless you know Johnson. He is not a big man. He is a small man. He hadn't got the depth of mind nor the breadth of vision to carry great responsibility. Any floor leader of a Senate majority party looks good, no matter how incompetent he may be. Johnson is superficial and opportunistic."

Johnson's nomination had not been executed with any degree of skill. Yet Democrats now had an unusually utilitarian ticket, one that in its own creaking way was strong enough to resuscitate FDR's long-dormant New Deal coalition of big-city Catholics, Southern whites, and disaffected rural interests. It was, once all the grime had been rinsed off everyone's hands, a good day's work. "Don't worry, Jack," Joe Kennedy reassured his son before departing California. "Within two weeks they'll be saying it's the smartest thing you ever did."

What Johnson said to the convention mattered little. What JFK might say could set the entire tone of the campaign to come. His acceptance was to be a bit of the extravaganza, held not within sports arena confines, but outdoors, at the immense hundred-thousand-seat Los Angeles Memorial Coliseum. Despite the added attraction of a Hollywood star–filled warm-up act, filling so many seats proved difficult. Thousands of attendees had to be swept toward the podium to create even the illusion of a full house.

Jackie watched from Hyannis, on a rented seventeen-inch TV set, in the company of her mother and stepfather. Joe Kennedy, already back across the country, had pretty much invited himself to Henry Luce's for a lobster dinner. To Luce, JPK let his hair down, opening up as he could not in Beverly Hills, where he had been surrounded by eggheads and union leaders. "There was no respect for those liberals [Stevenson, Humphrey, Freeman]," recalled Henry Luce III. "He just thought they were all fools on whom he had played this giant trick."

Luce and Kennedy felt each other out about how Luce's publishing empire and Joe Kennedy's son might co-exist during the campaign. "Well, now, Joe," said Henry Luce, "I suppose you are interested in the attitudes *Time* and *Life*, and I, might take about Jack's candidacy. As to domestic affairs, of course Jack will have to be left of center—"

"How can you say that?" JPK interrupted. "How can you think that any son of mine would ever be a ——ing liberal?"

Luce apologized that he meant nothing personal—merely that any Democrat nominee would have to comport himself in a certain way. "Now on the foreign matter," he continued. "If he shows any signs of weakness, in general, towards the anti-Communist cause, or to put it more positively, any weakness in defending and advancing the cause of the free world, why then we'll certainly be against him."

"Well," Joe reassured him, "there's no chance of that. You know that! I just want you to know that I, or we, are very grateful for all that you've done for Jack."

Henry Luce's fears might not have been relieved, however, by what now appeared on the screen: Adlai Stevenson, introducing Joe Kennedy's son to the coliseum crowds.

Jack Kennedy was exhausted, both physically and emotionally, from what he and Lyndon Johnson had just endured. "It was not one of his better speeches—he was tired," Kenny O'Donnell admitted, "and the setting sun was shining into his eyes." JFK began in proper fashion, a series of gracious introductions and references—to LBJ, Stevenson, Symington, Humphrey ("my traveling companion in Wisconsin and West Virginia") and even to Harry Truman—that played well. Then came a string of churlish cheap shots ("the political career of their candidate has often seemed to show charity toward none and malice for all. . . . Mr. Nixon may feel it is his turn now, after the New Deal and the Fair Deal—but before he deals, someone had better cut the cards") and odd historical references ("Richard Cromwell was not fit to wear the mantle of his uncle") that did not. But, ultimately, JFK's address provided the tone, not just for a campaign but for an administration. As he informed a nation:

> We stand today on the edge of a New Frontier, the frontier of the 1960s, a frontier of unknown opportunities and perils, a frontier of unfulfilled hopes and threats. But the New Frontier of which I speak is not a set of promises—it is a set of challenges. It sums up not what I intend to offer the American people, but what I intend to ask of them. It appeals to their pride, not their pocketbook—it holds out the promise of more sacrifice instead of more security. Beyond that frontier are uncharted areas of science and space, unsolved problems of peace and war, unconquered pockets of ignorance and prejudice, unanswered questions of poverty and surplus.
>
> It would be easy to shrink from that frontier, to look to the safe mediocrity of the past, . . . but I believe the time demands invention, innovation, imagination, decision. I am asking each of you to be new pioneers of that New Frontier.

And in the setting California sun and the ringing summonses to idealism and adventure, no one remembered Lyndon Johnson—but he remained as real as anything Jack Kennedy said that evening. And as JFK hoped to use him, he still hoped to use JFK.

"Clare," Lyndon Johnson would inform Henry Luce's wife, Clare Boothe Luce, on the way to a grander ceremony the following January, "I looked it up; one out of every four presidents has died in office. I'm a gamblin' man, darling, and this is the only chance I got."

CHAPTER TWENTY

"A two-fisted, four-square liar"

DESPITE ALL THE HUMDRUM and rote found in any convention's format, Democrats had surprisingly succeeded in delivering five days of suspense, intrigue, and, on occasion, even high idealism.

The GOP's forthcoming assemblage, on the other hand, promised Richard Nixon on the first ballot.

Such were the drawbacks of a primary season bereft of actual competition. The limelight had receded from the Republican Party, and when it returned, in Chicago two weeks after the Democrats had adjourned, it promised to switch back on with only the dimmest candlepower.

And so it would have, but for Nelson Rockefeller—who, after all, craved attention not for his party, but for himself.

Two factors made Rockefeller's belated gambit not merely feasible but, in a perverse way, wildly successful: first, a document, which, by rights and custom, should have rated mere sedate oblivion—the Republican Party platform; and, second and more significant, competitor Richard Nixon's hitherto unknown, but evidently finely tuned, sense of panic.

That Nelson Rockefeller had grasped the inherent possibilities for mischief lying dormant within the GOP's work-in-progress platform should hardly have been a total surprise. Fixated as he (and, to a lesser extent, the nation) was with defining national goals, it was indeed only natural that at some point he would have eyed the possibilities inherent within a party platform.

It was by no means a right-wing document. Crafted under the direction of forty-year-old Bell & Howell executive Charles Percy, its draft was a carefully kneaded portion of Eisenhower Republicanism leavened with a proper handful of nods to a more progressive future—counterbalanced, of course, with sprinklings of old Republican chestnuts.

Nonetheless, from Albany, on Friday, July 22, Rockefeller press secretary Robert L. McManus, a former Harriman staffer, released word that his chief found the nascent document, in any number of areas—defense, foreign policy, medical care, civil rights—"still seriously lacking in strength and specifics."

"The Governor is convinced," McManus continued, "that vigorous and forthright positions in all these areas—and in the particularly crucial case of civil rights—are vital for both the nation and the Republican party."

Hardly a "Cross of Gold" moment, but words that touched sensitive chords within the always careful, increasingly paranoid mind of Richard Nixon. For, just the previous day, the *New York Times* had noted: "But if Mr. Rockefeller finds the platform substantially short of what he feels the party should stand for, he now plans to let his name go before the convention in opposition to the Vice President, even if his delegate potential seems too low for any realistic hope of victory."

In 1960, Nixon coveted, to the point of obsession, a controversy-free, stage-managed coronation. He had progressed this far with little overt competition and wanted none now. He wanted no platform planks that might rile key voting groups—primarily white Southerners and Northern blacks. And of course he wanted nothing that would provide fodder for JFK that fall. Thus demanding and attempting to secure a convention free of pitfalls, Richard Nixon fell into one of the deepest of his pitfall-strewn career.

Nixon's inner circle—Robert Finch, Leonard Hall, and Herb Klein—remained sanguine. They had the votes, for both the platform and the nomination. Nelson Rockefeller could make all the noise he wished. He'd done so for months, if not years, without much effect. Beyond that, the latest Gallup poll showed Nixon leading Rocky 75 percent to 13 percent. Nixon's men saw no cause for alarm.

But Nixon himself did. Consulting no one, he telephoned former attorney general Herbert Brownell, a pillar of New York's Republican establishment, requesting to meet with Rockefeller at Brownell's Manhattan apartment.

Rockefeller's staff saw their opportunity. Rockefeller adviser Emmet Hughes demanded a whole series of conditions for a Rockefeller-Nixon summit. Nixon must grovel. He must personally call Rockefeller. The session must be held not at Brownell's—neutral ground—but rather literally on Rocky's home turf, his thirty-two-room 810 Fifth Avenue triplex apartment. When it was all over, Rockefeller—not Nixon—would announce the results, and the press release would be no tame listing of papered-over topics, but instead a detailed discussion of the issues in play. Last, but not least, that announcement would pointedly mention that it was front-runner Nixon—not also-ran, never-ran Nelson Rockefeller—who had requested the session.

It was a humiliating series of conditions. Richard Nixon agreed to each and every one. Still acting in secret from even his closest advisers, he arrived in New York at 7:30 that evening, his first priority not the platform but the ticket. A Nixon-Rockefeller slate might revive flagging GOP hopes throughout the populous Northeast, particularly in crucial New York. On July 20, just two days previously, Arthur Burns had written to Nixon suggesting Rockefeller as someone who "would add more strength to the Republican ticket than anyone else."

Yet, even Burns added a caveat: "I do not quite trust [Rockefeller]. . . . What I fear is that if you offered him the second spot he might turn it down, and then tell the entire world about it, and in the process cheapen the Vice Presidency for the man who is finally selected."

Nixon should have heeded Burns's warning. He didn't, not only offering Rockefeller the second slot but tendering him a package without precedent: the ability to dictate the platform *and* foreign policy, and to control federal patronage in New York.

Rockefeller said no.

In hindsight, Nixon recognized just how fortunate he indeed was: "Rockefeller's independent temperament would have made him a much more difficult running mate for me to deal with than Johnson would be for Kennedy."

Nixon's original plan possessed some logic: sensing Rockefeller's desire for action on the platform, he would give it to him—but in exchange for Rocky propping up the ticket. Nixon might then have retrieved his marbles, thanked his host for a fine meal, and departed. He still, however, feared a belated Rockefeller candidacy. He also feared that with Rockefeller empowered to authorize the conference's official public account, Richard Nixon, now so very close to convention eve, lay even more defenseless to Rocky's well-known penchant for ruthless bomb throwing.

Nixon remained. For three hours he and Rockefeller went back and forth on their statement—significantly working from a draft supplied by

Rockefeller staff. At midnight, a conference call: Nixon and Rocky, nego-
tiating for three hours more, this time with Chuck Percy and Emmet
Hughes (euphemistically and inaccurately identified in the subsequent
memorandum as "other members of the Platform committee") hooked up
from Chicago.

Nixon departed at 3:20 a.m. Only then did Nixon have Colonel
Hughes inform his own staff of events. At 5 a.m. Rockefeller's tireless—
and numerous—minions distributed mimeographed copies of what
would soon be known, either famously or infamously, as the "Compact
of Fifth Avenue."

Somehow, news of Nixon's activities failed to reach Herb Klein.
Pressed by the *New York Times'* James "Scotty" Reston, Klein denied that
any such sort of unlikely event was occurring. Reporters branded Klein
a liar.

Soon everyone knew what Scotty Reston knew and Herb Klein didn't.
Rockefeller's mimeographed sheets were flooding New York,
Washington, and Chicago. Their fourteen separate points were, at their
most, benign, a helpful listing of government initiatives. But at the compact's most mischievous level, and that is how Dwight Eisenhower rightly
saw them, they represented indictments of his administration for not
undertaking them.

Seven points involved domestic matters—ranging from farm policy to
federal health insurance to collective bargaining to school aid construction, and culminating in a grandiose restructuring of the federal government. Most controversial among Rockefeller's domestic planks was that
involving civil rights. Here, Rockefeller was pushing the envelope in a
most dangerous way. The GOP was poised to make significant gains in
the white South. At the very least it desired to retain Southern states that
Dwight Eisenhower had carried four years previously. The original platform draft had been decidedly more moderate, avoiding any specific mention of the controversial recent sit-in phenomenon or of any federal
intervention to end discrimination. Rockefeller's plank now paralleled the
just-adopted Democratic plank that had so inflamed Southerners. If
adopted, it threatened any GOP hope for carrying the South. If rejected,
it would alienate blacks. "Nixon made his choice, I believe, more out of
conscience than out of strategy," noted Theodore White, but the original

plank, "as written, would almost certainly have carried the Southern states for Nixon and, it seems in retrospect, might have given him victory."

If Rockefeller's civil rights plank inflamed crucial Southern sensibilities, his seven military planks provided even greater aggravation for Dwight Eisenhower—they denigrated nearly every aspect of his foreign and defense policies. Eisenhower was incensed. He didn't particularly relish criticism of his domestic agenda, but *this* was beyond the pale. "That section," he recorded in his memoirs, "seemed somewhat astonishing, coming as it did from two people who had long been in administration councils and who had never voiced any doubt—at least in my presence—of the adequacy of America's defenses."

Ike's office had learned of events at eight o'clock on Saturday morning. "That section is unacceptable," his press secretary, a terse Jim Hagerty, phoned back to Chicago. "We'll call you later with some changes."

"If our rockets only had the same thrust that the President developed on Saturday morning," recalled General Lucius Clay, "we would not have to worry about Khrushchev."

The enraged Ike soon grilled Nixon, who alibied that Rockefeller had unilaterally issued the offending proposals. "What I'm trying to do," Nixon went on, "is to find some ground on which Nelson can be with us and not against us." Eisenhower might sympathize with that. He knew how difficult Rockefeller could be, but he also knew that Nixon had botched the job. In the face of intense pressure from Eisenhower ("I left no doubt that it would be difficult for me to be enthusiastic about a platform which did not reflect a respect for the record of the Republican administration"), various offending passages were smoothed over, most notably in regard to defense. Article 7, for example, now read: "There *is* [emphasis added] no price ceiling on America's security. The United States can and must provide whatever is necessary to insure its own security and that of the free world, to provide any necessary increased expenditures to meet new situations. . . . To provide more would be wasteful. To provide less would be catastrophic."

Less easily patched up was the compact's impact upon the party itself. The 103 members of the platform committee, their work tossed away in the dead of night, had been made to feel like fools. The remaining 1,331 delegates barely felt better.

Conservatives, whose nerves already went taut at the very mention of Nelson Rockefeller's name, felt even angrier. They had swallowed Tom Dewey and Dwight Eisenhower, but now to have the tax-raising former New Dealer Nelson Rockefeller dictate their platform—that was simply beyond what they felt necessary to endure.

Barry Goldwater was their spokesman.

The Republican Party—the conservative party—had become suddenly bereft of conservative leadership. Worse, once one advanced beyond Eisenhower and Nixon, it appeared to have no leadership at all—unless one counted Nelson Rockefeller, too liberal and too new and too abrasive for anyone in the party to follow.

Into the breach stepped Goldwater, representing a new breed of conservatism and a reborn old breed of Republicanism.

Born to a prominent Phoenix department store family, Barry Morris Goldwater never pretended to have excelled at scholarship, preferring instead to tinker with such avocations as ham radio, photography, aviation, and even studies of the region's American Indians. Following his father's 1929 death, Barry dropped out of the University of Arizona to assist in running the family department store. By 1937 he was its president. In World War II, he piloted planes across the Atlantic and over the Himalayas. At war's end, like Kennedy and Nixon, he stood ready to enter politics.

Already an ideological conservative, well-read in such authors as Burke and Locke, he won election to the Phoenix city council, managed a successful gubernatorial campaign, and, in 1952, narrowly won election to the U.S. Senate, not only defeating that body's majority leader but also becoming the state's first Republican senator.

In Congress, Goldwater favored a strong anti-communism abroad and less government at home. He strenuously opposed big labor. Though he and JFK invariably found themselves on opposite sides, Jack Kennedy found Goldwater to be (in Arthur Schlesinger's words), "a man of decency and character."

"When you compare Nixon and Goldwater," JFK would privately comment, "Goldwater seems like Abraham Lincoln."

Yet, Goldwater would start projects and not finish them—among these, an investigation of UAW violence, a filibuster against Kennedy's labor reform bill. "Charming though Goldwater was," thought Robert Novak, "was he serious?"

Even in his first term, Goldwater established himself as a persistent Eisenhower critic. In 1958, when it seemed every other Republican was losing, Goldwater easily won re-election, and, beyond that, assumed leadership of the Republican Senatorial Campaign Committee, providing him with national contacts and exposure.

By 1959 Goldwater's tough talk won him a column in the *Los Angeles Times*. By July 1960, "How Do You Stand, Sir?" ran in 50 papers; by year's end, 140. Barry Goldwater was the voice of the new conservatism.

Admirers praised his refreshing candor. Detractors accused him of shooting from the hip. "If I could saw off the Eastern Seaboard and let it float out," he had famously stormed, "I sometimes think the country would be better off."

As 1960 began, his presidential poll numbers generally hovered from 1 percent all the way up to 2 percent. But beneath the surface, a Goldwater movement was indeed forming, aided immeasurably by the March 1960 publication of his ideological manifesto, *The Conscience of a Conservative*. Goldwater being Goldwater, the book was barely his. Former Notre Dame Law School dean Clarence Manion conceived of the project. William F. Buckley Jr.'s thirty-four-year-old brother-in-law L. Brent Bozell wrote it. Conservatives, hungry for ideas, starving for leadership, purchased *The Conscience of a Conservative* by the carload: ten thousand copies that month, more than fifty thousand by May, and three and a half million copies by 1964.

In May, conservative activists had formed Youth for Goldwater, their goal being not a presidential nomination, but a far humbler vice-presidential nod. In April a poll of 3,405 GOP county chairmen actually favored Goldwater for the vice presidency—257 to 251 to Henry Cabot Lodge.

As Youth for Goldwater formed and Rockefeller carped at Eisenhower from the left, Goldwater snarled at him from the right. Toward Richard Nixon, however, the Arizonan had long displayed more faith than he might have. "I believe you are the person who must select the spot on which the party is going to stand," he wrote to Nixon after 1958's election debacle, "put the flag there; and then rally the forces around it."

News of Nixon's Fifth Avenue "surrender" and the "Munich of the Republican Party" unleashed a stream of Goldwater anger, both at Rocky ("Governor Rockefeller," he fumed, "is out to destroy the Republican Party") and at Nixon. Previously, Nixon had promised Goldwater, always fanatical on labor issues, that he would support a right-to-work plank. After Fifth Avenue, he reversed himself (in truth, he might well have anyway).

"The man," a disappointed Goldwater confided to his private journal, "is a two-fisted, four-square liar."

Sammy Davis Jr.'s marriage to Swedish starlet May Britt would be postponed to accommodate JFK's political needs. He told the black press, "I . . . would do all in my power to help him even if I were called upon to make a great personal sacrifice." (COLLECTION OF THE AUTHOR)

A forlorn JFK event in Maine. Not every parade was ticker tape. "This is my time," JFK would say on the campaign stump. "My time is now." (COLLECTION OF THE AUTHOR)

Yonkers, New York, greets JFK. "Kennedy," noted the Associated Press, "has an edge among the jumpers, the shriekers and the squealers." (COLLECTION OF THE AUTHOR)

Pamela Turnure
Press Sec to the First Lady

Pierre Salinger
Press Secretary

above left:
JFK press secretary Pierre Salinger. "I've never
lacked for self-confidence . . . and at thirty-four
I had an enviable record of achievement," the
hyperkinetic, fast-talking Salinger would recall.
"But I was an outsider—indeed . . . the only
outsider. . . . I think it's fair to say that for
quite some time I walked on eggshells."
(Collection of the author)

above right:
Pamela Turnure. JFK staffer—and mistress.
Subject of an ill-fated, but potentially
dangerous, blackmail scheme.
(Collection of the author)

right:
Richard Nixon's political fortunes returned with
his "Kitchen Debate" against Nikita Khrushchev—
as this Republican ad noted.
(Collection of the author)

Pierre Salinger
Press Secretary

Pamela Turnure
Press Sec to the First Lady

above left:
JFK press secretary Pierre Salinger. "I've never lacked for self-confidence . . . and at thirty-four I had an enviable record of achievement," the hyperkinetic, fast-talking Salinger would recall. "But I was an outsider—indeed . . . the only outsider. . . . I think it's fair to say that for quite some time I walked on eggshells." (COLLECTION OF THE AUTHOR)

above right:
Pamela Turnure. JFK staffer—and mistress. Subject of an ill-fated, but potentially dangerous, blackmail scheme. (COLLECTION OF THE AUTHOR)

right:
Richard Nixon's political fortunes returned with his "Kitchen Debate" against Nikita Khrushchev— as this Republican ad noted. (COLLECTION OF THE AUTHOR)

David Powers
Assistant to the President

Longtime Kennedy aide—and friend—Dave Powers. "Dave was the first staffer to see [Kennedy] up in the morning," said Pierre Salinger, "and the last person to see him at night." (COLLECTION OF THE AUTHOR)

Theodore C. Sorensen
Spec Counsel to President

Theodore C. Sorensen. JFK's top speechwriter and rhetorician, his go-to guy for research, Ted Sorensen was—in JFK's own words—his "intellectual blood bank." "When Jack is wounded," said one observer, "Ted bleeds." (COLLECTION OF THE AUTHOR)

Myer Feldman
Mr. Sorensen's office

JFK's Chief of Legislative Research Myer "Mike" Feldman. His "Nixopedia" helped JFK prep for the "Great Debates." (COLLECTION OF THE AUTHOR)

Lawrence F. O'Brien
Spec Asst to the President

Kennedy aide Lawrence O'Brien. "Jack Kennedy was a remarkable fellow and I had great admiration for him," O'Brien would recall, "or I wouldn't have gone through all I did with him on these things." (COLLECTION OF THE AUTHOR)

Richard N. Goodwin
Mr. Sorensen's office

left:
JFK speechwriter Richard Goodwin. "An Iago in permanent pursuit of an Othello," observed Gore Vidal. (COLLECTION OF THE AUTHOR)

below left:
JFK aide Kenny O'Donnell. "You see Kenny over there," JFK once remarked. "If I woke up and asked him to jump out of this plane for me, he'd do it. You don't find that kind of loyalty easily." (COLLECTION OF THE AUTHOR)

below right:
JFK's loyal secretary Evelyn Lincoln. (COLLECTION OF THE AUTHOR)

Evelyn Lincoln
The President's office

A look at the record shows:

Wars ride hand-in-hand with Democratic Presidents

Wilson, Roosevelt, Truman--three Democrats--three Wars

Woodrow Wilson campaigned in 1916 on a program of "I will keep you out of war." He stated: "I will not allow your sons to be used as cannon fodder" and "There is such a thing as being too proud to fight." Two months after his inaugural, we were engaged in World War I.

Franklin Roosevelt in a campaign speech in 1940 at a time when he knew from his confidential intelligence reports that we were on the brink of war, declared: "I have said this before, but I shall say it again and again and again: Your boys are not going to be sent into any foreign wars."

What fatally has dogged the United States in this century when a Democrat was elected President? Can it be laid to bungling and bosses, or was it blind fate? How was it that the country has had peace and, for the most part, an ever-growing prosperity under all Republican Presidents of our modern era? Was it good management — or just good luck?

Whatever the reason, the facts remain — Democrats, war — Republicans, peace.

How will your ballot be cast on November 8 — to send your son to war or keep the peace? It should be for the experience, ability and proven know-how of Vice President Richard M. Nixon, a Republican.

Which President Will You Choose?

NIXON....OR KENNEDY

PRESIDENT EISENHOWER HAS SAID OF DICK NIXON:

"There is no man in the history of America who has had such a careful preparation as Vice President Nixon for carrying out the duties of the Presidency. There hasn't been a principal administrative meeting among the heads of government that he has not attended as an active participant. In every country that he has visited the United States has gained many additional friends. The esteem attached is a tribute to his dedication and to his wisdom."

SUPPORTERS OF JACK KENNEDY are on the record, too!

HARRY TRUMAN WONDERED ... "Senator, are you certain that you are quite ready for the country and that the country is ready for you in the role of President in January, 1961? I am greatly concerned and troubled about the situation as we are applied in the world and in the immediate future. That is why I would hope that someone with the greatest possible maturity and experience would be available at this time." (New York Herald Tribune, 7/5/60)

LYNDON JOHNSON OBJECTED ... "I am not prepared to apologize to Mr. Khrushchev — we yield I am not prepared to send regrets to Mr. Khrushchev — we yield (Speaking to a Washington State Democratic Convention at Spokane) (New York Times, 7/11/60)

ADLAI STEVENSON WORRIED ... "The amount of money being spent on Kennedy's campaign is phenomenal, probably the highest amount spent on a campaign in history." (Newsweek, 7/25/60)

HENRY WALLACE SAYS: "The (Democratic) program would increase prices to you by 25%."

HUBERT HUMPHREY WARNED ... "My opponent and his campaign aides may feel it is possible to buy a state, but they certainly won't have to win by such tactics in November." (Washington Post, 7/9/60)

WAYNE MORSE CHARGED ... "His statement in regard to campaign expenses are further evidence as to his lack of qualifications for the Presidency. The American people should make clear to Senator Kennedy that the White House will never be put up for sale ... It is obvious that the truth is not in him." (Baltimore Sun, 7/27/60)

VOTERS FOR NIXON, Henry Clock, Chairman — John C. Langan, Treasurer — Ruth Todd, Secretary — Long Beach Headquarters, Wilton Hotel Bldg.

Jack Kennedy's hawkish views caused the GOP to remind voters of past Democratic presidents—and past wars. (COLLECTION OF THE AUTHOR)

Richard Nixon lacked the advantage of JFK's large, photogenic family—but *Good Housekeeping*, nonetheless, gave its seal of approval to his seventy-five year old mother, Hannah Milhaus Nixon. (COLLECTION OF THE AUTHOR)

In 1960 recently installed Cuban dictator Fidel Castro visited the United Nations—inflaming American opinion. No fan of Richard Nixon, Castro also blasted JFK as an "illiterate and ignorant millionaire." (COLLECTION OF THE AUTHOR)

An anti-JFK, anti-Catholic ad that ran in West Virginia papers during that state's Democratic primary. (COLLECTION OF THE AUTHOR)

TWENTY-ONE

"The man who will succeed Dwight D. Eisenhower... Richard E. Nixon"

THE ILL-CONSIDERED WORDS of the Nixon-Rockefeller Compact of Fifth Avenue would soon be interred under a never-ending avalanche of still more words. At 10 a.m. on Monday, July 25, the 1960 Republican National Convention convened at Chicago's twelve-thousand-seat International Amphitheater, its participants focused now not nearly so much on platforms but on any convention's real purposes—speeches, bands, hoopla, funny hats, an elephant parading down Michigan Avenue—and, somewhere along the way, nominating its presidential and vice-presidential candidates.

The number of votes this convention needed to nominate Richard Nixon was 666.

Various Nixons had arrived in Chicago on Sunday, July 24. In these hectic times for them, this passed for a family reunion—seventy-five-year old Hannah Nixon ("Well, I never called him Dick. He just looks like a Richard to me"); forty-five-year-old brother Donald and his matronly looking wife, Clara; thirty-year-old brother Edward, a navy lieutenant, and his redheaded wife Gay Lynne and their daughters; and, most prominently, Richard Nixon's daughters, Patricia ("Tricia"), fourteen and "daringly" wearing red lipstick, and twelve-year-old Julie (less daringly in braces). Asked what she most wished to see in Chicago, Tricia, parked for the last month alongside her sister in a Santa Barbara summer camp, responded, "My parents."

Tricia and Julie's parents touched down at O'Hare the following morning, greeted by three thousand admirers. Whisked by helicopter to Meigs Field for a rally hosted by Illinois governor William G. "Billy the Kid" Stratton, they were then motorcaded to the Sheraton-Blackstone Hotel through crowds so immense that their limousine could not traverse the last block—the Nixons proceeded the rest of the way on foot. The sight of them so vulnerable so upset Herb Klein that, as he recalled, "I stepped hard on the foot of someone who was grabbing them by the arm. To my embarrassment, it turned out later that this was John Nidecker, a new advance man, and I had broken his foot."

Richard Nixon was a busy man—hammering out remaining platform questions, anointing a running mate, drafting his acceptance speech—but Nixon also peered nervously over his shoulder at John Kennedy and Lyndon Johnson. The Democrats' untidy gathering had, nonetheless, provided JFK with a traditional convention "bump," his early July 52 percent–to–48 percent edge now swelling to 55 percent to 45 percent. More ominously, by a 41 percent–to–25 percent margin the public now believed that Democrats would better facilitate world respect for the United States. Four years previously, Republicans had enjoyed a 35 percent–to–26 percent edge. Americans even viewed Democrats as better for business:

	Democrats Better	Republicans Better	No Difference, No Opinion
Overall	32%	24%	44%
White-collar workers	45%	20%	35%
Farmers	34%	21%	45%
Manual workers	43%	17%	40%

Dwight and Mamie Eisenhower arrived on Tuesday morning, July 26, a helicopter ferrying them from O'Hare to Meigs Field, and from there the obligatory motorcade escorted their Lincoln bubbletop six miles past a million cheering Chicagoans, a thousand Chicago police detectives, patrolmen stationed every twenty feet, and two teenagers who managed to obtain sufficient proximity to the president of the United States to toss rice in his face. At the Sheraton-Blackstone Hotel, a crowd fifteen thousand strong surged past police, enveloping the presidential limousine. The Eisenhowers did not walk the last block.

A marvelous triumph (save for the rice), but also one illustrating the strangely unbridgeable gulf separating president from vice president. Dwight Eisenhower had proceeded triumphantly past a million cheering souls—but Richard Nixon had not accompanied him. Instead, Ike shared his vehicle with two politicians not even running that year—Thruston Morton and stentorian conservative Illinois U.S. senator Everett McKinley Dirksen. Nixon merely awaited Ike at the Sheraton. True, Nixon—seemingly unperturbed, even strangely jovial as he waited, performing a little jig out on Balboa Drive—commandeered the conductor's baton to lead the Chicago Board of Trade Band. It was all very nice. But it would've been nicer still had Dick Nixon shared an enormous spotlight with Dwight Eisenhower.

That evening Ike addressed the convention. He discussed public policy, attacking socialism's "soaring record of suicides, drunkenness and lack of ambition"—and the Danish and Swedish press took umbrage. He downplayed obvious party divisions ("Within this Convention, I hear that there is some dispute among the delegates concerning the platform. Now there is nothing wrong in this. It is good! . . . There is room for healthy argument within our party"). But his primary goal, as ever, was to defend not Dick or Rocky, but his own record—"In the successes of the past seven and a half years, you have a solid foundation on which to build toward new levels of attainment. But thank God there is no smugness or complacency about your accomplishments."

"Every Republican," he lectured, "every independent, every discerning Democrat should be appealed to on the basis that we are truly a middle-of-the-road party"—a middle-of-the-road Dwight David Eisenhower party.

His speech, Nixon later wrote, was "one of the most effective political speeches he had ever made."

And yet Dwight Eisenhower never once criticized John F. Kennedy or Lyndon Johnson or even mentioned Richard Nixon by name, or even alluded to him. And when he was done, Eisenhower, not waiting for Richard Nixon's own address to the convention or even for Nixon's nomination, simply left town—and went back on vacation.

Nelson Rockefeller, having finally consented to attend the proceedings, remained. His phantasmagoric candidacy on hold for this campaign season, he continued to plump for his own ideas on the platform, further alienating not only Republicans of a conservative bent but those still loyal to the administration.

On the right, a small but growing number of delegates, centered in South Carolina, Louisiana, Texas, and Arizona—unimpressed by Nixon and almost itching for a fight—plotted the nomination of Barry Goldwater. But Goldwater, wary of appearing as quixotic as Rockefeller, drew back. "Get me three hundred names of delegates on paper," he barked at supporters. "Show me." Though 287 eventually signed on, Goldwater remained unconvinced.

Yet the nascent Goldwater movement possessed real significance. Unlike Adlai Stevenson's convention forces, Goldwater's battalions foreshadowed the explosion of a new movement rather than the last noisy gasp of one merely expiring on national television. It was not, however, something Richard Nixon (or anyone else, for that matter) yet recognized as particularly significant. Nixon himself was still peering backward—to a Republican Party still dominated by Eastern liberals such as Rockefeller and Dewey and Lodge.

Barry Goldwater's emerging voice was blunt. To the press he blasted JFK as "immature." Texan LBJ, he charged, was "not a conservative. Johnson is as far to the left as Humphrey or anyone else in the Democratic Party." Although Goldwater's Western feistiness only endeared him to an increasingly dissatisfied segment of the party, to Northeastern patricians such as Joe Alsop, "Senator Goldwater's issues and ideas belong to a world that never was, or at least a world that died at end of the 19th century." Goldwater publicly ordered supporters to withdraw his largely symbolic nomination. They moved forward anyway. A boisterous twelve-minute demonstration—featuring red-white-and-blue cardboard hats and a Yuma Indian band—greeted his name being placed before the convention. Some Goldwaterites complained of being jostled and restrained by convention guards. A flag-waving Texan was shoved out the door, a woman pushed to the floor.

When Louisiana cast ten votes for Goldwater—and then, under pressure, polled itself on whether to change to Nixon—Arizona moved to make Nixon's nomination unanimous. As Nelson Rockefeller chatted with his press secretary Robert McManus, the convention erupted in "ayes." Startled, Rocky looked up, said nothing, and tossed his Nixon imitation straw hat away.

Goldwater carried few votes, even temporarily. But the exercise allowed him to address the convention—in fact, his nomination had been a charade designed for just that purpose. His gruff charisma energized the convention in a way that little else had. Goldwater, noted Indianapolis journalist M. Stanton Evans, was engulfed "in bedlam. A great wave of sound exploded into the vaulted regions of the [hall]. . . . [T]he ovation . . . was real and deep and it was overwhelming."

"Republicans," Goldwater shouted not just to the convention but to the entire party behind it, "have not been losing elections because of more Democratic votes, we have been losing elections because conservatives often fail to vote. . . . Let's grow up, conservatives. . . . If we want to take this party back—and I think we can some day—let's get to work."

He had issued a call that would soon transform his party—and American politics as a whole. "Nineteen-sixty-four is another year," Goldwater had promised even before ordering conservatives to grow up. "I am not through by any means."

Still, the GOP needed to nominate Richard Nixon—that task officially falling to thirty-eight-year-old Oregon governor Mark O. Hatfield, one of the party's few winners in 1958's debacle. The heavily made-up Hatfield—as handsome as a TV Western gunslinger, in CBS News correspondent Charles Collingwood's estimation—proved nearly as terse, his 288-word address among the shortest nominating addresses ever.

Once again, Nixon had leaned leftward. Not only was Hatfield among the party's more pronounced liberals; so were Nixon seconders Senators Tom Kuchel and Jacob Javits. If anyone missed Nixon's point, one last seconder drove it home: FDR's youngest son, John Roosevelt.

Neither Goldwater nor Rocky had entered the vice-presidential sweepstakes, though numerous others fancied themselves at least VP timber. Interior secretary Fred A. Seaton, a former Nebraska newspaperman (and briefly a U.S. senator), and Grand Rapids congressman Gerald R. Ford both opened headquarters. The forty-seven-year-old Ford enjoyed not just the solid backing of his forty-six-vote home-state delegation, but also the support of Seaton's cabinet colleague Postmaster General Arthur Summerfield (a fellow Michigander). Ford, his campaign manager John B. Martin bragged, possessed "the most dark horse power" and so rated a slot on Nixon's "acceptable list."

Less acceptable was Indiana's Wendell Willkie Jr., son of the GOP's 1940 candidate. "I'm a farm boy from the streets of New York," he crowed. "I'm an Ivy Leaguer with an Indiana drawl." Willkie conceded, however, that he didn't have any *delegates* and that his chances stood somewhere around 1 percent.

Illinois governor William Stratton ("Illinois is absolutely necessary to the election of a Republican President") insisted that a Midwesterner receive consideration. If not, Stratton would nominate Everett Dirksen. Other names percolating included Treasury secretary Anderson and Pennsylvania's liberal U.S. senator Hugh Scott.

Nixon himself was rumored to be considering only Lodge, Morton, Ford, Seaton, Labor secretary Mitchell (Ike's most liberal cabinet member— "Some people think I'm kind of a welfare-stater"), and Minnesota congressman Dr. Walter Judd (the convention's fiery keynote speaker). Soon Nixon's list narrowed to just three: Lodge, Morton, and Judd.

Fifty-two-year-old Republican national chairman, Senator Thruston Morton, a moderate in the Nixon mold (albeit minus Nixon's penchant for controversy and acrimony), had definite possibilities. A proven border-state vote getter, Yale graduate Morton won election to both the House and the Senate by defeating incumbents (in the latter case, deputy majority leader Earle Clements). To this he had added a stint in Eisenhower's State Department. "Morton," as Richard Nixon recalled, "wanted the position badly."

Sixty-one-year-old Walter Judd, the sole conservative in Nixon's final mix, possessed a distinctly unusual résumé. In the 1920s and '30s he had served as a Congregational Church medical missionary to China, leaving that troubled country the first time after contracting malaria and the second following Japan's invasion. Elected to the House in 1942, Judd had sponsored the first legislation banning racial discrimination in immigration and naturalization as well as measures that eventually distributed seventeen billion dollars in surplus food abroad.

Judd, however, may have proven too right of center for Nixon's tastes (a situation perhaps compounded when Goldwater partisans moonlighted with a Judd-for-VP boomlet). No conservative had won a place on any Republican national ticket since Ohio senator John Bricker, Tom Dewey's running mate sixteen years before.

Henry Cabot Lodge, of course, was JFK's old adversary. Since then he had served, quite effectively, as Dwight Eisenhower's United Nations ambassador. In May 1960, his visibility—and his stock—rose appreciably when, in the wake of the U-2 debacle, he displayed before the UN Security Council particularly damning evidence of Soviet bloc eavesdropping—electronic devices secreted inside a carved wooden great seal of the United States, "a gesture of friendship" presented to Ambassador Averell Harriman in 1945. It had hung inside America's Moscow embassy for seven years.

Lodge, however, came with some foreboding negatives. Die-hard Robert Taft supporters still despised him for steamrolling their man in 1952. But even before that, Lodge had shown himself to be decreasingly Republican, voting just 56 percent with the GOP in his final congressional session.

With Rockefeller demurring, Nixon had largely decided on Lodge— he had even discussed with him the probability of his selection as early as that spring. Nonetheless, ever nervous regarding his status within the party, Nixon sought precedents to legitimize his actions, turning finally to the pattern of his own 1952 smoke-filled-room anointing. Just after midnight on the morning of Thursday, July 28, in a first-floor Sheraton-Blackstone suite, thirty-eight Republicans—senators (but not Goldwater), congressmen (including Gerald Ford but not Walter Judd), governors (no Rockefeller), cabinet members, state chairmen, and various elder statesmen (including Dewey, John Bricker, and the president's academician younger brother Milton)—convened to assist Richard Nixon in selecting his running mate.

Unlike 1952, however, this conclave was a sham, mere window dressing to anoint not a candidate but Richard Nixon's selection of a candidate. Nixon laid down the usual qualifications for a vice president, but with a crucial difference: His selection must add foreign policy strength to the ticket, as Nixon deemed foreign affairs essential to GOP victory. Democrats, Nixon argued, could never be outbid domestically. They would invariably promise more programs and benefits than Republicans would ever dare, but the GOP might still win if the campaign centered on Cold War battlefields. Only the dimmest party chieftain would not see Nixon's words as a powerful hint that he preferred UN ambassador Lodge to RNC chairman Morton.

Nixon was the nominee and might very well be the next president, but Illinois governor Stratton clearly rejected his reasoning. "You can say all you want to about foreign policy," Stratton countered, "but what's really important is the price of hogs in Chicago and St. Louis."

It fell once more to Dewey to provide guidance. "If we want to send the delegates home happy, we ought to agree on Morton," he advised. "But if we want to make the people happy, it should be Lodge. . . . He would make a superb Vice President, and he would put the emphasis on foreign policy, where it should be."

Morton folded, throwing his support to Lodge. But powerful antipathy remained toward Nixon's presumed choice. East Tennessee congressman B. Carroll Reece, the late Robert Taft's 1952 campaign manager, rose to speak, averring that while he personally had forgiven Lodge, many old Taftites might not. Then John Bricker—Taft's closest ally—surprised everyone by quickly interjecting that Lodge had been, in his estimate, "largely forgiven."

At 2:25 that morning Nixon pronounced his choice—Lodge—and rushed to phone Beverly, Massachusetts, to congratulate his new running mate. But his call generated an ominous omen—operators reported that Lodge's phone was either out of order or "off the hook." Lodge was, in fact, in New York.

Barry Goldwater would later brand Nixon's choice "a disastrous blunder," and JFK privately jibed, "That's the last Nixon will ever see of Lodge. If Nixon ever tries to visit Lodge at Beverly, they won't let him in the door."

Ideology aside, Nixon's choice puzzled many. Dirksen (Illinois—twenty-seven electoral votes), Judd (Minnesota—eleven electoral votes), Ford (Michigan—twenty electoral votes), or Scott (Pennsylvania—thirty-two electoral votes) all hailed from crucial swing states. Even Morton, from border state Kentucky, might prove a useful bridge to winning Southern votes. Alone among the hopefuls, Henry Cabot Lodge—from John Kennedy's Massachusetts—possessed no discernable hope of delivering his home state, significantly influencing the voting in his region, or even swinging a single state into the Nixon column.

Nixon, so often a cold, dispassionate judge of electoral strategies, had flung logic out the window. Instead, his choice was dictated both by a deep-seated obsession to curry favor with the party's still influential Rockefeller-Dewey Eastern wing and by deep-seated social insecurity—

an idea that by placing the ultra-Brahmin Lodge on his ticket he might compensate for his own filling station–grocery store origins, particularly against the Harvard–Palm Beach Kennedy organization. "The Kennedys," as Cowles Publishing correspondent Fletcher Knebel observed, "might be of Boston Society. The Lodges were Boston society."

"Wild Bill" Stratton continued lobbying for Everett Dirksen. Aside from Henry Cabot Lodge's weaknesses, Stratton had his own reasons (in many cases self-serving) for displeasure, but also highly relevant to the national ticket. "Illinois is absolutely necessary to the election of a Republican President," Stratton had warned. But a strong national ticket was also vital for Illinois GOP success. Stratton himself faced re-election, with chances that were less than stellar (he had won by just 36,877 votes in Ike's 1956 sweep). The party's challenge to incumbent Democratic senator Paul Douglas seemed hopeless. But most crucial of all may have been the fate of Cook County state's attorney Benjamin S. Adamowski, a former Democrat and now a confirmed foe of the Daley machine. If Dick Daley wanted *anyone* defeated in 1960, it was his erstwhile ally Adamowski—and he was working overtime to see that it happened.

To rescue his foundering ticket—and Illinois's twenty-seven electoral votes—Stratton proposed adding favorite-son Dirksen to the national slate. Dirksen (a winner in 1956 by 357,569 votes) might save everything, Stratton argued, while uninspiring New England liberal Lodge might lose them the whole ball game.

Indiana governor Harold W. Handley supported Stratton, as did numerous frustrated Illinois delegates. "I saw Lodge on television," fumed Centralia attorney James B. Wham, "and he'll run like a dry creek. The party is about to be swallowed up by destiny."

Lodge, already running like a dry creek (he had delayed his departure to the convention to preside at a rather mundane State Department award ceremony), finally arrived in Chicago, where Walter Judd, good soldier to the end, nominated him, speaking for fifteen minutes when asked to speak five (and, for good measure, praising Nixon as "the best candidate for President since George Washington"). Jerry Ford, vice-presidential ambitions on hold, provided the eighth of eight Lodge seconding addresses.

Lodge now pledged to "expend every ounce of energy" to help the ticket. Unfortunately, the new candidate possessed exceedingly limited amounts of energy—at least the energy he *expended* was limited.

Possessing much more energy—along with sudden enthusiasm for things Republican—was Nelson Rockefeller, though his miraculous transformation into the personification of party loyalty struck some as a tad ungainly. But it fell to Rocky—and he accepted the assignment—to introduce the newly nominated Nixon to an adoring convention. Very carefully, drawing near to his climax, the dyslexic Rockefeller carefully enunciated each and every syllable, "and the man who will succeed Dwight D. Eisenhower next January—Richard *E.* Nixon."

Richard *M.* Nixon had spent the previous three nights virtually without sleep, complicating the drafting of an acceptance address. Moreover, he had decided against reading it. For the first time since Harry Truman in 1948, an acceptance speech would be delivered "off the cuff." It was, to say the least, an extremely risky stratagem. At worst, Nixon might flub the entire attempt, faring no better than Nelson Rockefeller had with that errant *E.* At best, Nixon might merely be passable—and with John Kennedy off and running, Nixon couldn't afford mere mediocrity.

Remarkably, he delivered his valedictory in an even, conversational tone (perhaps from his immense weariness)—a stark contrast with Jack Kennedy's often shrill and theatrical effort. Nixon's wasn't just one of *his* better addresses; it was what many then claimed was among the better acceptances in convention history. It concluded with these words:

> One hundred years ago, in this very city, Abraham Lincoln was nom-
> inated for President. . . . The question then was freedom for the
> slaves and survival of the nation. The question now is freedom for all
> mankind and the survival of civilization. . . .
>
> What we must do is wage the battles for peace and freedom with
> the same . . . dedication with which we wage battles in war. . . .
> The only answer to a strategy of victory for the Communist world is
> a strategy of victory for the free world. Let the victory we seek . . .
> be the victory of freedom over tyranny, of plenty over hunger, of
> health over disease, in every country of the world.

When Mr. Khrushchev says our grandchildren will live under Communism, let us say his grandchildren will live in freedom.

Our answer to the threat of the Communist revolution is renewed devotion to the great ideals of the American Revolution . . . that still live in the minds and hearts of people everywhere.

I believe in the American dream, because I have seen it come true in my own life.

Abraham Lincoln was asked during the dark days of the tragic War between the States whether he thought God was on his side. His answer was, "My concern is not whether God is on our side, but whether we are on God's side." My fellow Americans, may that ever be our prayer for our country. And in that spirit—with faith in America, with faith in her ideals and in her people, I accept your nomination for President of the United States.

Such oratory impressed even those not normally impressed by the orator. "I remember thinking," said Ezra Taft Benson, "if he can give the American people this kind of inspiration throughout the campaign, he'll win, and win big."

The *New Republic* waxed enthusiastic regarding one of the magazine's least favorite politicians. Nixon, its columnist TRB wrote, "sent millions into raptures. . . . [It was] one of the most impressively effective fifty minutes we ever witnessed. He rang every bell." Ted Sorensen termed the address "brilliant."

"I have an announcement to make," Nixon now boomed to the convention, "a sure indication that we are on the way to victory! Five minutes before Ambassador Lodge was nominated he became a grandfather for the eighth time!"

Which no doubt only aggravated the foul mood festering in novelist Norman Mailer, there to fashion a feature for *Esquire* magazine. The disgusted Mailer would write:

"Yes," Nixon said, naturally but terribly tired an hour after his nomination, the TV cameras and lights and microphones bringing out a sweat of fatigue on his face, the words coming very slowly from the tired brain, somber, modest, sober, slow, slow enough so that one could touch emphatically the cautions behind each word, "Yes, I want to say," said Nixon, "that whatever abilities I have, I got from my mother." A tired pause . . . dull moment of warning, ". . . and my father." The connection now made, the rest comes easy, ". . . and my school and my church." Such men are capable of anything. . . .

Dwight Eisenhower expressed himself with less of the flavor of the West Village and more of West Point. "Charlie," the president told his friend Charles McAdam, "we nominated the wrong man."

TWENTY-TWO

"Why do you think they did that, Sammy?"

THE KENNEDYS were no strangers to Hollywood. Joe Kennedy was *of* Hollywood, investing first in the low-end but profitable Film Booking Offices (FBO) studios, and later in such operations as Pathé and Radio-Keith-Orpheum (RKO). Kennedy's actual tenure as a film executive was brief, only about three years, but while on the West Coast he developed an appreciation, even an obsession, for filmdom's growing influence on public tastes—and how stars were both made and unmade.

"There are only two pursuits that get in your blood," he once informed FDR's oldest son, James, "politics and the motion picture business."

In 1932, Joe Kennedy combined obsessions. That year he sat down with other Democratic Party powerhouses—Al Smith and national party chairman John Jacob Raskob, as well as several of Governor Franklin Roosevelt's top advisers—and with movie moguls Jack and Harry Warner. The pitch was made: Help elect Roosevelt. The Hollywood establishment of Louis B. Mayer, Irving Thalberg, Adolph Zukor, and Sam Goldwyn was still largely Republican—as were the Warners, but, as studio magnates went, they were still outsiders. So the Warners signed on to the Roosevelt cause. Jack Warner chaired the Roosevelt campaign's motion picture division, even organizing a huge, searchlight-illumined rally for FDR. Roosevelt carried normally Republican California by half a million votes.

By 1960 the great bulk of Hollywood stars were loyal and enthusiastic Democrats, and Joe worked assiduously to guarantee that they supported his son—a star in his own right—with proper enthusiasm. It was not always easy going. As late as the 1960 Democratic National Convention, stars such as Henry Fonda, Robert Ryan, Shirley MacLaine, Jessica Tandy, Vincent Price, Phyllis Kirk (Peter Lawford's erstwhile co-star on NBC's *Thin Man* series), Jan Sterling, Howard Duff, Ann Miller, and Diana Lynn all remained solidly for Stevenson.

But the Kennedys possessed one tremendous advantage: the Peter Lawford–Frank Sinatra connection.

Sinatra's involvement in Democratic politics was of long standing, his mother having been an active Democratic precinct worker back in their hometown of Hoboken. In 1948 Frank's Democratic loyalties translated into a bet that long-shot Harry Truman would win the presidential election. Sinatra won twenty-five thousand dollars. In 1956 he sang the national anthem at the Democratic National Convention, and when Sam Rayburn solicited him to croon "The Yellow Rose of Texas," he merely snarled, "Get your hands off the suit, creep." It was there, however, that Sinatra first took notice of Jack Kennedy, at thirty-nine less than two years younger than Sinatra himself. He viewed JFK as an attractive, glamorous Democratic rising star, sharing not just political but lifestyle philosophies with him. JFK returned the attention. As Peter Lawford phrased it, "Let's just say the Kennedys are interested in the lively arts and that Sinatra is the liveliest art of all." But it was not until Sinatra crossed paths with Lawford, at a Gary Cooper house party in the summer of 1958, that the alliance began cementing itself. By that October Walter Winchell was reporting that Sinatra ("Senator Kennedy is a friend of mine") was flying to Boston to campaign for Kennedy. Within days, Frank had publicly endorsed JFK for the presidency.

Facilitating Kennedy-Sinatra communications was JFK brother-in-law Lawford's acceptance into Sinatra's famed Rat Pack (Sinatra, Lawford, Dean Martin, Sammy Davis Jr., and comic Joey Bishop). Lawford's relationship with Frank had improved significantly since an early 1950s contretemps when Sinatra had found out that Lawford had dated Ava Gardner—about whom Sinatra felt especially possessive. "Do you want your legs broken, you ——?" Frank had snapped. "Well, you're going to get them broken, if I ever hear you're out with Ava again. So help me, I'll kill you."

Campaigning for JFK significantly improved Sinatra's often testy disposition. "I had never seen Mr. S happier since I began to work for him," recalled valet George Jacobs. "He was in even better spirits than when he won the Oscar. Now he had a purpose, a higher purpose than Hollywood stardom."

Sinatra recorded JFK's campaign theme song, music borrowed from Frank's 1959 hit "High Hopes" (Joe Kennedy had picked that out), with new lyrics composed to boost JFK:

K-E-double-N-E-D-Y,
Jack's the nation's favorite guy.
Everyone wants to back Jack.
Jack is on the right track.
And he's got high hopes,
He's got high hopes,
He's got high-apple-pie-in-the-sky hopes.

Yet while "High Hopes" blared from sound trucks in Wisconsin, the campaign vetoed importing the Rat Pack itself. "Senator Humphrey's boys," Lawford recalled, "had passed out pamphlets saying Jack's glamorous friends from Hollywood were coming to bedazzle the voters. Jack's advisers thought it might cause hard feelings, so we didn't go into the state."

The decision may very well have emanated from Bobby Kennedy. "He [RFK] was courteous, appreciative, but all business," Sammy Davis Jr. would write, "and I had the feeling that though he recognized our value at rallies he also saw a negative that our flashy show business association brought to the campaign."

Flashiness rarely proved detrimental in Los Angeles, however, and Sinatra's Rat Pack was accordingly employed to add proper glitz to his party's 1960 convention. They entertained first on Sunday, July 10, at a hundred-dollar-a-plate gala for 2,800 at the Beverly Hilton Hotel featuring not only Sinatra, Martin, and Sammy Davis Jr., but also Judy Garland, Angie Dickinson, Milton Berle, George Jessel, Tony Curtis, Janet Leigh, Mort Sahl, Joe E. Lewis, and Tony Martin. Then, to officially open the convention, Democrats scheduled a thirty-star chorus (including Sinatra, Davis, and Lawford—but not Martin; he was at the Sands—Curtis, Jessel, Nat King Cole, Jan Sterling, Shelley Winters, Edward G. Robinson, Shirley MacLaine, Myrna Loy, Charlton Heston, Vanessa Brown, Gogi Grant, Janet Leigh, Ralph Bellamy, Vincent Price, Gene Kelly, Barry Sullivan, Mercedes McCambridge, and Richard Conte) to perform "The Star-Spangled Banner."

As the old joke about Philadelphia audiences goes, they're so tough, they boo the national anthem. But, Philadelphia audiences aside, that's exactly what happened in Los Angeles in July 1960.

Applause greeted Sammy Davis Jr. when he advanced to sing his portion of the lyrics, but then it started. From Mississippi's delegation emanated long, loud, sustained, ugly booing. Davis couldn't believe it. His head snapped back to see where it was coming from. Others listened, too. No one did a thing about it. No one could, really. Davis stepped back, shaken, staring at a massive flag hanging at the back of the hall, "torn to shreds inside, hurt and naked in front of thousands of people."

Frank Sinatra, standing beside Sammy, advised, "Those dirty sons of bitches! Don't let 'em get you, Charley." Tears streamed down Davis's face. Sinatra kept reassuring him, "Hang on, Charley. Don't let it get you."

The assembled convention now sang the remainder of the nation's anthem. Davis stood frozen with hurt. "How can anyone hate me so much," Davis asked himself, "that they'd let the rest of the free world see the men who might be selecting the next President of the United States are men who feel such racial prejudice?"

The anthem over, Davis retreated offstage. Reporters cornered him. "Why do you think they did that, Sammy?" they asked, knowing the answer lay in two words: May Britt, the five-foot-six-inch, thirty-four-year-old Davis's five-foot-seven-inch, blond, Swedish, twenty-four-year-old—and, above all, *white*—fiancée. Sammy sidestepped them. "What can you say when people boo you?" was all he'd say. To Sinatra, Davis confessed he couldn't stand staying. Frank understood. Sammy caught a cab and then a plane for Boston. He didn't even stop to say good-bye to May.

Frank Sinatra remained at the convention, blackening the peak of his balding head so overhead cameras wouldn't reveal his epidermis as he prowled the convention floor. As Wyoming propelled JFK over the top, Frank jumped up and down like a jack-in-the-box, pounding Lawford on the back, booming, "We're on our way to the White House, buddy boy! We're on our way to the White House!"

That day, to paraphrase a future Sinatra hit, "was a very good day" for the Chairman of the Board. In Carson City, Nevada, Bert "Wingy" Grober, in hock to the IRS to the tune of $800,000, divested himself of 57 percent of the posh Cal-Neva Lodge resort and casino, which since the

1950s had boasted one Joseph P. Kennedy as part owner. Officially, Frank Sinatra would now own 25 percent of the Cal-Neva; Hank Sanicola, a long-time Sinatra crony, 16 percent; Atlantic City nightclub owner Paul "Skinny" D'Amato, 13 percent; and Dean Martin, 3 percent. *Officially.* Unofficially, Sinatra split his share with Sam Giancana—who had made the entire deal possible at the bargain price of just $250,000.

It was perhaps such events that inspired Dean Martin—again, that very night—to inform his Sands audience, "I'd like to tell you some of the *good* things the Mafia is doing."

But Sammy Davis Jr. was *not* having a good day, and the booing was just the tip of the iceberg. It was a lot easier to send someone an anonymous piece of hate mail than to have the guts to boo him in person, even from the safety of a crowd, and Davis received all manner of hate mail. It might be a cartoon showing Davis as a butler, standing before "Massa JFK" with a tray piled high with watermelon and fried chicken. Or for those taking pen to hand, the message might read, "Dear Nigger Bastard, I see Frank Sinatra is going to be the best man at your abortion. Well, it's good to know the kind of people supporting Kennedy before it's too late [signed] An ex-Kennedy voter."

With the formerly solid South in jeopardy (and the Davis-Britt romance controversial not merely in Dixie), the Davis wedding (and all its connections to Sinatra and from there to JFK) was a ticking political time bomb. "Public opinion experts," noted one article (and it was hardly unique), "say that when Frank Sinatra appears at pal Sammy Davis Jr.'s interracial marriage it will cost Kennedy as many votes (maybe more) as the crooner has been able to swing via his immensely successful JFK rallies."

The Davis nuptials were scheduled for October 16—not long after Britt's marriage to actor Eddie Gregson formally dissolved on September 28, and less than a month before Election Day. All sides— the Kennedys, Sinatra, Davis—fretted over how to proceed. Rumors flew that Dean Martin would stand in for Sinatra, if Frank were suddenly, conveniently, taken "ill."

"I have had the pleasure of knowing John personally and have met with him as a social equal," Davis had informed the black press. "His ideas are tremendous and it will be the greatest thing for this country if he puts them into effect.

"But if I feel that my appearance on John's behalf would cost him a single vote I would remain silent. I admire the man just that much and would do all in my power to help him even if I were called upon to make a great personal sacrifice."

Sammy meant it. Phoning Sinatra, Davis began, "Frank, we're going to have to put the wedding off. You wouldn't believe the problems a poor soul has trying to get married: there's a hitch getting the Escoffier Room for the reception, the rabbi's booked for a bar mitzvah. . . . I don't know when it'll be but I'll give you plenty of notice."

Sinatra knew a lie when he heard one. "Look," Sammy continued, "what the hell, it's best that we postpone it until after the election." Sinatra protested, then dissolved in tears. It was left to Peter Lawford ("Frank can't talk any more") to finish the phone call.

Sammy Davis had informed his best man before he had informed his bride.

Davis's official excuse involved neither Escoffier Rooms nor rabbis, but, rather, the difficulties of ending his fiancée's first marriage via Mexican divorce. "That was the lie," Davis would write, "and that's how we told it."

And so, it was the best of times and the worst of times for the Rat Pack, their joys tempered by the realities of what they—and the nation— truly were. Frank Sinatra had nearly worked his way out of the Kennedy campaign even before the convention—though not from any racial or mob- or lifestyle-related issues.

That controversy was purely artistic—and political.

By early 1960 Sinatra had decided to direct his first film, settling not on any Rat Pack–oriented fluff such as *Oceans 11*, but instead upon a serious drama—the true story of World War II PFC Eddie Slovik, the only American soldier executed for desertion since the Civil War. The film, to be called *The Execution of Private Slovik*, and based on William Bradford Huie's 1954 book of the same name, was not to be written by the conservative Huie, however. Instead, Sinatra had recruited blacklisted "Hollywood Ten" screenwriter Albert Maltz—who, in 1945, had written the award-winning, Sinatra-narrated, eleven-minute anti-discrimination documentary *The House I Live In*.

By 1960, numerous blacklisted screenwriters had returned to Hollywood studios, though always under assumed names. Not until

Kirk Douglas engaged Maltz's fellow Hollywood Ten writer Dalton Trumbo (a secret Oscar winner in 1956 for *The Brave One*) to pen the screenplay of *Spartacus* were any formerly barred communists openly returned to duty.

Maltz, who had also worked covertly on a few films in the 1950s, such as 1953's *The Robe*—a story of Christ—might soon have joined Trumbo in a return to respectability had it not been for Frank Sinatra's status as Hollywood's premier JFK cheerleader. Democrats could not afford to be seen as soft on communism. Part of Jack Kennedy's political charm was his reputation as a hardline anti-communist. While Republicans might deride Adlai Stevenson as a pinko, pinning the left-wing tag on JFK was far harder . . . unless Frank Sinatra made it easier for them.

Sinatra attorney Martin Gang phoned Maltz, inquiring if Sinatra's announcement of Maltz's engagement might be delayed until after the March 1960 New Hampshire primary. Maltz then called Sinatra (who was appearing at Miami's Fontainebleau) and asked him point-blank if Frank feared financing might disappear if a blacklisted writer was involved. Sinatra said not to worry, and in late March 1960 the announcement was indeed made.

Hollywood conservatives Ward Bond and John Wayne quickly jumped on Sinatra's decision. Wayne wrote an open letter to Sinatra, tying JFK into the mess:

> I wonder how Sinatra's crony, Senator John Kennedy, feels about him hiring such a man? I'd like to know his attitude because he's the one who is making plans to run the administrative government of our country.

That merely started the imbroglio. Veterans groups and newspaper columnists chimed in from coast to coast. "What kind of thinking," queried Hearst's tabloid *New York Mirror*, "motivates Frank Sinatra in hiring an unrepentant enemy of his country—not a liberal, not an underdog, not a free thinker, but a hard revolutionist who has never done anything to remove himself from the Communist camp or to disassociate himself with the Communist record?"

Gossip columnist Walter Winchell displayed sympathy for Sinatra (and, by his excitable standards, remarkable restraint), but, nonetheless, joined the chorus condemning his controversial move:

> Frank Sinatra is one of the most human men I know. He's always for the underdog. I differ with him in that I think the former Commy sympathizers who consider themselves underdogs sometimes deserve what they get. That's why I think Sinatra is making a Big, Big Boner in this matter. A very considerable body of public opinion is against his hiring this alleged "former" Red. As his friend, I am concerned that it will hurt Sinatra more than it will help Maltz. Frank, why do the picture at all? You need the money?

Sinatra's initial reaction—as it often did—proved combative. From Miami Beach he issued a public statement:

> Under the Bill of Rights, I was taught that no one may prescribe what shall be orthodox in politics, religion, or matters of opinion. . . . As the producer of the film I and I alone will be responsible for it. I accept that responsibility. I ask only that judgment be deferred until the picture is seen.
>
> I would also like to comment on the attacks from certain quarters on Senator John Kennedy by connecting him with my decision on employing a screenwriter. . . . I make movies. I do not ask the advice of Senator Kennedy on whom I should hire. Senator Kennedy does not ask me how he should vote in the Senate. . . . I spoke to many screen-writers, but it was not until I talked to Albert Maltz that I found a writer who saw the screenplay in exactly the terms I wanted. . . .
>
> I and I alone will be responsible for it. I am concerned that the screen-play reflects the true pro-American values of the story. I am prepared to stand on my principles and to await the verdict of the American people when they see *The Execution of Private Slovik*. I repeat: In my role as a picture-maker, I have—in my opinion—hired the best man to do the job.

For good measure, Sinatra reprinted his statement in Hollywood trade paper ads—merely amplifying a fracas that, if left to its own devices, might have quickly expired. Now, not only were columnists and veterans and John Wayne excised, so was Colonel Tom Parker—who threatened to yank his client Elvis Presley from appearing on the Rat Pack's upcoming *Welcome Home* television special, showcasing the twenty-five-year-old Elvis's return from the army.

Sinatra's longtime manager Nick Sevano recalled, "General Motors called me up—we had three Pontiac specials set—and they said . . . [if Sinatra] doesn't fire [Maltz] in the next twenty-four hours, we're canceling all our business dealings. I had recently gone back into business with Frank, and I had $250,000 at stake in those GM specials, so [we] flew to Palm Springs to try to talk Frank into firing Maltz, but he wouldn't budge. '—— 'em,' he said. 'There will be other specials.' When I pleaded with him to change his mind, he got so mad he fired me, and we had to break up our management company."

This was bad enough, but now Kennedy was tied into the whole affair. "The situation," reported Broadway columnist Dorothy Kilgallen, "was becoming especially delicate in Massachusetts, where rather important church figures don't quite understand the Sinatra-Kennedy connection."

"That's when old Joe called Frank," recalled Peter Lawford, "and said, 'It's either Maltz or us. Make up your mind.' He felt that Jack was getting rapped for being a Catholic and that was going to be tough enough to put to rest. He didn't want him to get rapped for being pro-Communist as well, so Frank caved in, and dumped Maltz that day."

A new Sinatra ad ran in the April 12 *New York Times*, 180-degrees from his previous apologias. Sinatra dropped the project, dropped Maltz, dropped everything. "God, was that a mess," Lawford added. "The ambassador took care of it in the end, but it was almost the end of old Frankie-boy as far as the family was concerned."

The ambassador had read Sinatra the riot act, "What is this commie Jew shit?" he screamed over the phone. "You stupid guinea!"

That was it. "Mr. S," recalled George Jacobs, "justified dropping Maltz (he paid him in full [$75,000]) and the project on the grounds of helping Jack, but it still killed him to have to eat Joe's humble pie and give up his own dream. He went on a three-day Jack Daniel's binge and totally destroyed his office at the [2666] Bowmont [Drive, Beverly Hills] house. 'Who gives a ——! I'm outta this ——ing business!' he screamed, ripping up books and scripts, hurling over bookcases. This time I felt his rage and frustration were understandable."

Three days of Jack Daniel's removes only so much frustration. A month later Sinatra attended a hundred-dollar-a-plate benefit for children with mental retardation at Sunset Boulevard's Moulin Rouge nightclub. In attendance were Jack Benny, Milton Berle, Gary Cooper, Sammy Davis Jr., comedian George Goble, the Marge and Gower Champion dance team, Dean Martin—and John Wayne.

Sinatra, a large part of the evening's entertainment, had been drinking heavily. In the Moulin Rouge parking lot afterward, the five-foot-seven-inch, 150-pound Sinatra confronted six-foot-four-inch, 225-pound Wayne, sputtering, "You seem to disagree with me."

"Now, now, Frank," the Duke responded, "we can discuss this somewhere else."

Wayne's equanimity merely inflamed Sinatra further. Friends pulled Frank back. Wayne calmly walked away. Sinatra, now mad at the world, snapped at a nearby reporter, "I guess you'll write all this down."

Lurching forward, he stepped into the path of an oncoming car. Brakes squealed. The car halted just two feet from him, and Sinatra screamed at its driver, twenty-year-old parking lot attendant Clarence English: "Hey, Charley! You almost hit me! You know what I'm insured for?" Then he reached into the car, attacking the kid and ripping his shirt—"Can you fight? You'd better be able to."

"Aw, Frank," protested twenty-one-year-old lot attendant Edward E. Moran, "he wasn't trying to hit you with the car. He's only trying to make a living."

Sinatra turned on Moran: "Who the —— are you?" he said, and then starting pushing him. Moran hit back, and Sammy Davis Jr.'s 220-pound bodyguard, Big John Hopkins, began working Moran over. "Tell that guy not to sue me if he knows what's good for him!" Sinatra yelled. "I'll break both his legs."

Two other parking attendants pulled Hopkins off Moran. Hopkins and Sinatra jumped into Davis's Rolls-Royce, leaving Moran to be treated for bruises about his left temple and ear at Hollywood Receiving Hospital. Moran charged Sinatra and Hopkins with battery and later sued Sinatra for $100,000.

"No comment," said John Wayne.

Buffeted by the Davis-Britt controversy and still smarting from his *Private Slovik* fiasco, Sinatra resented John Wayne and Walter Winchell and hordes of Legionnaires. But his real bitterness festered most against the one man who had really made him back down—his supposed friend Joe Kennedy. As George Jacobs explained:

> Although Mr. S would never talk back to Joe Kennedy, he soon vented his spleen on Teddy Kennedy, who showed up at a campaign appearance in Honolulu with three of the cheesiest-looking bimbos. . . . Even if they weren't hookers, they *looked* like hookers. Mr. S had a strong sense of decorum. He was outraged that Teddy could do something that would make his brother look bad. But I think he was really reacting to Joe's abuse of him. . . . So he reamed Teddy out, cursing him at the top of his lungs, right in the middle of the hotel suite in front of dozens of high-level workers and donors. Teddy got scared and disappeared. I think he flew back to the mainland that night. And Teddy gave Mr. S a wide berth after that.

Beyond that, the Rat Pack fought on a comic-opera third front: the battle of Lady May Lawford. May had never relinquished either her eccentric, outspoken ways (she had once informed Louis B. Mayer that she should be placed on his MGM payroll to "supervise" her "homosexual" son) or her antipathy to her son's Gaelic in-laws ("barefoot Irish peasants" and "bogrotters"), and as the *New York Herald Tribune*'s Earl Mazo reported, the Rat Pack was working from the convention onward to keep Lady Lawford quiet—particularly regarding Joe Kennedy.

As one gossip column noted:

> Peter Lawford's mother, Lady Lawford, telling tales out of school about her son's marriage to Pat Kennedy. Before their engagement party, Lady Lawford tells it, "Joe Kennedy told me he was sorry his daughter was going to marry an actor—and an English actor at that!"

And, in Walter Winchell's column, *New York Mirror* columnist Lee Mortimer, substituting for Winchell, cheerfully noted:

> No love lost between the Kennedy clan and Lady Lawford, Peter's mother, who writes me nice letters of congratulation for going after the eggheads and New Dealers.

For the Chairman of the Board, the cost of political idealism, its frustrations and its risks, grew higher by the day. Better not to care—to take the money and run (or in a celebrity's case, to take the money and endorse). As Colonel Tom Parker responded when columnist Art Buchwald inquired who Elvis Presley might ultimately endorse: "Whoever pays the largest personal appearance fee."

But Francis Albert Sinatra, for all his faults, never cared about the fees.

TWENTY-THREE

"Nothing takes precedence over his oath to uphold the Constitution"

MORE SIGNIFICANT even than Hollywood was Rome.

In a sense, it was all very ironic, for JFK displayed far keener interest in show business than in Roman Catholicism (Judy Campbell: "He loved gossip. I used to tell him, 'Go out and buy a movie magazine.' He used to ask a lot about Frank, what Frank was doing, who Frank was seeing"). For JFK, his religion was not something he chose, but rather something he was born with, akin to being Irish—something occasionally politically convenient, sometimes politically and socially inconvenient. Unlike many Catholics of his generation, educated in a wide-ranging network of parochial schools and Catholic universities, Jack Kennedy had not (save for the normal family influences, primarily his pious mother's) particularly benefited from a Catholic upbringing. Nor did he exhibit any special interest in his faith, exhibiting far greater curiosity in items historical—especially England's storied past. "While we were reading *Lives of the Saints*," observed sister Eunice, "Jack was reading Carlyle."

He did not even date a Catholic until he was twenty-two.

He had doubts about his faith, and though even saints may doubt, Jack's doubts seem to have been substantial. At Harvard he attended Mass only under duress—"This is one of the things I do for my father." To family friend Kay Halle, he confessed, "I wish we could start a new religion that would bring all people together." Once, upset by Francis Cardinal Spellman's actions, he fumed, "I'm going to quit the Church"—to which Jackie added, "*I'm* going to quit the Church."

"No," Joe Kennedy said, "neither of you can quit the Church—but I can, and I'm *really* going to quit the Church."

JFK once asked Chuck Spalding, "How do you come out on religion?"

"Well," Spalding responded, "I can't get an answer."

"That's where I am."

As president, he attended Mass with some (but compared to most contemporary Catholics, not nearly enough) regularity, the *New York Times* tallying that in 1962, his only full year in the White House, he attended Sunday Mass at least thirty-three Sundays.

"I want them to believe in me as a free thinking individual," he had told Judith Campbell—herself a lapsed Catholic, divorced, and significantly angry at the Catholic Church—"and not to worry about the influence of the Pope. The issues I'm interested in have nothing to do with religion."

As Joe Kennedy wrote to Jack's sister Kathleen before her 1948 death in a plane crash: "I am not particularly impressed with the depth of [Jack's] Catholic faith."

"I think it's so unfair of people to be against Jack because he is a Catholic," Jackie once complained to Arthur Krock at a Washington party. "He's such a poor Catholic. Now if it were Bobby, I could understand it."

Still, there remained elements of Catholic attitudes and practices that JFK could not, and did not, reject. "He'd be on his knees every night," recalled Dave Powers. "Nobody saw him more often than I did, except Jackie, so I know. Now sometimes when I go to bed, I'll say my prayers in bed, lying down. But he was always on his knees, every night that I saw him."

"In general," observed his wartime comrade Paul Fay, "Jack felt about his religion as many Catholics his age feel. Life was full and demanding and the need for religion generally seemed remote. But the basic faith acquired as a child in a Catholic family instilled in him a total allegiance to his faith that only real faith brings . . . [but h]is faith did not keep him from questioning his Church on positions that seemed in conflict with the needs of society."

Well before 1960, Jack Kennedy had begun separating what he termed his "private" faith from his "public" responsibilities as an officeholder—and not just separating them, but raising democracy above dogma. On Sunday, November 24, 1957, when he was interviewed on ABC TV's *Look Here!*, JFK argued that there was no reason a Catholic couldn't be president—in essence because he, JFK, would not allow his faith to intrude upon his politics: "Now, what church I go to on Sunday or what dogma of the Catholic Church I believe in is a personal matter. It does not involve public matter. It does not involve public questions of policy or as the Constitution defines responsibilities of the President, Senator, or member of the armed forces."

To the Catholic Church and its followers, of course, there existed no mere "personal matters" to be conveniently and allowably junked when in conflict with public office, livelihood, or relationships. But by March 1959, in an interview conducted by *Look* magazine's Fletchel Knebel, JFK had advanced his hypothesis one giant step further: "Whatever one's religion in his private life may be, for the officeholder nothing takes precedence over his oath to uphold the Constitution and all its parts—including the First Amendment and strict separation of church and state."

In practical terms, that meant that JFK, now running beyond the confines of heavily Catholic Massachusetts, could, and probably would, jettison any number (if not all) of the positions a Catholic politician might normally be expected to advance. In JFK's case, that meant aid to parochial schools and the appointment of an American ambassador to the Vatican ("I am flatly opposed to appointment of an ambassador to the Vatican. Whatever advantages it might have in Rome—and I'm not convinced of these—they would be more than offset by the divisive effect at home").

Thrilled to have one of their own finally in the hunt, most American Catholics ignored the import of Kennedy's remarks—that Catholics indeed might seek office but only if they were prepared to not act upon their faith once having gained it. But some did take exception. Noting that the Catholic conscience took precedence over all matters of state, the Reverend Edward H. Flannery, editor of the Diocese of Providence's weekly newspaper, *The Providence Visitor*, pointedly observed that the time may have come for Catholics to look beyond merely supporting their own in electoral races.

More significant was reaction from two national Catholic journals, *America* and *Commonweal*, neither particularly conservative. "We do not agree," argued *America*, "with the . . . statement that, in the forthcoming campaign, 'A Catholic would have to give his views on his religion.' This kind of cross-examination directed as it is solely to Catholics, as Catholics, is discriminatory, insulting and without pertinence in terms of the U.S. Constitution." *America* went on to criticize JFK's "efforts to appease bigots," taking particular issue with his statement "Whatever one's religion in his private life nothing takes precedence over his oath." *America* lectured, "Mr. Kennedy doesn't really believe that. No religious man, be he Catholic, Protestant or Jew, holds such an opinion. A man's conscience has a bearing on his public as well as his private life."

Commonweal added, "Senator Kennedy should have made the elementary point that there is no 'Catholic position' on these matters [school aid and relations with the Vatican], that they are not doctrinally religious questions at all, merely points of Constitutional interpretation and practical judgment, on which Catholics are perfectly free to disagree and on which they often disagree."

Such objections, however, were lost in the larger praise for the senator's stance. Cardinal Cushing rushed to pronounce Kennedy blameless on the matter, as did C. Stanley Lowell, associate director of Protestants and Other Americans United (POAU) ("a courageous stand," Lowell said of Kennedy's position). Of course the secular press, viewing the issue with secular eyes, saw nothing at all amiss.

Complicating Kennedy's situation, however, was a May 1960 pronouncement from the semi-official Vatican newspaper *L'Osservatore Romano*. Focusing primarily on events in Italy (and its large communist voting bloc), but not excluding its universal application, *L'Osservatore Romano* decried "the great confusion of ideas that is spreading, especially in some nations, among Catholics with regard to the relations between Catholic doctrine and social and political activities, and between the ecclesiastical hierarchy and the lay faithful in the civil field." The paper condemned detaching "the Catholic from the ecclesiastical hierarchy [and] proclaiming the believer's full autonomy in the civil sphere. . . . The Catholic may never disregard the teaching and directions of the church but must inspire his private and public conduct in every sphere of his activity by the . . . teachings of the hierarchy."

More trouble arrived in early July, this time from two Puerto Rican bishops (oddly enough named Davis and McManus) instructing their respective flocks not to vote for Governor Luis Muñoz Marín. Again,

Cardinal Cushing attempted damage control, but as Jack Kennedy remarked to aides, "If enough voters realize that [Puerto Rico] is American soil, this election is lost."

"Now I understand," Kennedy moaned to Ted Sorensen, only half in jest, "why Henry VIII set up his own church."

JFK faced anti-Catholic sentiment on two great fronts. History easily recalls the strain he encountered in West Virginia, that of hard-shell, often rural, often fundamentalist Protestantism. But there was also another very different sort of anti-Papist sentiment, equally if not more dangerous to him—that existing in his party's liberal wing. As historian Peter Viereck so famously observed, "Catholic baiting is the anti-Semitism of the liberals."

Many on the left viewed the Catholic Church as among society's more reactionary forces, theologically, morally (still influential enough in 1960 to effect the ban of contraceptives in Massachusetts and Connecticut), and, yes, politically. Any Catholic politician might arouse suspicions, but a Catholic like JFK—with an isolationist, anti-Semitic father and an ambiguous record on McCarthyism—could count on increased scrutiny, even when running for so innocuous an office as vice president in 1956. As California Democratic activist Frederick G. Dutton recalled, "[T]here was a lot of anti-Catholic prejudice in the bickering small talk. Everybody was very careful to keep it out of press comments, but you only had to move around that [19]56 delegation . . . to hear a bunch of anti-Catholic cracks that were pretty tough. They came from some of the most liberal people on the delegation."

Among Kennedy's more open liberal critics was *Nation* editor Paul Blanshard, author of four books dissecting Catholic attitudes, practices, and, above all, influence. Less liberal, though more personally anti-JFK, was Baptist (formerly Dutch Reformed) clergyman Daniel A. Poling, longtime editor of the monthly *Christian Herald* (circulation 427,000). Poling's quite personal animus originated in the course of the so-called Chapel of the Four Chaplains Incident. In February 1943, four naval chaplains—Methodist, Dutch Reformed, Catholic, and Jewish—perished when German U-boat U-223 torpedoed the U.S. Army transport ship the *USAT Dorchester*. Each gave his life jacket and his place in the lifeboats to save others. In 1950, the Reverend Poling, father of one of the four (the

Dutch Reformed lieutenant Clark V. Poling), invited Kennedy (as "a spokesman for the Roman Catholic faith") to participate in ceremonies dedicating a chapel memorializing the now-famous "Four Chaplains." JFK accepted, then begged off, explaining that Philadelphia archbishop William Cardinal Dougherty had asked him not to attend—and only reinforcing the belief of many Protestants that he took orders from the Catholic Church's hierarchy.

"The problem really was that the chapel was located in the sacristy of the Baptist Church [and not a public space]," Kennedy explained to the National Press Club in January 1960, "[and a Catholic's presence there] . . . is against the rules, customs, procedures of the Catholic Church. . . . I was invited to speak as the representative, according to Dr. Poling's words . . . , of the Catholic faith. I was not invited as a public officer. I was not invited as a member of congress."

Poling remained unconvinced—as did the most prominent of liberal anti-Catholics, Eleanor Roosevelt. She had first publicly crossed swords with JFK in December 1958, on ABC TV, jibing that she "would hesitate to place the difficult decisions that the next President will have to make with someone who understands what courage is and admires it but has not quite the independence to have it"—adding for good measure that Joe Kennedy had been "spending oodles of money all over the country" to promote his son's ambitions and "probably has paid representatives in every state by now," a situation she would have found "perfectly permissible" had JFK undertaken such activities on his own. JFK wrote to Eleanor, protesting his own—and his family's—innocence. She didn't buy his denials.

Undergirding Mrs. Roosevelt's hostilities was a latent, though quite firm, anti-Catholicism. "Somewhere," observed her biographer (and former lover) Joseph P. Lash, "deep in her subconscious was an anti-Catholicism which was a part of her Protestant heritage." As the campaign progressed, it did not diminish. In January 1960 Eleanor's friend Mary Lasker sent Eleanor news of a Gallup poll that revealed that 20 percent of the American public would still not elect a Catholic president. Mrs. Lasker was shocked that 20 percent would be so bigoted at such a late date. ER scribbled back that she was shocked that 80 percent *would* vote Catholic.

Following JFK's nomination, however, ER would be numbered among that 80 percent. She—and her compatriots—had nowhere else to go. Richard Nixon was out of the question. It was time for all good men—and women—to come to the aid of the Democratic Party.

That was not the case on the political spectrum's right side. Midwestern Protestants of both parties and conservative Southern Democrats (increasingly dissatisfied, in any case, with their national home) remained open to a Republican alternative. In August, two dozen American Protestant leaders conferred secretly in, of all places, Montreux, Switzerland, pondering how to block JFK's ever-likely election. That same month, the Minnesota Baptist Convention pronounced a Catholic president as "serious a threat to America as atheistic communism." In September, Arkansas's Baptist state convention vowed: "We cannot turn our government over to a Catholic President who would be influenced by the Pope and by the power of the Catholic hierarchy."

Condemning JFK's candidacy as a "hellish, world-wide plot to enslave men and women," Baptist preacher James C. Honeycutt Jr., from Stanley, North Carolina, circulated a bogus Knights of Columbus oath, disowning allegiance to "any heretical king, prince or state" and "obedience to any of their laws." Soon informed that the oath was a hoax, Honeycutt quickly apologized—but hastened to add that he *still* opposed any Catholic assuming the presidency.

The Reverend Honeycutt was small potatoes. The Reverend Norman Vincent Peale, best-selling author (*The Power of Positive Thinking*), publisher of *Guideposts* magazine, and America's second-best-known Protestant clergyman (next to Billy Graham), wasn't. On September 7, Peale headed a group of 150 clergymen (among them Daniel Poling) from thirty-seven different Protestant denominations—the National Council of Citizens for Religious Freedom—in raising questions regarding a Catholic presidency. Couching their statement in the mantle of reasonableness, decrying bigotry (no person should engage in hate mongering, bigotry, prejudice, or unfounded charges), tossing in an occasional patronizing compliment to Catholics ("persons of the Roman Catholic faith can be just as honest, patriotic, and public spirited as those of any other faith"), and even toward JFK (pointing out he was the only Catholic senator to vote against Wayne Morse's 1960 bill to aid parochial schools), the National Council for Religious Freedom nonetheless raised this question:

By recommendation, persuasion and veto power, the President can and must shape the course of legislation in this country. Is it reasonable to assume that a Roman Catholic President would be able to withstand altogether the determined efforts of the hierarchy of his church to gain further funds and favors for its schools and institutions, and otherwise breach the wall of separation of church and state?

The document's measured tone fooled no one. It was the same anti-Catholic mentality that had dogged Al Smith in 1928 and still festered in both shouted Southern sermons and discreet Northern whispers, and earned Peale and company almost universal condemnation. The *Christian Century* characterized it as "a disservice to American Protestantism."

"I find Paul appealing," jibed Adlai Stevenson, "and Peale appalling."

Eleanor Roosevelt joined the chorus—but by now her song sounded slightly more akin to "Ave Maria" than "Give Me That Old Time Religion." As she noted in her daily newspaper column:

Religious freedom cannot just be Protestant freedom. It must be freedom for all religions. It is a long time since I sat in my office and read the scurrilous literature that came into Democratic headquarters in Alfred E. Smith's campaign. Nothing quite so bad is reaching me now. But some of the letters sound hysterical and purely emotional. . . .

To tell a man he cannot run for any office in this country because he belongs to a certain religion or is a member of another race—even though he is required to fulfill all the obligations of citizenship, including fighting and dying for his country—is completely illogical and unconstitutional.

"I was not duped," said Peale, who soon abandoned the group. "I was just stupid."

Stupid or not, Joe Kennedy professed outrage. "All I can say," Joe wrote to his friend Lord Beaverbrook, "is that they have a hell of a nerve talking about freedom for the world when we have this condition right here in our own country. It seems to me more important than ever to fight this thing with everything we have and that's what we are going to do." Of course, however, while JPK decried Protestants questioning the role of the Catholic hierarchy in American politics, he questioned it, as well—in his case, he found it inexcusable that the hierarchy of the Catholic Church had not done *more* to support his son. Particularly negligent was New York's Francis Cardinal Spellman. Following the fifteenth annual Alfred E. Smith Memorial Foundation Dinner at the Waldorf-Astoria that October, Joe Kennedy phoned Spellman, absolutely enraged, charging him with favoring Richard Nixon. "That is a truly evil man," Spellman later muttered about Kennedy Sr.

Joe displayed far more affection for Boston's immeasurably more pliant Richard Cardinal Cushing. Their relationship, according to investigative journalist and author Peter Maas, may even have extended to a particularly inventive money-laundering scheme. If, say, diocesan collections amounted to $950,000 on a given Sunday (almost all of it in cash back then), JPK would graciously write the diocese a million-dollar check—while pocketing Cushing's cash. Both sides won—Cushing by $50,000 and Kennedy by a huge tax deduction plus the availability of a fortune in untraceable funds.

Democrats may not have desired any scrutiny of such Kennedy-Cushing connections (and who knew of them at the time?), but they certainly evinced interest in linking such ministers as Peale and Poling to the GOP. The Fair Campaign Practices Committee (FCPC) would ultimately identify more than three hundred different items of anti-Catholic literature circulating during the 1960 campaign—literally millions of copies of individual materials. Obviously, someone paid for them, and, if it could be proven that the GOP, rather than a mere aggregation of grassroots crackpots, was at work, well then, so much the better. RFK publicly accused Republicans of spending a million dollars on such screeds—a charge the FCPC later found baseless. Democratic national chairman Henry Jackson denounced the National Council of Citizens for Religious Freedom, demanding to know who drafted its controversial manifesto, and further demanding that Richard Nixon renounce it and its pronouncements. "Who used [Peale]?" Adlai Stevenson queried. "Who was really calling the shots?" So interested were Democrats in unraveling such questions that they engaged private investigators to resolve them—one gumshoe ultimately swearing that illegal wiretaps had been utilized.

Nixon, however, refused to play the religion card, whether from political calculation or from principle, though the latter seems the more likely. "Nixon was dead serious about it," recalled Bob Finch. "There were many in the South who wanted some kind of tacit approval to use it [the religion issue] and I made a number of calls [to stop it]."

Henry Cabot Lodge spoke personally to the issue, pronouncing, "I absolutely refuse to admit that my three Roman Catholic grandsons will be debarred from the Presidency on those grounds or, for that matter, my two Episcopal grandsons."

Whether or not Republicans were involved, the issue remained real—and perilous—for JFK, particularly in Dixie. It unduly jeopardized his chances of reclaiming electoral votes previously lost to Eisenhower, negating the advantages of adding LBJ to the ticket. *Lubbock Avalanche-Journal* editor Charley A. Guy contended, "The big issue in Texas—and Jerry Mann, the Kennedy-Johnson campaign manager in Texas says the same thing is true all over—is that of church and state. It is running deep. Just as deep—and maybe deeper than in 1928—and I went through that one in Texas, too." In Arkansas, *Hope Star* editor A. H. Washburn mused that the GOP might carry his state for the first time in history.

And then there was Billy Graham, whose father-in-law was among the 150 signing the Reverend Peale's statement. Publicly, Graham displayed official neutrality. Secretly, he worked strenuously to prevent Pennsylvania Avenue from falling into the hands of the papacy.

During West Virginia's primary, Pierre Salinger had chanced upon Graham aboard a railroad dining car, in transit from Bluefield, West Virginia, to Indianapolis. The Kennedy camp was then in the process of rounding up clergy in support of a statement urging tolerance in the upcoming election. Graham pledged participation but later ducked calls from Ted Sorensen on the issue. Ultimately, he begged off, arguing that it behooved him to maintain strict neutrality.

Yet, as Richard Nixon pretended to struggle over his choice for vice president, Graham, warning Nixon that JFK stood to "capture the Catholic vote," urged former Protestant missionary Dr. Walter Judd's selection—a decision that might well have only exacerbated already tense national religious feelings. And despite Graham's assurances to Sorensen and Salinger, at the campaign's end he appeared at a Columbia, South

Carolina, statehouse rally alongside Nixon, lamely contending that his appearance should not be "politically interpreted." Had Nixon not vetoed the idea, Graham would have endorsed the Republican ticket ("unqualifiedly and enthusiastically," in Nixon's words) in a *Life* magazine article.

Kennedy's boldest move on the religious issue was his acceptance of an invitation to appear before the Greater Houston Ministerial Association on Monday night, September 12. Joe Kennedy adamantly opposed attending. Baptist Sam Rayburn ("They hate your guts") concurred.

Though his hosts desired merely a question-and-answer session, Kennedy insisted on delivering an opening statement—drafted by the Unitarian Sorensen and studiously delivered word for word by JFK. He also demanded that a wide diversity of ministers be present, and that he would appear alone—for dramatic purposes, to increase his already formidable presence—on the stage of the Rice Hotel's Crystal Ballroom.

Sam Rayburn still shook his head as the event began. "This is the biggest mistake he's made in this campaign."

And yet, it was not *all* risk. Kennedy's audience certainly included its share of hard—and vocal—cases, but also included those willing, even eager, not only to extend JFK a chance, but also to support him. "What's the mood of the ministers?" JFK had asked Salinger beforehand, and his press secretary answered, "They're tired of being called bigots."

Kennedy, somberly attired in ministerial black suit and tie, elected a grand—and yet disarmingly humble—entrance, approaching the podium not from back stage as any speaker might normally do but from the rear of the auditorium, alone, without aides or entourage, not smiling yet not afraid, confident, almost daring attack, drawing strength from his vulnerability.

JFK had done it all before. In April 1959—like other presidential aspirants—he had appeared before the fifty-one-member Council of Methodist Bishops. Unlike the others, he had been subjected to questioning regarding his religion.

"I believe in an America," Kennedy now said in Houston, "where the separation of church and state is absolute—where no Catholic prelate would tell the President (should he be a Catholic) how to act and no Protestant minister would tell his parishioners for whom to vote—where no church or church school is granted any public funds or political preference—and where no man is denied public office merely because his religion differs from the President who might appoint him or the people who might elect him."

Kennedy had wanted Sorensen to provide a local touch, and nothing could be more local or sacred to Texans then the Alamo. Sorensen, on such short notice, failed to discover how many Catholics had died defending the Alamo (quite a number had certainly died capturing it), but even that failure had utility. "Side by side with Bowie and Crockett died McCafferty and Bailey and Carey," Kennedy informed the three-hundred-odd ministers present, "but no one knows whether they were Catholics or not. For there was no religious test at the Alamo."

Once more JFK carefully distanced himself from Catholic positions and interests:

I am not the Catholic candidate for President. I am the Democratic Party's candidate for President who happens also to be a Catholic.

I do not speak for my church on public matters—and the church does not speak for me.

Whatever issue may come before me as President, if I should be elected—on birth control, divorce, censorship, gambling, or any other subject—I will make my decision in accordance with these views, in accordance with what my conscience tells me to be in the national interest, and without regard to outside religious pressure or dictate. And no power or threat of punishment could cause me to decide otherwise.

And then, his trump card:

[I]f the time should ever come—and I do not concede any conflict to be remotely possible—when my office would require me to either violate my conscience or violate the national interest, then I would resign the office; and I hope any other conscientious public servant would do likewise.

Exceedingly more problematical was the question-and-answer session that followed, with ministers peppering him with largely hostile, often very precise, queries regarding theological points. Occasionally Kennedy claimed ignorance; in other cases, he misstated facts (primarily by claiming that Pius IX's 1864 encyclical, "The Syllabus of Errors," was "centuries old"). But, by and large, he acquitted himself with his usual magnificently effective combination of charm and sangfroid. "So I want you to know that I am grateful to you for inviting me tonight," he concluded. "I'm sure that I have made no converts to my Church,"—here his audience laughed, and it was not a nervous or polite laugh, but rather one revealing he had achieved a remarkable degree of empathy with them—"but I do hope— I do hope that at least my view, which I believe to be the view of my fellow Catholics, who hold office, . . . may be of some value in at least assisting you to make a careful judgment."

It had been a triumph, capped by a standing ovation. "As we say in my part of Texas," Sam Rayburn exclaimed, "he ate 'em blood raw. This young feller will be a great President."

Twenty Texas television stations broadcast the event live, and the Kennedy camp had filmed it verbatim for nationwide broadcast. Rigorously limited to just a half hour, it was perfect for television—particularly in heavily Catholic areas. JFK's campaign expended more on broadcasting his Houston speech than on any other item of campaign material.

Not everyone, of course, was impressed. "Senator Kennedy is either a poor Catholic," stewed persistent Kennedy critic W. A. Criswell of Dallas's twelve-thousand-member Free Baptist Church of Dallas—the nation's largest Southern Baptist congregation—"or he is stringing people along."

Also numbered among the unimpressed, but for quite different reasons, was Larry O'Brien. "I was with him," recalled O'Brien. "I never accepted the feeling that he had turned something around. No. I was with him, and I remember being in the elevator with him and going to the hall. You could always depend upon Kennedy to acquit himself well. . . . I certainly didn't have any feeling that it was going to be otherwise. Obviously, the Houston ministers conference was going to treat him cordially. There wasn't going to be any conflict. He'd make his presentation and leave. But I never accepted that it impacted on the election."

★ ★ ★

And, after all the interviews and meetings and opinion polls and thousands of words recorded on the subject, the nation still knew no more than what it would have learned had it listened in to one very brief conversation.

"What kind of Catholic are you?" John F. Kennedy was once asked.

JFK answered as Lyndon Johnson or Richard Nixon or Dwight Eisenhower or Harry Truman might have answered regarding their own faith.

"I go to church on Sunday."

Thirty-three out of fifty-two times a year.

"Matt Dillon ain't popular for nothing"

JACK KENNEDY HAD INDEED plotted his circumstances wisely to ensure that his Greater Houston Ministerial Association appearance would prove successful.

A key circumstance was Lyndon Johnson's absence. Lyndon Johnson— JFK's host on this Texas tour, his anointed running mate—would not accompany JFK. LBJ's assistant Bill Moyers was instructed to keep LBJ at arm's length—away from the stage, away from the very occasion. It made some sense, of course, to focus the spotlight solely upon JFK, to create not just another event, but an iconic image—a man alone against the crowd, a man of courage and dignity, the quintessential Texas showdown.

And yet it signified something deeper, something that began nearly as soon as this awkward partnership had awkwardly commenced—that LBJ, formerly the nation's most powerful Democrat, now waited at Jack Kennedy's beck and call.

LBJ's first warning had not been long in coming. On Friday morning, July 16—with Lyndon nominated the night previously and JFK yet to summon Americans to a "New Frontier"—Kennedy convened the Democratic National Committee to elect Washington's senator Henry Jackson as its new chairman, albeit a stopgap one. A promise JFK had tendered to David Lawrence to ultimately appoint Connecticut's John Bailey remained in place—but Bailey was a Catholic, and JFK wanted a Protestant occupying the post, at least during the campaign. JFK never shared a word of Jackson's appointment with LBJ. Lyndon Johnson learned about it from reporters.

"I think I'll go back to Texas," sighed LBJ, "make a couple of speeches, and the hell with it."

Numbered among Lyndon's many difficulties were those of explaining to fellow Texas Democrats (to many of whom "LBJ" now stood for "Let's Beat Judas"), to his Southern Senate colleagues, and, yes, to himself, what he had done. The process proved particularly painful with his Georgia

259

mentor Richard Russell, who declared to Johnson's assistants that he viewed both Democratic and Republican Party platforms as "reprehensible and socialistic," and, worse, that the Democratic edition might ensure "a second Reconstruction." Personally, Russell wanted to assist his boy LBJ. With this platform, he couldn't.

Russell's angst, however, was mild compared with Johnson's. The immediate post-VP-announcement period comprised what some termed "the heaviest period of boozing" in LBJ's life, his staff working overtime to transform him once more into something "functional." Particularly vexing was this incident (observed by George Reedy): an evening wandering hotel halls, so drunk ("an incredible toot") that he ensconced himself in his secretary's bed and wrapped himself "into her arms the same way a small child will snuggle into its mother's arms."

Following his unfortunate convention, Johnson sought shelter first at his Texas ranch, then in a brief Acapulco working vacation, accompanied by Reedy, Homer Thornberry, and a few staff members. There, he resolved to make the best of what he recognized already to be a bad situation, a mistake he had blundered into that might save the Democratic ticket yet damn himself. "I want you and your agency to handle all the advertising, media selection, and TV production for the Kennedy-Johnson ticket in Texas," he instructed Jack Valenti two weeks after the convention. "I aim to carry Texas for this ticket."

If RFK had loathed LBJ previously, he disliked him yet more after flying home from the convention with *Chicago Sun-Times* correspondent Peter Lisagor. RFK demanded that Lisagor verify rumors Bobby had heard of disparaging LBJ pre-convention comments regarding brother Jack. Lisagor begged off ("I don't see why I should tell that story now. You're all in bed together now. He's your vice presidential candidate"), but Bobby insisted. Eventually Lisagor relented, repeating LBJ's description of JFK as a "little scrawny fellow with rickets and God knows what other kind of diseases."

"'Have you ever seen his ankles?'" Lisagor quoted LBJ as saying. "'They're about so round.'" Lisagor also quoted LBJ predicting how, if JFK won, "'Old Joe Kennedy would run the country.'"

"I knew he hated Jack," said Bobby, "but I didn't think he hated him that much."

Against such background, the two candidates rendezvoused at Hyannis Port on Friday evening, July 29—an inauspicious beginning, starting with the charter aircraft carrying Johnson, Lady Bird, and an entourage of forty being delayed two and a half hours by fog. It turned out to be a rather perfunctory meeting, of no great substance. As Jack and Lyndon circled each other, so did Jacqueline and Lady Bird. Neither woman seemed particularly interested in speaking with the other. Jackie recalled Lady Bird making some remarks to her, "but she was kind of listening to Jack talking with her husband. Yet she would sit talking with us, looking so calm. I was very impressed by that."

"Jack Kennedy could not have been more gracious," remembered Lady Bird aide Betty Hickman. "He came over three or four times. 'Betty, can I get you more coffee? What can I do?' But Jacqueline didn't even speak to Lady Bird. She hardly acknowledged we were in the room."

JFK and LBJ, accompanied by Jim Rowe (now Johnson's scheduler) and Myer "Mike" Feldman (JFK's chief of legislative research), adjourned to discuss campaign matters—largely a matter of LBJ droning through a prepared memo. *Time* magazine's Hugh Sidey and the *Wall Street Journal*'s Robert Novak eavesdropped outside, unsuccessfully trying to catch a word—or a scoop. Between drawl and drone, they discovered precious little, learning only later that, as expected, JFK wanted his partner's campaigning restricted to Southern states. Sidey and Novak enjoyed better fortune (and acoustics) when LBJ adjourned to his room at a nearby hotel to discuss media matters with George Reedy and Pierre Salinger. They overheard an embarrassing session. Johnson puffed himself up by quoting *Denver Post* publisher Palmer Hoyt, who had supposedly recently told Lyndon, "You got a little maturity and all that, but what makes people holler when you walk by is [you're] six-foot-three inches, good looking, [a] broad-shouldered Texan. You ought to capitalize on that. Matt Dillon [Dodge City marshall in CBS's popular Western series *Gunsmoke*] ain't popular for nothing." Novak mused that the simile sounded suspiciously like a Johnson concoction.

Worse still was LBJ's invariably churlish behavior toward Reedy. Somehow, LBJ had concluded that JFK's popularity with the press stemmed not from any innate Kennedy charm, but rather from the rotund

Salinger's special skills. It all translated into a protracted indictment of Reedy, who sat glum, suffering in captive, depressed silence.

All of Congress sat depressed that August. Prior to Los Angeles, Johnson, throwing his weight around, ordered that a special congressional session would commence on Monday, August 8, ostensibly to deal with a handful of key issues such as health care, the minimum wage, housing, and civil rights. In reality, it was a ploy to keep senators and congressmen under his thumb during the convention. In practice, however, the session proved the most dismal of flops, merely serving to mire JFK, LBJ, and Richard Nixon in pointless legislative deadlock, when they should have been out campaigning. Most damaged of all was Johnson.

While Congress bickered, the South fumed. "We are having a great deal of difficulty in the Southern states," RFK informed Sargent Shriver in early August, "on the grounds that Jack's views are socialistic, and he wants the state to control both man and business."

In Texas, *Dallas Morning News* political editor Alan Duckworth fumed after Lyndon's July 29 tête-à-tête with JFK:

In an historic ceremony at Hyannis Port today, Senator John F. Kennedy accepted the surrender of Senator Lyndon B. Johnson of Texas and told him, "The men may keep their horses for spring plowing."

It remained imperative that Johnson take the stump. Sometimes he did. Sometimes he didn't, canceling events previously consented to, scheduling others on the spur of the moment. It was all too much for Jim Rowe. "I was so exhausted after one week of scheduling Johnson that I quit," Rowe recalled. "Get somebody else. I've scheduled Adlai, Kefauver, and Kennedy, but all three gave me less trouble in the whole business than you've given me in one week."

The situation proved so frustrating that Rowe penned this blistering epistle to his longtime friend:

Somebody ought to tell you the truth occasionally—and there is no one around who does. I would tell you to your face but I have learned I can't get one word in edgewise with you. . . . Don't you ever pause for a moment and wonder why old and devoted friends—at least a quarter of a century apiece—like John Connally and Jim Rowe find it impossible to work for you? . . . I have not seen you pay one compliment, thank one person, be the sweet and kind and attractive Lyndon I used to know in all the time I have traveled with you. I have seen you do nothing but yell at them, every single one of them. . . . And most of the time you, LBJ, are wrong and they are right. . . . They bend their heads and wait for the blows to fall—like obdurate mules who know the blow is coming. It makes me so goddamn mad I'd like to sock you in the jaw.

The entire Democratic South sat teetering, for whatever reasons—race, religion, economics—ready to tumble into the Republican column, with Texas at the head of the line. Whether Lyndon Johnson might correct the situation remained questionable. Years of compromising—compromising with Eisenhower, compromising with Northern liberal Democrats, and compromising with his Southern brethren—had taken their toll. "If Kennedy advisers imagine the South has any deep affection for Lyndon Johnson they are wholly mistaken," wrote one Richmond editor. "He is widely regarded as a renegade, turncoat and opportunist who plays footsie with the liberals."

The usual intransigents—Virginia's Harry Byrd and former Texas governor Alan Shivers—remained intransigent, with Shivers endorsing Nixon in late September, as he had twice endorsed Eisenhower. It could have been worse, but Sam Rayburn and current governor Price Daniel held Lone Star State Democrats in line for the ticket, Daniel distancing himself from the national platform ("No one should interpret the support of these nominees as support of the platform that was written in Los Angeles") and Rayburn so desperate he threatened to destroy the sacro-sanct oil and gas depletion allowances if Texas's right-wing oil and gas magnates jumped the ticket. For Sam Rayburn, more than a national elec-tion was at stake. It was a question of local honor. Mr. Sam was not about to let his boy down.

When in doubt in the South, hammer Republicans. Lyndon fired both barrels, jibing that Ike and the GOP had used Dixie as a golf course for the last eight years. Cynically playing the race card, he reminded Southerners of Northern discrimination and vowed to protect "constitutional rights for all Americans, no matter where they lived," whether in growing Northern ghettos or restive Southern states.

And he *enjoyed* hammering Richard Nixon. In Culpepper, Virginia, he shouted to the crowd (liberally laced with Democratic congressional staffers): "You make us feel so wonderful to come out here and look us in the eye and press the flesh. . . . [N]ow, what has Dick Nixon ever done for Culpepper?" It was vintage Johnson, and the only thing wrong with it—and indicative of the campaign's great vulnerability—was that Richard Nixon carried Culpepper that November.

In late September, two influential Southerners who might have jumped the party—and taken the region with them—announced they were remaining on board. Richard Russell and his segregationist Georgia colleague Herman Talmadge were backing the JFK-LBJ slate, unenthusiastically providing grudging endorsements, but that was enough. And from Mississippi, arch-segregationist U.S. senator James Eastland (personally close to JFK) took to the television airwaves for an hour to inform constituents, "Lyndon Johnson took everything relating to integration out of those civil rights bills. He has always opposed Congress's implementation of the segregation decisions of the Supreme Court."

It was nothing the campaign would have wanted broadcast outside Dixie, and, in truth, it was not anything LBJ would have been personally comfortable with, for no matter how much he compromised with the Southerners and, when convenient, comported as one of their own ("we of the South"), he cared far more about economics than race, about helping the disadvantaged than segregating them. Campaigning in Nashville, LBJ spied some racist graffiti and informed Bill Moyers, "I'll tell you what's at the bottom of it. If you can convince the lowest white man that he's better than the best colored man, he won't notice you picking his pocket. He'll give you somebody to look down on, and he'll empty his pockets for you."

On Monday, October 10, LBJ initiated a five-day, 3,500-mile, whistle-stop tour of eight Southern states—his eleven-car "Cornpone Special"—with his theme, "The Yellow Rose of Texas," blasting from loudspeakers. It was, however, more than a Harry Truman whistle-stop tour. It was also a mobile version of the famous "Johnson Treatment," extending a firm handshake, a stiff drink, and a few well-chosen words to each of the estimated 1,247 Southern politicos that came aboard.

Johnson recognized the immensity of his task. Mississippi Democrats had instructed their electors not to vote for Kennedy (they would ultimately vote for Harry Byrd). Georgia's and Louisiana's had mulled the same tactic. So, nervous regarding what response his tour might generate, Johnson preceded it with another junket headed by Louisiana's Lindy Boggs, wife of Congressman Hale Boggs. "In the South," Mrs. Boggs recalled, "in a year when there were civil rights difficulties, the only way he could send a team out and be sure it was met with politeness was if it had women on it. What Southern gentleman is not going to receive Southern ladies when they are coming to his state and his city?"

Lyndon was finally again in his element. Even so, he remained jumpy, volatile, insecure. Campaigning at New Orleans's train station before an immense throng, LBJ, noted Senator George Smathers, could look out to see "at least a thousand signs, 'Kennedy/Johnson, Kennedy/Johnson.'"

"We were doing great"; then LBJ "jumped like he was shot [nervously exclaiming] 'Look at that son of a bitch! Look at that sign there!' There was one [unfavorable] sign! It wasn't a foot high. There were thousands of signs and that was the one he picked out. 'Goddamit it! Look at that sign!' I thought, this is the damndest fellow I had ever seen in my life, here we had all this, and all he could see was [this one sign]. But that was typical Johnson. . . . It had to be unanimous as far as he was concerned."

Outside Dixie, LBJ remained largely invisible—largely by design. "Our polls," Sorensen would note, "showed that voters were making up their minds based on the presidential candidates not the vice-presidential candidates. . . . To the extent that Johnson appeared in local TV in the South which would shore up his natural constituency . . . fine."

Whether North or South, Johnson hammered the religious issue. At one stop he proclaimed, "If . . . people do apply a religious test as a qualification for office, then we tear up the Bill of Rights and throw our Constitution into the wastebasket. In the next election, the Baptists will be out, and next a Jew or a Methodist or a Christian cannot be President, and soon we will disqualify everyone who believes in God and only the atheists will be left as eligible, and that's not the American way."

JFK, nonetheless, wanted no part of showcasing Lyndon. "During the campaign," recalled veteran LBJ associate James Blundell, "Johnson kept saying to me, 'Nixon and Lodge are always making joint appearances.

When am I going to appear with Jack?' I could tell he was very sensitive about it.

"I don't think Jack ever said this or felt it, but some members of the Kennedy staff felt that Johnson wasn't as refined as Kennedy and maybe they shouldn't appear together. . . . [T]here was some of that feeling."

Nor was JFK interested in any vice-presidential debate, LBJ versus Lodge. For that matter, neither was Johnson. Hearing of such a possibility, he angrily phoned CBS president Frank Stanton: "If you're behind this, I just want you to know I'm going to fight you. I don't want to debate, and I don't look upon this as a friendly thing."

Such a low profile was fine—as long as nobody noticed. But people were noticing, and not just that LBJ was not visible, but that he had become the Kennedy campaign's virtual un-person. In early September, the Associated Press's Jack Bell wrote, "The voters of Washington, Oregon and Idaho—as well [as others]—who have heard the Massachusetts Senator speak in the last five days could be excused if they thought Kennedy was running alone on the Democratic ticket."

Two weeks later, speaking in New York City, Arthur Schlesinger unleashed this barb: "Johnson has dropped out of the campaign, but it does not really matter. No one hears from him any more, but it doesn't make much difference."

Obviously, Professor Schlesinger had misspoken. "I wired Senator Johnson," he would write, "that what I meant to say . . . was that the decisive race in this election is really between the presidential nominees and not the vice-presidential candidates. That is historically true." Not exactly a denial—or an apology.

Equally prickly was JFK's visit to Texas that September—the one bringing him to the Greater Houston Ministerial Association. The acrimony had begun, as was so often the case, with Bobby. LBJ campaign coordinator John "Dub" Singleton tendered to RFK, for his review and JFK's issuance, a rather innocuous statement on the federal oil depletion allowance, an issue one ignored in Texas at significant risk. "We're not going to say anything like that," RFK pronounced frigidly, tearing up the offending document as he spoke, letting it tumble piece by piece to the tarmac. "We put that son of a bitch on the ticket to carry Texas, and if you can't carry Texas, that's y'all's problem."

Robert Francis Kennedy, concluded Dub Singleton, was "the most arrogant person I had ever met in my life."

Meanwhile, Johnson was as nervous as a cat, pestering JFK that he should confer with Mr. Sam, more jittery than even his normal state. "I believe you're cracking up," JFK told him. Lyndon's mood merely worsened after being excluded from the Houston ministers' meeting. That morning, called upon to present JFK at an El Paso breakfast, a miffed LBJ produced a decidedly terse introduction. JFK proved typically unflappable. "I was just relaxing to hear Lyndon Johnson make a fifteen to twenty minute speech here this morning," he told the crowd. "I can see it will be a hard day for me."

The weeks flew by. Johnson—and Kennedy—worried that their great bargain might prove a great failure. "I am deeply disturbed about Texas," LBJ wrote John Connally in mid-October. "The Belden poll concerns me a great deal. Won't you give your best thoughts to what should be done—when, where, and how. We just must not win the nation and lose Texas. Imagine how the new administration will look upon us."

He continued, "If you could take charge the last month of the campaign, it might well make the difference. We have good people, but we haven't got anybody qualified to mastermind it as you can. The Senator is probably not going to run for Vice President but once."

Four days later, Lady Bird's eighty-one-year-old father, T. J. Taylor, died, bringing about a time for reflection on higher meanings. Among the mourners was an East Texas congressional administrative assistant and an associate of Johnson, Monk Willis. "The burial was over in the cemetery in Marshall," Willis recalled, "a few miles away. We went over to the cemetery. There wasn't any order—you know how you walk up to a grave. I happened to stand right next to Lyndon during the committal service. I've forgotten the prayers—very simple, 'earth to earth, ashes to ashes, dust to dust,' and all that. And then the grace of the Lord, the Benediction. The minister said, 'Amen.'

"Johnson looked up and said to me, 'Monk, how's that damn county of yours doing?'"

Lyndon Johnson was not about to lose Texas for JFK—or himself.

TWENTY-FIVE

"Nixon did everything but sweep out the plane"

LYNDON JOHNSON no longer controlled his own fate, but Richard Nixon now did his . . . or so he fancied.

For too many years, Nixon had played—and *been*—the underdog. Dwight Eisenhower's easy smile won voters' hearts. Few other Republicans had. For Nixon, the preceding four years had produced a series of polling numbers ranging from guardedly hopeful to merely disastrous. Now, following a relatively calm national convention and a widely praised acceptance address, Richard Nixon was for once . . . ahead.

He enjoyed a 51 percent–to–49 percent lead. Within ten days—according to George Gallup—it built to a commanding 53 percent–to–47 percent margin.

All Richard Nixon had to do was not blow it.

He would re-invent himself once more. There would be no slash-and-burn campaign against John F. Kennedy, no little digs at his wealth, no aspersions regarding his philandering or his health.

"For whatever reason," wrote journalist and commentator Chris Matthews decades later, "Nixon never once unleashed the kind of scorched-earth raid on the enemy that had made him such a ferocious campaigner in the past. . . . [He] never did get all that tough with Jack Kennedy."

Instead, Nixon attempted to craft a more statesmanlike, even somewhat liberal, persona—in hope of materializing as a younger, brainier, more hirsute edition of Ike. What emerged, however, was merely a shifty, ill-shaven—but still pompous—Adlai, an apparition hardly capable of mollifying even the most gullible liberals, but fully capable of disturbing—or at least mystifying—the less gullible of those to his right.

Richard Nixon would be folksy, a calm man in a calm mode, stressing his experience like an earnest employee going hat in hand to his employer for a promotion. No longer was Richard Nixon a Joe McCarthy in a clean shirt; now he was a Dwight Eisenhower with a good ticker, a candidate both professional and reassuring—and, trapped in the rhetoric of (and by the praise extended to) his acceptance address, truth be told, somewhat dull.

★ ★ ★

Both candidates—Kennedy and Nixon—spoke bravely of new leadership for the 1960s, but both campaigns looked backward to the preceding decade's tendencies toward conformity and playing it safe. Both steered a course free of ideology, piloting the ship of state straight down the middle, though sometimes that meant steering wildly left to right and back again. In Los Angeles on Friday, October 14, Nixon described himself as a "practical progressive." Five months earlier he had characterized himself as an "economic conservative."

"I cannot believe," chided Kennedy, "that the American people in these difficult times will choose a man with this fuzzy image of his own political philosophy."

Privately, JFK informed John Kenneth Galbraith that he "felt sorry for Nixon because he does not know who he is, and at each stop he has to decide which Nixon he is at the moment, which must be very exhausting."

Neither the left nor the right wing of the GOP was entirely satisfied with Nixon. Nelson Rockefeller promised to campaign strenuously for his former rival, but he merely went through a series of well-choreographed motions, convinced that Nixon was doomed no matter what anyone did. "It looks very much," Rocky informed the *Wall Street Journal*'s Robert Novak, "as though Nixon is going to lose the election for failing to pick up enough electoral votes in the big industrialized states. He's losing the big industrialized states, because he's chasing a will-o'-the wisp trying to capture Southern states. No matter how hard he tries, Nixon can't win the South. But he can alienate the North, which is attainable—and absolutely necessary."

Conservatives remained skeptical of Nixon, recalling his roles in torpedoing Robert Taft and Joe McCarthy, his public trumpeting of Eisenhower's foreign aid program, his decreased enthusiasm for fighting right-to-work battles. They were suspicious of his views on all sorts of domestic issues (in the course of the campaign he endorsed New York senator Jacob Javits's federal health insurance plan—which JFK would blast as too expensive—and the still moribund Equal Rights Amendment) and aghast at his pallid recent positions regarding Castro's Cuba. At William F. Buckley's *National Review*, only one senior editor, the former Trotskyite James Burnham, advocated endorsing him. The others, including Buckley and L. Brent Bozell, favored no endorsement—and carried the day.

Much farther to the right, longtime superpatriot and anti-Semite Gerald L. K. Smith fulminated that Richard Nixon was a "super-beatnik who seems to be a cross between Elvis the Pelvis and Franklin D. Roosevelt." In 1960, relatively few people knew how crazy Robert Welch's nascent John Birch Society was—or even what it was. But to Birchers, while Nelson Rockefeller was "definitely committed to trying to make the United States a part of a one-world socialist government," and JFK a "stooge" of the UAW's Walter Reuther, Richard Nixon was merely another so-called Republican who had helped scuttle Robert Taft eight years previously.

Barry Goldwater, for all his blunt bluster, was much more grounded in political realities. He played a far cagier game, akin to Nelson Rockefeller's, ostensibly supporting the 1960 ticket but looking with hard eyes toward 1964. "I summon Conservatives of both parties," he wrote in the conservative weekly *Human Events* in August, "to get behind Nixon and work tirelessly to give him the victory America needs. . . . What other choice have we? . . . In short, for Conservatives there exists no alternative to Nixon."

Like Rockefeller, however, Goldwater also wrote off Nixon's chances, though for reasons diametrically opposite. "Nixon made his basic mistake," he privately informed Bob Novak, "by moving to the left to woo an urban Democratic vote and particularly a Negro vote that was irrevocably Democratic. . . . Nixon's gestures toward the left . . . had not only lost Nixon his golden opportunity to become the first Republican in a generation to bring out the full conservative vote but also had botched up the chance to sweep all or most of the segregationist South."

But Barry's subtlety, as well as his public forbearance, never knew great limits. By early October he had already announced, "I'm for Dick Nixon [but should he lose] I will not hesitate to submit in 1964 for the Presidential nomination."

Some folks sniped at Dick Nixon. Some employed more direct action.

Thursday, October 27, was a particularly ugly day, with hecklers tossing eggs at Nixon at a rally in Muskegon, Michigan, and Nixon barking back, "And I would also suggest, while I am talking about manners, incidentally, that I have been heckled by experts. So, don't try something on me or we'll take care of you. All you do is to show your own bad manners when you do that." Earlier that day, authorities had discovered a plot to derail the Nixon campaign train near Fort Wayne, Indiana.

★ ★ ★

In 1960, Richard Nixon could not hope to match the Democrats' roster of Hollywood talent. While A-list celebrities for Nixon included John Wayne, Gary Cooper, Kirk Douglas, James Stewart, Jerry Lewis, Walt Disney, Sam Goldwyn, and Johnny Mathis, the truth was that much, if not most, of Nixon's stars' glamour had long since started to dim.

Such a description certainly described forty-nine-year-old former second-tier Warner Bros. star Ronald Wilson Reagan, now ensconced as host of CBS television's popular Sunday evening anthology, *GE Theater*. A seven-term president of the Screen Actors Guild, the increasingly conservative Reagan nonetheless technically remained a Democrat. "In watching him," his wife Nancy observed, "I discovered that changing party affiliation could be as difficult as changing one's religion."

Reagan had campaigned for Helen Gahagan Douglas in 1950, and though he endorsed Eisenhower in both 1952 and 1956 (originally he had urged Ike to run as a Democrat) and admired Nixon's tough talk during 1959's Kitchen Debate with Khrushchev, as 1960 approached he still considered Nixon somewhat the "villain." That changed when General Electric president Ralph Cordiner ("I think you might be wrong about Nixon") suggested otherwise. Reagan now not only endorsed Nixon; he contemplated changing parties. Nixon dissuaded Reagan, preferring the actor to campaign as a Democrat for Nixon. Rumors of Reagan's defection soon reached Joe Kennedy. Kennedy "asked to see me," Reagan recalled. "He tried to persuade me to change my mind and support his son but I turned him down."

Reagan considered Kennedy's "New Frontier" hardly new, but merely a repackaging of decades-old big-government schemes. "Under the tousled boyish hair cut," Reagan scoffed, "it is still old Karl Marx—

271

first launched a century ago. There is nothing new in the idea of a government being Big Brother to us all. . . . [T]he American people do not want the government paid services at 'any price' and if we collectively can't afford 'free this and that' they'd like to know it before they buy and not after it is entrenched behind another immovable government bureau."

Inevitably, Nixon's and JFK's Hollywood factions took to lobbing verbal grenades at each other. "We're the opposite of the Ratpack," jibed crooner-turned-hardboiled-movie-detective-turned-television-producer Dick Powell. "We've tried to get the most reputable movie people. They may not be the most popular at the moment, but they have dignity and the right image. If I were working for Kennedy I would try to stay away from the element that is supporting him. I'm good friends with most of them, but I think these people hurt Kennedy by their cheap publicity."

Columnist Art Buchwald conveyed Powell's comments to Peter Lawford, and Lawford exploded: "It's just sour grapes on Powell's part. They have no talent on their side so they call themselves respectable. . . . We've got the talent so our Ratpack is abused. . . . We have all the talent on our side. They'd give $100,000 just to get one of our people. The stars for Nixon are not entertainers. When we send our people out for Jack they entertain the people—and don't bore them."

John Wayne being John Wayne, he of course elevated his activism to a slightly higher, more combative—*more John Wayne*—level than did other celebrities for Nixon. The year 1960 saw Wayne complete work on what he considered his magnum opus, his film homage to the fight for Texas independence—*The Alamo.* As both the woefully overbudget twelve-million-dollar epic and the campaign rolled on, the Duke purchased a $152,000 three-page, red-white-and-blue ad in the Fourth of July issue of *Life* to promote the film—and to launch a not-very-veiled jab at the Democratic frontrunner:

Very soon the two great political parties of the United States will nominate their candidates for President. One of these men will be assigned the awesome duties of the White House. . . . In this moment when eternity could be closer than ever before, is there a statesman who for the sake of a vote is not all things to all men; a man who will put America back on the high road of security and accomplishment; without fear of favor or compromise; a man who wants to do the job that must be done and to hell with friend or foe who would have it otherwise; a man who knows that the American softness must be hardened; a man who knows that when our house is in order no man will ever dare to trespass. . . . There were no ghostwriters at the Alamo. Only Men.

★ ★ ★

At its most cohesive, Jack Kennedy's staff seemed (particularly to the outside world) a veritable band of brothers. The Nixon staff appeared (often to itself) a veritable band of in-laws, held together by a domineering, suspicious great-aunt.

It was not that the Nixon team lacked talent. Already, in 1960, it contained the nucleus—Bob Haldeman, John Ehrlichman, Chuck Colson (recommended, oddly enough, by Tip O'Neill), publicist William Safire, L. Patrick Gray (just retired from the navy to work for Nixon), Herb Klein, Bob Finch—of the juggernaut that would twice elect a U.S. president.

But while Robert Kennedy freed brother Jack to be simply the Candidate, there was no one on the Nixon team who so enjoyed Nixon's confidence. Murray Chotiner might have filled that role, but Chotiner—his ethical baggage making him anathema to the public—had long since forfeited such privilege. The Nixon camp did have an excellent potential replacement, however—former Republican national chairman Len Hall. Hall had proven useful—and loyal—to Nixon throughout the 1950s, particularly in mobilizing against the looming Rockefeller threat. But, noted historian David Halberstam, "There was . . . precious little gratitude on the part of Nixon for that help. Len Hall would not be his campaign manager. Nixon himself would be filling that position."

Nixon could not formally designate himself, but he could appoint an unworkable two-headed leadership that would leave him de facto in charge. Hall, then, would be "campaign chairman," while Robert Finch would be designated "campaign director." The thirty-five-year-old former Marine Finch seemed almost the anti-Nixon: handsome, personable, photogenic, in Ralph de Toledano's words, "shrewd, attractive, easy of manner, able, and lacking the introversion that made Nixon such an enigma to the average politician."

"There was a warmth about [Finch]," wrote Teddy White, "a vivid concern for people in his politics."

Yet behind the attractive facade was a severely limited talent. "In Congress," John Ehrlichman added, "it seems to help if you're a little scattered and disorganized, and Bob Finch was that. He had no talent whatever for running a campaign, or running the Department of Health, Education and Welfare, or running anything else requiring much consistency and firmness."

The overlap between Hall and Finch spawned inefficiencies. Approach Hall's people with a question, and you might be told it fell under Finch's authority. Approach Finch, and you might be informed it was Hall's responsibility. In fact, many items—far too many—fell under Richard Nixon's gaze: scheduling, logistics, speechwriting. He could not let go of details. Hours might be spent drafting not only speeches and statements but exhaustive answers to the dozens of questionnaires that flooded the campaign. "I felt it was my clear responsibility to review each answer in detail," he rationalized in his memoirs, "because they had asked for my views, not those of my staff. . . . I had to work literally night and day to catch up on this backlog and still keep current on the . . . speeches that had to made daily."

"Nixon did everything but sweep out the plane," recalled Finch. "He even insisted on sitting in the back of the plane and painstakingly writing his own speeches. We had people who were supposed to do that. They'd leave the plane after a week to ten days because they were not being utilized to the extent they wanted to be."

And, yet, that is not to say there was no role for staff—although that role might assume an odd, awkward, dysfunctional, buffering form. "As the campaign wore on," Teddy White would remember, "[Nixon developed] a strange reclusiveness. He would sit in the back seat of the campaign plane while Governors and eminent politicians sat forward. Nixon wanted their views and advice brought to him through intermediaries. He felt that the prince should not be open to a tug-of-war between his advisers, that an important man was too often apt to be swayed by the last advocate who caught his ear. He wanted information filtered as it came to him—and he wanted his filterers to filter his will back to those whom he must direct."

Hall's and Finch's influence waned. H. R. "Bob" Haldeman's grew. Beginning the year as Nixon's equivalent of JFK's Jerry Bruno, overseeing eighteen advance men, Haldeman would steadily accrete power, ending the exercise in a position very much like Nixon's Robert Kennedy.

Haldeman played to Nixon's preference for remoteness, for playing the selfless, godlike leader, keeping his own counsel, functioning in monklike isolation—and Haldeman would also play to his ego. "Nixon gets irritated by petty annoyances," Haldeman would recall at the peak of his power. "In 1960 we ran it badly and he was always angry with the need of dealing with petty details that were handled badly. He has no time for small talk, or the ordinary kind of bull when people get together. He's best when he's dealing with problems—you have to keep people off his back and let him deal with larger things. . . . Basically, there are ordinary people and extraordinary people, and he's one of the extraordinary ones; it's the way his mind works, the way he can soak up a whole range of opinions."

"It was an 'iron curtain,'" complained Nixon television adviser Ted Rogers. "Haldeman came between me and the candidate and between everyone else, including [Nixon secretary] Rose Mary Woods and the candidate. That was the beginning of the end of anyone's access to Nixon."

"Nixon was by nature an excluder," observed campaign research chief Jim Shepley (on leave from his position as chief of *Time-Life* domestic correspondents). "Haldeman liked to exclude people. When Nixon's need met Haldeman's abilities, you had the most perfect formula for disaster."

Nixon and Haldeman, mourned Len Hall, was "darkness reaching for darkness."

Oddly enough, Hall's alter ego Bob Finch disagreed. "The Nixon of 1960 and in his vice-presidential days," said Finch, "was if anything overly accessible. In that sense Haldeman was probably right in husbanding his time [later]."

Haldeman made the planes run on time, but the process was not without its bumps. At the close of one particularly grueling day, completed with an interminable airport receiving line, Nixon, zombielike, muttered to Haldeman, "Bob, from now on I don't want to land at any more airports." In New Jersey, that September, Haldeman advance men—former Justice Department attorney (and future U.S. senator) John Warner—so alienated the locals that sixteen county chairmen threatened to cancel their cooperation. In Iowa, Nixon's infamous dark temper exploded as he wasted valuable hours riding through empty corn-lined country roads (a trip planned by John Ehrlichman). Remembered Haldeman:

> Nixon seethed with anger. He was riding in an open convertible and Air Force Major Don Hughes, Nixon's military aide, was in the seat directly in front of Nixon's. Suddenly—incredibly—Nixon began to kick the back of Hughes's seat with both feet. And he wouldn't stop! Thump! Thump! Thump! The seat and the hapless Hughes jolted forward jaggedly as Nixon vented his rage. When the car stopped at a small town in the middle of nowhere, Hughes, white faced, silently got out of the car and started walking straight ahead, down the road and out of town. He wanted to get as far away as he could from the Vice-President. I believe he would have walked clear across the state if I hadn't set out after him and apologized for Nixon and finally talked him into rejoining us.

Yet, to the outside observer, the swing seemed flawless. "One could learn much," Teddy White recorded quite without irony, "from a day like the day that followed as the Nixon cavalcade crossed into Iowa."

★ ★ ★

Henry Cabot Lodge was much like that day in Iowa. On the surface he seemed quite impressive—articulate, handsome, experienced, a true public servant from one of the nation's most distinguished families. But in the long history of vice-presidential nominees, Lodge—though scoring extremely well in abstract popularity polls—ranked as among the more puzzling of selections, unable to carry his home state, nearly powerless to affect any outcome in his region, a toxin to his party's conservative base, and, ultimately, a drag upon the ticket in a region—the South—where real breakthroughs might yet be gained.

But even beyond his geographical and ideological deficiencies, Lodge suffered from two additional glaring deficiencies. The first was an aloof personality that, despite the glorious résumé fastened to it, alienated first the media (addressing reporters as "my good man") and then the public. "He was," Teddy White wrote of Lodge, "like medicine—good for you, but hard to take."

Lodge "looked like what you would expect an American statesman to look like," noted Nixon campaign television adviser Gene Wyckoff. "But when he opened his mouth and when he interacted with people on television, there was something not so attractive—something in his demeanor, a touch of hauteur, arrogance, aloofness, or condescension perhaps. His characterization did not ring true."

Everything about the Lodge choice seemed star-crossed—particularly on a single day in Indiana when the candidate had his right index finger smashed in a car door and then found himself trapped between floors in a hotel elevator.

Lodge clearly *hated* campaigning. His memoirs, for all their brevity, recount an unusually ill-tempered litany of carping regarding uncomfortable, noisy hotel rooms, bumpy airplane rides, rushed, bad meals, and annoying local politicians. It does not appear that Henry Cabot Lodge very much missed elected office at all.

He lay down on the job—literally—canceling afternoon appearances, taking hour-long after-lunch naps, refusing to appear after 6 p.m. He had his excuses. "There are really two essential things in campaigning," Lodge rationalized. "First, you must be in good humor. If you're going to be irascible, you ought to stay home. Second, you ought to make sense in your speeches. These are the two things you must do. Unless you're a saint, you can't be in good humor when you're exhausted."

True enough, but Lodge had exceeded the limits. "We didn't mind him having a nap in the afternoon," growled one veteran GOP operative, "but why did he have to put on his pajamas?"

★ ★ ★

Media-wise, Lodge proved wretched. Producing Lodge-centered television spots was nearly impossible—from virtually every angle. "My camera crews, trailing [Lodge] for footage," noted Gene Wyckoff, "reported difficulty in finding enthusiastic crowds." Before the cameras, Wyckoff noted, he "could not or would not perform." In Los Angeles, on Saturday morning, October 1, the campaign engaged a studio for Lodge to film material for a paid half-hour television show, *The Danger Spots*, to be aired on CBS that Monday night. With studio time running at nearly a thousand dollars an hour, Lodge proceeded to re-edit the script on site—and then botch his delivery of the message (Wyckoff: "[W]henever the film came up on the monitor to illustrate one of the trouble spots, he would start to watch it and lose his place in the script"). Almost nothing usable was shot. The show was scrapped.

There were other attempts—all equally dismal. "A few direct-to-camera commercials were also made of Ambassador Lodge," Wyckoff continued, "showing him at his worst: fidgeting in a chair, squinting at some cue cards that were probably lying on the floor under the camera, and reading as if he was seeing the words for the first time and was not sure what they meant."

★ ★ ★

As Robert Taft had discovered in 1952, however, one underestimated Lodge's capacity for intrigue at one's own peril. The year 1960 found Lodge attempting his own deal with the devil. In February, Lodge—"a man who deeply hopes for good relations between the U.S.S.R. and the United States"—journeyed to Moscow. Cognizant of what effects foreign affairs might have, and had had, on the upcoming campaign, Lodge made a secret pitch to neutralize Nikita Khrushchev, informing the volatile Soviet that "there is always a minimum of flexibility in foreign relations in the United States in an election year. What is hard or impossible to do in 1952 or 1956 or 1960 is often quite susceptible of accomplishment in 1953 or 1957 or 1961."

Lodge dangled a significant, though vague, carrot before Khrushchev. "Don't pay any attention to the campaign speeches," Lodge advised. "Remember, they're just political statements. Once Mr. Nixon is in the White House, I'm sure—I'm absolutely *certain*—he'll take a position of preserving and perhaps even improving our relations." Stateside, Lodge confided to Nixon that he had "had a talk with Khrushchev . . . not reported to the State Department."

Lodge may not have taken nyet for an answer. That autumn, an unidentified top Republican—said to have been a person with whom Khrushchev "had established not bad relations . . . at the time of my trip to the U.S.A." (Lodge escorted Khrushchev on his September 1959 American visit)—conferred with Soviet ambassador Mikhail Menshikov (the same Menshikov who had carried Khrushchev's embarrassing offer of support to Adlai Stevenson) and held out a pledge of new Nixon policies toward the Soviets if U-2 pilot Francis Gary Powers and two other American fliers shot down that July were released before the election. The Soviets wanted no part of the deal—or of assisting "that son of a bitch Richard Nixon."

"We, of course, understood," Khrushchev would later say, "that Nixon wished to make political capital out of this for himself in advance of the elections. . . . Nixon wanted to make it appear as if he had already arranged certain contacts with the Soviet government."

"We would never give Nixon such a present," the Soviet boss had informed his colleagues at the time. "If we give the slightest boost to Nixon, it will be interpreted as an expression of our willingness to see him in the White House."

★ ★ ★

Nixon's speechifying, conducted at a frantic pace, proved less impressive as his campaign ground on. More relaxed and polished than Kennedy when he began, even then Nixon suffered from a certain banality, a studious avoidance of substance. "The Vice President," noted Secretary of Agriculture Benson, who refused to introduce him in Salt Lake City, "embarked on a campaign of 'sweetness and light,' apparently attempting thereby to destroy the image of himself as a ruthless political opportunist with an 'instinct for the jugular,' which the Democrats and some of the press had for ten years and more labored to create. . . . He seemed to think he could be, politically speaking, all things to all men."

If Nixon's rhetoric distressed conservative Republican Benson, it sickened more liberal observers. "I have not only liked and admired Nixon," Joe Alsop wrote to a friend on October 6, "[I] have also helped considerably to build him up as a man who has grown great with experience." Nonetheless, Alsop found Nixon's speeches to be "a steady diet of pap and soothing syrup," with "the approximate content of a television commercial."

"You should read the texts of these Nixon utterances," publicly fumed *New York Times* correspondent James Reston. "They are as thin and similar as a pack of cigarette papers, but he got away with them . . . before anybody had time to report just how bad they were."

The media hated Richard Nixon, and he hated them ("He took everything critical as a personal blast at him," said William Safire)—and, after a while, that was all you needed to know. Certainly most of the press corps was to Nixon's left, which explained some, but not all, of the animus. Reporters could not stand his style—his personal manner and the uptight, uncommunicative persona that poisoned his entire campaign apparatus.

"He was always posing. He kept crossing and uncrossing his legs," recalled Carl Rowan, then a *Minneapolis Tribune* reporter. "He almost never looked me in the eye, acting as though he were reading answers to my questions off the wall or ceiling."

For two weeks, Ben Bradlee toured with Nixon's entourage, curious about that camp, eager to see what made Nixon tick. He found Finch and Herb Klein accessible but the remainder of the staff—and Nixon himself—off limits, distant, even combative. "When I went back," Bradlee recalled, "Kennedy peppered me with questions about what Nixon's operation was like. Different, joyless, strangely dull, almost hostile, was my answer."

Of course, there were reasons for that hostility—the press's outright, undisguised cheerleading for Nixon's opponent and its barely hidden contempt for his efforts. Among examples of what caused Nixon's angst: On November 2, Nixon, Lodge, and Ike rode in a tickertape parade in New York City, buffeted by truly massive crowds. The AP reported, "The total turnout seemed larger for Nixon than the one for Kennedy"—but not until the story's ninth paragraph.

"Ninety per cent of this press corps," contended *Chicago Tribune* correspondent Willard Edwards, "which ranged between 50 and 100 at various periods in the campaign, were all-out supporters of Kennedy. They were not only opposed to Nixon, they were outspoken in their hatred and contempt of him . . . it was loud and open. When Nixon was making a speech, there was a constant murmur or ridicule from many in the press rows just beneath the platform."

Asked if he minded being assigned to the Republican effort, gruff-voiced *New York Times* reporter Bill Lawrence growled, "No, I think I can do Jack more good when I'm with Nixon."

"[Nixon] accused the press of being on Kennedy's side," recalled CBS's Charles Kuralt. "I am sure he was right. I have believed that the outcome of that election might have been different had Nixon been able to put his feet up at the end of the day and relax with the reporters, explaining his positions over a glass of scotch and a cigar. But he was not the drinking, smoking, explaining sort, or the relaxing sort either. I think it cost him the Presidency in 1960."

At a mutually hostile September 20 Scranton press conference, a quartet of reporters—Bill Lawrence, NBC's Sander Vanocur, the *Baltimore Sun*'s Philip Potter, and *Newark News*'s Arthur Sylvester—seemed intent on tripping up Nixon regarding JFK's recent comments regarding Khrushchev and the Soviets. Nixon—thin-skinned anyway—vowed that would be his last campaign-trail press conference. Only Herb Klein's urgings prevented Nixon from canceling the next day's press conference in Springfield, Missouri, and creating yet another negative story for Nixon's interrogators to report. Springfield turned out to be as ugly as Scranton—and the campaign's last scheduled news conference.

If it seemed that press relations could not get much worse, they did—particularly on the day when an infuriated Rose Mary Woods finally had enough of Bill Lawrence's waspish comments—and poured her drink upon his brush-cut head.

TWENTY-SIX

"I seen him, I seen him"

ELEANOR ROOSEVELT needed wooing.

On Sunday, August 14, Jack Kennedy flew into Hyde Park, ostensibly to mark the twenty-fifth anniversary of the Social Security program before twenty-five hundred members of the Golden Ring Council of Senior Citizens. In reality, he arrived to negotiate peace with Eleanor. In one sense, the timing could have been better. In another, it couldn't have been. Two days previously, Eleanor's thirteen-year-old granddaughter, Sara Delano "Sally" Roosevelt (daughter of Eleanor's Republican son, John), had died falling off a horse at an Adirondack camp, curtailing ER's involvement in anything more than the granddaughter's funeral and a properly subdued private lunch with Jack and his aide Bill Walton. The circumstances provided JFK with a rare opportunity to reach out to his longtime antagonist on a personal level, calling Eleanor with sympathy before his arrival, adding more sympathy once he arrived. "That young man behaved with such sensitivity and compassion throughout that whole day," she would exclaim, "he gave me more comfort than almost anyone around me, my family or anybody else. The manner in which he treated me during the day of his visit won me—as did the many things he believed in and what he wanted to do."

Yet it was not an altogether easy meeting. Old wounds—and some not so old—remained open. "Pigheaded, mean, and spiteful" is how Jackie Kennedy characterized ER's more pungent remarks regarding her husband.

Eleanor and her camp maintained an exaggerated view of their own importance. "This meeting for Mr. Kennedy," Eleanor's physician, confidant, and Manhattan housemate Dr. David Gurewitsch gushed to Gore Vidal as they awaited JFK at the Dutchess County Airport, "is the most important meeting of his life. I hope he understands that."

"I said," recalled the always ironic Vidal, "that I thought he would rise to the occasion."

JFK continued playing the right notes, sharing with Eleanor a story of his meeting with Florida governor-elect C. Farris Bryant, who informed him, "I am a conservative and I am against integration and for right-to-work laws."

"Then why don't you become a Republican?" JFK told ER he had responded.

Eleanor had her own reasons for wanting the session to succeed, aside from Jack's concern over a granddaughter's death, aside from everyone's obsession with defeating Richard Nixon. Though she remained somewhat miffed with Adlai Stevenson ("I've come to believe Governor Stevenson may not have some of the characteristics I thought he had"), she still sought to lobby the nominee on her friend's behalf. Not that she was trying to force any appointments on Kennedy—she conceded that a new president should have independence in that regard ("And I believe that very sincerely"), but she made her pitch for Adlai as secretary of state anyway, and concluded the meeting feeling that JFK would appoint her old comrade to the post.

As for Kennedy, as Dave Powers remembered it, "The Senator came out of there like a boy who has just made a good confession. It was a great load off his mind."

ER became a fan. John, who had seconded Richard Nixon's nomination, did not, accusing JFK of being "a whiz kid who makes snap judgments and should not be entrusted with the leadership of the nation."

"He has matured," Eleanor countered. "He has the qualities of a scholar, and a sense of history. He will make a very good president, if elected."

To her friend Mary Lasker, she wrote, "I also had the feeling that he was a man who could learn. I liked him better than I ever had before because he seemed so little cock-sure, and I think he has a mind that is open to new ideas." She concluded, "My final judgment is that here is a man who wants to leave a record (perhaps for ambitious personal reasons, as people say) but I rather think because he really is interested in helping the people of his own country and mankind in general. I will be surer of this as time goes on."

The Kennedy touch with crowds—a growing, noticeable phenomenon—also impressed her. "I don't think anyone in our politics since

Franklin had the same vital relationship with crowds," Eleanor informed Arthur Schlesinger. "Franklin would sometimes begin a campaign weary and apathetic, but . . . would draw strength and vitality from the audiences, and would end in better shape than he started. I feel that Senator Kennedy is much the same—that his intelligence and courage elicit emotions from his crowds which flew back to him, and sustain him and strengthen him."

She continued lobbying for Adlai, perhaps a tad undiplomatically, writing in her August 17 column: "Kennedy has a quick mind, but I would say that he might tend to arrive at judgments almost too quickly. [He might better rely on Adlai Stevenson's] more judicial and reflective type of mind. I was pleased to learn that the Senator already had made plans much along these lines. It gave me a feeling of reassurance. . . . I think Kennedy is anxious to learn. I think he is hospitable to new ideas. He is hard-headed. He calculates the political effect of every move."

Her heart belonged to Adlai. But her vote now belonged to JFK.

★ ★ ★

Harry Truman may not have invented grudges, but he may well have perfected the art form. "I recognize the type now," observed Hearst columnist Westbrook Pegler (no Francis of Assisi himself) as far back as 1949. "You see them out west. Thin-lipped, a hater, a bad man in any fight. Malicious and unforgiving and not above offering you his hand to yank you off balance and work you over with a chair leg, pool cue or something out of his pocket."

Among Truman's more persistent vendettas was that held toward Joseph P. Kennedy. "It's not the pope I'm afraid of," Harry had said not long before Los Angeles, "it's the pop."

The feud dated from at least 1944, when vice-presidential nominee Harry Truman, campaigning in Boston, was visited by Joe Kennedy. "Harry," snarled Joe, "what the hell are you doing campaigning for that crippled son of a bitch that killed my son Joe?" Truman wanted to toss Kennedy Sr. out of his Ritz-Carlton hotel room window.

Nor did the ex-president favor JFK's brother Robert. "I just don't like that boy," said Harry, "and I never will. He worked for old Joe McCarthy, you know, and when old Joe was tearing up the Constitution and the country, that boy couldn't say enough for him."

It was, however, possible that Harry Truman liked neither brother nor pop *nor* pope. Rumors of Truman's Ku Klux Klan membership were persistent—though HST persistently denied them. In 1944, Republicans produced a man swearing that Truman had once attended a Missouri Klan meeting, and another who said that Truman had *addressed* a KKK Klonvocation. A third report contended that former Grand Kleagle Harry Hoffman had sworn Truman into the organization in 1920. Truman branded such tales "lies," and countered that in September 1921 he had supported an anti-Klan membership resolution among the Missouri Grand Lodge of Masons.

Grudge or not, it was time for Harry Truman to endorse his party's nominee, who, for his part, appeared to view the former president as somewhat of an eccentric relative—not to be overtly bashed, but not to be taken quite seriously, either.

To reconcile Missouri and Massachusetts, JFK dispatched an envoy, Governor Abe Ribicoff, to visit Truman. Noted Kenny O'Donnell: "The choice of Ribicoff, the Jewish governor of Connecticut, as his emissary to call upon the Masonic, Baptist Truman was not accidental and gave JFK a certain satisfaction."

"I never liked Kennedy," Truman fumed to Ribicoff. "I hate his father. Kennedy wasn't so great a Senator. . . . However, that no good son-of-a-bitch Dick Nixon called me a Communist and I'll do anything to beat him."

And so it was that HST unhappily endorsed JFK. To Dean Acheson, he penned (but never sent) these words:

> You and I are stuck with the necessity of taking the worst of two evils or none at all. So—I'm taking the *immature* Democrat as the best of the two. Nixon is impossible. So, there we are. . . .
>
> I'm afraid that this immature boy who was responsible for picking out five great Senators may not know any more about the Presidency that he will occupy than he did about the great Senators. Only one, Henry Clay, belonged in the list. I sent him a list of a dozen or so but it wasn't used. So, what the hell, you and I will take it and not like it but hope for the future.

On Saturday, August 20, the presidential hopeful and the presidential veteran conferred at Truman's Independence home. To pronounce Truman's public endorsement of JFK as "grudging" would be charitable, as this exchange with reporters indicates:

QUESTION: What caused you to decide that Senator Kennedy was ready for the country?

MR. TRUMAN: When the Democratic National Convention decided to nominate him for President. That is all the answer you need. The National Democratic Convention is the law for the Democratic party. I am a Democrat and I follow the law.

QUESTION: On July 2, I believe you said that you thought the Convention was fixed. Have you changed your opinion?

MR. TRUMAN: I did not say that. I said it looked to me as if the Convention was already made up the way it was supposed to go, and that is what the trouble was. And it was, and it has been done all right, and they nominated this man, and I am going to support him.

What are you going to do about that? . . .

QUESTION: You say that as a good Democrat, you of course will support Senator Kennedy. You told us out here before Los Angeles that you felt that Senator Kennedy was too young and inexperienced.

MR. TRUMAN: I said the National Democratic Convention solved that, and that is all there is to that.

QUESTION: You now feel that he is?

MR. TRUMAN: That is all there is to that.

It was, as Thruston Morton quipped, "the second Missouri compromise."

Harry Truman hated Richard Nixon—and, in fact, hated all Republicans (save, inexplicably, for Herbert Hoover)—more than he hated even the worst of the Kennedys. "If Nixon had to stick to the truth he'd have very little to say," Truman railed to Texas voters. "You don't set a fox to watch the chickens just because he has had a lot of experience in the henhouse. . . . Nixon has never told the truth in his life. . . . He is against the small farmer. He is against small business, agriculture, public power. I don't know what the hell he's for, and that bird has the nerve to come to Texas and ask you to vote for him. If you do you ought to go to hell."

"I have noted with interest," JFK wired Harry, "your suggestion as to where those who vote for my opponent should go. While I understand and sympathize with your deep motivation, I think it is important that our side try to refrain from raising the religious issue."

★ ★ ★

By now, Jack Kennedy also had the unions on his side, particularly the most political union of all, Walter Reuther's United Auto Workers. Reuther's 1,250 locals tossed their considerable muscle behind JFK. Hundreds of full-time UAW representatives and thousands of its rank and file volunteered for Kennedy. The UAW's journal, with a circulation of one and a half million, carried a drawing of a hooded Statue of Liberty captioned "Which do you choose, liberty or bigotry?"

For all his recent efforts, however, Reuther may still not have earned the Kennedys' personal respect. Traveling to Hyannis in early August, the fifty-four-year-old Reuther, barely ten years older than JFK, was startled by Jackie's query regarding how "his generation" handled public life.

Reuther harangued JFK and his economic staff regarding policy issues, cavalierly informing Kennedy regarding any economic statements that his campaign might issue: "Anything that you do, just send it down to our boys and we'll fix it up for you."

"Forget it," Kennedy later tersely informed his staff.

★ ★ ★

Labor Day, September 4, in Detroit witnessed a very significant occurrence—the creation of the Kennedy "crowd" phenomenon. Kennedy had always attracted good, enthusiastic crowds, and he relished them. They were important to him. He drew energy from them. That, after all, is why he employed advance man Jerry Bruno.

But in Detroit, something new happened. Kennedy arrived late from Metropolitan Airport. A crowd—not very large by Kennedy standards, only about five or six thousand people—had gathered, and as they waited, their enthusiasm only grew. Bruno's people possessed only a rickety snow fence to restrain them. When Kennedy appeared, the throng pushed forward, toppling the barrier, mobbing their standard-bearer. It was all very pre-Beatles Kennedymania, and when Kennedy reviewed film of the event, he was impressed.

"My God," JFK said to Bruno, "I can't believe that crowd. How did you do it?"

Bruno hadn't done anything, but he knew he had to do it again.

From that point on, Bruno stationed two men holding a rope, to restrain admirers until Kennedy appeared. The rope dropped. The crowd surged. And once it happened a few times, it happened every time. Crowds *knew* they were *expected* to rush the candidate. The bandwagon rolled.

"The jumpers," noted Theodore White,

> were, in the beginning, teen-age girls who would bounce, jounce and jump as the cavalcade passed, squealing, "I seen him, I seen him." Gradually over the days their jumping seemed to grow more rhythmic, giving a jack-in-the-box effect of ups and downs in a thoroughly sexy oscillation. Then, as the press began to comment on the phenomenon, thus stimulating more artistic jumping, the middle-aged ladies began to jump up and down too, until, in the press bus following the candidate, one would note only the oddities: the lady, say, in her bathrobe, jumping back and forth; the heavily pregnant mother, jumping; the mother with a child in her arms, jumping; the row of nuns, all jiggling under their black robes, almost (but not quite) daring to jump; and the double-jumper teenagers who, as the cavalcade passed, would turn to face each other and, in ecstasy, place hands on each others' shoulders and jump up and down together as a partnership.

"John F. Kennedy treated southern Ohio," columnist Murray Kempton wrote following one such episode,

> as Don Giovanni used to treat Seville. His progress, as ever, was an epic in the history of the sexual instinct of the American female. Outside Dayton, a woman of advanced years but intact instinct sat with her dog. Kennedy passed, she waved; he waved back; in that moment of truth she clasped her dog and kissed his wet muzzle. Jack

Kennedy is starting to enjoy these moments, and he is starting to enjoy them as a man of taste. He turns back now and goes on waving; the lingering hand gestures and the eye follows; its object is always a quietly pretty girl and the hand says that, if he did not have miles to go and promises to keep, he would like to walk with her where the mad river meets the still water.

"Kennedy," noted the Associated Press's Relman Morin, "has an edge among the jumpers, the shriekers and the squealers—mainly teenagers and excitable young women." Though Morin conceded, "Nixon seems to be ahead with the that's righters—the person who quietly murmurs 'that's right' when either candidate makes a point in a speech."

And it was not always teenage girls. In Pennsylvania's coal country, reporter Chuck Roberts noticed that Kennedy's right hand was bleeding. "Those ——ers," Kennedy explained. "When they shake hands, they really shake hands."

Wednesday, October 19, saw Kennedy reach Manhattan. The previous day he had campaigned just north of the city, in Yonkers. Forty thousand cheered him, plus another twenty thousand who had lined the three-mile parade route (still only 70 percent of the crowds that had greeted Ike four years previously). In New York, in cloudy weather, a fifty-piece marching band led Kennedy's cavalcade from Whitehall Street to Rockefeller Center past a million people downtown under threatening skies—fifty thousand at city hall alone. It was, inaccurately proclaimed New York mayor Robert Wagner, "the greatest reception anybody has ever received in this section of the city in its history." JFK, thanking Wagner for inviting him, informed the crowd that Wagner "has promised to do the same for the Vice President some time late in November or December." Wagner said it was news to him.

When JFK reached Rockefeller Center the heavens opened. Still, crowds pressed forward, frightening nearly eight-months-pregnant Jackie, causing her to fear that the "sides of the car seemed to be buckling in." The throng smashed a wooden platform attached to their Chevrolet convertible, as well as its antenna.

The next day, the Sanitation Department collected a hundred tons of refuse.

Estimating crowds was always a challenge, with Kennedy (or Nixon) functionaries rarely undercounting, and sometimes so egregiously not undercounting that generally favorable reporters—including Ben Bradlee—called them to task. Responding to Bradlee's query as to how the campaign arrived at its tallies, JFK retorted, "Plucky [Pierre Salinger] counts the nuns, and then multiplies by 100."

"By so deprecating the crowd count," Bradlee observed, "and making a joke about a subject that was sensitive, to say the least, Kennedy made the reporters laugh, and probably avoided a story about inflated crowd counts by his staff. Questioning of a crowd count given by a member of the Nixon team usually brought a lecture about bias."

Crowds, however, were not votes, and, certainly teenage girls were not votes. Larry O'Brien knew that all too well, recalling how in 1928 Al Smith had drawn the biggest crowd his hometown of Springfield had ever drawn—fifty thousand persons, fully twice what Herbert Hoover would soon attract. But when November came, Hoover swept Springfield.

Larry O'Brien was *very* skeptical of the significance of crowds—though they were indeed very large and would get larger. But not until *after* the debates.

TWENTY-SEVEN

"You bombthrowers probably lost the election"

THE BLACK VOTE was up for grabs—and with millions of African Americans now living *and voting* in the North—it was *worth* grabbing.

By 1950 more blacks (4.8 million) resided in the North than in the old Civil War Confederacy (4.4 million). In the two decades preceding 1960, the black non-Southern population had skyrocketed from 4 million to 9 million—with 1.1 million blacks in New York City alone. Non-Southern African Americans now comprised 48 percent of the nation's total black population.

Beyond that, the black vote was not only growing and strategically situated; it was in play. Historically, African Americans had voted with the Party of Lincoln—and against Southern Democrats—aligning themselves with Democrats only in recent decades. In 1952 and 1956 they wavered. For all his liberal credentials, Stevenson, often counting on white Southern delegates for support, rarely displayed great interest in black concerns. In February 1956, he warned that the nation must "proceed gradually" on desegregation and set the hundredth anniversary of Lincoln's Emancipation Proclamation—1963—as the year public schools might finally be desegregated. Stevenson's prediction was not that far off, but black patience was starting to wear thin. In 1956, 39 percent of blacks—and 47 percent of Southern urban blacks—voted for Eisenhower.

"Of all the major groups in the nation's population," George Gallup reported, "the one that shifted most to the Eisenhower-Nixon ticket was the Negro voter."

An April 1960 Gallup poll found that, by a 28 percent–to–25 percent margin, voters thought the GOP was doing more for the Negro. That was more curse than blessing, however, as most white Southerners thought the GOP was more pro-Negro, while most blacks thought the Democratic Party, the party of the "little person," favored them.

Black votes—scarce in Massachusetts—now spelled both opportunity and danger for JFK. He had skillfully courted Southern Jim Crow votes (at the 1956 convention, George Wallace escorted Eunice Kennedy Shriver to address Alabama's delegation), and blacks noticed. Even passages in *Profiles in Courage* seemed suspect, as JFK branded Reconstruction "a black nightmare the South could never forget," excoriating "the more radical Republican leaders who sought to administer the downtrodden South as conquered provinces."

As segregationist *Birmingham Post-Herald* syndicated columnist John Temple Graves (a great-grand-nephew of U.S. senator John C. Calhoun) observed, "[JFK] is too honest and New England-bred—and political—to take the Southern position on the race question, but he will never be a fanatic against us as Reuther or Nixon." When Graves observed that Kennedy might prove a "living antithesis of Earl Warren," Kennedy dispatched a gracious thank-you note to Graves, indicating his pleasure in adopting a "moderate philosophy on behalf of the national interest," as he did indeed "feel a common bond with many Southerners."

In 1957 JFK exacerbated black fears by informing the American Association of School Administrators that he favored "leaving all control over education itself, of course, in local hands"—to blacks, code words for segregation. In August 1957 he voted—with Southern Democrats—to allow jury trials in federal civil rights cases.

In June 1959 Kennedy invited the militantly segregationist Alabama governor John M. Patterson and his aide Sam Englehardt, leader of the local White Citizens Council, to breakfast at his Georgetown home. When Patterson jumped the gun and immediately endorsed Kennedy's presidential bid, blacks were enraged. "It is very difficult," worried the NAACP's Roy Wilkins, "for thoughtful Negro leaders to feel at ease over the endorsement of Senator Kennedy by Governor Patterson."

Chastened, JFK furiously courted the black vote. Through Joe Kennedy's lobbying, in May 1960, he hired Notre Dame University's Harris Wofford to command his campaign's civil rights section: "We really don't know much about this whole thing," JFK admitted. "I haven't known many Negroes in my life. . . . It's up to you. Tell us where we are and go to it."

When, however, the white Wofford suggested that *blacks* should assume a position of authority on Kennedy's campaign civil rights staff, RFK put his foot down. "The time isn't right," he said. "We'd lose the election."

But the ensuing campaign only convinced JFK of the importance of African American votes. Theorizing that he had garnered black support in West Virginia because of KKK alumnus Robert Byrd's opposition, he became convinced it was "absolutely fatal to have Southern support. I want to be nominated by the liberals. I don't want to go screwing around with all those Southern bastards."

At Los Angeles, as at previous Democratic conventions, the civil rights plank threatened to be the platform's most contentious and dangerous section. Anticipating Southern resistance, Wofford and Chester Bowles (chairman of the resolutions committee) loaded up their draft with everything civil rights advocates might want (and more), calculating that they would have to bargain away its more advanced recommendations—if they could even sneak them past JFK. Kennedy backed them to the hilt. "When I finally got to Bowles to tell him that the Kennedy word was out to support his *maximum* plank," Wofford recalled, "he couldn't believe it."

Nonetheless, JFK continued playing a double game, simultaneously courting black integrationists and Jim Crow Southerners. His selection of Lyndon Johnson only confirmed that to suspicious blacks and liberals. To Virginia governor Lindsay Almond, JFK pledged respect for the "principles Virginians stand for." In August, JFK privately vowed to Georgia governor Ernest Vandiver (married to Richard Russell's niece) never to send federal troops into his state (à la Eisenhower in Little Rock) to enforce integration.

Back and forth, back and forth, the Kennedys maneuvered. Robert Kennedy viewed unregistered blacks as a key component of his plan to register millions of new Democratic voters. In New York he hired twenty-eight-year-old East Harlem attorney Herman Badillo to do the job, and Badillo increased registration by 48 percent. But not every old-line politician appreciated RFK's move. "Kennedy is an asshole for sending in all these jerks to register the niggers," one St. Louis labor leader complained to Tip O'Neill.

Yet blacks remained wary. LBJ's nomination rankled—their fears perhaps compounded by unseemly stories emanating from Washington and Texas. "He especially liked to call me 'nigger,'" recalled Robert Parker, Johnson's bartender, waiter, and chauffeur, "in front of Southerners and racists like Richard Russell." Once, LBJ inquired if Parker wanted to be called by name. He replied affirmatively. "Let me tell you one thing, nigger," LBJ snapped, "as long as you are black, [and] you're gonna be black till the day you die, no one's gonna call you by your goddamn name. . . . Just pretend you're a piece of furniture."

Also counterproductive were Harry Truman's recent statements that the sit-in movement was communist influenced. And though history has largely forgotten it, there remained the issue of black anti-Catholic bigotry. "I'll tell you why I'm really voting against Kennedy," said one Harlem bartender to a reporter. "I'm a Baptist. Do I have to say any more?"

Exceedingly standoffish—but morally flexible—was controversial Harlem Democratic congressman Adam Clayton Powell Jr., who was for Eisenhower in 1956 and for Symington and then LBJ in 1960 before Los Angeles (Powell had been promised chairmanship of the House Education and Labor Committee). When Kennedy got the nomination, Powell demanded three hundred thousand dollars to campaign for him. He settled for fifty thousand dollars for ten campaign speeches. Powell wasn't the only one with his hand out. Said *Chicago Defender* editor Louis Martin, virtually JFK's only significant black adviser: "Those [black] papers aren't going to do a damn thing for you unless you pay [them] some money."

At Mayor Daley's urging, JFK engaged seventy-four-year-old Chicago South Side congressman William Levi "The Man" Dawson—perhaps as big a crook as Powell—to chair his campaign's Civil Rights Section (CRS). RFK regarded Dawson as "senile," particularly when Dawson advanced ideas such as renaming the CRS the "Minorities Section" (its old title) for fear of "offend[ing] our good Southern friends." Dawson was dispatched to an office, derisively known to Kennedy staffers as "Uncle Tom's Cabin," and ignored until the campaign's end.

More influential, certainly, than either Powell or Dawson was the Reverend Martin Luther King Jr. Until recently, Kennedy had not recognized King's value. As singer Harry Belafonte recruited black entertainers for JFK, he told Kennedy he ought to get to know King. "Why do you see him as important?" Kennedy shot back. "What can he do?"

And what *would* he do? "It is an open secret among many Negroes," noted *The Reporter* magazine in October 1960, "that the Reverend Martin Luther King, if he were to speak out on the subject, would probably indicate a preference for Nixon over Kennedy."

Nonetheless, JFK courted King, meeting with him for ninety minutes in June at Joe Kennedy's Fifth Avenue apartment. King, with little expectations, was pleasantly surprised—almost shocked—by Kennedy's attitude. Still he remained neutral—even following a second late-September meeting.

Increasingly nervous regarding the black vote, Kennedy now desired a *public* meeting with King. MLK countered by suggesting a joint King-Kennedy-Nixon summit in Florida (both candidates were in Miami for a mid-October American Legion convention). "The hell with that," JFK shouted at Harris Wofford. "Nixon might be smart enough to accept. If he does, I lose votes. I'm taking a much greater risk in the South than Nixon, but King wants to treat us as equals. Tell him it's off."

Which left King no excuse not to remain in Atlanta for an October 19 sit-in at Rich's Department Store—something MLK wanted to delay until after the election. Arrested with thirty-five others, King refused bail. Anticipating a quick release, he spent his first night ever behind bars. Back on September 23, however, he had received a twenty-five-dollar fine for traffic violations (expired plates and an expired Alabama license) plus twelve months' probation—predicated on his not violating "any Federal or State penal statutes or municipal ordinances." Now segregationist DeKalb County judge J. Oscar Mitchell, ruling that King had violated those terms, sentenced him to four months' hard labor at remote Reidsville Penitentiary.

Fears grew that Dr. King might not survive Reidsville's harsh regimen. And national Democrats feared that black voters might blame their party for Mitchell's outrage.

A distraught Coretta Scott King ("They are going to kill him. I know they are going to kill him"), six months pregnant, phoned Harris Wofford begging for help. Unable to reach JFK, Wofford had Chester Bowles phone his sympathies (Adlai Stevenson refused a similar request). Wofford and Sargent Shriver sped to catch JFK before his departure from

Chicago, tracking him down at a motel outside O'Hare Airport. "Why don't you telephone Mrs. King and give her your sympathy?" Shriver pled. "Negroes don't expect everything will change tomorrow no matter who's elected, but they do want to know whether you care. If you telephone Mrs. King, they will know that you understand and will help. You will reach their hearts and give support to a pregnant woman who is afraid her husband will be killed."

It was a simple act, marvelously compassionate and effective, but not without risks (King had been stopped in September basically for driving with a white woman). JFK, rather casually, agreed to it. "I want to express my concern about your husband," JFK, sprawled on his hotel bed, reassured Mrs. King. "I know this must be very hard on you. I understand you are expecting a baby, and I just wanted you to know that I was thinking about you and Dr. King. If there is anything I can do to help, please feel free to call me."

"It certainly made me feel good," Coretta King informed reporters, "that he called me personally and let me know how he felt. I had the feeling that if he was that much concerned, he would do what he could so that Dr. King was let out of jail. I have heard nothing from the vice president or anyone on his staff. Mr. Nixon has been very quiet."

Had the incident ended there, it might have produced merely marginal effects on the election, but a second act to the drama would soon transpire. Learning of his brother's actions, RFK exploded at Shriver and Wofford: "You bombthrowers probably lost the election. . . . You've probably lost three states and . . . the civil rights section isn't going to do another damn thing in this campaign.

"Do you know that three Southern governors told us that if Jack Kennedy supported Jimmy Hoffa, Nikita Khrushchev, or Martin Luther King, they would throw their states to Nixon? Do you know that this election may be razor close and you have probably lost it for us?"

RFK's second reaction was a deeper, more principled, outrage. He decided to call Judge Mitchell directly, phoning him from a New York pay phone. "Yes, it just burned me all the way up here on the plane," RFK recalled. "It grilled me. The more I thought about the injustice of it, the more I thought what a son of a bitch that judge was. I made it clear to him that it was not a political call; that I am a lawyer, one who believes in the right of all defendants to make bond and one who had seen the rights of defendants misused in various ways . . . and I wanted to make it clear that I opposed this. I felt it was disgraceful." Mitchell, publicly complaining of Bobby's "heavy pressure," nonetheless released King on a two-thousand-dollar bond.

That is the *legend* of Bobby Kennedy's call. The truth is more prosaic, more nuanced, more Machiavellian.

That RFK would make a volte-face so quickly and spontaneously seems problematical. That hard-shell segregationist Judge Mitchell would not tell Bobby what to *do* with his outrage seems only more so.

In actuality, it was JFK—not RFK—who maintained momentum, phoning Georgia governor Ernest Vandiver (the same Vandiver to whom JFK had promised never to send troops into Georgia), requesting Vandiver's assistance in securing King's release ("if I called the judge, . . . he thought that the judge would let Martin Luther King off, and that that would be helpful"). Once Vandiver assented, JFK requested that the governor phone Bobby to suggest he then phone Mitchell.

The reasons for such circumnavigation are obvious: to protect both JFK and Vandiver from political fallout. Segregationist Vandiver ("Wherever M. L. King, Jr., has been there has followed in his wake a wave of crimes including stabbing, bombings, and inciting of riots, barratry, destruction of property and many others. For these reasons, he is not welcome to Georgia") wanted no credit for freeing agitator King—he thought it would be "political suicide." And JFK, his candidacy hanging by a thread, wanted deniability if the episode blew up in everyone's face.

Vandiver's brother-in-law and political ally Bob Russell suggested that Georgia Democratic party secretary George D. Stewart (who had originally secured Oscar Mitchell's judicial appointment) act as Vandiver's go-between with Mitchell—adding yet more deniability to events. Stewart phoned Mitchell, secured his support, perhaps dangling a federal judgeship before him, and reported back to Vandiver, who then, per JFK's instructions, contacted Bobby (RFK was, said Vandiver, "expecting my call"). Thus, by the time Bobby finally called Mitchell, all the heavy lifting had been done.

"Bob," said Judge Mitchell to RFK, "it's nice to talk to you. And I don't have any objection about doing that [releasing King]."

The white press—even in the South—paid scant attention to the incident (seriously overshadowed as it was by the fourth Kennedy-Nixon debate and its aftershocks). But word quickly rippled through the black community, a situation assisted by the distribution of two million copies of a blue-colored four-page pamphlet, *The Blue Bomb*. Crafted by Wofford and Louis Martin and headlined "The Case of Martin Luther King, Jr.," it contrasted "'No Comment' Nixon versus 'A Candidate with a Heart,' Senator Kennedy." Millions of blue bombs detonated in black neighborhoods the Sunday before Election Day.

On black radio stations, the JFK team ran this ad:

Listen to Dr. Ralph Abernathy: "I honestly and sincerely feel that it is time for all of us to take off our Nixon buttons because Kennedy did something great and wonderful when he personally called Mrs. Coretta King and helped free Dr. Martin Luther King, Jr. This is the kind of act I was waiting for. It was not just Dr. King on trial. America was on trial. Mr. Nixon could have helped but he refused to even comment on the case. Since Kennedy showed his great concern for humanity when he acted first without counting the cost, he has my whole hearted support. This is the kind of man we need at this hour."

Dr. King's father, "Daddy" King, Baptist—and anti-Catholic to the core—had planned on voting for Nixon. The incident turned him—and others like him—around. "I had expected to vote against Senator Kennedy because of his religion," King Sr. bluntly admitted ten days before Election Day. "But now he can be my President, Catholic or whatever he is. It took courage to call my daughter-in-law at a time like this. He had the moral courage to stand up for what he knows is right. I've got all my votes, and I've got a suitcase, and I'm going up there and dump them in his lap."

"He was going to vote against me because I was a Catholic," Jack Kennedy marveled to Arthur Schlesinger Jr., "but since I called his daughter-in-law, he voted for me! That was a helluva bigoted statement, wasn't it?"

"Imagine, Martin Luther King having a bigot for a father." JFK grinned. "Well, we all have fathers, don't we?"

TWENTY-EIGHT

"The most dangerous man in America"

MARTIN LUTHER KING *Sr.* had endorsed Jack Kennedy, but Martin Luther King *Jr.* studiously never endorsed either Kennedy or Nixon, which meant that in 1960 the candidate enjoying the most prominent black advocate was . . .

. . . Richard Nixon.

The vice president's prominent ally was Jack Roosevelt "Jackie" Robinson, the first African American in twentieth-century Major League Baseball and the very embodiment not merely of postwar integration, but also of the great tension gripping blacks as they struggled with issues of accommodation and resistance, of principle and practicality—issues that could chew up a man and make him angry.

They made Jackie Robinson *very* angry.

Before Robinson joined Brooklyn in 1947, Dodgers general manager Branch Rickey (an active Republican and teetotaling Methodist) had counseled him that forbearance would be his lot, at least at first. "I'm looking for a ball player with guts enough not to fight back," Rickey warned, and through his first Brooklyn season Robinson contained his temper and his rage. But, forever after, he would not suffer fools or racists or halfhearted reformers gladly, on the ballfield or on the political field.

And in 1960 he would be supporting Richard Nixon.

★ ★ ★

By 1950s standards Richard Nixon exhibited remarkably liberal tendencies on race. An honorary NAACP member, he impressed American blacks during a March 1957 eight-nation African tour. More substantively, in 1957 Nixon issued rulings from his Senate presiding officer's chair to limit filibusters and to allow civil rights measures to bypass Mississippi arch-segregationist James Eastland's Judiciary Committee and move directly to the floor.

Clouding everything, however, was Nixon's connection to the Eisenhower administration's go-slow policies. Worse, when a black reporter queried Nixon regarding his earlier opposition to the Humphrey-Ives Fair Employment Practices Bill, he retorted, "I'll have you know I voted against it and if it comes up again, I'll do the same."

Nonetheless, with Jack Kennedy's weaknesses so visible, Richard Nixon remained a viable option for black voters—particularly for Jackie Robinson. Retired from baseball following the 1956 season, Robinson secured employment as personnel director for the New York–based Chock full o'Nuts coffee company, and, commencing in April 1959, as a thrice-weekly columnist for the *New York Post*. All the while, his activism grew.

Of all major national figures, Robinson disliked two in earnest: Dwight Eisenhower ("more interested in golf than he is in civil rights") and Jack Kennedy (for his pattern of accommodation toward Southern Democratic segregationists). Robinson never forgave JFK's ill-advised June 1959 breakfast with Alabama governor Patterson. "I cannot move [that] barrier," Robinson wrote to Chester Bowles, "that was placed before me."

But as 1960 began, Robinson—often Republican leaning, but actually a registered independent—faced a decision regarding his presidential preferences. Richard Nixon remained an option, as did Hubert Humphrey. Humphrey "impresses me," thought Robinson, "as a man you can trust." Jack Kennedy did not.

In March 1960 Robinson campaigned for Humphrey in Wisconsin. RFK charged that Robinson was financially compensated for his efforts. "Whoever originated such a story," Robinson fumed, "is a liar."

JFK, desiring a truce, conferred with Robinson at Chester Bowles's Georgetown home on Wednesday evening, June 29. Rarely did Kennedy's charm fare so poorly. "You've got to look them in the eye," Robinson would later complain—and JFK did not. Robinson expected straightforward answers, and felt he had not received them. "I had to challenge Kennedy six times."

"Mr. Robinson," Kennedy said in expiation, "I don't know much about the problems of the colored people since I come from New England."

"I figured the hell with that," Robinson fumed. "Any man in Congress for fifteen [*sic*] years ought to make it his business to know colored people."

Kennedy asked what Robinson needed to come on board. "I don't want your money," Robinson exploded. "I'm just interested in helping the candidate who I think will be best for the black American."

JFK, attempting damage control, soon wrote to Robinson, reiterating his commitment to civil rights ("If anyone expects the next Democratic Administration to betray the cause of human rights, he can look elsewhere for leadership"), rationalizing his notorious breakfast with Governor Patterson, and reiterating his goal of "an end to all discrimination—in voting, in education, in housing, in employment, in the administration of justice, and in public facilities, including lunch counters."

Kennedy's letter mollified Robinson only temporarily, as their truce exploded with JFK's selection of LBJ as his running mate. That left Richard Nixon—by now paralyzed by indecision in many areas, not the least of these being race—as Robinson's only option. Nixon knew he must retain a significant portion of the black vote—crucial in key Northern states—though marvelous vistas seemed to be opening to him in the South, which was skittish regarding both the Democratic platform and Kennedy's religion. The largest crowd Richard Nixon would attract in his entire campaign was on August 26, at downtown Atlanta's Five Points intersection, overflowing Woodruff Park, spilling out onto Peachtree Street—a massive 150,000 persons, most, though not all, white. Dwight Eisenhower had already achieved remarkable inroads in the normally solid South:

SOUTHERN VOTING

	Democratic	Republican
1928	48%	52%
1932	76%	24%
1936	76%	24%
1940	73%	27%
1944	69%	31%
1948	70% (incl. Dixiecrats)	30%
1952	51%	49%
1956	49%	51%

Now, the remarkable sight of 150,000 cheering Georgians reinforced Richard Nixon's already burgeoning hopes of carrying the South. He would do nothing to jeopardize his historic chance—he might, after all, *exceed* what Ike had already accomplished. "The South," concluded Ralph de Toledano, "seemed solidly his."

It was heady stuff, and as Nixon maneuvered a middle line between the races, he ultimately satisfied no one. Nonetheless, he was not Jack Kennedy, and he was not entirely without merit, so Jackie Robinson signed on to the Nixon team. "Jack thought blacks should have a say in both parties," his wife Rachel later remembered. "That was his main reason for supporting Nixon. I remained a Democrat, and we often argued about that."

Richard Nixon was also not *Robert* Kennedy, who on WMCA's *Barry Gray Show* now charged not only that Jackie's politics were harming American blacks but also that Chock full o'Nuts owner William Black was a reactionary, anti-labor Republican Nixon backer. Robinson countered that Black was, in fact, a registered Liberal Party member and a five-thousand-dollar donor to Humphrey's effort. "If [RFK] is going to resort to lies," Robinson stormed, "then I can see what kind of campaign this is going to be. I don't see where my company has anything at all to do with his brother's . . . breakfast with . . . the racist Governor of Alabama."

"To me," Robinson added, "the most revealing [item] was Robert Kennedy's reference to 18 million Negro Americans as 'his Negroes'—meaning Jackie Robinson's. . . . I don't run any plantation and I suggest to Kennedy that he stop acting as if he did."

Meanwhile, Nixon steadily frittered away his advantages vis-à-vis blacks. Handed an issue—such as that the Kennedy family's largest real-estate holding, the four-million-square-foot Chicago Merchandise Mart, hired blacks only in the most menial of positions—Nixon refused to touch it, arguing that he would campaign only against JFK and not against his family (a decision "I take sole responsibility for"). What Nixon said was true—he had eschewed *any* attacks on Joe or Bobby. Consistency, however, did nothing to help him in the black community.

Nor did lack of effort. "No literature, no workers, no assistants," is how Nixon's top black aide E. Frederic Morrow, a former NAACP field secretary on leave from the White House, described the Nixon campaign's minority outreach. "Unlike the Eisenhower campaigns . . . I was never seen with the Vice-President. I rode in caravans in a rear car and was never called into parleys or strategy meetings. . . . I never had a dime to spend for anything other than personal expenses." Nixon failed to appear before an all-black group until September 13.

Worse still was the cancellation of a scheduled Nixon appearance before black Chicago clergy and business leaders. As Bob Haldeman crudely informed veteran Nixon aide James Bassett, "The boss says he ain't going to do that nigger thing in Chicago." When Bassett (generally convinced that Nixon was "consciously colorblind") resisted, Haldeman reiterated, "The boss says he ain't going to do that nigger thing."

In Harlem, unknown forces (most likely connected to Adam Clayton Powell) circulated a reproduction of a covenant to Nixon's Washington home, prohibiting its sale or lease to "Negroes, or to any person or persons of Negro blood or extraction, or to any person of the Semitic race. . . ." Such covenants had been dead letters—struck down by the Supreme Court—for three years before Nixon signed his deed. The attack may have been unfair—but it was effective.

Henry Cabot Lodge was not effective. At an East Harlem rally, on Wednesday evening, October 12, Lodge outlined the ticket's civil rights program to a largely uninterested, largely Puerto Rican crowd. He spoke of the need to desegregate the entire national school system or its public facilities. And then he said: "There should be a Negro in the Cabinet. . . . That is our program . . . a pledge that will be redeemed."

Lodge's was an ambitious, enthusiastic move, with none of the usual hedging that often marked either ticket's civil rights posturing. Had it been followed up on, it might have captured significant portions of the black electorate. Yet it was fraught with strategic peril. Not cleared with Nixon, Lodge's statement jeopardized any hoped-for Southern exodus to the GOP. "Whoever recommended that Harlem speech ought to have been thrown out of an airplane from 25,000 feet," grumbled one Virginia Republican. Particularly controversial was Lodge's pledge of a black cabinet member. It was this promise, rather than his call to desegregate the school system, that ignited widespread debate.

"With respect to any appointments to the Cabinet," Nixon, campaigning in California, quickly backtracked, "I will attempt to appoint the best man possible without regard to race, creed or color"—strictly speaking, a not offensive or illogical position, but with an aide quickly chiming in that Nixon would not appoint a black just to appoint a black, Nixon appeared to be in full, panicked retreat mode.

"This," noted Jackie Robinson, no doubt with understatement, "did not sit well with me."

Democrats gleefully pointed to Republican disunity, smugly capitalizing on the dangerous civil rights issue. Lodge's pledge, charged JFK, was "racism in reverse at its worst."

"Will we have Mr. Lodge passing out cabinet posts," Johnson asked on a rare Northeastern campaign swing, "and Mr. Nixon turning them down?"

Meanwhile the Nixon-Lodge campaign fumbled attempts at damage control. Conferring with Republican leaders at Hartford's Hotel Bond, Lodge exited claiming his pledge "wasn't even mentioned." Nixon ("We talked about that") departed, claiming otherwise.

And then, Detroit Democratic representative Charles C. Diggs Jr. charged that the Eisenhower administration's highest ranking black, assistant labor secretary J. Ernest Wilkins, "was thrown out" so Lodge's son George might occupy his twenty-thousand-dollar-a-year post. Lodge denied the accusation, but, also facing Diggs's charges of reneging on his Harlem pledge, he now reiterated his earlier controversial promise: "If Richard Nixon is elected, there will be a qualified Negro on the Cabinet."

"Let [Kennedy] declare where he stands," jeered Lodge. "If he's against it, let him say it."

JFK didn't bite.

Lodge's lone-ranger gambit "hurt us in the South unquestionably," Nixon later reflected, "and it did us no good in the North. To Negroes . . . it appeared to be a crude attempt to woo [them] without regard to the qualifications an individual might have for high office—something that Lodge had never remotely intended to suggest." What had really hurt the ticket with blacks, however, was how Nixon had fled from the pledge. But that fumble proved a mere innocent prologue to one that Nixon would soon commit with no help whatsoever from Lodge— Nixon's inaction following Martin Luther King's arrest.

Nixon had first met King in Accra, Ghana, in 1957. In September 1958, King wrote to Earl Mazo, praising Nixon: "Nixon would have done much more . . . in race relations than President Eisenhower. . . . Much of the tension in the south and many of the reverses . . . could have been avoided [with] a strong, positive stand. . . . Nixon, I believe, would have done that."

Yet something—a lot of things—bothered King about Nixon. He continued: "Nixon has a genius for convincing you he is sincere. When you are close to Nixon he almost disarms you with his apparent sincerity. . . . [I]f Richard Nixon is not sincere, he is the most dangerous man in America."

On their own, perhaps neither Kennedy nor Nixon would have intervened to free Dr. King. Both were urged to do so by advisers. Kennedy did. Nixon didn't.

Campaigning for Nixon in the Midwest, Jackie Robinson importuned fellow Nixon aide Leonard Garment. "He has to call . . . right now; I have the number of the jail." Frederick Morrow felt the same. Yet when Herb Klein asked Nixon how to respond, Nixon blandly answered: "I think Dr. King is getting a bum rap. But despite my strong feelings in this respect, it would be completely improper for me or any other lawyer to call the judge. And Robert Kennedy should have known better than to do so." Klein told reporters, "No comment."

Nixon looked to the administration for cover, requesting Attorney General Rogers to have Eisenhower press secretary Jim Hagerty issue a statement. The White House refused, but even if it had, Jim Hagerty wasn't the candidate on the spot. Richard Nixon was, and, in the eyes of American blacks, he had failed the test.

"I had known Nixon longer," King would write. "He had been supposedly close to me, and he called me frequently for my advice. And yet, when this moment came it was like he had never heard of me. . . . I considered him a moral coward and one who was unwilling to take a courageous step and take a risk."

Frederick Morrow jumped ship. Jackie Robinson nearly did—prominent black psychologist Dr. Kenneth Clark lobbied him to do so. Robert Kennedy and reporter Carl Rowan lobbied Rachel Robinson. Branch Rickey convinced Robinson otherwise.

"It is easy . . . to make . . . a 'grandstand play,'" Nixon wrote Robinson, "but you and I know that real progress in the civil rights field is best advanced by the day to day, consistent application of the principles which we know are sound."

This was small comfort for Jackie Robinson, who had been suspended from his *New York Post* column (never to be rehired) for supporting a candidate—one he now no longer believed in.

"He thinks calling Martin would be grandstanding," Robinson mourned. "Nixon doesn't deserve to win."

TWENTY-NINE

"No one could tell him anything"

AT 8 P.M. CDT, Monday, September 26, 1960, Politics As Usual expired.

Cause of Death: four one-hour television broadcasts.

The Suspects: one Act of Congress, two presidential candidates, three television networks, four moderators, sixteen panelists, and (give or take ten million viewers) seventy million men, women, and children, hunkered down in America's living rooms—alternately transfixed by the spectacle before them and desiring nothing more (or less) than a return to their regularly scheduled programming.

The age of the presidential debate had arrived.

Face-to-face. Hour-long. One following upon the other. Careening from topic to topic. Jettisoning nuance for slogan. Public policy ruled by the tick of the second hand.

Government by gotcha.

Lights. Camera. Rhetoric . . .

. . . and, of course, a novelty that changed the course of the 1960 election and almost every presidential campaign since.

Presidential debates.

Superficially, a hankering to air the day's vital issues had propelled the demand for debates. In actuality, issues provided a mere excuse. What America truly craved was the bare-knuckle collision of personalities—not political scientists' facts and economists' figures but lacerated flesh and spurting blood; not the snippy, measured repartee of oak-paneled academic halls or the carefully calibrated logic of official white papers but the drama of the prizefight ring, the nail-biting tension of quiz-show isolation booths.

At the very moment of Richard Nixon's nomination, NBC chairman Robert W. Sarnoff had telegraphed both Nixon and JFK, inviting their participation in the "Great Debate" (Sarnoff coined the phrase)—an invitation initially garnering just three paragraphs on page 14 of the *New York Times*. Kennedy—veteran of debates against Humphrey in Wisconsin and

Johnson in Los Angeles, as well as Lodge on live TV in October 1952—
hesitated not an instant. Had Sarnoff not acted, Kennedy would have.
Pierre Salinger recalled:

> I took the telegram to [Kennedy]. He made an immediate reaction—
> "Why not?" . . . Within twenty minutes . . . we had sent off a
> telegram . . . saying we wanted to do it. The feeling was that we had
> absolutely nothing to lose by a debate with Nixon. If we accepted right
> away, that would put Nixon in a position where he had to accept.
> Everybody just felt that the debates would be most helpful to Kennedy.

And helpful to the networks. CBS and ABC quickly came aboard,
as did Richard Nixon—at least in principle. But the devil resided, as
ever, in the details. Even with everyone's tentative agreement, nothing
could really move forward until Congress suspended Section 315 of the
Federal Communications Act of 1934—the Equal Time Rule—which
it did that August, though only for the 1960 election and only for
national candidates.

Details now mattered, but few meaningful precedents existed. Would
Americans now witness an actual debate, as Tom Dewey and Harold
Stassen had battled back in the 1948 Oregon primary, one candidate hammering the other? Who would moderate? What powers might that moderator possess? How long would the debates last? NBC and CBS had
originally offered eight hours; ABC proposed nine (with segments alternating between networks). What would the internal time limits be? The
locations? The stage layouts? If candidates took questions—from whom?
From which networks? From radio? TV? Or the print media? Or why
limit questions to the press? Nixon's people toyed with the idea of questions from representatives of various interest groups. But which groups?
When would debates begin? Or end? All such questions meant that the
decision-making process wasn't just Kennedy versus Nixon but CBS
versus NBC versus ABC and radio versus television and electronic media
versus print. To complicate matters further, at one point Sarnoff even proposed commercial sponsorship.

The Great Debate—brought to you by the Chicago Merchandise
Mart.

It's a wonder debates were ever held.

But they were. Because ultimately everyone, no matter how reluctantly, wanted them staged. Everyone needed them. The media had its reasons—ratings and circulation and prestige. So did the candidates. John Kennedy had to demonstrate that he—an inexperienced, some said unqualified, contender—could survive, toe to toe, against tough, seasoned debater Nixon. Nixon needed to prove he wasn't afraid of the glamorous upstart Kennedy. He also needed, after all, to entice a minimum of five million Democrats and independents to cross over to him. He wasn't Eisenhower. It wasn't a matter of merely retaining support. Richard Nixon, upstart in his own right, had yet to gain it.

At least, that was how he eventually saw it. Originally, Nixon strongly opposed debating. So did his advisers. Debates would merely raise Kennedy's profile, inflate his still meager stature. Nixon, however, thought he might yet dance around the subject. Herb Klein recalled, "We . . . would tepidly support [suspending] Article 315. . . . While we gave lip service to the change in law, we had met with Nixon on it, and he had been an outspoken, strong advocate of avoiding a debate on the principle that a President or Vice-president is in a position where he cannot answer all the questions fully because of his knowledge of security information."

Very sound reasoning—that imploded in the wake of Robert Sarnoff's very public, very high-profile challenge. Suddenly Nixon—as so often in his career, with trips to Nelson Rockefeller's Fifth Avenue triplex, to Mao and Peking, to the Lincoln Memorial at midnight, with the institution of wage and price controls and affirmative action—shifted gears so quickly they smoked and stripped. Abruptly, at a Blackstone Hotel press conference in the wake of his nomination, Richard Nixon proclaimed he would debate, not even deigning to inform his closest advisers of his radical volte-face.

As Herb Klein remembered:

I was standing a few feet away from him . . . and almost fell over. . . . Len Hall [heard] it from a reporter and Bob Finch from me. Nixon avoided all discussion with us as to why he had changed his mind or at exactly what moment he had made the decision. I could attribute the reversal only to the fact that he did not want his manhood sullied by appearing as if he were afraid to debate his opponent face-to-face, and he was confident that he could win. . . . On the other hand, he rightfully believed that a refusal to debate would be used by Kennedy as an issue and would be heavily emphasized by network newsmen, who . . . were pressing hard for . . . debates.

Klein thought Nixon viewed the issue as one of "manhood," but such an emotion-based rationale excludes the ever-present question of cool, "flexible" Nixon calculation. Nixon knew he was a skilled, effective debater. It was not mere ego or fear at work. He had distinguished himself in high school, and at Whittier and Duke: He was an expert, prize-winning debater. He had advanced up the political ladder by demolishing Jerry Voorhis and Helen Gahagan Douglas in face-to-face debates.

Yes, Richard M. Nixon could debate.

However, he had something to prove in high school and college and against Voorhis and Douglas. Now, he was vice president of the United States, with little or nothing to establish upon the debate platform. Beyond that, John Kennedy, no matter how lackadaisical his congressional reputation, was no pushover—no Voorhis or Douglas, or any of the hapless academic debaters Nixon had so easily demolished.

The John Kennedy of 1960 was simply *not* the John Kennedy of 1947—all skin and bones and shyness and lacking in real purpose beyond the ambitions his father and the ghost of his older brother had pushed upon him.

This debater, this current version of John F. Kennedy, was a very different and very dangerous opponent.

Richard Nixon was different, too. Yes, he was now engaged in creating the first (or was it the first? It was difficult to tell) "New Nixon"—less edgy and slashing, more mellow, mature, and diplomatic. He would not blast Jack Kennedy (at least not to his face) for JFK's softness on communism or the unions or big spending or inflation. Even if Nixon wanted to, those charges would stick far less easily than those hurled at Voorhis or Douglas—not only by reason of Kennedy's at best tepid liberalism, but also because of Kennedy's cool, almost uncanny ability to laugh off opponents' barbs, to evade an awkward question, to make adversaries appear foolish and small. Lyndon Johnson knew that all too well and would, certainly, never bring up attendance and quorum calls again—at least, not to Jack Kennedy.

Richard Nixon was mellower—and Jack Kennedy unlike any opponent Richard Nixon, mellow or not, had yet confronted. But Kennedy, for all his flair and wit and intelligence, suffered from his own weaknesses—and before his legend took shape and transformed Kennedy's oddities of manner, accent, and delivery into Camelot glamour, they remained very real deficiencies. As Nixon biographer Fawn Brodie summarized, "Nixon dismissed the Kennedy wit as pedantic. . . . Kennedy when speaking was inclined to rush, and to keep his voice too high. His only gesture was a monotonous poke with his forefinger. Nixon was a seasoned orator with a fine baritone voice."

And beyond all that, television had created—or, at least, repeatedly saved—Richard Nixon. Thirty minutes of the Checkers speech had rescued him when all his friends in the Republican Party wished to pitch him overboard—or at least stand, gaze averted, while someone else did. His televised "kitchen debate" against Khrushchev similarly salvaged his once more sinking fortunes. Reporters, Richard Nixon calculated, might filter and distort his message, demean his character and motives, but live, unedited television and radio radically diminished a hostile media's influence, beaming a direct line to the voters. As 1960 began, remarkable as it seems today, Richard Nixon was *the* candidate of the television age.

Beyond all such factors, however, was a far larger question not of style but of substance, not of tactics but of strategy. In 1946, 1950, and 1952, Richard Nixon had been able to seize the offensive, decrying each New and Fair Deal failure, every communist, every Democratic pinko and egghead. Now, as in 1958's midterm fiasco, Dick Nixon would have to defend Dwight Eisenhower's faltering administration in a world of Castro and Khrushchev and the Congo, of anti-American riots in Caracas and Japan, of falling farm prices and two recessions, of missile gaps and Sputniks and U-2s. Grinning, grandfatherly Dwight Eisenhower's personal popularity had never diminished. That of his administration had.

Nixon could dodge those issues on the campaign trail, or he could frame them in ways he wished them framed. But on a debate stage, live, before millions, Jack Kennedy and a panel of reporters—those damn reporters—would never concede him that privilege. Richard Nixon had to ask himself if he was that good, that skilled, a debater.

And, ultimately, he answered yes—yes, he was.

Even those who agreed with Nixon's assessment of his skills—and many did—viewed his move as abysmally wrongheaded. If Nixon won, he proved what everyone already "knew," thus, he won nothing.

If he lost . . .

That's what Eisenhower thought. So, too, did Jack Kennedy, confiding to aides that his opponent was "a damn fool to agree to debate me on an equal-time TV basis. Just imagine if Eisenhower had had to do this against Stevenson in 1952 and 1956. He would have looked silly."

As quickly as Nixon announced his decision, he regretted it. "Kennedy has everything to gain and very little to lose," he informed Ralph de Toledano, arguing against what he, nonetheless, knew he must do. "I'm better known than [JFK] is and I'm the front-runner. By appearing with me, he'll get far greater exposure than he would on paid television time and alone. And how do I handle him? If I hit him hard, he'll have the sympathy of the audience. If I don't, then I'll look weak."

Nixon, wracked by indecision, reached out to exiled Murray Chotiner, now practicing law in Los Angeles. Chotiner similarly advised against debating JFK "for exactly the same reasons I wanted him to debate Voorhis. He was giving away points to the lesser well-known man." Beyond that, Chotiner believed, Nixon would have to defend the rapidly tarnishing Eisenhower record. It hadn't sold well in 1958. There was nothing to suggest it was any more popular in 1960. But not debating was no longer a real option, and both Nixon and Chotiner knew it. Once committed, Nixon was trapped.

When Nixon formally agreed to Robert Sarnoff's challenge (four days after Sarnoff issued it and four days after JFK formally agreed), he did so by telegram, his key stipulations being for the "full and free exchange of views without prepared texts or notes and without interruption. I think it also is desirable that some of the time offered by the networks be used for individual appearances of the candidates both the uninterrupted expression of their views and for questioning by panels of accredited journalists."

Nixon's initial requests were, thus, rather modest, though had he demanded that the journalistic panel consist of Murray Chotiner, Pat

Nixon, and Checkers, the Kennedy team would probably have acquiesced, desperate as they were to secure Nixon's consent to a face-off. Just staging debates was a Kennedy victory. What the debates were mattered less than that they were held at all.

"I'm not really concerned about the program," JFK's radio and television strategist, J. Leonard Reinsch (on loan from Cox broadcasting), had told Kennedy over clam chowder at Hyannis, just after coming on board. "All I want is a picture of you and Nixon on the same television tube. We'll take it from there."

Nixon and Kennedy functionaries (along with network representatives) conferred a full fifteen times, including three sessions at New York's Waldorf-Astoria, hammering out details. JFK's side, eager to maximize their charismatic and self-assured candidate's exposure, pressed for five debates. Beyond that, although the Kennedy family was rich, the Democratic Party was not. Compared to the Republican Party, it enjoyed relatively little funding for national television. In this sense alone, the debates—roughly two million dollars in free radio and television airtime—were a Democratic Party godsend.

Nixon's camp insisted on a maximum of three debates (Nixon staffer Fred Scribner Jr. thought two would suffice; another staffer just one—"If they [the Democrats] weren't scared, why wouldn't they be willing to pin everything on one show?"), and that they be finished with them relatively early, demanding an October 21 end date. Nixon would later write: "The question we faced was not whether to debate, but how to arrange the debates so as to give Kennedy the least possible advantage."

The logical—and actual—compromise: four one-hour broadcasts, ending on Friday, October 21.

JFK's people expressed no problem with Nixon's ban on "prepared texts or notes." Nor did either side want candidates posing questions and challenges to each other; that would be left to reporters. Recalled *The Reporter* magazine's Douglas Cater, both camps feared "that the candidates would be 'too polite' if they interrogated each other. . . . [S]ince nobody likes the prosecuting-attorney type on television, it was better to turn this thankless task over to others."

Next—settled with precious little controversy—was the issue of who might be present in the studios. As Herb Klein summarized, "We insisted that there be no live audience . . . because we feared a "Kennedy clique" would have emotional impact. Even the press was kept in a separate room, although I escorted pool reporters in and out of the studio at the start and at the conclusion. . . . [R]eporters watch[ed] television monitors, not the actual physical debate."

Nixon demanded one additional condition. Debates two and three would be topically open-ended. Debates one and four would be more specific, one confrontation devoted wholly to domestic issues, the other to foreign affairs. Nixon, in the driver's seat regarding debate formats, got to select which topic would kick-start the series and which would close it. He wrote: "Foreign affairs was my strong suit, and I wanted the larger audience for that debate. I thought most people would watch the first one. . . . Most of my advisors believed that interest would build . . . and that the last program . . . would be the most important one. I yielded to their judgment and agreed."

And so, for once, Richard Nixon, the candidate taking no counsel but his own, heeded his no doubt amazed advisers. Their reasoning discounted the lure of the new and the fragility of public attention, particularly in a format where both candidates—in 1960 and in any year, in any contest—tend to play it safe, to regurgitate stump speech bromides, to quickly erode their welcome. Beyond all this, the Nixon camp had also miscalculated on a very basic level. The first debate was on a Monday, the fourth on a Friday. *People stay home on Monday nights. They go out on Fridays*—even during presidential debates.

Richard Nixon should have listened to his own calculating little heart.

Four dates, four debates in four different cities, hosted by all three television networks, were decided upon:

Monday, September 26, at 9:30 p.m. (Eastern time)—Chicago—CBS
Friday, October 7, at 7:30 p.m.—Cleveland—NBC
Thursday, October 13, at 7:30 p.m.—Nixon in Hollywood; Kennedy in New York City—ABC
Friday, October 21, at 8 p.m.—New York City—ABC

Besides Leonard Reinsch and Pierre Salinger, Kennedy turned to television producer Bill Wilson. Just twenty-nine, Wilson was nonetheless a veteran of both Stevenson campaigns, and while his Stevenson credentials made him more than somewhat suspect to longtime Kennedyites (RFK: "Well, okay, but you better not —— up"), he proved to possess the experience and talent for the job, eventually maneuvering his way close to (though not fully into) the campaign's inner circles. He liked Jack Kennedy's confidence levels—Wilson had no reluctant performer on his hands. JFK oozed self-assurance. He *knew* he could take Nixon, and his aura motivated Bill Wilson to create the circumstances that would make JFK's planned triumph easier.

Beyond Bill Wilson, JFK also had a very special sort of television adviser: brother-in-law Peter Lawford. "Don't be afraid of the camera," Lawford told Jack. "Look directly into it, as though it were a friend across the dinner table. You'll be making contact with millions of people at the same moment, but each one will feel as though you're talking only to him."

It was different in the Nixon camp. For once, Ike offered assistance—the expertise of his own longtime television adviser, the veteran film actor and television and Broadway producer Robert Montgomery. Nixon turned Eisenhower down.

Nixon already had a TV guru, though their relationship lacked—well, it lacked just about everything. Murray Chotiner had lured the largely apolitical thirty-one-year-old Edward A. "Ted" Rogers into Nixon's 1950's Senate campaign, and two years later Rogers produced Nixon's pivotal "Checkers" telecast. Initially, Rogers considered Nixon easy to work with, but the more Dick Nixon learned about the medium, the less he thought others knew. Following his "Checkers" triumph, Nixon proved increasingly uncooperative. In the 1956 campaign, he even physically attacked Rogers, having to be pulled off him by *Baltimore Sun* reporter Phil Potter. By 1960, Rogers loathed Nixon. But, "volunteered" by his present employer, Desilu, he nonetheless returned to action. But even with his impressive title of television adviser, he enjoyed little access to his candidate. Reduced to leaving messages with Nixon's campaign plane, he never knew if Nixon saw them. Ted Rogers was not a happy warrior.

June 1960 witnessed another painful episode. Nixon assembled his campaign staff—Rogers included—to devise strategies for the coming general election. Rogers presented his ideas on streamlining the upcoming convention, enjoyed the session's give-and-take, and thought everything went well. Then he received a call from an embarrassed Len Hall: Nixon didn't like Rogers's ideas. He also didn't appreciate Rogers's manner (not respectful enough), and would henceforth make all the big decisions himself. Rogers (along with a fellow top campaign aide, the *Los Angeles Times* reporter Jim Bassett) wanted to quit. "Rogers [was] staggered by the transformation," David Halberstam would write. "Nixon had changed in a decade from a reasonably approachable young man to a political megalomaniac. No one could tell him anything. He had decided he was the ultimate politician."

Thus, as the campaign roared forward and the debates approached, Richard Nixon had a television adviser who could no longer stomach him, who enjoyed limited access to him, and whose advice Nixon would not take anyway. And, being the great debater that Nixon knew he was, he would do nothing to prepare for his confrontation with Kennedy—not in terms of issue-oriented preparation, nor of physical pacing, nor in review of the telecast's technical details.

He had, nonetheless, been warned.

Nixon may no longer have respected fellow politicians or professional media advisers, but he did respect sports figures. He loved sports, and when, just following the Chicago convention, West Point's legendary football coach Earl "Red" Blaik wrote to Nixon advising him to pace himself, Richard Nixon took notice.

"It is just as important to plan your campaign with the understanding of possible physical attrition as it is to plan the presentation of issues," Blaik wrote, specifically noting the importance of television and warning that a candidate "must always project as the relaxed, confident, fresh and unwearied candidate. . . . [Y]ou must have sufficient rest, diversion and change of pace to eliminate fatigue which comes to us all, but in far greater degree to those whose daily routine is a repetition of speaking engagements, a matter of meeting individuals by the score, endless hours of flying, and the daily planning which is required for victory."

"Fatigue, strain, and just plain being worn out," Blaik summarized, "are all common denominators to the team that should have won but did not."

Nixon read Blaik's letter, thought his counsel reasonable, scrawled "Right" in its margin, and then proceeded to ignore it.

Not all of Nixon's problems resulted from bad judgment. Some resulted from bad luck, compounded by bad judgment, compounded by bad luck. Such a malevolent chain reaction seriously drained his energies as his first confrontation with Kennedy beckoned.

On Wednesday, August 17, Nixon campaigned in Greensboro, North Carolina. Jostled by a large, enthusiastic crowd, he slammed his left knee against his limousine door. Nothing seemed amiss until four days later, when, after bowling with his family at Camp David, he found that his joint had become sore and swollen.

He hobbled back onto the campaign trail, where the pain and swelling only increased. Finally, he consulted White House physician Dr. Walter Tkach, former air force base flight surgeon, who diagnosed the malady as hemolytic staphylococcus, which destroys red blood cells and can permanently destroy cartilage. He told Nixon, "We want you to come out to the hospital right away."

Nixon, being Nixon, and being in the midst of a national campaign, protested. The forty-three-year-old Tkach held firm. "Look, I know what your schedule is," he commanded, "and I'm just as anxious as you are to keep it, but you had better get out to the hospital or you will be campaigning on one leg."

Nixon checked into Walter Reed Army Hospital—its thirty-four-dollar-a-day, second-floor presidential suite—where he was told he'd be in traction for two full weeks. He received treatments of erythromycin, penicillin, and three other antibiotics—as well as visits from Dwight Eisenhower, Nelson Rockefeller (who flew to Washington in his private plane, a button proclaiming "I'm for Nixon" on his lapel), Everett Dirksen, and Lyndon Johnson.

Jack Kennedy, for all his prattling about Nixon's lack of "class," merely sent a telegram. Henry Cabot Lodge didn't show, either.

Doctors released Nixon from Walter Reed two days early, on Friday, September 9—and Nixon struggled desperately to recapture lost time. Kennedy had inched into the lead (51 percent) while Nixon was hospitalized. Dick Nixon had to get moving—and *keep* moving.

Remaining home on Saturday, he appeared on *Meet the Press* on Sunday morning, flying out of Baltimore that Monday, heading for Indianapolis, then to Dallas and San Francisco the same day. The next morning it was Portland, Oregon, then Vancouver, then Washington State and Boise, Idaho. Wednesday saw him in Grand Forks, Peoria, and St. Louis—a grueling schedule for a man just out of a hospital bed. On the flight from Fargo to Peoria he caught cold. Arriving in St. Louis after 11 p.m., he nonetheless worked before turning in, finally getting to bed at 3 a.m.

At 3:30 a.m., he woke up burning with a 103-degree fever. He summoned his campaign physician, Long Beach surgeon Dr. Malcolm C. Todd, demanding to be made healthy enough to speak at 8:30 a.m. to the national convention of the International Association of Machinists, which Kennedy had addressed just the day before. "I don't see how you can possibly do it," Todd responded, but Nixon insisted the convention speech was "essential." In fact, it wasn't. The machinists were going to endorse Kennedy, and nothing Nixon or Lodge or even Eisenhower could do would change that. Still, Nixon told himself—and Todd—that his appearance was "essential," and Todd dutifully pumped enough aspirin and antibiotics into his patient to get him—less feverishly and quite sleeplessly—through the night and the quite pointless event. "I don't know when I have ever felt so weak," Nixon recalled of his trek to the speaker's podium that morning.

Remarkably, miraculously, Nixon performed brilliantly. Yes, Kennedy strolled away with the machinists' endorsement—by a ten-to-one margin—but Richard Nixon, desperately sick as he was, dazzled the hostile labor crowd with his performance and arguments. The *New York Times* reported:

> [I]f the 1,500 convention delegates had been awarding a prize for showmanship, Vice President Nixon almost certainly would have won the honors.
>
> A great majority of the unionists came here preferring the Democratic nominee and they did not waver. . . . They held fast despite a widespread readiness to acknowledge that the Republican candidate had done a more impressive job of stating his viewpoint . . . than their favorite had from the same rostrum twenty-four hours earlier.

Pushing on, Nixon flew to address Republican women in Atlantic City, then to a rally of thirteen thousand at a Roanoke football stadium, and then on to Omaha and Des Moines, reaching Iowa at 1:30 in the morning to deliver a major farm policy speech at 8 a.m. . . . and on . . . and on . . . until he flew out of Washington, D.C., and touched down at Chicago's Midway Airport at 10:30 p.m. CST Sunday night, September 25, having lost ten pounds from his normal, never-heavy frame. Exhausted and worn, Richard Nixon was—worse still—*looking it*.

THIRTY

"He felt cool, calm, and very alert"

DEBATING JOHN FITZGERALD KENNEDY the next evening, Nixon had a plan: to be in bed by midnight.

He wasn't.

Ten thousand Republicans greeted him on the Midway tarmac. He could not properly leave without saying a few words, though there never was such a thing in politics. Three fifteen-minute stops en route to the hotel later, and Richard Nixon's seventy-five-car motorcade arrived at the Pick-Congress Hotel blearily, not sharply, at 1:00 a.m.

Minus a raging fever, it was a virtual repeat of his baleful St. Louis experience—in late and rising early, all for a pointless speech to a hostile labor union. That morning, at Chicago's Morrison Hotel, he would address the United Brotherhood of Carpenters and Joiners.

Unlike Richard Nixon, Jack Kennedy approached this first debate with appropriate seriousness, respecting boundaries of geography and time but also the thresholds of his own constitution—of any human's limitations—within a national campaign's grueling context, and the crucial need for sufficient rest. Cognizant of this debate's high stakes, and having endured a lifetime of bad health, he knew too well how he must pace himself—as did everyone around him. This was particularly true of JFK's own father, who, even under normal circumstances, phoned each night to ensure that the family standard-bearer receive sufficient rest and proper medication.

So while Nixon, who had enjoyed a lifetime of remarkably good health (recent events notwithstanding), even now ignored the limits of human endurance, Kennedy didn't. *The Caroline* landed in Chicago, not at the midnight hour preceding the Great Debate, but two full days earlier. Kennedy arrived fast asleep at Midway from Salt Lake City at 4:15 a.m., Saturday morning, and scheduled no public appearances that day. Then on Sunday he arose at 6 a.m. for an early Mass and a quick round-trip to Cleveland, where at a Euclid Beach Amusement Park steer roast with Mike DiSalle he addressed 120,000 persons (his largest crowd yet; twenty-eight-year-old speechwriter Richard Goodwin thought him visibly preoccupied by the debate). Returning to Chicago, he avoided exhausting motorcades, instead helicoptering into lakefront Meigs Field for a brief rally. On Monday, the day of the debate, he slept in, not appearing before the United Brotherhood of Carpenters until 2:30 that afternoon—and then husbanding his energies by speaking for only fifteen minutes. Nixon wasted thirty-five minutes of time and precious energy speaking to yet another union that would never endorse him.

Beyond that, JFK conferred with aides in preparation for the debate, something the cocksure Nixon did not do. On Monday morning, three key Kennedy staffers—the indispensable Ted Sorensen, Richard Goodwin, and the bespectacled forty-six-year-old Myer "Mike" Feldman—arrived at Kennedy's Ambassador East Hotel suite armed with a footlocker full of research material, three-by-five index card after three-by-five index card, to prime their candidate on the issues of the day—and, perhaps more importantly, on Richard Nixon (Feldman termed his research the "Nixopedia"). They proceeded to force-feed the candidate (always a very quick study) what he needed to know and say, and, just as significantly, what strategic pitfalls he needed to avoid. Starting on the Ambassador Hotel rooftop, then moving to Kennedy's sitting room, they concentrated first on Kennedy's eight-minute opening address (he didn't like what they presented—"too rhetorical"), then spent a full morning drilling facts into Kennedy's head. At midday, JFK dispatched Goodwin and Feldman to research questions the session had developed; he lunched with Sorensen, RFK, and pollster Lou Harris before addressing the Brotherhood of Carpenters.

Harris suggested—as part of a stratagem to deflect any questions about his client's age and maturity—that JFK answer any question in three-part fashion in order to project a warmer image. He urged JFK to slow down his delivery.

Returning to his bedroom, the candidate "napped."

"I go by his door," Harris recalled, "and . . . he's playing Peggy Lee records. So I asked him if he'd taken a nap. He said 'no' and asked where Bobby was. So I went next door and had a hell of a time getting Bobby up. Bobby had taken a nap, which was typical. Bobby was a true believer."

With Goodwin, Feldman, Sorensen, Harris, and Bobby returned to the suite, Jack—flat on his back in T-shirt and khakis—continued cramming.

At debate's end it would, however, be as much about dreams as about factoids, about big pictures as well as little lined, white cards. "We need someone," Henry Kissinger had advised Arthur Schlesinger over lunch in late August, "who will take a big jump—not just improve on existing trends but produce a new frame of mind, a new national atmosphere. If Kennedy debates with Nixon on who can best manage the status quo, he is lost. The issue is not one technical program or another. The issue is a new epoch. If we get a new epoch and a new spirit, the technical programs will take care of themselves."

New epochs. New spirits. New frontiers. Jack Kennedy was good at that.

But Jack Kennedy also possessed an additional advantage beyond Kissingerian *neu epoche politik* and the collected works of Peggy Lee: the glories of speed.

Wearied from months of campaigning, JFK required, for want of a better word, renewed "vigor." To his assistance came forty-two-year-old friend and campaign aide Chuck Spalding, who informed Kennedy of a doctor he had consulted back in Manhattan—hulking, potbellied, heavily accented sixty-year-old German-born Dr. Max Jacobson, aka "Miracle Max," aka "Dr. Feelgood."

"I was working at the J. Walter Thompson advertising agency in New York," Spalding would recall, "and going through a messy divorce that left me just exhausted. A family friend suggested . . . Jacobson, so I went. Well, I walked into his New York office and everybody was sitting in the waiting room—Eddie Fisher, Alan Jay Lerner, Zero Mostel, Johnny Mathis, and several actresses. They were all patients of his, plus half of Hollywood!

"Max was a strange man—loud, arrogant, kind of a mad scientist type. But I was desperate, and I let him give me a shot. Well, I went over the top of the building! I felt wonderful, full of energy—capable of doing just about anything. I didn't know exactly what he was giving me, but it was a magic potion as far as I was concerned."

It was, indeed, *black* magic. Jacqueline Kennedy biographer Barbara Leaming vividly described Dr. Jacobson's malevolent hold upon his cast of celebrity patients:

Some people saw Jacobson as a savant, even a god; others as "cunning and relentless," "corrupt to the core," "a ruiner of lives." His modus operandi was to make his patients so dependent on his injections that they could no longer function independently. When that point was reached, more often than not those lives veered tragically off course. The central element of the Jacobson experience was what actor Patrick O'Neal described as the doctor's desire to make each injection a rite, in which he fostered the grotesque illusion that he was having sex with the patient via his needle.

Once, Spalding absented himself from the campaign trail, on assignment in New York. Again, he visited Dr. Jacobson and returned "raring to go. Jack and I had both been to a party the night before, and he was pooped. 'Where do you get all this energy?' he asked, and when I told him he said he wanted some.

"That made me nervous. I told him, 'If you're thinking of doing it, I'm going to tell Bobby. I can't be responsible.' He said, 'Fine,' and I did. So Bobby knew all about it."

Spalding was right to be nervous. Bobby should have been. Aside from the too-good-to-be-true nature of what Jacobson was peddling, "Miracle Max" was far worse than merely "loud" or "arrogant"—worse even than what Barbara Leaming and Patrick O'Neal described. His office was dirty, littered, and disheveled, his personal hygiene deplorable. "Many of Max's patients ended up with hepatitis," a Jacobson assistant revealed, "because the office was filthy." A Jacobson nurse described him as a "quack," a "butcher," "out of his mind"—on drugs himself.

Cleanliness may be next to godliness, but who cared about cleanliness when you felt godlike after receiving Dr. Feelgood's elixirs. And besides, someone else was recommending Max: Mark Shaw, *Life*'s thirty-eight-year-old staff photographer covering Kennedy's campaign. Shaw, however, was more than a photographer. He and his twenty-six-year-old wife, Broadway star ("Flower Drum Song") Pat Suzuki, were social friends of the Kennedys—as well as Jacobson patients. Shaw—destined to die of a drug overdose—enthusiastically seconded Spalding's recommendation.

Kennedy was sold. After all, Dr. Feelgood wasn't doing anything yet illegal. It just felt that way.

On Wednesday, September 14 (ironically, the day Nixon contracted the flu in Fargo)—two days after JFK's Houston ministers speech and twelve days preceding the first debate—Kennedy, under strict secrecy, alone and having ditched his Secret Service escort, surreptitiously slipped into Jacobson's 155 East Seventy-second Street offices. Jacobson's normally crowded practice was emptied of patients. Only his wife Nina and a nurse remained. Kennedy complained of feeling drained, of losing concentration.

"The demands of his political campaign were so great he felt fatigued," Jacobson recalled. "His muscles felt weak. It interfered with his concentration and affected his speech. I was not at all surprised. These constituted the most common symptoms of stress."

Jacobson injected Kennedy with a mysterious concoction of drugs (generally conceded to be 75 percent amphetamines—largely Dexedrine, steroids, calcium, animal placentas, and vitamins; Jacobson by and large favored Vitamin B).

A warm rush exploded through Kennedy's body.

"After his treatment," Jacobson concluded, "[JFK] told me that his muscle weakness had disappeared. He felt cool, calm, and very alert. I gave him a bottle of vitamin drops to be taken orally."

It would not be the last time Max Jacobson would treat John F. Kennedy.

Inside the Ambassador East, JFK's cramming continued. Instinctively, the Kennedy team understood how to win in a format not yet invented. In this televised presidential "debate," soaring rhetoric remained essential, but wouldn't by itself turn the trick. Kennedy had to master the dynamics of one of early TV's most popular—and, already, most disgraced—formats, the quiz show. He would need to marshal a semester's quotient of seemingly arcane facts, factoids, slogans, and figures, all to be disgorged at the flick of a reporter's query. It was the type of minutiae that, in real management, a chief executive left to his subalterns.

Finally, there was more to JFK's long Chicago weekend than campaigning and cramming; there was also time for socializing. On Saturday,

JFK visited with Chicagoans Sargent and Eunice Shriver and their three children, Robert, Maria, and Timothy. But, as usual, Jack Kennedy may have had "other" forms of human interaction in mind.

More likely, however, he did not.

The story goes like this, and while many wild and unlikely stories about JFK in the end prove unfortunately, sordidly true, this one falls into the highly doubtful category. But as the years progress, and as it becomes more and more entrenched in the canon of political literature, it deserves to be noted—and questioned. The story first surfaced in C. David Heymann's 1989 best-selling Jackie Kennedy biography, *A Woman Named Jackie*. It was attributed to Langdon P. Marvin Jr., FDR's godson, a Harvard honors graduate, onetime JFK roommate, and longtime friend of JFK. Marvin allegedly informed Heymann:

> The night before the debate, Jack said to me, "Any girls lined up for tomorrow?" So I called Bobby and made arrangements to have a girl waiting for him in a room at the Palmer House. I took him down there about ninety minutes before airtime, rode up in the elevator with him, introduced him to the girl (she'd been prepaid for her services), then stood guard in the corridor outside the hotel room. Jack evidently enjoyed himself, because he emerged fifteen minutes later with an ear-to-ear grin on his face.
>
> During the debate he looked the picture of self-assurance and good health. Nixon, meanwhile, looked like an escaped convict—pallid, perspiring, beady-eyed. Jack was so pleased by the results he insisted we line up a girl for him before each of the debates.

Why would Marvin's spicy narrative prove dubious?

The reasons, it transpires, are numerous, ranging from motive to internal inconsistencies to points in between.

Internal inconsistencies: First, the Palmer House is situated nowhere near either the Ambassador or the debate studios. Visiting the Palmer House involved not only substantial risk but also a significant detour—one bringing Kennedy perilously near to Richard Nixon's Pick-Congress quarters. There are risks, there are John Kennedy risks, and there are risks not even a Jack Kennedy would take.

Beyond that, Marvin also noted, "We had recently returned from New Orleans, where Jack spent 20 minutes making love to stripper Blaze Starr in the closet of a hotel suite while her fiancé, Governor Earl Long, held a party in the next room. In the closet, Jack found the time to tell Blaze the story of President Warren G. Harding's making love to his mistress Nan Britton in a White House closet." If that incident happened at all, it didn't happen "recently." Long had left office that May. Worse, he had been dead since September 5.

Fast-forward: "[H]e insisted we line up a girl for him before each of the debates." Again, unlikely, as Jackie Kennedy joined him in New York for both debates three and four.

Motive: Langdon Marvin may have once been JFK's pal, but by the time David Heymann's book appeared, he'd long had reasons to hold a grudge against the Kennedys. The reasons remain mysterious, but, unlike virtually everyone else in JFK's considerable entourage, Marvin, an aviation consultant by profession, received no government position in Camelot. In fact, he became persona non grata. When airline industry representatives warned the White House against appointing Marvin to anything affecting their industry, Bobby Kennedy responded—*in writing*—with unusual bluntness:

> I assure you that Langdon Marvin will not be a part of the administration. He will not have a job of any kind and will play no role, directly or indirectly, in the policies of the administration.
>
> Your sentiments regarding Mr. Marvin are exactly in accord with mine, and I assure you that, when I say that Langdon Marvin will have nothing to do with the government for the next four years, I mean what I say.

Langdon Marvin's story is a good story. Repeating it uncritically is not very good history.

Richard Nixon's day proved less prone to Kennedyesque rumors. With his pointless Carpenters and Joiners appearance complete, he finally commenced debate preparation, cramming for a full five hours. Unlike his rival, he prepped alone. Unlike Kennedy, he concentrated not on debate give-and-take, but rather on his opening and closing statements.

He also now had time to visit the television studio where the contest would take place, to case it for whatever might be amiss—podium and camera placement, lighting, temperature, to obtain a feel for battlefield terrain. He didn't.

Kennedy *had* rendezvoused with CBS producer Don Hewitt, to discuss those issues, a week earlier. The thirty-seven-year-old Hewitt, a veteran of the *CBS Evening News* and Edward R. Murrow's *See It Now* series, had met JFK at a Midway Airport hangar—Kennedy having purposely flown into Chicago to personally review debate guidelines and logistics. "Where do I stand?" JFK kept asking. "Do I stand? Do I sit? How much time do I have to answer? Can he interrupt? Can I interrupt?"

"Kennedy," Hewitt would recall, "took the thing far more seriously" than Nixon.

Nixon didn't bother to see Ted Rogers (and hadn't since Rogers had flown to Kansas City a few days earlier to strategize about the upcoming debate). He largely ignored a questions-and-answers book that campaign research chief Jim Shepley had prepared for him. "We kept pushing for him to have some give-and-take with either somebody from the staff . . . anything," a frustrated Bob Finch recalled. "He hadn't done anything except to tell me that he knew how to debate. He totally refused to prepare. After all, he was the master debater. Who were any of us to presume to insist?"

Nixon did, however, heed counsel from Henry Cabot Lodge. Phoning from Texas, Lodge bluntly told Nixon to "erase the assassin image." Attorney General Bill Rogers (no relative of Ted Rogers) offered similar guidance, advising Nixon to be "the good guy."

The candidate received different advice from sixty-six-year-old author, screenwriter, and journalist Adela Rogers St. John, who wrote: "God will go with you tonight when you walk before that camera. . . . Don't mention Kennedy by name. Call him my opponent. SMILE OH PLEASE PLEASE SMILE. . . . They [Las Vegas bookmakers] say you can swing the odds back to yourself IF YOU ARE NIXON TONIGHT IF YOU TAKE CHARGE IF YOU ARE ON THE OFFENSIVE."

But what did she know compared to seasoned politicians like Lodge and Bill Rogers? Take-no-prisoners debater Nixon would traverse the high road.

On Monday morning, CBS newsman Howard K. Smith—that night's moderator—rode a hotel elevator with Pierre Salinger. "Are you ready for tonight's bout?" Salinger inquired.

"I don't matter," responded Smith, angling for information. "What matters is, is your man ready?"

"Ready?" the bluff Salinger shot back. "He's been up shadow-boxing since daybreak."

Intellectually, JFK *was* ready; emotionally, he harbored churning knots of doubt. Not helping was Dave Powers. As JFK dressed to leave for WBBM's McClurg Court studio, he likened himself to a boxer climbing into the ring at Madison Square Garden. Powers, ever the baseball fan, corrected his boss. "No, Senator," he advised, "it's more like the opening-day pitcher in the World Series—because you have to win four of these."

And so JFK remained edgy, silent, and tense riding to WBBM, snarling at traffic lights, cutting short advice on how to comport himself.

Meanwhile, Ted Rogers finally gained access to Richard Nixon—at 4:30 p.m.—and for a mere half hour. About all Nixon wanted to know was the length of the ride to WBBM (it was ten minutes). Rogers had warned Nixon (or, at least, tried to warn him—he never knew what got through) to arrive in Chicago early, to husband his strength, to rest—Kennedy's strategy. Now Rogers knew how right he had been. David Halberstam would write, "Rogers was shocked; the candidate looked better suited for going to a funeral, perhaps his own, than to a debate. His face was sickly gray and seemed to sag. He was nearly exhausted. He had lost some twenty or thirty pounds [actually only ten] and his frame had hardly been robust to begin with. . . . Rogers was stunned; this was a sick man and nobody had said anything."

The vice president now departed the Pick-Congress. Klein, riding with Nixon, advised him to come out swinging, to take it to Kennedy. Nixon distrusted such counsel, fearing it might be something that CBS president Frank Stanton had put in Klein's ear. Fights make good television. Good television was in Frank Stanton's interests—not necessarily Richard Nixon's.

Klein, who should have seen it much sooner, now suddenly realized how badly Nixon's appearance had deteriorated. "I thought he looked bad wearing a shirt which was too large," Klein recalled, "but it seemed like no time to disturb the candidate with such impressions. He was tense and silent. I briefed him on the procedures which would follow our arrival . . . and left him to his own thoughts."

Outside WBBM's Studio 1, Kennedy partisans—largely college students, both male and female—outnumbered Nixon's. Three GOP women carried signs reading "Vote Republican. Experienced Leadership." Outraged Kennedy people jeered them mercilessly. Two Democratic women grabbed one sign-bearer's placard and ran down the street with it, ripping it apart as they went.

Studio 1's layout was less like a campaign stop, with all its hustle and jostling, and more like a quiz-show isolation booth. Both candidates and their top aides would be ushered into a special "red zone"—quarantined from the 250-plus reporters nervously herded, just fifty feet away, in their own area, which was chockablock with monitors and phones. Photographers could enter the "red zone" only briefly before hostilities opened.

Nixon's two-car motorcade arrived first, entering through a freight entrance, then up a ramp directly to WBBM's garage. Exiting, Nixon slammed his knee on the limousine door. His face turned "chalk white," betraying incredible pain and worse fear. Ted Rogers asked if it was the same knee that had hospitalized him. It was.

Nixon had not previously been to WBBM. But Ted Rogers had, and in fact he had dealt with any number of potentially troublesome issues. As fate would have it, though, nothing Rogers had done had much effect.

Temperature was an issue for each face-to-face debate. Nixon sweated—a lot—his hypersensitivity to temperature heightened by stress. Hot studio lights were not for him. "Air conditioning," the *Los Angeles Times* reported, "will be turned up . . . to ensure that neither man breaks out in sweat during the program." Rogers prayed that would do the trick.

Lighting was also important. Rogers, fretting that Nixon's deep-set eyes would televise poorly, positioned two small spotlights ("inkies") to offset that risk, and CBS had transported a lighting expert from New York to ensure that all went well. Kennedy said his lighting was fine.

And then there was the set itself. Its color proved to be yet another controversy, a growing tempest in a gray teapot. CBS had promised a dark gray background, and Nixon's strategists calculated that a light blue–gray suit, pale blue shirt, and dark blue tie would contrast nicely with it. Unfortunately, CBS hadn't painted the set *dark* gray. CBS painted it *light* gray, and a light blue–gray-clad Nixon juxtaposed against the light gray background was not a good idea, particularly on black-and-white television. He could only look washed out, undistinguished, like part of the furniture. Desperately, Ted Rogers ordered the set repainted, each time a slightly darker shade (at airtime it remained slightly wet to the touch), all to no avail. Light gray it started; light gray it ended. On this set, Jack Kennedy—deeply tanned and dark suited—would be the picture. Gray-faced, gray-suited Richard Nixon comprised part of the frame.

Nixon, Klein, and Rogers now arrived. Nixon, oozing bonhomie, finally tried the stage on for size. Eight minutes later, Kennedy's entourage—JFK, RFK, Salinger, Sorensen, Kenny O'Donnell, Larry O'Brien, Bill Wilson—pulled in. "Nixon was sitting in a chair," CBS's Frank Stanton recalled, "under the microphone giving some sound levels when he saw Senator Kennedy come in. So he jumped up to speak to him, and the microphone hit on his head and it sounded like somebody dropped a watermelon. It was terrible."

Kennedy looked great—rested, confident, tanned. Even Nixon admitted his opponent never "look[ed] more fit." Howard K. Smith was even more impressed. Kennedy, he later posited, "entered . . . looking like a young athlete come to receive his wreath of laurel. Addison's disease made him look bronzed. . . . Steroids . . . caused him to fill out to an attractive manliness."

"Glad to see you," said Kennedy. The two opponents grasped each other's hands. Nixon attempted small talk: "I heard you had a big audience in Cleveland." JFK merely nodded. Nixon complimented Kennedy on his color: "I suppose you get it the same way I do—riding around in convertibles. You know, it's the wind that burns you, not the sun." Kennedy said something about getting tanned in Nixon's home base of Southern California, his voice nearly inaudible.

As the two rivals posed for pictures, a Nixon aide asked Bobby Kennedy his thoughts regarding Nixon's appearance. "Terrific! Terrific!" RFK responded. "Wouldn't change a thing!"

CBS staff carefully explained debate ground rules. To ensure equal time, a system of "traffic lights" governed events: Green meant the candidate had sixty seconds left; amber meant thirty seconds; red meant stop. If a candidate didn't stop, moderator Smith was empowered to gavel him to silence.

A CBS functionary informed the candidates, "If you have to go for water you will be off camera."

"Will you do the same thing if I have to dab my lips?" Nixon inquired. "I perspire a lot."

"The vice president," the Associated Press reported, "was assured that he would be off camera while dabbing his lips."

But CBS's assurances, it would turn out, would be honored more in the breach than in the studio.

Then came the question of makeup—for Nixon, one possessing unusual significance. "He has very translucent, almost blue-white skin," Ted Rogers recalled. "You can actually see the roots of his beard beneath his skin. TV is just an electronic development that goes beyond x-rays and radar. This x-ray like quality of television made Nixon a bad visual candidate for television."

Rogers advised makeup, and the Nixon campaign had imported BBD&O advertising agency executive Everett "Ev" Hart for the job. Don Hewitt had also made available CBS makeup staff—including the very skilled, thirty-nine-year-old, Max Factor–trained Frances "Frannie" Arvold—to both candidates. The petite, soft-spoken Ms. Arvold was familiar with challenging, high-profile assignments: She had made-up President Eisenhower; each week she tackled Edward R. Murrow's five o'clock shadow. Nixon, however, was aware that during West Virginia's televised debate, Humphrey had worn makeup and JFK hadn't, and Kennedy forces had subsequently criticized Humphrey for such unmanly artifice. "To Nixon," Herb Klein recalled, "this made it look like [Humphrey] lacked macho, and Nixon was a very macho man."

So when Jack Kennedy answered Don Hewitt, "No, thank you, not really," Dick Nixon declined as well. Hewitt, however, still fretted over how wan Nixon appeared, and fretted more that he might catch blame for it. "Frank," he called to Frank Stanton, "you better look at this." Stanton saw what Hewitt saw. Warily, almost plaintively, he inquired of Ted Rogers, "Are you satisfied [with] the way your candidate looks?"

"Yeah," said Rogers, "we think he looks great."

Stanton surrendered. He motioned Hewitt to join him outside in the hallway. "It's none of our business," he advised Hewitt. "That's the way they want . . ."

Nixon did, however, agree to something called a "beard stick"—exactly what Frannie Arvold used on Murrow. Everett Hart applied some beard stick—a brand called Lazy Shave—to the vice president. Ralph de Toledano thought it only made Nixon look worse.

Nixon, mike and lighting checks complete, retreated to his green room, jauntily calling to supporters, "See you later." AP's Arthur Edson sensed "a false heartiness in his voice."

Kennedy remained on the nondescript, green-carpeted studio stage, posing for the camera. "He too looked nervous and ill at ease," reported the AP. Twice, Bobby appeared, conferring edgily with his brother. Kennedy performed his own mike check, intoning, "It's a pleasure to be here in this situation for what is sometimes known as the great debate." CBS technicians lowered his sound levels, and then pronounced everything satisfactory. JFK headed to his own anteroom.

His volume was right. His attire was wrong—specifically a white shirt that Don Hewitt pointed out would unduly reflect harsh studio lighting. An aide hightailed it back to the Ambassador East to fetch one of pale blue.

Earlier Frank Stanton had noticed another item amiss in the normally fastidious Kennedy wardrobe. Stanton recalled:

> [I]n the warm-up, if you will . . . Jack Kennedy had socks on about this long [very short], and he was sitting in the chair, and of course his trousers came up, and he had the bare legs. . . . I said as a friendly thing . . . we ought to make sure that his people know. . . . Because otherwise he'd have been naked there and it would have been a distraction. No question about that . . . . I got hold of . . . Leonard Reinsch. . . . He got one of the junior people to take his socks off and give them to [JFK]. I said, "Can you get somebody at the hotel to bring out some long socks[?]" . . . But little things like that make a difference.

In his dressing room, JFK confided that he too considered his adversary's appearance wretched. "He [Nixon] just looked awful," Pierre Salinger recalled. "Not that [Kennedy] was not confident already, but it gave him an extra bit of confidence. He walked out of there knowing that he had him. . . . I think he thought Nixon was afraid."

Conversation within the Kennedy camp nonetheless remained awkward. Kennedy's confidence might be returning, but his men remained obviously edgy. Talk turned to the obsession du jour—makeup. Someone speculated that Nixon would not emerge from his dressing room until Kennedy did—meaning that JFK would have to go first to Frances Arvold for makeup. History has generally recorded that JFK—bronzed from Addison's disease, tanned from campaigning out West and from rooftop debate prep—didn't require makeup and didn't resort to it. But virtually all television performers do. Bill Wilson knew it. Jack Kennedy knew it. JFK asked Wilson if reporters were outside, watching. Wilson indicated they were. "——— 'em, I won't do it," Kennedy spat back, not wanting to draw criticism for using makeup—particularly following the stink his people had launched against Humphrey. Wilson, however, wouldn't give up—Kennedy needed to reduce glare and shine. JFK finally asked Wilson if he could do it. Wilson could, but he needed supplies and wasn't about to ask CBS for them. Having once been employed at WBBM, however, Wilson knew where to find what he needed. Sprinting two blocks to a drugstore, he returned with a compact of Max Factor Creme Puff.

"Do you know what you're doing?" Kennedy demanded.

"Yes," Wilson said, preparing to gently dab the powder upon the candidate's pores.

"Okay," JFK, still very relaxed, agreed—and won the war of the makeup.

Max Factor Creme Puff or not, inside the Kennedy green rooms, the tension built. Larry O'Brien remembered:

> I remember there were some sandwiches and tea, and Kennedy did pour a cup of tea for himself. Nobody else touched anything. . . . I was a wreck.
>
> [N]ow you're just checking your watch. And there [was] probably between fifteen and ten minutes to air time. There was no outward

indication at least of any Kennedy concern. He was very self-composed. But there wasn't a normal conversation taking place, and I really couldn't stand it, so I walked out of the room and strolled down the hall. Down the hall a short distance, I realized that was the door to the studio, so I opened the door, walked in, closed the door and stood there. There were a number of staff people, camera crews and all that, finalizing everything, checking the lights, et cetera.

And I looked across this very large studio and noted a fellow pacing up and down alone, and it was Nixon. As I watched him, at one point he went over and checked the podium, where his position would be, and he went back. And even with my rather poor eyesight I could see that this man was heavily made up. He just didn't quite look like Nixon in a way. But clearly I was observing a fellow that was terribly uptight.

Then the countdown over the loudspeaker began, and I am still standing there. Nixon hasn't left the studio. And the countdown came and I don't recall the exact minutes, but four minutes to air time there's no Kennedy. Three minutes to air time, there's no Kennedy. At which point I'm semi-hysterical standing there, and I'm just about to say, "God, didn't you hear the—?" And at perhaps two minutes to air time the door opened, Kennedy walked in, moved directly to the podium and stood. Nixon, looking ill at ease, took his position, attempted to speak to Kennedy—Kennedy nodded. And they were on the air.

THIRTY-ONE

"They've embalmed him before he even died"

SHOWTIME.

At stage center, moderator Howard K. Smith hunched stiffly behind a truncated little desk that looked, at best, like something to be found in the more progressive grade schools—and at worst like a dime-store version of a butcher block. At stage left sat John Fitzgerald Kennedy, at stage right, Richard Milhous Nixon, both looking less like aspirants for the Free World's highest honor than like patients in an otherwise empty waiting room, the tiny end tables next to them bereft of even the oldest magazines. Beyond the candidates and their barren end tables stood spindly podiums, from which they would issue their respective statements and responses.

Backs to the television audience, facing Smith and Kennedy and Nixon, and just below them, sat the evening's journalistic panel. From left to right: ABC's bespectacled Washington bureau chief Robert Fleming, CBS's Stuart Novins (host of *Face the Nation*), Mutual's Washington bureau chief Charles Warren, and NBC's political correspondent and former *New York Times* reporter Sander Vanocur.

And outside the studio—in comfortable suburban homes, in cramped city apartments, in sedate clubs and smoky barrooms—somewhere between sixty-five and eighty million Americans watched on flickering, often snow-speckled, cathode-ray screens. The best guess was seventy million viewers—60 percent of U.S. households, the biggest television market share in history. Nobody really knew for sure how many watched—or how many more listened on radio. But everyone knew it was immense, the biggest thing yet to hit broadcasting—or politics.

White maned at just forty-six, Howard K. Smith began tersely, matter-of-factly, almost anti-climactically. "The candidates need no introduction," stated Smith, not bothering to provide much more than the sparest setup for what might follow.

Kennedy went first. The first debate, as Smith had bothered to reiterate, was restricted to "internal or domestic American matters." Nonetheless, JFK quickly dragged in foreign affairs, employing the words "communist" or "communists" thrice, "Khrushchev" three times, and, for good measure, "Soviet" three more times, injecting the specter of a looming (if not already existing, at least in terms of growth rates) economic gap with Moscow. Nikita Khrushchev, JFK argued, "maintains the Communist offensive throughout the world because of the productive power of the Soviet Union itself."

Considering what is now known regarding Soviet "productivity," Kennedy's proposition was laughable. In 1960, however, nobody, neither Birchers nor Democrats nor Republicans, was laughing at the men with bad haircuts and ill-fitting suits inhabiting the Kremlin, launching Sputniks into space, shooting down U-2s.

Even ever-loyal Ted Sorensen had to admit that his "tense and unsmiling" chief had delivered his eight-and-a-half-minute opening statement "perhaps too rapidly and undramatically." But Kennedy nonetheless proved effective, forcefully restating his trademark, though maddeningly vague, theme that America could "do better"—while providing very deft, specific, and, yes, even moving, examples of how the last eight years had failed Negroes, Puerto Ricans, and Mexicans, Georgia peanut farmers and Wisconsin and Minnesota dairy farmers, as well as the malnourished, poverty-stricken children of West Virginia. For good measure, he again unfurled Franklin Roosevelt's still widely admired New Deal banner—his Good Neighbor policy, the Tennessee Valley Authority, and, of course, Social Security—and, for good, nonpartisan, measure, even a nod toward Abraham Lincoln.

His effort comprised, in the aggregate, a competent, successful, if not overwhelming, performance.

He wasn't bad.

What followed was.

For all the Monday-morning quarterbacking about Richard Nixon's physical appearance, all scrawny and wan, it was not his makeup or weight or shirt size or suit color that did him in. His manner and his words failed him—particularly his grotesquely weak, defensive, and artlessly constructed and wretchedly delivered opening statement.

"Mr. Smith, Senator Kennedy," Richard Nixon began, "the things that Senator Kennedy has said many of us can agree with," thus instantly validating Kennedy's remarks and stature, and, worse, setting the tone for a remarkable string of similar toadying. A few sentences later, it was "I subscribe completely to the spirit that Senator Kennedy has expressed tonight," and throughout Richard Nixon's wet-dishrag opening statement, his forlorn, deferential, defensive, Uriah Heep–like obsequiousness slunk listlessly, steadily, spinelessly forward, periodically, almost compulsively, inserting aversions of agreement with his charismatic foe:

Senator Kennedy has suggested that he believes he knows the way. I respect the sincerity which he—which he makes that suggestion.

Here again, may I indicate that Senator Kennedy and I are not in disagreement as to the aims.

We both want to help the old people. We want to see that they do have adequate medical care.

Let us understand throughout this campaign that his motives and mine are sincere.

I know Senator Kennedy feels as deeply about these problems as I do.

Even when Nixon rebutted Kennedy's charges, rattling off a reasonable complement of facts and figures, and compared Eisenhower's record to Harry Truman's less successful tenure ("[Y]our wages have gone up five times as much in the Eisenhower Administration as they did in the Truman Administration. What about the prices you pay? We find that the prices you pay went up five times as much in the Truman Administration as they did in the Eisenhower Administration. What's the net result of this? This means that the average family income went up fifteen per cent in the Eisenhower years as against two per cent in the Truman years"), he blunted his message with asides like "good as this record is, may I emphasize it isn't enough." Attempting to articulate Republicans' values, he retreated into the fog-shrouded confines of the most painful generalities:

"What kind of programs are we for? We are for programs that will expand educational opportunities, that will give to all Americans their equal chance for education, for all of the things which are necessary and dear to the hearts of our people. We are for programs, in addition, which will see that our medical care for the aged are—is—are much—is much better handled than it is at the present time."

Beyond substance was style. Nixon's approach was halting, his voice weak, his manner uncertain. While Kennedy spoke, the camera shifted to Nixon, who looked jarringly . . . shifty. When Nixon spoke, the camera switched to Kennedy, studiously jotting notes. The implication: What Nixon said was dubious, and Kennedy would soon rebut it.

Eighteen minutes into the first of four great debates, Jack Kennedy had accomplished everything he set out to do. He had stood up to Nixon, projected a mature and presidential image—tough, yet not unduly combative—gesturing with choppy little hand motions, staring straight ahead through the rotating lenses of CBS cameras and into the eyes of scores of millions of Americans. But most of all, JFK had trumped his opponent's vaunted high card of "experience"—though he had not done that on his own, and certainly not without help from Richard Nixon.

And, yes, Nixon did look physically bad.

"When I first saw the pictures in the control room," recalled Bill Wilson, "I thought one [Nixon] looked same old, same old, and the other guy looked great and new."

"I couldn't believe it when the thing went on and he looked so haggard," echoed Bob Finch. "I saw he didn't have any makeup on."

In the pressroom, liberal syndicated columnist Doris Fleeson stared incredulously at the bank of monitors before her. "Why, Nixon has lost the thing," she exclaimed, stunned by his wretched, uncomposed appearance. "He sat there spraddled out almost as if his fly were open."

Spraddling compounded by painfully obvious sweating. Cooling Studio 1 hadn't worked. Nixon still perspired badly, beads of perspiration particularly obvious on his chin and nose, causing his Lazy Shave makeup to run, but, worse still, causing him to mop his brow as Kennedy spoke. He thought the cameras wouldn't catch him. They did, making a bad situation worse.

In the question-and-answer session, Nixon again got out of the box with a major stumble, failing to respond to Kennedy's spirited defense of his own experience and his attack on the historical Republican Party record. It made for perhaps the most stupefying moment of Nixon's entire career.

> MR. KENNEDY: Well, the Vice President and I came to the Congress together in 1946; we both served in the Labor Committee. I've been there now for fourteen years, the same period of time that he has, so that our experience in uh—government is comparable. Secondly, I think the question is what are the programs that we advocate, what is the party record that we lead? I come out of the Democratic party, which in this century has produced Woodrow Wilson and Franklin Roosevelt and Harry Truman, and which supported and sustained these programs which I've discussed tonight. Mr. Nixon comes out of the Republican party. He was nominated by it. And it is a fact that through most of these last twenty-five years the Republican leadership has opposed federal aid for education, medical care for the aged, development of the Tennessee Valley, development of our natural resources. I think Mr. Nixon is an effective leader of his party. I hope he would grant me the same. The question before us is: which point of view and which party do we want to lead the United States?
> MR. SMITH: Mr. Nixon, would you like to comment on that statement?
> MR. NIXON: I have no comment.

The sullen, Fifth Amendment–invoking Hollywood Ten, defying the House Committee on Un-American Activities, provided more cooperative and sympathetic answers. From such a stunning nolo contendere, Nixon, despite the occasional sojourn into me-tooism ("I agree with Senator Kennedy's appraisal generally in this respect"), could only rebound upward, though even when he succeeded in marshaling facts and figures, he could never summon the sense of poetry and mission that Jack Kennedy so readily radiated—his Harvard Yard aura of sophistication, his steely resolve, his raw sex appeal. Unlike Nixon, Kennedy proved unafraid, unhesitant, to chisel sharp demarcations between himself and his opponent. It was the mark of leadership—or, at least, of a man comfortable enough to portray himself in that role—and Jack Kennedy flaunted leadership, the necessity for choice, whenever possible. During the course of the sixty-minute contest, he regularly expressed disagreement with his wan opponent.

The Vice President and I disagree on this.

On that question the Vice President and I disagreed.

On that question the Vice President and I disagreed. I voted in favor of that proposal and supported it strongly, because I think that that provided assistance to our teachers for their salaries without any chance of federal control and it is on that vote that—Mr. Nixon and I disagreed, and his . . . breaking the tie defeated the proposal.

Meanwhile, war raged in Don Hewitt's control room, as Bill Wilson and Ted Rogers battled to make their respective candidates look good, particularly in the realm of those now crucial "reaction shots," particularly as sweat continued to almost cascade down Richard Nixon's wan face. In pre-debate planning, Rogers and Wilson had each demanded reaction shots. CBS resisted, fearing criticism from whichever candidate emerged looking the worse. Richard Nixon was now clearly looking beyond worse, his situation incalculably aggravated by CBS having broken its word that its cameras would discretely avert their gaze during such awkward moments.

As David Halberstam would write:

[S]omething curious happened in the control booth: Wilson and Rogers switched sides. Whereas in the earlier moments Wilson had been demanding reaction shots of Kennedy (cool, patrician, slightly disdainful as Nixon talked), now he was demanding more reaction shots of *Nixon*, and Rogers was demanding more of *Kennedy*, anything to get that brutal, relentless, unsparing camera off the face of Nixon. It was a madhouse in the control room. Wilson pointing at his sheet, shouting at Hewitt, "You owe us two more of Nixon, you've had sixteen of Kennedy and only fourteen of Nixon," and Rogers shouting, "No, no," and Hewitt yelling at both of them to keep quiet so that he could work.

Toward the close of Nixon's painfully deflating hour, one last sweeping curveball eluded him, this one thrown by NBC's Sander Vanocur:

MR. VANCOUR: Now, Republican campaign slogans say it's experience that counts. . . . Now, in his news conference on August twenty-fourth, President Eisenhower was asked to give one example of a major idea of yours that he adopted. His reply was, and I'm quoting; "If you give me a week I might think of one. I don't remember." Now that was a month ago, sir, and the President hasn't brought it up since. . . . [W]hich version is correct—the one put out by Republican campaign leaders or the one put out by President Eisenhower?

MR. NIXON: Well, I would suggest, Mr. Vanocur, that if you know the President, that was probably a facetious remark. I would also suggest that insofar as his statement is concerned, that I think it would be improper for the President of the United States to disclose uh—the instances in which members of his official family had made recommendations, as I have made them through the years to him, which he has accepted or rejected. The President has always maintained and very properly so that he is entitled to get what advice he wants from his cabinet and from his other advisers without disclosing that to anybody—including as a matter of fact the Congress. Now, I can only say this. Through the years I have sat in the National Security Council. I have been in the cabinet. I have met with the legislative leaders. I have met with the President when he made the great decisions with regard to Lebanon, Quemoy and Matsu, other matters. The President has asked for my advice. I have given it. Sometimes my advice has been taken. Sometimes it has not. I do not say that I have made the decisions. And I would say that no president should ever allow anybody else to make the major decisions. The president only makes the decisions. All that his advisers do is to give counsel when he asks for it. As far as what experience counts and whether that is experience that counts, that isn't for me to say. I can only say that my experience is there for the people to consider; Senator Kennedy's is there for the people to consider. As he pointed out, we came to the Congress in the same year. His experience has been different from mine. Mine has been in the executive branch. His has been in the legislative branch. I would say that the people now have the opportunity to evaluate his as against mine and I think both he and I are going to abide by whatever the people decide.

It was an inept response, worsened immeasurably by an unnecessary validation of Jack Kennedy's assertion of equivalent experience—"we came to the Congress in the same year."

JFK concluded the evening, once again in the airy rhetoric that in less artistic hands seemed more windy than soaring: "If we fail, if we fail to move ahead, if we fail to develop sufficient military and economic and social strength here in this country, then I think that the tide could begin to run against us. And I don't want historians, ten years from now, to say, these were the years when the tide ran out for the United States. I want them to say these were the years when the tide came in; these were the years when the United States started to move again."

For all of Nixon's blunders and all of Kennedy's patrician grandeur, his Ciceronian, Sorensenian oratory, if one examines the Chicago debate in its totality, balanced point against point, miraculously Nixon ends up doing not too badly. More surprisingly still, much of the not particularly pro-Nixon national press corps initially reached that conclusion. Buffeted by ham-fisted gaffes, Lazy Shave–stained perspiration, and shifty, beady-eyed glances, Richard Nixon's not inconsiderable rhetorical skills had still not completely abandoned him.

"Nixon *looked* terrible but performed rather well," thought *New York Times* reporter Tom Wicker. "At the time of the debate, I was . . . traveling with Lodge . . . and I came away from the television screen—underestimating what I had *seen* as against what I had heard—with the impression that the debate had been a dead heat."

"It was not much of a debate," admitted Howard K. Smith. "Because the reporters on the panel were not allowed to pose follow-up questions, both candidates shamelessly slid by questions rather than answering them. I . . . thought Nixon was marginally better."

"After last night's debate," scoffed CBS's Edward R. Murrow, "the reputation of Messrs. Lincoln and Douglas is secure."

"I thought Kennedy looked amazingly cool and unrattled," recalled Ben Bradlee. "And . . . Nixon . . . looked like an awkward cadaver. When it was over, I wanted to check my own feeling that Kennedy had wiped the floor with Nixon, and went to . . . listen to what the big boys were saying. Marquis Childs[,] Scotty Reston, Roscoe Drummond[,] and columnist Joe Alsop were declaring the debate dead even. Perhaps, I realized only later, because they too were afraid of the consequences of declaring the debate a victory for an upstart they liked over a sitting vice president they didn't like."

Perhaps, but perhaps they got it wrong because they saw two Nixons that night. The first Nixon was the "live" Nixon. Reporters were acclimated to the "live" Nixon, and, through the decades, on any given night, the "live" Nixon never looked nearly as shabby or unpleasant as the "television" Nixon. Their accumulated image of the "live" Nixon bled into the night's "television" Nixon, particularly when both Nixon personas co-existed so very close by the other, blurring the "television" Nixon and making his sweaty imperfections less significant—at least, to them.

The *New York Times'* Russell Baker missed it, too, not really concentrating on the studio TV monitor, merely listening to the words and hastily scribbling them down. "I thought Nixon had a slight edge," he later wrote, "but as I talked to more and more people it was clear they thought Kennedy had won a great victory. . . . I missed it completely because I had been too busy taking notes and writing to get more than fleeting glimpses of what the country was seeing on the screen. That night television replaced newspapers as the most important communications medium in American politics."

Sixty or seventy or eighty million Americans had never seen the "live" Nixon. All they saw was this wan "television" Nixon.

The reporters heard words but not poetry, saw old politicians and not new heroes. Professor John Hellman analyzed the two contrasting performances, examining Studio 1's jousting not through prisms of mundane electioneering, but rather from those of actual—or, at least, Hollywood—courtship. "By all signals of appearance and mannerism available to viewers," wrote Hellman, "watching two rival suitors in a Hollywood romantic comedy, Nixon was obviously the wrong one."

Nixon stalwart Arthur Burns put it in less flowery terms: "[W]hat Mr. Kennedy said in substance was: we have a wonderful country, a beautiful country, a great tradition, and our task is to make our country more beautiful, more wonderful still. . . . When Mr. Nixon responded by tackling specific issues such as agriculture and citing statistics . . . I knew he had lost the debate then and there."

Not everyone in the studio got it wrong. The technicians and politicians knew what they saw, and they knew who triumphed.

"I left the studio thinking, 'My God, we don't have to wait until election day,'" Don Hewitt recalled. "'We have a president.' That's bad. Nobody should be elected president of the United States because he's a better TV performer than the guy he's running against."

"My God!" Dick Daley exclaimed. "They've embalmed him before he even died."

"What we saw on Nixon's face that night," recalled Richard Goodwin, "was the panic in his soul."

The debate over, the cameras and mikes and floodlights clicked off, Frank Stanton trundled down toward the candidates' holding area. "Well, there's his coat," a Secret Service agent informed Stanton, speaking of the vice president. "He was in a hurry to get out. He was very quick to leave." Bobby Kennedy, standing out in the hallway, motioned Stanton to enter his brother's area:

> I said that I appreciated the fact that he had participated. And he said, "Oh, you know Dick Daley, don't you?" . . . And I said, "Yes." I didn't see that Daley was in the room, in the shadows. And I did know him, so he came over, and I said, well, I was going back to my hotel. Daley said, "I'll take you into the city." . . .
>
> So I went in with Daley, and Daley said, "What did you think of that young man?" And I said, "He did an excellent job."
>
> "Well," he said, "it's changed my mind about him."

Daley meant what he said. Buttonholing Leonard Reinsch, he demanded, "How many of these debates do we have? Buy the time for more if you don't have any free ones. The debates will make Kennedy President."

Outside Chicago, people knew, too.

In California, Pat Nixon's brother, Bill Ryan, watched, disconcerted by the stark, unflattering contrast between his brother-in-law and his opponent. "Dick looked so haggard," Ryan recalled, "so strangely dark." Bill Ryan's reaction was more ironic than most. His job at Universal Studios: lighting expert.

From New York, John Hall, business agent of the Make-up and Hair Stylist Union local, told the *Chicago Daily News*, "We all say a

Democratic make-up artist made [Nixon] up. They loused him up so badly that a Republican couldn't have done that job."

Pat, Julie, and Trisha Nixon watched in Washington. Bothering Pat more than her husband's appearance was Sander Vanocur's dredging up Eisenhower's "give me a week" gaffe. To reporters, she announced that she—ironically, like Ike—had "no comment."

Rose Mary Woods's parents phoned from Sebring, Ohio, solicitously inquiring if her boss was well. She conveyed their remarks. Nixon asked her what she thought. Rosemary confessed she agreed with them.

Hannah Nixon called. She, too, asked if her son was "feeling all right."

Rose Kennedy, maternal instincts finely tuned, could only say, "I felt so sorry for Nixon's mother tonight."

When the debate ended, Henry Cabot Lodge, patrician purveyor of bad advice, snapped, "That son-of-a-bitch just lost us the election!"

Jackie Kennedy watched in Hyannis, in hardly the intimate setting she would have preferred. True, Arthur and Marian Schlesinger were among the scheduled attendees, and they were fine, but also invited were the Democratic national committeewomen (and their husbands) from the six New England states plus New York—plus any number of reporters.

Arthur had been in Manhattan regarding publication of his fifty-one-page campaign effort *Kennedy or Nixon: Does It Make Any Difference?* With Hyannis's airport heavily fogbound, he never made it, but Jackie's television set did, one rented for the occasion. "I own one in Washington," she explained, "but we don't have one here. I rented one for the conventions and then again when Jack began campaigning. I guess I'll have to break down and buy one."

The *Christian Science Monitor* chronicled the house party with the proper deference due to the future rulers of media-driven Camelot:

> [Jackie's] only jewelry was a three-strand necklace of costume pearls, a gold bracelet, and a plain gold wedding band.
>
> Except for celebrities present, the pleasant homey living room . . . looked much like millions of others last night. Guests were sitting about informally, some on the floor.
>
> The lemon-yellow linen couch had to be moved around to face the television screen. And when it was, everybody laughed.

Underneath were two dollies—a reminder that 2½-year[-old] Caroline was upstairs sleeping through one of the great events of her father's career.

Not all members of the press proved so charmed. *Boston Herald-Traveler* reporter Mary Tierney sputtered:

[We] all had to sit there and watch her reactions to the debate. She did a lot of hand-wringing. She was like a silly schoolgirl, saying, "What do I say? What do I do?" It was so ridiculous. She was such a jerk.

We'd ask her, "Well what do you think, Jackie?" And she'd say, "Well . . . you know." She took the most inane, baby doll approach to this thing.

But at evening's end, Jacqueline Bouvier Kennedy managed to say, "My husband was brilliant. I'm very proud of him." And that got printed, and that was more than sufficient.

Jackie and Pat and Hannah and Rose had all watched on television. On radio, more than seventeen million listeners heard—*heard*—something very different. Despite all of Richard Nixon's diffidence and "agreeability," he projected fairly well when people merely heard the words, when they didn't see one man tanned, another perspiring, one man serious and purposeful, another shifty, trying too hard to smile, to desperately effect a friendly, plain-folks mien.

In Texas, Lyndon Johnson listened—but did not see. "I was with LBJ the night of the first debate," thirty-three-year-old CBS News correspondent Nancy Hanschmann (CBS's first female reporter—better remembered as Nancy Dickerson) recalled. "We were listening on a car radio. Johnson was distressed that Kennedy had blown it. 'The Boy didn't win,' he kept saying. That's how LBJ referred to Jack, you know, 'The Boy.'"

"Nixon was best on radio," said Earl Mazo, "simply because his deep resonant voice carried more conviction . . . than Kennedy's higher-pitched voice and his Boston-Harvard accent. But on television, Kennedy looked sharper . . . the image of the man who could stand up to Khrushchev."

That very evening, the virtually all-Democrat Southern Governors' Conference met in Hot Springs, Arkansas. Taking time from whatever Southern governors otherwise do, at 9 p.m. they checked out events from Chicago. Democrat though they were, save for North Carolina's moderate Luther Hodges, they still feared to publicly endorse their youthful Catholic, Yankee, and increasingly liberal standard-bearer. Earlier in the day, Hodges had circulated a pledge supporting JFK. *Nobody* but Hodges, not even Alabama's John Patterson or Florida's LeRoy Collins, would sign. But then came nine o'clock. Hot Springs' TV stations presented their broadcast on a one-hour time delay, forcing the Southern governors to first listen on radio. They remained unimpressed. An hour later came the telecast. Hodges retrieved his document. Ten of his eleven fellow Democratic governors telegraphed Kennedy their support.

Small and old, Richard Nixon had limped off the stage, not realizing how small, old, shriveled, and reptilian he looked. He shook JFK's hand, made conversation, posed with him once more for photographers. Kenny O'Donnell asked JFK what they had discussed. "Oh, I don't know," JFK answered, "just the usual small talk. I wasn't listening to him. But while he was talking about the weather . . . he was watching the photographers out of the corner of his eye. When one of them was taking a picture of us, he would put a stern expression on his face and start jabbing his finger into my chest, so he would look as if he was laying down the law to me about foreign policy or Communism. Nice fellow."

The Kennedys were nice fellows, too. As reporters swarmed around Kennedy and Nixon, and Nixon looked so sternly at his opponent, a woman, ostensibly a Nixon supporter, broke through the throng, cooing to him a solicitous, "That's all right. You'll do better next time!" She wasn't for Nixon at all. Kennedy operative Dick Tuck—a master of campaign dirty tricks, engaged at Bobby Kennedy's behest—had hired her expressly to shed her very public crocodile tears.

A pay phone rang backstage. CBS's Don Hewitt took the call. "How the guy got that number," Hewitt recalled, "I don't know. It was [JFK's] father who called to tell him how good it was."

"It's all over," Joe Kennedy crowed, delighted by the slaughter he had witnessed.

JFK made his own call. Fifteen minutes after the debate ended, long before Jackie, so often ignored, expected anything, he phoned her, clearly elated.

Jack Kennedy had won—and he knew it, too.

THIRTY-TWO

"The bones of a single American soldier"

NO JOY DWELT WITHIN the Republican high command. Political failure radiates its own special, rotting aura—the awkward sideways glances, the mumbled replies, the congratulatory phone calls neither made nor received, and, finally, angry recriminations, merciless second-guessing. Failure, not joy, nor hope, dwelt within Richard Nixon's camp; downcast pessimism permeated it, from its inner councils to its remotest hinterlands—and, certainly, it hung like an anchor around the heart of Herb Klein:

> I accompanied Nixon . . . in virtual silence. He was clearly exhausted. At the hotel he quickly went to bed and then called several of us in individually to discuss the event. I think he felt he had done well, and none of us disillusioned him that evening. When I departed from his suite, I left . . . to find as many reporters as we could. I thought it was highly important to put on a confident front and to find out what they really thought as we sipped a drink in the bar of two or three hotels. Most of them had concentrated so much on the content of the debate that they offered few opinions on the outcome. . . . It was only later when the public opinion favoring Kennedy started seeping in that the press began its interpretation of the debate's negative consequences on Richard Nixon's campaign for the presidency.

The damage was done.

Tom Wicker discovered that soon enough. "When I boarded Lodge's press bus the next morning," he would write, "the gloomy demeanor of his aides quickly disabused me of [any idea] the first match had been a draw."

Ike phoned Nixon. Though Ike hadn't actually bothered to view the debate (he was in New York to address the National Council of Catholic

349

Charities), he had, nonetheless, formed his own opinions. They weren't noticeably positive. "Once in a while," he advised, "try not to appear to be quite so glib, to ponder and appear to think about something before answering a question."

"Nixon had been hurt, but not too badly," Ralph de Toledano observed. "The effect[s] on his advisers and his campaign staff were the major factors in what followed. Until the first debate, they had seen Nixon as the winner. After that they were thrown into a mood of depression that communicated itself to the candidate. And Republican leaders, disconcerted by what they considered to be Nixon's gentle treatment of his opponent and his 'me too' approach, descended on him with angry criticism. He had, they said, thrown away the opportunity to let 120 million Americans know that there was a difference between the two parties."

Typical was this exasperated letter from a rank-and-file California Nixon supporter: "You are running for President, not Mr. Eisenhower. . . . It is fine to agree with Kennedy, but we are not interested in agreements. The differences are the real issue. . . . Last night was not a great debate. Dick Nixon wasn't the man who demolished Jerry Voorhees [sic] and smashed Helen Gahagan into oblivion. That's the man we want to vote enthusiastically for."

"Well, Joe," said TR's irascible seventy-six-year-old daughter, Alice Roosevelt Longworth, in a phone call to her cousin Joe Alsop, "your man's in, my man's finished. I don't see why they bother to go on with the election. Dick has finished himself off."

British prime minister Harold Macmillan, originally hopeful of a Nixon victory and in Manhattan to address the United Nations General Assembly, had watched on American television. The following morning, he and Ike breakfasted at the Waldorf-Astoria. "Your chap's beat," said Macmillan bluntly, but Ike already knew that. "In his heart," Macmillan confided to his diary, "it seemed as if the President thought that Mr. Nixon might lose."

Waves of enthusiasm now cascaded upon the Kennedy shoreline, in cheering, jumping, screaming crescendos. JFK embarked for Ohio, flying out of Chicago at 2 a.m., resuming his campaign just five hours later, at a breakfast just west of Cleveland at a lobster and fillet mignon kind of joint called Hellriegel's Inn. In flight aboard *The Caroline*, he tried relaxing over a glass of beer and a bowl of tomato soup. He couldn't. The debate, his triumphs, and his shortcomings replayed constantly in his mind. Demanding better material for debate two, just two weeks hence, he projected merely guarded reserve. Staffer Richard Goodwin did not. Pumped up, smelling victory, young Goodwin wanted to crow. "We've got it all won now," he fairly blurted out.

"It was all right," JFK replied with the slightest smile. He knew the truth lay somewhere in between.

Immense crowds had greeted JFK in Ohio just forty-eight hours earlier. Now greater still, their enthusiasm assumed fever pitch. Jack Kennedy was no longer just a candidate for president. He was a TV star, a movie star, a young Frank Sinatra making bobby-soxers swoon at Manhattan's Paramount Theater, someone they had entertained in their living rooms, the winning pitcher in game one of the World Series, the heavyweight champion of debates. "Hey, you really did a job on him last night," they'd scream, pushing wildly, recklessly toward his motorcade. "You really got him last night."

The politicians, once so noncommittal, now felt the same way. In Ohio, where the Kennedys had concentrated on strong-arming Governor Mike DiSalle into submission, they had initially ignored the state's very popular, *very* conservative, Democratic U.S. senator Frank Lausche. Lausche returned the favor, snubbing the JFK-LBJ ticket, refusing to stump for it, avoiding Kennedy's massive pre-debate Sunday rally.

That was Sunday. On Tuesday, Frank Lausche materialized quite unannounced, wanting to board the Kennedy bandwagon.

The disheartened Nixon campaign took stock. Everyone offered answers, excuses, scapegoats, solutions. Bob Haldeman's answer was that Herb Klein had allowed the press too much access to Nixon, wearing him down. Dr. Malcolm Todd advised, "You looked weak and pale and tired tonight on TV because, in fact, you *are* weak and pale and tired—even though you don't feel that way at all, in your own mind. We have to lighten up the schedule, get more food into you, and get you up to par before the next debate."

Ted Rogers had much the same thing to say, insisting:

Please back off the man-killing schedule. For God's sake, no more buffalo burger barbecues in Sullivanville Illinois! . . . Please give us time for make-up and lighting tests. It's now a matter of life and death we have these. . . . Richard Nixon is not the same man he was June 1. . . . Richard Nixon did not look his usual self because he was not in top shape. Instead of a contrast between experience and youth, the debate became one of health vs. fatigue.

Nixon stepped on the scales, shocked to learn he had dropped ten pounds to 160 pounds, reluctantly admitting that his clothes hung loose about his neck. Dr. Todd prescribed a milkshake ("I had not had one for years") at each meal, plus one each afternoon, for the next two weeks.

Nixon had lost more than pounds. He had lost points in the polls. A Gallup poll released the day before the first debate found Nixon marginally ahead:

Prefer Nixon-Lodge	45%
"Lean to" Nixon-Lodge	2%
Undecided	7%
Prefer Kennedy-Johnson	45%
"Lean to" Kennedy-Johnson	1%

When Gallup factored everything in, Nixon led 51 percent to 49 percent, but drilling deeper into Gallup's results revealed trouble on the Nixon horizon. By party affiliation the 7 percent undecided broke down thusly:

Democrat	50%
Independent	33%
Republican	17%

Superficially, Gallup's extrapolation that a population cohort that was three-to-one Democratic would break for Nixon—it simply defied logic. Yet, drilling down further, among undecided respondents Gallup discovered the following "enthusiasm levels" for the individual nominees:

Nixon	24%
Lodge	33%
Kennedy	22%
Johnson	20%

Following debate one, Nixon's situation seemed markedly worsened. Gallup released these figures (not bothering to separate "prefer" from "lean to"):

Prefer Kennedy-Johnson & "Lean to" Kennedy-Johnson	49%
Prefer Nixon-Lodge & "Lean to" Nixon-Lodge	46%
Undecided	5%

Fueling Nixon's five-point decline was, of, course, public perception of who had triumphed upon the light gray battlefields of Studio 1:

Kennedy won	43%
Nixon won	23%
Same	29%
No opinion	5%

Nonetheless, Nixon's situation was not nearly as downbeat as first reports held. Dr. Gallup wouldn't report it for two weeks, but he had also developed a formula for determining *likely* voters, and regarding likely voters—even after Nixon's lackluster performance—it was a dead heat, a 48 percent–to–48 percent tie.

Carrying Jack Kennedy's prizefight analogy a step further, JFK had staggered Nixon, bloodied him, but failed to deliver the knockout blow.

Now came debate two, scheduled to be held in Cleveland at 7:30 p.m. on Friday, October 7—Eleanor Roosevelt's seventy-sixth birthday— the event to be hosted by NBC. Except that no one had quite realized how small television studios were in Cleveland and how large a circus a two-man presidential debate might be. NBC decided to shift everything to WRC's northwest Washington, D.C., Studio A, and Richard Nixon shifted tactics.

First, of course, came makeup. The *Times'* Russell Baker reported:

Mr. Nixon will be using a new make-up man . . .

His regular man, Everett Hart, handled the job in Chicago. Mr. Hart's absence this week will have nothing to do with the "sabotage" charges, Nixon aides say. Mr. Hart is reported ill and unable to come to Washington.

Mr. Nixon's aides here say he will probably use a studio make-up man. Mr. Kennedy's aides insist that their man requires no make-up.

Oddly enough, Ev Hart's health never sufficiently recovered for him to resume his makeup duties.

Nixon regained the ten pounds he had lost prior to the first debate, but he only marginally kept his vow of sufficient rest prior to the Washington face-off, furiously campaigning in Nashville and Cleveland the previous day, drawing huge crowds, and not arriving home until midnight, spending all day Friday cramming once more.

His strategy, however, had mercifully changed. In Ohio, *Cleveland Press* editor Louis Selzer had advised him, "Don't pay any attention to the critics who talk about a New Nixon and an Old Nixon. These men are not your friends anyway. . . . Take the offensive from the first, with the gloves off."

But Dick Nixon already knew that by now.

He also knew he would avoid looking directly at Kennedy. Since Chicago—and he had done a lot of thinking since Chicago—he realized that directly looking at an opponent only increased his nervousness. Tonight, Richard Nixon would gaze into the camera, at his interrogators, at anyone but Jack Kennedy. Richard Nixon would speak to America.

The set had changed, too. Nixon's people complained that CBS's Chicago stage had looked stark. NBC replied with earth tones, a brown background flecked with green on textured grass cloth. Also new was a wedgelike desk shared by the candidates and the evening's moderator— this time NBC's Frank McGee—a contrivance that Russell Baker thought looked like a "boomerang." Two American flags now decorated the stage. People had called to complain about Old Glory's absence in Chicago.

The format changed. No opening or closing statements. Reporters could pose whatever questions they wished, on topics either foreign or domestic. A candidate had two and a half minutes to respond; his opponent, one and a half minutes to rebut.

Roles seemed reversed from the beginning. Jack and Bobby Kennedy arrived first, at 6:28 p.m. Nixon, with military aide Don Hughes in tow, followed at 6:52 p.m., made up at his home by his new makeup artist, "card-carrying Republican" Stan Lawrence.

And now it became Kennedy's turn to complain: about the studio's bracing sixty-four-degree temperature and about the four five-hundred-watt spotlights illuminating his position ("When I saw all these lights, I decided that NBC had chosen its candidate"). NBC doused one spotlight and jacked the thermostat to seventy degrees. All Nixon got was his spotlights accidentally knocked off-kilter by photographers jostling for pre-debate pictures.

Unlike in Chicago, little repartee and no pre-debate posing occurred. Both candidates retreated to their respective green rooms. Kennedy reemerged at 7:28 p.m., Nixon a minute later, just sixty seconds before airtime. Kennedy reached over, extended his hand. Nixon shook it but didn't stand. Reporters speculated that he recalled how he had hit his head—"like . . . a watermelon"—the last time he had risen to greet his adversary.

Nixon took the first question from CBS's Paul Niven regarding Kennedy's recent comments comparing "the loss of Cuba" to "the loss of China." Nixon came out of the box running, not about to tumble into the same over-obliging trap he had created for himself in Chicago: "Well, first of all, I don't agree with Senator Kennedy that Cuba is lost and certainly China was lost when this Administration came to power in 1953. . . . Now I'm very surprised that Senator Kennedy, who is on the Foreign Relations Committee, would make such a statement. . . . I don't think this kind of defeatist talk by Senator Kennedy helps the situation one bit."

The tone had been set: Nixon aggressive, Kennedy oddly defensive—at times, almost aping the feeble first-debate Nixon ("I have no disagreement with the Vice President's position on that. My view is the same as his"). The two antagonists had somehow switched personas, and there was no question which was the winning approach.

ABC's mustachioed and dapper Edward P. Morgan, three-point handkerchief peeking nattily from breast pocket, queried Kennedy regarding his suggestion in May that President Eisenhower apologize to Premier Khrushchev for the U-2 overflight. Kennedy dismissed Nixon's criticism of his statement as "distorted," and recited a list of Cold War apologies already issued by the administration. Again, Nixon struck back hard, unapologetically and effectively:

> We all remember Pearl Harbor. We lost three thousand American lives. We cannot afford an intelligence gap. And I just want to make my position absolutely clear with regard to getting intelligence information. I don't intend to see to it that the United States is ever in a position where, while we're negotiating with the Soviet Union, that we discontinue our intelligence effort. And I don't intend ever to express regrets to Mr. Khrushchev or anybody else if I'm doing something that has the support of the Congress and that is right for the purpose of protecting the security of the United States.

Beyond questions of substance—and the reinvigoration of Richard Nixon—Jack Kennedy was clearly off his game, regressing to uningratiating habits of talking too fast and too coldly. The press certainly thought so. Columnist Roscoe Drummond, while conceding that JFK remained "very attractive and impressive," criticized his inclination to speak "at a rapid rate in an almost tense monotone with little change of tenor or tempo."

The *Chicago Tribune*'s Willard Edwards said much the same—and more:

> Kennedy, who wore no make[up], according to an aide, looked the same as before, his chin lifted, his face earnest as he answered questions put by [the panel]. . . . But he raced through his words, swallowing some of them, and was obviously much less at ease than in Chicago. . . .
>
> During the time they were on view, Nixon looked at Kennedy only once when the senator accused [him] of "distorting" a statement. Kennedy seemed fascinated by Nixon, regarding him with almost an incredulous look, so fixedly that a studio attaché once whispered to him to speak directly into the microphone.

Even normally difficult-to-please Dwight Eisenhower seemed, by his standards, impressed. "The second debate," he would record with, nonetheless, noticeable understatement, "made us feel much better."

Kennedy's unease stemmed largely from questions surrounding Quemoy and Matsu, Nationalist-held islands just miles off the central Red Chinese coast. For nearly a decade, American policy had been officially hazy regarding these heavily fortified islands. While a formal congressional resolution committed the United States to defending Nationalist Formosa (Taiwan) and the reasonably adjacent Pescadores islands, it did not formally bind America to defending Quemoy and Matsu. It nonetheless did "include the securing and protection of such related positions and territories of that area now in friendly hands." And two Senate amendments to specifically exclude Quemoy and Matsu from Formosa's defense perimeter had met overwhelming defeat. Many strategists feared that if America specifically stated it would not defend Quemoy and Matsu, it would only invite Red Chinese aggression.

The controversy had commenced at Hyannis Port on Friday, September 30, as NBC news anchors Chet Huntley and David Brinkley taped a nearly hour-long interview with JFK for Frank McGee's weekly *The Campaign and the Candidates* series. Huntley inquired if Kennedy agreed with the "present policy [*sic*] with which it seems to me we are committed now to the defense of the tiny islands off the coast of China, Quemoy and Matsu?"

"I have always thought that was an unwise place to draw the line," Kennedy responded. "We should draw the line . . . so that any aggressor knows that if he moves into this area that it would mean war. . . . Under the Eisenhower doctrine, we have stated we would defend Quemoy and Matsu if it was part of an attack on the island of Formosa. How are we going to make that judgment? . . . Quemoy and Matsu are not essential to the defense of Formosa."

As soon as debate two neared closure, ABC's Edward P. Morgan queried Kennedy, "[Y]ou had always thought that Quemoy and Matsu were unwise places to draw our defense line in the Far East. . . . [C]ouldn't a pullback from those islands be interpreted as appeasement?"

Since the Truman administration, Democrats had awkwardly defended their opposition to and attitude toward Soviet and Chinese communism, with JFK among his party's more aggressive Cold Warriors, a picture of anti-Red resolve. The U-2 and Quemoy and Matsu exchanges, while cementing his newfound alliance with party liberals, jeopardized his appeal to the electorate's still strongly anti-communist majority, wary of losing still more territory and people to the Reds. Nonetheless, once having revived the issue, JFK had to defend his position: "I do not believe that that line in case of war should be drawn on those islands but instead on . . . Formosa. And as long as they are not essential to . . . Formosa, it's been my judgment ever since 1954 . . . that our line should be drawn in the sea around the island itself."

Again, Nixon responded like the Nixon of old, dredging up Truman administration missteps, out-hawking the normally "bear any burden" Kennedy:

> I disagree completely. . . . South Korea was supposed to be indefensible as well. Generals testified to that. And Secretary Acheson made a very famous speech at the Press Club, early in the year that [the] Korean War started, indicating in effect that South Korea was beyond the defense zone of the United States. I suppose it was hoped when he made that speech that we wouldn't get into a war. But it didn't mean that. We had to go in when they came in. . . . [T]he question is not these two little pieces of real estate—they are unimportant. . . . It's the principle. . . . If we do that we start a chain reaction; because the Communists aren't after Quemoy and Matsu, they're after Formosa. . . . [T]his is the same kind of woolly thinking that led to disaster for America in Korea.

As it happened, fortune finally smiled on Kennedy, the luck of the draw granting him the evening's closing remarks—and once again he played his strongest trump card, the majority status of his Democratic Party:

> [P]arties are important in that they tell something about the program and something about the man. . . . The Democratic party in this century has stood for something. It has stood for progress; it has stood for concern for the people's welfare. It has stood for a strong foreign policy and a strong national defense, and as a result, produced Wilson, President Roosevelt, and President Truman. The Republican party has produced McKinley and Harding, Coolidge, Dewey, and Landon. They do stand for something. They stand for a whole dif-

ferent approach to the problems facing this country at home and abroad. That's the importance of party; only if it tells something about the record. And the Republicans in recent years—not only in the last twenty-five years, but in the last eight years—have opposed housing, opposed care for the aged, opposed federal aid to education, opposed minimum wage and I think that record tells something.

It was over. Kennedy, with a talk to deliver that night at Washington's all-black Howard University, bolted from WRC's studio, barely pausing to shake Nixon's hand. To the *Chicago Tribune*'s Willard Edwards, he looked "irritated [and] anxious to get away" and had little more to offer than "We had a fine exchange," and to agree with Nixon that "We'll know on November 8 who won."

Nixon, heartened by the recovery of his trademark form, proved more talkative: "It was a good sharp debate—certainly not dull. . . . It was a faster and better way to stage such a meeting. Of course the time was too short. I had so much more I wanted to say."

Rose Kennedy thought her son had done fine. No doubts resided in her mind. To her diary she confided: "He looked more assured than Nixon and looked better physically. Jack seemed to have all the initiative and once or twice rose to inspiring heights of oratory. . . . Jack really looks, sounds, and acts like young Lincoln."

A day later came validation of her maternal judgments: "The policeman came into the hairdresser's and said . . . that Jack had won the debate, or rather people had liked him better."

More likely, they merely liked him better; few really thought he had won. Debate one had elevated expectations. JFK now had to do more than break even, and few felt he had, particularly in the face of Richard Nixon's improvement. James Reston found Nixon "[m]ore composed this time, and much more political in his answers. . . . At . . . the first debate, his supporters were discouraged; tonight when the lights went out, they were pleased and even delighted."

In the pressroom, Reston surveyed his peers: eleven thought Nixon won, eleven scored it a tie, and a mere five awarded the night to Kennedy.

Reston concluded that the vice president "clearly made a comeback, came out ahead." The *New York Herald-Tribune* proclaimed that Nixon had "clearly won the second round." Roscoe Drummond announced Nixon was "now back on even terms . . . [his] candidacy [given] a new lift, an indispensable lift."

In crude mathematics, the score now stood one-even, but to equate debate two's impact to that of the first was foolhardy. Most importantly, viewership had dropped by approximately ten million viewers. For another, each debate triggered reactions—elations—of widely different stripes. Nixon's victory was a relief, all too much akin to the great, slow exhale following a successful biopsy. Kennedy's victory was a thrill, a jump-up-and-down moment in national history. It had made him not just cancer free. It made him a star.

And, perhaps, that is why Nixon stonewalled Kennedy's call for a fifth debate. The idea was tempting, and Nixon had even summoned the exiled Murray Chotiner for advice. Chotiner said go for it. "I thought," Chotiner recalled, "he was coming on."

Nixon said no. Instead, he proposed expanding the final fourth debate to two hours—another proposal that ultimately went nowhere.

A mere six days separated debates two and three. Gone was Kennedy's cocksureness, his sense of inevitable triumph. The afternoon of debate three found John Kenneth Galbraith on New York's Upper East Side, where he was scheduled to speak at the Carlyle Hotel. Kennedy ordered Galbraith to cancel his talk, summoning him instead to his top-floor, duplex suite in that very same hotel to confer for debate prep. They lunched with Ted Sorensen and Arthur Schlesinger, but JFK, Galbraith sensed, was

> visibly ill at ease. Occasionally he would propose a likely question for discussion and then change the subject before the answer. Once he was distracted by where he had put a check handed to him a few minutes earlier . . . "I must learn to be more careful with money."
>
> Kennedy, too nervous to concentrate on anything, signaled an end to the gathering. As the party rode down the elevator together, Kennedy muttered, "I keep saying to myself, 'Kennedy, you're the only thing that stands between Nixon and the White House.'"

Debate three featured yet another new format. Candidates would not resolutely stare—or irresolutely sweat—across the confines of a single stage. This time, courtesy of campaign scheduling difficulties, an entire continent separated them—Nixon was stationed in Hollywood, JFK on Manhattan's West Side. Each would have identical studios, with carbon-copy lighting and game show–style podiums, each performing before a bank of four cameras.

Temperatures? Not identical. Kennedy's studio remained seasonably toasty, Nixon's cranked down to sixty or sixty-two—some even said fifty-eight. Still, Nixon sweated profusely. Off camera, he repeatedly dabbed his upper lip.

In Hollywood, Nixon had yet another new makeup artist, NBC's Claude Thompson. No one quite understood why NBC's head makeup man had materialized at rival ABC. Nobody bothered to explain.

In New York, a half hour before airtime, JFK again arrived wearing a white shirt and, once more, changed to blue.

Jackie attended—she would rent no television this evening. ABC staffers served the Kennedys sandwiches, canapés, coffee, and tea. The senator hadn't eaten dinner. Too nervous now, he merely sipped tea.

Each candidate awaited airtime in relative comfort. In New York and in Hollywood, ABC had constructed two-room, twelve-by-twenty-four apple green prefabricated cottages, each complete with a roof, easy chairs, desks, five phones, and even a red carpet from the studio entrance to its homey front door.

Originally, this intercontinental session was to feature repeated split-screen shots simultaneously showing both candidates. The idea was a bad one. Split screens had been feasible when both men shared the same stage and wasn't a good idea even then. ABC director Marshall Diskin dismissed the concept as merely "distracting" and sent the split-screen gimmick into the ashcan of debate history.

Debate three did, however, utilize debate two's no-opening-or-closing-statements, all-questions-allowed format, lurching more stolidly than nimbly from topic to topic—from defending West Berlin to compulsory arbitration to the chaos-plagued former Belgian Congo to the U-2 to government spending to the oil depletion allowance (of major importance in pivotal Texas; Kennedy proved oddly noncommittal; Nixon voiced support), but only two exchanges seemed to catch anyone's attention: Harry Truman's vocabulary and, once again, Quemoy and Matsu.

As previously noted, Tuesday, October 11, had found former presi-dent Truman campaigning in San Antonio, blasting Nixon and all things GOP, testily instructing local Democrats, "If you vote for Nixon, you ought to go to hell." Republicans demanded that Truman apologize. Truman refused, for good measure, laughingly instructing reporters, "Tell them to go to hell."

So it was that thirty-four-year-old panelist Charles Von Fremd of CBS asked of John Kennedy, "Thruston Morton, declared . . . that you owed Vice President Nixon and the Republican party a public apology for some strong charges made by former President Harry Truman, who bluntly suggested where [they] could go. Do you feel that you owe the Vice President an apology?"

Kennedy responded, as he often did when at his best, skillfully mixing dollops of wit, self-deprecation, and the principle of not-really-going-near-the-question:

> Well, I must say that Mr. Truman has his methods of expressing things; he's been in politics for fifty years; he's been president of the United States. They . . . are not my style. But I really don't think there's anything that I could say to President Truman that's going to cause him, at the age of seventy-six, to change his particular speaking manner. Perhaps Mrs. Truman can, but I don't think I can. I'll just have to tell Mr. Morton that. If you'd pass that message on to him.

Nixon, however, retreated to Nixon at his worst, or at least his most mediocre, responding ponderously, humorouslessly, self-righteously, and—bottom line—for far too long:

> I just do want to say one thing, however. We all have tempers; I have one; I'm sure Senator Kennedy has one. But when a man's president of the United States, or a former president, he has an obligation not to lose his temper in public. One thing I've noted as I've traveled around the country are the tremendous number of children who come out to see the presidential candidates. I see mothers holding their babies up, so that they can see a man who might be president of the United States. I know Senator Kennedy sees them, too. It makes you realize that who-

ever is president is going to be a man that all the children of America will either look up to, or will look down to. And I can only say that I'm very proud that President Eisenhower restored dignity and decency and, frankly, good language to the conduct of the presidency of the United States. And I only hope that, should I win this election, that I could approach President Eisenhower in maintaining the dignity of the office; in seeing to it that whenever any mother or father talks to his child, he can look at the man in the White House and, whatever he may think of his policies, he will say: "Well, there is a man who maintains the kind of standards personally that I would want my child to follow."

Observers who chose to comment merely scoffed.

Nixon fared better with old standbys Quemoy and Matsu. He had struck a public nerve with his debate two comments advocating their defense. And Peking had helpfully inflamed tempers by shelling the islands within twenty-four hours of the Washington debate, their heaviest bombardment since resuming offensive action that June. In the intervening week, Nixon similarly shelled Kennedy for his paucity of resolve. From Hollywood, he reiterated:

What I object to here is the constant reference to surrendering these islands. Senator Kennedy quotes the record [of the Senate's 1955 Senate vote] . . . but what he forgets to point out is that the key vote . . . where he was in the minority [74–13] was one which rejected his position. Now, why did they reject it? For the very reason that those Senators knew, as the President of the United States knew, that you should not indicate to the Communists in advance that you're going to surrender an area that's free. Why? Because they know as Senator Kennedy will have to know that if you do that you encourage them to more aggression.

Kennedy countered that a "trigger-happy" defense of Quemoy and Matsu would initiate a "massive nuclear holocaust." From ABC's West Sixty-sixth Street studio he twitted Nixon and the Republicans for being more concerned about Quemoy and Matsu than in far more significant pieces of real estate that had fallen, or were falling, into communist hands:

He didn't take that position on Tibet. He didn't take that position on Budapest. He doesn't take that position that I've seen so far in Laos. Guinea and Ghana have both moved within the Soviet sphere of influence in foreign policy; so has Cuba. I merely say that the United States should meet its commitments to Formosa and the Pescadores. But as [former commander of the Asiatic Fleet] Admiral [Harry E.] Yarnell has said, and he's been supported by most military authority, these islands that we're now talking about are not worth the bones of a single American soldier; and I know how difficult it is to sustain troops close to the shore under artillery bombardment. And therefore, I think, we should make it very clear the disagreement between Mr. Nixon and myself. He's extending the Administration's commitment.

It received relatively little notice, but Kennedy's citation of Admiral Yarnell's comments was a strange and slender reed upon which to hang an otherwise defensible policy. The admiral had been dead since July 1959. A veteran of the previous century's Spanish-American War, he had been retired since 1939—and eighty years of age when he made the statement at a 1955 symposium with twelve other military leaders. The other eleven had disagreed with him.

"Why doesn't the Senator quote Admiral Dewey while he's at it?" jibed Nelson Rockefeller.

In the end, Nixon won again, and not just marginally as in the second debate, but rather obviously and overwhelmingly. His polling operation, Claude Robinson's Opinion Research Corporation, reported he had proven more effective in the third debate than had Kennedy in the first. This was, grudgingly admitted Teddy White, "Nixon's best performance in terms of impact on the audience. . . . [I]t was as if, separated by a continent from . . . his adversary, Nixon were more at ease and could speak directly to the nation that lay between them."

Kennedy's stature was rapidly unraveling, his persona more testy than tested. James Reston thought JFK "more confident—even cocky," but that seemed a minority opinion. New York Herald-Tribune television critic John Crosby, listening on radio, observed that "Kennedy sounded frequently, quite angry and, for the first time, on the defensive. . . . Of the two, Kennedy seemed more tense. Kennedy hasn't the breath control of

Nixon and this is far more noticeable on radio than on TV. He talks too fast on both TV and radio, but again, it's more noticeable on radio."

As the debates dragged on, their novelty rapidly evaporating, it became painfully evident that the format itself left much to be desired. There was, of course, plenty of blame to assign. Reporters blamed the format. Others blamed the reporters. Ted Sorensen eventually concluded that the panelists had been the weakest link in the whole system, finding their questions "unimaginative . . . increasingly inept . . . rarely [with] continuity in a single debate but . . . repetitious in the course of all four."

But if the reporters could no longer make the debates interesting, Richard Nixon would.

THIRTY-THREE

"Senator Kennedy is in clear violation of the spirit of the law"

IT WAS GETTING HOTTER, and for once it was Richard Nixon turning up the thermostat, a task made so much more convenient by controversies both small and large—particularly when ABC's cameras caught Jack Kennedy cheating.

Debaters were not to employ notes. Nixon's initial response to NBC's Robert Sarnoff's call for debates clearly spelled out his desire for a "full and free exchange of views without prepared texts or notes." But during debate three (the only venue where JFK and Dick Nixon did not share a studio), Jack Kennedy possessed not one note, not even *one stack* of notes, but rather *two stacks*, and, worse (certainly from his standpoint), he dropped a note and picked it up off the floor—and the camera caught him.

"I couldn't have been more shocked," Richard Nixon exclaimed, sounding far too much like Claude Rains in *Casablanca* for his own good. "All my statements were from memory, without notes. That was the rule to be followed. I never complain about debates after they are over but before the next debate, we had better settle on rules."

For good measure, Bob Finch proclaimed that, in resorting to such contraband, JFK had, in effect, employed "a ghost writer." Finch didn't say "yet again." He didn't have to.

Kennedy responded with a written statement (perhaps, come to think of it, ghostwritten) that was properly assertive—yet that notably neglected to deny either any agreement or the violation thereof:

> I quoted from a photostat . . . regarding our treaty relationships around Formosa.
>
> If the President . . . is to be quoted on a matter involving our security he should be quoted accurately. I think quoting the record accurately is in the interest of these debates.

It fell to Pierre Salinger to issue denials, his job complicated by ABC vice president John Daly's recollection that both men would speak "ad lib"—"without prepared text or notes."

The days proceeded. Tempers frayed like a cheap suit. Two days in advance of debate four, the Democratic National Committee released a five-minute television commercial highlighting the first Kennedy-Nixon confrontation—nothing surprising there, little about which Republicans might gripe. But the DNC played it cute, cobbling together otherwise disjointed footage of Kennedy into neat little narratives where none had existed previously. Worse still, interspersed with these creations were shots, wrenched from their context, of Richard Nixon smiling or solemnly nodding agreement. Faking a celluloid Richard Nixon worse than the real debate one version seemed beyond unfair: It was egregiously unnecessary. Bob Finch blasted the Democrats' "alteration and tampering with the honest sequence of appearances [and] vicious political trickery," calling the commercial "a throwback to old political tricks such as cropped or trick photographs."

The best response the increasingly embattled Salinger could now muster was the gaucherie that his candidate may have indeed looked better in the spot "because we paid for it."

But cribbed notes and clipped films were nothing compared to what now transpired regarding an actual, increasingly grave, public-policy question: Fidel Castro's Cuba.

The bearded, fatigue-clad, thirty-two-year-old revolutionary Castro had seized power on New Year's Day 1959, leading his band of revolutionary guerrillas out of the Sierra Maestra and into Havana, overthrowing corrupt longtime dictator Fulgencio Batista. Tossing away a reservoir of American goodwill, Castro soon sent his relations with the United States spiraling downward in an avalanche of overheated Marxist rhetoric, the extinction of private property and free speech, the jailing of dissidents, and the sharp retort of firing squads at mass executions. By 1960 Castro's nation had lurched dangerously nearer the Soviet orbit—and in September of that year Castro launched his own gaudy personal invasion of the American mainland.

The occasion was that year's United Nations General Assembly, already a media circus thanks to Nikita Khrushchev's bumptious, shoe-thumping antics. Castro, however, made Khrushchev seem sedate as he and his gun-toting eighty-five-person entourage held court at Harlem's seedy and hitherto-segregated Hotel Theresa. Haranguing the General Assembly for four and a half hours, Castro lacerated everything Norte Americano, including John Kennedy, whom he derided as an "illiterate and ignorant millionaire."

It was not something Americans were used to, being spat at on their own soil—and, thanks to the protocols of the United Nations, being unable to prevent it. But while this treatment was unfamiliar to Americans, they were becoming unpleasantly used to Castro's heavy-handed economic policies. On October 14, 1960, Havana nationalized 382 businesses, including the remainder of the country's 161 sugar mills and virtually the remainder of its banks and textile mills—nearly two billion dollars' worth of property in all.

John F. Kennedy had been slow in arriving at the anti-Castro game. His latest published effort, *The Strategy of Peace*, a "selection of speeches and statements" issued in late March 1960, had sympathetically described the vituperative new Cuban despot in oddly idealized, strangely heroic terms:

> Fidel Castro is part of the legacy of [Simon] Bolivar who led his men over the Andes Mountains, vowing "war to the death" against Spanish rule. . . . Castro is also part of the frustration of that earlier revolution which won its war against Spain but left largely untouched the indigenous feudal order. . . .
>
> Whether Castro would have taken a more rational course after his victory had the United States Government not backed the dictator Batista so long and so uncritically, and had it given the fiery young rebel a warmer welcome in his hour of triumph, especially on his trip to this country, we cannot be sure.

Such lyrical paeans to despotism, admitted Ted Sorensen, proved an ultimate embarrassment to a presidential candidate, though not enough for JFK to officially repudiate. But as the campaign reached a crescendo, the hour for extolling "fiery young rebels" had long passed. As Richard Goodwin would recall, "Everywhere—in the Dakotas as well as Florida—

there were more questions about Cuba and Castro than about any other matter of foreign policy."

JFK increasingly busied himself hammering the administration, Richard Nixon in particular, for its actions and inactions on Castro, trumpeting loudly and with more than some justification, "The people of the United States would like to hear [Nixon] discuss his views on an island not four miles off the coast of China [Quemoy], but 90 miles off the Coast of the United States—Cuba."

In actuality, Kennedy wasn't exactly sure himself what he would do regarding Cuba or what Eisenhower or Nixon might do. But what, after all, had that to with the business at hand? "As the pace of the campaign quickened," Arthur Schlesinger would ultimately gingerly concede, "politics began to clash with Kennedy's innate sense of responsibility."

On Thursday, October 20, the eve of debate four—and the same day the United States recalled its ambassador from Havana—JFK raised the stakes, issuing a position paper basically calling for a U.S.-backed overthrow of Havana's Marxist dictatorship. To the casual observer the document merely appeared because it appeared, because Cuba was increasingly at the center of the news and because the next president, whoever he might be, must deal with the Castro regime. In actuality, it was directly related to debate three and the drubbing administered to Jack Kennedy over two other islands half a world away. Because Kennedy had looked "soft" in the China straits, Arthur Schlesinger would later explain, he must now look tough ("take the offensive") in the Caribbean.

In part, too, it was also a defensive move. From Washington on October 19, Kennedy research aide forty-eight-year-old Harvard Law professor Archibald Cox had written to Richard Goodwin, warning that Richard Nixon was "willing to take action which disregards the [Organization of American States] charter and endangers our relations with other Latin American states for the sake of some supposed political advantages." Nixon, Cox continued, was "willing to endanger our position in the world and risk war . . . to get votes. It is time for us to take away the claim that the Republicans are the party of peace. No one will suppose that Senator Kennedy is an appeaser."

Anti-communism was good politics. Even liberals recognized that. A Democrat could only lose by looking weak on defense, irresolute against

Moscow and Havana. Even the notorious egghead Chester Bowles (an isolationist America Firster in pre–Pearl Harbor days) recognized that. "You have been brilliantly successful in building up our position in regard to American military strength," Bowles congratulated Jack Kennedy just before debate four, "to a point where no one can call us 'soft on Communism.'"

And having established that reputation, Kennedy was not about to fling it away for a portfolio of real estate called Quemoy and Matsu. He needed to change the subject. Accordingly, on that October 20, Kennedy's white paper contained this fateful clause: "We must attempt to strengthen the non-Batista democratic anti-Castro forces in exile, and in Cuba itself, who offer eventual hope of overthrowing Castro."

And then he took a swipe at the Eisenhower administration: "Thus far these fighters for freedom have had virtually no support from our government."

In fact, the Eisenhower White House *was* plotting Castro's overthrow (Americans were not parachuting into Cuba for sport), and Richard Nixon (for obvious reasons) counted himself among the administration's most aggressive advocates of prompt action. An invasion had originally been planned for September 1960, but disunity among Cuban exile groups as to who might lead any resulting government forced the CIA to abandon that date. As John Kennedy would in time discover, organizing a coup was not the same as wanting one.

Beyond that, in July and again in September, CIA director Allen Dulles had personally briefed Kennedy on intelligence matters. Nixon, believing that JFK now officially knew that a coup was in the works, concluded that Jack Kennedy was purposefully playing the most cynical politics with national security. He was outraged. "For the first and only time in the campaign," he would write, "I got mad at Kennedy— personally. . . . And my rage was greater because I could do nothing about it."

His rage had been building for quite some time. On Sunday, October 9, the Nixon campaign had a forced day off, stuck in Billings, Montana, in the rain. Nixon nervously paced the deserted city streets. He stopped for hotcakes, country sausage, milk, and coffee in a diner, eating it alone in a booth, having borrowed $2.50 from a cop to pay for it, chatting with strangers—"Didn't you recognize me by my big nose?" He slipped into the First Methodist Church to attend services, witnessing five baptisms, autographing Bibles, returning to his hotel to compose upcoming speeches, watching the World Series (Pirates 3, Yankees 2) on television, and, finally, had Herb Klein summon the *Chicago Tribune*'s Willard Edwards for a private little talk that turned into a great unburdening.

Eventually, the conversation turned to Kennedy and Cuba. Nixon confided that the CIA was already training a Cuban exile invasion, and that Kennedy knew about it—but, aware that Nixon could not counter him, JFK kept jabbing away.

As Edwards's notes indicate, Nixon explained that he "was in a position" to discomfort Kennedy "by revealing that the Eisenhower administration was planning an action more bold against Castro than any Kennedy had suggested. He simply could not do so."

"The gag was the more infuriating," Edwards continued, "because Nixon was becoming increasingly angry over Kennedy's refusal to attribute to his Republican opponent the same good motives Nixon freely accorded to his rival. Nixon had accused Kennedy of naivety, recklessness, gullibility, and extreme bad judgment, but always interpolated in his speeches a reminder that he thought Kennedy's goals the same as his.

"But Kennedy, beginning with his acceptance . . . in which he assailed Nixon as a man with 'malice for all, charity for none,' had never once conceded that Nixon's motives might be good."

Willard Edwards departed, concluding that Nixon's Cuban apologia was "off the record," though Nixon had never said anything explicitly to that effect. It was all, in Edwards's mind, "implicit."

"If Nixon couldn't talk about it," he would write, "neither could I."

Yet, the question remains: Had Nixon meant to leak this state secret, to blow Kennedy out of the water, employing Edwards as a conduit? In 1960 reporters could, and did, retain a confidence if national security was at stake, and not only did Edwards maintain the vice president's secret; he telegraphed to Jack Kennedy that Richard Nixon would keep silent. On Wednesday, October 12, Edwards proceeded as far as he dared and wrote, "Nixon's position . . . has both advantages and disadvantages. In the field of foreign policy, he is privy to certain government operations which he may not discuss when Kennedy attacks the administration for inaction. He accepts this frustration as a penalty of his office."

Did Edwards's words embolden Kennedy's team to push even further than they had on Cuba—particularly when they needed a quick bounce to slide past the Quemoy-Matsu imbroglio?

We may never know. But we do know that years later, Kennedy's men, still jealously guarding his reputation, would claim he fell victim not to his own cynicism but rather to their ineptitude. Kennedy, they averred, had *never seen* the controversial October 20 statement prior to its release. Richard Goodwin, working on it since October 19, ran it past Sorensen and Salinger. They pronounced it fine, clearly within the parameters of the candidate's recent statements on the subject, merely requiring the candidate's OK.

"It was very late at night," Goodwin would later explain.

I called . . . to read it to Kennedy, but . . . we decided not to wake him. Not knowing about the Bay of Pigs invasion plans, which I didn't know but Kennedy may very well have known [in his memoirs Goodwin flatly states JFK did know], the statement didn't have any implication for me that it took on immediately in the press. He had been . . . giving speeches saying we ought to do something to help the anti-Castro forces. So it didn't appear to me to be anything much different from what he had been saying either. . . . However, a particular phrase, one or two words used, did in fact suggest the force of military action from the outside, which was not in my mind, to tell you the truth. And I certainly knew nothing about the plans.

"It was," Goodwin also contended (and Arthur Schlesinger made a similar assertion), "the only public statement by the candidate in the entire campaign that he had not personally reviewed."

Given the demands and realities of a presidential (or even a non-presidential) campaign, Goodwin and Schlesinger's protestations—that this was the *only* campaign statement JFK never saw—strike one as a bit fanciful, though even if awake Kennedy might well have blundered down the same path. "In all probability," Schlesinger coyly confessed, "Kennedy would have approved the text, though he told me he would have changed the phrase 'fighters for freedom' to 'forces of freedom.'"

The Goodwin-Schlesinger "While Kennedy Slept" defense rings false on several levels. Kennedy biographer Herbert Parmet notes:

> [T]he release was issued not during the night, Goodwin remembers, or even the next morning. The early release on the twentieth . . . was the three-thousand-word refutation of Nixon's criticism of Kennedy's "misstatements." The Cuban comments were, instead, handed to the press on the evening of the twentieth . . . to make the morning papers of the twenty-first. If Kennedy was asleep at a crucial point, taking his customary afternoon nap, there was still enough time between then and that evening for him to have cleared the statement.

And Kennedy had indeed already issued similar statements. "The forces fighting for freedom in exile and in the mountains of Cuba," he had asserted, "should be sustained and assisted." As far back as October 6, in Cincinnati, he had pledged himself to a policy of "encouraging those liberty-loving Cubans who are leading the resistance to Castro."

So Kennedy may—or may not—have erred, may or may not have slept, and Nixon may have been—and probably was—miffed. Mistakes happen. People get angry. Not easily understandable is what followed Nixon's anger: If Kennedy had sabotaged a covert operation, by *supporting* it, Nixon would now undermine it by *opposing* it.

In his first memoir, *Six Crises*, he wrote, "There was only one thing I could do. The covert operation had to be protected at all costs. I must not even suggest by implication that the United States was rendering aid to rebel forces. . . . In fact, I must go to the other extreme: I must attack the Kennedy proposal to provide such aid as wrong and irresponsible because it would violate our treaty commitments."

On the face of it, Nixon's tactic made no sense. It must have resulted from blind rage. His actions would only make any later armed intervention impossible. His actions could only—in the long term—torpedo what he claimed to advocate.

"Nixon's response," wrote Tom Wicker, "remains hard to understand or justify."

Unless, of course, one reads between the lines.

Meanwhile, as his crucial last debate drew nearer, Senator Kennedy remained keyed up, edgy, less willing than ever to assume that victory belonged to him by divine right of his being a Kennedy. Index cards and suntans would no longer turn the trick. For debates three and four, ABC allowed both candidates full access to its studios for up to thirty-six hours prior to airtime. Kennedy, according to ABC's Tom Moore (later network president), rehearsed in excess of seven hours for each session. Beyond that, he engaged noted television (*Producer's Showcase* and *Playhouse 90*) and theatrical (*The Miracle Worker*) producer Fred Coe to supervise his tune-ups. Nixon, win or lose, ahead or behind, ignored ABC's offer.

For debate four, Nixon pulled into the studio with barely eight minutes to go. Kennedy, fresh from a shave and sunlamp treatment at the Waldorf, arrived just after him, with the vice president barely having begun his light tests. Though Kennedy had spent so much time in these studios, even debating there previously, he still complained about the lighting—and got it dimmed.

And, again, the battle over temperature: Kennedy insisted the studio be seventy-two degrees. Reporters noted it registered at seventy-one and a half.

ABC's Quincy Howe moderated. CBS's Walter Cronkite, NBC's John Chancellor, ABC's John Edwards, and Mutual's Frank Singiser would pose questions.

Nixon won the coin toss. He would speak first—and last—crucial advantages made all the more significant by the fact that the night's audience had yet again soared to the gargantuan seventy-million level of their first encounter.

Kennedy remained noticeably edgy. Standing at his podium, he drew three great breaths, so great the press could not fail to notice them.

The show began.

Limited to foreign policy, debate four careened from antipode to antipode—from Quemoy and Matsu to who might emerge as the next secretary of state to affairs at the United States Information Agency to limiting atomic testing to freeing Eastern Europe. Yet its brightest spotlight fell upon a single portion of the world stage: Cuba.

It must have surprised Jack Kennedy when Cold Warrior Richard Nixon attacked his Cuban position with unbridled vehemence, particularly when he knew that he and the Eisenhower administration were basically on the same page. Nixon later damned his task as "the most uncomfortable and ironic duty I have had to perform in any political campaign," but he executed it with as much force as he had yet mustered in these debates:

> Senator Kennedy's policies and recommendations . . . are probably the most dangerously irresponsible recommendations that he's made during the course of this campaign. . . . We have five treaties . . . in which we have agreed not to intervene in the internal affairs of any other American country.
>
> The Charter of the United Nations . . . also provides that there shall be no intervention by one nation in the internal affairs of another. . . . If we were to follow [Kennedy's] recommendation . . . we would lose all of our friends in Latin America, we would probably be condemned in the United Nations, and we would not accomplish our objective.

Kennedy responded mildly, merely questioning administration diplomatic efforts to coordinate an international economic boycott. In doing so, he ignored what was at best Nixon double-talk, and at worst a Nixon slip—revealing what actual national policy was:

> Now, what can we do? Well, we can do what we did with Guatemala. There was a Communist dictator that we inherited from the previous Administration. We quarantined Mr. [Jacobo] Arbenz. The result was that the Guatemalan people themselves eventually rose up and they threw him out. We are quarantining Mr. Castro today.

Read between the lines, and not very deeply between them, and what Nixon said was this: The United States would deal with Castro the same way it had disposed of far-left Arbenz in June 1954. We would *indeed* help overthrow Fidel. We'd just keep our mouths shut about it.

Then Kennedy let slip an "ugly-American"-style line. Usually careful to advocate a more sophisticated strategy toward Cuba—an amalgam of economic, diplomatic, and propaganda tactics—he now lectured Nixon: "In

1957 I was in Havana. I talked to the American Ambassador there. He said that he was the second most powerful man in Cuba." JFK had employed this anecdote on the stump, sometimes modifying it ("Probably he [the ambassador] shouldn't be"), but here, nervous and rushed, before his largest audience, before tens of millions of liberals at home and sensitive Latin Americans abroad, he did not. Neither group could have relished it.

It was, when all was done, arguably "mission accomplished" for Richard Nixon. True, near the end he made a (perhaps Freudian) little gaffe ("America cannot stand pat") that provided otherwise unsatisfied Democrats with a cause for titters. But overall he had succeeded once more.

"I felt that I had made as good a case as possible for my point of view," he would write. But he also had a cause for concern. His position was not the emotionally popular stance. "I had no illusion about the effect on the public generally," he recalled. "I was in the ironic position of appearing to be 'softer' on Castro than Kennedy . . . the opposite of the truth. . . . My attack was effective but with the wrong audience."

There was, of course, more to the debate. JFK scored with his usual thrusts about American prestige in decline, its diplomatic fumbling—particularly with Africa's emerging nations—and, finally, regarding one of the key points in the Democratic campaign: America's alleged missile gap. Remarkably, for all the controversy surrounding this supposed national peril, the word "missile" did not appeared in the debates until debate three, and even then rather perfunctorily. In debate four, Kennedy warned, quite unnecessarily as it turned out,

> Mr. Nixon talks about our being the strongest country in the world. I think we are today. But we were far stronger relative to the Communists five years ago, and what is of great concern is that the balance of power is in danger of moving with them. They made a breakthrough in missiles, and by nineteen sixty-one, two, and three, they will be outnumbering us in missiles. I'm not as confident as he is that we will be the strongest military power by 1963.

When it was over, it was all pretty tense. No facades of friendliness survived between the two combatants, at least in the case of Jack Kennedy.

They shook hands, exchanged farewells. Nixon made one last attempt at small talk: "It sure goes by fast, doesn't it?" JFK merely nodded, said nothing, and rushed off. Some said his performance so angered and disappointed him that he punched his apple green cottage wall before departing. Whether America could stand her or not, Richard Nixon returned to Pat, across town at the Waldorf-Astoria.

Nixon felt good about things. But the liberal press did not, disconcerted as they were to find themselves preferring Richard Nixon's words to John Kennedy's—certainly so regarding Cuba. The senator from Massachusetts, the Democratic nominee, hell-bent on jingoism? Richard Nixon, HUAC inquisitor, five-o'clock-shadowed proto-McCarthyite, counseling restraint and the rule of international law? The election might be just around the corner, but Kennedy's heresy could not pass unnoticed.

Walter Lippmann, the seventy-one-year-old dean of liberal columnists, perceptively (or perhaps just reflexively) saw through Nixon's "false and insincere" position, but nonetheless chided Kennedy, gently but publicly, for blundering into yet another foreign policy trap: "He [JFK] made a mistake. . . . Mr. Kennedy, who would, I believe, make the better president, is not infallible. He is human and it is human to err."

"I really don't know what further demagoguery is possible from Kennedy on this subject," sneered the *New York Post*'s Murray Kempton, "short of announcing that, if elected, he will send Bobby and Teddy and Eunice to Oriente Province to clean Castro out."

James Reston, while easily seeing through Richard Nixon's gossamer-thin Guatemalan subterfuge, felt no better about Kennedy's penchant for creating—or at least aggravating—foreign policy entanglements: "Senator Kennedy made what is probably his worst blunder of the campaign . . . a clear violation of the inter-American treaty prohibition against intervention in the internal affairs of the hemisphere republics."

And then, the final irony: Nixon challenged Kennedy to a fifth debate—and Kennedy ultimately demurred.

By now, many, if not most, observers had recognized that a fifth debate, whether in the manner of the first and fourth confrontations or the second and third, would accomplish nothing. "The fourth debate was the dreariest," Theodore White would write, "[because] both candidates had by now almost nothing new left to say." And certainly no one would have anything new to say in the disjointed, unilluminating, jump-from-topic-to-topic format everyone had already beaten to death.

What Richard Nixon now proposed was something completely new—and completely cynical. It was completely new (at least, in 1960) in that he proposed a debate, much like the Lincoln-Douglas face-off (it was always better to compare yourself to Lincoln and Douglas, rather than Dewey and Stassen), on "one subject of great immediate public interest on which the candidates completely disagree with each other." The question being: "What should the United States Government do about Castro?"

Answering his own question, Nixon proposed "a political and economic quarantine," arguing that Kennedy's call for anti-Castro action would violate five treaties America was signatory to, alienate our Latin American allies, and, most presciently, "give Mr. Khrushchev a valid excuse to intervene in Cuba . . . saying that the United States had intervened in violation of its treaty obligations in trying to overthrow the existing government. If this happened, your policy could lead to World War III."

Now, of course, Nixon would later write so passionately of his discomfort in arguing against armed intervention. Yet here he was, as bold as brass, demanding another hour on national television to argue what he would claim to so vehemently oppose, and which, he would further claim, would deprive him of votes he could ill afford to lose.

It remains all very confused.

And it grew yet more perplexing: Here was Jack Kennedy, who had previously clamored for a fifth session, his party being short of money for last-minute airtime, now dodging pallid, wan, shifty Dick Nixon's offer.

Why?

JFK might have been wary of alienating his party's left wing (Stevenson found JFK's comments "appalling"), the permanent Washington and New York punditocracy, the Restons and Lippmanns ("So far I have not met anyone who heard the fourth debate and is yearning to have a fifth") to whom Nixon's arguments (if not Nixon himself) sounded so reasonable and true. It might not take much for the Adlais and Eleanors to bolt. They were a skittish bunch—particularly where Joe Kennedy's progeny was concerned.

And so Jack Kennedy quickly backpedaled regarding arming Cuba's exiles and dissidents. "If I win this thing, I won it," he informed Goodwin and Sorensen, "but if I lose it, you guys lost it."

From Milwaukee, two days following the debate, JFK telegraphed Richard Nixon: "I have never advocated and I do not advocate, intervention in Cuba in violation of our treaty obligations." He contended that he had merely spoken in favor of utilizing "all available communications—radio, television and the press—and the moral power of the American government to let the forces of freedom in Cuba know that we believe that freedom will again rise in that country."

JFK had a way of grabbing grandeur from mishap.

But privately he needed to grovel—if not directly, then at least through surrogate grovellers. Still in Milwaukee, he dispatched Arthur Schlesinger to phone Scotty Reston and Walter Lippmann to explain that he had never meant what Richard Nixon—*and they*—said he said. Schlesinger had trouble contacting Reston, then aboard the Nixon campaign train, but reached Lippmann. Lippmann, Schlesinger later wrote, "thought the Kennedy people were trying to play the issue both ways and deserved to be called on it."

"In any case," Schlesinger also revealed, "Kennedy thereafter dropped Cuba and concentrated for the rest of the campaign on his central themes."

Before the episode concluded, however, came an additional chiding—this one from the *New York Times*. "It is Senator Kennedy who overextended his lines," the *Times* editorialized, and then let him off the hook he had himself baited. "It is fortunate that he has quickly seen and understood his own error, and has now climbed onto more solid ground."

Or perhaps having failed to win any of the last three debates—and perhaps even having lost all three—Jack Kennedy had no stomach for further frustration. It was one thing to have sunk one PT boat, another to lose three.

Perhaps even more mysteriously, in the end what did Richard Nixon really feel about Castro or Cuba? In *Six Crises*, he describes the debates at length, particularly debate four's wrangling over Castro, and his discomfort in arguing against overthrowing Castro. He covers the same ground in his second memoir, *RN*.

And, not very surprisingly, in *Six Crises*, he offers recommendations for conducting future debates: a two-hour format, no moderators, and debates "limited to specific subjects." Yet nowhere does he mention his idea for a fifth debate where he would again argue for "a political and economic quarantine" and against arming anti-Castro exiles.

What *had* Richard Nixon really believed? In overthrowing Castro? In not overthrowing Castro? What made Dick Nixon advocate another debate based on defending a cause that pained him—a position he claimed wouldn't win him votes anyway? Had the debates taught him that issues *really* didn't matter? That what counted was coming across better on the tube (and, in the last three debates, he had indeed looked better)? That in October 1960's mini–Cuban crisis, he had been, at least publicly, *resolute*, while Senator John F. Kennedy had shifted awkwardly from position to position, exhibiting not the toughness he had originally aimed at projecting but instead a weakness that compelled him to state, re-state, and then finally junk major positions within just a few days—hardly the vigorous statesmanship he promised or America wanted?

Whatever the case, it appears that Richard Nixon came to fully comprehend what each successful politician instinctively comprehends: It's not the snake oil that matters; it's the salesman. It's the *pitch*. "Issues," Red Blaik had written him, after all, "are important, but far more important is the impression created by the candidate."

Tricky Dick had become even trickier.

THIRTY-FOUR

"They know not what they do"

ILLINOIS WAS A KEY STATE, and as much as Richard Daley had been annoyed and insulted and disrespected by Jack Kennedy in the closing hours of the Democratic National Convention, he still had work to do. Dick Daley was, however, not entirely altruistic, not entirely forgiving. He had his reasons for wanting to do right by Jack Kennedy. If JFK lost Illinois, he might drag the Democratic ticket down with him. Daley wanted his man Judge Otto Kerner as governor, and, more importantly, his man Daniel Ward, dean of the DePaul University College of Law, in the Cook County state's attorney post. A state's attorney could cause a lot of trouble for a politician like Dick Daley. A friendly state's attorney could make life a lot easier. Dan Ward, despite his respectable credentials, would make a *very* accommodating state's attorney.

On Friday night, November 4, JFK hit Chicago, where a crowd estimated at a million and a half persons cheered his torchlit parade as it wended its way from Grant Park to the packed six-thousand-seat Chicago Coliseum at Wabash and Sixteenth Streets, where, at a podium festooned with JFK, LBJ, and Dick Daley banners, Kennedy would deliver a slashing, nationally televised campaign speech. Another twenty-eight thousand Democrats gathered for a show boasting 110 entertainers—headlined by Gene Kelly, Joey Bishop, Vic Damone, and Myrna Loy—at the Chicago Stadium.

Not everyone participated of his or her own free will. Attendance was often mandatory. If you were part of the machine or depended on the machine for livelihood, survival, or peace of mind, it was best you attend—or else. As black South Side alderman Claude Holman ("God bless Richard J. Daley, the greatest mayor in the history of the world, the best friend the black man ever had") ordered—in writing—to his Fourth Ward friends and associates, "You must be present at 4654 Cottage Grove, Democratic Headquarters at 4:30 p. m. Friday. I personally will receive you aboard the bus."

Newsmen were skeptical of the million-and-a-half-person esti-mate, but the turnout was indeed massive. So was security. The coli-seum had been closed tighter than a drum for twenty-four hours, Kennedy's convertible under guard in a local garage. Still, there was trouble. As Kennedy neared the coliseum, twenty-three-year-old machinist Jaime Cruz Alejandro maneuvered through the crowd, trying to get as close as he could, pushing so furiously that he caught the attention of patrolman Vincent Moretti—as did the bulge in Alejandro's coat pocket. Moretti approached. Alejandro ran. Five other cops joined Moretti in running down Alejandro, who had immigrated from Puerto Rico just six years before. Police slammed him to the pavement. It took all six cops to finally subdue Alejandro, but when they had, they found a loaded .25-caliber automatic pistol in his pocket. The pro-Kennedy crowd screamed, "Kill him, kill him." Alejandro protested that he carried the gun only for protection, meant JFK no harm, and planned on voting for him.

Literally moments later, the Reverend Israel Dabney, a sixty-one-year-old black minister, approached a coliseum gate carrying a paper bag containing a loaded .38-caliber revolver. Dabney said he lived in a gang-ridden neighborhood and, like Alejandro, protested that he carried his weapon for self-protection.

The sixties, it appeared, were a more dangerous time than America was bargaining for.

★ ★ ★

The days dwindled down to a precious few. The number of places in which one had to be only grew. Richard Nixon—despite the two weeks he had lost to illness—decided in the campaign's final days to honor his con-vention pledge to campaign in all fifty states, a commitment now taking him to Alaska—a state with only three electoral votes. The decision stunned savvy observers. Even the friendly *Los Angeles Times* jibed that the move "demonstrate[ed] his new found confidence by wasting twelve hours in a 6 to 1 [*sic*; it was 2 to 1] Democratic stronghold."

While few seemed to notice, similar scheduling snafus vexed Jack Kennedy, who was scheduled to slog through Eastern states no longer in play. "I'll be wasting my time in New York. I've got New York and I've got

Connecticut," he stormed at Kenny O'Donnell. "But I haven't got California. Give me those two days in California and I'll win there."

O'Donnell protested that it was too late to change the schedule.

"You and your damned schedule," JFK yelled. "If we lose California, it will be your thick-headed fault."

★ ★ ★

Meanwhile, Richard Nixon's association with New York psychotherapist Dr. Arnold Hutschnecker had become known to the Kennedy camp, which meant it had the excellent possibility of soon becoming known to others. Joe Kennedy, bragging that he had "a whole dossier" on the relationship, utilized Frank Sinatra to plant stories in the press, and hints of Nixon's treatment ran in Walter Winchell's syndicated column. The Sunday preceding the election, the Associated Press phoned Hutschnecker, inquiring if Nixon was in "good health."

But the Hutschnecker story didn't have legs. The "Nixonburgers" story, however, did.

Kennedy family attorney James M. McInerney—the James M. McInerney who had handled the Kater affair—had unearthed a $205,000 December 10, 1956, loan from the Hughes Tool Co. (an arm of reclusive billionaire Howard Hughes's financial empire) to Richard Nixon's not particularly reputable brother Donald—to finance Donald's small chain of "Nixonburgers" restaurants. Hughes's loan was secured by a Nixon family lot in Whittier, assessed at thirteen thousand dollars and worth no more than fifty-two thousand. Don Nixon eventually went bankrupt, and the loan was never repaid. McInerney's story was now leaked to columnist Drew Pearson, who wondered aloud "that thereafter Hughes' problems with various government agencies [the Justice Department and the Civil Aviation Board] improved. Whether the improvement was connected with the loan is not known." Pearson added ominously that the loan came at Hughes's behest "with the approval and knowledge of the Vice President."

Nixon, barnstorming through Ohio, refused comment. Bob Finch slammed Pearson's charges as "an obvious political smear in the last two weeks of the campaign," claiming that any suggestions "that we in any way had anything to do with the Hughes Tool Co. receiving any so-called government benefits is pure libel." Almost instantly, the Justice Department dismissed Pearson's charges as baseless. Nothing was ever proven against Nixon—no connection ever made to any action benefiting Hughes—even by Robert Kennedy's Justice Department. At such a late hour, in such a tight race, however, such charges could not but hurt.

★ ★ ★

Nixon, receiving reports of JFK's hands shaking on the campaign trail—a symptom of Parkinson's disease—resisted raising JFK's uncertain medical history. But *somebody* thought otherwise. The public rumblings began at a Mount Clemens, Michigan, Lions Club meeting on Thursday, November 3, when FDR's Republican son John demanded to know if JFK suffered any adrenal deficiency "as a result of Addison's disease." Soon Thruston Morton was demanding "a full disclosure to the voters," charging that Drs. Travell and Cohen's July statement on Kennedy's health was insufficient, and recalling that in 1956 Ike "had his physicians release a complete, detailed report on his health a week before voters went to the polls."

"Vice President Nixon," said Morton, "has now directed his doctors to disclose all the records of his physical condition. Senator Kennedy has been unwilling to disclose these facts to the voters. I hope that Senator Kennedy will reconsider his indicated intention and make a full disclosure to the voters."

Also galloping to the attack was Congressman Walter Judd—*Dr.* Walter Judd—also questioning the Travell-Cohen statement ("Any layman, let alone a doctor, can read it and see the political nature of the omissions"). "Addison's Disease," Judd pointedly noted, "tends to create the adrenal insufficiencies that are disturbing to physical and mental health. If drugs of the large dosage indicated were required some years ago, it is not unreasonable to suppose that even more massive and critical dosages are required today. This is the sort of fact voters are entitled to have and to have now."

Nixon meanwhile was proposing that Ike himself remind voters of his own 1956 medical disclosures and challenge both Kennedy and Nixon to do likewise (as Roosevelt and Morton had already challenged the candidates). The Eisenhower White House once more stiff-armed Richard Nixon when he needed help. Press Secretary Jim Hagerty derided Nixon's idea as a "cheap, lousy, stinking political trick." Ike standoffishly refused to be "a party to anything that has to do with the health of the candidates."

"It was," noted Pierre Salinger, with, no doubt, much relief, "too little and too late."

* * *

It was still not too late, however, for Nixon to make use of Dwight David Eisenhower.

Ike had rarely gone to bat for his junior partner, and when he had, it had invariably been done artlessly, bereft of discernable enthusiasm. Instructive was an incident concerning the filming of two Nixon campaign documentaries. Recalled Nixon television adviser Gene Wyckoff:

[T]he hardest ingredient to find for these two films was the voice of President Eisenhower lauding Nixon and Lodge. I have no doubt that the President would have recorded this specially for the sound track, but . . . Jim Hagerty told us that Eisenhower would not do any active campaigning until he was asked by the Vice-President and for reasons of his own, Nixon was not yet asking. Fortunately, all public utterances of a President are recorded. [We located] a dinner speech during which the President had praised the Republican candidates in detail. Hagerty's office provided a tape of this speech. After a few hours of editing to clear up the President's diction by snipping out mispronounced words and replacing them with properly pronounced words from other portions of the speech, we had quite an acceptable film narration by Eisenhower.

But as the campaign progressed, and Ike came to realize that the alternative to Richard Nixon was not Robert Anderson or a dozen other Republicans, but, rather, Jack Kennedy ("the young genius"), his interest finally intensified. "I'm going to make eight to ten appearances during the campaign," Ike confided to an associate on August 19. "Motorcades kill me, but I'm going to do them to try to arouse enthusiasm."

From Philadelphia on Friday evening, October 28, Ike delivered a thirty-minute TV address for Nixon, producing the highest audience of any ad in the campaign—a 33 percent audience share, a full 18 percent of all TV households. From Wichita Falls and San Diego and Roanoke, JFK jeered at Ike's appearance ("I don't care how many rescue squads they send"), but he was too intelligent, and too realistic, a politician not to realize the truth. "With every word he utters," he informed Red Fay, "I can feel the votes leaving me. It's like standing on a mound of sand with the tide running out. If the election were held tomorrow, I'd win easily, but six days from now, it's up for grabs."

On Monday afternoon, October 31, Nixon was to discuss with Ike the possibility of adding additional stops—Michigan, upstate New York, and downstate Illinois—to the late-starting Ike juggernaut. But before they conferred, Pat Nixon received a call ("Ike must never know I called you") from Mamie Eisenhower (never a great Nixon fan) informing Pat that Ike's health would not allow any such burst of activity, and begging Pat to intercede to halt her husband's plan. Soon, Dick received confirmation from Ike's personal physician, Major General Howard Snyder: "I know what he *wants* to do, and he usually won't take my advice. Please, either talk him out of it or just don't let him do it—for the sake of his health."

"Dick looked like he had been hit by an ax," recalled Interior Secretary Fred Seaton. "He turned to me and said, 'I'm going to go in there and knock down any suggestions anybody has except to keep the dates already committed.'"

"It was not easy," Seaton added. "The boss was all fired up and steamed up for campaigning and he had his spurs on."

When they met, Nixon sputtered a few lame excuses as to why Ike should not expend any more effort on his behalf. "He was confused—to put it mildly," Nixon recalled. "At first he was hurt and then he was angry."

"Why didn't Dick pay attention to what I was saying?" Eisenhower sputtered to Len Hall after Nixon had departed.

"He was uptight, Mr. President."

"Goddammit," Ike stormed, "he looks like a loser to me!"

★ ★ ★

In Dallas, on Friday afternoon, November 4, LBJ and Lady Bird arrived to address two thousand supporters at an Adolphus Hotel luncheon, freshening up beforehand at the Baker Hotel across Commerce Street. Waiting to pounce upon the Johnsons was Texas's single

Republican congressman, Dallas's Bruce Alger, armed with a hand-lettered sign reading "LBJ Sold Out to Yankee Socialists"—and accompanied by hundreds of truly frenzied Nixon supporters. Lyndon and Lady Bird would have to proceed through this angry, screaming, spitting (but well-dressed) mob, and the situation only worsened when the Johnsons reached the elegant Adolphus lobby.

It was here that LBJ saw his great opportunity.

With cameras rolling, Lyndon Johnson slowed to a crawl, shooing away aides and then police ("I told the police to stand aside"), taking his great, molasses-slow time to traverse the Adolphus lobby and step into the safety of its elevators. "LBJ and Lady Bird could have gone through that lobby and got on that elevator in five minutes," recalled Sam Rayburn aide D. B. Hardeman, "but LBJ took thirty minutes to go through that crowd, and it was all being recorded and photographed for television and radio and the newspapers, and he knew and played it for all it was worth. They say he never learned how to use the media effectively, but that day he did."

"If he could have thought this up," said Bill Moyers, "he would have thought it up. Tried to invent it. But the moment it happened he knew."

Lyndon Johnson knew that it was time not only to display his own bravery, but to play the great, never-failing trump card of Southern gallantry. "If the time has come," he proclaimed, "when I can't walk through the lobby of a hotel in Dallas with my lady without a police escort, I want to know about it."

And he wanted others to know it. "One thing about Texas," Jack Valenti observed, "particularly old fashioned Texans and Southerners, is they don't want women treated in a disparaging, discourteous way. You could spit on Johnson and get away with it, but you couldn't spit on the wife of a candidate. And that cost [Alger] a lot of votes in the Dallas area."

Bruce Alger's "mink coat riot" also cost the GOP ticket the South, as Richard Russell—so long aloof from the campaign, and now so outraged by events—took the stump for LBJ. "Although we have had our differences," Russell now proclaimed, "I have never been disappointed in Lyndon Johnson."

A day later Johnson himself campaigned in South Texas: "I looked at them [the rioters]," LBJ told his audience, "and thought of what the Good Book says: 'Forgive them, O Lord, for they know not what they do.'"

★ ★ ★

Jack Kennedy spent the Monday before Election Day squandering precious time on friendly New England turf, in Providence, Rhode Island, and in Springfield, Massachusetts; then in still quite amenable Connecticut and in less hospitable, less Catholic, less Democratic, but still winnable Vermont; and finally in Manchester, New Hampshire (where he had already campaigned on September 2). His party suffered an hour-and-a-half-long delay in Massachusetts, causing Kennedy to scrub an appearance just across the Connecticut border, in Thompsonville, a carpet-manufacturing mill town where three to five thousand chilled supporters still waited to see him as his convertible moved past on its way to Enfield and then south onto the crowd-lined Springfield-Hartford expressway to Hartford's Atheneum Square, where a huge throng had begun forming a good two hours before JFK's scheduled noon appearance. Waiting, they chanted "We want Jack!" or sang campaign songs—led by two hundred costumed college girls, the Governor's Foot Guard Band, and Mayor James H. Kinsella, who clearly loved being mayor of Hartford (but not so much that he wasn't busy running for district probate judge).

Five hundred state and local police patrolled the huge crowd—estimated at between seventy and a hundred thousand persons—maintaining order, though their yoke was light enough to allow the crowd to attack the few hardy souls bearing Nixon-Lodge signs, snatch those signs from their grasp, smash them to the ground, and rip them apart.

Awaiting Kennedy was State Chairman Bailey and Governor Ribicoff. As Kennedy's caravan approached the square, suddenly the sun broke through the clouds, eliciting lusty cheers. As Jack approached the platform, the crowd surged toward him, nearly separating a mother from her baby carriage. A Connecticut state trooper bounded over the barricade, took the four-month-old from the carriage, and cradled it in his arms until Kennedy finally departed.

Meanwhile, nerves frayed on the Kennedy staff. Pierre Salinger snapped at reporters. Larry O'Brien was similarly surly. The atmosphere proved so tense that even the normally forgiving Teddy White was forced to note it.

From there it was on to an outdoor rally in Manchester, where the weary JFK noted that his sisters Jean, Eunice, and Patricia had campaigned with him "in all 55 states." He was, however, not so punchy that he could not rebound to quip, "[W]ell, it seemed like 55."

He ended the day—and the campaign—back home, before a huge, adoring Boston Garden crowd, telling the cheering throng, "I do not run for the office of the Presidency after fourteen years in Congress with any expectation that it is an empty or an easy job. I run for the Presidency of the United States because it is the center of the action, and in a free society the chief responsibility of the President is to set before the American people the unfinished public business of the country."

But he also shared this secret reason for coveting the White House. The presidency, Honey Fitz's grandson slyly informed his fellow Bostonians, was a good-paying job with no heavy lifting.

And they cheered that, too.

★ ★ ★

While the Kennedys had campaigned as a family unit—nearly as a military unit—the Nixons had done things differently. Fourteen-year-old Tricia and twelve-year-old Julie had never been out on the presidential campaign trail. They had not even seen their father—save for Sundays—since September 12. But with just a week left, Pat Nixon finally relented to her daughters' pleas and allowed them a sabbatical from classes—though, until the day before the balloting, they had still not witnessed Richard Nixon live on the stump.

That Monday, in San Diego, postal authorities discovered a liquid aluminum bomb mailed to Nixon. Wrapped in brown paper, about the size of a jar of instant coffee, and marked "pull string to open," its detonation would have been fatal to a range of twenty-five feet. Federal postal officials ordered increased vigilance regarding packages to all four major candidates.

On late Monday afternoon Nixon staged a four-hour "telethon" from Detroit's ABC affiliate, WXYZ. Not having slept for more than three hours at a stretch since his Alaska junket, he was tired and cranky—and, at least off camera, he acted it. "God damn it!" he screamed at studio staff. "Can't you stupid bastards do anything right?" And then he settled in for four hours of a remarkably effective performance. With the GOP not having purchased the time slots regularly reserved for commercials, however, ABC ran its usual ads, including one for cranberry sauce. Master of ceremonies Roy Rowan (categorized by the *Chicago Tribune* as "somewhat hysterical"), presumably meaning to praise events as "amazing," instead earnestly pronounced that "the response to this program is simply appalling."

But it was neither as amazing nor as appalling as what transpired in El Cajon, California, the following Saturday, when Victor and Norma Rae Rojas disagreed over what to watch on TV. The forty-four-year-old Mr. Rojas, a Democrat, wanted to watch JFK. Thirty-four-year-old Norma, a Republican, preferred Lawrence Welk. They argued. She seized a paring knife and stabbed him in the chest. He was dead by the time police arrived.

From Detroit, Nixon—still alive—flew to Chicago's O'Hare Airport. His motorcade sped at a sixty-to-seventy-miles-per-hour clip past knots of supporters, waiting and waving and cheering on roadways and overpasses, to WBBM, where searchlights, the twenty-five-member Chicago Board of Trade American Legion band, several thousand shivering supporters, and far too many Republican dignitaries (nearly a hundred) waited to see Dick Nixon before he moved inside for one last national TV hookup—this one with Eisenhower in Washington and Lodge in Boston. "We want Nixon; win with Nixon," the crowd chanted in thirty-seven-degree weather.

"It's cold out here," Nixon declared, "but I don't care. I just don't want any of you voters to catch pneumonia and not be able to vote tomorrow." The crowd spilled out from the parking lot, onto McClurg Court. People wobbled on boxes for better views. Some climbed trees.

With Nixon's ten-minute telecast over—and the campaign nearly spent—his five-car motorcade raced back to O'Hare, where fifty to seventy-five chilled supporters kept vigil. The Nixons climbed the gangway into their plane—but then emerged for one final wave. That was, after all, the thing about politics. Waving and smiling was exhausting but addictive, and what was worse than the crowds and the events and the speeches was their absence—the abrupt, sudden silence of empty, littered auditoriums, of suddenly empty lives.

The Nixons came out for one last wave.

"I'm just out for a little ride"

IT WAS, SAID EVERYONE, VERY CLOSE.

On election eve, CBS's Roper's poll had Nixon leading 49 percent to 47 percent with 4 percent undecided, up from a 46 percent–to–44.5 percent Nixon lead with a substantial 9.5 percent still up for grabs. That was Nixon's good news. Factoring in undecideds, however, Roper pronounced Kennedy "slightly ahead."

The Princeton Research Service called it 52 percent to 48 percent for Kennedy. George Gallup forecast 49 percent to 48 percent for Kennedy, with 3 percent undecided, deeming the race too close to call. California's Field poll revealed Kennedy ahead among that state's likely voters 49 percent to 47 percent, with 4 percent undecided—though warning that a last-minute Nixon surge could carry him over.

Bookies seemed less willing to hedge their bets. In New York, odds were Kennedy 3-1, in the Midwest 11-5, in Vegas 9-5.

The unions—save, of course, for the Teamsters and, mysteriously, the left-wing International Longshoremen's and Warehousemen's Union—backed Kennedy. Newspapers—57 percent of them—supported Nixon, the smallest percentage supporting a GOP candidate since 1932, when 55 percent had endorsed doomed Herbert Hoover.

One newspaper *not* supporting Nixon was Cuba's official paper *Revolucion*, which compared Nixon and Kennedy to two brands of soap in "different wrappers": "No matter which candidate is elected, he can be summed up in one word: Nothing." *Revolucion* exhibited particular offense regarding Vice President Nixon's recent remarks that if Cuba improved its attitude toward the United States, "we might change ours with respect to the Cuban sugar quota." *Revolucion* dismissed that as "blackmail." For good measure, it published on its back page a photo of two hooded Klansmen, claiming they supported Nixon.

Eighty-four million registered voters were eligible to go to the polls and elect a president, a vice president, twenty-seven governors, thirty-four U.S. senators, and 437 House members, with polls open from 4 a.m. EST in Tennessee to 2 a.m. EST in Alaska.

Voting started, however, at the stroke of midnight, in a tiny, newly incorporated (just a month and four days previously) hamlet in north-ernmost New Hampshire—Dixville Notch. All nine voters braved two inches of snow and nine-degree weather to reach first town moderator Neil Tillotson's white frame inn, The Balsams, and cast their ballots before anyone else in the country. The sixty-one-year-old Tillotson went first, dropping his paper ballot into a wooden box on a simple table before a roaring fireplace. Tillotson voted for Nixon. *Everyone* in Dixville Notch voted for Nixon.

Just afterward, Hart's Location, New Hampshire, voted seven to five for Nixon. In 1956, Stevenson carried the place by five votes to three. In the dark New England night, two more towns, Waterville and Millsfield, followed. Nixon swamped Kennedy twenty to two in Waterville (seven-teen to zero for Ike in 1956) and four to one in Millfield (five to two for Ike in 1956—two folks had moved away).

In Connecticut, the Windsor Town Democratic Committee ran this brief ad:

FOR LADIES ONLY—This year we are asking the ladies to wear their high heels to the polls. The democrats are using the top lever and we don't want anyone to fail to reach it. Go Kennedy! *Go* all the way! Go Democratic!

On Long Island, ninety-five-year-old Linn B. Young traveled the five miles from his Baiting Hollow farm to the polling place at Riverhead Town Hall, told his daughter to vote for Nixon, went into the voting booth, came out, walked toward his car—and promptly dropped dead.

In Atlanta, life began. Mrs. Frank Maloof, pregnant with her fourth child, voted on her way to the hospital and announced that if it were a boy she would name him either Kennedy Nixon Maloof or Nixon Kennedy Maloof. Her fellow voters cheered.

In Syracuse, New York, thirty-three-year-old Democratic poll watcher Daniel Patrick Moynihan ostentatiously demanded that a locked room on the premises be opened. The trench-coated, tweed-hatted

Moynihan had become convinced it concealed Republican evildoing. It took a while to locate the key—to an otherwise empty room.

President Eisenhower, accompanied by his son, thirty-eight-year-old colonel John Eisenhower, helicoptered into Gettysburg from Washington, arriving on the Barlow Fire Hall front lawn at 6:55 a.m.—precisely five minutes before the polls opened, a fact that elections judge Mrs. Fred Swisher carefully pointed out to him. "I've got to make it legal," Ike replied. "I don't want to come this far and lose my vote."

Finally admitted, he perused the propositions on the ballot ("My goodness, that's technical"), spending forty-five seconds in the booth itself. Reporters asked Ike how he voted, and he pointed to his wristwatch and the tiny photos of his four grandchildren set in its face. "That's who I voted for," he said, once again missing a chance to boost Nixon.

Jackie Kennedy, very pregnant and fighting a cold for a solid month, awoke at Hyannis at 6 a.m. She had a two-hour drive ahead of her to Boston, to her husband, and to voting. JFK had spent the night at Boston's Statler-Hilton Hotel, and as he exited through its lobby and the crowd of three hundred that awaited him, few noticed a woman in a bright purple coat and black leather beret—his wife—until Jack took her arm. Sensing Jackie's vulnerability in this crowd, he held his arm before her, protecting her from whatever violence or force—however innocent—might disturb her.

They voted at 8:46 a.m. at the Third Ward, Sixth Precinct polling place, Boston's West End Library. Registrar Evelyn M. Hiltz asked both for identification. "John F. Kennedy, 122 Bowdoin Street," the candidate responded. "Jacqueline," she murmured.

Jackie—number 85—voted first. Jack whispered in her ear and then informed reporters, "I told her how to operate the machine." Still, she stood there. Jack repeated his instructions. A poll worker entered the black-curtained booth with her to ensure she knew how to vote for her husband. "I hope it worked," Jackie said as she emerged. Asked if she had voted "a straight ticket," she wrinkled her nose and managed a weak smile.

Jack—number 86—entered another of the library's six booths, exiting in thirty seconds. For all her uncertainty, Jackie exited in fifteen.

Actually, it was fake, at least on Jackie's part. She had already voted by absentee ballot (the only absentee in the district)—and she hadn't voted a straight ticket. She later told Arthur Schlesinger she had voted solely for her husband, ignoring the rest of the slate: "It is a rare thing to be able to vote for one's husband as President of the United States, and I didn't want to dilute it by voting for anyone else." That wasn't true either. She had voted for one other Democrat—Eddie McLaughlin, an old JFK navy buddy, for lieutenant governor—ignoring even Congressman Tip O'Neill.

"Well, this is it," Kennedy answered reporters wanting to know his plans. "Just go home and see my daughter."

They boarded the *Caroline* for Hyannis—a pleasant flight filled with champagne and song and chicken Kiev—pleasant, that is, for all save the baggage handler making the one-hour flight trapped inside the *Caroline*'s luggage compartment. At Hyannis they were met by a hundred local police plus an enthusiastic crowd of two hundred, including a group of girls from the Cape Cod Secretarial School wielding a large banner optimistically proclaiming, "Welcome home, President Jack." JFK's twenty-five-year-old cousin Ann Gargan drove them home, past small, scattered crowds. All minds had been made up, all votes decided, but JFK kept in practice, waving to them all.

Up the Atlantic coast, Henry Cabot and Emily Sears Lodge had spent the preceding night at their Beverly, Massachusetts, home. Election morning, their police-escorted motorcade arrived at the Cove Montserrat Elementary School—on Eisenhower Avenue—to vote. A crowd of five hundred, including two hundred schoolchildren, cheered their arrival. Seventeen voters waited ahead of them in line. The checker couldn't find Lodge's name on the list. He assured her it was there. It indeed was. He told reporters he anticipated a reasonably close race, no landslide. Back in their car, the Lodges headed for a flight that would take them to Washington to await results.

Lyndon Johnson's ranch was located in two counties—Republican Gillespie County and Democratic Blanco County. He voted—number 99—in Blanco County at 10 a.m. in Johnson City at the Pedernales Electric Cooperative building. Lady Bird followed, and when someone asked how he voted, he flashed a big grin and said simply, "Democratic."

Anyone thinking Lyndon Johnson would return home to placidly await results did not know Johnson. He would be on the phone, hammering away, hectoring supporters, checking and double-checking, nagging and pleading. No election was ever over for Lyndon Johnson, even with the mixed emotions he now felt. "Tommy the Cork" Corcoran, knowing those feelings very well, wrote to LBJ that day, "I know you didn't like what I said to you [several months ago] about escaping from the cage of Texas, but your subconscious knew even then it was true. . . . No matter how the votes fall today, you are a free force in the world, free to be right, free to be a national statesman, free to be a world statesman, free to free the greatness that FDR saw in you."

Truman voted in Independence. Stevenson voted in Libertyville, before taking a call from Marlene Dietrich. He wrote her back, "Your telephone calls delighted me. I am flattered and grateful—and all I ask now is that you stop off for a visit with me."

Eleanor Roosevelt voted early in Hyde Park before returning to her limestone Manhattan townhouse at 55 East Seventy-fourth Street. Two days previously, she had remarked to a Republican friend, "we both believe that our particular man is the best man for the country," only to receive the reply, "They are both too young. I don't believe either of them will be good for the country." The thought astonished ER.

Richard J. Daley voted at the firehouse at Thirty-fifth and Lowe, half a block from his 3536 South Lowe home. Following a quick detour to the Eleventh Ward headquarters, he headed to City Hall, not so much for city business, but for more important business.

Herbert Hoover arose early, trudging from his Waldorf Towers suite to Cathedral High School on Manhattan's East Fiftieth Street. He voted straight Republican. "Any man who has been President of the United States at the hands of his party always sticks with his party," he informed reporters, but refused to make any predictions, explaining, "I'm not a prophet." Exiting Cathedral High, he came across his East Side neighbor James A. Farley, Franklin D. Roosevelt's former postmaster general—and Joe Kennedy Jr.'s choice for president at the 1940 Democratic Convention. Glad to see each other—time heals some wounds—Hoover and Farley shook hands. Farley predicted a Kennedy landslide, no more than fifteen states for Nixon.

Ike had issued an invitation to fifty-three United Nations member nations to observe U.S. elections firsthand. Nine accepted, though most pled insufficient staff and time to prepare. Cuba and the Soviet Union refused. Generalissimo Francisco Franco's Spain posted its staff in Whittier. Nigeria and Ghana chose Atlanta.

Martin Luther King could not vote. Having relocated from Montgomery to Atlanta in February 1960, he had not held Georgia residency long enough to vote there. He announced plans to cast an absentee ballot in Montgomery, but having paid no poll taxes since 1958, he proved ineligible there as well.

In County Wexford, the Kennedys' ancestral Irish home, two cables went out to America on behalf of town inhabitants from the Newcross harbor commissioners: the first to JFK himself; the second to the Wexford Men's Association in New York. That one read, "If Kennedy is elected, victory bonfires will blaze along the Wexford Coast."

At a salon named Alexandre's, Rose Fitzgerald Kennedy got her hair done—praying the Rosary all the while.

Richard Nixon arrived at his polling station, a green stucco tract house—10651 Avonbury Avenue, East Whittier, the home of Mr. and Mrs. Roger McNey and their six children—at 7:15 a.m. The actual voting occurred in the McNeys's twelve-by-fifteen-foot family room, which, crowded with two Nixons, seven McNeys (Mr. McNey had been transferred by his employer, a chip-beef packager, back to Texas), five voting inspectors, and a full complement of reporters and photographers, quickly resembled a subway car at rush hour. Mrs. McNey, an Irish Catholic, but a Nixon supporter nonetheless, offered her visitors coffee. Mrs. Nixon, attired in an olive dress and matching jacket, declined. Her husband protested that he didn't normally drink coffee but had some anyway—and fulsomely praised it.

The Nixons surrendered their unmarked absentee ballots. Everyone wanted a picture of them casting ballots, but the crush made that impossible. Nixon assumed control, suggesting that still photographers remain in the room, then vacate it for a reenactment staged for newsreel and TV cameramen. That stretched out the Nixons' voting to a full half hour.

Five minutes into the event, Pat Nixon felt something: a hand belonging to Mrs. Jarri Pietrowski. Trapped inside the booth by all the hubbub, she had reached out to tap Mrs. Nixon on the shoulder. "My gosh, there's a voter caught back here," Pat Nixon exclaimed. Mrs.

Pietrowski said not to worry ("I don't mind at all") and remained inside for another twenty-five minutes.

Nixon voted, handed out pens bearing his signature to the McNey children, and exited past five hundred onlookers into a caravan scheduled to return him to Los Angeles' Hotel Ambassador.

Three blocks later, he ordered it to pull over. With his military attaché Major Don Hughes and Secret Service agent Jack Sherwood, Nixon scampered from his black Cadillac into a white convertible driven by a Los Angeles Police Department bunco squad officer, John DiBetta. Nixon, taking the wheel, drove off, with the press just behind.

He ditched them.

He stopped at his mother's home in nearby La Habra, white stucco, with an orange grove out front, his late father's name still on the mailbox. He spent fifteen minutes there. Hannah had already voted.

He drove south, south, ever southward, along the coast, with no particular destination in mind. Ninety miles from Whittier, in Oceanside, California, he stopped for gas. "I'm just out for a little ride," he informed attendant Cliff Edwards. "It's the only way I could get some rest."

Meanwhile Herb Klein was left to explain to reporters his boss's disappearance, noting that Nixon often preferred such private moments. Private moments turned into private hours, and with the candidate still absent, Klein, attempting to appear calm, theorized that Nixon was driving "just around without any destination."

It was not always easy being Herb Klein.

Southward sped Nixon, Hughes, Sherwood, and DiBetta. Around San Diego someone mentioned Tijuana. Hughes commented that he had never been there. Nixon chimed in that he hadn't been there in twenty-five years and—why not?—let's go.

Richard Nixon—the ultimate control freak—was winging it on the most important day of his life.

Lunchtime. Crossing into Mexico, DiBetta inquired of Border Patrol agents where to find the best Mexican food. They recommended a place run by a German called Old Heidelberg. That probably made as little sense to Nixon as it did to anyone else, but, being trusting souls, they (along with Tijuana mayor Xicotencati Leyva Aleman, who had quickly learned of Nixon's presence in his city) lunched on enchiladas *und* cerveza at Old Heidelberg.

In the meantime, Nixon had Major Hughes phone Los Angeles to inform Bob Finch of their whereabouts. Finch was properly amazed.

A Tijuana police car, sirens sounding and lights flashing, escorted Nixon's car back to the border. U.S. immigration agent John Martin, thinking an ambulance might be approaching, opened another lane. When the white convertible reached his booth, he was shocked to see the vice president of the United States in the front passenger seat.

"Hello," said Nixon, proceeding to shake hands with Martin and another equally surprised immigration agent. Pleasantries aside, Martin had duties to perform.

"Are you all citizens of the United States?"

"Yes, I am, but I don't know about that man in the back," Nixon joked.

North of San Diego, the convertible turned inland. Nixon wanted to show his traveling companions "one of my favorite Catholic places," the Spanish colonial Mission of San Juan Capistrano. The place was pretty much empty, with a half dozen visitors on the grounds. Nixon conducted an informal tour, past its elementary school—where a nun flashed Nixon a V sign—and into the mission chapel itself. "For a few minutes," he recalled, "we sat in the empty pews for an interlude of complete escape."

Back in Los Angeles, Dick Nixon had some explaining to do. "It wasn't planned," he told reporters. "We just started driving and that's where we wound up."

In Hyannis that afternoon, each Kennedy arrived. It was a desultory, awkwardly nervous day, a late breakfast for JFK, the receipt of a ten-foot good-luck rose horseshoe from neighbors, a reunion with Caroline (and a bag of toys for her collected on the road), touch football with Bobby. Author Cornelius Ryan, then a Kennedy staffer, chatted with JFK about World War II and Normandy and Rommel—and longest days.

Bobby retreated to his own cottage, where a bank of four Teletype machines and thirty telephones received returns and rumors of returns— that day's phone bill would run to ten thousand dollars. "Bobby was in total command of the situation," Ryan recalled. "He was very crisp. Curiously, one of the strange things I noticed was that there was very little communication between Jack and Bobby. Jack would come into the breakfast room and stand with his back against the wall, just listening. Bobby would be at the far end of the table, surrounded by telephones. There were calls from political leaders all over the country. Bobby would say, 'How are things going there?' He had that particular Massachusetts twang in his voice, which always seemed . . . when he got tensed up . . . [to become] terribly pronounced."

Joe Kennedy was finally back on the scene. It seemed safe for that now, and reporters—from a distance—watched gray-flannel-suited father and sweater-clad son conversing privately, at length, and not without tension, in the nippy November air.

And then, at 3:30 that afternoon, John F. Kennedy, herald of a New Frontier, apostle of the vigorous life . . . took a nap.

THIRTY-SIX

"The help of a few close friends"

WITHIN THE RED, gold, violet, and pink confines of the Ambassador Hotel's Royal Suite, Richard Nixon also napped. There, along with Pat, Trisha, Julie, his South Florida millionaire friend Bebe Rebozo, Murray Chotiner, mother Hannah, brothers Don and Ed and their wives, various in-laws, and a few others, he would receive returns, await his fate.

Waiting. That is what he and JFK—hunkered down with all the other Kennedys at Hyannis—now had in common. Those who could not rest for this past year now could do nothing but rest. And wait and hope and pray.

Lyndon Johnson received returns at the Provincial Suite of Austin's historic Driskill Hotel. A tan phone provided direct access to Hyannis Port, a black one to the Democratic National Committee in Washington. A third linked Johnson to state headquarters—he was, after all, also running for the U.S. Senate.

Henry Cabot Lodge took returns at Washington's Sheraton Park Hotel. Ike would meet him there at 7:30 p.m., then informally address campaign workers at 7:50 p.m., before returning to the White House. Press Secretary Jim Hagerty announced that Ike would not wait up for results. He didn't, being in bed by 11:00.

★ ★ ★

NBC, with Huntley and Brinkley at the helm, and CBS, with Walter Cronkite, commenced their coverage at 7:30 p.m. Eastern time; ABC's John Daly started an hour later—that network opting to leave *Bugs Bunny* and *The Rifleman* on the air in lieu of tedious fragmentary returns. Each network now increasingly relied upon computers to project results. ABC had the veteran Univac, used already in four national elections; NBC had the RCA 501; and CBS had the brand-new IBM 7090. CBS News president Sig Mickelson hoped to know the winner by 7:30.

He was crazy.

At first, however, he seemed prescient. John Bailey's Connecticut flopped into JFK's corner, by a far wider margin than expected. "Fantastic," crowed JFK, as he lit a big cigar. Eunice Shriver broke into "When Irish Eyes Are Smiling."

As early as 5:30 p.m., internal network projections forecast a Kennedy win. At 6:30 p.m. NBC calculated the odds as 15 to 1 against Nixon. The *New York Times* went to press with headlines heralding JFK's triumph . . . and then . . . the tide slowly started to shift. Now, it looked like a horse race. The *Times* stopped its presses.

Popular vote margins decreased to the vanishing point. State after key state tightened—Ohio, Michigan, Illinois, Wisconsin, New Jersey, Minnesota, California. "I see *you* are losing Ohio," LBJ called to say. "*I* am carrying Texas and we are doing pretty well in Pennsylvania."

Despite his bravado, the import of his choice still haunted Johnson. "The night he was elected vice-president," recalled journalist Margaret Mayer, "I don't think I ever saw a more unhappy man. . . . There was no jubilation. Lyndon looked as if he'd lost his last friend on earth, and later he was rude to me, very rude, and I tried to remind myself that he was very unhappy."

The union vote held for JFK, with 73 percent of UAW members voting Democratic. He lost popular votes in the South (by 16.5 percent, by one estimate) but no electoral votes. Kennedy took 70 percent of the black vote—up from Stevenson's 62 percent four years earlier. Outside the South, JFK's religion gained him an estimated 1.6 percent of the popular vote—and crucial electoral votes. Some estimated that he bumped the Democratic Catholic vote up from 50 percent in 1956 to 80 percent—the best ever for a presidential candidate.

★ ★ ★

The tension grew. A Kennedy victory no longer seemed assured. A landslide was a dream extinguished. With 0.3 percent of returns in, ABC's Univac called it for Nixon, pegging odds of a Nixon victory at a solid 10 to 1. Electoral votes that Kennedy had hoped for—Iowa's, Florida's, and, especially, Ohio's, tumbled into the Nixon column. Other states JFK had counted on—Michigan, Minnesota, Alaska, Wisconsin, Illinois, Missouri, New Mexico,

California, South Carolina, and Texas—hung precariously in the balance.

Nearly every state Teddy Kennedy oversaw had been lost. "I'm worrying about Teddy," Bobby confided to Kenny O'Donnell. "We've lost every state [except Hawaii] that he worked in out west. Jack will kid him, and that may hurt Teddy's feelings." Yes, Jack was a kidder, even in times like these—often a cruel one. "He's lost another state," JFK had ribbed old classmate Lem Billings. "His record is still minus one hundred percent. He's lost every county and every state of which he was supposed to be in charge." Billings dissolved in tears.

Kennedy lost Hyannis Port's Barnstable Township 4,515 to 2,783. In Texas, Johnson—for the Senate—won handily (58 percent) against thirty-five-year-old Midwestern University economics professor John Tower. In Minnesota, Hubert Humphrey trounced Minneapolis mayor P. Kenneth Peterson. Massachusetts Republicans re-elected U.S. senator Leverett Saltonstall and recaptured the governor's mansion. Wild Bill Stratton lost in Illinois, and congressional aspirant Gore Vidal was swamped in upstate New York. Jack Kennedy's hopeless trio of Midwestern vice-presidential hopefuls—Freeman of Minnesota, Loveless of Iowa, and Docking of Kansas—all met defeat.

One by one the Kennedys slipped out of the increasingly suffocating atmosphere to walk the Nantucket Sound shore alone with their thoughts. Jackie pondered not only losing but—even more fearfully—winning. "I feel," she thought, "as though I had just turned into a piece of public property. It's really frightening to lose your anonymity at thirty-one."

"Everybody would be walking back and forth from house to house," Eunice remembered. "Jack was over at our father's house a lot, and back to Bobby's to see what was on there, and now and then over to his house to check there, and to sit and rest awhile."

By midnight the atmosphere in Hyannis was funereal. "Their bigots," somebody mourned, "beat our bigots."

★ ★ ★

At 2:00 a.m. Mayor Daley called.

"With a little bit of luck," he reassured Jack Kennedy, "and the help of a few close friends, you're going to carry Illinois."

It might have been more than luck.

★ ★ ★

Dick Daley had more at stake in this election than the White House. Wanting Cook County state's attorney Ben Adamowski swept from office before Adamowski did serious damage to his machine, he would do anything to accomplish that goal. And if his anti-Adamowski juggernaut swept Illinois into the Kennedy column, well, then, so much the better.

Daley's efforts were like a storm gathering across the prairies, inevitable and unstoppable. Everyone saw them coming. In October, former Chicago Corporation Counsel David H. Brill announced the formation of a group titled the Committee on Honest Elections, designed to ferret out the growing number of "deadheads, ghosts, and phantoms" infesting city voter lists.

Before long, Brill was hauling evidence of irregularities in six wards to a grand jury. On November 3 Brill issued a report contending that 10 percent of the lists were irregular. Voters were listed as living in vacant lots, barbershops, taverns, and stores where no living quarters existed. Some were registered two or three times. Some had moved away as long as "15 years ago." And, of course, some were simply "dead for a long time."

Brill's investigators compiled an unending list of irregularities. In one district alone they discovered 108 votes cast from unregistered voters. In the Sixth District of Alderman Claude Holman's Fourth Ward, they found forty-five "floaters"—voters who not only weren't properly registered; they simply did not exist at all.

★ ★ ★

Jack Kennedy also had other friends in Chicago.

In the winter of 1959–60, Chicago mob attorney Robert J. McDonnell helped arrange a conference between Sam "Momo" Giancana and Joe Kennedy. Giancana, recalled McDowell, "had so many assets in place. They were capable of putting drivers in every precinct to help out the precinct captains, to get the voters out. And they had the unions absolutely going for Kennedy. . . . There was no ballot stuffing. I'm not suggesting that. They just worked—totally went all out. He [Kennedy] won it squarely, but he got the vote because of what Mooney [Giancana] had done. I'm convinced in my heart of hearts that Mooney carried the day for John F. Kennedy."

Momo Giancana's godson and brother recorded this about their family's activities: "To assure the election's outcome, guys either trucked people from precinct to precinct and poll to poll so they vote numerous times or stood menacingly along voting booths, where they made it clear to prospective voters that all ballots were to be cast for Kennedy."

"Beyond doubt," congressional investigator Robert Blakey would contend, "in my judgment . . . enough votes were stolen—let me repeat that—stolen in Chicago to give Kennedy a sufficient margin that he carried the state of Illinois."

"The presidency," bragged mobster Mickey Cohen, "was really stolen in Chicago."

★ ★ ★

The earmarks of fraud were not hard to find. In Chicago's Sixth Ward, Thirty-eighth Precinct, after forty-three voters had cast their ballots, the machine tally read 121 total votes. In the Second Ward, Fiftieth Precinct, only twenty-two voters were on the official list; seventy-seven individuals voted. In one Southside district, twenty-two voted. Kennedy triumphed seventy-one to three.

JFK rolled through Chicago by 456,312 votes, receiving 1,378,343 votes in total, more than he received in any *state* save California, Michigan, Ohio, New York, and Massachusetts, and just 7,072 votes less than he received in all of New Jersey, and 10,776 more than he received in Lyndon Johnson's Texas.

"Listen, honey," Sam Giancana would later boast to Judith Campbell, "if it wasn't for me, your boyfriend wouldn't even be in the White House."

★ ★ ★

JFK had friends elsewhere as well. In one St. Louis neighborhood, completely bulldozed for urban renewal, returns were, nonetheless, heavy for Kennedy. And in Lyndon Johnson's Texas, equally suspicious events transpired. In Fannin County (Sam Rayburn's home county), 4,895 registered voters cast 6,138 ballots. In Angela County's Twenty-seventh

Precinct, 86 individuals voted—Kennedy won 147 to 24. Nixon carried one Fort Bend County precinct 458 to 350, and 182 ballots were declared void. Kennedy won another by 68 to 1; all were upheld.

JFK carried Texas by 46,267 votes.

★ ★ ★

In his fourth-floor suite, Nixon watched little television, receiving returns instead from wire services and phone calls. By midnight California time (3 a.m. in Hyannis), with his situation worsening (results from Pennsylvania and Texas had been particularly discouraging; California, Minnesota, Illinois, and Michigan still provided slim reeds of hope), but by no means entirely settled, Richard Nixon reluctantly decided to appear before the Ambassador Hotel ballroom crowd. Prior to that unfortunate errand, however, he had another, far harder, visit to make: to his two daughters, still ignorant of where their family future lay.

"Hi, Daddy, how is the election going?" Tricia asked.

"I'm afraid we lost, honey," he blurted out. Tricia burst into tears. "I'm not crying because of myself but for you and Mommy," she explained. "You have worked so hard and so long."

His daughter's tears dried, Nixon explained to Pat, "I don't intend to make an outright concession, but the least I can do is to indicate that, if the present trend continues, Kennedy will be elected."

She was less resigned to defeat than he. "I simply cannot bring myself to stand there with you," Pat countered, "while you concede the election to Kennedy."

The Nixons and their three Secret Service men departed for a statement he did not want to make. Pat gave each of their security men a little kiss, struggling to control her own feelings, mastering them enough to joke, "I guess I'll have to get a teaching job again."

At 12:15 a.m. they entered the Ambassador Ballroom. A thousand supporters remained, desperate for encouragement. Nixon was devastated, but he knew what he had to do. Smiling and waving, he played the role of a man still controlling events, but eventually he reached the real point of his mission. "If the present trend continues," said Nixon, "Senator Kennedy will be the next President of the United States."

"You're still going to win!" the crowd shouted. "Don't give up!"

Pat didn't want to hear it either. She kept smiling. She knew what she had to do, too. The smile remained frozen on her face—but only between tears and sobs.

At Bobby's house, Jackie Kennedy watched Dick Nixon on television. "Does this mean you're president, Bunny?" she asked.

"No," JFK replied, "it's too early yet."

"Why don't you give up?" someone shouted at the screen.

"Why should he?" JFK interjected. "I wouldn't, in his place."

Henry Cabot Lodge came on TV. "Cabot looks like he's having a hard time staying awake," jibed Kennedy.

The Kennedys ducked into the kitchen for something to eat. Pierre Salinger wanted Jack to hike down to the Hyannis Armory, where all the TV crews had gathered, to issue his own statement. Kennedy, recalling how bone weary Nixon had looked, answered, "You want me to put on a performance at this hour of the night? Not me. I'm going to bed, and all of you better do likewise."

"How can you go to bed now?" Dave Powers demanded.

"Because," JFK responded, "it's too late to change another vote. But next time, we'll go to bed early."

With that, he left through Bobby's kitchen door, heading for his own home, just next door. Behind JFK was a Secret Service agent. Voices called into the Cape Cod darkness: "Good night, Mr. President."

And so John Fitzgerald Kennedy, truly not knowing if he was Mr. President or not, went to bed.

Bobby remained awake, receiving more returns, analyzing results, making calls. But even he had his limits.

Joe Kennedy did not, waiting until everything had been nailed down—it was Michigan at 5:45 a.m. that put his son over the top, made him president. Only then did Joe retire. Years later, reading of another multimillionaire, Ross Perot, Rose Kennedy informed a grandson, "I read in the paper that he was going to spend $100 million to buy the election. Your grandfather only spent ten."

★ ★ ★

The amazing thing was that Nixon came so close. So much had gone against him, some items beyond his control, many decisions of his own sorry making, blown up in his Lazy Shave made-up face—the debates, Ike's "give me a week" gaffe and his general absence from the campaign, the King arrest and release, Cuba, his choice of Lodge, the craven idiocy of his capitulation to Rockefeller, Norman Vincent Peale's gaucherie, lying bedridden for two weeks with his bad knee, campaigning with a 103-degree fever, the fifty-state strategy, micromanaging his campaign to death. He had started from behind. He should have fallen even further behind. Jack Kennedy should have strolled to victory.

Conversely, JFK seemed to have done everything right. He had swept the primaries. Picked the "right" vice-president. Remained healthy enough so no one noticed his infirmities. Charmed the press. Held the Stevenson liberals in check. Swung the black vote while retaining the white South. Demolished Nixon's claim of "experience." Run to his right on Cuba. Been Catholic but not *too* Catholic.

With the country still exceedingly more Democratic than Republican, why had the race proven so *damn* close? Ralph de Toledano observed that, in the end, issues proved unimportant; voters merely decided they liked Kennedy better. Yes, but not by much. They *should* have liked the exceedingly charismatic Kennedy far more than the shifty Nixon, whom they just barely liked better than Hubert Humphrey two elections later. No, there was simply something about JFK that disturbed 1960's voters. His age? His religion? His money? His never-ending horde of nouveau riche relations posing as America's new royalty? That cold glint in the Kennedy eye, the passionless passion in his voice that supporters portrayed as sureness of purpose but that may have merely betrayed ruthless lust for power?

Nixon with a tan and a shave, Tammany in a Brooks Brothers suit.

★ ★ ★

It was close, not merely nationally; it was excruciatingly close in state after state. Kennedy won New Jersey, Illinois, and Hawaii with less than 50 percent of the vote. He won Delaware, Michigan, Hubert Humphrey's Minnesota, Harry Truman's Missouri, Lyndon Johnson's

Texas, and New Mexico, Hawaii, and Arkansas with less than 51 percent. He won Pennsylvania, Nevada, and Solid South South Carolina with less than 52 percent. He won only nine states with more than 52 percent, just six outside New England.

Kennedy carried supposedly virulently anti-Catholic West Virginia by 52.7 percent—his seventh-highest margin. The Mountain State had gone for Eisenhower in 1952. Kennedy's percentage exceeded Stevenson's in 1952.

Where Nixon won, he won bigger. Nixon captured twenty of his twenty-six states with more than 52 percent of the vote. Only in California, Alaska, and Washington did he win with less than 51 percent. In Montana, Wisconsin, and Florida he won with less than 52 percent.

In Georgia, where Richard Nixon had drawn 150,000 supporters in Atlanta and seen dreams of luring the white South into his camp take shape, Kennedy drew 62.54 percent of Peach State votes—second only to the 63.63 percent he had attracted in Rhode Island, the nation's most Catholic state. Indeed, as Ernest Vandiver had confidently predicted, Georgia would indeed vote for a Democrat for president *even* if he were a "one-legged Chinaman who couldn't speak English."

Nixon captured only Virginia, Tennessee, and Florida in the old Confederacy. He narrowly fell short in Arkansas, South Carolina, North Carolina, Louisiana, and Texas (Ike had taken the latter two states four years earlier). The Solid South had remained solid. Nixon had tossed away the African American vote essentially for a chimera.

Worse than a chimera. Kennedy's newly energized black vote had helped move Illinois, Michigan, and New Jersey, Missouri, and, quite possibly, Texas and Pennsylvania into the Democratic column. That meant 76 electoral votes even without Texas and Pennsylvania, a whopping 132 votes with them, minimally short-circuiting an easy victory for Richard Nixon (285 to 227 electoral votes), perhaps even an absolute landslide (351 to 171).

★ ★ ★

The morning came. Before 6:00 a.m., a distraught Julie Nixon jolted her father awake. "What are we going to do?" she wailed. "Where are we going to live? What kid of job are you going to be able to get? Where are we going to school?"

Pierre Salinger had not been asleep for more than an hour, at the nearby Yachtsman motel, when the phone jangled him awake at 8:30 a.m. It was the Associated Press, demanding, "It's all over. . . . How fast will you have a statement from him?"

Secret Service agents—already guarding the president-elect—waved Salinger into the Kennedy compound, where he found Ted Sorensen already present, reading to JFK (soaking in a tub in his second-floor bathroom) the latest returns.

"Any[thing] new from Nixon yet?" JFK demanded. Salinger said no. He threw Kennedy a towel as JFK continued to ponder events. His victory's infinitesimal margin had left Jack Kennedy more shaken than elated.

Hours passed. Time drew near for Dick Nixon to concede. But he had not as yet heard from Dwight Eisenhower. Ike was busy—he had meetings.

The Nixons checked out of the Ambassador. Donald Nixon approached, near to tears, "I hope I haven't been responsible for your losing the election." Richard reassured him that he had not.

The final returns: Jack Kennedy by 303 to 219 in the electoral college, winning 34,220,984 to 34,108,157 in the popular vote—though because of a muddled situation on Mississippi ballots, the *Congressional Quarterly* calculated that Nixon had actually captured the popular vote by 58,181. Suffice it to say, it was close, and, suffice it to say, Jack Kennedy had won.

At 9:45 a.m. PST Herb Klein—not Richard Nixon—stood before the cameras to announce that the great chase had ended, just as he—not Richard Nixon—had so casually announced it had begun ten months earlier to the day. In Hyannis, at Joe's white clapboard Marchant Avenue home, the Kennedys watched on TV. JFK spied Klein's trim looks and fashionable wardrobe. "He looks," the president-elect kidded the pudgy, often-disheveled Salinger, "more like a New Frontiersman than you do."

Klein read Richard Nixon's terse concession—a telegram Nixon had already sent to Kennedy: "I want to repeat through this wire the congratulations and best wishes I extended to you on television last night. I know that you will have the united support of all Americans as you lead the nation in the cause of peace and freedom in the next four years."

It was over.

Someone in Hyannis mentioned that Nixon should have issued the statement himself—at least for the sake of his supporters. JFK pondered his rival's disconcerting absence. And then, Jack Kennedy—who himself had fled from voters the night of what he thought would be a similar debacle, the night of West Virginia's primary—spoke.

"He went out," sneered JFK of his vanquished rival, "the way he came in . . . no class."

THIRTY-SEVEN

"*Dies irae*"

THE AMERICAN DREAM—the great, grand Kennedy dream—had reached fruition, shattering boundaries that might circumscribe others. Not only was Jack president, but, just as family "jokes" had foretold, Bobby, so very young, assumed the attorney generalship, and, Teddy, so young he had to wait two years before reaching the constitutional threshold, reclaimed Jack's former U.S. Senate seat.

It was only right.

At Jack's inaugural, old Robert Frost, blinded by sun reflecting off January snow, his vision already dimmed by his eighty-five years, fumbled through a poem. Marian Anderson sang the national anthem (Jackie's idea). Richard Cardinal Cushing droned on in prayer ("the most grating priestly voice in Christendom," McGeorge Bundy once noted), and those of a mind to believe in omens might have noticed that as Cushing implored God "for a divine spark," wisps of blue smoke wafted before him. His podium, experiencing an electrical short, came dangerously near to erupting into flames. Jack Kennedy gritted his teeth, pretended not to notice—and, tempting fate, vowed to "pay any price, bear any burden, meet any hardship."

Flames aside, Camelot began with more hubris than eventual success. Sorensen, O'Donnell, O'Brien, Salinger, Schlesinger, Goodwin, Cox, Wofford, Feldman, and Powers all received properly significant appointments. Sargent Shriver helped initiate the new Peace Corps. Adlai Stevenson went not to the State Department, but to the United Nations; John Kenneth Galbraith went further still, to the U.S. embassy in India. "Brilliant people circulated," historian Garry Wills noted, "telling each other how brilliant they were."

Not so brilliant, however, as to prevent the Bay of Pigs, the Berlin Wall, JFK's own disastrous summit at Vienna, the murder of Vietnam's Diem brothers, and an October world brought to the brink of nuclear winter—the Cuban missile crisis. Watching all this, no doubt pondering that they might do better, were Lyndon Johnson and Richard Nixon, though how they might ever be tendered that chance seemed more than fanciful. Johnson, accursed by a faltering physical heart, was now beset with a shattered political heart, chafing under the burdens of a burdenless, powerless office and the sight—and slights—of administration favorites from Robert Kennedy on down, though RFK, by himself, would have been sufficient to plunge Lyndon Baines Johnson into despondency's nadir. Daily, the Oval Office slithered increasingly beyond his grasp for 1968, and—if rumors were to be believed—even the lowly vice presidency might not remain his in 1964.

Richard Nixon? His comeback trail lurched into disastrous detour in 1962, as he failed, rather badly, rather gracelessly, to unseat Pat Brown from California's governorship. "You won't have Nixon to kick around any more, gentlemen," he snarled to reporters, perhaps drunkenly ("with lubrication but without grace," as John Ehrlichman phrased it), the most sincere—though hardly the most prophetic—words he ever spoke.

"I must remember to smile when I get defeated," JFK chuckled to Earl Warren aboard Air Force One, on hearing news of his rival's self-immolation. Journalist Mary McGrory could not discern who—president or chief justice—relished Nixon's pain more, but she recalled two "heads together over the clippings . . . laughing like schoolboys."

There was no laughter in Palm Beach. There, Joe Kennedy, in December 1961, had suffered a debilitating stroke, surviving speechless and paralyzed on his right side. He had worked so hard, accomplished so much, sinned gravely and often against God and against man to steal fame and power and treasure from the grasp of a hostile world. Now he enjoyed not fame or power or treasure, or much of anything else, and his suffering removed much of power's pleasure from his now powerful sons.

Their missteps, and an ominous grassroots dissatisfaction within the GOP, fueled a revived, militant conservatism. JFK had barely carried Texas in 1960. Against Barry Goldwater's rising star, his 1964 chances there grew exceedingly dicey—a mere 38 percent rating in one Texas poll.

So, in November 1963, Jack Kennedy traveled to San Antonio and Houston and Fort Worth—and Dallas, where, if all went according to plan, he would proceed by motorcade to the Dallas Trade Mart and deliver a speech ending with the 124th Psalm: "Except the Lord keep the city," JFK would have said, "the watchman woke but in vain."

Friday morning, November 22, saw paths intersect in unlikely nexus at Dallas' Love Field: Richard Nixon, alone, his electoral career in tatters, in town for a mundane board meeting of the Pepsi-Cola Company, embarking in glum anonymity for New York; and JFK and LBJ, ascendant, but nervous regarding their futures, arriving from nearby Fort Worth, cheered by enthusiastic crowds.

Dallas was not numbered among JFK's favorite locales ("nut country," he jeered), being the heart of Texas's opposition to him, his New Frontier, and all things liberal. It was there in 1960 that Congressman Alger had unleashed his "mink-coat riot." It was in Dallas, less than a month before JFK's visit, that an angry anti-UN crowd had jostled and spat upon Adlai Stevenson. Now handbills bearing JFK's likeness and captioned "WANTED FOR TREASON" littered Dallas streets.

Premonitions filled Jack Kennedy's heart.

In Houston, as JFK spoke, his hands shook so violently, he nearly dropped his index card notes.

"Jackie," he told his wife, inside their Fort Worth hotel suite, "if somebody wants to shoot me from a window with a rifle, nobody can stop it, so why worry about it?"

Yet JFK did worry. "You know," he continued, pacing like a man trapped by fate, "last night would have been a hell of a night to assassinate a president. I mean it. There was the rain, and the night, and we were all jostled. Suppose a man had a pistol in a briefcase." He went through the motions of imitating his own assassination—"Then he could have dropped the gun and the briefcase—and melted away in the crowd."

Jack Kennedy peered out from his Texas Hotel window, at the speaker's stand below him, repeating to Larry O'Brien, "Just look at that platform. With all those buildings around it, the Secret Service couldn't stop someone who really wanted to get you."

He kept repeating himself, as if obsessed, as if somehow *knowing*. To Kenny O'Donnell, just before leaving for Dallas, he reiterated, "[I]t was not a very difficult job—all one had to do was get a high building someday with a telescopic rifle, and there was nothing anybody could do."

Yet, within Dallas itself, with Lyndon Johnson and Johnson's henchman John Connally (now governor of Texas, previously JFK's secretary of the navy) in tow, JFK enjoyed a warm, encouraging, enthusiastic welcome. "You can't say Dallas doesn't love you today," chirped John Connally's wife, Nellie. JFK might as well have been in Massachusetts.

Save, of course, seconds later, for a twenty-four-year-old ex-Marine sharpshooter, ex–Soviet defector, ex-nobody named Lee Harvey Oswald and a mail-order, 6.5-mm Mannlicher-Carcano rifle.

Richard Cardinal Cushing, as he had performed JFK's wedding and baptized his children, and officiated at his inaugural, now offered the requiem for the soul of the departed, a Mass that included the *Dies Irae*, a dirgeful, six-century-old Latin prayer that began:

Dies irae! dies illa
Solvet sæclum in favilla
Teste David cum Sibyllâ
[Day of wrath and terror looming!
Heaven and earth to ash consuming,
David's word and Sibyl's truth foredooming!]

★ ★ ★

Lyndon Johnson was already president. Robert Kennedy was already on the way out. In 1964, unwilling to serve LBJ, unable to stomach him, RFK would depart the new administration, winning a Senate seat from New York.

That election, finally a true landslide for "Landslide Lyndon," provided Johnson with the mandate his predecessor never enjoyed, and which would propel his Great Society: the war on poverty, Medicare, Medicaid, the Civil Rights Act of 1965, the Job Corps, the Model Cities Program, food stamps, VISTA, Upward Bound, the National Endowment for the Arts. Lyndon Johnson, observed David Brinkley, "seemed really to believe in a radical notion: that it is possible for the mass of mankind to be happy."

Lyndon Johnson had now become much more than the heir to John F. Kennedy. He was now legatee to Franklin Roosevelt. Yet, in the long run, it was his inheritance from the hated JFK that would prove his true legacy, would fuel his undoing, his immediate, precipitous descent from grace, power, and posterity.

Vietnam.

Urban unrest helped generate massive Republican congressional gains in 1966. Vietnam finished the job—and Lyndon Johnson—forty-eight months later. Eugene McCarthy, rousing himself from eight torpid, resentful years in the Senate, stirred himself to challenge LBJ's handling of the war, and when Clean Gene's New Hampshire primary effort bore surprising fruit, Robert Kennedy entered 1968's fray.

Johnson ("I shall not seek, and I will not accept, the nomination of my party for another term as your President") stunned the nation by withdrawing from the race. Lyndon Johnson, after all, never was very interested in presidential primaries.

Dies irae! dies illa
Solvet saeclum in favilla

Vice President Hubert Humphrey replaced him, but when an escaped convict's .30-06 rifle bullet smashed into Martin Luther King's face, and America's cities erupted into arson, riots, and violence, the nation seemed headed for chaos.

Dies irae! dies illa
Solvet saeclum in favilla

Vying for the growing anti-war vote, RFK vanquished McCarthy in the California primary and might have reclaimed the presidency, if not in 1968, then in 1972—but for his exit following his victory celebration through the kitchen of Los Angeles's Ambassador Hotel (site of Richard Nixon's concession speech eight years earlier, and where he had retreated after the Checkers speech several political lifetimes before), and but for a twenty-four-year-old Palestinian immigrant named Sirhan B. Sirhan.

Dies irae! dies illa
Solvet saeclum in favilla

Lyndon Johnson retained enough political clout to bestow the Democratic nomination, for what it was now worth, on Hubert Humphrey, and Richard J. Daley ("The policeman is not there to create disorder. The policeman is there to preserve disorder") retained enough physical clout to ensure that a Democratic convention might actually be held in an increasingly turbulent year.

Among the Republicans, Nelson Rockefeller (damaged by his 1963 divorce from Tod Rockefeller and his indecorously hasty remarriage to Margaretta "Happy" Murphy) demonstrated once more that, despite all his energy, resources, and knish-eating prowess, he possessed not the semblance of an idea of how to become his party's nominee—at least, not against Richard Nixon, who, although he would not debate in 1968, went on to an eerie repeat of his 1960 squeaker, the outcome decided by less than 1 percent of the popular vote. In 1968 Nixon took Illinois—and the presidency.

Aided by H. R. Haldeman and John Ehrlichman and a new recruit to his inner circle, Henry Kissinger, Richard Nixon moved to shut down John Kennedy's Vietnam War but not Lyndon Johnson's Great Society ("We get the action," crowed GOP liberal Hugh Scott, "and the conservatives get the rhetoric"). Richard Nixon might have faced another Kennedy—Teddy—in 1972. Chappaquiddick intervened. Mary Jo Kopechne drowned, and Edward Kennedy's chances for the presidency sank with her.

Dies irae! dies illa
Solvet saeclum in favilla

Against the inept and unpopular Democratic George McGovern–Sargent Shriver ticket, Richard Nixon now coasted to his own landslide, as great as Lyndon's—larger, even more satisfying, than Ike's—but in the course of his triumph, his campaign aides broke into the Watergate offices of Democratic national chairman Larry O'Brien, some said (among many theories) in search of incriminating material regarding Nixon's connections with, and payments from, Howard Hughes. Connections with Hughes had helped sink Nixon in 1960—and again in 1962. In June 1972, with McGovern not yet nominated, another Hughes entanglement might prove potentially as damaging as the first two.

A few inches of duct tape discovered in a Watergate doorjamb, however, proved more damaging still. Haldeman and Ehrlichman, mourned by few, resigned and went to jail, and Richard Nixon walked up the stairs to a Marine Corps helicopter waiting on the White House South Lawn, held his head as high as could, extended his arms in an ironic V, waved good-bye, and traveled through sky and time into exile and disgrace.

"Always remember," Richard Nixon had advised his staff minutes before, "others may hate you, but those who hate you don't win unless you hate them, and then you destroy yourself."

Dies irae! dies illa
Solvet saeclum in favilla

Notes

Chapter One: January

1   Announcement. *New York Times*, 2 January 1960, p. 6; *Washington Post*, 3 January 1960, pp. 1, 12; *New York Times*, 3 January 1960, pp. 1, 44; *Chicago Tribune*, 3 January 1960, pp. 1–2; *Christian Science Monitor*, 4 January 1960, p. 3; Sorensen, *Kennedy*, pp. 122–23; Fairlie, pp. 64–65; Dallek, *Unfinished Life*, pp. 243–44; O'Brien, *Kennedy*, pp. 443–44.

Chapter Two: "My son will be President in 1960"

3   "Honey Fitz." Burns, pp. 11–12; Goodwin, *Fitzgeralds*, pp. 92–173, 190–205, 245–52; Maier, pp. 53–59, 201–2, 218–19; Parmet, *Jack*, pp. 7–9; Schwarz, pp. 30–36, 65–71; Hersh, *Camelot*, pp. 35–41; McCarthy, pp. 30–32; Madsen, pp. 48–49, 55.

3   Patrick J. Kennedy. Burns, pp. 4–10; Goodwin, *Fitzgeralds*, pp. 98, 100, 226–32, 253–57; Schwarz, pp. 23–30; Koskoff, pp. 5–13; Russell, pp. 326–31; O'Brien, *Kennedy*, pp. 9–10; Maier, pp. 42–45; Kessler, pp. 8–12; Madsen, pp. 45–48.

3   Boston Latin. Whalen, *Founding Father*, pp. 31–32; Russell, pp. 326–31.

3   "The measure . . . raised." Whalen, *Founding Father*, p. 31.

3   125 pounds. O'Brien, *Kennedy*, p. 70.

3   Grades. O'Brien, *Kennedy*, p. 62.

3   Class standing. Friedenberg, p. 32; O'Brien, *Kennedy*, p. 75.

4   JPK strings. Blair and Blair, pp. 41; O'Brien, *Kennedy*, p. 77; Hamilton, pp. 143–45.

4   "whose body . . . dreams." Madsen, p. 188.

4   Father's insistence. Blair and Blair, p. 86.

4   No Irish spouses. Wills, *Kennedy Imprisonment*, p. 65.

4   "either [Joe Jr.'s] . . . States." Schlesinger, *Robert Kennedy*, p. 13; Goodwin, *Fitzgeralds*, p. 468; Burns, p. 30.

5   "You would . . . come." Carr, p. 112; Russell, p. 366; Schoor, p. 153.

5   *Why England Slept*. Kennedy, *Why England Slept*, *passim*; *New York Times*, 3 August 1940, p. 17; *New York Times*, 11 August 1940, p. 79; Burns, pp. 39–45; Blair and Blair, pp. 106–9; O'Brien, *Kennedy*, pp. 84–86; Hamilton, pp. 325–38; Schoor, pp. 98–100.

5   Lowest honor grade. Blair and Blair, pp. 80–81; Hamilton, p. 321.

5   Krock. Krock, pp. 343, 350; Blair and Blair, pp. 81–82, 84–85; Collier and Horowitz, *Kennedys*, p. 85; Parmet, *Jack*, pp. 55, 72, 75; Wills, *Kennedy Imprisonment*, pp. 134–35; Ritchie, p. 18.

5   Klemmer. O'Brien, *Kennedy*, p. 108.

5   "What do . . . it!" Martin, *Hero*, p. 136.

5   "It was . . . that." Morrow, *Best Year*, p. 190; Reeves, *Character*, p. 67.

6   Navy and Marine Corps Medal. *Hartford Courant*, 15 August 1944, p. 2; Russell, p. 363; Maier, p. 167; Schwarz, p. 316.

6   "The medal . . . battle." Reeves, *Character*, p. 66.

6   "It was . . . out." Morrow, *Best Year*, p. 191; Maier, p. 170.

6   "The biggest . . . bomb." Renehan, p. 304; Goodwin, *Fitzgeralds*, p. 688.

6   Death of Joe Jr. *New York Times*, 15 August 1944, p. 18; *Hartford Courant*, 15 August 1944, p. 2; *Hartford Courant*, 16 August 1944, p. 6; McCarthy, pp. 24, 80–81, 83; Schoor, pp. 147–50; Renehan, pp. 303–5; Russell, pp. 363–64; Dallek, *Unfinished Life*, pp. 106–7.

6   "Joe's worldly . . . things." Russell, p. 364; Bryant, p. 14.

6   "You know . . . him." Dallek, *Unfinished Life*, p. 107.

7   "I can . . . ahead.'" Fay, p. 152; Russell, p. 367; Dallek, *Unfinished Life*, pp. 117–18; Kessler, p. 288; Thomas, p. 48.

7   Hearst. Burns, pp. 55–56; Carr, p. 78; Schoor, pp. 154–56; Sorensen, *Kennedy Legacy*, p. 27; O'Brien, *Kennedy*, pp. 180–88; Ritchie, pp. 145–46.

7   Lieutenant governorship. O'Donnell, Powers, and McCarthy, p. 47; Goodwin, *Fitzgeralds*, pp. 709–10; O'Neill, pp. 76–77; Blair and Blair, pp. 430–31; Parmet, *Jack*, p. 143; Kessler, pp. 290–91; Hamilton, pp. 746–77; O'Brien, *Kennedy*, p. 194.

7   Curley. *Berkshire Eagle*, 19 January 1946, pp. 1–2; Burns, p. 60; Russell, p. 367; Blair and Blair, p. 415; O'Neill, p. 28; Carr, pp. 79–80. Curley's exit was hardly accidental. Joe Kennedy tendered him twelve thousand dollars to run for mayor and vacate the congressional seat.

7   "Miami candidate." Wills, *Kennedy Imprisonment*, p. 62; Dallek, *Unfinished Life*, p. 126; McCarthy, p. 91; Carr, p. 81.

7   Poor speaker. Carr, p. 81; Parmet, *Jack*, p. 150; Dallek, *Unfinished Life*, p. 124; Martin, *Hero*, p. 202; Martin, *Destruction*, p. 139.

7   Neville. Carr, p. 80; Whalen, *Founding Father*, p. 391; O'Donnell, Powers, and McCarthy, pp. 48, 69–71; Blair and Blair, p. 421; Goodwin, *Fitzgeralds*, p. 710; Dallek, *Unfinished Life*, p. 131.

7   "The first . . . money." Russell, p. 368; Lasky, *JFK*, p. 98; Maier, p. 204; Parmet, *Jack*, p. 148; Hersh, *Camelot*, p. 42; O'Brien, *Kennedy*, p. 196.

7   "We're going . . . flakes." Russell, p. 373; Bryant, p. 14; Hamilton, p. 753; Kessler, p. 367; Thomas, p. 48; Collier and Horowitz, *Kennedys*, p. 206; Heymann, *RFK*, p. 151. Various authors place this statement at varying mileposts along the Kennedy career. If it was not said in 1946, it certainly applies to 1946.

8   "Joe Kennedy . . . later." O'Neill, p. 77; Dallek, *Unfinished Life*, p. 130; Kessler, p. 297.

8   Ten-dollar bill. Lasky, *JFK*, p. 95; Savage, p. 5.

8   Primary opposition. Carr, p. 80; O'Donnell, Powers, and McCarthy, p. 69; Parmet, *Jack*, p. 152; Russell, p. 369; Blair and Blair, p. 464; Dallek, *Unfinished Life*, p. 123; Martin, *Destruction*, p. 147; O'Brien, *Kennedy*, p. 194.

8   "You're Jack . . . smile." Goodwin, *Fitzgeralds*, p. 708; Maier, p. 204.

8   PT-109. *New Yorker*, 17 June 1944, pp. 31–43; *Reader's Digest*, August 1944, pp. 75–80; Burns, p. 67; McCarthy, p. 93; Carr, p. 82; Renehan, pp. 285–87; Carr, p. 82; Dallek, *Unfinished Life*, pp. 106, 130; Hamilton, pp. 652–54.

8   "My story . . . great." Goodwin, *Fitzgeralds*, p. 714; Lasky, *JFK*, p. 94; Maier, p. 170; O'Brien, *Kennedy*, p. 199.

9   "fighting conservative." *Look*, 11 June 1946, pp. 32–36; Reeves, *Character*, p. 82; Lasky, *JFK*, p. 95.

9   "Why[,] you . . . in 1960." Dallek, *Unfinished Life*, p. 126.

9   1946 primary returns. *Berkshire Eagle*, 19 June 1946, p. 1; *Fitchburg Sentinel*, 19 June 1946, p. 1; *New York Times*, 23 June 1946, p. E6; Carr, p. 83.

9   1946 general election returns. *Berkshire Eagle*, 6 November 1946, p. 1.

9   Wardrobe. Burns, p. 71; Morrow, *Best Year*, p. 58.

9   "Gorgeous George." Evans and Novak, p. 99.

9   "If you . . . seen." Blair and Blair, p. 524.

9   "began at . . . it." Hellmann, p. 57; Martin, *Destruction*, p. 169.

10 "I will . . . convention." Russell, p. 372.

11 Lodge-Taftite antipathy. *New York Times*, 28 February 1985, pp. 1, A21; *Washington Post*, 28 February 1985, pp. 1, C5; *Chicago Tribune*, 28 February 1985, p. A10; Whalen, *Lodge, passim; Current Biography 1943*, pp. 449–53; Friedenberg, p. 34.

11 Lodge-McCarthy antipathy. Reeves,, *McCarthy*, pp. 442–44; Cohn pp. 67–68.

11 "be a sensation." Whalen, *Founding Father*, p. 416; Parmet, *Jack*, p. 173; Maier, pp. 271–72; Cohn, p. 73.

11 Pat Kennedy. Parmet, *Jack*, p. 172; Cohn, p. 73; Heymann, *RFK*, p. 69.

11 Eunice Kennedy. Parmet, *Jack*, p. 172; Kessler, p. 343; Reeves, *Character*, p. 120; Martin, *Destruction*, p. 180.

11 McCarthy wedding. Thomas, pp. 357–58.

11 Godfather. Heymann, *RFK*, p. 69; Lasky, *RFK*, p. 81; Martin, *Destruction*, p. 180.

11 McCarthy contribution. Whalen, *Founding Father*, pp. 416–17; Pilat, p. 20; Dallek, *Unfinished Life*, p. 191.

11 *Boston Post*. Whalen, *Lodge*, pp. 127–33; Burns, pp. 110, 132–33; Parmet, *Jack*, pp. 241–43, 511; McCarthy, pp. 106–7; Goodwin, pp. 764–65; Koskoff, pp. 415–16; O'Brien, *Kennedy*, pp. 256–57; Carr, pp. 91–92; Jamieson, p. 125.

12 "He was . . . campaigner." O'Brien, *Kennedy*, pp. 247–48.

12 1952 returns. *New York Times*, 6 November 1952, pp. 1, 25; *Hartford Courant*, 6 November 1952, pp. 1, 17; Burns, p. 115.

12 "I never . . . people." Schlesinger, *Thousand Days*, p. 13; Matthews, p. 100; Carr, p. 116.

12 RFK-McCarthy. *New York Times*, 1 August 1953. p. 9; *Washington Post*, 1 August 1953, p. 4; *Current Biography 1958*, p. 220; Cohn, pp. 68–72; McCarthy, p. 128; Schlesinger, *Robert Kennedy*, pp. 98–118; Schlesinger, *Thousand Days*, p. 12; Thomas, pp. 64–66; Heymann, *RFK*, pp. 63–88; Lasky, *RFK*, pp. 81–97; Hersh, *Bobby and J. Edgar*, pp. 138–39; Sorensen, *Kennedy Legacy*, pp. 34–35.

12 "Joe McCarthy . . . Boston." Dallek, *Unfinished Life*, p. 190.

12 "made no . . . [McCarthy]." Sorensen, pp. 46–47.

12 1954 surgery. *New York Times*, 11 October 1954, p. 39; *Hartford Courant*,

21 October 1954. p. 1A; Burns, pp. 156–60; Blair and Blair, pp. 556–79; Sorensen, pp. 38–42; McCarthy, pp. 114–15, 117–18; Parmet, *Jack*, pp. 307–11; Gilbert, pp. 142–48; Goodwin, *Fitzgeralds*, pp. 774–76; Dallek, *Unfinished Life*, pp. 195–96; Smith, *Grace and Power*, pp. 32–33; O'Brien, *Kennedy*, pp. 279–84; Martin, *Hero*, pp. 95–97; Martin, *Destruction*, pp. 196–97.

13 "Jack was . . .pain." Goodwin, *Fitzgeralds*, p. 774; Dallek, *Unfinished Life*, p. 196.

13 "Jack had . . . scene." Martin, *Hero*, p. 95.

13 Travell, 1955. *Current Biography 1961*, pp. 457–58.

14 "There wasn't . . . lucky." Goodwin, *Fitzgeralds*, p. 776.

14 "New England . . . primary." Sorensen, p. 80.

14 Nominating speech. Burns, p. 186; Carr, p. 107; Sevareid, pp. 183–84; McCarthy, p. 121; Schlesinger, *Thousand Days*, pp. 7–8; Watson, *Vista*, p. 5.

14 Film. Sevareid, p. 184; McCarthy, p. 121; Carr, p. 107; Parmet, *Jack*, p. 367; Goodwin, p. 782.

14 Vice-presidential contest. Goodwin, *Fitzgeralds*, p. 783; Reeves, *Character*, p. 135.

14 "If we . . . Kennedy." Schlesinger, *Thousand Days*, p. 7; Friedenberg, p. 41; Lesher, p. 114.

14 "the most . . . Senate." Donaldson, p. 29.

14 "Improve . . . record." Boyle, p. 139; Thomas, p. 86.

15 "With only . . . marbles." O'Donnell, Powers, and McCarthy, p. 146; Jamieson, p. 123; Martin, *Hero*, p. 130.

15 *Profiles in Courage*. *New York Times*, 12 May 1957, p. E2; Burns, pp. 160–63; Parmet, *Jack*, pp. 393–97; McCarthy, pp. 115–17; Carr, pp. 105–6; O'Brien, *Kennedy*, pp. 331–39; Wills, *Kennedy Imprisonment*, pp. 139–42; Kennedy, *Profiles in Courage*, *passim*; Sorensen, pp. 66–70; Lasky, *JFK*, pp. 162–63; Parmet, pp. 320–33, 394–97.

15 Drew Pearson. *Current Biography 1961*, pp. 234–35; Burns, p. 163; Abell, pp. 405, 418–19; Sorensen, pp. 69–70; Wallace and Gates, pp. 6–13; Clifford, pp. 306–10.

15 "I've never . . . work." O'Neill, p. 87.

15 "John Kennedy . . . leaders." Sorensen, p. 43.

15 Algeria. Kennedy, *The Strategy of Peace*, pp. 66–80; Burns, pp. 195–96; Goodwin, *Fitzgeralds*, p. 790.

15 "Every time . . . crowd." Boyle, p. 140; Schlesinger, *Robert Kennedy*, pp. 261–85.

16 1958 returns. O'Donnell, Powers, and McCarthy, p. 166; McCarthy, p. 133.

16 "LeMoyne, . . . him. 'Mr. President.'" Heymann, *Jackie*, p. 212; Collier and Horowitz, *Kennedys*, p. 199; Pitts, pp. 152–53.

16 "Jack is . . . him." Russell, p. 384; Hersh, *Camelot*, p. 89.

16 "I never . . . talker." O'Neill, p. 86.

17 "With a . . . positions." Lincoln, p. 41.

17 "He is . . . others." *Hartford Courant*, 15 July 1960, p. 18.

17 "America's . . . favorite movie." Wills, *Kennedy Imprisonment*, p. 20.

17 "would hesitate . . . it." *Chicago Defender*, 9 December 1958, p. 4;

Schlesinger, *Thousand Days*, p. 14; Lash, p. 280.

18   "I know . . . people." Martin, *Hero*, p. 149.

18   Gallup poll. *Hartford Courant*, 12 July 1960, p. 9.

18   "Yes . . . they are." Bradlee, *Conversations*, p. 16; Bradlee, *Life*, p. 206.

Chapter Three: "Independent as a hog on ice"

19   "the Johnsons . . . down." Caro, *Ascent*, p. 7; Caro, *Path*, p. 92.

19   Senator prophecy. *Abilene Reporter–News*, 20 July 1948, p. 5; Mooney, *The Lyndon Johnson Story*, p. 8; Caro, *Path*, p. 3; Conkin, pp. 17, 27; Unger and Unger, p. 4.

19   "nothing . . . drunkard." Caro, *Path*, p. 93.

19   Road crew. White, *The Professional*, pp. 63–64; Dugger, pp. 100–105; Goodwin, *Johnson*, pp. 42–44; Conkin, pp. 32–36; Dallek, *Lone Star Rising*, p. 60; Woods, pp. 44–49; Miller, *Lyndon*, pp. 25–27.

20   "When he . . . poverty." Unger and Unger, pp. 27–28; Miller, *Lyndon*, pp. 32–33. As a teacher, Johnson was no practitioner of multi-culturalism, forcefully insisting his students speak English at all times, even on the playground.

20   High school teaching. Conkin, pp. 56–57; Unger and Unger, p. 32; Woods, pp. 70–71; Miller, *Lyndon*, p. 35.

20   Stealing elections. Conkin, pp. 55–56.

20   "Everyone knew . . . it." Caro, *Ascent*, p. 8; Goodwin, *Johnson*, pp. 56–60; Unger and Unger, pp. 25–26, 28; Conkin, pp. 48–51.

20   KKK. Caro,, *Path*, pp. 160–65, 172–73; Caro, *Ascent*, p. 8; Conkin, pp. 49–50; Johnson, *My Brother Lyndon*, pp. 29–31.

20   Kleberg. *New York Times*, 5 November 1931, p. 1; White, *The Professional*, p. 70; Evans and Novak, p. 6; Caro, *Path*, pp. 313–22; Dugger, pp. 127–29; Dallek, *Lone Star*, pp. 91–96; Goodwin, *Johnson*, p. 70; Jobe and Muslin, pp. 36–37; Woods, pp. 73–78, 104; Haley, p. 11. Kleberg's election in a special election to succeed Texas's lone GOP representative, Harry Wurzbach, had special significance, giving the Democrats 218 House seats to 214 for the Republicans with one Farmer-Labor seat and two remaining vacancies finally guaranteeing their control of the House.

20   "He had . . . less." Dugger, p. 167; Unger and Unger, p. 36.

20   Little Congress. Caro, *Ascent*, p. 8.

20   Fired by Kleberg. Jobe and Muslin, pp. 39–40; Unger and Unger, p. 52; Dallek, *Lone Star Rising*, pp. 123–24; Dallek, *Lyndon B. Johnson*, p. 18; Miller, *Lyndon*, p. 49. LBJ must not have completely worn out his welcome with Kleberg, as he was able to cajole his old boss into hiring his younger brother, Sam Houston Johnson, as his replacement. Miller, *Lyndon*, p. 49; Conkin, p. 74; Johnson, *My Brother Lyndon*, p. 54.

21   NYA. *Current Biography 1951*, p. 308; Evans and Novak, p. 6; Dugger, pp. 185–90; Conkin, pp. 74–75; Caro, *Path*, pp. 340–44; Goodwin, *Johnson*, pp. 84–86; Miller, *Lyndon*, pp. 53–57; Jobe and Muslin, p. 40; Steinberg, p. 159.

21   Congressional victory. *New York Times*, 11 April 1937, p. 1; *Port Arthur News*,

11 April 1937, pp. 1–2; *Hartford Courant*, 11 April 1937, pp. 1, 10; *Current Biography 1951*, p. 308; Miller, *Lyndon*, pp. 57–62; Dugger, pp. 190–200; Conkin, pp. 79–84; Goodwin, *Johnson*, pp. 86–87; Evans and Novak, p. 7.

21   "Don't forget . . . liberal." Caro, *Ascent*, p. 15; Dallek, *Lone Star Rising*, pp. 168–69; Unger and Unger, p. 79.

21   REA. Caro, *Ascent*, pp. 576–77; Dallek, *Lone Star Rising*, p. 18; Woods, p. 134.

21   Mentors. Evans and Novak, pp. 9–11.

21   "Lyndon . . . go." Unger and Unger, p. 77.

22   "a damn . . . ice." Caro, *Path*, p. 618; Unger and Unger, p. 77; Dallek, *Lone Star Rising*, p. 194; Steinberg, p. 159.

22   1941 defeat. *New York Times*, 30 June 1941, p. 19; *New York Times*, 2 July 1941, pp. 20, 46; *Chicago Tribune*, 2 July 1941, p. 11; *Hartford Courant*, 15 July 1941, p. 3; Mooney, *The Lyndon Johnson Story*, pp. 43–44; Evans and Novak, p. 14; Caro, *Path*, pp. 739–40; Dallek, *Lone Star Rising*, pp. 207–24; Dugger, pp. 226–36; Caro, *Path*, pp. 389–436; Johnson, *My Brother Lyndon*, p. 72; Goodwin, *Johnson*, pp. 93–94; Unger and Unger, pp. 102–4; Woods, pp. 154–55. Fort Worth's O'Daniel, a radio performing, flour manufacturing down-home politician with a predilection for hillbilly bands, served as the model for governor Pappy O'Daniel in the 2000 Coen Brothers' film *O Brother, Where Art Thou?*

22   Christadelphian. Conkin, p. 27.

22   Brown & Root. Miller, *Lyndon*, pp. 114–16; Dallek, *Lone Star Rising*, pp. 175–76, 198; 208, 245–46; Conkin, pp. 91–96; 104–5, 109; Caro, *Ascent*, pp. 273–74, 285–86. Brown & Root is now owned by the Halliburton Co.

23   "in the . . . blood." Caro, *Ascent*, p. 19.

23   "[H]e wouldn't . . . coward." Caro, *Ascent*, p. 37; Morrow, *Best Year*, p. 209.

23   First enlistee. *New York Times*, 12 December 1941, p. 4; Mooney, *The Lyndon Johnson Story*, p. 44; White, *The Professional*, p. 96; Miller, *Lyndon*, p. 91; Unger and Unger, p. 108.

23   "if Mr. . . . accordingly." Caro, *Ascent*, p. 31.

23   Combat, medal. Mooney, *The Lyndon Johnson Story*, p. 46; Caro, *Ascent*, pp. 44–45; Miller, *Lyndon*, p. 99; Conkin, p. 108; Connally and Herskowitz, p. 103; Goodwin, *Johnson*, pp. 94–95; Caro, *Master*, pp. 622–23; Morrow, *Best Year*, pp. 205–8; Reston, *Lone Star*, pp. 82–84.

24   FDR order. *New York Times*, 10 July 1942, p. 7; Caro, *Ascent*, p. 45; Dallek, *Lone Star Rising*, pp. 241–42; Miller, *Lyndon*, p. 100; White, *The Professional*, p. 96.

24   KTBC. Conkin, pp. 111–12; Goodwin, *Johnson*, pp. 98–100; Caro, *Ascent*, pp. 82–88; Evans and Novak, pp. 22–23; Unger and Unger, pp. 117–21; Haley, pp. 60–67; Woods, pp. 172–74.

24   "He was . . . always." Evans and Novak, p. 19; Dugger, pp. 262–63; Caro, *Path*, p. 766; Dallek, *Lone Star*, pp. 265–66; Brinkley, *Brinkley's Beat*, p. 61; Woods, p. 179; Mooney, *The Lyndon Johnson Story*, pp. 52–53.

24   "They called . . . word." *New York Times*, 13 April 1945, p. 3; Evans and

Novak, p. 21.

25   "Johnson's . . . death." Evans and Novak, p. 21.

25   "I never . . . liberal." Caro, *Path*, p. 765.

25   "On many . . . minority." Caro, *Ascent*, p. 15; Dallek, *Lone Star Rising*, p. 278.

25   "an errand . . . contractors." Caro, *Ascent*, p. 136.

25   "If the . . . fortune?" Conkin, pp. 113–14; Caro, *Ascent*, pp. 135–36;
        Morrow, *Best Year*, p. 45.

26   "leave more . . . knew" *New York Times*, 16 June 1993, p. D25.

26   "Labor's . . . fart." Baker and King, p. 40.

26   "The civil . . . hire." *Journal of Negro History*, January 1977, p. 34; Miller,
        Lyndon, p. 118. A slightly different version of this statement occurs in White,
        America in Search of Itself, p. 109.

26   Helicopter. *Brownsville Herald*, 25 June 1948, p. 12; *San Antonio Express*, 6
        July 1948, p. 22; *Abilene Reporter–News*, 20 July 1948, p. 5; Caro, *Ascent*, pp.
        209–23, 228–34, 247–49; Miller, *Lyndon*, pp. 119–20; Morrow, *Best Year*,
        pp. 272–74; Conkin, pp. 116–17; Reston, *Lone Star*, pp. 135–36; Johnson,
        My Brother Lyndon, p. 74.

26   "old . . . job done" *Abilene Reporter–News*, 20 July 1948, p. 5.

26   Seventy-eight votes. *Chicago Tribune*, 14 September 1948, p. 5.

26   "My state . . . caveman." Baker and King, p. 40.

27   1952 VP. Dugger, pp. 375–77.

27   Senate Democratic Leadership. Goodwin, *Johnson*, pp. 107–8; Evans and
        Novak, pp. 51–52.

27   "That was . . . sleep." O'Brien, *Victories*, pp. 36–37; Evans and Novak, p. 52;
        Caro, *Master*, p. 475.

27   "I think . . . people." Lash, pp. 246, 350; Unger and Unger, p. 198; Dallek,
        Lone Star Rising, p. 497.

27   Heart attack. *New York Times*, 3 July 1955, pp. 1, 22; Mooney, *The Lyndon
        Johnson Story*, pp. 126–28; Evans and Novak, pp. 91–94; Miller, *Lyndon*, pp.
        179–83; Baker and King, pp. 150–52; Caro, *Master*, pp. 618–32; Goodwin,
        Johnson, p. 125; Steinberg, p. 298; White, *The Professional*, pp. 132–33.

28   "more than . . . day." *Brainerd Dispatch*, 9 November 1960, p. A-4.

28   "an incredibly . . . practice." Donaldson, p. 24.

28   "I've talked . . . bear!" Alsop Interview I, LBJ Library, p. 8.

28   "Why members . . . needed." Reedy, p. 57.

28   Attitudes, wardrobe. Reedy, pp. 21–22.

29   "a magnificent . . . plaid." Lamb, p. 334.

29   1956 attempt. *New York Times*, 12 March 1956, pp. 1, 12; *New York Times*,
        23 May 1956, pp. 1, 32; Connally and Herskowitz, p. 133; Evans and Novak,
        p. 258; Miller, *Lyndon*, p. 198; Caro, *Master*, pp. 820–21; Steinberg, p. 306.

29   "my son . . . mate." Watson, *Chief of Staff*, p. 26; Hersh, *Edward Kennedy*, p. 123*fn*.

29   LBJ refuses JPK. Martin, *Destruction*, p. 203.

29   JFK-Corcoran. Caro, *Master*, pp. 646–47; Watson, *Chief of Staff*, p. 26;
        Miller, *Lyndon*, p. 238; Thomas, p. 96.

29   LBJ-Stevenson. Krock, p. 360; Woods, p. 310.

29   LBJ-Kefauver. Miller, *Lyndon*, p. 200; Evans and Novak, p. 72.

29   "proudly casts . . . battle." Burns, p. 189; Evans and Novak, p. 238; Schlesinger, *Robert Kennedy*, p. 132; Mooney, *The Politicians*, pp. 247–48.

30   Senate liberals. Evans and Novak, p. 200; Caro, *Master*, pp. 1615–17; Goodwin, *Johnson*, pp. 135–36; Dallek, *Lone Star*, pp. 548–49, 551–52.

30   "I am . . . advocate." *Journal of Negro History*, January 1977, p. 41.

30   Southern Manifesto. *New York Times*, 12 March 1956, pp. 1, 19; *New York Times*, 15 March 1956, p. 18; Miller, *Lyndon*, pp. 187–88; Fite, pp. 333–36; Unger and Unger, p. 431; Caro, *Master*, pp. 785–88; Baker and King, p. 71.

30   1957 Civil Rights Act. Evans and Novak, pp. 124–40; Caro, *Master*, pp. 863–1012; Unger and Unger, pp. 203–16; Dallek, *Lone Star Rising*, pp. 517–27; Miller, *Lyndon*, pp. 204–12. Among Southern senators only LBJ, Gore, Kefauver, Smathers, and Texas's Ralph Yarborough voted for the bill.

30   "The Negroes . . . again." Fite, p. 376; Goodwin, *Johnson*, p. 148.

30   "Bobby . . . the presidency." Miller, *Lyndon*, p. 236; Baker and King, p. 43.

31   LBJ-Schlesinger. Schlesinger, *Thousand Days*, p. 10; Evans and Novak, p. 105; Caro, *Master*, p. 833.

31   "The Democratic . . . run." Dallek, *Unfinished Life*, p. 269.

31   "Lyndon . . . be elected." Miller, *Lyndon*, pp. 235–36; Seshol, p. 44; Dallek, *Unfinished Life*, p. 269.

31   "[He] fluctuates . . . thinker." *Chicago Tribune*, 3 August 1959, p. 6.

31   "He is . . . two." Miller, *Lyndon*, p. 235.

31   Eleanor Roosevelt. Lash, p. 279; Dallek, *Lone Star*, pp. 552–53; Unger and Unger, p. 237.

31   Rowe. *San Mateo Times*, 23 March 1959, p. 18; Evans and Novak, p. 245; Dallek, *Lone Star*, pp. 544–45.

31   Senate re-election. Caro, *Master*, pp. 1035–36; Dallek, *Lone Star Rising*, p. 546. To minimize his risks, LBJ cajoled the Texas legislature into allowing a candidate to run for two offices simultaneously.

32   "Johnson for President Committee." *New York Times*, 18 October 1959, pp. 1, 52; Miller, *Lyndon*, p. 237; Davis, *Politics*, p. 398.

32   "All this . . . nomination." Dallek, *Lone Star*, p. 545.

32   "Johnson . . . seriously." Lincoln, pp. 41–42; Woods, p. 353.

32   "Before the . . . responsibilities." Reedy, p. 56. Reedy may have been alluding to a rumored LBJ affair with a young Texas-born staffer. Parmet, *JFK*, p. 14; Unger and Unger, p. 228.

32   "I've already . . . pot." Baker and King, p. 119.

Chapter Four: "You're my boy"

33   "the most . . . conceived." Rovere, p. 299.

34   Yorba Linda. Nixon, *RN*, p. 3; Brodie, pp. 36, 67–68; Parmet, *Nixon*, p. 55.

34   "Preachers . . . than sheriff." Parmet, *Nixon*, p. 54.

34   Frank Nixon. Keough, pp. 19–20; Kornitzer, p. 38; Costello, pp. 21–22; Sevareid, pp. 74–75; Nixon, *RN*, pp. 5–6; Brodie, pp. 37–38.

34   "stern disciplinarian." Nixon, *RN*, pp. 6–7.

34 "I tried . . . him." Sevareid, p. 75; Nixon, *RN*, p. 7; Ambrose, *Nixon*, pp. 25–26.

34 "Nixon's father . . . importance." Summers, p. 92.

34 "My mother . . . saint." *New York Times*, 10 August 1974, p. 4; Parmet, *Nixon*, p. 56; Brodie, p. 53; Summers, p. 483.

34 "Fear was . . . downfall." Summers, p. 13.

35 Oratory. *Los Angeles Times*, 3 April 1928, p. A7; *Los Angeles Times*, 28 May 1929, p. A9; Keogh, pp. 23–24; Costello, pp. 22–23; Sevareid, p. 74; Ambrose, *Nixon*, pp. 46–49; Brodie, pp. 47–48.

35 "I came . . . do." Ambrose, *Nixon*, p. 102; Mazo, p. 26.

35 FBI. Mazo, pp. 26–27; Sevareid, p. 84; Gellman, pp. 5–8.

35 Private practice. *Current Biography 1958*, p. 310; Costello, pp. 27–28; Ambrose, *Nixon*, pp. 91–92; Parmet, *Nixon*, p. 85.

35 Pat Nixon background. Nixon, *RN*, pp. 28–30; Kornitzer, pp. 131–34; Costello, pp. 28–29; Eisenhower, *Pat Nixon*, pp. 17–70; Parmet, *Nixon*, pp. 87–88; Morrow, *Best Year*, pp. 118–21; Anthony, pp. 331–32, 487.

35 "From the . . . too." Eisenhower, *Pat Nixon*, p. 68; Morrow, *Best Years*, p. 119; Morris, *Nixon*, p. 227; Anthony, p. 487; Halberstam, *Fifties*, p. 319.

36 Letter soliciting candidacy. Nixon, *RN*, p. 40.

36 Socialist. Brodie, p. 172.

37 "A vote . . . Line!" Greenberg, p. 25; Costello, pp. 54–55.

37 Debates. Costello, pp. 56–57; Sevareid, p. 83.

37 "Jerry . . . you." Costello, p. 57; Greenberg, p. 25; Matthews, pp. 38–39.

37 1946 returns. *New York Times*, 7 November 1946, p. 4; Costello, p. 58; Mazo, p. 48; Parmet, *Nixon*, p. 113; Brodie, p. 182; Gellman, p. 82; Bochin, p. 22; Matthews, p. 41.

37 "I know . . . treason." Parmet, *Nixon*, p. 170.

37 Hiss case. Parmet, *Nixon*, pp. 161–81.

38 "the only . . . to." Morris, *Nixon*, p. 588.

38 "Let's Look . . . Loves!" *New York Times*, 31 January 1974, p. 36; Keough, pp. 44–45; Mazo, pp. 79–81; Parmet, *Nixon*, p. 195; Morris, *Nixon*, pp. 579–81.

38 "Pink Lady." *Los Angeles Times*, 30 August 1950, p. 8; *Los Angeles Times*, 1 November 1950, p. 21; Costello, pp. 64–67; Parmet, *Nixon*, pp. 186–215; Brodie, pp. 241–42; Matthews, pp. 72–73. For his part, Marcantonio could not stand Douglas and privately referred to her as a bitch. Mazo, p. 81*fn*; Brodie, p. 237.

38 "Tricky Dick." Costello, p. 68; Bochin, p. 27; Brodie, p. 238; Summers, p. 86; Matthews, p. 72.

38 Thousand-dollar contribution. *Chicago Tribune*, 25 July 1960, p. 3; *Chicago Tribune*, 26 July 1960, p. 10; Nixon, *RN*, pp. 91–92; Nixon, *In the Arena*, p. 223; Mitchell, pp. 99–100, 248; Gellman, pp. 306–7. Following Nixon's victory, JFK informed a Harvard audience of his personal pleasure in Mrs. Douglas's defeat.

38 $150,000. O'Neill, p. 81.

38   1950 election returns. *Los Angeles Times*, 8 November 1950, pp. 1–2; *New York Times*, 8 November 1950, pp. 1, 11; *Chicago Tribune*, 8 November 1950, p. 1; Costello, p. 73; Keough, p. 45; Mazo, p. 83; Brodie, p. 244; Ambrose, *Nixon*, p. 223; Morris, *Nixon*, p. 611.

38   "I was . . . vote." Fay, p. 62; Mitchell, p. 248.

39   Earl Warren. Mazo, p. 82; Brodie, p. 250.

39   Dewey, VP deal. Brodie, p. 252; Summers, p. 117.

39   Dewey suggests Nixon. Mazo, p. 96; White, *1960*, p. 225; Ambrose, *Nixon*, pp. 262–63; Eaton, pp. 451–53; Manchester, *Glory*, p. 619; Summers, pp. 117–18.

39   "a little . . . way" Parmet, *Nixon*, p. 232; Halberstam, *Fifties*, p. 314.

39   "That's . . . me." Eaton, p. 453.

39   "Dear Dick . . . Kennedy." Nixon, *RN*, p. 112.

39   "Eisenhower . . . point man." Nixon, *RN*, p. 108.

40   "If the . . . hatchet!" *Fresno Bee-Republican*, 3 September 1952, p. 9-A; *Abilene Reporter-News*, 17 September 1952, p. 4B; Brodie, p. 273.

40   *New York Post*. Kornitzer, p. 188; Keough, pp. 48–49; Mazo, p. 109; Morris, *Nixon*, pp. 762–63; Parmet, *Nixon*, p. 239; Whitman, *Profile*, pp. 93–94.

40   Sherman Adams. Wicker, p. 160.

40   "I think . . . me." Nixon, *Six Crises*, p. 98; Nixon, *RN*, p. 119; Morris, *Nixon*, p. 803; Wills, *Nixon Agonistes*, p. 102; Witcover, p. 117.

41   "If my . . . pot." Nixon, *Six Crises*, p. 100; Nixon, *RN*, p. 120; Alsop, p. 192; Brodie, p. 281; Parmet, *Nixon*, p. 245; Wicker, p. 94. As surprising as Nixon using such language to Eisenhower is his using it in his memoirs *RN*—though not in *Six Crises*.

41   "Just tell . . . too!" Nixon, *RN*, p. 126; Nixon, *In the Arena*, p. 201; Parmet, *Nixon*, p. 245; Wicker, p. 97; Morris, *Nixon*, p. 823.

41   58 million. Brodie, p. 271; Parmet, *Nixon*, p. 238.

42   "Pat . . . anything." *New York Times*, 24 September 1952, p. 22; Keough, p. 57; Mazo, pp. 129–30.

42   "It was . . . it." *New York Times*, 24 September 1952, p. 22; Keough, p. 57; Mazo, p. 130; Ambrose, *Nixon*, pp. 288–89; Greenberg, pp. 32–33; Morris, *Nixon*, p. 832; Wicker, p. 98.

42   "I don't . . . America." *New York Times*, 24 September 1952, p. 22; Kornitzer, pp. 204–5; Keough, p. 58; Alsop, pp. 65–66; Costello, p. 108; Mazo, pp. 130–31.

42   "The telephone . . . tree." Mazo, pp. 130–31; Nixon, *Six Crises*, p. 118; Morris, *Nixon*, p. 835.

43   "He was . . . on." Alsop, pp. 64–65.

43   Wheeling rendezvous. *Oakland Tribune*, 25 September 1952, p. 5; *Lowell Sun*, 25 September 1952, p. 1; Keough, p. 59; Costello, p. 110; Mazo, p. 134; Kornitzer, p. 205; Nixon, *Six Crises*, p. 123; Nixon, *RN*, pp. 131–32; Morris, *Nixon*, pp. 847–49; Ambrose, *Nixon*, p. 292; Ambrose, *Eisenhower: Soldier and President*, p. 282; Summers, pp. 121, 138; Wills, *Nixon Agonistes*, p. 113.

43   "When they . . . man." Summers, p. 82.

43   "And incidentally . . . Communists?" *Charleston Gazette*, 14 March 1954, p. 6;

Brodie, p. 301.

44   "Eisenhower was . . . up." Summers, p. 147.

44   Offer to Anderson. Wicker, pp. 190–93.

44   Eisenhower VP choices. Ambrose, *Nixon*, p. 548

44   Ileitis. *Chicago Tribune*, 9 June 1956, pp. 1–2; *New York Times*, 11 June 1956, pp. 1, 18, 19, 20; *New York Times*, 12 June 1956, pp. 1, 21; Costello, p. 148; Eisenhower, *Waging Peace*, p. 9; Nixon, *RN*, pp. 212–13.

44   Gallop poll—Nixon-Stevenson. *Hartford Courant*, 29 January 1960, p. 24; Rovere, p. 294; Costello, p. 68.

44   Eisenhower-Stassen. Alsop, p. 70; Nixon, *Six Crises*, pp. 160–62.

45   Frank Nixon. *Chicago Tribune*, 5 September 1956, p. 1; *New York Times*, 5 September 1956, p. 27; Kornitzer, p. 83; Nixon, *RN*, p. 216.

45   "president of . . . years." Witcover, pp. 132–33.

45   "I do . . . shallowness" Parmet, *Nixon*, p. 59.

45   "We were . . . thing." Martin, *Destruction*, p. 254.

45   "Isn't it . . . him?" Martin, *Destruction*, p. 242.

46   "I think . . . opportunist." Blair and Blair, p. 526; Summers, p. 201.

46   "The Vice-President. . . one." Halberstam, *Fifties*, p. 730; Ambrose, *Nixon*, p. 564; Ambrose, *Eisenhower: The President*, p. 601.

46   "the most . . . evaluation." De Toledano, pp. 297–98.

46   "Having made . . . impulse." White, *1960*, p. 71.

47   "I was . . . do it." Nixon, *RN*, p. 246; Ambrose, *Nixon*, p. 493.

47   1958 election. Nixon, *RN*, p. 246; Costello, p. 174.

47   June 1957 Gallup poll. *Syracuse Herald-Journal*, 10 December 1958, p. 36; De Toledano, p. 292.

47   Len Hall. De Toledano, pp. 292–93.

47   "persuade . . . Republican," Lurie, pp. 252–53.

48   "Boy, I'd . . . help." Perret, *Eisenhower*, p. 596.

48   "Boy . . . in 1960!" Parmet, *Eisenhower*, p. 527; Manchester, *Glory*, p. 879.

48   "I'll quit . . . help." Perret, *Eisenhower*, p. 596.

48   "Those . . . against it." Lurie, p. 251.

48   Caracas. *New York Times*, 14 May 1958, pp. 1, 9; Kornitzer, pp. 278–92; Costello, pp. 254–59; Mazo, pp. 219–52; Nixon, *Six Crises*, pp. 210–27; Nixon, *RN*, pp. 232–38; Alsop, pp. 74–76; Nixon, *In the Arena*, pp. 204–7.

48   Kitchen debate. *New York Times*, 26 July 1959, pp. 1–2, E3; Nixon, *The Challenges We Face*, pp. 219–27; Kornitzer; pp. 293–316.

48   "truths . . . exchanges." Ambrose, *Nixon*, pp. 532–33; Abell, p. 538.

48   Gallup poll—Nixon-JFK. *Hartford Courant*, 1 April 1960, p. 15; Lurie, p. 252; Manchester, *Glory*, p. 879; Witcover, p. 136.

49   Gallup poll—Nixon-Stevenson. *Hartford Courant*, 1 May 1960, p. 37A; *Hartford Courant*, 5 June 1960, p. 4B.

49   1947 debate. Mazo, pp. 49–50; McCarthy, p. 99; Gellman, pp. 102–3; Nixon, *In the Arena*, p. 216; Silvestri, p. 29; Perret, *Jack*, p. 142.

49   Burning Tree. Matthews, p. 91; Summers, p. 201.

49   Nixon tears. Beran, p. 11; Black, p. 401; Summers, p. 202.

49   Fruit basket. Burns, p. 169; Carr, p. 106.

49   "Nixon is . . . him." Ambrose, *Nixon*, p. 564; Summers, p. 201.

49   "You have . . . disgusting." Matthews, p. 123.

50   "Jack told . . . Nixon." Anderson, p. 202.

50   "When . . . Mr. Nixon." Matthews, p. 124.

50   Wilson and Roosevelt. Lurie, pp. 251–52.

50   Federal aid to education. *Hartford Courant*, 23 March 1960, p. 14.

50   "The Vice . . . President." *Hartford Courant*, 23 March 1960, p. 14.

50   "It seems . . . world." McKeever, p. 419.

51   "her tension . . . remote" Summers, p. 38.

51   Agreement with Pat. Mazo, p. 139; Alsop, pp. 70–71; Ambrose, *Nixon*, pp. 350–51.

52   "The political . . . abuse." Coolidge, p. 229.

Chapter Five: "Kicked in the head by a horse"

53   Harriman, Williams. Sevareid, pp. 330–42.

54   "Mr. Morse . . . virtue." *New York Times*, 23 July 1974, p. 40.

55   "back some . . . horse." *New York Times*, 29 April 1959, p. 12; *New York Times*, 23 July 1974; p. 40; Smith, *Tiger in the Senate*, pp. 48–49.

55   Pique. Parmet, *Jack*, pp. 496–97.

55   Television show. *New York Times*, 8 January 1960, p. 12.

55   "highly reactionary . . . taxes." Reeves, *Character*, p. 168.

55   Morse invective. Smith, *Tiger in the Senate*, p. 399.

55   "I am not . . . nomination." *New York Times*, 22 July 1959, p. 14; Smith, *Tiger in the Senate*, p. 401.

55   "Half the . . . house." Schlesinger, *Thousand Days*, p. 21; Schlesinger, *Journals*, p. 66.

55   "presidential campaign . . . dinner." *New York Times*, 24 January 1960. pp. 1, 46; Smith, *Tiger in the Senate*, p. 402.

56   Georgetown neighbors. *Sheboygen Press*, 5 April 1960, p. 22.

56   "He never . . . missiles." *Idaho State Journal*, 1 July 1960, p. 2.

56   66.4 percent. Eaton, p. 491.

56   "the most . . . politicians." Mcfarland, p. 104.

56   "[Symington], . . . on Symington." Dallek, *Unfinished Life*, p. 245.

56   "liked Stuart . . . reporters." Bradlee, *Conversations*, p. 18.

57   Truman. Mcfarland, p. 106.

57   Acheson. Mcfarland, p. 106; Evans and Novak, p. 246.

57   Clifford. Frantz and McKean, p. 153; Mcfarland, p. 106; Friedenberg, p. 43 Mooney, *The Politicians*, p. 322.

57   "Your strength . . . untouched." Frantz and McKean, p. 153.

57   "What . . . could." Mcfarland, p. 106.

57   "Funny thing . . . cows." Mcfarland, p. 106.

58   "Childhood came . . . house," *Current Biography 1966*, p. 189.

58   Mayoral elections. *Current Biography 1966*, p. 190; Solberg, p. 109.

58   1948 election. *New York Times*, 3 November 1948, p. 2; *Winona Republican–*

Herald, 3 November 1948, pp. 1, 8; *Chicago Tribune*, 7 November 1948, p. 45; *Current Biography 1966*, p. 190; Solberg, p. 128; Amrine, p. 14.

59   "Be civilized . . . Neanderthals." Berman, p. 60.

59   Stevenson. Berman, p. 62.

59   "the spark of greatness." *Chicago Defender*, 9 December 1958, p. 4; Lash, p. 279.

59   "had never . . . hear." Dallek, *Unfinished Life*, p. 245.

59   UAW. *Chicago Tribune*, 16 October 1959, p. 8; Boyle, p. 141.

59   Humphrey entering primaries. *New York Times*, 15 July 1959, p. 14; *New York Times*, 15 August 1959, p. 8; *New York Times*, 31 December 1959, p. 10; *New York Times*, 11 January 1960, pp. 1, 31; *Chicago Tribune*, 12 January 1960, p. 2.

59   "a series . . . rug" *Chicago Tribune*, 6 January 1960, p. 3.

60   *Congressional Quarterly* poll. *Chicago Tribune*, 6 December 1960, p. D36.

60   "I don't . . . dead." Dallek, *Unfinished Life*, p. 245.

60   "There were . . . time." Miller, *Lyndon*, p. 236; Woods, pp. 353–54.

60   Rowe. *New York Times*, 9 August 1959, p. SM10; Dallek, *Lone Star Rising*, p. 544: Solberg, p. 201.

Chapter Six: "When Bobby hates you, you stay hated"

61   "What's $100 million . . . Jack?" Kessler, p. 369.

61   "For the . . . between." Whalen, *Founding Father*, p. 438; Newfield, p. 42; Krock, p. 338; Whalen, *Kennedy versus Lodge*, p. 12.

61   *Current Biography 1958*, p. 220; Schlesinger, *Robert Kennedy*, pp. 73–76, 90.

61   "absolute . . . disaster." Schlesinger, *Robert Kennedy*, p. 94; O'Donnell, Powers, and McCarthy, p. 96.

61   "Those politicians . . . did." Tanzer, p. 197.

61   McClellan's palms. Hersh, *Bobby and J. Edgar*, p. 141.

61   Talbott. *Current Biography 1958*, p. 221; Schlesinger, *Robert Kennedy*, pp. 117–18; Lasky, *RFK*, pp. 100–101; Heymann, *RFK*, p. 93.

62   Chotiner. *New York Times*, 8 June 1956, p. 38; *Current Biography 1958*, p. 221; *New York Times*, 31 January 1974, p. 36; Parmet, *Nixon*, pp. 271, 426; de Toledano, p. 304; Summers, pp. 51–52.

62   McClellan Committee. Kennedy, *The Enemy Within*, pp. 160–61.

62   "As Mr. . . . evil." *New York Times*, 28 February 1960. p. BR22; Kennedy, *The Enemy Within*, p. 162; Sloane, p. 159; Schlesinger, *Robert Kennedy*, p. 163; Talbot, p. 128.

62   "Here's a . . . this?" Schlesinger, *Robert Kennedy*, p. 153; Beran, p. 40.

62   *The Enemy Within*. Kennedy, *The Enemy Within*, *passim*; *New York Times*, 26 January 1960, p. 30; *New York Times*, 28 February 1960, p. BR22.

62   Wicker basket. Thomas, p. 88.

63   "like a . . . be?" *Hartford Courant*, 15 July 1960, p. 18.

63   "To me . . . pol" O'Neill, p. 83.

63   "Tip, let . . . them." O'Neill, pp. 82–83; Heymann, *RFK*, p. 108.

63   "That young . . . them." Hersh, *Bobby and J. Edgar*, p. 6.

63   "The first . . . Cabinet." Sorenson, *Kennedy*, p. 34.

63   "I want . . . eyes." Martin, *Hero*, p. 126.

63   McCarthy services. Lasky, *RFK*, p. 110; Thomas, p. 88.

63   "I was . . . diplomat!" Heymann, *RFK*, p. 145.

64   "You can . . . hated." O'Neill, p. 83. It 1960, Joe would deny having made such comments, but, nonetheless, boasted "hard as nails" Bobby was "like me." Schlesinger, *Robert Kennedy*, p. 97; Woods, p. 372.

64   "Robert Kennedy . . . fellow." Heymann, *RFK*, p. 84.

64   "Inside the . . . line." Schlesinger, *Robert Kennedy*, p. 193.

64   "He was . . . echelon." Schlesinger, *Robert Kennedy*, p. 213.

64   "the most . . . it." Schlesinger, *Robert Kennedy*, p. 213.

64   "Bob could . . . brother." O'Brien, *Victories*, p. 62.

64   "Jack was . . . the guy?'" Thomas, p. 91.

64   Senate cafeteria. Thomas, p. 96.

65   RFK-LBJ hunting incident. Seshol, p. 10; Caro, *Lone Star Rising*, p. 559; Dallek, *An Unfinished Life*, p. 269; Dallek, *Lyndon B. Johnson*, p. 113; Woods, p. 357; Thomas, p. 96.

Chapter Seven: "I am not a candidate for the vice presidency of anything"

66   Rockefeller fortune. Alsop, p. 34.

66   "Make all . . . can." Alsop, p. 102.

67    $17,500. Sevareid, p. 44.

67   "Open Skies." Morris, *Nelson Rockefeller*, pp. 301–3; Alsop, p. 94; Gervasi, pp. 174–75. The "Open Skies" concept was originally Henry Kissinger's.

68   "Why don't . . . board?" Reich, p. 662.

68   "He has . . . people." Isaacson, p. 91. Kissinger remained on Rockefeller's payroll during the 1960 campaign, earning twelve thousand dollars that year. Isaacson, p. 92.

68   "Because Nelson's . . . President." Alsop, p. 141.

69   11,125 votes. Sevareid, p. 48.

69   "He was . . . politics." Reich, p. 674.

69   "Don't worry . . . you," Reich, p. 674.

69   Rockefeller electoral possibilities. Reich, p. 684; Gervasi, p. 203; Alsop, p. 92.

69   "I think . . . City!" Persico, p. 38; Reich, p. 688; Wagner, p. 125.

69   Humphreys. Alsop, pp. 79–80, 98; Gervasi, pp. 21, 186.

70   "A wooden . . . democracy." Isaacson and Thomas, p. 585.

70   "The deciding . . . Rockefeller." Gervasi, p. 22.

70   Tammany. Gervasi, pp. 220–21; Collier and Horowitz, *Rockefellers*, p. 331; Kramer and Roberts, pp. 205–6; Allen, *The Tiger*, pp. 273–79.

70   "If Len . . . me." Reich, p. 705.

71   "Nelson Rockefeller . . . America." Nissenson, p. 191.

71   Rockefeller-Weaver. Reich, p. 689; Wagner, p. 125. Pat Weaver was actress Sigourney Weaver's father.

71   "He made . . . self–conceived." Gervasi, p. 219; Kramer and Roberts, p. 205.

71   Tod Rockefeller. Reich, pp. 752–54; Persico, p. 42; White, *1964*, pp. 79–80.

71   Nixon, Rockefeller allies. Sevareid, p. 26; Reich, p. 758; Mazo, pp. 5–6.

72   Keating. Morris, *Nelson Rockefeller*, pp. 327–28; Sevareid, pp. 56–57; Gervasi, pp. 221–23; Mazo, pp. 264–66; Reich, pp. 758–59.

72   "Honestly and . . . Governor." Reich, p. 759; Sevareid, p. 57.

72   Suez, *New York Post*. *New York Times*, 4 November 1958, pp. 1, 21; Morris, *Nelson Rockefeller*, p. 329; Reich, p. 761; Nissenson, p. 188; Kramer and Roberts, p. 207.

72   Margin. *New York Times*, 5 November 1958, pp. 1, 27, 32, 34; Sevareid, p. 26; Reich, p. 765; Parmet, *Nixon*, p. 345; White, *1960*, p. 68.

72   Fourteen GOP governors. Bryant, p. 100.

72   Taxes. Parmet, *Nixon*, p. 369.

72   "spend the . . . Albany." de Toledano, p. 293.

73   1958 Gallup poll. *Syracuse Post-Standard*, 23 January 1959, p. 3; *Hartford Courant*, 20 January 1960, p. 13; *Washington Post*, 24 May 1960, p. A2; *Hartford Courant*, 24 July 1960, p. 12A; Costello, p. 14.

73   Rocky-Stevenson. *Syracuse Post-Standard*, 11 January 1959, p. 5; *Nevada State Journal*, 16 January 1959, p. 4; *Fresno Bee-Republican*, 31 January 1959, p. 20.

73   "I hate . . . States." de Toledano, p. 298; Collier and Horowitz, *Rockefellers*, p. 339; Kramer and Roberts, pp. 221–22.

73   "Most of . . . too." *Fresno Bee-Republican*, 31 January 1959, p. 20.

73   "What Rocky . . . charge." Ambrose, *Nixon*, p. 536.

73   "under certain . . . anything." *Chicago Tribune*, 23 August 1959, p. 6.

73   Rockefeller trips. *Wisconsin Rapids Daily Tribune*, 21 December 1959, p. 9.

74   New Jersey. *Bridgeport Post*, 27 December 1959, p. C8.

74   "perhaps 70 per cent." *Wisconsin Rapids Daily Tribune*, 21 December 1959, p. 9.

74   Dartmouth. *Los Angeles Times*, 27 December 1959, p. 12.

74   "the ablest . . . labors" White, *1960*, p. 68.

74   "Nixon . . . counted." Aitken, p. 267.

74   Hall. Halberstam, *Powers*, p. 334.

75   "in size . . . conventions." *Chicago Tribune*, 25 December 1959, p. A10; White, *1960*, pp. 75–76.

75   "The great . . . final." *New York Times*, 27 December 1959, p. 37; *Chicago Tribune*, 27 December 1959, p. 2; White, *1960*, pp. 82–84; Kramer and Roberts, p. 225.

75   "I shall . . . vice-presidency." *New York Times*, 27 December 1959, p. 37; *Chicago Tribune*, 27 December 1959, p. 2.

75   "The tone . . . it." Kramer and Roberts, p. 226.

76   "The more . . . general." de Toledano, p. 299.

76   "We've just . . . groin." de Toledano, p. 299.

Chapter Eight: "An independent merchant competing against a chain store"

77   "For fifty . . . primary." Lincoln, p. 42.

77   "My chief . . . manipulation." Lincoln, p. 43.

78   JPK's states. Hersh, *Edward Kennedy*, 123*fn*; Leamer, *Kennedy Men*, p. 434.

78   "a man . . . pear." *New York Times*, 6 January 1960, p. 27.

78   California pro-Stevenson. O'Brien, *Victories*, p. 58.

78   DiSalle, Symington. *The Reporter*, 3 March 1960, p. 21; O'Donnell, Powers, and McCarthy, pp. 169–70; Schlesinger, *Robert Kennedy*, p. 194.

79   "It had . . . them." O'Donnell, Powers, and McCarthy, p. 169; Friedenberg, p. 44.

79   Harris poll, Ohio. Lasky, *JFK*, p. 323.

79   Pittsburgh meeting. *Nevada State Journal*, 12 July 1960, p. 4; *The Reporter*, 4 August 1960, p. 30; Sorensen, p. 131; Lasky, *RFK*, pp. 142–43.

79   "Bailey subsequently . . . capitulated." Dallek, *Unfinished Life*, p. 247; Heymann, *RFK*, p. 146.

79   DiSalle delegates for JFK. *Lincoln Evening Journal*, 5 January 1960, p. 1; *New York Times*, 6 January 1960, pp. 1, 27; *Hartford Courant*, 6 January 1960, pp. 1, 7, 8; *Chicago Tribune*, 6 January 1960, p. 3; Schlesinger, *Robert Kennedy*, p. 194; Heymann, *RFK*, p. 146.

79   "favorite son . . . stooge." *The Reporter*, 3 March 1960, p. 21; Lasky, *JFK*, p. 325.

79   Harris poll. *New York Times*, 20 January 1960, p. 1; *Appleton Post-Crescent*, 6 April 1960, p. 2; Lasky, *JFK*, p. 329; Wofford, p. 41.

79   "You've got . . . choice." Whalen, *Founding Father*, p. 438; Wofford, p. 41; Martin, *Hero*, p. 152; Martin, *Destruction*, p. 244.

80   JFK-Brown. O'Donnell, Powers, and McCarthy, pp. 117–18.

80   Chessman. *Modesto Bee*, 3 March 1960, p. 26.

80   Brown announcement. *New York Times*, 20 January 1960, p. 16; *New York Times*, 22 January 1960, p. 10.

80   California to JFK. O'Donnell, Powers, and McCarthy, p. 148; O'Brien, *Victories*, p. 78; Dallek, *Unfinished Life*, p. 247.

80   JPK, California. Whalen, *Founding Father*, p. 439; Dallek, *Unfinished Life*, p. 247.

80   California Democratic Council. *New York Times*, 14 February 1960, p. 46; *Chicago Tribune*, 14 February 1960, p. 34.

81   New Jersey. Davis, *Politics*, pp. 431–32; Koskoff, p. 422.

81   NYS Democratic leaders. O'Donnell, Powers, and McCarthy, pp. 198–99; Koskoff, pp. 384, 422; Schwarz, p. 388; Maier, p. 490; Russell, *President Makers*, p. 386; Whalen, *Founding Father*, p. 435; Lasky, *RFK*, p. 144.

81   "a bootlegger . . . pimp." Grondahl, p. 184; Lasky, *JFK*, p. 351.

81   "I don't . . . 1964." *Weirton Daily News*, 23 March 1960, p. 4.

81   "He is . . . it." Whalen, *Founding Father*, p. 438; Lasky, *RFK*, pp. 143–44; Parmet, *Jack*, p. 510.

81   County office building. Grondahl, p. 184; Lasky, *JFK*, p. 351.

81   "Joe Kennedy . . . it." Mcfarland, pp. 106–7.

81   Other New Hampshire candidates. *Lincoln State Journal*, 30 January 1960, p. 1; *Newark Advocate*, 3 March 1960, p. 17; *Charleston Daily Mail*, 6 May 1960, p. 12.

82   Fisher—stalking horse? *Chicago Tribune*, 6 March 1960, p. 7; *Chicago Tribune*, 7 March 1960, p. C5; O'Brien, *Victories*, pp. 62–64. Fisher went on to

invent one of the most successful ballpoints ever, the "Fisher Space Pen," which accompanied the Apollo 11 astronauts to the moon.

82   Powell. *Facts on File*, 3–9 March 1960, p. 80; *Chicago Tribune*, 9 March 1960, p. 2; *Hartford Courant*, 9 March 1960, pp. 1, 22.*Christian Science Monitor*, 9 March 1960, p. 8; *Lowell Sun*, 9 March 1960, p. 1.

82   New Hampshire results. *Chicago Tribune*, 9 March 1960, p. 1; *Portsmouth Herald*, 9 March 1960, p. 1; *New York Times*, 10 March 1960, p. 22; *Facts on File*, 9 March 1960, p. 79.

82   "Wisconsin's Third Senator." O'Donnell, Powers, and McCarthy, p. 150; Collier and Horowitz, *Kennedys*, p. 207; O'Brien, *Kennedy*, p. 444; Schwab and Shneidman, p. 91.

82   JFK, agriculture. *Madison Capital-Times*, 5 April 1960, p. 22; O'Brien, *Kennedy*, pp. 426–27.

83   "[B]y taking . . . symbol." Goodwin, *Remembering*, p. 79.

83   February 1960. Gallup poll. *Hartford Courant*, 28 February 1960, p. 3B.

84   Gallup poll—Nixon vs. JFK or Stevenson *Hartford Courant*, 28 February 1960, p. 3B.

84   Gallup poll—South. *Hartford Courant*, 16 March 1960, p. 32.

84   Gallup poll—JFK vs. LBJ or Stevenson. *Hartford Courant*, 6 March 1960, p. 23A.

85   "Bobby didn't . . . could." O'Brien, *Kennedy*, p. 446.

85   "I went . . . campaign." *Wisconsin State Journal*, 15 February 1960, p. 2; Hersh, *Edward Kennedy*, pp. 129–30; Leamer, *Kennedy Men*, p. 420.

85   "I don't . . . rest." Leamer, *Kennedy Men*, pp. 419–20.

85   "They're all . . . time." O'Donnell, Powers, and McCarthy, p. 180; Schlesinger, *Robert Kennedy*, p. 195; O'Brien, *Kennedy*, p. 246; Martin, *Destruction*, p. 246.

86   "I don't . . . people." Bruno and Greenfield, p. 40.

86   *Caroline. Lima News*, 25 September 1960, p. C14; *Holland Evening Sentinel*, 29 September 1960, p. 9; Kessler, pp. 377–78; Carr, p. 117; O'Brien, *Kennedy*, p. 437.

86   "Come down . . . fair." Humphrey, p. 208; Schlesinger, *Robert Kennedy*, p. 195.

86   "I cannot . . . store." *Sheboygen Press*, 5 April 1960, p. 13; Humphrey, p. 208; Sorensen, p. 135; Solberg, p. 205; Lasky, *RFK*, p. 146; Schlesinger, *Robert Kennedy*, p. 195; Goodwin, *Remembering*, p. 83; Davis, *Kennedys*, p. 285; Schwab and Shneidman, p. 92.

86   "So many . . . machine!" Martin, *Hero*, p. 160.

87   JFK–old woman. Collier and Horowitz, *Kennedys*, p. 207; Martin, *Hero*, p. 142; Maier, p. 332.

87   "That might . . . it." Salinger, *PS:*, p. 71.

87   "this sort . . . it" Reeves, *Character*, p. 159; Anderson, p. 204.

87   "My speech . . . time." Martin, *Hero*, p. 149.

87   De Gaulle's memoirs. Carr, p. 118; Heymann, *Jackie*, p. 208.

88   "Acapulco!" Heymann, *Jackie*, p. 196; Martin, *Destruction*, p. 244.

88   Jackie—Poles. Fay, pp. 17–18; Heymann, *Jackie*, pp. 204, 218–19, 241.

88   Pregnancy. O'Donnell, Powers, and McCarthy, pp. 178–79.

88   "While [Smith . . . thought." Anderson, p. 202.

89   32 percent Catholic. *Facts on File*, 31 March–6 April 1960, p. 112; *Hayward Daily Review*, 4 April 1960, p. 3; *Sheboygen Press*, 5 April 1960, p. 1; Solberg, p. 204.

89   "Square Deal for Humphrey Committee." *Oakland Tribune*, 31 March 1960, p. 14; *Madison Capital-Times*, 1 April 1960, pp. 1, 4; *Stevens Point Journal*, 1 April 1960, p. 2; Solberg, pp. 205, 207; Silvestri, p. 103. Many suspected Teamster involvement in the ad, and clues pointed to a low-level Humphrey worker named Charlie Greene. During the primary RFK charged the Teamsters were pouring $1.2 million into Humphrey's Wisconsin campaign, a laughable figure. The "Square Deal" ad cost only $2,500.

89   Anti-Catholic mailings. Lasky, *Watergate*, pp. 35–37; Summers, p. 210; Heymann, *RFK*, pp. 148–50; Leamer, *Kennedy Men*, p. 421.

89   Corbin-Keyes. Schlesinger, *Robert Kennedy*, p. 196; O'Donnell, Powers, and McCarthy, p. 158.

90   "They say . . . civilization." Schlesinger, *Robert Kennedy*, p. 197; Heymann, *RFK*, p. 148.

90    $116,500. Alexander, p. 19.

90    $1 million. Dallek, *Unfinished Life*, p. 235.

90   "Humphrey's [staffs] . . . boss." Berman, p. 75.

90   Staffer-JFK, dirt on HHH. Goodwin, *Remembering*, pp. 82–83.

91   "There weren't . . . nominee?" Kennedy, *Remember*, p. 366.

91   Bowles demurs. Wofford, pp. 41–42; Bowles, p. 288; Schaffer, pp. 171–72: Stossel, p. 144; Beran, p. 72.

91   Draft Bowles. Schaffer, pp. 172–73; Bowles, pp. 292–93.

91   Shriver. Wofford, pp. 41–42; Stossel, p. 142.

91   RFK. Halberstam, *Best*, p. 19; Beran, p. 72.

91   "I was . . . Kennedy." Bowles, p. 294.

91   Bayley. Salinger, *With Kennedy*, p. 56; White, *1960*, p. 102.

91   JFK, Bradlee predictions. Bradlee, *Conversations*, p. 17.

92   "Stevenson Jew." Lasky, *RFK*, p. 145; Lasky, *JFK*, p. 328; Lasky, *Watergate*, p. 37.

92   JFK, HHH promises. *Madison Capital-Times*, 5 April 1960, p. 4.

92   Turnout. *Sheboygen Press*, 5 April 1960, p. 1.

92   Hotel Phister. Bradford, p. 126; Goodwin, *Remembering*, p. 83.

92   HHH lead. Lasky, *RFK*, p. 150.

92   Volunteers. Lasky, *JFK*, p. 331; Lasky, *RFK*, p. 148.

92   Wisconsin returns. *Facts on File*, 31 March–6 April 1960, p. 112; *New York Times*, 19 April 1960, p. 29.

92   Districts. White, *1960*, pp. 102–3; Stossel, p. 145.

93   "We carried . . . up." *Appleton Post–Crescent*, 6 April 1960, p. 2.

93   Harris poll. Salinger, *With Kennedy*, pp. 57–58.

93   Gravy. *Appleton Post-Crescent*, 6 April 1960, p. 1.

93   "I suppose . . . well." *Appleton Post-Crescent*, 6 April 1960, p. 1.

93   "In the . . . Virginia." Miller, *Lyndon*, p. 236.

93   "What does . . . Johnny?"; "It means . . . convention." White, *1960*, p. 103; O'Donnell, Powers, and McCarthy, p. 183; Salinger, *PS:*, p. 73.

Chapter Nine: "The rich man's Harold Stassen"

95   Klein. *New York Times*, 10 January 1960, p. 1; *Chicago Tribune*, 10 January 1960, pp. 1, 5.

96   "Anyone who . . . liar." *New York Times*, 9 January 1960, p. 12; *New York Times*, 12 January 1960, p. 15.

96   "Dinner with Ike." *New York Times*, 28 January 1960, pp. 1, 19; *Chicago Tribune*, 28 January 1960, p. 7.

96   New Hampshire primary. *New York Times*, 9 March 1960, p. 22; *Portsmouth Herald*, 9 March 1960, p. 1.

96   January 1960 press conferences. *New York Times*, 1 February 1960, p. 34.

96   February 3, 1960 press conference. *New York Times*, 4 February 1960, pp. 12, 14; *Chicago Tribune*, 4 February 1960, p. 3; Ambrose, *Eisenhower: Soldier & President*, pp. 500–501; Ambrose, *Eisenhower: The President*, pp. 559–60.

96   Gridiron Club, March 16, 1960 press conference. *Berkshire Eagle*, 15 March 1960, p. 1; *Hartford Courant*, 16 March 1960, p. 22A; *New York Times*, 17 March 1960, pp. 1, 16; *Chicago Tribune*, 17 March 1960, p. 1; *San Antonio Express*, 17 March 1960, p. 4-A; *Bridgeport Telegram*, 17 March 1960, p. 27; *Hartford Courant*, 20 March 1960, p. 16A.

97   "I came . . . great." Buckley, pp. 284–85.

98   Individual primary results. *Facts on File*, 31 March–6 April 1960, p. 112; *Facts on File*, 28 April–4 May 1960, p. 150; *Facts on File*, May 25, 1960, p. 180; *Oakland Tribune*, 6 April 1960, pp. 1, 4; *New York Times*, 19 April 1960, p. 29; *Chicago Tribune*, 27 April 1960, p. 3; *New York Times*, 27 April 1960, p. 25; *New York Times*, 28 April 1960, p. 21; *Chicago Tribune*, 1 May 1960, p. 7; *Oakland Tribune*, 4 May 1960, p. 6; *Washington Post*, 5 May 1960, p. A2; *New York Times*, 4 May 1960, pp. 1, 29; *New York Times*, 5 May 1960, p. 27; *Chicago Tribune*, 7 May 1960, p. 4; *New York Times*. 7 May 1960, p. 47; *San Mateo Times*, 8 June 1960, p. 12; *Chicago Tribune*, 12 June 1960, p. 8; *Charleston Daily Mail*, 12 May 1960, p. 8; *New York Times*, 22 May, p. 63. Black Indianapolis attorney Frank Beckwith secured 20,000 votes in Indiana's Republican primary.

98   "Khrushchev will . . . U.N." *Western Political Quarterly*, March 1961, p. 310.

99   Nixon primary totals. *Chicago Tribune*, 12 June 1960, p. 8. Nixon did not, however, best the total of all Democratic primary hopefuls. Additional votes included Paul Fisher's 6,784 New Hampshire votes, Mike DiSalle's Ohio totals, and California pension advocate George McLain's 634,950 votes.

99   Morton. *New York Times*, 13 February 1960, p. 14.

99   Dewey. *New York Times*, 28 March 1960, pp. 1, 17; *New York Times*, 2 April

1960, p. 1; *Hartford Courant*, 17 April 1960, p. 3B.

99   Numerous Rocky-for-VP advocates. *New York Times*, 8 April 1960, p. 16; *Hartford Courant*, 11 April 1960, p. 14.

99   "When I . . . myself." *Hartford Courant*, 20 March 1960, p. 16A.

99   *Denver Post*. *New York Times*, 14 April 1960, p. 21; *Hartford Courant*, 17 April 1960, p. 5A.

100   Rockefeller tours. *New York Times*, 15 April 1960, pp. 1, 10; *Hartford Courant*, 15 April 1960, p. 2.

100   Burns. *Journal of Economic History*, June 1990, p. 419; de Toledano, p. 300. In April Nixon confided to British Foreign Secretary, Selwyn Lloyd that barring any recession he thought he could defeat any Democratic contender, save for JFK. "About him he seemed doubtful," Lloyd noted. Aitken, p. 268.

100   "Mr. Nixon . . . go." *Hartford Courant*, 3 April 1960, p. 2B.

100   "It is . . . leadership." *New York Times*, 5 May 1960, pp. 1, 24; *Chicago Tribune*, 5 May 1960, p. 3; White, *1960*, p. 198.

100   Chair or keynote. *Chicago Tribune*, 10 May 1960, p. 1; *Hartford Courant*, 10 May 1960, p. 15; White, *1960*, p. 198; Collier and Horowitz, *Rockefellers*, p. 341.

100   Rocky not attending. *New York Times*, 5 May 1960, pp. 1, 24; *Chicago Tribune*, 15 May 1960, p. 1; White, *1960*, p. 198.

101   "both agreed. . . electorate." Benson, p. 518.

101   Rockefeller-Benson. Benson, pp. 519–20.

101   May 1960 Gallup poll. *Hartford Courant*, 22 May 1960, p. 34A.

101   Second May 1960 Gallup poll. *Hartford Courant*, 25 May 1960, p. 7; *Hartford Courant*, 5 June 1960, p. 4B.

101   "I would . . . resign." Ambrose, *Eisenhower: The President*, p. 575.

102   "It would . . . unity." *Washington Post*, 24 May 1960, p. A2; *New York Times*, 24 May 1960, pp. 1, 17; *Hartford Courant*, 24 May 1960, p. 1; Kramer and Roberts, p. 227.

102   Stassen. *Washington Post*, 26 May 1960, p. A2.

102   "these are . . . times." *New York Times*, 26 May 1960, pp. 1, 20, 32; *Washington Post*, 26 May 1960, p. A1; *Hartford Courant*, 26 May 1960, p. 1A; *Hartford Courant*, 27 May 1960, p. 20.

102   "well trained"; "know what . . . qualified." *New York Times*, 27 May 1960, p. 15; *Chicago Tribune*, 27 May 1960, p. 4.

102   McCrary. Parmet, *Nixon*, p. 385.

103   "How about . . . integrity." Ambrose, *Nixon*, p. 540; Ambrose, *Eisenhower: The President*, p. 560.

103   "I was . . . irresistible." Ehrlichman, p. 19.

103   "She stood . . . asked." Ehrlichman, p. 21.

104   "Oh, it . . . one asked." Rather and Gates, p. 140.

104   "I had . . . asked." Ehrlichman, p. 22.

104   Breakfast. *New York Times*, 8 June 1960, pp. 1, 29; *Hayward Daily Review*, 8 June 1960, p. 1; Eisenhower, *Waging Peace*, p. 592; Wagner, p. 126.

104   "[T]hose now . . . mark." *New York Times*, 9 June 1960, pp. 1, 16; *Hartford*

Courant, 9 June 1960, pp. 1, 8; White, *1960*, pp. 200–202; Kramer and Roberts, p. 227; Mooney, *The Politicians*, p. 340; Persico, p. 41.

104    $3.5 billion. Ambrose, *Eisenhower: The President*, p. 595; Wagner, p. 127.

105   "I've spent . . . anybody." *New York Times*, 14 January 1960, p. 14; *Chicago Tribune*, 14 January 1960, p. 4; Ambrose, *Eisenhower: The President*, p. 560.

105   "By getting . . . unconscionable." Ambrose, *Eisenhower: The President*, p. 560.

105   "I suspect . . . advisers." Eisenhower, *Waging Peace*, p. 593; Ambrose, *Eisenhower: The President*, p. 595.

105   Suspected Hughes. *New York Times*, 20 September 1982, p. B13; Kramer and Roberts, pp. 225–26.

105   "I see . . . this." Kramer and Roberts, pp. 227–28.

105   "The tenor . . . ambitions." Persico, p. 41.

105   "does not . . . him." *Hartford Courant*, 10 June 1960, pp. 1–2; Parmet, *Nixon*, p. 386.

106   Rocky-Ike phone call. Eisenhower, *Waging Peace*, p. 593; Ambrose, *Eisenhower: The President*, p. 595; Wicker, pp. 222–23; Wagner, p. 127. Whitman became Rockefeller's executive assistant in 1965. *New York Times*, 17 October 1991, p. B12.

106   Hobby. Ambrose, *Eisenhower: The President*, p. 595.

106   Rockefeller poll. *The Reporter*, 1 September 1960, p. 31.

106   "I don't . . . campaigner." *The Reporter*, 1 September 1960, p. 31.

106   "the rich . . . Stassen." *Hartford Courant*, 12 June 1960, p. 33A.

106   "The President . . . opposite." Ambrose, *Eisenhower: The President*, pp. 595–96.

107   "the feeling . . . party.'" Ambrose, *Eisenhower: The President*, pp. 595–96.

107   "That's exactly . . . also." Benson, p. 527.

107   Governors' Conference. *Hartford Courant*, 27 June 1960, pp. 1, 6; *Facts on File*, June 23–29, 1960, p. 220.

107   "I don't . . . ambition." Ambrose, *Nixon*, p. 547.

107   Phoned Hague. Wicker, p. 223; Ambrose, *Nixon*, p. 547.

107   "I told . . . it." Eisenhower, *Mandate*, pp. 594–95; Wicker, p. 223.

108   "was far . . . realized" Eisenhower, *Waging Peace*, pp. 594–95; Lurie, p. 252.

108   Kissinger. Schlesinger, *Journals*, p. 84.

Chapter Ten: "Committing a sin against God"

109   1958 Harris poll. White, 1960, p. 110; Parmet, *JFK*, p. 39.

109   December 1959 Harris poll. *Hartford Courant*, 10 May, 1960, p. 18; Sorensen, *Kennedy*, p. 139; O'Donnell, Powers, and McCarthy; p. 183; White, *1960*, p. 110; O'Brien, *Victories*, p. 67.

109   Kanahwa Hotel meeting. Schlesinger, *Robert Kennedy*, p. 198.

109   "There's only . . . problem"; "I looked . . . ashes." Martin, *Destruction*, p. 249; Maier, p. 333.

109   "It can't . . . Hubert." O'Donnell, Powers, and McCarthy, pp. 160–61; Loughry, p. 4; Friedenberg, pp. 47–48.

110   Pressuring HHH. O'Donnell, Powers, and McCarthy, pp. 161–62.

110   Gaitskell. *Hartford Courant*, 9 May 1960, p. 14.

110   HHH 60 percent. *Charleston Daily Mail*, 12 May 1960, p. 6; Sorensen, *Kennedy*, p. 139; White, *1960*, pp. 110–11; Parmet, *JFK*, p. 39; O'Brien, *Kennedy*, p. 449. Harris, "rather lamely, I thought," recalled Larry O'Brien, blamed the sudden massive shift on anti-Catholic sentiment, implying rather strongly that Harris's shifting numbers resulted more from faulty polling methodology, rather than from realities on the ground. In view of Harris's poor performance in Wisconsin, this cannot entirely be discounted. O'Brien, *Victories*, p. 67.

110   March 1960 Gallup poll. *Hartford Courant*, 27 March 1960, p. 21A.

111   Illinois. *Facts on File*, 7–13 April 1960, p. 124; *Chicago Tribune*, 7 May 1960, p. 4; Lincoln, p. 44; http://www.ourcampaigns.com/RaceDetail.html ?RaceID=35921.

111   New Jersey primary. *New York Times*, 20 April 1960, p. 1.

111   Massachusetts primary. *New York Times*, 27 April 1960, p. 25; *Washington Post*, 27 April 1960, p. A10; *New York Times*, 28 April 1960, p. 21; Silvestri, p. 112; http://www.ourcampaigns.com/RaceDetail.html?RaceID=35925.

111   Pennsylvania primary. O'Brien, *Victories*, p. 78; Lasky, *JFK*, p. 325.

111   Pennsylvania results. *New York Times*, 27 April 1960, p. 25; *Washington Post*, 27 April 1960, p. 1; *New York Times*, 28 April 1960, p. 21; Evans and Novak, p. 259; Silvestri, p. 112.

112   "I called . . . impressed." O'Brien, *Victories*, p. 78.

112   Precinct captain. O'Brien, *Victories*, p. 78.

112   Hartke. Evans and Novak, pp. 248–49; Lincoln, p. 44.

112   Harris poll. Lincoln, p. 44; Evans and Novak, p. 257.

112   Symington above fray. Olson, p. 345; Frantz and McKean, p. 153.

112   Symington announces. *New York Times*, 25 March 1960, pp. 1, 16, 26; *Hartford Courant*, 25 March 1960, p. 1A; *New York Times*, 26 March 1960, p. 9; Alexander, p. 19; Olson, p. 355.

112   Daly. *Chicago Tribune*, 18 April 1978, pp. 1, 10; *New York Times*, 19 April 1978, p. B10; *Chicago Tribune*, 22 April 1978, p. F2.

112   Latham. *Oakland Tribune*, 4 May 1960, p. 6; *Washington Post*, 5 May 1960, p. A2; *Facts on File*, 28 April–4 May 1960, p. 150; http://www.ourcampaigns.com/ RaceDetail.html?RaceID=35931.

112   19 percent against JFK. *Washington Post*, 5 May 1960, p. A2. *New York Times*, 4 May 1960, p. 30; *Washington Post*, 5 May 1960, p. A2; *New York Times*, 5 May 1960, pp. 27, 28.

113   District of Columbia primary. *Facts on File*, 28 April–4 May 1960, p. 150; *New York Times*, 4 May 1960, p. 31; *Oakland Tribune*, 4 May 1960, p. 6; Smith, *Tiger in the Senate*, pp. 403–5; Miller, *Lyndon*, p. 236; Alexander, p. 24.

113   Food allotments. *New York Times*, 2 May 1960, p. 14.

113   "I remember . . . face." Stossel, p. 147.

113   "My first . . . were." Stossel, p. 146.

113   "Imagine, just . . . milk." White, *1960*, p. 116; Heymann, *RFK*, p. 152.

114   "Until [JFK] . . . jobs." Bruno and Greenfield, p. 43.

114 JFK-miner meeting. Collier and Horowitz, *Kennedys*, p. 207.

114 "There was . . . her." Leamer, *Kennedy Women*, p. 505; Heymann, *RFK*, p. 153.

115 "The staff . . . her." Bradford, p. 126.

115 "West Virginia . . . country." Graham, pp. 260–61; Leamer, *Kennedy Women*, p. 493; Anderson, p. 207; Dallek, *Unfinished Life*, p. 254.

115 95 percent. *New York Times*, 25 April 1960, pp. 1, 16.

115 "It's a . . . thing." Bradlee, *Conversations*, p. 26*fn*; Martin, *Destruction*, p. 247; Hersh, *Bobby & J. Edgar*, p. 194.

115 "Old-Time Religion." O'Donnell, Powers, and McCarthy, p. 166.

115 "We were . . . religion." Goodwin, *Remembering*, p. 85.

115 Bethany College address. Goodwin, *Remembering*, p. 87.

116 "I don't . . . not." *Charleston Gazette*, 20 April 1960, pp. 1, 10.

116 "I refuse . . . mission." White, *1960*, p. 117; O'Brien, *Victories*, pp. 166–67; O'Donnell, Powers, and McCarthy, p. 166; Leamer, *Kennedy Men*, p. 429; Watson, *Vista*, p. 6; Heymann, *RFK*, p. 150.

116 JFK-O'Brien. O'Brien, *Victories*, p. 167.

116 "[W]hen . . . Bible." *Charleston Daily Mail*, 30 April 1960, p. 3; *New York Times*, 9 May 1960, p. 23; Sorensen, *Kennedy*, p. 145; White, *1960*, p. 117; O'Donnell, Powers, and McCarthy, p. 168.

117 "Joseph Alsop . . . Pope-haters." *Charleston Gazette*, 16 April 1960, p. 14.

117 "Let me . . . hilt." Heymann, *RFK*, p. 150.

118 HHH cabinet. *Charleston Gazette*, 12 April 1960, pp. 1, 4; *Morgantown Post*, 12 April 1960, p. 1; *Beckley Post-Herald*, 12 April 1960, p. 1.

118 Pressure on HHH contributors. *New York Times*, 22 April 1960, p. 17; White, *1960*, p. 119; Mooney, *The Politicians*, pp. 328–29; Solberg, p. 210.

118 "I have . . . them." *New York Times*, 8 May 1960, pp. 1, 47; Sorensen, *Kennedy*, p. 141; Novak, p. 63.

118 No Wisconsin debate. *Chicago Tribune*, 24 April 1960, p. 20; *Charleston Daily Mail*, 6 May 1960, p. 12.

118 Sorensen advice. O'Brien, *Kennedy*, p. 454.

118 May 4 debate. *Charleston Gazette*, 5 May 1960, pp. 1, 11A–11B.

118 Food package. O'Donnell, Powers, and McCarthy, p. 170; Watson, pp. 6–7; O'Brien, *Kennedy*, p. 454.

119 "rambling . . . conclusion." *Chicago Tribune*, 2 May 2, 1960, p. 2.

119 "boring gabfest." *Charleston Gazette*, 5 May 1960, p. 1.

119 "cannot win . . . him?" *Brainerd Daily Dispatch*, 11 October 1960, p. 15; Heymann, *RFK*, p. 152.

119 "If Johnson . . . primary?" O'Donnell, Powers, and McCarthy, pp. 168–69.

119 "It has . . . doing." *New York Times*, 1 May 1960, p. 54.

119 "Poor little . . . votes?" *Raleigh Register*, 11 April 1960, p. 1; *Charleston Gazette*, 12 April 1960, p. 1; Dallek, *Unfinished Life*, p. 256.

120 "Gutter politics . . . campaign." *Hartford Courant*, 9 May 1960, p. 1A.

120 "I'd suggest . . . open." *Chicago Tribune*, 1 May 1960, p. 3; Dallek, *Unfinished Life*, p. 256.

120 "Johnson is . . . chance." *Charleston Gazette*, 12 April 1960, p. 1; Mooney,

The Politicians, p. 326; Dallek, *Lone Star Rising*, pp. 566–67; Lincoln, p. 63.

120   "If they . . . themselves?" Mooney, *The Politicians*, p. 326.

120   "He just . . . him." Heymann, *RFK*, pp. 149–50.

120   "The effort . . . candidate." *New York Times*, 19 April 1960, p. 29.

120   Byrd, KKK. *Charleston Gazette*, 12 April 1960, p. 1; *Hartford Courant*, 22 April 1960, p. 31D.

Chapter Eleven: "A little black bag and a checkbook"

121   "There were . . . time." Goodwin, *Fitzgeralds*, p. 799.

121   FDR Jr., 1952. Schlesinger, *Robert Kennedy*, p. 94.

121   JPK, FDR Jr. Schlesinger, *Robert Kennedy*, p. 199; O'Donnell, Powers, and McCarthy, p. 165; Kennedy, *Remember*, p. 369.

121   "You know . . . you." Schlesinger, *Robert Kennedy*, p. 200. It was also Joe who thought to have FDR Jr.–related literature mailed to West Virginia homes bearing a Hyde Park postmark. O'Donnell, Powers, and McCarthy, p. 165; O'Brien, *Kennedy*, p. 452; Kelley, *His Way*, p. 271.

121   "I think . . . known." Kessler, p. 107.

121   "with a . . . it." Martin, *Hero*, p. 139.

122   "While Kennedy . . . idol." Goodwin, *Fitzgeralds*, p. 799.

122   "Sure am . . . bedroom." *New York Times*, 29 April 1960, p. 22.

122   "God's son . . . do." Dallek, *Unfinished Life*, p. 255; Maier, p. 335.

122   "His father . . . close." O'Donnell, Powers, and McCarthy, p. 165; Kennedy, *Remember*, p. 370; Jamieson, p. 127.

122   "Tell Hubert . . . him." Hodgson, p. 100.

122   HHH 4-F. O'Brien, *Victories*, p. 72.

123   West Virginia servicemen. Silvestri, pp. 110, 111.

123   "Nightly I . . . attack." O'Brien, *Kennedy*, p. 454.

123   "Hubert Humphrey . . . War II." FDR on HHH. *Charleston Gazette*, 9 May 1960, p. 15; *Wisconsin Rapids Daily Tribune*, 7 May 1960, p. 9; *Weirton Daily Times*, 28 July 1960, p. 4; Schlesinger, *Robert Kennedy*, p. 201; Leamer, *Kennedy Men*, p. 426; Bradlee, *Conversations*, p. 26; O'Brien, *Kennedy*, p. 453; Heymann, *RFK*, pp. 153–54.

123   "It is . . . forces." *Raleigh Register*, 9 May 1960, p. 1.

123   "Any discussion . . . campaign." Goodwin, *Fitzgeralds*, p. 799; Dallek, *Unfinished Life*, pp. 256–57; Heymann, *RFK*, p. 154; Goodwin, *Remembering*, p. 88.

123   "Of course . . . smile." Heymann, *RFK*, p. 154; Solberg, p. 209; Miller, *Lyndon*, p. 237; Schlesinger, *Robert Kennedy*, p. 201. FDR Jr. apologized to Humphrey during the Los Angeles convention, terming his comments "unnecessary and unwarranted." His apology may have stemmed from JFK eying the delegates HHH still controlled. *Weirton Daily Times*, 28 July 1960, p. 4; Lasky, *JFK*, p. 350.

123   West Virginia Teamsters. *Charleston Daily Mail*, 2 May 1960, p. 4; *New York Times*, 2 May 1960, p. 14; *Chicago Tribune*, 2 May 1960, p. 2; Heymann, *RFK*, p. 152.

123   "Jimmy Hoffa . . . nomination." *Morgantown Post*, 6 May 1960, p. 4; Lasky,

RFK, p. 151.

123 "I can't . . . it." *Charleston Gazette*, 27 April 1960, pp. 1, 4; Schlesinger, *Robert Kennedy*, p. 200; O'Brien, *Victories*, p. 69.

124 United Mine Workers. *Charleston Daily Mail*, 8 April 1960, p. 4; *Charleston Daily Mail*, 15 April 1960, p. 3; *Morgantown Post*, 13 May 1960, p. 6; Kelley, *His Way*, p. 271.

124 UAW endorsement. Boyle, p. 140; *Charleston Daily Mail*, 8 April 1960, p. 4.

124 "Walter's . . . sheriff." Lichtenstein, p. 355; Boyle, p. 142.

124 "didn't go . . . win." Lichtenstein, p. 355.

124 Spending. Solberg, p. 210; Alexander, p. 19; O'Brien, *Victories*, p. 69; Dallek, *Unfinished Life*, p. 257.

124 "Most of . . . money." Dallek, *Unfinished Life*, p. 257.

124 Eddie Ford. O'Neill, pp. 91–92; Kessler, p. 376.

125 "They passed . . . seen." Martin, *Destruction*, pp. 249–50.

125 "Votes were . . . today." Lasky, *JFK*, p. 328; Martin, *Destruction*, p. 248; Novak, p. 65.

125 Smith. Lasky, *JFK*, p. 347.

125 "Every time . . . bagman." Hersh, *Camelot*, p. 96.

125 "I keep . . . candidate." Humphrey, p. 217; Solberg, p. 210; Kessler, pp. 379–80; Martin, *Hero*, pp. 156–57; Hersh, *Camelot*, p. 100.

125 O'Brien. O'Brien, *Victories*, pp. 68, 74; Heymann, *RFK*, p. 151*fn*.

125 Gabriel, Spalding, RFK. Hersh, *Camelot*, p. 97.

126 Chafin. Leamer, *Kennedy Men*, pp. 423–24; Loughry, pp. 10–11; Campbell, pp. 243–44.

126 Southern West Virginia totals. *Charleston Daily Mail*, 20 May 1960, p. 6; Loughry, p. 12; Campbell, p. 244.

126 "flagrant vote-buying . . . it." Loughry, p. 7.

126 "two dollars . . . vote." Davis, *Kennedys*, p. 286; Martin, *Destruction*, p. 248; Klein, *Human*, p. 234.

126 "I know . . . election." Hersh, *Camelot*, p. 95.

126 Fontainebleau meeting. *Washington Monthly*, December 1999; Spada, pp. 254–55.

126 "We need . . . Humphrey." Interview with Don Hewitt, JFK Library.

126 Adonis. Giancana and Giancana, p. 284; Hersh, *Camelot*, p. 100; Summers and Swan, p. 271; Schwarz, p. 411; Van Meter, p. 174; Hersh, *Bobby and J. Edgar*, p. 195; Leamer, *Kennedy Men*, p. 465; Heymann, *RFK*, p. 145*fn*. Some say JPK met instead with Skinny D'Amato. Adonis never did return home. He died in Milan in 1972.

126 "We even . . . President." Giancana and Giancana, p. 284.

126 D'Amato. Jacobs and Stadiem, p. 167; Loughry, p. 23; Hersh, *Camelot*, p. 100; Kelley, *His Way*, p. 270; Summers and Swan, pp. 271–72; Heymann, *Jackie*, p. 232*fn*.

127 "put in . . . money," Giancana and Giancana, p. 284.

127 Davis, Lawford. Davis, *Why Me?*, p. 108; Summers, *Sinatra*, pp. 271–72.

127 Dexter, Sinatra. Summers and Swan, p. 272.

127 $750 check. White, *1960*, p. 120; Solberg, pp. 211–12.

127 "'Dear Jack . . . a landslide." *Charleston Daily Mail*, 20 May 1960, p. 6; Whalen, *Founding Father*, p. 440; Brodie, p. 417.

128 "You git . . . hear?" White, *1960*, p. 121; O'Donnell, Powers, and McCarthy, p. 169.

128 HHH telethon. White, *1960*, pp. 120–22; O'Donnell, Powers, and McCarthy, p. 169; Watson, p. 7.

128 Otten. *Hartford Courant*, 6 May 1960, p. 18.

128 Wesleyan. *Hartford Courant*, 12 May 1960, p. 12D.

128 "Our people . . . Constitution" White, *1960*, p. 115.

128 30–27. *Hartford Courant*, 15 April 1960, p. 18; *Charleston Daily Mail*, 15 April 1960, pp. 1, 4.

128 Salinger. Salinger, *PS:*, p. 77.

128 McDonough. O'Donnell, Powers, and McCarthy, p. 170.

129 JPK New York meeting. Whalen, *Founding Father*, pp. 439–40.

129 "poor mouth." *Chicago Tribune*, 2 May 1960, p. 2; *New York Times*, 6 May 1960, p. 12; *Charleston Gazette-Mail*, 8 May 1960, p. 14-A.

129 Fayette County poll. *New York Times*, 6 May 1960, pp. 1, 13; *Charleston Daily Mail*, 12 May 1960, p. 5.

129 "My poll . . . optimistic." Leamer, *Kennedy Men*, p. 422.

129 April 30 Harris poll. *New York Times*, 1 May 1960, p. 57.

129 Harris discounted. O'Donnell, Powers, and McCarthy, p. 170.

129 Slight lead. O'Donnell, Powers, and McCarthy, p. 170. Conversely, Judith Campbell, who visited Jack at Georgetown on April 6, contended, "There was no question in Jack's mind that he would win in West Virginia, regardless of the religious issue." Exner, p. 130.

129 Crowds. *New York Times*, 1 May 1960, p. 57.

129 O'Donnell. O'Donnell, Powers, and McCarthy, p. 170.

130 "a moral . . . Wisconsin." O'Brien, *Victories*, p. 75; O'Brien Interview I, LBJ Library, p. 16.

130 Times, precincts. *New York Times*, 10 May 1960, p. 1; *Chicago Tribune*, 10 May 1960, p. 12.

130 "If we . . . Humphrey!" O'Donnell, Powers, and McCarthy, p. 171; Martin, *Hero*, p. 156.

130 *Private Property. Washington Post*, 10 May 1960, p. B9; White, *1960*, p. 124; O'Donnell, Powers and McCarthy, p. 196; Bradlee, *Conversations*, p. 27; Bradlee, *Life*, p. 208.

130 Flying to Wheeling. Bradlee, *Life*, p. 208; White, *1960*, p. 124; O'Donnell, Powers, and McCarthy, p. 196; O'Brien, *Kennedy*, p. 455.

130 Returns. *Charleston Daily Mail*, 12 May 1960, p. 1; O'Brien, *Victories*, pp. 75–76; Sorensen, *Kennedy*, p. 146.

130 "How the . . . now!" Martin, *Destruction*, p. 252.

130 "I had . . . prejudice." *Charlestown Daily Mail*, 11 May, 1960, p. 1.

Chapter Twelve: "All the eggheads are for Stevenson"

131   "Stop-JFK." Miller, *Lyndon*, p. 237.

131   HHH quits. *New York Times*, 11 May 1960, p. 1; *Chicago Tribune*, 11 May 1960, pp. 1–2.

131   Muriel Humphrey. Martin, *Destruction*, p. 252; Miller, *Lyndon*, pp. 236–37; Solberg, p. 212; Schlesinger, *Robert Kennedy*, p. 202*fn*; Woods, p. 354. In an instructive passage, Teddy White merely describes the tense RFK visit as a "graceful thank-you call." White, *1960*, p. 123.

131   "I'm for . . . me." Kuralt, p. 54.

132   Parking ticket. *Charleston Daily Mail*, 12 May 1960, p. 8; *Sitka Sentinel*, 12 May 1960, p. 6.

132   "Jack the Dwarf Killer." *Morgantown Post*, 13 May 1960, p. 6. HHH won June 1960's South Dakota primary, but he was unopposed.

132   *CQ* survey. *Chicago Tribune*, 6 December 1960, p. D36.

132   *Hartford Courant*, 18 December 1959, p. 25; *Hartford Courant*, 29 January 1960, p. 24.

133   Gallup poll. Kastenmeier. *New York Times*, 23 February 1960, p. 18.

133   Stevenson background. *Chicago Tribune*, 26 September 1928, p. 28; *Chicago Tribune*, 2 December 1928, p. 28.

133   1948. Whitman, p. 28.

133   Two percent. *Hartford Courant*, 29 January 1960, p. 24.

134   "[M]y opponent . . . backbone" Whitman, *Portrait*, p. 100.

134   "He has. . . mind . . ." Halberstam, *Fifties*, p. 235.

134   "One reason . . . believe." Schlesinger, *Thousand Days*, p. 31.

134   "like a . . . Korea." *Hartford Courant*, 26 September 1952, p. 14.

134   "Sure. All . . . there." *Hartford Courant*, 26 September 1952, p. 14; Halberstam, *Fifties*, p. 235; Manchester, *Glory*, p. 625.

134   Landslide. Manchester, *Glory*, p. 639.

135   "If the . . . sheriff." Woods, p. 308.

135   "an alien . . . disapproval." Schlesinger, *Robert Kennedy*, p. 133; Beran, p. 72.

135   "Nobody asked . . . run." White, *1960*, p. 269.

135   RFK vote. Schlesinger, *Robert Kennedy*, p. 136; Beran, p. 72.

136   "I don't . . . up." Dallek, *Unfinished Life*, p. 236.

136   "The Catholic . . . nominated." Dallek, *Unfinished Life*, p. 236.

136   "He wanted . . . it." Martin, *Hero*, pp. 171–72.

136   "He wishes . . . him." McKeever, pp. 428–29.

137   "I get . . . confidence." Beschloss, *The Crisis Years*, p. 33.

137   "I've got . . . them." Reston, *Deadline*, p. 277.

137   "another chance in 1960" Davis, *Politics*, p. 400.

137   "I have . . . offered." *New York Times*, 10 February 1960, p. 2; *Hartford Courant*, 10 February 1960, p. 1A.

137   Castro. *Hartford Courant*, 20 March 1960, p. 11A.

137   "the amount . . . history." *New York Times*, 19 February 1960, p. 13; Martin, *Adlai Stevenson*, p. 480.

137   Stevenson for President Committee. *New York Times*, 12 April 1960, pp. 1, 24; McKeever, p. 438.

138   "If I . . . evader,'" *New York Times*, 12 April 1960, pp. 1, 24.

138 May 19. *New York Times*, 20 May 1960, pp. 1, 6; *Chicago Tribune*, 20 May 1960, pp. 1, 2; McKeever, pp. 446–47; Martin, *Adlai Stevenson*, pp. 504–5.

139 "talk and . . . not.'" *New York Times*, 2 June 1960, pp. 1, 6; *Chicago Tribune*, 2 June 1960, pp. 1, 8; Whitman, p. 206.

139 Oregon primary. McKeever, p. 448.

139 "That was . . . it." Reston, *Deadline*, p. 278.

139 "Now that . . . leader." *New York Times*, 12 June 1960, p. 51; *Chicago Tribune*, 12 June 1960, p. 20; *New York Times*, 17 June 1960, p. 18; Schlesinger, *Thousand Days*, p. 29; Schlesinger, *Robert Kennedy*, pp. 203–4; Whitman, *Profile*, p. 208.

140 "S is . . . anyone." Schlesinger, *Robert Kennedy*, p. 203; Dallek, *Unfinished Life*, p. 238.

140 "Jack invited . . . stubborn." Martin, *Hero*, p. 139. Equally stubborn for Adlai was Arthur Schlesinger's wife, Marian Cannon, prompting a note from RFK: "Can't you control your own wife—or are you like me?" Schlesinger, *Robert Kennedy*, p. 204.

140 "So far . . . Stevenson." *New York Times*, 10 June 1960, p. 14; Lash, pp. 287–88.

141 ER declares. *Chicago Tribune*, 13 June 1960, p. 1.

141 "My message . . . it?" *New York Times*, 13 June 1960, pp. 1, 19; Lash, p. 290; Whitman, p. 209.

141 Hyde Park. Vidal, p. 343.

142 "[Stevenson] is . . . north." Schlesinger, *Robert Kennedy*, pp. 202–3.

142 "Their relationship . . . more." Sorensen, *Kennedy Legacy*, p. 66.

142 "leaned forward . . . man." Dallek, *Unfinished Life*, p. 237.

142 "Let Adlai . . . Stevenson!" Lasky, *RFK*, pp. 155–56; Martin, *Hero*, p. 144.

142 "They're not . . . Adlai." Thomas, p. 134.

142 RFK suggestion. Lasky, *RFK*, p. 154.

142 "against . . . judgment." O'Brien, *Victories*, pp. 79–80.

143 "If I . . . you." Schlesinger, *Robert Kennedy*, p. 203.

143 JFK-Minow. McKeever, p. 448; Dallek, *Unfinished Life*, p. 259; Parmet, *JFK*, p. 14; Martin, *Adlai Stevenson*, p. 506.

143 "I told . . . them." Schlesinger, *Robert Kennedy*, p. 203; Martin, *Adlai Stevenson*, p. 509.

143 "I have . . ."; ". . . gutter talk." O'Brien, *John F. Kennedy*, pp. 459–60.

143 "Why doesn't . . . himself." O'Brien, *John F. Kennedy*, pp. 459–60.

143 "No, certainly . . . up" McKeever, p. 448; Martin, *Adlai Stevenson*, p. 506; Dallek, *Unfinished Life*, p. 259.

143 "Guess who . . . Daddy." McKeever, p. 448; Martin, *Adlai Stevenson*, p. 510; Dallek, *Unfinished Life*, p. 259.

Chapter Thirteen: "They were a dime a dozen"

145 "I was . . . serious." Goodwin, *Fitzgeralds*, 724; Kessler, p. 303; Morrow, *Best Year*, p. 185.

145 Prostitute. Goodwin, *Fitzgeralds*, p. 465; Wills, *Kennedy Imprisonment*, pp. 28–29.

145 Gonorrhea. Kessler, p. 381.

145 Chlamydia. Pottker, p. 152.

145 Arvad background. Wills, *Kennedy Imprisonment*, pp. 19–20.

146 "There was . . . self-centeredness." Blair and Blair, p. 142; Wills, *Kennedy Imprisonment*, p. 31.

146 "One of . . . like." *Charleston Daily Mail*, 13 January 1942, p. 10; Dallek, *Unfinished Life*, p. 84.

146 "Damn it . . . married." Parmet, *Jack*, p. 90.

146 Hoover. Blair and Blair, pp. 145–46; Parmet, *Jack*, pp. 91–92; Davis, *Kennedys*, pp. 111–12; Hamilton, pp. 453–55, 471–72, 474; O'Brien, *Kennedy*, pp. 120–24; Maier, p. 163; Kessler, pp. 260–65.

146 Gene Tierney. *San Antonio Light*, 19 January 1976, p. 3; Parmet, *Jack*, pp. 131, 167; Goodwin, *Fitzgeralds*, p. 723; O'Brien, *Kennedy*, pp. 210–11. Regarding Hollywood actresses: Marilyn Monroe is not included in this work, due to the difficulty, if not impossibility, in determining when her affair with JFK began. Authors Sarah Bradford, Barbara Leaming, and James Spoto all date the first JFK-Monroe meeting as occurring in 1961. Lawford biographer James Spada and Kennedy family chronicler Nellie Bly have Monroe trysting with JFK during the 1960 convention. Jackie biographer David Heymann places their introduction at the Lawfords' in 1957, with the affair not beginning until 1959. Monroe biographer Donald H. Wolfe places it as far back as 1951. Jackie and Marilyn biographer Donald Spoto dates the affair to a one-time event (at Bing Crosby's) in March 1962. Anthony Summers cites a variety of versions and dates from the early 1950s through 1961. Churchwell, p. 213; Spada, p. 257; Bradford p. 222; Heymann, *Jackie*, p. 233; Spoto, p. 155; Bly, pp. 108–9.

146 Pregnancy, 1946. Kessler, p. 300.

146 Durie Malcolm. Hersh, *Camelot*, pp. 326–31; Blair and Blair, pp. 499–502; Bradlee, *Conversations*, pp. 43–49; Martin, *Destruction*, pp. 306–7; Bly, pp. 124–27.

146 "I went . . . dozen." Wills, *Kennedy Imprisonment*, p. 28–29; Goodwin, *Fitzgeralds*, pp. 724–25; Leamer, *Kennedy Men*, p. 249; Morrow, p. 184. Horton, with Lem Billings, accompanied JFK to that fateful Harlem brothel years before. Wills, *Kennedy Imprisonment*, p. 28; Goodwin *Fitzgeralds*, p. 465.

147 "He wanted . . . him." Kessler, p. 391.

147 "There was . . . sure." Leamer, *Kennedy Men*, p. 429.

147 Bonus. Schwarz, p. 408; Davis, *Kennedys*, p. 274.

147 "He's gone . . ."; "No." Leamer, *Kennedy Women*, p. 49.

148 "only until . . . is over." Fay, pp. 180–81.

148 Bobby Baker, April 8. Leamer, *Kennedy Men*, p. 422; Hersh, *Camelot*, pp. 115–16.

148 "I talked . . . details." Heymann, *RFK*, p. 422. Alsop well knew the dangers of political blackmail, having been photographed by KGB agents in a sexual assignation with another man during an early 1957 trip to Moscow. Alsop refused to play the Kremlin's game. Yoder, pp. 153–56.

148 Darr. Hersh, *Camelot*, pp. 111–20; Parmet, *Jack*, p. 168; Heymann, *RFK*,

pp. 422–23.

149 "public knowledge . . . water." Heymann, *RFK*, p. 423; Hersh, *Camelot*, p. 117; Frantz and McKean, p. 156.

149 "I had . . . it." Hersh, *Camelot*, p. 117.

149 "I told . . . McInerney." Hersh, *Camelot*, p. 117.

149 McInerney, 1953. Hersh, *Camelot*, pp. 86–87.

149 Kater. O'Brien, *Kennedy*, pp. 440–42; Dallek, *Unfinished Life*, p. 406; Hersh, *Camelot*, pp. 107–10; Leamer, *Kennedy Women*, p. 499; Anderson, pp. 195–96; Leaming, *Mrs. Kennedy*, p. 17; Bly, pp. 100–101.

150 "Lyndon loved . . . people." Caro, *Master*, p. 654; Unger and Unger, p. 431.

150 Helen Gahagan Douglas. Caro, *Master*, pp. 144–45; Unger and Unger, p. 82.

150 "sufficiently enchanted . . . Bird." Parmet, *JFK*, p. 14; and what of Richard Nixon? Well, not much. Bill Clinton's chief counsel Lloyd Cutler narrated a tale of "a little volunteer investigative work" in 1960 with *Miami News* editor, and JFK partisan, Bill Baggs, who, Cutler contended, "was especially interested in the weekend parties that Richard Nixon used to attend at Bebe Rebozo's house in Key Biscayne. . . . Bill found some call girls in Miami who claimed to have been at these parties. It was all going to make a very good story about Richard Nixon until we learned that among the people who were frequently in the house was Senator Kennedy, so we dropped the story. We never did find out whether Mr. Nixon had gone upstairs." Summers, *Arrogance*, p. 211.

150 *Washington Star*. Hersh, *Camelot*, pp. 108–9; Bly, p. 101.

150 Blackmail ring. Hersh, *Camelot*, p. 113. By a strange coincidence, in February 1961 RFK appointed Edwyn Silberling, a prosecutor in that 1952 blackmail case, to head the Justice Department's newly formed Organized Crime and Racketeering Section. *New York Times*, 2 February 1961, pp. 1, 13; Lasky, *RFK*, p. 168.

151 Giancana's $500,000. Giancana and Giancana, p. 284.

151 "went to . . . $500,000." Hersh, *Camelot*, p. 112; Martin, *Destruction*, p. 306; Frantz and McKean, p. 156.

151 "went to . . . crime." Hersh, *Camelot*, p. 114.

151 D'Amato theory. Van Meter, p. 173.

152 Giancana meeting. *Washington Monthly*, December 1999; O'Brien, *Kennedy*, p. 685. Campbell had JFK requesting a meeting with Giancana on the evening of April 6, two days before Baker supposedly informed JFK of the plot. It is not terribly unlikely that either she or JFK were off by a day or two, either in Campbell's recollections or in JFK's dating of the memo at the time.

152 Campbell introduction. Schwarz, p. 406; Scheim, p. 89; Kelley, *His Way*, p. 269; Summers and Swan, p. 264; Leamer, *Kennedy Men*, pp. 409–10; Giancana and Giancana, p. 282; Kessler, p. 375; Spada, p. 254.

152 "She was . . . point." Jacobs and Stadien, p. 133.

152 "I . . . next morning." Martin, *Hero*, p. 199; Summers and Swan, pp. 262–63.

Journalist Mary McGrory also accompanied JFK.

152 "I was at . . . Jack." Summers and Swan, p. 264; Exner, p. 86; Leamer, *Kennedy Women*, p. 489. Campbell claimed that even before JFK hit on her on that night, Teddy Kennedy ("You can't blame a guy for trying") had—and failed. Exner, pp. 86–89; Hersh, *Camelot*, p. 298; Bly, p. 105.

153 "the world's . . . listener." Exner, p. 87.

153 "an almost . . . was." Exner, p. 90.

153 "Sam Flood." Exner, p. 116; Summers and Swan, p. 265; Klein, *Human*, pp. 230–31; Hersh, *Camelot*, p. 299; Blakey and Billings, p. 380; Leamer, *Kennedy Men*, p. 412; Leamer, *Kennedy Women*, p. 490; Levy, p. 162.

153 "chief gunman . . . mob." Schlesinger, *Robert Kennedy*, p. 164.

153 "I thought . . . Giancana." *Chicago Tribune*, 10 June 1959, p. 1, 8; Heymann, *RFK*, p. 157; Thomas, p. 67.

153 Roselli. Leamer, *Kennedy Men*, p. 411; Hersh, *Camelot*, p. 294; Heymann, *Jackie*, p. 231; Bradford, p. 223; Hersh, *Bobby and J. Edgar*, p. 292.

153 "With . . . to Sinatra." Summers and Swan, pp. 263–64. Walters also heard reports of Kennedy cocaine use.

154 "in Miami . . . companion." Leamer, *Kennedy Men*, p. 408; Smith, *Grace and Power*, p. 9.

154 "Frank's got . . . them." Giancana and Giancana, p. 281.

154 "I've already . . . box." Giancana and Giancana, p. 280. Mickey Cohen biographer Brad Lewis contends that Campbell's first Kennedy family dalliance was not with Jack but Joe. Lewis, p. 267.

154 "I know . . . thought." Blakey and Billings, p. 378; Scheim, p. 88; Summers, p. 217; Bly, pp. 211–12. Cohen also claimed to have donated five thousand dollars to Richard Nixon's 1946 campaign and raised seventy-five thousand dollars for his 1950 effort. Summers, pp. 54–57; Lewis, pp. 52, 264.

155 Darr blackmail. In her most peculiar allegation, Judith Campbell claimed to have transported two satchels full of cash *from* JFK to Sam Giancana. As JFK or Giancana hardly knew Campbell at this time, and as the Kennedys had any number of ways to transport funds to Chicago, or, more logically, even from within Chicago itself, i.e., from the Merchandise Mart, to Giancana, her claim makes little sense. Beyond that, if Giancana was blackmailing the Kennedys, it was not cash that drove him, but power and immunity once the family occupied the White House. Hersh, *Camelot*, pp. 303–4; Leamer, *Kennedy Men*, pp. 413–14.

155 "You . . . fatal flaw." Blakey and Billings, p. 382; Scheim, pp. 88–89; Lewis, p. 267.

155 West Virginia. Bradford, p. 128.

155 "If I . . . you." Klein, *Human*, p. 233.

156 "Today's our . . . it." Pottker, p. 170.

Chapter Fourteen: "A clean bill of health"

157   Tawes. *New York Times*, 25 January 25, 1960, p. 1; Lasky, *JFK*, p. 327.

157   Maryland primary. *Charleston Daily Mail*, 12 May 1960, p. 1; O'Brien, *Victories*, p. 77; Smith, *Tiger in the Senate*, p. 405; Dallek, *Unfinished Life*, p. 258.

157   Oregon primary. Lincoln, p. 45.

157   "of course . . . Nixon." *New York Times*, 22 May 1960, p. 63.

157   May Gallup poll. *Hartford Courant*, 4 May 1960, p. 13; *Hartford Courant*, 15 May 1960, p. 3B; *Hartford Courant*, 20 May 1960, p. 22.

157   "Well, the . . . Jack." Goodwin, pp. 799–800.

158   California primary. http://www.ourcampaigns.com/RaceDetail.html?RaceID= 55200.

158   "California Democrats . . . story." Novak, p. 66.

158   "When we . . . school." Martin, *Hero*, pp. 160, 193.

158   Joan Kennedy. Martin, *Hero*, p. 194.

159   Daley. O'Donnell, Powers, and McCarthy, pp. 199–200.

159   RFK-Lehman exchange. Thompson and Myers, p. 204; Whalen, p. 445; Lasky, *RFK*, p. 142; Parmet, *JFK*, p. 21; Heymann, *RFK*, p. 175.

160   Joe Clark. O'Neill, pp. 90–91.

160   NBC News estimate. *New York Times*, 13 June 1960, p. 55.

160   "Well, that's . . . majority." Collier and Horowitz, *Kennedys*, p. 211.

160   "I am not . . . you?" *New York Times*, 31 May 1960, p. 23; Dallek, *Unfinished Life*, p. 260; Dallek, *Lone Star Rising*, p. 569.

160   "The summit . . . it." *New York Times*, 31 May 1960, p. 23.

160   "The most . . . man." *New York Times*, 31 May 1960, p. 23.

160   Citizens Committee for Lyndon Johnson, *Chicago Tribune*, 3 June 1960, p. 5.

161   April 1960 Gallup poll. *Hartford Courant*, 20 April 1960, p. 12; *New York Times*, 24 April 1960, p. E3.

161   Gallup poll–South. *Hartford Courant*, 21 April 1960, p. 25.

161   New Mexico. *Hobbs News-Sun*, 5 June 1960, pp. 1, 3; *Deming Headlight*, 9 June 1960, p. 2; White, *1960*, p. 156.

162   "There I . . . gone." *Tucson Daily Citizen*, 29 April, 1960, p. 4; *Tucson Daily Citizen*, 30 June 1960, p. 16; *Arizona Daily Sun*, 2 May 1960, p. 3; Evans and Novak, pp. 253–54; Miller, *Lyndon*, p. 242.

162   "Lyndon all . . . Kennedy." O'Donnell, Powers, and McCarthy, p. 200.

162   Minnesota Democrats. Miller, *Lyndon*, p. 239.

162   "The Kennedys . . . funny." Miller, *Lyndon*, pp. 238–39.

162   "Mr. Johnson . . . toadstools." Lincoln, p. 51.

162   "the requisite . . . Angeles." Hersh, *Camelot*, p. 337*fn*.

162   "Little Lyndon . . . me." Baker and King, pp. 118–19; Novak, p. 66.

163   "Clark Clifford . . . me." Acheson Interview, JFK Library, pp. 2–3.

164   "Senator . . . be patient." *New York Times*, 3 July 1960, pp. 1, 18, 19; *Oakland Tribune*, 3 July 1960, p. 5; *Facts on File*, 30 June–6 July 1960, p. 230; Mcfarland, p. 106; Jamieson, pp. 139–40.

164   "good men" *New York Times*, 3 July 1960, pp. 1, 18, 19; *Oakland Tribune*, 3 July 1960, p. 5; *Facts on File*, 30 June–6 July 1960, p. 230; Mcfarland,

p. 106; Jamieson, pp. 139–40; Reeves, *Character*, pp. 168–69.

164   Sorensen. *New York Times*, 5 July 1960, p. 20; Sorensen, *Kennedy*, p. 152.

164   Washington staff. *New York Times*, 3 July 1960, p. 19; *Oakland Tribune*, 3 July 1960, p. 5.

164   White, *1960*, pp. 162–63; Sorensen, *Kennedy*, pp. 151–52.

164   "If we . . . America." *New York Times*, 5 July 1960, pp. 1, 20; *Oakland Tribune*, 5 July 1960, pp. 1, 5; *Galveston News*, 5 July 1960, pp. 1–2; Lasky, *JFK*, p. 373; Sorensen, *Kennedy*, pp. 152–53; Jamieson, pp. 140–41; Reeves, *Character*, pp. 170–71; O'Brien, *Kennedy*, p. 461. JFK was, of course, fortunate that HST did not skewer him à la Lloyd Bentsen, "Senator, I served with FDR. I knew FDR. Franklin Roosevelt was a friend of mine. Senator, you're no Franklin Roosevelt."

165   "studies all . . . advice." *New York Times*, 5 July 1960, p. 20; *Oakland Tribune*, 5 July 1960, p. 5; Jamieson, p. 140.

165   Truman didn't watch. *Oakland Tribune*, 5 July 1960, p. 1; *Burlington Times–News*, 5 July 1960, p. 1.

165   "We all . . . harm." Lash, p. 292.

165   June Gallup poll. *Hartford Courant*, 17 June 1960, p. 30.

166   Symington. Mcfarland, p. 109.

166   51 percent. *Hartford Courant*, 12 June 1960, p. 34A.

166   51 percent to 49 percent. *Hartford Courant*, 5 June 1960, p. 4B.

166   LBJ press conference. Graham, p. 261.

166   "I am . . . Americans." *Oakland Tribune*, 5 July 1960, pp. 1, 5; Evans and Novak, pp. 265–66; Dallek, *Lone Star Rising*, p. 571; Mooney, *The Politicians*, p. 330.

166   "I am . . . store." *Facts on File*, 30 June–6 July 1960, p. 230; *Oxnard Press– Courier*, July 5, 1960, p. 1; Evans and Novak, p. 266.

167   "Tell your . . . Boston." Lasky, *JFK*, p. 375.

167   Rovere. Vidal, *Palimpsest*, pp. 343–44.

167   Jenkins and Cook. Reston, *Lone Star*, pp. 189–91.

167   "Let me do . . . me." Reston, *Lone Star*, p. 191; Woods, pp. 357–58.

167   "Doctors have . . . youth." *New York Times*, 5 July 1960, p. 18; *Galveston News*, 5 July 1960, pp. 1–2; *Facts on File*, 30 June–6 July 1960, p. 230; *Frederick Post*, 1 December 1960, p. 17; Evans and Novak, p. 272; Sorensen, *Kennedy*, p. 39; Salinger, *With Kennedy*, p. 65.

168   Connally. *Oakland Tribune*, 5 July 1960, pp. 1, 5; Lasky, *JFK*, p. 373; Dallek, *Lone Star Rising*, p. 572; Reston, *Lone Star*, p. 191; Schlesinger, *Robert Kennedy*, pp. 204–5.

168   "So far . . . down." Reston, *Lone Star*, pp. 192–93.

168   "It's that . . . [Kennedy]." Lasky, *RFK*, p. 157.

168   RFK-Baker confrontation. *Syracuse Post–Standard*, 15 July 1960, p. 6; *Portsmouth Herald*, 15 July 1960, p. 4; *Florence Morning News*, 15 July 1960, p. 6; Lasky, *RFK*, p. 157.

168   "John F. . . . malaria." *New York Times*, 5 July 1960, p. 18; *Oakland Tribune*, 5 July 1960, p. 1; Lasky, *JFK*, p. 376; Blair and Blair, pp. 575–76; O'Brien,

Kennedy, p. 462.

168   "It is a . . . convention." *Galveston News*, 5 July 1960, pp. 1–2; Reston, *Lone Star*, p. 192.

169   "All the . . . about." *New York Times*, 3 May 1973, p. 33; Summers, p. 211. The Long Beach offices of Richard Nixon's personal physician Dr. John Lungren were burglarized in September 1972. *San Antonio Express*, 4 May 1974, p. 1.

169   June 11 letter. *Burlington Times–News*, 5 July 1960, pp. 1, 5A; *Frederick Post*, 1 December 1960, p. 17.

169   "I sat . . . right.'" Martin, *Destruction*, p. 254.

169   "Your fine . . . function." *Lowell Sun Press*, 5 July 1960, p. 6; Lasky, *JFK*, pp. 376–77.

169   Judd-LBJ exchange. Dallek, *Lone Star Rising*, p. 572; O'Brien, *Kennedy*, p. 452.

Chapter Fifteen: "First blood for Kennedy"

170   "The vice-presidency . . . training." *Washington Post*, 9 July 1960, pp. 1, A2, A9; *Chicago Tribune*, 9 July 1960, pp. 1, 4; Miller, *Lyndon*, p. 243.

171   "I was . . . them." Martin, *Destruction*, p. 255; Anderson, pp. 208–9.

171   "Jealous . . . tiddly-winks." Miller, *Fishbait*, pp. 306–7.

171   "I was . . . leper." Valenti interview, JFK Library, p. 4.

171   "It's all . . . landslide." Graham, p. 261.

171   "Jack Kennedy . . . here.'" Lasky, *JFK*, p. 380*fn*.

171   Daley. *Chicago Tribune*, 11 July 1960, pp. 1, 5.

171   *New York Times*, 8 July 1960, p. 49; Sorensen, *Kennedy*, p. 155.

171   Iowa. *Los Angeles Times*, 11 July 1960, p. 3; *Wall Street Journal*, 11 July 1960, p. 3; *Washington Post*, 12 July 1960, pp. 1, A13; Sorensen, *Kennedy*, p. 155; Watson, *Chief of Staff*, p. 32; Mooney, *The Politicians*, p. 334.

172   "Don't ask . . . you." Miller, *Lyndon*, p. 250.

172   "They would . . . at all." Galbraith, *Life*, p. 382. Both Docking and Loveless later received positions in Kennedy's administration.

172   Alaska. Watson, *Chief of Staff*, p. 33.

172   "The Kennedys . . . department." Martin, *Hero*, p. 167; Martin, *Destruction*, p. 244.

172   "I particularly . . . persuasion." Miller, *Lyndon*, p. 250.

172   Iowa, Kansas, Alaska. *Delta Democrat-Times*, 10 July 1960, p. 21.

172   Black delegates. *Pittsburgh Courier*, 16 July 1960, p. 10; Bryant, p. 140.

172   Rostenkowski. O'Donnell, Powers, and McCarthy, p. 201.

173   59½-6½-2. *Chicago Tribune*, 11 July 1960, pp. 1, 5; McKeever, p. 455; Davis, *Politics*, p. 430.

173   "First blood . . . Kennedy." White, *1960*, p. 175.

173   Pennsylvania caucus. *Washington Post*, 12 July 1960, pp. 1, A13; *New York Times*, 12 July 1960, p. 20; *Facts on File*, 7 July–13 July 1960, p. 235; White, *1960*, p. 176; Davis, *Politics*, p. 431.

173   "Sorry, I'm . . . steady." *Washington Post*, 12 July 1960, p. A13.

173   "concern for . . . country" Sorensen, p. 155; Lasky, *JFK*, pp. 390–91.

173 "Hubert, we . . . hell." Martin, *Destruction*, p. 255.

173 "I'm going . . . you." Lasky, *RFK*, p. 163.

173 "You know . . . Hubert." Lasky, *JFK*, p. 391; Lasky, *RFK*, p. 163.

173 "I should . . . Kennedy." Schlesinger, *Robert Kennedy*, p. 195; Hodgson, p. 99.

174 "Well, Joe . . . car." Schlesinger, *Robert Kennedy*, p. 195.

174 McCarthy. Miller, *Lyndon*, p. 247.

174 "leaning tower . . . putty." *Hartford Courant*, 28 October 1966, p. 22; Lasky, *RFK*, p. 163.

174 Eleanor at airport. *Los Angeles Times*, 11 July 1960, pp. 1, 14; *Long Beach Press–Telegram*, 11 July 1960, p. A2; *Fresno Bee*, 11 July 1960, p. 6; Lash, pp. 292–93.

175 Eleanor-Brown. *Los Angeles Times*, 12 July 1960, pp. 1, 3.

175 "unselfishness and . . . vote." *New York Times*, 12 July 1960, p. 23; *Los Angeles Times*, 12 July 1960, p. 1; *Chicago Tribune*, 12 July 1960, p. 8; *Bridgeport Post*, 12 July 1960, p. 8; Sorensen, p. 155; Lash, pp. 293–94.

175 "You've got . . . you." Baker and King, p. 118; Heymann, *RFK*, p. 164; Thomas, p. 97.

175 Bradlee on LBJ. Bryant, p. 139.

175 "But, Daddy . . . us." Schlesinger, *Robert Kennedy*, p. 205; Martin, *Hero*, p. 169.

175 "If you . . . you." Martin, *Destruction*, p. 255.

175 "A Negro . . . bed." White, *1964*, p. 431; Lincoln, p. 84; Woods, p. 359.

175 "What shall . . . say?" Martin, *Destruction*, p. 255; Martin, *Hero*, p. 169.

175 "I remember . . . twitch." Martin, *Destruction*, p. 255.

176 "When Jake . . . safe." Mooney, *The Politicians*, p. 332.

176 LBJ attack. *New York Times*, 13 July 1960, pp. 1, 18; Evans and Novak, p. 273; Heymann, *RFK*, p. 164; Dallek, *Unfinished Life*, p. 265; Dallek, *Lone Star Rising*, p. 573; Mooney, *The Politicians*, p. 332.

176 "I assume . . . Senate." *New York Times*, 13 July 1960, p. 1, 18; *Long Beach Press–Telegram*, 13 July 1960, p. A–4; *Facts on File*, 7 July–13 July 1960, p. 236; Evans and Novak, p. 273; Sorensen, p. 156; Lincoln, p. 86; O'Brien, *John F. Kennedy*, p. 463; Dallek, *Lone Star Rising*, pp. 573–74; Martin, *Hero*, pp. 169–70; O'Brien, *Victories*, p. 82.

176 "I yield . . . president." Valenti Interview, JFK Library, p. 2.

176 "That was . . . road." Reston, *Lone Star*, p. 194.

176 "When [JFK] . . . twitched." Martin, *Destruction*, p. 255.

Chapter Sixteen: "We had to win on the first ballot"

177 Antipathy to Schlesinger. Schlesinger, *Thousand Days*, pp. 33–34.

177 "Arthur's attitude . . . turmoil." Lasky, *JFK*, p. 305.

177 "an ingrate . . . leprous." Galbraith, *Life*, p. 379.

177 "The worst . . . history." Galbraith, *Life*, p. 381; Martin, *Adlai Stevenson*, p. 522.

177 "On arriving . . . Irish." Galbraith, *Life*, p. 379. Actually, Theodore

Chaiken Sorensen was half Jewish.

178 Hollywood Stevensonions. *New York Times*, 14 July 1960, pp. 1, 15.

178 "Catching contagion . . . itself." White, *1960*, p. 178.

178 Stevenson arrives. Lasky, *RFK*, p. 162.

178 Biltmore demonstration. *Los Angeles Times*, 12 July 1960, pp. 1, 9.

178 "the ablest . . . candidate." *Facts on File*, June 23–29, 1960, p. 220.

178 "There was . . . start." Martin, *Adlai Stevenson*, p. 524.

178 Convention floor demonstration. *Los Angeles Times*, 13 July 1960, p. 3; *Chicago Tribune*, 13 July 1960, pp. 1, 8; *Hartford Courant*, 13 July 1960, p. 2; White, *1960*, pp. 178–79.

179 "he acted . . . monsters." http://murrayfromson.com/fromsonfile/2004/07/ when-there-was-unforgettable-week-as.html.

179 Stevenson response. *New York Times*, 13 July 1960, pp. 1, 18; Martin, *Adlai Stevenson*, p. 525.

179 "Mrs. Roosevelt . . . him." Martin, *Adlai Stevenson*, p. 525.

179 "The woods . . . sleep." White, *1960*, p. 179; McKeever, p. 460; Davis, *Politics*, p. 436; Martin, *Adlai Stevenson*, p. 525.

179 "Governor, you're . . . got." White, *1960*, p. 182–83; O'Donnell, Powers, and McCarthy, p. 201; Cohen and Taylor, p. 259; Stossel, p.150; Davis, *Politics*, p. 437; Martin, *Adlai Stevenson*, p. 526.

180 JFK camp convention tactics. Salinger, *With Kennedy*, p. 64; Salinger, *PS:*, p. 78; Miller, *Lyndon*, p. 250; Graham, p. 261.

180 "the box." Salinger, *PS:*, pp. 78–79; Martin, *Destruction*, p. 254.

180 "[W]e developed . . . monitor." O'Brien Interview I, LBJ Library, p. 2.

180 "If any . . . now." Collier and Horowitz, *Kennedys*, p. 212; Lasky, *JFK*, p. 384.

181 "I didn't . . . else." Schlesinger, *Robert Kennedy*, p. 205.

181 "I want . . . ballot." Schlesinger, *Robert Kennedy*, pp. 205–6; Martin, *Hero*, p. 171.

181 "Kennedy's got . . . switchboard." Mooney, *The Politicians*, p. 333.

181 Press kits. Salinger, *With Kennedy*, pp. 62–63.

181 Daily newspaper. Salinger, pp. 63–64.

182 Murphy. Salinger, *With Kennedy*, p. 59; Salinger, *PS:*, p. 78.

182 Las Vegas. Dallek, *Lone Star Rising*, p. 572; Goodwin, *Fitzgeralds*, pp. 800–801.

182 Davies villa. Koskoff, p. 422; Smith, *Hostage*, p. 687; White, *1960*, p. 195; Whalen, *Founding Father*, p. 442; Lasky, *JFK*, p. 388; Fay, pp. 80–81; Koskoff, p. 422; Guiles, p. 370. Jack and Jackie had spent part of their honeymoon at Davies's Beverly Hills villa. The property can be seen in such films as *The Godfather*, *The Jerk*, and *The Bodyguard*. O'Brien, *John F. Kennedy*, p. 270.

182 Fay-Sidey-Kennedy exchange. Davis, *Kennedys*, p. 135; Kessler, p. 384.

182 522 North Rossmere. O'Donnell, Powers, and McCarthy, p. 209; O'Brien, *John F. Kennedy*, p. 461; Martin, *Hero*, pp. 170–71.

183 Winchell. Winchell, pp. 276–77; Schwarz, p. 408.

183 "It stunned . . . chance." Exner, p. 162. Peter Lawford biographer James Spada claims that Marilyn Monroe was among those with JFK, Lawford, and Kenny O'Donnell at that dinner and had had relations with JFK

beforehand. Spada, p. 257.

183   Ménage à trois. Exner, pp. 164–65; O'Brien, *Kennedy*, p. 684. http://www.findarticles.com/p/articles/mi_m1316/is_12_31/ai_58170292/pg_2.

183   "All I . . . me." Exner, p. 168; Wills, *Kennedy Imprisonment*, pp. 22–23.

183   "The Kennedy . . . organization." Ehrlichman, p. 22.

184   Platform staffing. Boyle, pp. 140–41.

184   JFK backs liberal planks. Johnson and Porter, pp. 574–600.

184   Southerners acquiesce. *Chicago Tribune*, 13 July 1960, pp. 1, 7.

184   Church. Nixon, *Six Crises*, p. 312.

184   "We can't . . . dead." Schlesinger, *Robert Kennedy*, p. 206; Martin, *Hero*, p. 171.

184   "We had . . . stable." Schlesinger, *Robert Kennedy*, p. 204.

185   "And suddenly . . . calculate." http://www.esquire.com/features/superman-supermarket-3.

185   Nominations. *Chicago Tribune*, 14 July 1960, p. N5.

185   "I say . . . people." *New York Times*, 14 July 1960, pp. 1, 15; Whitman, pp. 212–16; McKeever, p. 462; Stossel, p. 150; Lasky, *JFK*, pp. 396–97; Davis, *Politics*, pp. 437–38.

185   "And so . . . man." *Chicago Tribune*, 14 July 1960, p. N5.

186   "Mike why . . . balconies." O'Brien Interview I, LBJ Library, p. 11.

186   "I've always . . . in." Miller, *Lyndon*, p. 252; Martin, *Hero*, p. 171.

186   Demonstration counterproductive. Miller, *Lyndon*, p. 252.

186   "I rode . . . funeral." Galbraith, *Life*, pp. 382–83.

186   LBJ drunk. Martin, *Hero*, p. 170; Heymann, *RFK*, p. 168.

186   Patterson. O'Donnell, Powers, and McCarthy, p. 207.

186   Florida. Sherrill, p. 170.

187   "It's your . . . chance!" Martin, *Hero*, p. 172.

187   "Go tell . . . over." Salinger, *With Kennedy*, p. 68.

187   Alabama. White, *1960*, p. 184; O'Donnell, Powers, and McCarthy, p. 215.

187   Blown fuse. *New York Times*, 19 July 1960, p. 24; O'Donnell, Powers, and McCarthy, pp. 187–88; Sorensen, *Kennedy*, p. 162.

188   McKracken-Teddy. Martin, *Hero*, pp. 172–73; Hersh, *Edward M. Kennedy*, pp. 137–38.

188   "Tell them . . . President." Salinger, *With Kennedy*, p. 68.

188   "You have . . . President." Fay, p. 49; Collier and Horowitz, *Kennedys*, p. 213; White, *1960*, p. 185; Sorensen, p. 161; Spada, p. 230. Ted Sorensen, who, after all, had a way with words, put it this way: "Wyoming [was] alerted to the important role it could play."

188   "Wyoming casts . . . States." White, *1960*, p. 185; Whalen, *Founding Father*, p. 443; Fay, p. 48; Salinger, *With Kennedy*, p. 68.

188   Totals. Eaton, p. 505. Barnett was Governor of Mississippi; Faubus of Arkansas; Rosellini of Washington.

188   JFK-Bobby. *Chicago Tribune*, 14 July 1960, p. 8; O'Donnell, Powers, and McCarthy, p. 216; Dallek, *Unfinished Life*, p. 266.

188   "When the . . . Massachusetts." Lincoln, p. 88.

189   Dozen roses. Exner, p. 170; Reeves, *Character*, p. 173.

189   "While he . . . Jackie." Martin, *Destruction*, p. 258.

189   "There will . . . nomination." Martin, *Hero*, p. 173.

Chapter Seventeen: "Too shallow a puddle"

190   Twenty-two possibilities. Sorensen, *Kennedy*, pp. 162–63.

190   "If they . . . in." Davis, *Politics*, p. 432; Lasky, *RFK*, p. 145.

190   "add more . . . else." Schlesinger, *Thousand Days*, p. 30.

190   "[Muriel] . . . Kennedy." Miller, *Lyndon*, p. 237; Solberg, p. 212.

191   RFK-Otten-Novak. Novak, p. 68; Sorensen, *Kennedy*, p. 165; Schlesinger, *A Thousand Days*, pp. 40–41; Seshol, p. 43.

191   RFK, Jackson. *New York Times*, 14 July 1960, p. 1.

191   Alsop. *Hartford Courant*, 14 July 1960, p. 14.

191   "Stuart Symington . . . nomination." Lincoln, pp. 92–93.

191   "I came . . . decoys." Novak, p. 68.

191   "We are . . . win." Frantz and McKean, p. 158.

192   "You didn't . . . years." Clifford, p. 317.

192   "I don't . . . down." Frantz and McKean, p. 158.

192   "We went . . . head." Mcfarland, p. 110.

192   "I will . . . Lyndon." Clifford, p. 318; Graham, p. 263; Mcfarland, p. 110.

192   Bowles-Humphrey. Bowles, pp. 293–94.

192   HHH-Stevenson. *New York Times*, 14 July 1960, p. 15.

192   Mansfield. *New York Times*, 14 July 1960, p. 15.

192   "Not you . . . ourselves." *Chicago Tribune*, 14 July 1960, p. S2; Dallek, *Unfinished Life*, pp. 266, 269; Cohen and Taylor, pp. 259–60.

192   "You know . . . Senate." Graham, p. 262; Sorensen, *Kennedy*, p. 165; O'Donnell, Powers, and McCarthy, pp. 189–90; Parmet, *JFK*, p. 23.

193   "I must . . . him." Clifford, p. 318; Frantz and McKean, p. 159; Mcfarland, p. 110; Olson, p. 359.

193   "He seemed . . . anyway" *Syracuse Post–Standard*, 15 December 1988, p. 22.

193   A hundred dollars. Clifford, p. 319; Olson, p. 360; Mcfarland, p. 110.

193   "I would . . . nominee." *Chicago Tribune*, 16 July 1960, p. S3.

Chapter Eighteen: "I'm not going to die in office"

194   "Well, that's . . . maybe." Miller, *Lyndon*, p. 253; Woods, p. 360; Mooney, *The Politicians*, p. 335; Mooney, *The Lyndon Johnson Story*, p. 160.

194   "But he'll . . . refuse." Bowles, pp. 293–94. There was little, if any support for LBJ in the JFK camp, but in June 1960 Pierre Salinger had volunteered a "hunch" to reporter Earl Mazo: a JFK-LBJ ticket. Seshol, p. 42.

194   Graham-Alsop-JFK. White, *1964*, p. 430; Graham, p. 262; Sorensen, *Kennedy*, p. 165; Seshol, p. 44; Dallek, *Unfinished Life*, p. 270; Dallek, *Lone Star Rising*, p. 574. Evelyn Lincoln reports that no record of a Monday Alsop meeting exists in her diary. She does report a Sunday meeting. Lincoln, pp. 96–97.

195   "Since writing . . . open." Miller, *Lyndon*, pp. 240, 248.

195   Rayburn. O'Neill, p. 94.

196   Graham-LBJ lunch. White, *1964*, p. 431; Graham, p. 262; Dallek, *Unfinished Life*, p. 271. Actually, Hiram Johnson rejected the vice presidency in 1920. Frank Lowden rejected it in 1924.

196   Corcoran-JFK. Seshol, p. 44; Dallek, *Unfinished Life*, p. 270; Dallek, *Lone Star Rising*, pp. 574–75.

196   O'Neill-JFK. O'Neill, pp. 94–95; Seshol, pp. 44–45; Heymann, *RFK*, p. 167.

196   Graham-JFK. Graham, p. 262. Evelyn Lincoln denies the existence of this Graham memo. Lincoln, p. 98.

196   Alsop column. *Hartford Courant*, 14 July 1960, p. 14.

197   LBJ joke. *Long Beach Press-Telegram*, 19 June 1960, p. B-2.

197   "I want . . . gavel." Mooney, *The Politicians*, p. 335; Sorensen, *Kennedy*, p. 165.

198   "Power is . . . goes." White, *1960*, p. 190; Evans and Novak, p. 280; Eaton, p. 505; Goodwin, *Johnson*, p. 161; Dallek, *Lone Star Rising*, p. 579. Among the most intriguing of theories that LBJ coveted the vice presidency is that proposed by Stuart Symington Jr. that he had heard reports that LBJ had threatened JFK that he would "take a walk if he did not get the nomination . . . and blackmailed Kennedy into it." Mcfarland, p. 111.

198   "The idea . . . it." Schlesinger, *Robert Kennedy*, p. 208.

198   "They would . . . all." Galbraith, *Life*, p. 382. Docking, Loveless, and Freeman all later received positions in Kennedy's administration.

199   Memo dictated to Lincoln. Lincoln, pp. 89–91; Dallek, *Unfinished Life*, p. 271; Martin, *Hero*, p. 174.

199   RFK-Rayburn. Watson, *Chief of Staff*, p. 35. Rayburn dictated an account of RFK's visit to Rayburn to his attorney Roland Boyd, which was later deposited with LBJ White House chief of staff Marvin Watson.

200   "Don't get . . . accept." Seshol, p. 45; Dallek, *Lone Star Rising*, p. 576. In every version of the vice-presidential story, accounts of events and times are often askew. LBJ put the time of Rayburn's advice at 2 A.M., which would *predate* RFK's visit. It is not impossible LBJ was slightly off in his recollection.

200   "If you . . . him." Lincoln, p. 94; Dallek, *Unfinished Life*, p. 271; Martin, *Hero*, p. 175.

200   Shriver. Parmet, *JFK*, pp. 24–25.

200   Lincoln-JFK. Lincoln, p. 95.

200   "my first . . . weeks." Mooney, *The Lyndon Johnson Story*, p. 160.

200   8 A.M. call. Miller, *Lyndon*, pp. 249–50; White, *1960*, p. 189.

200   Thornberry-LBJ. Miller, *Lyndon*, p. 250; Evans and Novak, p. 279.

200   "I was . . . it." Schlesinger, *Robert Kennedy*, p. 208; Thomas, p. 97; Dallek, *Lone Star Rising*, p. 578; Parmet, *JFK*, p. 21; Witcover, p. 153.

201   Boggs-Rayburn. Reston, *Lone Star*, p. 195; Krock, p. 363; O'Brien, *John F. Kennedy*, p. 466; Martin, *Hero*, pp. 174–75; Parmet, *JFK*, p. 27. Theodore White puts the JFK-Rayburn meeting in a corridor following JFK's first meeting with LBJ. White, *1960*, p. 190.

202   "Up until . . . [picture]." Mooney, *The Lyndon Johnson Story*, p. 161.

202 "This is . . . for?" O'Donnell, Powers and McCarthy, p. 221; Dallek, *Lone Star Rising*, p. 579; Martin, *Hero*, p. 178; Dallek, *Unfinished Life*, p. 272.

202 "I'm forty-three . . . on?" O'Donnell, Powers, and McCarthy, p. 221; Schlesinger, *Robert Kennedy*, p. 208; Hersh, *Camelot*, p. 130; Martin, *Hero*, p. 178; Collier and Horowitz, *Kennedys*, p. 213; Dallek, *Unfinished Life*, p. 272.

203 Union leaders. White, *1960*, p. 191; Sorensen, *Kennedy*, p. 165; Schlesinger, *Thousand Days*, pp. 51–52; O'Donnell, Powers, and McCarthy, pp. 222–23; Lasky, *Goldberg*, pp. 23–24.

203 "I don't . . . life." Heymann, *RFK*, p. 168.

203 "They were . . . windows," Heymann, *RFK*, p. 168.

203 "Dave Dubinsky . . . great!" Miller, *Lyndon*, p. 259; Martin, *Hero*, p. 179.

203 "Well, it . . . us." Martin, *Hero*, p. 179.

204 "No you . . . else." White, *1964*, p. 433; Miller, *Lyndon*, p. 260; Graham, p. 264.

204 "Do you . . . Stevenson?" White, *1964*, p. 434; Miller, *Lyndon*, p. 260; Graham, p. 265; Dallek, *Unfinished Life*, p. 271.

204 "Do you . . . me?" Dallek, *Unfinished Life*, p. 53; Dallek, *Lone Star Rising*, p. 580.

204 "You're young . . . now." Evans and Novak, p. 281; Dallek, *Lone Star*, p. 579.

204 "I know . . . happen." Miller, *Lyndon*, p. 257; Dallek, *Lone Star Rising*, p. 579. Not present, but also adamantly opposing LBJ going onto the ticket was another Johnson mentor, Georgia's Richard Russell. Fite, p. 376.

204 "We're not . . . here." Miller, *Lyndon*, p. 257; White, *1964*, p. 435.

204 "I'm a . . . night." Seshol, p. 45; Dallek, *Lone Star Rising*, p. 575; Witcover, p. 154.

204 "Lyndon, if . . . eyes." Miller, *Lyndon*, p. 257; Dallek, *Lone Star Rising*, p. 579.

204 "Graham, my . . . room." Miller, *Lyndon*, p. 261; Dallek, *Unfinished Life*, p. 54.

205 "I've never . . . confusion." Miller, *Lyndon*, p. 261.

205 RFK-Rayburn. Heymann, *RFK*, p. 169; Parmet, *JFK*, p. 29.

205 RFK-LBJ. Dallek, *Unfinished Life*, p. 54; Dallek, *Lone Star Rising*, p. 580; Miller, *Lyndon*, pp. 261–62; Thomas, p. 98; Witcover, p. 156.

205 "Jack, Bobby's . . . withdraw." White, *1964*, p. 436; Heymann, *RFK*, p. 169; Miller, *Lyndon*, p. 261; Dallek, *Unfinished Life*, p. 54.

205 "Oh, that's . . . happening." White, *1964*, p. 436; Dallek, *Unfinished Life*, pp. 54–55; Dallek, *Lone Star Rising*, p. 580.

205 "All right . . . accept." Miller, *Lyndon*, p. 262; Witcover, p. 157.

205 "There is . . . established." Parmet, *JFK*, p. 29.

206 "[Tommy] Corcoran . . . nominated." Martin, *Hero*, p. 164.

206 Rowe-RFK. Dallek, *Unfinished Life*, p. 55; Dallek, *Lone Star Rising*, p. 581; Miller, *Lyndon*, p. 262; Martin, *Destruction*, pp. 259–60; Witcover, p. 158.

206 "When Senator . . . no." Lincoln, p. 103.

206 "Yesterday was . . . life." Seshol, p. 57; Thomas, p. 98.

Chapter Nineteen: "He is not a big man"

207 "I have . . . morning." *Modesto Bee and News–Herald*, 14 July 1960, p. 8.

207 Eleanor leaves LA. Lash, p. 295.

207 Rauh. Martin, *Hero*, p. 168; Lasky, *RFK*, p. 168.

207 "This is . . . terms." Lincoln, p. 102.

207 "It is . . . hypocrite." Connally and Herskowitz, p. 166; Dallek, *Lone Star*, p. 578.

208 Luci Baines Johnson. *Los Angeles Times*, 15 July 1960, p. 1; Hewitt Interview, JFK Library, pp. 6–7.

208 "If *asked* . . . stayed." Martin, *Hero*, p. 181.

208 Rauh, Freeman. Dallek, *Lone Star Rising*, pp. 581–82.

208 "It is . . . struggle." Lichtenstein, p. 356; Boyle, p. 143.

209 "I . . . win." Lasky, *RFK*, p. 167.

209 Voice vote. *Chicago Tribune*, 15 July 1960, pp. 1–2; Dallek, *Lone Star Rising*, p. 582.

209 Morton. Nixon, *Six Crises*, p. 312; Ambrose, *Nixon*), 545; Lasky, *JFK*, p. 406.

209 Ike-Robinson. Ambrose, *Eisenhower: The President*, pp. 696–97.

210 "Don't worry. . . did." Schlesinger, *Robert Kennedy*, p. 211; Lasky, *RFK*, p. 148; Hersh, *Camelot*, p. 123; David and David, p. 112; Leamer, *Kennedy Men*, pp. 436–37; Thomas, p. 98; Parmet, *JFK*, p. 21.

210 Empty seats. O'Brien, *John F. Kennedy*, p. 468; Watson, *Vista*, p. 9; Davis, *Politics*, p. 440.

210 Rented TV. Bradford, p. 130.

210 "There was . . . trick." Collier and Horowitz, *Kennedys*, pp. 214–15; Dallek, *Unfinished Life*, p. 268; Whalen, *Founding Father*, p. 444; Lasky, *JFK*, p. 409.

210 "Well, there's . . . Jack." Kessler, pp. 383–84; Koskoff, pp. 422–23; Martin, *Hero*, p. 182.

211 "It . . . eyes." Sorensen, p. 167; O'Donnell, Powers, and McCarthy, p. 228; Fairlie, p. 82; Schlesinger, *Thousand Days*, pp. 60–61; Matthews, pp. 134–35.

211 Acceptance speech. *New York Times*, 16 July 1960, pp. 1, 6, 7; White, *1960*, pp. 191–92; Sorensen, *Kennedy*, pp. 165–67; Schlesinger, *Thousand Days*, pp. 59–60; O'Donnell, Powers, and McCarthy, pp. 228–29.

212 "Clare I . . . got." Martin, *Hero*, p. 181; Woods, p. 361.

Chapter Twenty: "A two-fisted, four-square liar"

214 "The Governor . . . party." *New York Times*, 23 July 1960, pp. 1, 6; *Chicago Tribune*, 23 July 1960, p. S2; Klein, *Perfectly Clear*, p. 100; White, *1960*, p. 215; Parmet, *Nixon*, p. 386; Kramer and Roberts, p. 231.

214 "But if . . . victory." *New York Times*, 22 July 1960, pp. 1, 9.

214 Gallup poll. *Hartford Courant*, 24 July 1960, p. 12A.

214 Meeting background. White, *1960*, p. 215; Collier and Horowitz, *Rockefellers*, p. 342.

215 Burns. Parmet, *Nixon*, pp. 385–86.

215 Nixon offer. Nixon, *RN*, p. 266; Gervasi, p. 239; Parmet, *Nixon*, p. 387; Schlesinger, *Journals*, p. 84. Henry Kissinger conveyed this information to

Arthur Schlesinger that August.

215 "Rockefeller's independent . . . Kennedy." Nixon, *RN*, pp. 265–66; Wagner, p. 128.

216 Conference call. *New York Times*, 24 July 1960, p. 38; *Chicago Tribune*, 24 July 1960, p. 2; White, *1960*, p. 424.

216 Civil Rights. *New York Times*, 24 July 1960, p. 38; *Chicago Tribune*, 24 July 1960, p. 2; White, *1960*, pp. 425–26.

216 "Nixon made . . . strategy." White, *1960*, p. 223.

217 "as written . . . victory." White, *1960*, pp. 222–23.

217 "That section . . . defenses." Eisenhower, *Mandate*, p. 595; Ambrose, *Eisenhower: The President*, p. 597; Black, p. 396.

217 "That section . . . changes." Eisenhower, *Mandate*, p. 595.

217 "If our . . . Khrushchev." Aitken, p. 270.

217 "What I'm . . .us" Eisenhower, *Mandate*, p. 596; Wagner, p. 130; Ambrose, *Eisenhower: The President*, p. 598.

217 "I left . . . administration." Eisenhower, *Mandate*, p. 596.

217 "There *is* . . . catastrophic." *Chicago Tribune*, 25 July 1960, p. 8; *Chicago Tribune*, 27 July 1960, p. 7; Eisenhower, *Mandate*, p. 596; Ambrose, *Eisenhower: The President*, p. 598.

218 "a man . . . character." Schlesinger, *Thousand Days*, p. 18. When JFK visited Phoenix in 1945, Joe Kennedy advised him to look up the Goldwaters. Blair and Blair, p. 368; Parmet, *Jack*, p. 131.

218 "When you . . . Lincoln." Martin, *Hero*, p. 222.

219 "Charming though . . . serious?" Novak, p. 54.

219 Goldwater column. Shadegg, p. 248; *Los Angeles Times*, 11 September 1960, p. B3; *New York Times*, 11 August 1963, p. 173.

219 Poll numbers. *Hartford Courant*, 20 January 1960, p. 13; Parmet, *Nixon*, p. 382.

219 *Conscience of a Conservative*. Schneider, pp. 26–27; Andrew, p. 46.

219 Youth for Goldwater. Schneider, p. 27.

219 GOP chairmen. *New York Times*, 11 April 1960, p. 18; *Amarillo Globe–Times*, 1 July 1960, p. 18.

219 "I believe . . . it." Ambrose, *Nixon*, p. 505.

220 "Governor Rockefeller . . . Party." *The Reporter*, 1 September 1960, p. 33; *Los Angeles Times*, 13 September 1960, p. B3; White, *1960*, p. 239; Gervasi, p. 239; de Toledano, p. 302; Kramer and Roberts, p. 233; Friedenberg, p. 75; Shadegg, p. 236.

Chapter Twenty-one: "The man who will succeed Dwight D. Eisenhower . . . Richard E. Nixon"

220 "The man . . . liar." Halberstam, *Fifties*, p. 313.

221 666. *New York Times*, 13 June 1960, p. 55; *New York Times*, 28 July 1960, p. 12.

221 Nixons arrive. *Chicago Tribune*, 25 July 1960, p. 21.

221 Motorcade. *Chicago Tribune*, 26 July 1960, p. 9.

222 "I stepped . . . foot." Klein, *Perfectly Clear*, pp. 101–2.

222 52 percent to 48 percent. *Hartford Courant*, 6 July 1960, p. 32.

222 55 percent to 45 percent. Nixon, *RN*, p. 266; Manchester, *Glory*, p. 1077.

222 World respect. *Hartford Courant*, 27 July 1960, p. 3.

222 Better for business. *Hartford Courant*, 29 July 1960, p. 36.

222 Eisenhower arrival. *New York Times*, 27 July 1960, pp. 1, 16; *Chicago Tribune*, 27 July 1960, pp. 1, 11.

223 "soaring record . . . ambition." *New York Times*, 29 July 1960, p. 11.

223 "Within this . . . party." *New York Times*, 29 July 1960, p. 11; Eisenhower, *Mandate*, p. 597.

223 "Every Republican . . . party." *New York Times*, 27 July 1960, p. 17; *Chicago Tribune*, 27 July 1960, pp. 8–9; Eisenhower, *Mandate*, p. 597.

223 "one of . . . made." Nixon, *Six Crises*, p. 316.

223 Eisenhower departs. *Chicago Tribune*, 28 July 1960, p. S5.

224 "Get me . . . Show me," *Chicago Tribune*, 25 July 1960, p. 20; *Tucson Citizen*, 27 July 1960, p. 1; White, *1964*, p. 93.

224 "not a . . . Party." *Chicago Tribune*, 25 July 1960, p. 30.

224 "Senator Goldwater's . . . century." *Hartford Courant*, 28 July 1960, p. 18.

224 Goldwater nomination. *New York Times*, 28 July 1960, p. 13; *Chicago Tribune*, 28 July 1960, p. 6; *Tucson Citizen*, 28 July 1960, p. 6; *Modesto Bee*, 28 July 1960, p. A-5; *Chicago Tribune*, 29 July 1960, p. 8; *Facts on File*, 21 July–27 July 1960, p. 256; White, *1960*, p. 225.

224 Rockefeller straw hat. *Modesto Bee*, 28 July 1960, p. A-5.

224 Charade. Brennan, p. 36; Reinhard, p. 154.

225 "in bedlam . . . overwhelming." Schneider, p. 29.

225 "Republicans have . . . work." *New York Times*, 28 July 1960, pp. 1, 14; *Chicago Tribune*, 28 July 1960, p. 6; Shadegg, p. 270; Perlstein, pp. 94–95; Wagner, p. 131; Andrew, p. 51; Reinhard, p. 155.

225 "Nineteen-. . . means." *Tucson Citizen*, 27 July 1960, p. 1.

225 Hatfield. *Bennington Banner*, 27 July 1960, p. 8.

225 Seconds. *New York Times*, 28 July 1960, p. 12; *Chicago Tribune*, 28 July 1960, p. W6.

225 "the most . . . list." *New York Times*, 23 July 1960, p. 6; *Chicago Tribune*, 25 July 1960, p. B14; *New York Times*, 27 July 1960, p. 16.

225 "I'm a . . . drawl." *New York Times*, 23 July 1960, p. 6.

226 Names percolating. *New York Times*, 22 July 1960, pp. 1, 8; *Chicago Tribune*, 22 July 1960, p. 3. Byrnes ran as a Wisconsin favorite-son candidate in 1964.

226 "Some people . . . welfare-stater." *El Paso Herald–Post*, 28 July 1960, p. 6.

226 Judd, keynoter. Nixon, *Six Crises*, p. 317; Nixon, *RN*, p. 266.

226 Narrows to three. Nixon, *RN*, p. 266.

226 Morton. Nixon, *RN*, p. 266.

226 Judd. *New York Times*, 15 February 1994, p. A19.

226 Lodge. *New York Times*, 27 May 27, 1960, p. 1, 5; *New York Times*, 27 May 28, 1960, p. 5.

227 Lodge voting record. Lodge, p. 262.

227   Decided in spring. Lodge, p. 183.

227   Sheraton-Blackstone meeting. *New York Times*, 29 July 1960, p. 8; *Galveston Daily News*, 3 August 1960, p. 4.

227   "You can . . . St. Louis." *Lima News*, 3 August 1960, p. 10; White, *1960*, p. 226.

228   "It we . . . be." *New York Times*, 29 July 1960, p. 8.

228   Morton suggests Lodge. Nixon, *RN*, p. 266.

228   Reece, Bricker. *Galveston Daily News*, 3 August 1960, p. 4.

228   2:25 call. Nixon, *RN*, p. 267; Lodge, p. 183.

228   Off the hook. *New York Times*, 24 September 1952, p. 21.

228   "a disastrous blunder." Goldwater, *With No Apologies*, p. 119; Aitken, p. 271.

228   "That's the . . . door." Matthews, p. 136.

229   "The Kennedys . . . society." Whalen, *Lodge versus Kennedy*, p. 8.

229   Stratton 1956 win. *Chicago Tribune*, 28 November 1956, p. B10.

229   Lodge delays departure. *Chicago Tribune*, 28 July 1960, p. W9.

229   "the best . . . Washington." *Chicago Tribune*, 29 July 1960, pp. 4, 8.

229   Ford seconds. *New York Times*, 29 July 1960, p. 8; *Chicago Tribune*, 29 July 1960, p. 4.

230   "expend every . . . energy" *New York Times*, 29 July 1960, p. 10; *Chicago Tribune*, 29 July 1960, pp. 1, 5.

230   "and the . . . Nixon." *Chicago Tribune*, 29 July 1960, p. 1.

230   Sleepless Nixon. Aitken, p. 271.

230   First since Truman. *Chicago Tribune*, 29 July 1960, p. 8.

230   "One hundred . . . States." *New York Times*, 29 July 1960, p. 9; Nixon, *Six Crises*, p. 319; de Toledano, p. 303.

231   "I remember . . . big." Benson, p. 532.

231   "sent millions . . . bell." *New Republic*, 8 August 1960, p. 2; *New Republic*, 7 November 1960, p. 2.

231   "brilliant." Matthews, p. 136.

231   "I have . . . time!" *Chicago Tribune*, 29 July 1960, p. 4. It was a girl.

231   "Yes . . . anything." http://journalism.nyu.edu/pubzone/weblogs/pressthink/2004/07/21/mailer_con_p.html.

232   "Charlie, we . . .man." Perret, *Eisenhower*, p. 597.

Chapter Twenty-two: "Why do you think they did that, Sammy?"

233   Joe Kennedy. Koskoff, pp. 27–41; Kessler, pp. 51–59; Schwarz, pp. 116–33, 268.

233   "There are . . . business." Whalen, *Founding Father*, p. 455.

233   Warner. Gabler, *Empire*, p. 317; Berg, p. 402.

233   Stevenson supporters. *Hayward Daily Review*, 22 June 1960, p. 48; *Long Beach Press-Telegram*, 14 July 1960, p. 4; *Chicago Tribune*, 16 October 1960, p. B16.

233   "Get your . . . creep." Kelley, *His Way*, p. 244; Levy, p. 69.

234   "Let's just . . . all." Levy, p. 72.

234   Cooper houseparty. Levy, p. 69.

234   Sinatra campaigning. *San Antonio Light*, 24 October 1958, p. 39.

234   Sinatra endorsement. Lasky, JFK, p. 352.

234   "Do you . . . you." Levy, p. 71.

234   "I had . . . stardom." Levy, p. 144.

235   Joe Kennedy, "High Hopes." Heymann, *Jackie*, p. 214.

235   "High Hopes" lyrics. *New York Times*, 21 March 1960, p. 24; Kelley, *His Way*, p. 270; Summers and Swan, p. 262.

235   Sound trucks. *The Reporter*, 17 March 1960, p. 30.

235   "Senator Humphrey's . . . state." Lasky, *RFK*, p. 149.

235   "He [RFK] . . . campaign." Davis, *Why Me?*, p. 112.

235   Gala. *Hayward Daily Review*, 22 June 1960, p. 48; *Chicago Tribune*, 16 October 1960, p. B16; Kelley, His Way, p. 276.

235   Anthem chorus. *Van Nuys News*, 14 July 1960, p. 24A; Tosches, p. 345.

236   Davis booing. *New York Times*, 12 July 1960, p. 23; *Chicago Tribune*, 12 July 1960, p. 3; *Chicago Defender*, 12 July 1960, p. 3; Davis, *Yes I Can*, pp. 548–49; Kelley, pp. 276–77.

236   Sinatra's head. Kelley, His Way, p. 277.

236   "We're on . . . House." Levy, p. 165.

236   Cal-Neva Lodge. Tosches, p. 345; Summers and Swan, p. 289; Levy, p. 244; Quirk and Schoell, p. 149.

237   "I'd like . . . doing." Tosches, p. 345.

237   Hate mail. Davis, *Sammy*, pp. 377–78; Levy, p. 67. When Sammy was scheduled to attend JFK's inaugural, Joe Kennedy's language wasn't much better, complaining to Sinatra about "the nigger bastard with the German [sic] whore." Jacobs and Stadiem, p. 163.

237   "Public opinion . . . rallies." Davis, *Why Me?*, p. 117; Davis, *Yes I Can*, p. 558; Davis, *Sammy*, p. 377.

237   Dean Martin. *El Paso Herald Post*, 5 September 1960, p. 6; Davis, *Yes I Can*, p. 562.

237   "I have . . . sacrifice." *Pittsburgh Courier*, 13 August 1960, p. 23.

238   "Look what . . . election." Davis, *Why Me?*, pp. 118–19; Davis, *Yes I Can*, pp. 563–64; Davis, *Sammy*, p. 379.

238   Informed Sinatra first. Davis, *Why Me?*, pp. 119–20; Davis, *Yes I Can*, p. 565; Davis, *Sammy*, pp. 379–80.

238   "That was . . . it." Davis, *Why Me?*, p. 120; Davis, *Sammy*, p. 380.

238   *The House I Live In*. Roberts and Olson, pp. 471–72; Quirk and Schoell, pp. 150–51; Kelley, *His Way*, p. 271.

239   Ward Bond. *Los Angeles Times*, 9 April 1960, p. 1.

239   "I wonder . . . country." *San Mateo Times*, 26 March 1960, p. 10; Kelley, *His Way*, p. 273; Levy, p. 158.

239   "What kind . . . record?" Kelley, *His Way*, p. 273.

240   "Frank Sinatra . . . money?" *Charleston Daily Mail*, 31 March 1960, p. 44.

240   "Under the . . . job." *Los Angeles Times*, 26 March 1960, p. 2; Rouverol, p. 241; Kelley, *His Way*, p. 273.

241   Elvis. Levy, p. 158.

241 "General Motors . . . company." Kelley, *His Way*, p. 274; Levy, p. 158.

241 "The situation . . . connection." *Coshocton Tribune*, 17 April 1960, p. 4; Lewis, p. 267.

241 "That's when . . . day." Kelley, *His Way*, p. 274.

241 April 12 ad. *Los Angeles Times*, 9 April 1960, p. 1; *New York Times*, 12 April 1960, p. 28; *Chicago Defender*, 12 April 1960, p. A16; Rouverol, pp. 241–42; Kelley, *His Way*, pp. 274–75.

241 "God . . . was concerned." Kelley, *His Way*, p. 271; Levy, p. 158.

241 "What is . . . guinea!" Levy, pp. 144–45.

241 "Mr. S" Jacobs and Stadiem, p. 472.

242 Children with mental retardation. *Los Angeles Times*, 16 May 1960, p. B1.

242 Hundred-dollar-a-plate. *Oakland Tribune*, 14 May 1960, p. 1; *Hartford Courant*, 15 May 1960, p. 7A.

242 Attendees. *Oakland Tribune*, 14 May 1960, p. 1; *Hartford Courant*, 15 May 1960, p. 7A; *Los Angeles Times*, 16 May 1960, p. B1.

242 Wayne-Sinatra. *Oakland Tribune*, 14 May 1960, p. 1; *Hartford Courant*, 15 May 1960, p. 7A; *Los Angeles Times*, 16 May 1960, p. B1; *Chicago Tribune*, 16 May 1960, p. 18; Kelley, p. 275; Levy, p. 159; Roberts and Olson, pp. 471–72.

243 "Although Mr. . . . that." Jacobs and Stadiem, p. 151.

243 Lady May Lawford-Mayer. Spada, pp. 93–95; Wayne, pp. 282, 287.

243 "barefoot Irish peasants" Lawford, *Symptoms of Withdrawal*, p. 10; Lawford, *Bitch!*, p. 62; Maier, p. 256; Wayne, p. 287; Leamer, *Kennedy Women*, p. 449.

243 "bogrotters." Spada, p. 263.

243 Mazo. Lasky, *RFK*, p. 141.

243 "Peter Lawford's . . . that!" *El Paso Herald Post*, 5 September 1960, p. 6.

244 "No love . . . Dealers." *Nevada State Journal*, 6 August 1960, p. 4.

244 "Whoever pays . . . fee." *Lowell Sun*, 23 October 1960, p. 3.

Chapter Twenty-three: "Nothing takes precedence over his oath to uphold the Constitution"

245 "He loved . . . seeing." Hersh, *Camelot*, p. 300.

245 "While we . . . Carlyle." Goodwin, p. 752.

245 Not until 22. Blair and Blair, pp. 68–71; Friedenberg, p. 33.

245 "This is . . . father." Reeves, *Character*, p. 57.

245 "I wish . . . together." Martin, *Hero*, p. 217.

245 JFK-JPK-Jackie. Martin, *Hero*, p. 216.

245 Spalding-JFK. Martin, *Hero*, pp. 216–17; Perret, *Jack*, p. 260.

246 Sunday Mass. Maier, p. 372. He may have attended more at Camp David.

246 "I want . . . religion." Exner, pp. 91–92.

246 "I am . . . faith." Schlesinger, *Robert Kennedy*, p. 55. On the other hand, JPK mistress Janet Des Rosiers was not impressed by *Joe's* Catholicism: "He never went to church, I don't think. He never talked about it . . . he did not go to confession. Oh God! If a priest heard his confession." Kessler, p. 328.

246 "I think . . . it." Wills, *Kennedy Imprisonment*, p. 61; Martin, *Hero*, p. 217;

Collier and Horowitz, *Kennedys*, pp. 207–8; Harper and Krieg, p. 287.

246   "He'd be . . . him." Martin, *Hero*, p. 217.

246   "In general . . . society." Fay, pp. 240–41.

247   "Now, what . . . forces." *New York Times*, 24 November 1957, p. 148; *New York Times*, 25 November 1957, p. 33.

247   *Look*, March 3, 1959, pp. 13–17; *Chicago Defender*, 17 February 1959, p. 5; Burns, p. 228; McCarthy, p. 137; Harper and Krieg, p. 287; Wofford, p. 38.

247   Flannery. *Lowell Sun*, 9 March 1959, p. 1.

247   *America, Commonweal. Charleston Gazette*, 2 March 1959, p. 25; *Morgantown Dominion-News*, 2 March 1959, pp. 1–2; *Florence Morning News*, 2 March 1960, p. 1; Burns, p. 228; McCarthy, pp. 137–38.

248   Cushing. *Bridgeport Post*, 9 March 1960, p. 2; *Lowell Sun*, 9 March 1960, p. 1; Burns, p. 229.

248   Lowell. Burns, p. 229.

248   *L'Osservatore Romano. Long Beach Press-Telegram*, 18 May 1960, p. A-8; *New York Times*, 15 January 1960, pp. 1, 14; Harper and Krieg, pp. 173–74; Ambrose, *Nixon*, p. 545. In his September 1960 meeting with the Greater Houston Ministerial Association, JFK remarkably claimed he was "not familiar with this statement." *New York Times*, 13 September 1960, p. 22.

248   Puerto Rico. *Facts on File*, 26 October 1960, p. 369; *The Reporter*, 27 October 1960, p. 26; *Western Political Quarterly*, December 1965, pp. 821–39; Sorensen, p. 209; Fuchs, pp. 183–85.

249   "Now I . . . church." Schlesinger, *Thousand Days*, p. 106; Sorensen, *Kennedy*, p. 148; Harper and Krieg, p. 275; Parmet, *JFK*, p. 38.

249   "Catholic baiting . . . liberals." Dallek, *Unfinished Life*, p. 232; Maier, p. 319.

249   Contraceptives. *New York Times*, 24 January 1960, p. BR32. The contraceptives issue briefly dogged JFK in 1959, during a debate over whether the U.S. should provide contraceptives as part of its foreign aid program. JFK, indicating opposition, faced the suspicion that he took orders from Rome. He was let off the hook when Ike announced his own opposition. McCarthy, pp. 139–40.

249   "There was . . . delegation." Interview of Frederick G. Dutton, Governmental History Documentation Project; Regional Oral History Office University of California, pp. 66–67.

249   "Chapel of the Four Chaplains" incident. *New York Times*, 15 January 1960, pp. 1, 14; *New York Times*, 13 September 1960, p. 22; Harper and Krieg, pp. 173–74; O'Brien, *Kennedy*, pp. 420–21.
        December 1958 ER-JFK clash. Lash, pp. 281–82.

250   "Somewhere deep . . . heritage," Lash, p. 282.

250   Roosevelt-Lasker. Lash, p. 282.

251   Montreux. Martin, *Destruction*, pp. 248–49.

251   "a serious . . . communism." Fuchs, p. 176; O'Brien, *Kennedy*, p. 473; Friedenberg, p. 51.

251   "We cannot . . . hierarchy." Fuchs, pp. 177–78; Friedenberg, p. 51.

251   Honeycutt. *Florence News* 21 July 1960, p. 5.

251   National Council of Citizens for Religious Freedom. *New York Times*, 8 September 1960, pp. 1, 25; *Los Angeles Times*, 9 September 1960, p. 8.

252   "By recommendation . . . state?" *New York Times*, 8 September 1960, p. 25.

252   "a disservice . . . Protestantism." *Fresno Bee*, 14 September 1960, p. 3–A.

252   "I find . . . appalling." *New York Times*, 26, December 1993, p. 40; Ambrose, *Nixon*, p. 564; O'Brien, *Kennedy*, p. 474. Stevenson, however, was not above remarking that he found the absence of discussion of Nixon's Quakerism "curious." *Chicago Tribune*, 12 September 1960, p. 8.

252   "Religious freedom . . . unconstitutional." Roosevelt, pp. 288–89.

252   "I was not . . . stupid." *Chicago Tribune*, 15 September 1960, p. Q3; O'Brien, *Kennedy*, p. 474.

252   "All I . . . do." Collier and Horowitz, *Kennedys*, p. 217

253   JPK-Spellman. Kessler, pp. 385–86; Collier and Horowitz, *Kennedys*, p. 217; Parmet, *JFK*, p. 38. Joe welshed on four hundred thousand dollars in pledges to New York archdiocesan charities and did not invite Spellman to the inauguration.

253   JPK-Cushing. Kessler, p. 379. In 1972 former Joe Kennedy aide Frank Morrissey revealed that he had once helped Joe remove over a million dollars in cash from the basement of his Hyannis Port home. "A big northeast storm was coming up," recalled Farrell, "The old man was afraid a lot of the cash would get wet." Kessler, pp. 385–86.

253   RFK. *New York Times*, 25 August 1960, p. 20; *Chicago Tribune*, 26 August 1960, p. 6; Lasky, *RFK*, p. 177; Lasky, *Watergate*, p. 45; Jamieson, p. 136; Silvestri, p. 118.

253   Jackson. *New York Times*, 13 September 1960, p. 25; *Fresno Bee*, 14 September 1960, p. 3–A.

253   "Who used . . . shots?" *Chicago Tribune*, 19 September 1960, p. 20.

253   Investigators. *Chicago Tribune*, 25 July 1973, p. 7; *Tucson Citizen*, 25 July 1960, p. 1; *Chicago Tribune*, 30 July 1973, p. 6; Lasky, *Watergate*, p. 48.

254   "Nixon was . . . calls" Jamieson, p. 127.

254   "I absolutely . . . grandsons." *New York Times*, 13 September 1960, p. 25.

254   *Lubbock Avalanche-Journal. Lima News*, 20 September 1960, p. 6.

254   *Hope Star. Lima News*, 20 September 1960, p. 6.

254   Graham-Salinger. Salinger, *With Kennedy*, p. 58; Salinger, *PS:*, pp. 74–75; Parmet, *Jack*, pp. 516–17.

254   Graham-Judd. Diamond, p. 104.

254   South Carolina rally. *New York Times*, 2 November 1960, p. 19; *Modesto Bee*, 3 November 1960, p. 6; *New York Times*, 4 November 1960, p. 1.

255   *Life*. Nixon, *Six Crises*, p. 365.

255   "They hate . . . guts." O'Brien, *Kennedy*, p. 475.

255   JPK, Rayburn opposed. Martin, *Hero*, p. 219. Nixon had refused a similar invitation. Silvestri, p. 119.

255   Q-and-A only. Friedenberg, p. 53.

255   "This . . . campaign." Martin, *Hero*, p. 219.

255   "What's the . . . bigots?" Friedenberg, p. 53.

255　1959 Methodist meeting. *New York Times*, 16 April 1959, p. 22; *New York Times*, 1 August 1960, p. 14; Burns, pp. 229–30.

255　"I believe . . . him." *New York Times*, 13 September 1960, p. 25; White, pp. 427–430; Davis, *Kennedys*, pp. 297–98; Fuchs, p. 179; Dallek, *Unfinished Life*, pp. 283–84.

256　"Side by . . . Alamo." *New York Times*, 13 September 1960, p. 22; O'Brien, *Kennedy*, pp. 476–77; Jamieson, p. 132; Reston, *Lone Star*, p. 198; Silvestri, "I am . . . otherwise." p. 126; Parmet, *JFK*, p. 42.

256　"If the . . . likewise." *New York Times*, 13 September 1960, p. 22; Friedenberg, p. 59; Silvestri, p. 126; Harper and Krieg, p. 278; Fuchs, p. 180.

257　Syllabus of Errors. Fuchs, p. 181; Lasky, *RFK*, p. 155.

257　"So I . . . judgement." *New York Times*, 13 September 1960, p. 25.

257　"As we . . . President." O'Donnell, Powers and McCarthy, p. 241; Lincoln, p. 123; Dallek, *Unfinished Life*, p. 284; Martin, *Hero*, p. 219; Steinberg, p. 331; Silvestri, p. 123.

257　Television. Jamieson, p. 136; Silvestri, pp. 123–24; Felknor, p. 91; Parmet, *JFK*, p. 44; O'Brien, *Kennedy*, p. 474.

257　"Senator Kennedy . . . along." *Galveston News*, 5 July 1960, p. 21; Moody, p. 346.

257　"I was . . . election." O'Brien Interview I, LBJ Library, p. 16.

258　"What kind . . ."; ". . . on Sundays." Martin, *Hero*, p. 217.

Chapter Twenty-four: "Matt Dillon ain't popular for nothing"

259　LBJ absent. Friedenberg, p. 54.

259　Jackson. Evans and Novak, pp. 289–90. Jackson became the first Protestant Democratic national chairman since Tennessee congressman Cordell Hull in 1925.

259　"I think . . . it." Evans and Novak, p. 290.

259　"Let's Beat Judas." Mooney, *The Politicians*, p. 349.

260　Russell. Fite, pp. 376–77.

260　LBJ drinking. Dallek, *Flawed Giant*, p. 4.

260　Acapulco. Evans and Novak, pp. 290–91.

260　"I want . . . ticket." Valenti, *A Very Human President*, pp. 16–17.

260　LBJ-Lisagor-RFK. Koskoff, pp. 423–24; Collier and Horowitz, *Kennedys*, p. 212; Miller, *Lyndon*, p. 241; Schlesinger, *Robert Kennedy*, p. 205; Dallek, *Lone Star Rising*, pp. 572–73; O'Brien, *Kennedy*, p. 462; Reston, *Lone Star*, p. 189; Martin, *Destruction*, p. 262; Leamer, *Kennedy Men*, p. 435; Dallek, *Flawed Giant*, pp. 33–34; Seshol, p. 59.

261　Fog. *San Antonio Express and News*, 30 July 1960, p. 1; *Bridgeport Telegram*, 30 July 1960, pp. 1–2; Parmet, *JFK*, p. 52.

261　"but she . . . that." Martin, *Destruction*, p. 263.

261　"Jack Kennedy . . . room." Woods, p. 366.

261　Eavesdropping. Novak, p. 71.

261　"You got . . . nothing." Evans and Novak, p. 293; Novak, p. 72.

261 Reedy, Salinger. Evans and Novak, p. 293; Novak, p. 72.

262 Special Session. *Winona Daily News*, 27 August 1960, p. 6. Lasky, *JFK*, pp. 418–26; Evans and Novak, pp. 291–92; Dallek, *Lone Star Rising*, p. 584; Nixon, *Six Crises*, p. 324; Eisenhower, *Mandate*, p. 598.

262 "We are . . . business." Parmet, *JFK*, p. 50.

262 "In an . . . plowing." Busby, p. 110.

262 "I was . . . week." Woods, pp. 372–73.

262 "Somebody ought . . . jaw." Woods, p. 373.

263 "If Kennedy . . . liberals." Lincoln, p. 125.

263 Byrd. Sorensen, *Kennedy*, p. 188; Lasky, *JFK*, p. 417.

263 Shivers. *Chicago Tribune*, 25 September 1960, p. 29; *Los Angeles Times*, 25 September 1960, p. C3.

263 "No one . . . Angeles." Parmet, *JFK*, p. 50.

263 Rayburn. Evans and Novak, p. 298.

263 Golf course. Mooney, *The Politicians*, p. 349.

263 "constitutional rights . . . lived." Mooney, *The Politicians*, p. 349.

264 Culpepper. Evans and Novak, p. 303; Dallek, *Lone Star Rising*, p. 586.

264 Russell, Talmadge. Fite, pp. 378–79; Henderson, p. 123; Dallek, *Lone Star Rising*, p. 584.

264 "Lyndon Johnson . . . Court." Lincoln, p. 125.

264 "we of . . . South." *Journal of Negro History*, January 1977, p. 37.

264 "I'll tell . . . you." Dallek, *Lone Star Rising*, p. 584; Woods, p. 367.

264 Cornpone Express. Dallek, *Lone Star Rising*, p. 586; Lincoln, p. 124; Mooney, *The Politicians*, p. 349.

264 1,247 politicians. Mooney, *The Politicians*, p. 349.

265 Georgia, Louisiana. *Winona Daily News*, 27 August 1960, p. 6; Henderson, p. 122.

265 "In the . . . city?" Donaldson, p. 135.

265 "We were . . . concerned." Caro, *Master*, p. 335.

265 "Our polls . . . fine." Jamieson, pp. 155–56.

265 "If it . . . way." *Hartford Courant*, 10 September 1960, p. 1; Evans and Novak, p. 299. Ironically, it was a vengeful LBJ who had initiated the most concrete action barring religious political activity. In 1954's Texas Democratic primary, two right-wing non-profit foundations—H. L. Hunt's Facts Forum and the New York–based Committee for Constitutional Government—had angered Johnson by aiding his primary opponent, thirty-one-year-old state senator Dudley T. Dougherty. That July, Johnson slipped a provision into the tax code stripping non-profits, and inadvertently churches), of their tax-exempt status if they became involved in politics. *Review of Religious Research*, September 1998, pp. 16–34.

265 "During the . . . feeling." Miller, Lyndon, p. 268.

266 JFK against VP debate. Sorensen, *Kennedy*, p. 197.

266 "If you're . . . thing." Stanton Interview, JFK Library, p. 13. Lodge, lazy as ever, wasn't interested either.

266 "The voters . . . ticket." *Long Beach Press Telegram*, 7 September 1960, p. 3;

Lasky, *JFK*, pp. 434–35.

266   Schlesinger-LBJ. *Elyria Chronicle Telegram* 30 September 1960, p. 2.

266   RFK-Singleton. Reston, *Lone Star*, pp. 196–97; Woods, p. 372.

267   "I believe . . . up." Dallek, *Lone Star Rising*, p. 587; Woods, p. 373.

267   "I was . . . me." Lincoln, pp. 103–4;
     http://www.jfklink.com/speeches/jfk/sept60/jfk120960_elpaso01.html.

267   "I am . . . once." Reston, *Lone Star*, p. 198.

267   "The burial . . . doing?" *New York Times*, 23 October 1960, p. 89; Miller,
     Lyndon, p. 272; Woods, p. 370.

Chapter Twenty-five: "Nixon did everything but sweep out the plane"

268   Nixon lead. *Hartford Courant*, 17 August 1960, p. 19; *New York Times*, 18
     August 1960, p. 1; *New York Times*, 21 August 1960. p. 47; De Toledano, p.
     303; Manchester, *Glory*, p. 1078; Brodie, p. 423.

268   "For whatever . . . Kennedy." Mathews, p. 178.

269   "I cannot . . . philosophy." *New York Times*, 16 October 1960, p. 52;
     http://www.jfklink.com/speeches/jfk/oct60/jfk151060_newcastle01.html.

269   "felt sorry . . . exhausting." Wicker, p. 257; Mathews, p. 147; Halberstam,
     Fifties, p. 722.

269   Rockefeller. Safire, p. 28.

269   "as though . . . necessary." Novak, p. 74.

269   ERA. *New York Times*, 3 September 1960, p. 18. The 1960 GOP platform
     also supported the ERA.

270   Buckley. Bridges and Coyne, p. 69.

270   "super-beatnik . . . Roosevelt" Jeansonne, p. 165.

270   JBS. *Appleton Post-Crescent*, 10 August 1960, p. 12.

270   "I summon . . . Nixon." Kolkey, p. 31.

270   "Nixon made . . . South." Novak, p. 75.

270   "I'm for . . . nomination." Cook, p. 129.

271   "And I . . . that." *Chicago Tribune*, 28 October 1960, p. S4; Committee on
     Commerce, p. 818; Klein, *Perfectly Clear*, p. 97.

271   Fort Wayne. *Chicago Tribune*, 28 October 1960, p. 1.

271   Entertainers. *New York Times*, 25 September 1960, p. X9; *Los Angeles Times*,
     27 September 1960, p. 10; *Lowell Sun*, 23 October 1960, p. 3; *Tucson Daily
     Citizen*, 29 October 1960, p. 43; *Bridgeport Post*, 29 October 1960, p. 17;
     Ada Evening News, 31 October 1960, p. 5; *Winona Daily News*, 5 November
     1960, p. 12; *Long Beach Press-Telegram*, 7 November 1960, p. A-12;
     Pasadena Star-News, 11 November 1960, p. 7; Ambrose, *Nixon*, pp. 562–63.

271   "In watching . . . religion." Reagan, *Nancy*, p. 154.

271   "I think . . . Nixon." *Van Nuys Valley News*, 4 November 1960, p. 7-A;
     Reagan, *Life*, pp. 133–34.

271   "He tried . . . down." Reagan, *Life*, pp. 133–34.

271   "Under . . . bureau." Ambrose, *Nixon*, p. 546; Black, p. 395.

272   "We're the . . . publicity." *Lowell Sun*, 23 October 1960, p. 3.

272   "It's just . . . them." *Lowell Sun*, 23 October 1960, p. 3.

272   "Very soon . . . Men." Roberts and Olson, pp. 473. Sammy Davis wanted a part in *The Alamo*. Though Wayne was interested, his Texas investors thought Davis was uppity and failed to appreciate his engagement to May Britt. The role went to Jester Hairston, a sixteen-year veteran of *The Amos and Andy Show*, and actually a small-scale Renaissance man of black performers—a Julliard-trained Tufts graduate, actor, songwriter, theatrical director, and conductor, composer of Harry Belafonte's 1956 hit "Boy Child Jesus" and Sidney Poitier's singing voice in *Lilies of the Field*. Roberts and Olson, p. 461.

273   Colson. O'Neill, p. 158.

273   Gray. White, *Breach*, p. 84.

273   "There was . . . position." Halberstam, *Powers*, p. 334.

273   Hall-Finch dichotomy. White, *Breach*, p. 84.

273   "shrewd, attractive . . . politician." de Toledano, p. 293.

274   "There was . . . politics." White, *1968*, p. 175.

274   "In Congress . . . firmness." Ehrlichman, p. 47.

274   Hall-Finch. de Toledano, p. 304.

274   "I felt . . . daily." Nixon, *Six Crises*, p. 330.

274   "Nixon did . . . be." Jamieson, pp. 151–52.

274   "As the campaign . . . direct." White, *Breach*, p. 84.

275   Eighteen advance men. White, *Breach*, p. 83.

275   Haldeman gains power. White, *Breach*, p. 85.

275   "Nixon gets . . . opinions." White, *1968*, pp. 174–75.

275   "It was . . . Nixon." Jamieson, p. 151.

275   "Haldeman liked . . . disaster." White, *Breach*, p. 84.

275   "darkness reaching for darkness." Halberstam, *Powers*, p. 335.

275   "The Nixon . . . [later]." Jamieson, p. 151.

276   "Bob, from . . . airports." Ehrlichman, p. 24.

276   Warner. Ehrlichman, p. 25.

276   "Nixon seethed . . . us." Haldeman, pp. 74–75; Ambrose, *Nixon*, p. 568.

276   "One could . . . Iowa." White, *1960*, pp. 276–78.

276   Lodge popularity. *Hartford Courant*, 17 August 1960, p. 19; *Hartford Courant*, 19 August 1960, p. 36.

277   "my good man." de Toledano, p. 303.

277   "He was . . . take." White, *1964*, p. 88.

277   "looked . . . true." Wyckoff, p. 49; Jamieson, p. 157.

277   Indiana. *Odessa American*, 23 September 1960, p. 1.

277   Lodge carping. Lodge, pp. 185–87.

277   Laziness. De Toledano, p. 303.

277   6 P.M. Brooke, p. 156.

277   "There are . . . exhausted." Whelan, *Lodge*, p. 174.

277   "We didn't . . . pajamas?" Whelan, *Lodge*, p. 174.

277   Wyckoff experiences. Wyckoff, pp. 46–49.

278   Lodge, Moscow. Beschloss, *The Crisis Years*, p. 35.

279   U-2 deal. Beschloss, *The Crisis Years*, p. 36.

279   Salt Lake City. Benson, pp. 542–43.

279   "The Vice President . . . men." Benson, p. 542.

279   "I have . . . commercial." Brodie, p. 421. *New York Times*, 9 September 1960, p. 28; *Los Angeles Times*, 9 September 1960, p. 2.

280   "He took . . . him." Greenberg, p. 134.

280   "He was . . . ceiling." Greenberg, pp. 134–35.

280   "When I . . . answer." Bradlee, *Life*, pp. 211–12.

280   *Modesto Bee*, 3 November 1960, p. A4; White, *1960*, p. 360.

280   "Ninety per . . . platform." *Human Events*, 17 February 1961, p. 213.

280   "No. I . . . Nixon." Novak, p. 73.

281   "[Nixon] . . . 1960." Kuralt, p. 55.

281   Scranton. Committee on Commerce, pp. 183–89; Klein, *Perfectly Clear*, pp. 88–91. Sylvester later joined the Kennedy administration. When Lawrence, a JFK golfing buddy, joined ABC News in 1961 he sought Kennedy's advice on the move. *Tucson Daily Citizen*, 3 March 1972, p. 38.

281   Springfield. Committee on Commerce, pp. 216–22; Klein, *Perfectly Clear*, pp. 91–92.

281   Woods. Klein, *Perfectly Clear*, p. 98; Ambrose, *Nixon*, p. 561.

Chapter Twenty-six: "I seen him, I seen him"

282   Sara Delano Roosevelt. *New York Times*, 13 August 1960, p. 12; *New York Times*, 14 August 1960, p. 25; *Troy Record*, 15 August 1960, pp. 1, 14; Martin, *Hero*, p. 221.

282   "That young . . . do." Martin, *Hero*, p. 220.

282   "Pigheaded, mean. . . spiteful." Martin, *Hero*, p. 220.

282   Gurevich, Vidal. Vidal, *Palimpsest*, p. 347.

283   Florida governor. ER to Mary Lasker, August 15, 1960; Perret, *Jack*, p. 259.

283   "I've come . . . had." Parmet, *JFK*, pp. 35–36.

283   Stevenson appointment. Lash, p. 297; Parmet, *JFK*, p. 36.

283   "The Senator . . . his mind." O'Donnell, Powers, and McCarthy, p. 233.

283   "He has . . . goes on." Martin, *Hero*, p. 220.

283   "I also . . ."; ". . . elected." ER to Mary Lasker, August 15, 1960; Parmet, *JFK*, pp. 35–36; Dallek, *Unfinished Life*, p. 278.

283   "I don't . . . him." Martin, *Hero*, pp. 220–21.

284   "Kennedy has . . . move." Lasky, *JFK*, pp. 415–16; Roosevelt, pp. 286–87.

284   "I recognize . . . pocket." *Middleton Times–Herald*, 24 January 1949, p. 4; Pilat, p. 13.

284   "It's not . . . pop." Miller, *Plain Speaking*, p. 187; McCullough, p. 970; Maier, p. 341; Summers and Swan, p. 270.

284   "Harry, what . . . Joe?" Miller, *Plain Speaking*, p. 186; Blair and Blair, p. 350; Madsen, pp. 191–92.

284   "I just . . . him." Miller, *Plain Speaking*, p. 409; Schlesinger, *Robert Kennedy*, p. 214; McCullough, p. 981.

285   KKK. *Lowell Sun*, 28 October 1944, p. 17.

285 "The choice . . . satisfaction." *New York Times*, 21 August 1960, p. 1; O'Donnell, Powers, and McCarthy, p. 232.

285 "I never . . . him." Dallek, *Unfinished Life*, p. 278. Nixon never did call Truman a communist. In Texas, in October 1952 he damned HST, Adlai Stevenson, and Dean Acheson as "traitors to the high principles in which many of the nation's Democrats believe" which Truman translated into actual traitors and finally into communists. *New York Times*, 28 October 1952, p. 14.

285 "You and . . . future." Ferrell, ed., pp. 390–91.

286 Truman Q and A. *New York Times*, 21 August 1960, pp. 1, 46; Lasky, *JFK*, pp. 416–17.

286 "the second . . . compromise." *Oshkosh Northwestern*, 23 August 1960, p. 6.

286 "If Nixon . . . hell." *New York Times*, 12 October 1960, p. 1; Reston, p. 196; Brodie, p. 422.

287 "I have . . . issue." *Oakland Tribune*, 20 October 1960, p. 3.

287 Reuther. Lichtenstein, pp. 356–57.

287 Detroit. *Los Angeles Times*, 5 September 1960, pp. 1, 2; Bruno and Greenfield, p. 47; Fairlie, p. 57.

288 "The jumpers . . . partnership." White, *1960*, p. 361.

288 "John F. . . . water." Wills, *Kennedy Imprisonment*, p. 14.

289 "Kennedy has . . . speech." *Portsmouth Times*, 3 November 1960, p. 33.

289 "Those ——ers . . . hands." Martin, *Hero*, p. 196.

289 NYC crowds. *New York Times*, 20 October 1960, p. 1, 25.

290 JFK, Bradlee. Bradlee, *Conversations*, p. 20.

290 O'Brien. O'Brien, *Victories*, p. 93.

Chapter Twenty-seven: "You bombthrowers probably lost the election"

291 Population. Franklin, p. 620; *Chicago Defender*, 26 November 1958, p. 4.

291 Stevenson. *Hartford Courant*, 24 May 1956, p. 14.

291 39 percent. *Hartford Courant*, 9 December 1960, p. 40; *Los Angeles Times*, December 9, 1960, p. 17; Bryant, p. 62; Hoff, p. 78.

291 47 percent. *Social Forces*, March 1962, p. 209.

291 "Of all . . . voter." *Social Forces*, March 1962, p. 209; Caro, *Master*, p. 842.

291 Gallup poll. *Hartford Courant*, 24 April 1960, p. 36A.

292 Wallace. Lesher, p. 114.

292 *Profiles in Courage*. Kennedy, *Profiles in Courage*, pp. 115, 140.

292 Graves. Bryant, pp. 61, 68.

292 "leaving all . . . hands." *Chicago Defender*, 2 March 1957, p. 6; Bryant, pp. 62–63.

292 Juries. *Chicago Defender*, 5 August 1957, p. 5; *Pasadena Star–News*, 2 August 1957, p. 3; Parmet, *Jack*, pp. 411–12; Caro, *Master*, pp. 945–47, 981–88; O'Brien, *John F. Kennedy*, pp. 371–73. Senators Johnson and Goldwater also voted aye. Senators Symington, Humphrey, and Morse voted nay. That only nine Democrats stood with them on this issue stunned blacks.

When the amendment passed, Senate minority leader Knowland wept.

292   Breakfast. *Chicago Defender*, 1 March 1960, p. A11; *Charleston Gazette*, 9 June 1960, p. 3; Bryant, pp. 103–4; Lasky, *RFK*, p. 138.

292   "It is . . . Patterson." Lasky, *RFK*, p.139.

292   "We really . . . it." Schlesinger, *Robert Kennedy*, p. 215.

293   "The time . . . election." Lasky, *RFK*, p. 182. RFK had proven bolder in his University of Virginia days, fighting to integrate an audience hearing black United Nations functionary Ralph Bunche. Bryant, p. 244.

293   Byrd. *New York Times*, 12 May 1960, p. 23; Schlesinger, *Robert Kennedy*, p. 215.

293   "When I . . . it." Schlesinger, *Robert Kennedy*, pp. 215–16.

293   Almond, Vandiver. *Journal of American History*, September 1997, pp. 591, 593; Henderson, p. 122; Bryant, p. 151.

293   Voter registration. Heymann, *RFK*, p. 177.

294   "He especially . . . furniture." Pipes, p. 210.

294   Truman. *New York Times*, 19 April 1960, p. 21.

294   "I'll tell . . . more?" *The Reporter*, 13 October 1960, p. 35.

294   Labor Committee. Bryant, p. 166; Sorensen, p. 156; Lincoln, p. 42; Stossel, p. 161.

294   Fifty thousand dollars. Leamer, *Kennedy Men*, p. 458; O'Brien, *John F. Kennedy*, p. 481; Wofford, p. 60; Sorensen, p. 172; Lasky, *RFK*, p. 182. Powell's vote had also been for sale in 1956. Facing income tax charges, he endorsed not only Ike but also Senate candidate Jacob Javits. The charges mysteriously disappeared. Miller and Leighton, pp. 210–11.

294   "those [black] . . . money." Leamer, *Kennedy Men*, p. 458.

294   Wofford, p. 61; Thomas, *RFK*, p. 84; O'Brien, *John F. Kennedy*, p. 481; Bryant, pp. 163–64; Stossel, pp. 161–62. Dawson's career was a microcosm of the shift of the black population from the GOP to the Democratic Party. He had twice run for Congress and had even served the Chicago City Council as a Republican. *Chicago Tribune*, 10 November 1970, p. A10; White, *1960*, pp. 254–55.

294   Belafonte. Heymann, *RFK* p. 177.

295   "It is . . . Kennedy." *The Reporter*, 13 October 1960, p. 36.

295   MLK-JFK meetings. King, pp. 143–44; Bryant, pp. 133, 180.

295   Florida meeting. King, p. 144; Bryant, p. 180.

295   "The hell . . . off." Leamer, *Kennedy Men*, p. 458; Bryant p. 180.

295   Atlanta arrest. *Wisconsin Rapids Daily Tribune*, 20 October 1960, p. 2; Bryant p. 180.

295   "any . . . ordinances." Garrow, pp. 142–43.

295   "They are . . . him." Garrow, p. 146; Schlesinger, *Robert Kennedy*, pp. 216–17.

296   "Why don't . . . killed." Matthews, p. 171.

296   "I want . . . me." Bryant, p. 184; Matthews, p. 171.

296   "It certainly . . . quiet." Matthews, p. 171; Schlesinger, *Robert Kennedy*, p. 217; Matthews, p. 171; Garrow, p. 147.

296   "You bombthrowers . . . us?" Schlesinger, , *Robert Kennedy*, p. 217;

Matthews, p. 171; Garrow, p. 147; Bryant, p. 184; Martin, *Hero*, p. 229.

296   "Yes, it . . . disgraceful." Schlesinger, *Robert Kennedy*, pp. 217–18.

297   JFK-RFK-Vandiver-Mitchell. *Journal of American History*, September 1997, pp. 583–95; Henderson, pp. 124–25; Branch, p. 377. RFK confirmed details of this version in a taped December 1964 interview. Vandiver also provided verification. Publicly, Vandiver blasted JFK's role in the King affair as disgraceful "when the Democratic nominee for the presidency makes a phone call to the home of the foremost racial agitator in the country."

298   "The Blue Bomb." *Journal of American History*, September 1997, p. 586; Stern, p. 37; Weisbrot, p. 48.

298   "Listen to . . . hour.'" Jamieson, p. 145.

298   "I had . . . lap." Martin, *Hero*, p. 229.

298   "Imagine Martin . . . we?" Schlesinger, *Robert Kennedy*, p. 218; White, *1960*, p. 352; Manchester, Glory, p. 1081; King, p. 149; Wicker, p. 241. Theodore H. White deleted "Daddy" King's anti-Catholic reports in *The Making of the President, 1960*.

Chapter Twenty-eight: "The most dangerous man in America"

299   "I'm looking . . . back," Robinson, p. 46; Allen, p. 75; Rampersad, p. 126.

299   NAACP. Lasky, *Watergate*, p. 46.

299   African tour. Pipes, p. 209.

299   1957 session. *New York Times*, 10 January 1957, pp. 1, 21; Mazo, p. 259; Long, pp. 38, 65; Nixon, *Six Crises*, p. 363; Parmet, *Jack*, pp. 408–10; Lasky, *JFK*, pp. 247–48.

300   "I'll have . . . same." *Chicago Defender*, 4 January 1958, p. 11; Long, p. 102.

300   Post baseball career. Long, p. 64. The column was ghostwritten.

300   "more interested . . . rights." *Wisconsin Daily Rapids*, 2 May 1960, p. 2.

300   Patterson. *Wisconsin Daily Rapids*, 2 May 1960, p. 2; Long, *passim*; Rampersad, pp. 343–44.

300   Robinson registration. Rampersad, pp. 340–41.

300   "impresses . . . trust . . ." Long, p. 67.

300   "Whoever . . . liar." Lasky, *RFK*, p. 149; Lasky, *Watergate*, pp. 33–34.

300   JFK-Robinson meeting. *Long Beach Press-Telegram*, 19 June 1960, p. B-2; *New York Times*, 2 July 1960, p. 6.

300   "You've . . . eye" *Oakland Tribune*, 15 October 1960, p. 3; Robinson, p. 149; Bryant, p. 135.

300   "I had . . . times." *Chicago Tribune*, 29 September 1960, p. S6.

300   "Mr. Robinson . . ."; ". . . colored people." Allen, p. 219; Lasky, *JFK*, p. 256; Robinson, p. 149.

301   "I didn't . . . American." Robinson, p. 150; Bryant, p. 135; Pipes, p. 270.

301   JFK letter. *New York Times*, 2 July 1960, p. 6; Long, pp. 107–9.

301   LBJ. Pipes, p. 270.

301   Voting. *Washington Post*, 11 September 1960, p. A2.

301   Atlanta. de Toledano, pp. 304–6.

302   "Jack thought . . . that." Allen, pp. 218–19.

302   WMCA. *New Castle News*, 5 October 1960, p. 4; Rampersad, p. 347; Lasky, *JFK*, pp. 432–33; Lasky, *RFK*, pp. 179–80.

302   Merchandise Mart. Martin, *Destruction*, p. 265; Bryant, p. 166.

302   Morrow background. *Los Angeles Times*, 10 September 1960, p. 16; Morrow, *Black Man*, p. 295.

303   "Unlike the . . . expenses." Morrow, *Black Man*, p. 295; Bryant, p. 166.

303   September 13. *Los Angeles Times*, 14 September 1960, p. 7.

303   "The boss . . . thing." Brodie, p. 430.

303   "Negroes, or . . . race." Lasky, *Watergate*, pp. 45–46; Wofford, p. 60.

303   "There should . . . redeemed." *New York Times*, 13 October 1960, pp. 1, 26; *New York Times*, 14 October 1960, p. 1; Nixon, *Six Crises*, p. 350; Robinson, p. 136; Brodie, p. 423.

303   "Whoever recommended . . . feet" *New York Times*, 14 October 1960, pp. 1, 24.

303   "With respect . . . color." *New York Times*, 13 October 1960, p. 26; *New York Times*, 14 October 1960, p. 24.

304   "This did . . . me." Robinson, p. 151.

304   "racism in . . . worst." *Nevada State Journal*, 18 October 1960, p. 7; *Hartford Courant*, 19 October 1960, p. 1A; Nixon, *Six Crises*, p. 365.

304   "Will we . . . down?" *Troy Record*, 19 October 1960, p. 12.

304   Hartford meeting. *Hartford Courant*, 16 October 1960, pp. 1, 2A; *Hartford Courant*, 17 October 1960, pp. 1, 7; *New York Times*, 17 October 1960, p. 1, 23.

304   "If Richard . . . Cabinet." *Chicago Tribune*, 19 October 1960, p. 8.

304   "Let [Kennedy] . . . it." *Troy Times–Record*, 18 October 1960, p. 14; *Hartford Courant*, 19 October 1960, p. 1A; *Chicago Tribune*, 19 October 1960, p. 8; Nixon, *Six Crises*, p. 350. Diggs, convicted of payroll kickbacks in 1978, resigned from Congress and served seven months in prison.

304   "hurt us . . . suggest." Nixon, *Six Crises*, p. 351; Whalen, *Lodge*, p. 174.

304   Accra. Bryant, p. 179.

305   "Nixon has . . . America." King, p. 149; Garrow, p. 119; Stern, p. 19.

305   "He has . . . jail." Rampersad, p. 351.

305   Nixon, Klein. Nixon, *Six Crises*, p. 362; Brodie, p. 431.

305   Rogers, Haggerty. Nixon, *Six Crises*, pp. 362–63.

305   "I had . . . risk." King, p. 148.

305   Morrow leaves. Stern, p. 36; Weisbrot, p. 46; Morrow, *Black Man*, p. 296; Branch, p. 375.

305   Lobbying Robinson. Rampersad, p. 351.

305   "It is . . . sound." Long, p. 115; Rampersad, p. 352.

306   *Post* firing. Long, pp. 115–17; Rampersad, pp. 348, 352–53.

306   "He thinks . . . win." Wicker, p. 240; Matthews, p. 172. Nixon had no trouble, however, telegraphing baseball commissioner Ford Frick regarding a forthcoming major league barnstorming trip to Japan. *Pasadena Star–News*, 15 July 1960, p. 19.

Chapter Twenty-nine: "No one could tell him anything"

307   Sarnoff. *New York Times*, 28 July 1960, p. 14; *Chicago Tribune*, 29 July 1960, p. 4; *The Reporter*, 10 November 1960, p. 19; Kraus, pp. 59–60, 74.

308   JFK-Lodge debate. Whalen, *Lodge*, pp. 98–101.

308   "I took . . . Kennedy." Salinger, *PS*, p. 83.

308   Commercial sponsorship. *Chicago Tribune*, 23 August 1960, p. A5.

309   "We had . . . information." Klein, *Perfectly Clear*, p. 101.

309   Nixon volte-face. *Chicago Tribune*, 28 July 1960, p. 4.

309   "I was . . . debates." Klein, *Perfectly Clear*, p. 102; Halberstam, *Powers*, p. 329.

309   "that the . . . others." *New York Times*, 25 July 1960, p. 47.

311   "Nixon dismissed . . . voice." Brodie, p. 424; Manchester, *Glory*, p. 882.

311   Eisenhower against. Eisenhower, *Mandate*, pp. 598–99; Sorensen, *Kennedy*, p. 196; Ambrose, *Nixon*, pp. 588–89.

312   Kennedy against. Martin, *Hero*, p. 222.

312   "Kennedy has . . . weak." de Toledano, p. 306.

312   Chotiner. Lurie, pp. 255–56.

312   "full and . . . journalists." *New York Times*, 1 August 1960, p. 9; *Chicago Tribune*, 1 August 1960, p. 1; Kraus, p. 129.

313   "I'm not . . . there." Watson, *Vista*, p. 9; Perret, *Jack*, p. 261.

313   Scribner. *The Reporter*, 10 November 1960, p. 20.

313   "If they . . . show?" White, *1960*, p. 310.

313   "The question . . . advantage." Nixon, *RN*, p. 268.

313   Four debates. Watson, *Vista*, p. 11.

313   "We insisted . . . debate." Klein, *Perfectly Clear*, p. 102; Salinger to Klein, 1 September 1960.

314   "Foreign affairs . . . agreed." Nixon, *Six Crises*, p. 324; Nixon, *RN*, pp. 268–69, 272; Klein, *Perfectly Clear*, p. 302; Silvestri, p. 130.

315   JFK confidence. Halberstam, *Powers*, pp. 336, 339; Klein, *Perfectly Clear*, p. 302.

315   Lawford. Spada, pp. 259–60.

315   Montgomery. Pipes, pp. 273–74; Ambrose, *Nixon*, pp. 558–59.

315   Rogers background. *Lima News*, 1 August 1960, p. 20; *New York Times*, 18 March 2003, p. C14; Halberstam, *The Powers That Be*, pp. 329–32.

316   "Rogers [was] . . . politician." Halberstam, *Powers*, p. 332.

316   Blaik letter. Ambrose, *Nixon*, p. 556.

317   Greensboro. *Chicago Tribune*, 18 August 1960, p. A10; *New York Times*, 30 August 1960, p. 1; *Chicago Tribune*, 30 August 1960, pp. 1, 6; *Chicago Tribune*, 31 August 1960, p. 10; Manchester, *Glory*, p. 1078.

317   "Look, I . . . leg." Nixon, *Six Crises*, p. 326; de Toledano, p. 306; Ambrose, *Nixon*, p. 563; Lungren, p. 67; Aitken, p. 276.

317   JFK. *Washington Post*, 30 August 1960, p. A1; *New York Times*, 31 August 1960, p. 1, 19; *Chicago Tribune*, 31 August 1960, p. 10; *Oakland Tribune*, 31 August 1960, p. 4; *New York Times*, 1 September 1960, p. 12; *Washington Post*, 1 September 1960, p. 16; *Washington Post*, 3 September 1960, p. A2; *New York Times*, 2 September 1960, p. 1; Ambrose, *Nixon*, pp. 563–64; Aitken, p. 276.

317   51 percent. Brodie, p. 424.

317   Post-hospital itinerary. Nixon, *Six Crises*, pp. 330–31; White, *1960*, pp. 299–300; Ambrose, *Nixon*, p. 566; Committee on Commerce, pp. xiv–xv.

318   Machinists. *Long Beach Independent–Press–Telegram*, 14 September 1960, p. A-11; *New York Times*, 16 September 1960, p. 20; Nixon, *Six Crises*, pp. 331–32; White, *1960*, p. 300; Ambrose, *Nixon*, p. 566; Committee on Commerce, pp. 108–16; Stephen Ambrose incorrectly identifies the physician then traveling with Nixon as Dr. John C. Lungren. It was, indeed, Dr. Todd. Dr. Lungren does not even mention this episode in his memoirs. Lungren, *passim*.

318   "If the . . . earlier." *New York Times*, 16 September 1960, p. 20. Nixon recounts this incident in *Six Crises*. Remarkably, he does not even hint at how well he performed.

Chapter Thirty: "He felt cool, calm, and very alert"

320   Nixon arrival. *Chicago Tribune*, 25 September 1960, p. 7; *Chicago Tribune*, 26 September 1960, p. 1; *Chicago Tribune*, 27 September 1960, pp. 1, 10; Nixon, *Six Crises*, p. 337; White, *1960*, p. 311; Nixon, *RN*, p. 27.

320   Carpenters and Joiners. *Chicago Tribune*, 25 September 1960, p. 7; *Los Angeles Times*, 27 September 1960, p. 11; Committee on Commerce, pp. 287–95.

321   JFK, 15 minutes. *Chicago Tribune*, 25 September 1960, p. 8; *Los Angeles Times*, 25 September 1960, p. 2; *Washington Post*, 26 September 1960, pp. A1–A2; *Chicago Tribune*, 26 September 1960, pp. 1, 2; *Chicago Tribune*, 27 September 1960, pp. 1, 10; *Los Angeles Times*, 27 September 1960, p. 11; White, *1960*, p. 311; O'Donnell, Powers, and McCarthy, pp. 242–43.

321   "napped." *Washington Post*, 3 March 2007, p. B06, *Current Biography 1966*, p. 156; White, *1960*, pp. 311–12; Sorensen, p. 198; Goodwin, *Remembering*, pp. 112–13; Salinger, *P.S.*, p. 83.

321   "I go . . . believer." Matthews, p. 146; Thomas, p. 106.

322   "We need . . . themselves." Schlesinger, *Robert Kennedy*, p. 219; Schlesinger, *Journals*, p. 89.

322   "I was . . . concerned." Anderson, p. 221; Leamer, *Kennedy Men*, p. 449.

322   "Some people . . . needle." Leaming, *Mrs. Kennedy*, p. 103.

322   "That made . . . it." Anderson, p. 221.

322   "Many of . . . filthy." Anderson, p. 303.

322   Nurse. Reeves, *Character*, pp. 295–96.

323   Shaw, Suzuki. *New York Times*, 28 January 1969, p. 43; Heymann, *Jackie*, p. 298; Smith, *Grace and Power*, p. 225; Anderson, p. 221; Spoto, p. 297; Leaming, *Mrs. Kennedy*, p. 104; Bly, p. 123. Mark Shaw ("laden with methamphetamine residue," said the official report) died of a drug overdose in January 1969. He was forty-seven.

324   JFK 9/14 visit. *New York Times*, 4 December 1970, pp. 1, 34, 81; Heymann, *Jackie*, pp. 297–98; Heymann, *RFK*, p. 238; Hersh, *Camelot*, pp. 234–37; Leaming, *Mrs. Kennedy*, pp. 103–4; Spoto, pp. 196–97; Gilbert, p. 167; Reeves, *Character*, pp. 295–96; Anderson, p. 222; Bradford, p. 160.

324   "The demands . . . stress." Anderson, p. 222.

324 "After his . . . orally." *New York Times*, 4 December 1960, pp. 1, 34, 81; *New York Times*, 28 January 1969, p. 43; Heymann, *Jackie*, p. 298; Heymann, *RFK*, p. 238; Spoto, pp. 196–97; Gilbert, p. 167.

325 Shrivers. *Chicago Tribune*, 25 September 1960, p. 8.
Watson background. *Bridgeport Telegram*, 16 June 1957, p. 45; *New York Times*, 2 February 1960, p. 71; *Oneonta Star*, 26 January 1961, p. 4; Leamer, *Kennedy Men*, p. 324.

325 "The night . . . debates." Heymann, *Jackie*, p. 242; Aitken, pp. 277–78; Heymann, *RFK*, p. 162; Anderson, p. 222.

326 Earl Long. *Bridgeport Post*, 8 May 1960, p. 5; *Pasadena Independent*, 6 September 1960, p. 4.

326 NYC Debates. *Chicago Tribune*, 14 October 1960, p. 11; *New York Times*, 22 October 1960, p. 10.

326 "I assure . . . say." *Oneonta Star*, 19 August 1963, p. 4; White House guards were also provided with photos of Marvin and ordered never to allow him entrance.

326 Opening and closing statements. *Chicago Tribune*, 25 September 1960, p. 7; *Chicago Tribune*, 26 September 1960, p. 18; *Chicago Tribune*, 27 September 1960, p. 18; *New York Times*, 27 September 1960, p. 30; *Chicago Tribune*, 27 September 1960, p. 18; White, *1960*, pp. 312–13; Nixon, *Six Crises*, p. 337; Klein, *Perfectly Clear*, p. 105.

327 Didn't visit studio. White, *1960*, pp. 312–13; O'Brien, *Kennedy*, pp. 479–80.

327 "Kennedy . . . more seriously." Hewitt Interview, JFK Library, p. 2; Hewitt, p. 72; O'Brien, *John F. Kennedy*, p. 481; Silvestri, p. 132. Nixon may not have been as formally prepped on debate details as JFK, but as debate one opened, JFK forgot to rise to answer questions. Nixon noticed and gingerly motioned to moderator Howard K. Smith to remind Kennedy of the ground rules.

327 Rogers and Shepley. de Toledano, p. 307; Klein, *Perfectly Clear*, p. 104; Halberstam, *The Powers That Be*, p. 337; Summers, p. 207.

327 "We kept . . . insist?" Matthews, p. 147; Summers, p. 207.

327 "erase . . . image." White, *1960*, p. 313; Barnouw, pp. 163–64; Brodie, p. 414; Silvestri, p. 131; Dallek, *Unfinished Life*, p. 285.

327 "the good guy." Matthews, p. 147; Summers, p. 206.

327 "God will . . . OFFENSIVE." Ambrose, *Nixon*, p. 571.

328 Smith-Salinger. Smith, *Death*, pp. 268–69.

328 "No, Senator . . . these." Sorensen, p. 198; Leamer, *Kennedy Men*, p. 450.

328 JFK tense. Sorensen, p. 198; White, *1960*, p. 312.

328 "Rogers was . . . anything." Halberstam, *Powers*, p. 338.

328 Nixon fears a fight. White, *1960*, p. 313.

328 "I thought . . . thoughts." Klein, *Perfectly Clear*, p. 104. A review of broadcast kinescopes indicates that Nixon's size-16 shirt fit reasonably well that night. It was his jacket collar that hung ridiculously loose upon his shrunken frame.

329 Outside WBBM, altercation. *Chicago Tribune*, 27 September 1960, p. 10.

329   "red zone." *Los Angeles Times*, 26 September 1960, p. 31; *Hartford Courant*, 26 September 1960, p. 5B. During the debate itself, two photographers, working without flashes, shot the event.

329   Nixon arrival, knee. Hewitt Interview, JFK Library, p. 2; *Chicago Tribune*, 27 September 1960, pp. 1, 10; *Los Angeles Times*, 27 September 1960, p. 2; *New York Times*, 27 September 1960, p. 29; White, *1960*, p. 313; de Toledano, p. 307; Hewitt, p. 71.

329   "Air conditioning . . . program." *Los Angeles Times*, 26 September 1960, p. 31; *Hartford Courant*, 26 September 1960, p. 5B.

329   Lighting. *Los Angeles Times*, 26 September 1960, p. 31; *Washington Post*, 1 October 1960, p. 1; *Chicago Tribune*, 1 October 1960, p. 5; Klein, *Perfectly Clear*. p, 105; White, *1960*, p. 314.

330   Gray set. *New York Times*, 27 September 1960, p. 28; Klein, *Perfectly Clear*, p. 105; Sorensen, *Kennedy*, p. 199; Bochin, p. 49; Barnouw, p. 163.

330   Nixon onstage. Klein, *Perfectly Clear*, p. 105.

330   "When [JFK] . . . terrible." *Chicago Tribune*, 27 September 1960, p. 1; *Washington Post*, 27 September 1960, p. A2; *Hartford Courant*, September 1960, p. 27; *Los Angeles Times*, 27 September 1960, p. 2; Stanton Interview, JFK Library, p. 4

330   "look[ed] more . . . manliness." Smith, *Death*, p. 263.

330   "Glad to . . . Cleveland." *New York Times*, 27 September 1960, p. 29; *Washington Post*, 27 September 1960, p. A2; Brodie, p. 426; Ambrose, *Nixon*, p. 571; Matthews, p. 148.

330   "I suppose . . . sun." *Hartford Courant*, 27 September 1960, p. 27; *Uniontown Evening Standard*, 27 September 1960, p. 7; *Chicago Tribune*, 27 September 1960, p. 1; Nixon, *Six Crises*, pp. 337–38.

330   "Terrific! . . . thing!" Martin, *Hero*, p. 222; David and David, p. 116; Summers, p. 207.

331   CBS functionary–Nixon. *Hartford Courant*, 27 September 1960, p. 27. The *Washington Post* supported the AP's account: "The crew explained to Kennedy and Nixon that if they took a drink of water or wiped the sweat off their brows the camera would look the other way." *Washington Post*, 27 September 1960, p. A2.

331   "He has . . . television." Jamieson, pp. 158–59.

331   Rogers advises. Nixon, *RN*, p. 270.

331   Hart. Klein, *Perfectly Clear*, p. 105.

331   Arvold. *New York Times*, 25 May 1958, p. X13; *New York Times*, 6 October 1960, p. 34; *Syracuse Post-Standard*, 11 October 1984, p. 1; Hewitt Interview, JFK Library, p. 2; Cronkite, p. 187; Barnouw, p. 163.

331   "To Nixon . . . man." Matthews, p. 149; Summers, p. 207.

331   Stanton-Hewitt. Hewitt Interview, JFK Library, p. 2; Matthews, p. 149; Halberstam, *Powers*, pp. 339–40; Watson, *Vista*, p. 12.

332   "beard stick." *New York Times*, 25 May 1958, p. X13; Nixon, *Six Crises*, p. 338; de Toledano, p. 307; Klein, *Perfectly Clear*, p. 105.

332   Edson. *Hartford Courant*, 27 September 1960, p. 27.

332 JFK on stage. *Hartford Courant*, 27 September 1960, p. 27.
332 Shirt. *Washington Post*, 27 September 1960, p. A2; *New York Times*, 8 October 1960, p. 12; Watson, *Vista*, p. 12; Klein, *Perfectly Clear*, p. 105.
332 "[I]n the . . . difference." Stanton Interview, JFK Library, p. 20.
333 "He [Nixon] . . . afraid." Salinger, *PS:*, pp. 83–84.
333 JFK-Wilson. Hewitt Interview, JFK Library, p. 2; Halberstam, *Powers*, p. 339; Hewitt, p. 73; Sorensen, *Kennedy*, p. 198; Parmet, *JFK*, p. 46.
333 "I remember . . . air." O'Brien Interview I, LBJ Library, p. 19; Matthews, pp. 149–50; O'Brien, *Victories*, pp. 92–93.

Chapter Thirty-one: "They've embalmed him before he even died"

335 Panel. *New York Times*, 23 September 1960, p. 19; *Los Angeles Times*, 25 September 1960, p. 3; *New York Times*, 27 September 1960, p. 29.
335 Audience. *Los Angeles Times*, 27 September 1960, p. 1; *Chicago Tribune*, 2 October 1960, p. W13; *New York Times*, 23 October 1960, p. 70; White, *America*, p. 403; Lurie, p. 256; Ambrose, *Nixon*, p. 580; Barnouw, p. 115*fn*.
336 "perhaps . . . undramatically." Sorensen, *Kennedy*, pp. 198–99.
336 JFK opens; Nixon defensive. *New York Times*, 27 September 1960, p. 28; *Washington Post*, 27 September 1960, pp. A10–A11; *Christian Science Monitor*, 27 September 1960, p. 16; *Chicago Tribune*, 27 September 1960, p. 6.
338 "What kind . . . time." *New York Times*, 27 September 1960, p. 28; *Washington Post*, 27 September 1960, p. A10; *Chicago Tribune*, 27 September 1960, p. 6.
338 "When I . . . new." http://www.msnbc.msn.com/id /16711248/site/newsweek/ page/2.
338 "I couldn't . . . on." Matthews, p. 150.
338 "Why, Nixon . . . open." Martin, *Hero*, p. 223; Summers, p. 208.
340 "On that . . . proposal." *New York Times*, 27 September 1960, pp. 28–29.
340 "reaction shots." Halberstam, *Powers*, pp. 336–37.
340 "[S]omething . . . work." Halberstam, *Powers*, p. 340.
340 Vanocur. *New York Times*, 27 October 1960, p. 29.
342 "If we . . . again. *New York Times*, 27 October 1960, p. 29.
342 "Nixon *looked* . . . heat." Wicker, p. 229.
342 "It was . . . better." Smith, *Events Leading Up to My Death*, pp. 262–63.
342 "After last . . . secure." Sperber, p. 604.
342 "I thought . . . like." Bradlee, *Life*, p. 211.
343 "I thought . . . politics." Watson, *Vista*, p. 13; Ritchie, p. 193.
343 "By all signals . . . one." Hellman, p. 128.
343 "[W]hat Mr. . . . there." Wicker, p. 228.
344 "I left . . . against." *Chicago Tribune*, 22 September 1960, p. D22.
344 "My . . . even died." Dallek, *Unfinished Life*, p. 286; Summers, p. 208.
344 "What . . . his soul." Goodwin, *Remembering*, p. 115.
344 Stanton. Stanton Interview, JFK Library, p. 4.
344 "How many . . . President." Wicker, pp. 228–29.
344 "Dick looked . . . dark." Eisenhower, *Pat Nixon*, p. 191.

344   "We all . . . job." *San Mateo Times*, 30 September 1960, p. 6; *Washington Post*, 1 October 1960, p. 1.

345   Pat Nixon. *Los Angeles Times*, 25 September 1960, p. 26; Eisenhower, *Pat Nixon*, pp. 191–92.

345   Woods. Nixon, *Six Crises*, p. 340; Eisenhower, *Pat Nixon*, p. 191.

345   "feeling all right." Nixon, *Six Crises*, p. 341; Nixon, *RN*, p. 271; Lurie, p. 256; Aitken, pp. 278–79.

345   "I felt . . . tonight." Salinger, *With Kennedy*, p. 72.

345   "That son . . . election!" Brodie, p. 427; Dallek, *Unfinished Life*, p. 286; Whalen, *Lodge*, p. 174; Summers, p. 208.

345   Schlesingers. Schlesinger, *Thousand Days*, p. 69; Schlesinger, *Journals*, p. 85.

345   Invitees. *Chicago Tribune*, 25 September 1960, p. 6; *Lima News*, 25 September 1960, p. C14; Heymann, *Jackie*, p. 242.

345   "I own . . . one." *Christian Science Monitor*, 27 September 1960, p. 6; Schlesinger, *Kennedy or Nixon, passim*.

345   "[Jackie's] only . . . career." *Christian Science Monitor*, 27 September 1960, p. 6.

346   "[W]e all . . . thing." Heymann, *Jackie*, p. 242.

346   "My husband . . . him." *Los Angeles Times*, 25 September 1960, p. 26; *Christian Science Monitor*, 27 September 1960, p. 6.

346   17.1 million. *Hartford Courant*, 19 October 1960, p. 6.

346   "I was . . . 'The Boy.'" Dickerson, p. 56; Anderson, p. 222; Matthews, p. 153.

346   "Nixon . . . to Khrushchev." O'Donnell, Powers, and McCarthy, pp. 245–46; Silvestri, p. 137; Martin, *Hero*, p. 223; Wyckoff, p. 216.

347   Southern Governors' Conference. *Stevens Point Journal*, 27 September 1960, p. 14; *Christian Science Monitor*, 28 September 1960, p. 14; *Los Angeles Times*, 28 September 1960, p. 6; White, *1960*, p. 319; Wyckoff, p. 216.

347   "Oh, I . . . fellow." O'Donnell, Powers, and McCarthy, pp. 244–45; Sorensen, *Kennedy*, p. 206.

347   Dick Tuck. Thomas, p. 106; Summers, pp. 208–9.

347   "How the . . . was." Hewitt Interview, JFK Library, p. 5.

347   "It's all over." Martin, *Hero*, p. 224.

348   Jackie. *Christian Science Monitor*, 27 September 1960, p. 6; Schlesinger, *Thousand Days*, p. 69.

Chapter Thirty-two: "The bones of a single American soldier"

349   "I accompanied . . . presidency." Klein, *Perfectly Clear*, pp. 102–6.

349   "When I . . . draw." Wicker, p. 229.

350   "Once in . . . question." Eisenhower, *Mandate*, p. 599; Ambrose, *Nixon*, p. 575; Ambrose, *Eisenhower: The President*, p. 601.

350   "Nixon had . . . parties." de Toledano, p. 308.

350   "You are . . . for." Ambrose, *Nixon*, p. 575.

350   "Well, Joe . . . off." Martin, *Destruction*, p. 265; Cordery, p. 451.

350   Macmillan. *New York Times*, 26 September 1960, p. 15; Leaming, *Jack Kennedy*, p. 116.

351   Goodwin-JFK. Goodwin, *Remembering*, pp. 115–16; Summers, p. 208.

351 "Hey, you . . . night." White, *1960*, p. 319; Halberstam, *Powers*, p. 340; Parmet, *JFK*, p. 44; Silvestri, pp. 136–37.

351 Lausche. *Chicago Tribune*, 26 September 1960, p. 2; O'Donnell, Powers, and McCarthy, p. 243; Parmet, *JFK*, p. 45.

351 Haldeman. Nixon, *Six Crises*, pp. 340–41; Rather and Gates, p. 123; Lurie, p. 256.

351 "You looked . . . debate." *Long Beach Independent-Press-Telegram*, 14 October 1960, p. A-11; Nixon, *Six Crises*, p. 341; Nixon, *RN*, p. 271.

352 "Please back . . . fatigue." Jamieson, pp. 152–53. Nixon ate only half his bison sandwich. As of February 2008, the remainder survived in the care of Steve Jenne, then a fourteen-year-old Sullivanville Eagle Scout. http://www.sun-sentinel.com/news/custom/fringe/sns-ap-il-Nixon-sandwich,0,2915104.story.

352 Milkshakes. Nixon, *Six Crises*, p. 341; Nixon, *RN*, p. 271; de Toledano, p. 308; Lurie, p. 256; Silvestri, p. 138; Bochin, p. 51.

352 Gallup poll; party affiliation. *Los Angeles Times*, 25 September 1960, pp. B1–B2. In his memoir *RN*, Nixon reverses these results, claiming *Kennedy was ahead 51 percent to 49 percent on the eve of the first debate.* Nixon, *RN*, p. 273.

352 "enthusiasm levels." *Los Angeles Times*, 25 September 1960, p. B2.

353 49 percent to 46 percent. *Los Angeles Times*, 12 October 1960, pp. 2, 9; *Hartford Courant*, 26 October 1960, p. 5.

353 43 percent to 23 percent. *Los Angeles Times*, 12 October 1960, pp. 2, 9; Summers, p. 208.

353 48 percent to 48 percent. *Los Angeles Times*, 26 October 1960, pp. 2, 10. Basically, what Gallup's numbers revealed was that almost everyone who thought the debate deadlocked voted for Nixon.

353 Cleveland debate shifted. *Washington Post*, 30 September, p. A16; *Chicago Tribune*, 2 October 1960, p. 5; *Washington Post*, 7 October 1960, p. A1.

354 "Mr. Nixon . . . make-up." *New York Times*, 6 October 1960, p. 34.

354 Nashville and Cleveland. *New York Times*, 7 October 1960, pp. 1, 26; *Chicago Tribune*, 7 October, p. 5; Bochin, p. 51; Ambrose, *Nixon*, p. 577.

354 "Don't pay . . . off." Nixon, *Six Crises*, p. 343; Bochin, p. 51.

354 New Nixon approach. *Stevens Point Journal*, 14 October 1960, p. 3.

354 New set. *New York Times*, 7 October 1960, p. 24; *Washington Post*, 7 October 1960, p. A1.

354 Flags. *New York Times*, 8 October 1960, p. 12; *Washington Post*, 8 October 1960, p. A1.

354 New format. *Washington Post*, 7 October 1960, p. A1; *Chicago Tribune*, 7 October 1960, p. 5.

355 Pre-debate details. *Chicago Tribune*, 1 October 1960, p. 5; *New York Times*, 7 October 1960, p. 24; *New York Times*, 8 October 1960, pp. 1, 12; *Washington Post*, 8 October 1960, pp. A1, N3; *Chicago Tribune*, 8 October 1960, p. N3; Nixon, *RN*, p. 271; Schlesinger, *Thousand Days*, pp. 70–71; Schlesinger, *Journals*, p. 87; Silvestri, p. 138; Watson, *Vista*, p. 14; Jamieson, p. 159.

355 "Well, . . . one bit." *New York Times*, 8 October 1960, p. 10; *Washington Post*,

8 October 1960, p. A8; *Chicago Tribune*, 8 October 1960, p. N1; Silvestri, p. 138; Bochin, p. 51; Parmet, *JFK*, p. 46.

356   "We all . . . States." *New York Times*, 8 October 1960, pp. 8, 10; *Washington Post*, 8 October 1960, p. A8.

356   "very attractive . . . tempo." *Washington Post*, 8 October 1960, p. A11.

356   "Kennedy, who . . . microphone." *Chicago Tribune*, 8 October 1960, p. N3.

356   "The second . . . better." Eisenhower, *Mandate*, p. 599.

357   Senate debate. *Washington Post*, 29 January 1955, pp. 1–2; Parmet, *Nixon*, p. 342.

357   Huntley-JFK. *New York Times*, 1 October 1960, p. 9; *New York Times*, 14 October 1960, p. 32; *New York Times*, 15 October 1960, p. 11; Lasky, *JFK*, p. 439; Brooks and Marsh, p. 127; http://www.jfklink.com/speeches/joint/joint011060_nbctv03.html. The interview aired October 1.

358   "I disagree . . . Korea." *New York Times*, 8 October 1960, pp. 1, 11; *Washington Post*, 8 October 1960, p. A9; Sorensen, *Kennedy*, p. 204; Bochin, pp. 51–52.

358   "[P]arties . . . something." *New York Times*, 8 October 1960, p. 11; *Washington Post*, 8 October 1960, p. A9.

359   JFK leaves. *Washington Post*, 8 October 1960, p. A1.

359   "irritated . . . who won." *Chicago Tribune*, 8 October 1960, p. N3.

359   "It was . . . say." *Washington Post*, 8 October 1960, p. A1.

359   "He looked. . . Lincoln." Kennedy, *Remember*, p. 374.

359   "The policeman . . . better." Kennedy, *Remember*, p. 374.

359   "More composed . . . delighted." *New York Times*, 8 October 1960, p. 10.

359   Pressroom survey. *New York Times*, 8 October 1960, p. 10; Nixon, *Six Crises*, p. 344.

359   "clearly . . . out ahead." *New York Times*, 8 October 1960, p. 10; Nixon, *Six Crises*, pp. 344–45; Nixon, *RN*, p. 271; Bochin, p. 52.

360   "clearly won . . . round." Nixon, *Six Crises*, p. 344; Nixon, *RN*, p. 271; Bochin, p. 52.

360   "now look . . . lift." *Washington Post*, 8 October 1960, p. A11; Nixon, *Six Crises*, p. 345.

360   Viewership drops. *New York Times*, 14 October 1960, p. 21; Nixon, *RN*, p. 271; Bochin, p. 52.

360   Fifth debate. *New York Times*, 12 October 1960, pp. 1, 33; Watson, *Vista*, p. 14.

360   "I thought . . . on." Lurie, p. 257.

360   Two-hour debate. *Los Angeles Times*, 9 October 1960, pp. E6, 26; *New York Times*, 12 October 1960, pp. 1, 33; *Chicago Tribune*, 12 October 1960, p. 7; *New York Times*, 13 October 1960, p. 24; *Chicago Tribune*, 18 October 1960, p. 6.

360   JFK-Galbraith. Galbraith, *Life*, p. 385.

361   Identical studios. *New York Times*, 12 October 1960, p. 32; *New York Times*, 14 October 1960, p. 22.

361   Temperatures, sweat. *Chicago Tribune*, 14 October 1960, p. 6.

361   Claude Thompson. *Kingsport News*, 14 October 1960, p. 6.

361 White shirt. *Stevens Point Journal*, 14 October 1960, p. 3.

361 Cottages. *Chicago Tribune*, 14 October 1960, p. 11.

361 Split-screen. *New York Times*, 14 October 1960, p. 22.

362 "If you . . . hell." *New York Times*, 12 October 1960, p. 1; Reston, p. 196.

362 "Tell them . . . hell." *Washington Post*, 13 October 1960, p. A25.

362 "Thurston . . . apology?" *Washington Post*, 14 October 1960, p. A18; *Chicago Tribune*, 14 October 1960, p. 10.

362 "Well, I . . . him." *Washington Post*, 14 October 1960, p. A18; *Chicago Tribune*, 14 October 1960, pp. 7, 10; Sorensen, *Kennedy*, p. 203.

362 "I just . . . follow'" *Washington Post*, 14 October 1960, p. A18; *Chicago Tribune*, 14 October 1960, p. 10.

363 PRC shelling. *Los Angeles Times*, 9 October 1960, p. E6.

363 Nixon attacks JFK. *Los Angeles Times*, 9 October 1960, p. 26; *Washington Post*, 12 October 1960, p. A2; *Hartford Courant*, 13 October 1960, p. 1; *New York Times*, 13 October 1960, p. 25; Committee on Commerce, *passim*.

363 "What I . . . aggression." *Washington Post*, 14 October 1960, p. A18; *Chicago Tribune*, 14 October 1960, p. 10.

363 "massive nuclear holocaust." *Washington Post*, 13 October 1960, pp. A1–A2; *New York Times*, 13 October 1960, p. 24.

364 "He didn't . . . commitment." *Washington Post*, 14 October 1960, p. A18; *Chicago Tribune*, 14 October 1960, p. 10.

364 Yarnell background. *New York Times*, 18 October 1955, p. 17; *New York Times*, 8 July 1959, p. 29; *Van Nuys Valley News*, 3 November 1960, p. 32–A; Lasky, *JFK*, p. 441.

364 "Why . . . at it?" *New York Times*, 30 October 1960, p. 65. And why, one might ask, did Richard Nixon not subject Kennedy to well-deserved ridicule regarding the mysterious, superannuated, and highly dead, Admiral Yarnell in debate four?

364 Robinson. Nixon, *Six Crises*, p. 347; Bochin, p. 53.

364 "Nixon's . . . them." White, *1960*, p. 318.

364 "more confident . . . cocky." *New York Times*, 14 October 1960, p. 22.

364 "Kennedy sounded . . . radio." *Hartford Courant*, 19 October 1960, p. 6.

365 "unimaginative . . . all four." Sorensen, *Kennedy*, pp. 199–200.

Chapter Thirty-three: "Senator Kennedy is in clear violation of the spirit of the law"

366 "full and . . . notes . . ." Watson, *Vista*, p. 9; Perret, *Jack*, p. 261.

366 "All my . . . rules." *Chicago Tribune*, 14 October 1960, p. 1.

366 "a ghost writer." *Chicago Tribune*, 14 October 1960, p. 1; *Troy Record*, 14 October 1960, p. 19.

366 "I quoted . . . debates." *Washington Post*, 14 October 1960, p. A2; *Chicago Tribune*, 14 October 1960, p. 1.

367 Salinger. *Washington Post*, 14 October 1960, p. A2; *Chicago Tribune*, 14 October 1960, p. 1.

367 "without prepared . . . notes" *Chicago Tribune*, 14 October 1960, p. 1.

367　"alteration and . . . photographs." *New York Times*, 22 October 1960, p. 12; *Chicago Tribune*, 22 October 1960, p. 5, Jamieson, pp. 159–60.

367　"because we . . . it." *New York Times*, 22 October 1960, p. 12; *Chicago Tribune*, 22 October 1960, p. 5. "It is too bad that that was done," admitted Ted Sorensen, "I can see where the Republicans felt it was misleading." Jamieson, pp. 160–61.

367　Castro. Quirk, pp. 334–43; Beschloss, *Crisis Years*, p. 23.

368　Expropriations. *New York Times*, 15 October 1960, pp. 1, 6; *Washington Post*, 15 October 1960, pp. A1, A5; *Chicago Tribune*, 15 October 1960, pp. 1–2; O'Brien, *Kennedy*, p. 492; Blight and Kornbluh, p. 161.

368　"Fidel Castro . . . sure." *New York Times*, 13 March 1960, p. BR8; *New York Times*, 30 March 1960, p. 34; Kennedy, *The Strategy of Peace*, pp. 132–33.

368　Sorensen. Sorensen, *Kennedy*, p. 205. Ted Sorensen alibied that the "Bolivar" comments were composed by a "junior staff member who had written them from a wholly different perspective."

368　"Everywhere . . . foreign policy." Goodwin, *Remembering*, p. 124.

369　"The people . . . Cuba." O'Brien, *Kennedy*, p. 492; Lasky, *RFK*, p. 181.

369　"As the . . . responsibility." Schlesinger, *Thousand Days*, p. 224.

369　"take the offensive." Schlesinger, *Thousand Days*, p. 225; Blight and Kornbluh, p. 161. Kennedy had personally instructed Goodwin to "get ready for a real blast at Nixon." Goodwin, *Remembering*, p. 125; Beschloss, *Crisis Years*, p. 28.

369　"willing to . . . appeaser." Parmet, *JFK*, pp. 47–48.

370　"You have . . . Communism.'" Parmet, *JFK*, p. 49.

370　"We must . . . government." *New York Times*, 21 October 1960, pp. 1, 18.

370　Anti-Castro coup. Ambrose, *Eisenhower: The President*, p. 557; Ambrose, *Nixon*, p. 550.

370　Dulles briefing. *Tucson Citizen*, 19 July 1960, p. 3; Nixon, *Six Crises*, p. 354; Lurie, p. 258; O'Brien, *Kennedy*, p. 493; Blight and Kornbluh, p. 160. Alabama governor John Patterson had also informed JFK of invasion preparations, warning of their political effects. "If [an invasion] occurred before the election, I believed Nixon would win. I recall watching him very closely. He heard me out and thanked me." O'Brien, *Kennedy*, p. 494; Leamer, *Kennedy Men*, p. 456; Hersh, *Camelot*, pp. 176–78.

370　Billings. *Chicago Tribune*, 10 October 1960, pp. 10, 11; *New York Times*, 10 October 1960, p. 17; *Washington Post*, 10 October 1960, p. A2; Klein, *Perfectly Clear*, pp. 94–95. Controversy remains—though it shouldn't—regarding what Kennedy knew and when he knew it. Tom Wicker, *One of Us*, p. 232, Ted Sorensen, *Kennedy*, p. 205, and Michael O'Brien, *Kennedy*, p. 494, provide Kennedy with the benefit of the doubt, but Herbert Parmet, *JFK*, pp. 47–49, lays out compelling reasons for believing otherwise. Goodwin's later statements, in his 1988 memoir, support Parmet's view. Beyond that, General Andrew Goodpaster informed author Michael Beschloss that he had briefed JFK "about the planning, which was to form the unit and train the unit, that this was what had been approved."

Beschloss, *Crisis Years*, pp. 29–30*fn.*

371 "Nixon's position . . . office." *Chicago Tribune*, 12 October 1960, p. 6; Klein, *Perfectly Clear*, p. 95.

372 Goodwin. Blight and Kornbluh, p. 39.

372 "It was . . . plans." Parmet, *JFK*, p. 49; Goodwin, *Remembering*, p. 125.

372 Schlesinger. Schlesinger, *Thousand Days*, p. 73.

372 "It was . . . reviewed." Goodwin, *Remembering*, pp. 124–26; Parmet, *JFK*, p. 48.

372 "In all . . . freedom.'" Schlesinger, *Thousand Days*, p. 73; Wicker, *One of Us*, p. 232.

373 "[T]he release . . . statement." Parmet, *JFK*, p. 48.

373 "The forces . . . assisted." Parmet, *JFK*, p. 47.

373 "encouraging . . . to Castro." *Washington Post*, 7 October 1960, pp. A1–A2; Parmet, *JFK*, p. 47; http://www.jfklink.com/speeches/jfk/oct60/jfk061060 _cincinatti02.html.

373 "There was . . . commitments." Nixon, *Six Crises*, p. 355.

373 "Nixon's . . . or justify." Wicker, *One of Us*, p. 232.

374 JFK prep. Watson, *Vista*, p. 14.

374 Pre-debate details. *Connellsville Daily Courier*, 21 October 1960, p. 1; *Washington Post*, 22 October 1960, p. A8; *New York Times*, 22 October 1960, p. 10; *Chicago Tribune*, 22 October 1960, p. 5; *New York Times*, 23 October 1960, p. 70.

374 Limited to foreign policy. *New York Times*, 22 October 1960, pp. 8–9; *Washington Post*, 22 October 1960, pp. A8–A9.

375 "the most . . . campaign." Nixon, *RN*, p. 272.

375 "Senator . . . objective." *New York Times*, 22 October 1960, p. 8; *Washington Post* , 22 October 1960, p. A8; *Chicago Tribune*, 22 October 1960, p. 6; Nixon, *Six Crises*, p. 355; Schlesinger, *Thousand Days*, p. 226.

375 "Now what . . . today." *New York Times*, 22 October 1960, p. 8; *Washington Post*, 22 October 1960, p. A8; *New York Times*, 24 October 1960, p. 21.

375 "In 1957 . . . Cuba." *New York Times*, 22 October 1960, p. 8.

376 "Probably he . . . be" *New York Times*, 25 August 1960, p. 20; O'Brien, *Kennedy*, p. 492; Ambrose, *Nixon*, p. 570.

376 "America . . . stand pat." *Washington Post*, 22 October 1960, p. A9.

376 "I felt . . . audience." Lurie, p. 259.

376 "Mr. Nixon . . . 1963." *Washington Post*, 22 October 1960, p. A8.

377 "It sure . . . it?" *Chicago Tribune*, 22 October 1960, p. 5.

377 Punches wall. Klein, *Perfectly Clear*, pp. 102–6.

377 "He [JFK] . . . err." *Winnipeg Free Press*, 26 October 1960, p. 2; *Charleston Gazette–Mail*, 30 October 1960, p. 12A.

377 "I really . . . out"; "Senator Kennedy . . . republics." Lasky, *JFK*, p. 454; Hersh, *Camelot*, p. 181; *New York Times*, 23 October 1960, p. E10; *Oswego Palladium Times*, 4 November 1960, p. 14; Goodwin, *Remembering*, p. 126; Leamer, *Kennedy Men*, p. 454.

377 "The fourth . . . say." White, *1960*, p. 318.

378 "What should . . . III." *New York Times*, 24 October 1960, pp. 1, 18;

Washington Post, 24 October 1960, p. A7; Committee on Commerce, pp. 715–18.

378   JFK dodges fifth debate. *New York Times*, 25 October 1960, p. 28. JFK argued that other issues should also be a part of the event.

378   "appalling." Beschloss, *Crisis Years*, p. 30.

378   "So far . . . fifth." *Winnipeg Free Press*, 26 October 1960, p. 2.

379   "If I . . . it." Schlesinger, *Thousand Days*, p. 73; Goodwin, *Remembering*, p. 126.

379   "I have . . . country." *New York Times*, 24 October 1960, p. 19; *Washington Post*, 24 October 1960, p. A7; *New York Times*, 25 October 1960, p. 34; http://www.jfklink.com/speeches/jfk/oct60/jfk231060_telegram.html.

379   Lippmann. Schlesinger, *Thousand Days*, p. 73; Schlesinger, *Journals*, p. 91.

379   "In any . . . themes." Schlesinger, *Thousand Days*, p. 73.

379   "It is . . . ground." *New York Times*, 25 October 1960, p. 34.

380   Recommendations. Nixon, *Six Crises*, p. 355.

Chapter Thirty-four: "They know not what they do"

381   "God bless . . . had." Fremon, p. 40.

381   "You must . . . bus." Cohen and Taylor, p. 264.

382   Dabney. *New York Times*, 5 November 1960, p. 14; *Chicago Tribune*, 5 November 1960, p. 1; *Oakland Tribune*, 5 November 1960, p. 2; *Columbus Daily Telegram*, 5 November 1960, p. 9; *Winnipeg Free Press*, 5 November 1960, p. 4. Authorities released Alejandro and Dabney on five-hundred-dollar bond each. *Chicago Tribune*, 7 November 1960, p. A9; *Lowell Sun*, 7 November 1960, p. 24.

382   Alaska. *Los Angeles Times*, 7 November 1960, p. 1. JFK also campaigned in Alaska, visiting Anchorage on September 3. *Los Angeles Times*, 4 September 1960, pp. 1, 4.

383   California. O'Brien, *Kennedy*, p. 494.

383   Hutschnecker. Summers, p. 219.

383   Nixonburger loan. Summers, pp. 155–57; Higham, pp. 187–88; Barlett and Steele, pp. 203–4; Mathews, pp. 177–78.

383   Bankruptcy. Barlett and Steele, pp. 203–4.

383   Pearson. *Portsmouth Herald*, 27 October 1960, p. 4; *Hayward Daily Record*, 27 October 1960, p. 3; *Burlington Times-News*, 28 October 1960, p. 3A; *Arizona Daily Sun*, 31 October 1960, p. 5; Mathews, pp. 177–78.

383   No comment. *Hayward Daily Record*, 27 October 1960, p. 3.

383   "an obvious . . . libel." *Chicago Tribune*, 31 October 1960, p. 17; Mathews, pp. 177–78; Parmet, *Nixon*, p. 409.

384   Justice Department. *Burlington Times-News*, 28 October 1960, p. 3A.

384   No proof. Ambrose, *Nixon*, pp. 599–600.

384   Shaking. Aitken, p. 276.

384   Roosevelt. *Syracuse Post-Standard*, 5 December 1960, p. 1.

384   Morton. *Los Angeles Times*, 7 November 1960, p. 6.

384   Judd. Lasky, *JFK*, pp. 377–78; Sorensen, p. 39; Salinger, *With Kennedy*, p. 65.

384   Hagerty, Ike. Ambrose, *Nixon*, p. 601.

385 "It was . . . late." Salinger, *With Kennedy*, p. 65.

385 "[T]he . . . Eisenhower." Wyckoff, pp. 50–51.

385 "the young genius." Wicker, p. 242; Perret, *Eisenhower*, p. 597.

385 "I'm going . . . enthusiasm." Eisenhower, *Mandate*, p. 597.

385 TV. Jamieson, p. 150.

386 "I don't . . . send." *Oakland Tribune*, 5 November 1960, p. 2B; White, *1960*, p. 373.

386 "With every . . . grabs." Fay, p. 65; Mathews, p. 175.

386 Mamie. Nixon, *RN*, p. 274; Anthony, p. 596. Mamie's call was barely a month after her own mother had passed away.

386 "I know . . . health." Nixon, *RN*, p. 274.

386 "Dick looked . . . on." Jamieson, p. 148.

386 "He was . . . angry." Jamieson, p. 148. Tom Wicker and David Halberstam strongly impugn Nixon's contention in his autobiography *RN* that he kept Ike out of the campaign out of concern for the general's health, painstakingly noting it was not issued until all the principals—Ike and Dr. Snyder—were dead or—in Mamie's case—almost dead. But Fred Seaton's corroboration of Nixon's contention was given in 1966—three years before Eisenhower's passing, four years before Snyder's, and thirteen years before Mamie's. Wicker, pp. 242–43.

386 Ike, Hall. Wicker, pp. 242–43; Halberstam, *Powers*, p. 336; Perret, *Eisenhower*, p. 598; Summers, p. 206.

386 Adolphus luncheon. *Syracuse Post-Standard*, 1 November 1960, p. 1; Evans and Novak, p. 302; Mooney, *The Politicians*, p. 350.

387 "I told . . . aside." *Syracuse Post-Standard*, 1 November 1960, p. 1.

387 "LBJ and . . . did." Miller, *Lyndon*, p. 271.

387 "If he . . . knew." Miller, *Lyndon*, p. 271.

387 "If the . . . it." *New York Times*, 5 November 1960, p. 1; Reston, *Lone Star*, pp. 198–99; Dallek, *Lone Star*, pp. 587–88; Woods, p. 373.

387 "One thing . . . area." Valenti Interview, JFK Library, p. 5.

387 "Although, we . . . Johnson." *New York Times*, 8 November 1960, p. 17.

387 "I looked . . . do.'" *New York Times*, 8 November 1960, p. 17.

388 Nerves. White, *1960*, p. 373.

389 55 states. *Modesto Bee*, 8 November 1960, p. A3;http://www.jfklink.com/speeches/ jfk/nov60/jfk071160_manchester01.html.

389 "I do . . . country." White, *History*, p. 478; http://www.jfklink.com/speeches/ jfk/nov60/jfk071160_boston02.html.

389 Heavy lifting. Galbraith, *Name Dropping*, p. 102.

389 Tricia, Julie. *Chicago Tribune*, 8 November 1960, p. 6.

389 Bomb. *Chicago Tribune*, 8 November 1960, p. 4; *Galveston News*, 8 November 1960, p. 1.

389 "God damn . . . right?" *Washington Post*, 8 November 1960, pp. 1, 2A; *Modesto Bee*, 8 November 1960, p. A-3; Novak, p. 76.

390 Commercials. *New York Times*, 8 November 1960, p. 23.

390 "the response . . . appalling." *New York Times*, 8 November 1960, p. 23;

Chicago Tribune, 8 November 1960, p. 4; *Modesto Bee*, 8 November 1960, p. A-3; Committee on Commerce, pp. 1082–1116; Wyckoff, p. 56.

390 Rojas. *Long Beach Independent*, 7 November 1960, p. 1; *San Mateo Times*, 7 November 1960, p. 22.

390 Chicago. *Chicago Tribune*, 8 November 1960, p. 5; *Modesto Bee*, 8 November 1960, p. A3; Committee on Commerce, pp. 1117–19.

Chapter Thirty-five: "I'm just out for a little ride"

391 Polls. *Washington Post*, 8 November 1960, p. A17; *Los Angeles Times*, 7 November 1960, pp. 1, 28; *Hartford Courant*, 8 November 1960, p. 1; Crespi and Mendelsohn, pp. 80–81, 110; Brodie, p. 432.

391 Odds. *Long Beach Press-Telegram*, 4 November 1960, p. 30.

391 Unions, newspapers. *Long Beach Press-Telegram*, 4 November 1960, p. 30.

391 *Revolucion*. *Los Angeles Times*, 8 November 160, p. D10; *Humboldt-Eureka Standard*, 8 November 1960, p. 1.

391 Election details. *Hartford Courant*, 8 November 1960, p. 15B.

392 Early voting. *New York Times*, 8 November 1960, p. 22; *Chicago Tribune*, 8 November 1960, pp. 1, 2; *Hartford Courant*, 8 November 1960, p. 15; *Los Angeles Times*, 8 November 1960, pp. 1, D1; *Humboldt-Eureka Standard*, 8 November 1960, p. 1.

392 Windsor. *Hartford Courant*, 8 November 1960, p. 14.

392 Young. *Los Angeles Times*, 9 November 1960, p. 16.

392 Maloof. *Los Angeles Times*, 9 November 1960, p. 6.

392 Moynihan. Hodgson, p. 69.

393 Eisenhower. *Los Angeles Times*, 8 November 1960, pp. D3, 6; *Hartford Courant*, 8 November 1960, p. 5; *Modesto Bee*, 8 November 1960, p. A-3; *Valparaiso Vidette-Messenger*, 9 November 1960, pp. 1, 6; Mamie, evidently not an early riser, motored into Gettysburg that afternoon to cast her ballot.

393 JFK votes. *Modesto Bee*, 8 November 1960, p. A2; *Washington Post*, 9 November 1960, p. D1; O'Donnell, Powers, and McCarthy, p. 255; Carr, p. 126.

393 Jackie votes. O'Neill, p. 100; Heymann, *Jackie*, p. 245. Because Jackie had cast the *only* absentee, everyone knew precisely for whom she had voted— *and not voted*. "I was crushed," O'Neill recalled, "and I couldn't understand how she could do that to me."

394 "Well, this . . . daughter." *Modesto Bee*, 8 November 1960, p. A2; *Washington Post*, 9 November 1960, p. D1; O'Donnell, Powers and McCarthy, p. 255.

394 Hyannis arrival. *Humboldt–Eureka Standard*, 8 November 1960, p. 1; *Modesto Bee*, 8 November 1960, pp. 1, A2; *Hartford Courant*, 8 November 1960, p. 5.

394 Lodge. *New York Times*, 8 November 1960, p. 21; *Washington Post*, 8 November 1960, p. A5; *Los Angeles Times*, 8 November 1960, p. D2; *Hartford Courant*, 8 November 1960, p. 5; *Oakland Tribune*, 8 November 1960, p. 2E.

394 LBJ. *Hartford Courant*, 8 November 1960, p. 5; *Washington Post*, 8 November

1960, p. A12; *Washington Post*, 9 November 1960, p. A5.

395 "I know . . . you." Woods, p. 376.

395 Truman. *Hartford Courant*, 8 November 1960, p. 5.

395 "Your telephone . . . me." Martin, *Hero*, pp. 550–51.

395 Roosevelt. http://www.gwu.edu/~erpapers/myday/displaydoc.cfm?_y=1960 and_f=md004874.

395 Daley. Cohen and Taylor, p. 264.

395 Hoover, Farley. *New York Times*, 9 November 1960, p. 13; *Washington Post*, 9 November 1960, p. A5; *Los Angeles Times*, 8 November 1960, p. D3.

395 UN. *New York Times*, 8 November 1960, p. 16; *New York Times*, 9 November 1960, p. 2.

396 King. *Modesto Bee*, 3 November 1960, p. 5; Branch, p. 374.

396 Wexford. *Hartford Courant*, 8 November 1960, p. 8.

396 Rose. Russell, p. 391.

396 Nixon votes. *Los Angeles Times*, 8 November 1960, p. D2; *Chicago Tribune*, 8 November 1960, p. 6; *Hartford Courant*, 8 November 1960, p. 5; *Modesto Bee*, 8 November 1960, p. 1; *Washington Post*, 9 November 1960, p. D1; Nixon, *Six Crises*, pp. 376–77. Like Kennedy, Nixon's voting residence was fictitious. He and Pat were registered at F. Donald Nixon's house at 13844 East Whittier Boulevard.

397 The Ambassador was a Schine hotel, owned by the family of G. David Schine, a former aide to Senator Joe McCarthy and one of the causes of his downfall.

397 Ditches. *Modesto Bee*, 8 November 1960, pp. 1–A2.

397 Mother. *Chicago Tribune*, 24 July 1960, p. 6; *Los Angeles Times*, 8 November 1960, p. 4.

397 "I'm just . . . rest." *Modesto Bee*, 8 November 1960, p. 1; *Washington Post*, 9 November 1960, p. D1; de Toledano, p. 309.

397 Klein. *Modesto Bee*, 8 November 1960, p. A2.

398 Finch. *Modesto Bee*, 8 November 1960, pp. 1, A3; Nixon, *Six Crises*, pp. 377–78; Summers, p. 231.

398 Border. *Los Angeles Times*, 8 November 1960, p. 2D.

398 San Juan Capistrano. Nixon, *Six Crises*, p. 378; Summers, p. 231.

398 "It wasn't . . . up." *Modesto Bee*, 8 November 1960, p. 1; *Washington Post*, 9 November 1960, p. D1.

398 Afternoon. Carr, pp. 126–27; White, *1960*, pp. 7–8; O'Brien, *Victories*, p. 95; Brodie, p. 420.

398 "Bobby was . . . pronounced." Martin, *Destruction*, p. 272.

399 JPK. Carr, pp. 126–27; White, *1960*, p. 8.

399 Nap. White, *1960*, p. 8.

Chapter Thirty-six: "The help of a few close friends"

400   Nixon. *Hartford Courant*, 8 November 1960, p. 5; *Washington Post*, 9 November 1960, p. D1; Summers, p. 231.

400   LBJ. *New York Times*, 8 November 1960, p. 17; *Hartford Courant*, 8 November 1960, p. 5; *Washington Post*, 9 November 1960, p. A5.

400   Lodge, Ike. *Hartford Courant*, 8 November 1960, p. 5; *Modesto Bee*, 8 November 1960, p. 1; Eisenhower, *Mandate*, p. 601.

400   ABC. *Brainerd Dispatch*, 9 November 1960, p. 16.

400   Mickelson. *Los Angeles Times*, 8 November 1960, p. A6.

401   Connecticut. *Hartford Courant*, 9 November 1960, p. 11B; *Chicago Tribune*, 9 November 1960, p. 1; Martin, *Destruction*, p. 273.

401   NBC. de Toledano, p. 309.

401   *Times*. Martin, *Destruction*, p. 273.

401   "I see . . . Pennsylvania." White, *1960*, p. 25; O'Donnell, Powers and McCarthy, p. 257; Sorensen, *Kennedy*, p. 211; Woods, p. 375.

401   "I don't . . . unhappy." Miller, *Lyndon*, p. 273; Woods, p. 375.

401   UAW. Boyle, p. 145.

401   Catholics. Jamieson, p. 135*fn*; Bochin, p. 54.

401   Projections. *Los Angeles Times*, 8 November 1960, p. D1; Schoor, p. 188.

402   "I'm worrying . . . feelings." Martin, *Destruction*, p. 273.

402   "He's lost . . . charge." Martin, *Hero*, p. 235.

402   Hyannisport. Carr, p. 126; White, *1960*, p. 6; White, *In Search of History*, p. 491; Sorensen, p. 36; Schwab and Shneidman, p. 100.

402   "I feel . . . thirty–one." Anthony, p. 597.

402   "Everybody . . . awhile." Kennedy, *Remember*, p. 376.

402   "Their bigots . . . bigots." Bowles, p. 297; Martin, *Hero*, p. 235.

402   "With a . . . Illinois." Bradlee, *Conversations*, p. 33.

403   Brill. *Chicago Tribune*, 28 October 1960, p. 10; Campbell, p. 246; Gumbel, p. 163.

403   November 3 report. *Chicago Tribune*, 4 November 1960, p. 8.

403   Irregularities. *Chicago Tribune*, 20 October 1960, p. A2; *Chicago Tribune*, 28 October 1960, p. 10; *Chicago Tribune*, 4 November 1960, p. 8; *Chicago Tribune*, 26 November 1960, p. 2.

403   "had so . . . Kennedy." Hersh, *Camelot*, p. 136; Gumbel. p. 165.

404   "To assure . . . Kennedy." Lewis, pp. 264–65.

404   "Beyond doubt . . . Illinois." Hersh, *Camelot*, p. 140.

404   "The presidency . . . Chicago." Blakey and Billings, p. 377; Bly p. 111; Gumbel, p. 167.

404   Wards. de Toledano, p. 311; Heymann, *RFK*, p. 182.

404   "Listen, honey . . . House." Exner, p. 194; Gumbel, p. 166.

404   Missouri, Texas. de Toledano, p. 311; Campbell, pp. 255–56.

405   "I simply . . . Kennedy." Nixon, *Six Crises*, pp. 386–87.

405   "I guess . . . again." *Hartford Courant*, 10 November 1960, p. 7.

405   Rally. *New York Times*, 9 November 1960, p. 20; *Washington Post*, 9 November 1960, pp. 1, A5; *Hartford Courant*, 10 November 1960, p. 7; Nixon, *RN*, p. 276.

406   Tears. *New York Times*, 9 November 1960, p. 1; *Hartford Courant*, 10 November 1960, p. 7; Brodie, pp. 432–33.

406   Bunny. White, *1960*, p. 20; Carr, p. 127; O'Donnell, Powers, and McCarthy, p. 258.

406   "Why don't . . ."; " . . . staying awake." O'Brien, *Victories*, p. 96.

406   Powers. Martin, *Hero*, p. 235.

406   "Good night, Mr. President." Kennedy, *Remember*, p. 377.

406   RFK. Martin, *Hero*, p. 235.

406   "I read . . . ten." Martin, *Destruction*, p. 274.

408   "one-legged . . . English." Henderson, p. 124. Ironically, despite his fumbling of King's Atlanta arrest, Nixon carried Atlanta's largely black districts. Branch, p. 376.

408   "What are . . . school?" *New York Times*, 9 November 1960, pp. 1, 42; Nixon, *Six Crises*, p. 392.

409   Salinger. Salinger, *With Kennedy*, p. 74; Sorensen, *Kennedy*, p. 212.

409   Ike. *New York Times*, 9 November 1960, p. 1; *New York Times*, 10 November 1960, p. 42.

409   "I hope . . . election." Lurie, p. 262.

409   *CQ*. Parmet, *Nixon*, p. 355.

409   "I want . . . years." *New York Times*, 10 November 1960, p. 1.

410   "He went . . . class." *New York Times*, 9 November 1960, p. 1; *Hartford Courant*, 10 November 1960, p. 7; Salinger, *With Kennedy*, p. 76; Matthews, p. 179.

Chapter Thirty-seven: "*Dies irae*"

411   "the most . . . Christendom." Manchester, *Death*, p. 586.

411   JFK inauguration. *New York Times*, 21 January 1961, pp. 8, 12; *Long Beach Independent*, 20 January 1961, pp. 1, 4; Manchester, *Glory*, pp. 889–90; Bradford, p. 165; Heymann, *RFK*, p. 198; Taraborrelli, p. 35; Smith, *Grace and Power*, p. 66.

411   "Brilliant people . . . were." Wills, *Kennedy Imprisonment*, p. 144.

412   "You won't . . . gentlemen" *New York Times*, 8 November 1962, pp. 1, 18; Nixon, *RN*, p. 303; Parmet, *Nixon*, pp. 429–30.

412   "with lubrication . . . grace." Summers, p. 232.

412   "heads together . . . schoolboys." Parmet, *Nixon*, p. 437.

412   38 percent. Blakey and Billings, p. 3.

412   "Except the . . . vain." *New York Times*, 23 November 1963, p. 11; *New York Times*, 24 November 1963, p. 12; Sorensen, *Kennedy*, p. 751.

413   Nixon. Nixon, *RN*, pp. 311–12.

413   "nut country." O'Donnell, Powers, and McCarthy, p. 25; Bradford, p. 266; Leamer, *Kennedy Men*, p. 734.

413   Stevenson. *Amarillo Globe–Times*, 25 October 1963, pp. 1–2; Warren Commission Report, pp. 30, 41, 292; Martin, *Adlai Stevenson*, pp. 774–75.

413   WANTED FOR TREASON. Warren Commission Report, pp. 30, 41, 292; Manchester, *Death*, p. 64.

413   Index cards. Smith, *Grace and Power*, p. 494.

413   "Jackie . . . about it?" O'Donnell, Powers, and McCarthy, p. 25; Schlesinger, *Thousand Days*, p. 1024.

413   "last night. . . crowd." Manchester, *Death*, p. 121; Leamer, *Kennedy Men*, pp. 734–35.

413   "Just look . . . you." O'Brien, *Victories*, p. 157; Maier, p. 455.

413   "[I]t was . . . do." Warren Commission Report, p. 42.

414   "You can't . . . today," *San Antonio Express–News*, 21 November 1965, p. 2–D; Warren Commission Report, p. 48; Manchester, *Death*, p. 153.

414   "seemed really . . . happy." Brinkley, *Brinkley's Beat*, p. 57.

415   "I shall . . . President." *New York Times*, 1 April 1968, p. 1, 27.

415   Ambassador Hotel. *Long Beach Press-Telegram*, 7 November 1960, p. A-12; Manchester, *Glory*, pp. 632–33; Ehrlichman, pp. 25–26; Wicker, p. 100; Mazo, p. 122.

415   "The policeman . . . disorder." Cohen and Taylor, p. 482.

417   "Always remember . . . yourself." *New York Times*, 23 April 1994, p. 13.

Bibliography

Abell, Tyler, ed. *The Drew Pearson Diaries 1949–1959*. New York: Holt, Rinehart, Winston, 1974.

Aitken, Jonathan. *Nixon: A Life*. Washington, DC: Regnery, 2007.

Alexander, Herbert E. *Financing the 1960 Election*. Princeton, NJ: Citizens' Research Foundation, 1962.

Allen, Maury. *Jackie Robinson: A Life Remembered*. New York: Franklin Watts, 1987.

Alsop, Stewart. *Nixon and Rockefeller: A Double Portrait*. Garden City, NY: Doubleday, 1960.

Ambrose, Stephen E. *Eisenhower: The President*. New York: Simon & Schuster, 1984.

Ambrose, Stephen E. *Eisenhower: Soldier and President*. New York: Simon & Schuster, 1990.

Ambrose, Stephen E. *Nixon: The Education of a Politician 1913–1962, Volume I*. New York: Simon & Schuster, 1987.

Anderson, Christopher. *Jack and Jackie: Portrait of an American Marriage*. New York: William Morrow, 1996.

Anderson, Jack, and James Boyd. *Confessions of a Muckraker*. New York: Random House, 1979.

Andrew, John A., III. *The Other Side of the Sixties: Young Americans for Freedom and the Rise of Conservative Politics*. New Brunswick, NJ: Rutgers University Press, 1997.

Anthony, Carl Sferrazza. *First Ladies: The Saga of the Presidents' Wives and Their Power 1789–1961*. New York: William Morrow, 1990.

Baker, Bobby, and Larry L. King. *Wheeling and Dealing: Confessions of a Capital Hill Operator*. New York: W. W. Norton, 1978.

Barlett, Donald L., and James Steele. *Howard Hughes: His Life and Madness*. New York: W. W. Norton, 1979.

Barnouw, Erik. *A History of Broadcasting in the United States. Volume III: From 1953*. New York: Oxford University Press, 1970.

Benson, Ezra Taft. *Cross Fire: The Eight Years with Eisenhower*. Garden City, NY: Doubleday, 1962.

Beran, Michael Knox. *The Last Patrician: Bobby Kennedy and the End of American Aristocracy*. New York: St. Martin's Press, 1998.

Berman, Edgar. *Hubert: The Triumph and Tragedy of the Humphrey I Knew*. New York: G. P. Putnam's Sons, 1979.

Beschloss, Michael R. *Mayday: Eisenhower, Khrushchev, and the U-2 Affair*. New York: HarperCollins, 1987.

Beschloss, Michael R. *The Crisis Years: Kennedy and Khrushchev 1960–1963 Affair*. New York: HarperCollins, 1991.

Black, Conrad. *Richard M. Nixon: A Life in Full*. New York: PublicAffairs, 2007.

Blair, Joan, and Clay Blair Jr. *The Search for J.F.K.* New York: Berkley Publishing, 1976.

Blakey, G. Robert, and Richard N. Billings. *The Plot to Kill the President*. New York: Times Books, 1981.

Blight, James G., Peter Kornbluh, eds. *Politics of Illusion: The Bay of Pigs Invasion Reexamined.* Boulder, CO: Lynne Rienner, 1999.

Bly, Nellie. *The Kennedy Men: Three Generations of Sex, Scandal, and Secrets.* New York: Kensington Books, 1997.

Bochin, Hal W. *Richard Nixon: Rhetorical Strategist.* Westport, CT: Greenwood Press, 1990.

Bowles, Chester. *Promises to Keep: My Years in Public Life.* New York: Harper & Row, 1971.

Boyle, Kevin. *The UAW and the Heyday of American Liberalism, 1945–1968.* Ithaca, NY: Cornell University Press, 1995.

Bradford, Sarah. *America's Queen: The Life of Jacqueline Kennedy Onassis.* New York: Viking, 2000.

Bradlee, Benjamin C. *A Good Life: Newspapering and Other Adventures.* New York: Simon & Schuster, 1995.

Bradlee, Benjamin C. *Conversations with Kennedy.* New York: W. W. Norton, 1975.

Branch, Taylor. *Parting the Waters: America in the King Years, 1954–63.* New York: Simon & Schuster, 1989.

Brennan, Mary C. *Turning Right in the Sixties: The Conservative Capture of the GOP.* Chapel Hill: University of North Carolina Press, 1995.

Bridges, Linda, and John R. Coyne Jr. *Strictly Right: William F. Buckley Jr. and the American Conservative Movement.* Hoboken: John Wiley & Sons, 2007.

Brooke, Edward W. *Bridging the Divide: My Life.* New Brunswick, NJ: Rutgers University Press, 2007.

Brooks, Tim, and Earle Marsh. *The Complete Directory to Prime Time Network TV Shows 1946–Present.* New York: Ballantine Books, 1981.

Bruno, Jerry, and Jeff Greenfield. *The Advance Man.* New York: William Morrow, 1971.

Bryant, Nick. *The Bystander: John F. Kennedy and the Struggle for Black Equality.* New York: Basic Books, 2006.

Buckley, William F., Jr., ed. *Odyssey of a Friend: Whittaker Chambers' Letters to William F Buckley, Jr. 1954–1961.* New York: G. P. Putnam's Sons, 1969.

Burns, James MacGregor. *John F. Kennedy: A Political Profile.* New York: Avon Books, 1959.

Busby, Horace. *The Thirty-first of March: An Intimate Portrait of Lyndon Johnson's Final Days in Office.* New York: Farrar, Straus & Giroux, 2006.

Campbell, Tracy. *Deliver the Vote; a History of Election Fraud, an American Political Tradition 1742–2004.* New York: Carroll & Graf, 2005.

Caro, Robert A. *The Power Broker: Robert Moses and the Fall of New York.* New York: Random House, 1974.

Caro, Robert A. *The Path to Power.* New York: Vintage Books, 1983.

Caro, Robert A. *Means of Ascent.* New York: Alfred A. Knopf, 1990.

Caro, Robert A. *Master of the Senate.* New York: Alfred A. Knopf, 2002.

Carr, William A. *JFK: An Informal Biography.* New York: Lancer Books, 1962.

Chalmers, David M. *Hooded Americanism: The History of the Ku Klux Klan.* Chicago: Quadrangle Books, 1968.

Churchwell, Sarah. *The Many Lives of Marilyn Monroe*. New York: Picador, 2004.

Clifford, Clark. *Counsel to the President: A Memoir*. New York: Random House, 1991.

Cohen, Adam, and Elizabeth Taylor. *American Pharaoh: Mayor Richard J. Daley—His Battle for Chicago and the Nation*. Boston: Little, Brown, 2000.

Cohen, Dan. *Undefeated: The Life of Hubert H. Humphrey*. Minneapolis: Lerner Publications, 1978.

Cohn, Roy. *McCarthy*. New York: New American Library, 1968.

Collier, Peter, and David Horowitz. *The Kennedys: An American Drama*. San Francisco: Encounter Books, 2002.

Collier, Peter, and David Horowitz. *The Rockefellers: An American Dynasty*. New York: Simon & Schuster, 1976.

Committee on Commerce, United States Senate. *Final Report of the Subcommittee on Communications Part II: The Speeches, Remarks, Press Conferences, and Study Papers of Vice President Richard M. Nixon August 1 through November 7, 1960*. Washington, DC: U.S. Government Printing Office, 1961.

Conkin, Paul K. *Big Daddy from the Pedernales*. Boston: Twayne Publishers, 1986.

Connally, John, with Mickey Herskowitz. *In History's Shadow: An American Odyssey*. New York: Hyperion, 1993.

Cook, Fred J. *Barry Goldwater: Extremist of the Right*. New York: Grove Press, 1964.

Coolidge, Calvin. *The Autobiography of Calvin Coolidge*. New York: Cosmopolitan Book Corporation, 1929.

Cordery, Stacy A. *Alice: Alice Roosevelt Longworth, from White House Princess to Washington Power Broker*. New York: Viking, 2007.

Costello, William. *The Facts About Nixon*. New York: Viking Press, 1960.

Crespi, Irving, and Harold Mendelsohn. *Polls, Television and the New Politics*. Scranton: Chandler Publishing, 1970.

Cronkite, Walter. *A Reporter's Life*. New York: Alfred A. Knopf, 1996.

Dallek, Robert. *An Unfinished Life: John F. Kennedy, 1917–1963*. Boston: Little, Brown, 2003.

Dallek, Robert. *Flawed Giant: Lyndon Johnson and His Times, 1961–1973*. New York: Oxford University Press, 1998.

Dallek, Robert. *Lone Star Rising: Lyndon Johnson and His Times, 1908–1960*. New York: Oxford University Press, 1991.

Dallek, Robert. *Nixon and Kissinger: Partners in Power*. New York: HarperCollins, 2007.

Davis, John H. *The Kennedys: Dynasty and Disaster*. New York: S. P. I. Books, 1992.

Davis, Kenneth S. *The Politics of Honor: A Biography of Adlai E. Stevenson*. New York: G. P. Putnam's Sons, 1967.

David, Lester. *The Lonely Lady of San Clemente*. New York: Crowell, 1978.

David, Lester, and Irene David. *Bobby Kennedy: The Making of a Folk Hero*. New York: Dodd, Mead, 1986.

Davis, Sammy, Jr., and Jane and Burt Boyar. *Sammy: The Autobiography of Sammy Davis Jr.* New York: Farrar, Straus & Giroux, 2000.

Davis, Sammy, Jr., and Jane and Burt Boyar. *Why Me? The Sammy Davis Jr. Story*. New York: Farrar, Straus & Giroux, 1989.

Davis, Sammy, Jr., and Jane and Burt Boyar. *Yes I Can*. New York: Farrar, Straus & Giroux, 1965.

De Toledano, Ralph. *One Man Alone: Richard Nixon*. New York: Funk & Wagnalls, 1969.

Diamond, Sara. *Roads to Dominion: Right-Wing Movements and Political Power in the United States*. New York: Guilford Press, 1995.

Donovan, Robert J. *PT 109: John F. Kennedy in World War II*. New York: McGraw-Hill, 1961.

Dugger, Ronnie *The Politician: The Life and Times of Lyndon Johnson, The Drive for Power, from the Frontier to Master of the Senate*. New York: W. W. Norton, 1982.

Eaton, Herbert. *Presidential Timber: A History of Nominating Conventions, 1886–1960*. London: Free Press of Glencoe, 1964.

Eisenhower, Dwight D. *Mandate for Change: The White House Years, 1953–56*. Garden City, NY: Doubleday, 1963.

Eisenhower, Dwight D. *Waging Peace: The White House Years, 1956–1961*. Garden City, NY: Doubleday, 1965.

Eisenhower, Julie Nixon. *Pat Nixon the Untold Story*. New York: Simon & Schuster, 1986.

Emblidge, David, ed. *My Day: The Best of Eleanor Roosevelt's Acclaimed Newspaper Columns, 1936–1962*. New York: DaCapo Press, 2001.

Erlichman, John. *Witness to Power: The Nixon Years*. New York: Simon & Schuster, 1982.

Evans, Rowland, and Robert Novak. *Lyndon B. Johnson: The Exercise of Power*. New York: New American Library, 1966.

Exner, Judith Campbell, with Ovid Demaris. *Judith Exner: My Story*. New York: Grove Press, 1977.

Fairlie, Henry. *The Kennedy Promise: The Politics of Expectation*. Garden City, NY: Doubleday, 1973.

Fay, Paul P., Jr. *The Pleasure of His Company*. New York: Harper & Row, 1966.

Falkner, David. *Great Time Coming: The Life of Jackie Robinson from Baseball to Birmingham*. New York: Simon & Schuster, 1995.

Farrell, John Aloysius. *Tip O'Neill and the Democratic Century*. Boston: Little, Brown, 2002.

Felknor, Bruce L. *Political Mischief: Smear, Sabotage and Reform in U.S. Elections*. Westport, CT: Praeger Publishers, 2002.

Ferrell, Robert H., ed. *The Eisenhower Diaries*. New York: W. W. Norton, 1981.

Fite, Gilbert C. *Richard B. Russell, Jr.: Senator from Georgia*. Chapel Hill: University of North Carolina Press, 1991.

Franklin, John Hope. *From Slavery to Freedom: A History of Negro Americans*. New York: Vintage Books, 1969.

Frantz, Douglas, and David McKean. *Friends in High Places: The Rise and Fall of Clark Clifford*. Boston: Little, Brown, 1995.

Fremon, David K. *Chicago Politics: Ward by Ward*. Bloomington: Indiana University Press, 1988.

Friedenberg, Robert V. *Notable Speeches in Contemporary Presidential Campaigns.* Westport, CT: Praeger, 2002.

Friendly, Fred W. *Due to Circumstances Beyond Our Control . . .* New York: Alfred A. Knopf, 1967.

Fuchs, Lawrence H. *John F. Kennedy and American Catholicism.* New York: Meredith Press, 1967.

Gabler, Neal. *An Empire of Their Own: How the Jews Invented Hollywood.* New York: Crown, 1988.

Gabler, Neal. *Winchell: Gossip, Power and the Culture of Celebrity.* New York: Alfred A. Knopf, 1994.

Galbraith, John Kenneth. *A Life in Our Times.* New York: Houghton-Mifflin, 1981.

Galbraith, John Kenneth. *Name Dropping: From FDR On.* New York: Houghton-Mifflin, 1999.

Gates, Gary Paul. *Air Time: The Inside Story of CBS News.* New York: Harper & Row, 1978.

Gellman, Irwin. *The Contender: Richard Nixon: The Congress Years, 1946–1952.* New York: Free Press, 1999.

Gervasi, Frank. *The Real Rockefeller: The Story of the Rise, Decline and Resurgence of the Presidential Aspirations of Nelson Rockefeller.* New York: Atheneum, 1964.

Gilbert, Robert E. *The Mortal Presidency: Illness and Anguish in the White House.* New York: Basic Books, 1992.

Goldberg, Robert Alan. *Barry Goldwater.* New Haven, CT: Yale University Press, 1995.

Goldwater, Barry M. *With No Apologies: The Personal and Political Memoirs of United States Senator Barry M. Goldwater.* New York: Morrow, 1979.

Goodwin, Doris Kearns. *Lyndon Johnson and the American Dream.* New York: St. Martin's Press, 1991.

Goodwin, Doris Kearns. *The Fitzgeralds and the Kennedys.* New York: Simon & Schuster, 1987.

Goodwin, Richard. *Remembering in America: A Voice from the Sixties.* Boston: Little Brown, 1988.

Gormley, Ken. *Archibald Cox: Conscience of a Nation.* Reading, MA: Perseus Books, 1997.

Graham, Katherine. *Personal History.* New York: Alfred A. Knopf, 1997.

Greenberg, David. *Nixon's Shadow: The History of an Image.* New York: W. W. Norton, 2003.

Grondahl, Paul. *Mayor Erastus Corning: Albany Icon, Albany Enigma.* Albany, NY: Washington Park Press, 1997.

Guiles, Fred Lawrence. *Marion Davies.* New York: McGraw-Hill, 1972.

Gumbel, Andrew. *Steal This Vote: Dirty Elections and the Rotten History of Democracy in America.* New York: Nation Books, 2005.

Halberstam, David. *The Fifties.* New York: Villard, 1993.

Halberstam, David. *The Best and the Brightest.* New York: Modern Library Edition, 2001.

Halberstam, David. *The Powers That Be.* New York: Alfred A. Knopf, 1975.

Haley, J. Evetts. *A Texan Looks at Lyndon: A Study in Illegitimate Power.* Canyon, TX: Palo Duro Press, 1964.

Haldeman, H. R., and Joseph DiMona. *The Ends of Power.* Boston: W. H. Allen, 1978.

Hamilton, Nigel. *JFK: Reckless Youth.* New York: Random House, 1992.

Harper, Paul, and Joann P. Krieg, eds. *John F. Kennedy: The Promise Revisited.* New York: Greenwood Press, 1988.

Haygood, Wil. *In Black and White: The Life of Sammy Davis Jr.* New York: Alfred A. Knopf, 2003.

Hellmann, John. *The Kennedy Obsession: The American Myth of JFK.* New York: Columbia University Press, 1997.

Henderson, Harold P. *Ernest Vandiver: Governor of Georgia.* Athens: University of Georgia Press, 2000.

Hersh, Burton. *The Education of Edward Kennedy.* New York: William Morrow, 1972.

Hersh, Burton. *Bobby and J. Edgar: The Historic Face-Off Between the Kennedys and J. Edgar Hoover That Transformed America.* New York: Carroll & Graf, 2007.

Hersh, Seymour M. *The Dark Side of Camelot.* Boston: Little, Brown, 1997.

Hewitt, Don. *Tell Me a Story: Fifty Years and 60 Minutes in Television.* New York: PublicAffairs Books, 2001.

Heymann, C. David. *A Woman Named Jackie: An Intimate Portrait of Jacqueline Bouvier Kennedy Onassis.* New York: Lyle Stuart, 1989.

Heymann, C. David. *RFK: A Candid Biography of Robert F. Kennedy.* New York: Dutton, 1998.

Higham, Charles. *Howard Hughes: His Secret Life.* New York: G. P. Putnam's Sons, 1993.

Hodgson, Godfrey. *The Gentleman from New York: Daniel Patrick Moynihan: A Biography.* Boston: Houghton-Mifflin, 2000.

Hoff, Joan. *Nixon Reconsidered.* New York: Basic Books, 1994.

Humphrey, Hubert H. *The Education of a Public Man: My Life and Politics.* Garden City, NY: Doubleday, 1976.

Isaacson, Walter. *Kissinger: A Biography: An American Life.* New York: Simon & Schuster, 1992.

Isaacson, Walter, and Evan Thomas. *The Wise Men: Six Friends and the World They Made.* New York: Simon & Schuster, 1988.

Jamieson, Kathleen Hall. *Packaging the Presidency: A History of Presidential Campaign Advertising.* New York: Oxford University Press, 1996.

Jamieson, Kathleen Hall, and Paul Waldman. *The Press Effect: Politicians, Journalists and the Stories That Shape the Political World.* New York: Oxford University Press, 2003.

Jacobs, George, with William Stadiem. *Mr. S: My Life with Frank Sinatra.* New York: HarperCollins, 2004.

Jeansonne, Glen. *Gerald L. K. Smith: Minister of Hate.* New Haven, CT: Yale University Press, 1988.

Jobe, Thomas H., and Hyman L. Muslin. *Lyndon Johnson: The Tragic Self a Psychohistorical Portrait.* New York: Insight Books, 1991.

Kelley, Kitty. *His Way: An Unauthorized Biography of Frank Sinatra.* New York: Bantam Books, 1986.

Kelley, Kitty. *Jackie Oh!* New York: Lyle Stuart, 1978.

Kennedy, John F. *The Strategy for Peace.* New York: Harper, 1960.

Kennedy, John F. *Profiles in Courage.* New York: Harper, 1956.

Kennedy, John F. *Why England Slept.* New York: Wilfred Funk, 1940.

Kennedy, Rose Fitzgerald. *Times to Remember.* Garden City, NY: Doubleday, 1974.

Kennedy, William. *O Albany! Improbable City of Political Wizards, Fearless Ethnics, Spectacular Aristocrats, Splendid Nobodies, and Underrated Scoundrels.* New York: Viking Penguin, 1983.

Keogh, James. *This Is Nixon.* New York: G. P. Putnam's Sons, 1956.

Kessler, Ronald. *The Sins of the Father: Joseph P. Kennedy and the Dynasty He Founded.* New York: Warner, 1996.

King, Martin Luther, Jr. *The Autobiography of Martin Luther King, Jr.* Ed. Clayborne Carson. New York: Intellectual Properties Management in association with Warner Books, 1998.

Klein, Edward. *The Kennedy Curse: Why Tragedy Has Haunted America's First Family for 150 Years.* New York: St. Martin's Press, 2004.

Klein, Herbert G. *Making It Perfectly Clear: An Inside Account of Nixon's Love-Hate Relationship with the Media.* Garden City, NY: Doubleday, 1980.

Kornitzer, Bela. *The Real Nixon: An Intimate Biography.* New York: Rand-McNally, 1960.

Koskoff, David E. *Joseph P. Kennedy: A Life and Times.* Englewood Cliffs, NJ: Prentice-Hall, 1974.

Kramer, Michael, and Sam Roberts. *"I Never Wanted To Be Vice-President of Anything!": An Investigative Biography of Nelson Rockefeller.* New York: Basic Books, 1976.

Kraus, Sidney. *The Great Debates: Kennedy vs. Nixon, 1960.* Bloomington: Indiana University Press, 1977.

Krock, Arthur. *Memoirs: Sixty Years on the Firing Line* New York: Funk & Wagnalls, 1968.

Kuralt, Charles. *A Life on the Road.* New York: G. P. Putnam's Sons, 1990.

Lamb, Brian, ed. *Booknotes: Stories from American History.* New York: Penguin: 2002.

Lash, Joseph P. *Eleanor: The Years Alone.* New York: W. W. Norton, 1972.

Lasky, Victor. *Arthur J. Goldberg: The Old and the New.* New Rochelle, NY: Arlington House, 1971.

Lasky, Victor. *It Didn't Start with Watergate.* New York: Dell Publishing, 1977.

Lasky, Victor. *JFK: The Man and the Myth.* New York: Macmillan, 1963.

Lasky, Victor. *RFK: The Myth and the Man.* New York: Trident Press, 1968.

Leamer, Laurence. *The Kennedy Men: The Laws of the Father, 1901–1963.* New York: HarperCollins, 2002.

Leamer, Laurence. *The Kennedy Women: The Saga of an American Family.* New York: Villard Books, 1994.

Leaming, Barbara. *Jack Kennedy: The Education of a Statesman.* New York: W. W. Norton, 2006.

Leaming, Barbara. *Mrs. Kennedy: The Missing History of the Kennedy Years*. New York: Simon & Schuster, 2001.

Lesher, Stephan. *George Wallace: American Populist*. New York: Perseus Publishing, 1994.

Levy, Shawn. *Rat Pack Confidential: Frank, Dean, Sammy, Peter, Joey and the Last Great Show Biz Party*. New York: Doubleday, 1998.

Lewis, Brad. *Hollywood's Celebrity Gangster: The Incredible Life and Times of Mickey Cohen*. New York: Enigma Books, 2007.

Lichtenstein, Nelson. *The Most Dangerous Man in Detroit: Walter Reuther and the Fate of American Labor*. New York: Basic Books, 1995.

Lincoln, Evelyn. *My Twelve Years with Kennedy*. New York: D. McKay, 1965.

Lodge, Henry Cabot, Jr. *The Storm Has Many Eyes: A Personal Narrative*. New York: W. W. Norton, 1973.

Long, Michael G., ed. *First Class Citizenship: The Civil Rights Letters of Jackie Robinson*. New York: Times Books, 2007.

Loughry, Dr. Allen H. *Don't Buy Another Vote, I Won't Pay for a Landslide: The Sordid and Continuing History of Political Corruption in West Virginia*. Charleston, WV: McClain Printing Company, 2006.

Lowery, Charles D., and John F. Marszalek. *Encyclopedia of African-American Civil Rights: From Emancipation to the Present*. New York: Greenwood Press, 1992.

Lungren, John C., Jr. *Healing Richard Nixon: A Doctor's Memoir*. Lexington: University Press of Kentucky, 2003.

Lurie, Leonard. *The Running of Richard Nixon*. New York: Coward, McCann & Geoghegan, 1972.

Manchester, William. *The Death of the President*. New York: Harper & Row, 1967.

Manchester, William. *The Glory and the Dream: A Narrative History of America, 1932–1972*. Boston: Little, Brown, 1973.

Martin, Deana, and Wendy Holden. *Memories Are Made of This: Dean Martin through His Daughter's Eyes*. New York: Crown, 2004.

Martin, John Bartlow. *Adlai Stevenson of Illinois*. Garden City, NY: Doubleday, 1976.

Martin, Ralph. *Front Runner, Dark Horse: A Political Study of Senators Kennedy and Symington*. Garden City, NY: Doubleday, 1960.

Martin, Ralph G. *A Hero for Our Time: An Intimate Story of the Kennedy Years*. New York: Macmillan, 1983.

Martin, Ralph G. *Seeds of Destruction: Joe Kennedy and His Sons*. New York: Putnam Adult, 1995.

Matthews, Christopher J. *Kennedy and Nixon: The Rivalry That Shaped Postwar America*. New York: Touchstone, 1997.

Mazo, Earl. *Richard Nixon: A Political and Personal Portrait*. New York: Harper & Brothers, 1959.

McCarthy, Joe. *The Remarkable Kennedys*. New York: Popular Library, 1960.

McCullough, David. *Truman*. New York: Simon & Schuster, 1992.

McDougal, Dennis. *Privileged Son: Otis Chandler and the Rise and Fall of the L.A. Times Dynasty*. New York: Perseus, 2001.

McFarland, Linda. *Cold War Strategist: Stuart Symington and the Search for National Security*. Westport, CT: Praeger Publishers, 2001.

McKeever, Porter. *Adlai Stevenson: His Life and Legacy*. New York: William Morrow, 1989.

Mickelson, Sig. *From Whistle Stop to Sound Bite: Four Decades of Politics and Television*. New York: Praeger Publishers, 1989.

Miller, Merle. *Lyndon: An Oral Biography*. New York: G. P. Putnam's Sons, 1980.

Miller, Merle. *Plain Speaking: An Oral Biography of Harry S. Truman*. New York: Berkley Publishing, 1973.

Miller, William "Fishbait," and Frances Spatz Leighton. *Fishbait: The Memoirs of the Congressional Doorkeeper*. Englewood Cliffs, NJ: Prentice-Hall, 1977.

Mitchell, Greg. *Tricky Dick and the Pink Lady: Richard Nixon vs Helen Gahagan Douglas—Sexual Politics and the Red Scare, 1950*. New York: Random House, 1998.

Mooney, Booth. *The Politicians: 1945–1960*. Philadelphia: J. P. Lippincott, 1970.

Mooney, Booth. *The Lyndon Johnson Story*. New York: Farrar & Straus, 1964.

Morris, Joe Alex. *Nelson Rockefeller: A Biography*. New York: Harper & Bros., 1960.

Morris, Roger. *Richard Milhous Nixon: The Rise of an American Politician*. New York: Henry Holt, 1990.

Morrow, Lance. *The Best Year of Their Lives: Kennedy, Johnson and Nixon in 1948, Learning the Secrets of Power*. New York: Basic Books, 2003.

Morrow, E. Frederick. *Black Man in the White House: A Diary of the Eisenhower Years by the Administrative Officer for Special Projects, the White House, 1955–1961*. New York: Coward-McCann, 1963.

Mulvaney, Jay. *Kennedy Weddings: A Family Album*. New York: St. Martin's Press, 2002.

Newfield, Jack. *Robert Kennedy: A Memoir*. New York: Dutton, 1969.

Nissensen, Marilyn. *The Lady Upstairs: Dorothy Schiff and the New York Post*. New York: St. Martin's Press, 2007.

Nixon, Richard M. *In the Arena*. New York: Simon & Schuster, 1990.

Nixon, Richard M. *Six Crises*. Garden City, NY: Doubleday, 1962.

Nixon, Richard M. *The Challenges We Face*. New York: McGraw-Hill, 1960.

Nixon, Richard M. *RN: The Memoirs of Richard Nixon*. New York: Grosset & Dunlop, 1978.

Novak, Robert D. *The Prince of Darkness: 50 Years Reporting in Washington*. New York: Crown Forum, 2007.

O'Brien, Lawrence F. *No Final Victories: A Life in Politics from John F. Kennedy to Watergate*. Garden City, NY: Doubleday, 1974.

O'Brien, Michael. *John F. Kennedy: A Biography*. New York: Thomas Dunne Books, 2005.

O'Connor, Len. *Clout: Mayor Daley and His City*. Chicago: Henry Regnery, 1975.

O'Donnell, Kenneth P., David F. Powers, and Joe McCarthy. *"Johnny, We Hardly Knew Ye": Memories of John Fitzgerald Kennedy*. Boston: Little, Brown, 1972.

O'Neill, Thomas P. "Tip," with William Novak *Man of the House: The Life and Political Memoirs of Speaker Tip O'Neill*. New York: Random House, 1987.

Olson, James C. *Stuart Symington: A Life*. Columbia: University of Missouri Press, 2003.

Parmet, Herbert S. *Eisenhower and the American Crusades.* New York: Macmillan, 1972.

Parmet, Herbert S. *Jack: The Struggles of John F. Kennedy.* New York: Dial Press, 1980.

Parmet, Herbert S. *JFK: The Presidency of John F. Kennedy.* New York: Dial Press, 1983.

Parmet, Herbert S. *Richard Nixon and His America.* Boston: Little Brown, 1990.

Perret, Geoffrey. *Eisenhower.* New York: Random House, 1999.

Perret, Geoffrey. *Jack: A Life Like No Other.* New York: Random House, 2001.

Perlstein, Rick. *Before the Storm: Barry Goldwater and the Unmaking of the American Consensus.* New York: Hill & Wang, 2001.

Persico, Joseph E. *The Imperial Rockefeller: A Biography of Nelson A. Rockefeller.* New York: Simon & Schuster, 1982.

Pilat, Oliver. *Pegler: Angry Man of the Press.* Westport, CT: Greenwood Press, 1973.

Pipes, Kasey S. *Ike's Final Battle: The Road to Little Rock and the Challenge to Equality.* Los Angeles: World Ahead Media, 2007.

Pitt, David. *Jack and Lem: John F. Kennedy and Lem Billings: The Untold Story of an Extraordinary Friendship.* New York: Carroll & Graf, 2007.

Potter, Jeffrey. *Men, Money & Magic: The Story of Dorothy Schiff.* New York: New American Library, 1977.

Pottker, Jan. *Janet & Jackie: The Story of a Mother and Her Daughter, Jacqueline Kennedy Onassis.* New York: St. Martin's Press, 2001.

President's Commission on the Assassination of President Kennedy. *The Warren Commission Report.* New York: Barnes & Noble, 1992.

Quirk, Robert E. *Fidel Castro.* New York: W. W. Norton, 1995.

Quirk, Lawrence J., and William Schoell. *The Rat Pack: The Hey-Hey Days of Frank and the Boys.* Dallas: Taylor, 1998.

Rampersad, Arnold. *Jackie Robinson: A Biography.* New York: Alfred A. Knopf, 1997.

Rather, Dan, and Gary Paul Gates. *The Palace Guard.* New York: Harper & Row, 1974.

Reagan, Nancy. *Nancy.* New York: Morrow, 1980.

Reagan, Ronald. *An American Life.* New York: Simon & Schuster, 1990.

Reedy, George. *Lyndon B. Johnson: A Memoir.* Kansas City, MO: Andrews, McMeel, 1985.

Reeves, Richard. *President Kennedy: Profile of Power.* New York: Simon & Schuster, 1993.

Reeves, Thomas C. *A Question of Character: A Life of John F. Kennedy.* New York: Free Press, 1991.

Reeves, Thomas C. *The Life and Times of Joe McCarthy: A Biography.* New York: Stein & Day, 1982.

Reich, Cary. *The Life of Nelson A. Rockefeller: Words to Conquer 1908–1958.* New York: Doubleday, 1996.

Reinhard, David W. *The Republican Right Since 1945.* Lexington: University Press of Kentucky, 1983.

Renehan, Edward J., Jr. *The Kennedys at War: 1937–1945.* New York: Doubleday, 2002.

Reston, James "Scotty." *Deadline: A Memoir.* New York: Random House, 1991.

Reston, James, Jr. *The Lone Star: The Life of John Connally.* New York: HarperCollins, 1989.

Roberts, Randy, and James S. Olson. *John Wayne: American*. New York: Free Press, 1995.

Robinson, Jackie, with Alfred Duckett. *I Never Had It Made*. New York: G.P. Putnam's Sons, 1972.

Rouverol, Jean. *Refugees from Hollywood: A Journal of the Blacklist Years*. Albuquerque: University of New Mexico Press, 2000.

Rovere, Richard H. *The Eisenhower Years: Affairs of State*. New York: Farrar, Straus, and Cudahy, 1956.

Russell Francis. *The President Makers: From Mark Hanna to Joseph P. Kennedy*. Boston: Little, Brown, 1976.

Safire, William. *Before the Fall: An Inside View of the Pre-Watergate Nixon White House*. Somerset, NJ: Transaction Publishers, 2005.

Salinger, Pierre. *With Kennedy*. Garden City, NY: Doubleday, 1966.

Salinger, Pierre. *P.S.: A Memoir*. New York: St. Martin's Press, 1995.

Sandbrook, Edward. *Eugene McCarthy and the Rise and Fall of Postwar American Liberalism*. New York: Knopf, 2005.

Savage, Sean J. *JFK, LBJ, and the Democratic Party*. Albany, NY: SUNY Press, 2004.

Schaffer, Howard B. *Chester Bowles: New Dealer in the Cold War*. Washington, DC: Institute for the Study of Diplomacy, 1993.

Schlesinger, Arthur M., Jr. *A Thousand Days*. Cambridge: Houghton-Mifflin, 1965.

Schlesinger, Arthur M., Jr. *Journals: 1952–2000*. New York: Penguin Press, 2007.

Schlesinger, Arthur M., Jr. *Kennedy or Nixon: Does It Make Any Difference?* New York: Macmillan, 1960.

Schlesinger, Arthur M., Jr. *Robert Kennedy and His Times*. Cambridge: Houghton-Mifflin, 1978.

Schneider, Gregory L. *Cadres for Conservatism: Young Americans for Freedom and the Rise of the Contemporary Right*. New York: New York University Press, 1999.

Schoor, Gene. *Young John Kennedy*. New York: Macfadden-Bartell, 1963.

Schwab, Peter, and J. Lee Shneidman. *John F. Kennedy*. Boston: Twayne, 1974.

Schwarz, Ted. *Joseph P. Kennedy: The Mogul, the Mob, the Statesman, and the Making of an American Myth*. Hoboken, NJ: John Wiley & Sons, 2003.

Sheshol, Jeff. *Mutual Contempt: Lyndon Johnson, Robert Kennedy and the Feud That Defined a Decade*. New York: W. W. Norton, 1997.

Sevareid, Eric. *Candidates 1960: Behind the Headlines in the Presidential Race*. New York: Basic Books, 1959.

Shadegg, Stephen C. *Barry Goldwater: Freedom Is His Flight Plan*. New York: Fleet, 1962.

Sherrill, Robert. *Gothic Politics in the Deep South*. New York: Ballantine Books, 1969.

Silvestri, Vito N. *Becoming JFK: A Profile in Communication*. Westport, CT: Praeger, 2000.

Sinatra, Nancy. *Frank Sinatra: An American Legend*. New York: Simon & Schuster, 1985.

Smith, Amanda, ed. *Hostage to Fortune: The Letters of Joseph P. Kennedy*. New York: Viking, 2001.

Smith, A. Robert. *The Tiger in the Senate: The Biography of Wayne Morse*. Garden City, NY: Doubleday, 1962.

Smith, Howard K. *Events Leading Up to My Death*. New York: St. Martin's Press, 1996.

Smith, Sally Bedell. *Grace and Power: The Private World of the Kennedy White House*. New York: Random House, 2004.

Solberg, Carl. *Hubert Humphrey: A Biography*. New York: W. W. Norton, 1984.

Sorensen, Theodore C. *Kennedy*. New York: Harper & Row, 1965.

Spada, James. *Peter Lawford: The Man Who Kept the Secrets*. New York: Bantam Books, 1991.

Sperber, A. M. *Murrow: His Life and Times*. New York: Freundlich Books, 1986.

Spoto, James. *Jacqueline Bouvier Kennedy Onassis: A Life*. New York: St. Martin's Press, 2001.

Steinberg, Alfred. *Rayburn: A Biography*. New York: Hawthorn Books, 1975.

Stossel, Scott. *Sarge: The Life and Times of Sargent Shriver*. Washington: Smithsonian Books, 2004.

Summers, Anthony. *The Arrogance of Power: The Secret World of Richard Nixon*. New York: Viking Penguin, 2000.

Summers, Anthony, and Robbyn Swan. *Sinatra: The Life*. New York: Alfred A. Knopf, 2005.

Taraborrelli, J. Randy. *Jackie, Ethel, Joan*. New York: Warner Books, 2000.

Thomas, Evan. *Robert Kennedy: His Life*. New York: Touchstone, 2000.

Tosches, Nick. *Dino: Living High: The Dirty Business of Dreams*. New York: Doubleday, 1992.

Unger, Irwin, and Debi Unger. *LBJ: A Life*. New York: John Wiley & Sons, 1999.

Valenti, Jack. *A Very Human President*. New York: W. W. Norton, 1975.

Van Meter, Jonathan. *The Last Good Time: Skinny D'Amato, the Notorious 500 Club, and the Rise and Fall of Atlantic City*. New York: Crown, 2003.

Vidal, Gore. *Palimpsest: A Memoir*. New York: Random House, 1995.

Wagner, Steven. *Eisenhower Republicanism: Pursuing the Middle Way*. DeKalb: Northern Illinois University Press, 2006.

Wallace, Mike, with Gary Paul Gates. *Between You and Me: A Memoir*. New York: Hyperion, 2005.

Watson, Mary Ann. *The Expanding Vista: American Television in the Kennedy Years*. Durham, NC: Duke University Press, 1994.

Watson, W. Marvin. *Chief of Staff: Lyndon Johnson and His Presidency*. New York: St. Martin's Press, 2004.

Weisbrot, Robert. *Freedom Bound: A History of America's Civil Rights Movement*. New York: W. W. Norton: 1990.

Whalen, Richard J. *The Founding Father: The Story of Joseph P. Kennedy. A Study in Power, Wealth and Family Ambition*. New York: Signer, 1964.

Whalen, Thomas J. *Kennedy versus Lodge: The 1952 Massachusetts Senate Race*. Boston: Northeastern University Press, 2000.

White, Theodore H. *America in Search of Itself: The Making of the President, 1956–1980*. New York: Harper & Row, 1982.

White, Theodore H. *Breach of Faith: The Fall of Richard Nixon*. New York: Atheneum, 1975.

White, Theodore H. *In Search of History: A Personal Adventure.* New York: HarperCollins, 1978.

White, Theodore H. *The Making of the President, 1960.* New York: Atheneum, 1961.

White, Theodore H. *The Making of the President, 1964.* New York: Atheneum, 1965.

White, Theodore H. *The Making of the President, 1968.* New York: Atheneum, 1969.

White, William S. *The Professional: Lyndon B. Johnson.* New York: Crest, 1964.

Whitman, Alden, and the New York Times. *Portrait: Adlai E. Stevenson: Politician, Diplomat, Friend.* New York: Harper & Row, 1965.

Wicker, Tom. *One of Us: Richard Nixon and the American Dream.* New York: Random House, 1991.

Wills, Garry. *The Kennedy Imprisonment: A Meditation on Power.* Boston: Atlantic Monthly Press, 1961.

Wills, Garry. *Nixon Agonistes: The Crisis of the Self-Made Man.* Boston: Houghton Mifflin, 1969.

Winchell, Walter. *Winchell Exclusive: "Things That Happened to Me—And Me to Them."* Englewood Cliffs, NJ: Prentice-Hall, 1975.

Witcover, Jules. *Crapshoot: Rolling the Dice on the Vice Presidency.* New York: Crown, 1991.

Wofford, Harris. *Of Kennedys and Kings.* New York: Farrar, Straus, Giroux, 1980.

Woods, Randall. *LBJ: Architect of American Ambition.* New York: Free Press, 2006.

Wyckoff, Gene. *The Image Candidates: American Candidates in the Age of Television.* New York: Macmillan, 1968.

Oral History Interviews

Dean Acheson, 27 April 1964, for the John F. Kennedy Library.

Stewart Alsop, 15 July 1969, for the Lyndon Baines Johnson Library.

Frederick G. Dutton, "Democratic Campaigns and Controversies, 1954–1966," Governmental History Documentation Project: Goodwin Knight/Edmund Brown, Sr. Era, Regional Oral History Office University of California, Bancroft Library, Berkeley, California. Interviews conducted by Amelia R. Fry, 1977–1978.

Don Hewitt, 8 October 2002, the John F. Kennedy Library.

Roger Kent, "Building the Democratic Party in California, 1954–1966," Governmental History Documentation Project: Goodwin Knight/Edmund Brown, Sr. Era, Regional Oral History Office University of California, Bancroft Library, Berkeley, California. Interviews conducted by Anne H. Brower and Amelia R. Fry, 1976, 1977.

Larry O'Brien (Interview I), 18 September 1985, for the Lyndon Baines Johnson Library.

Frank Stanton, 26 August 2002, for the John F. Kennedy Library.

Jack Valenti, 25 May 1982, for the Lyndon Baines Johnson Library.

William S. White (Interview I), 25 May 1982, for the Lyndon Baines Johnson Library.

Newspapers

Abilene Reporter-News
Ada Evening News (OK)
Albany Times Union (NY)
Amarillo Globe-Times
Anniston Star (AL)
Appleton Post-Crescent (WI)
Arizona Daily Sun
Beckley Post-Herald (WV)
Bennington Banner (VT)
Berkshire Eagle (MA)
Billings Gazette (MT)
Boston Globe
Brainerd Daily Dispatch (MN)
Bridgeport Post (CT)
Bridgeport Telegram (CT)
Buffalo News
Burlington Daily Times-News (NC)
Charleston Gazette (WV)
Charleston Daily Mail (WV)
Chicago Daily Defender
Chicago Daily Herald
Chicago Daily Tribune
Clearfield Progress (PA)
Connellsville Daily Courier (PA)
Coshocton Tribune (OH)
Delta Democrat-Times (MS)
Deming Headlight (NM)
El Paso Herald-Post
Elyria Chronicle-Telegram (OH)
European Stars and Stripes
Fitchburg Sentinel (MA)
Florence Morning News (SC)
Frederick Post (MD)
Fremont-Newark Argus (CA)
Fresno Bee
Fresno Bee-Republican
Galveston Daily News
Greely Daily Tribune (CO)
Hammond Times (IN)
Hartford Courant
Hayward Daily Review (CA)
Hobbs Daily News-Sun (NM)
Holland Evening Sentinel (MI)
Houston Chronicle

Humboldt-Eureka Standard (CA)
Indiana Evening Gazette (PA)
Jefferson City News & Tribune (MO)
Kingsport News (TN)
Kingsport Times-News (TN)
Lawton Constitution-Morning Press (OK)
Lincoln Evening Journal (NE)
Lima News (OH)
Long Beach Press-Telegram (CA)
Los Angles Times
Lowell Sun (MA)
Madison Capital-Times (WI)
Maniwetoc Herald-Times (WI)
McKean County Democrat (PA)
Miami Times
Middlesboro Daily News (KY)
Middletown Times-Herald Record (NY)
Modesto Bee (CA)
Morgantown Post (WV)
Nevada State Journal
New York Post
New York Times
The New Yorker
Newsday
Oakland Tribune
Odessa American (TX)
Oshkosh Daily Northwestern (WI)
Oswego Palladium Times (NY)
Oxnard Press-Courier (CA)
Pacific Stars & Stripes
Palatine Herald (IL)
Pasadena Independent
Pasadena Star-News
Philadelphia Inquirer
Pittsburgh Courier
Port Arthur News (TX)
Portsmouth Herald (NH)
Raleigh Register (WV)
Redlands Daily Facts (CA)
San Antonio Express
San Antonio Express-News
San Francisco Chronicle
San Jose Mercury News
San Mateo Times (CA)
Schenectady Gazette (NY)

Sheboygen Press (WI)
Sitka Sentinel (AK)
Stevens Point Daily Journal (WI)
Syracuse Herald-Journal
Syracuse Post-Standard
Tri-State Defender (TN)
Troy Record (NY)
Uniontown Evening Standard (PA)
Valparaiso Vidette-Messenger (IN)
Van Nuys Valley News (CA)
Wall Street Journal
Washington Post
Washington Times
Watertown Times (NY)
Weirton Daily Times (WV)
Winnipeg Free Press
Wisconsin Rapids Daily Tribune (WI)
Wisconsin State Journal
Zanesville Times Recorder (OH)

Periodicals

Current Biography
Esquire
Facts on File
The Historian
Human Events
The Journal of American History
The Journal of Economic History
The Journal of Negro History
Life
Look
The Nation
Newsweek
Presidential Studies Quarterly
Reader's Digest
The Reporter
Review of Religious Research
Social Forces
Time
The Western Political Quarterly

Academic Paper

Davidge, Wendell Keith, and Kenneth C. Petress. "The 1960 Presidential Campaign's Pivotal Turning Point: John F. Kennedy's Speech to the Greater Houston Ministerial Association." Paper Presented at the Southern States/Central States Joint Communication Conference, Lexington, Kentucky, 16 April 1993.

Acknowledgments

Thanks go to the John F. Kennedy Presidential Library and Museum, the Lyndon Baines Johnson Library, the Harry S. Truman Library and Museum, the National Archives, the Schenectady County (NY) Library, the New York State Library, the New York State Legislative Library, the Saratoga Springs (NY) Public Library, the Begley Library of Schenectady County Community College, the Lucy Scribner Library at Skidmore College, the Williams College Library, the University at Albany Library, the Jared van Wagenen Jr. Library of the State University of New York at Cobleskill, and to the Folsom Library of Rensselaer Polytechnic Institute (RPI).

And thanks for the assistance of Dr. Ronald A. Faucheux and Larry Margolin and my friends Douglas R. Burgey, Robert Going, Cathy Harp, Herb Moss, and John Thorn.

And thanks to Philip Turner, my extremely supportive editor at both Carroll & Graf and Union Square Press, as well as to his always responsive editorial assistant Iris Blasi. Thanks are also extended to Union Square managing editor Rebecca Maines, transatlantic line editor James Morgan, freelance production editor Eileen Chetti, design manager Chrissy Kwasnik, and the team at Oxygen Design.

Thanks also to my agent Carol Mann at the Carol Mann Agency.

And, of course, to my beloved wife, Patty.

Index

ABC, 118, 246–247, 308, 331, 361, 367, 389–390, 400–401
Abernathy, Ralph, 298
Acheson, Dean, 57, 163, 206, 285, 358
Adamowski, Benjamin S., 229, 403
Adams, Sherman, 40, 47, 48
Adonis, Joey, 126
AFL-CIO, 89, 203
African Americans, 237, 291, 294, 303, 359, 408
Alaska, 172
Aldrich, Nelson Wilmarth, 67, 71
Alejandro, Jaime Cruz, 382
Aleman, Xicotencati Leyva, 397
Alger, Bruce, 387
Almond, J. Lindsay, 201, 293
Alsop, John, 134
Alsop, Joseph, xi, 17, 50, 117, 128, 134, 140, 148, 174, 191–192, 194, 196–197, 224, 279–280, 342, 350
Alsop, Stewart, 28, 134
Ameche, Alan "The Horse," 88
Anderson, Clinton, 161, 204
Anderson, Marian, 411
Anderson, Robert B., 44, 48, 102–103, 226, 385
anti-Catholicism, 89–90, 93, 109–110, 112, 120, 128, 195, 249, 294
anti-Communism, 9, 11, 37–39, 238–241
anti-Semitism, 90, 92
Arbenz, Jacobo, 375
Arizona, 218
Arvad, Inga, 145–146, 149
Arvey, Jacob M., 78, 181
Attwood, William, 142

Badillo, Herman, 293
Bailey, John M., 79, 259, 388, 401
Baker, Bobby, xi, 30–32, 148, 151–152, 162–163, 168, 175, 197, 204
Baker, Russell, 343, 353–354
Ball, George, 143
Ball, Joseph, 58
Barkley, Alben W., 134
Barnett, Ross, 188
Barr, Joseph, 78
Bartlett, Charles, 50
Bassett, James, 303, 316

Batista, Fulgencio, 367
Bayley, Edwin, 91
Bay of Pigs, 372, 411
Beaverbrook, Lord, 157, 252
Beck, Dave, 15, 62
Belafonte, Harry, 294–295
Belgian Congo, 361
Bell, Jack, 266
Bellamy, Ralph, 235
Bender, George H., 98
Benny, Jack, 242
Benson, Ezra Taft, 47, 100–101, 107, 231, 279
Benton, William, 118
Berle, Milton, 235, 242
Berlin, 361
Billings, Kirk LeMoyne "Lem," 14, 16, 402
Billings, Richard, 155
Bishop, Joey, 234, 381
Black, William, 302
Blaik, Earl "Red," 316, 380
Blair, James T., Jr., 185
Blair, William McCormick, Jr., 143–144
Blakey, G. Robert, 155, 404
Blanshard, Paul, 249
Blundell, James, 265–266
Boggs, Hale, 201–202, 265
Boggs, Lindy, 265
Bolivar, Simon, 368
Bond, Ward, 239
Bouvier, Jacqueline Lee, 147. *See also* Kennedy, Jacqueline Bouvier
Bowles, Chester Bliss, xi, 68, 80, 91, 122, 139, 164, 184, 192, 194, 293, 295, 300, 370
Bozell, L. Brent, 219, 270
Braden, Joan, 64
Bradlee, Ben, xi, 18, 56, 91, 130, 162, 175, 280, 290, 342
Bradlee, Tony, 130
Bricker, John, 226–228
Brill, David H., 403
Brinkley, David, 357, 400, 414
Britt, Elton, 81–82
Britt, May, 236, 237
Britton, Nan, 326
Brodie, Fawn, 311

Brown, Edmund G. "Pat," xi, 53, 55, 78, 80, 84, 98, 99, 111, 158, 161, 174, 175, 188, 412
Brown, George R., 27
Brown, Vanessa, 235
Brownell, Herbert, 214
Bruno, Jerry, 114, 125, 275, 287–288
Bryant, C. Farris, 283
Buchwald, Art, 244, 272
Buckley, Charles A., 81, 128–129, 159
Buckley, William F., Jr., 97, 219, 270
Bundy, McGeorge, 411
Burnham, James, 270
Burns, Arthur, 100, 215, 343
Burns, James McGregor, 14, 139
Bush, Prescott, 102
Byrd, Harry Flood, 30, 58, 263, 265
Byrd, Robert Carlyle, 120–121, 129–130, 293

Calhoun, John C., 292
California, 36, 77, 78, 80, 98, 158, 174
Campbell, Judith (Exner), xii, 126, 151–155, 183, 189, 245–246, 404
Cannon, Clarence, 209
Carlino, Joseph, 69
Cassini, Oleg, 146
Castro, Fidel, 102, 367–373, 375–380
Cater, Douglas, 313
CBS, 24, 163, 164, 186, 271, 308, 327, 329, 330, 335, 337, 340, 342, 355, 400
Celeste, Vincent J., 16
Central Intelligence Agency (CIA), 370
Cerrell, Joe, 158
Chafin, Raymond, 126
Chambers, Whitaker, 37, 97–98
Champion, Gower, 242
Champion, Marge, 242
Chancellor, John, 374
Chandler, Norman, 36
Chapman, Oscar, 161
Chase, Nick, 147
Chavez, Dennis, 161
Chessman, Caryl, 80
Chicago, Illinois, 381, 390, 403–404
Childs, Marquis, 342
China, People's Republic of, 363–364, 369
Chotiner, Murray M., xi, 38, 62, 273, 312, 360, 400
Chou En-lai, 98

Church, Frank, 184
civil rights, 25, 30, 60, 113, 184, 216–217, 299, 303–304, 414
Clark, Blair, 5, 152
Clark, Bob, 150
Clark, Joe (Pennsylvania senator), 159, 164
Clark, Joe (Pennsylvania state treasurer), 159–160
Clark, Kenneth, 305
Clay, Henry, 165, 285
Clay, Lucius, 68, 217
Clements, Earle, 204, 226
Clifford, Clark, xi, 15, 57, 112, 148–149, 163, 191–193, 199
Clift, Montgomery, 130
Cluster, Alvin Peyton, 6
Coe, Fred, 374
Cohen, Eugene J., 169, 384
Cohen, Mickey, 154, 404
Cohen, Wilbur, 20
Cohn, Roy, 12, 51
Cold War, 355–356
Cole, Nat "King," 235
Collingwood, Charles, 225
Collins, T. LeRoy, 164, 184, 209, 347
Colson, Chuck, 273
Columbus, Christopher, 165
Connally, John B., xi, 25–26, 32, 161, 166–168, 175, 176, 204, 205, 208, 263, 267, 413
Connally, Nellie, 208, 414
Connecticut, 392
Conte, Richard, 235
Conway, Jack, 110, 124
Cook, Don, 167
Coolidge, Calvin, 52, 358
Cooper, Gary, 234, 242, 271
Corbin, Paul, 89–90
Corcoran, "Tommy the Cork," 29, 196, 199, 201, 206, 395
Cordiner, Ralph, 271
Cotter, John, 9
Cox, Archibald, xii, 369, 411
Criswell, W. A., 257
Cronkite, Walter, 374, 400
Crosby, John, 364–365
Crotty, Peter J., 81
Cuba, 137, 364, 411
Curley, James Michael, 3, 7

Curtis, Tony, 235
Cushing, Richard Cardinal, xii, 125, 248, 249, 253, 411, 414

Dabney, Israel, 382
Daley, Richard J., xii, 78, 158–159, 162, 171, 179–180, 192, 294, 344, 381, 395, 402–403, 415–416
Dallek, Robert, 29
Dalton, Mark, 45
Daly, John, 400
Daly, Lar, 82, 112
D'Amato, Paul, 126, 151, 152, 237
Damone, Vic, 381
Daniel, Price, 204, 263
Darr, Alicia, 148, 150–151, 155
Davies, Marion, 182
Davis, Sammy, Jr., xii, 127, 234–238, 242
Dawson, William Levi, 294
Dean, James, 114
De Gaulle, Charles, 101
Democratic National Committee, 55, 259, 400
Democratic National Convention (1940), 395
Democratic National Convention (1948), 58
Democratic National Convention (1956), 63, 234
Democratic National Convention (1960), 88, 163–164, 170–212, 286
Democratic presidential primaries, 77, 78, 81–82, 111–113
De Sapio, Carmine, 70, 81, 121, 128, 159, 184
Des Rosiers, Janet, 86, 145
Dever, Paul, 12
Dewey, Thomas E., 18, 39–41, 69, 99, 226, 227, 308, 358, 378
Dexter, Brad, 127
DiBetta, John, 397
Dickerson, Nancy, 346
Dickinson, Angie, 235
Dietrich, Marlene, 395
Diggs, Charles C., Jr., 304
Dirksen, Everett McKinley, 223, 226, 228–229, 317
DiSalle, Michael V., 53, 78–79, 111, 113, 158, 192, 321, 351
Diskin, Marshall, 361
Disney, Walt, 271

District of Columbia, 77, 111, 113
Docking, George R., 172, 190, 402
Dougherty, William Cardinal, 250
Douglas, Helen Gahagan, 25, 38, 50, 150, 271, 310
Douglas, Kirk, 239, 271
Douglas, Melvyn, 38
Douglas, Paul, 229
Douglas, Stephen A., 378
Douglas, William, 195
Downey, Sheridan, 38
Drummond, Roscoe, 342, 356, 360
Dubinsky, David, 203
Duckworth, Alan, 262
Duff, Howard, 233
Dulles, Allen, 370
Dulles, John Foster, 33, 43
Dutton, Frederick G., 249

Eastland, James, 30, 264, 299
Ebbins, Milt, 152–153
Edson, Arthur, 332
Edwards, Cliff, 397
Edwards, India, 161, 162, 166–167
Edwards, John, 374
Edwards, Willard, 280, 356, 359, 371–372
Ehrlichman, John D., xii, 103, 183, 273–274, 276, 412, 416–417
Eisenhower, Dwight D., xii, 11, 12, 27–28, 30, 33, 38–45, 47–48, 50–51, 54, 67, 70–73, 95–99, 101–102, 104–108, 134, 135, 138, 160, 209, 216, 217, 219, 222–223, 232, 254, 263, 268–269, 280, 291, 293, 294, 300, 301, 304, 305, 317, 331, 337, 340–341, 349, 355–356, 363, 370–371, 375, 384–385, 393, 395, 400, 407, 409
Eisenhower, John, 393
Eisenhower, Mamie, 43, 222–223, 386
Eisenhower, Milton, 227
Englehardt, Sam, 292
English, Clarence, 242
Evans, M. Stanton, 225
Evans, Rowland, 24–25
Exner, Judith Campbell. See Campbell, Judith (Exner)

Farley, James A., 395
Faubus, Orval E., 188

Fay, Paul, 7, 38, 88, 148, 182, 246, 386
Federal Bureau of Investigation (FBI), 145–146, 148–149, 151, 154
Fejös, Paul, 146
Feldman, Myer, 261, 321, 411
Finch, Robert H., xiii, 74, 103, 183, 214, 254, 273–274, 280, 309, 327, 338, 366–367, 383–384, 398
Finletter, Thomas K., 179
Fisher, Eddie, 322
Fisher, Paul C., 82, 96
Fitzgerald, John, 3, 10
Flannery, Edward H., 247
Fleeson, Doris, 96, 338
Fleming, Robert, 335
Flemming, Arthur, 102
Foley, Edward H., 201
Fonda, Henry, 233
Ford, Eddie, 124–125
Ford, Gerald R., 102, 225–229
Fox, John, 11–12, 61
Franco, Francisco, 396
Freeman, Orville, 110, 164, 172, 174, 185, 191, 208, 402
Frost, Robert, 179, 411

Gabriel, Victor, 125
Gahagan, Helen, 350
Gaitskell, Hugh, 110
Galbraith, John Kenneth, xiii, 122, 139, 172, 177, 186, 198, 269, 360, 411
Gallup, George, 18, 268, 291, 352–353, 391
Gallup poll, 101, 157, 161, 165, 214, 250
Gang, Martin, 239
Gardner, Ava, 234
Gargan, Ann, 394
Gargan, Mary Elizabeth, 187
Gargan, William, 187
Garland, Judy, 235
Garment, Leonard, 305
Garner, Jack, 201
Giancana, Chuck, 127, 154
Giancana, Sam, xiii, 126–127, 150–152, 154–155, 237, 403–404
Gildes, Perry, 63–64
Glass, Alice, 150
Goble, George, 242
Goering, Hermann, 145–146
Goldberg, Arthur M., 139, 190, 203
Goldwater, Barry M., xiii, 27, 95–96,
101, 106, 218–220, 224–225, 227, 270, 412
Goldwyn, Sam, 233, 271
Goodwin, Richard, 82–83, 115, 321–322, 344, 351, 368–369, 372–373, 379, 411
Gore, Albert, Sr., 29, 54, 164
Graham, Billy, 251, 254–255
Graham, Philip, xiii, 166, 175, 192, 194–196, 199, 204–206
Grant, Gogi, 235
Graves, John Temple, 292
Gray, L. Patrick, 273
Green, Bill, 78, 111–112
Green, Dwight, 133
Green, Edith, 139
Gregson, Eddie, 237
Griffith, D. W., 139
Grober, Bert, 236–237
Gruenther, Alfred, 102
Gurewitsch, David, 282
Guy, Charley A., 254

Hagerty, Jim, 217, 305, 384–385, 400
Hague, Gabriel, 107
Halberstam, David, 273, 316, 328, 340
Haldeman, H. R., xiii, 103, 273, 275–276, 303, 351, 416–417
Haley, Jack, 183
Hall, John, 344
Hall, Leonard Wood, xiii, 47, 70, 74, 214, 273, 275, 309, 316, 386
Halle, Kay, 145, 245
Halleck, Charles, 102
Hamilton, Alexander, 165
Hand, Lloyd, 162
Handley, Harold W., 229
Hanschmann, Nancy, 346
Hardeman, D. B., 201, 387
Harding, Warren G., 31, 54, 326, 358
Harlow, Bruce, 106–107
Harriman, W. Averell, 53, 57, 70–72, 121, 173, 227
Harris, Lou, xiii, 79, 92–93, 109–110, 112, 128–129, 321–322
Hart, Everett "Ev," 331–332, 354
Hartke, Vance, 54, 112
Hatfield, Mark O., 225
Hayden, Carl, 162
Hearst, William Randolph, 182
Hellman, John, 343

Hersey, John, 8
Herter, Christian, 12, 72
Hesburgh, Theodore, 68
Heston, Charlton, 235
Hewitt, Don, xiv, 327, 331–332, 340, 343–344, 347
Heymann, C. David, 325
Hickman, Betty, 261
Hill, Lister, 27
Hiltz, Evelyn M., 393
Hiss, Alger, 37, 48
Hitler, Adolf, 146
Hobby, Oveta Culp, 102–103, 106
Hodges, Luther, 347
Hoffa, Jimmy, xiv, 15–16, 55, 62, 123–124, 157, 170, 296
Hoffman, Harry, 285
Hogan, Frank, 70
Holifield, Chet, 37
Hollers, Hardy, 25
Hollings, Ernest, 175
Holman, Claude, 381, 403
Holmes, Oliver Wendell, 133
Honeycutt, James C., Jr., 251
Hoover, Herbert, 163, 286, 290, 391, 395
Hoover, J. Edgar, xiv, 35, 50, 64, 145–146, 151, 154
Hopkins, Big John, 242
Horton, Ralph, 147
Howe, Quincy, 374
Hoyt, Palmer, 261
Hughes, Don, 355, 397–398
Hughes, Emmet John, 75, 105, 214, 216
Hughes, Howard, xiv, 383, 416
Huie, William Bradford, 238
Humphrey, Hubert H., xiv, 31, 54, 55, 57–60, 77, 80, 82–86, 89–93, 99, 109–111, 113, 115, 117–120, 122–132, 138, 139, 151, 157, 158, 160, 161, 173, 174, 188, 190–192, 197, 203, 206, 211, 235, 300, 307, 333, 402, 407, 415–416
Humphrey, Muriel, 58, 114, 131, 190
Humphrey, Nancy, 127
Humphreys, George, 69–70
Hunt, H. L., 176, 195
Huntley, Chet, 357, 400
Hutschnecker, Arnold A., xiv, 34–35, 44, 383
Hylton, Charles D., 126

Illinois, 77, 78, 98, 111, 133, 172–173, 403–404
Indiana, 77, 111, 112
International Association of Machinists, 318
International Longshoremen's and Warehousemen's Union, 391
Iowa, 171–172
Isaacson, Walter, 70
Israel, 72

Jackson, Harry E., 82, 95
Jackson, Henry, 62, 164, 191, 192, 203, 206, 253, 259
Jacobs, George, 152, 234, 241, 243
Jacobsen, Jake, 176
Jacobson, Max, xiv, 322–324
Jacobson, Nina, 324
Javits, Jacob, 225, 269
Jefferson, Thomas, 165
Jenkins, Walter, 32, 167
Jessel, George, 235
John Birch Society, 270
Johnson, Hiram, 78
Johnson, Lady Bird, xiv, 24, 150, 170, 186, 200, 204, 261, 386–388, 394
Johnson, Luci Baines, 170, 208
Johnson, Lynda Bird, 170
Johnson, Lyndon Baines, xv, 19–32
    and African Americans, 294, 304
    Arizona support for, 162
    birth and education, 19–20
    and Robert Byrd, 120–121
    California, 80, 158
    and civil rights, 263–264
    and Tommy Corcoran, 395
    in Dallas, Texas, 413
    Democratic National Convention, 170–171, 186–188
    Democratic presidential nomination, 82–85
    and Dwight Eisenhower, 223
    and election of 1960, 394–395, 400
    extramarital affairs, 150
    Gallup polls, 110, 161, 353
    and Barry Goldwater, 224
    health issues, 30–31
    and Hubert Humphrey, 58, 60
    and JFK, 27, 90, 119, 131, 166–171, 175–176, 310–311, 401
    and liberals, 138

and mink coat riot, 387–388
New Mexico support for, 161–162
New York delegate votes, 184
and Nixon, 222, 317
on Nixon-Kennedy debate, 346
as president, 414–415
presidential campaign, 259–267,
308
primary campaign, 77, 99, 110–112,
157
reaction to Pennsylvania delegate
decision, 173
and RFK, 64–65
rival presidential candidates, 54–55
Jackie Robinson reaction to, 301
Senate race (1941), 22
and South, 254
and Adlai Stevenson, 143
and Stuart Symington, 57
Texas campaign, 386–388
Truman's support for, 164–165
as vice president, 411–412
as vice-presidential candidate, 192,
194–211
West Virginia, 118, 124, 128
Judd, Walter, 169, 227–229, 254, 384

Kane, Joe, 7, 8
Kansas, 172
Kastenmeier, Robert W., 133
Kater, Florence M., 149
Kater, Leonard, 149
Keating, Kenneth B., 72
Kefauver, Estes, 14, 16, 29, 54, 82–84,
135, 168
Kelly, Gene, 235, 381
Kempton, Murray, 288, 377
Kennedy, Caroline, 115, 346
Kennedy, Edward M., xv, 3, 57, 59, 85–
86, 155, 158, 187, 188, 243, 377,
402, 411, 416
Kennedy, Ethyl, 63
Kennedy, Eunice, 3, 11, 377, 389
Kennedy, Jacqueline Bouvier, xv, 1, 87–
89, 114–115, 130, 142, 145, 155–
156, 164, 167, 183, 188–189, 210,
245, 246, 261, 282, 287, 289, 322–
323, 325, 326, 345–346, 348, 360,
393–394, 402, 406, 413
Kennedy, Jean, 3, 88, 389
Kennedy, Joan, 155, 158

Kennedy, John Fitzgerald, xv
and African American cabinet posts,
304
and African Americans, 292–298
assassination, 414
campaign schedule, 382–383
and Catholicism, 245–258. See also
Roman Catholicism
childhood and education, 2–5
congressional campaign, 7–9
and crowds, 287–290
Cuba, 367–373
delegate hunt, 157–166
and Democratic National
Convention, 170–175, 207–211
and election of 1960, 391–410
extramarital affairs, 145–156,
325–326
and Barry Goldwater, 218, 224
health issues, 13, 80, 87, 166–169,
384–385
and Hubert Humphrey, 59–60,
131–132
Illinois, 381–382
and Max Jacobson, 322–324
and Martin Luther King Jr., 294–299
and LBJ, 27, 31, 32, 166–169,
175–176, 194–206, 259–267
and liberals, 138–144
mob connection rumors, 126–127
and Wayne Morse, 54–55
New England, 388–389
and Nixon, 38, 39, 45–46, 49–50,
230, 268
Ohio, 350–351
in polls, 47, 222, 352–353
and Adam Clayton Powell Jr., 294
presidency, 411–414
presidential aspirations, 15–18
primary campaign, 77–94, 99,
109–130
and Jackie Robinson, 300–301
and Eleanor Roosevelt, 140–141,
282–284
and Franklin Roosevelt Jr., 121–122
Senate campaigns, 10–12, 16
and Frank Sinatra, 234–241
and Adlai Stevenson, 132–134, 136,
140, 142–144
and Stuart Symington, 56, 190–193
television debates, 307–313, 315,

Kennedy, John Fitzgerald *(continued)*
320–348, 353–367, 374–380
and Harry S. Truman, 284–287
vice-presidential bid, 29
and voting corruption, 124–130
in World War II, 5–7, 122–123
Kennedy, Joseph Patrick, Jr., 3–7, 79, 395
Kennedy, Joseph Patrick, Sr., xv, 2–6,
16, 29, 38, 61, 62, 64, 78, 81, 86,
90, 92, 115, 121–122, 125–130,
145–148, 157–158, 160, 170, 175,
182, 195, 205–206, 208, 210, 233,
235, 237, 241, 243, 245, 246, 250,
252–253, 255, 260, 271, 284, 295,
347, 378, 383, 399, 403, 406, 412
Kennedy, Kathleen, 3, 11, 146, 246
Kennedy, Patricia, 3, 11. *See also*
Lawford, Patricia Kennedy
Kennedy, Patrick J., 3
Kennedy, Robert Francis, xvi, 3, 12, 61–
65, 79, 85, 89–92, 119, 120, 123–
125, 129–131, 135, 142, 143, 145,
151, 153, 154, 162–163, 168, 172,
173, 175, 176, 180, 181, 184, 186,
187, 191, 197–200, 203–206, 235,
260, 262, 266–267, 273, 284, 293,
294, 296–297, 300, 302, 305, 321–
323, 326, 330, 344, 347, 355, 377,
384, 398–399, 402, 406, 411, 414,
415
Kennedy, Rose Fitzgerald, xvi, 2–3, 91,
188, 345, 359, 396, 406
Kennedy, Rosemary, 3
Keogh, Gene, 81
Kerner, Otto, 381
Kerr, Robert, 204
Keyes, Helen, 90
Khrushchev, Nikita, 48, 98, 101, 134–
138, 160, 231, 271, 278–279, 281,
296, 311, 336, 355–356, 367–368,
378
Kilgallen, Dorothy, 241
King, Coretta Scott, 295
King, Martin Luther, Jr., xvi, 294–299,
304, 396, 407, 415
King, Martin Luther, Sr., 298, 299
Kinsella, James H., 388
Kirk, Phyllis, 233
Kissinger, Henry, 68, 108, 322
Kleberg, "Miz Mamie," 20
Kleberg, Richard M., 20

Klein, Herbert G., xvi, 95, 164, 214,
216, 222, 273, 280, 281, 305, 309–
310, 313–314, 328–329, 349, 371,
397, 409
Klemmer, Harvey, 5
Knebel, Fletcher, 229, 247
Knight, William H. Y., 97
Knowland, William, 43, 78
Kopczynska, Barbara Maria, 148
Kopechne, Mary Jo, 416
Krock, Arthur, 5, 13, 62, 146, 246
Kuchel, Tom, 225
Ku Klux Klan, 112, 120, 285
Kuralt, Charles, 281

labor, 25, 55, 62, 190, 203, 318, 391. *See
also specific headings, e.g.,* United
Auto Workers (UAW)
LaFollette, Robert, 105
LaGuardia, Fiorello, 58
Landis, Jim, 140
Laos, 364
Lash, Joseph P., 250
Lasker, Mary, 31, 250, 283
Laski, Harold, 4
Latham, John Hugh, 112–113
Lausche, Frank, 351
Lawford, May, 243–244
Lawford, Patricia Kennedy, xvi, 183,
243, 389
Lawford, Peter, 126–127, 152, 183, 233–
236, 241, 272, 315
Lawrence, Bill, 281
Lawrence, David, 78, 160, 173, 259
Lawrence, David L., 111–112
Lawrence, Stan, 355
Lawrence, W. H., 92
Leaming, Barbara, 322–323
Lebanon, 341
Lehman, Herbert H., 70–71, 159
Leigh, Janet, 235
Lerner, Alan Jay, 322
Lewis, Jerry, 271
Lewis, Joe E., 235
Lewis, John L., 124
Liberal Party, 203, 302
Lilienthal, David, 172
Lincoln, Abraham, 230, 231, 291, 336,
378
Lincoln, Evelyn, 126, 147, 148, 152,
162, 188–189, 191, 199, 200

Lincoln-Douglas debates, 133, 342, 378
Lippmann, Walter, 37, 377–379
Lisagor, Peter, 60, 87, 121–122, 141, 260
Little, Herbert C., 117
Lodge, Emily Sears, 394
Lodge, George, 304
Lodge, Henry Cabot, Jr., xvi, 10–12, 27, 61, 102, 121, 219, 226–228, 230, 231, 254, 266, 276–280, 303, 308, 317, 327, 345, 349, 352–353, 394, 400, 406, 407
Lodge, Henry Cabot, Sr., 10
Loeb, William, 81
Long, Earl, 326
Long, Russell, 27
Longworth, Alice Roosevelt, 350
Loveless, Herschel C., 172, 188, 190, 402
Lowell, C. Stanley, 248
Loy, Myrna, 235, 381
Luce, Clare Boothe, 54–55, 212
Luce, Henry, 5, 55, 68, 210
Lynch, Pat, 158–159
Lynn, Diana, 233

Maas, Peter, 253
MacArthur, Douglas, 24
MacDonald, David, 182
MacLaine, Shirley, 233, 235
Macmillan, Harold, 101, 350
Magnusen, Warren, 160
Mailer, Norman, 17, 185, 231
Malcolm, Durie, 146
Maloof, Frank, 392
Maltz, Albert, 238–241
Manion, Clarence, 219
Mann, Jerry, 254
Mansfield, Mike, 192, 203
Marcantonio, Vito, 38
Marín, Luis Muñoz, 248
Markman, Sherwin J., 171–172
Marsh, Charles, 150
Martin, Dean, 154, 234, 235, 237, 242
Martin, Hershey, 207
Martin, John, 225, 398
Martin, Louis, 294, 298
Martin, Mayris, 207
Martin, Tony, 235
Marvin, Langdon P., Jr., 325–326
Marx, Karl, 271
Maryland, 77
Massachusetts, 7–12, 98, 175–176

Mathis, Johnny, 271, 322
Matsu Island, 341, 357, 361, 363–364, 370, 372, 374
Matthews, Chris, 268
Maverick, Maury, 20–21
Mayer, Louis B., 233, 243
Mayer, Margaret, 401
Mazo, Earl, 243, 304, 346
McAdam, Charles, 232
McCambridge, Mercedes, 178, 235
McCarthy, Eugene J., xvii, 54, 63, 122, 164, 173–174, 185–186, 415
McCarthy, Joseph R., 11–12, 27, 43, 56, 61, 90, 92, 93, 120, 134, 269, 284–285
McClellan, John, 61–62
McCormack, John W., 195–196, 209
McCoy, Ronald, 146
McCraken, Tracy, 188
McCrary, "Tex," 102
McDonnell, Robert J., 403
McDonough, Bob, 128
McElroy, Neil, 102
McFarland, Ernest, 27, 162
McGee, Frank, 354
McGee, Gale, 54
McGill, Ralph, 100
McGovern, George, 416
McGrory, Mary, 412
McInerney, James M., 149–150, 383
McKinley, William, 18, 358
McLain, George H., 158
McLaughlin, Eddie, 394
McLendon, Sarah, 105
McMahon, Patrick, 6
McManus, Robert L., 213–214, 224
McNey, Roger, 396
Meany, George, 203
Menshikov, Mikhail A., 136, 279
Merman, Ethel, 97
Meyer, Agnes, 136, 179
Meyer, Eugene, 136
Meyner, Robert B., 53, 55, 80–81, 84, 111, 164, 187, 188
Mikelson, Sig, 400
Miller, Ann, 233
Minnesota, 173–174, 251
Minow, Newton, 143
Mitchell, J. Oscar, 295–297
Mitchell, James P., 102, 226
Mitchell, Stephen A., 42
Monroe, Marilyn, 114

Monroney, A. S., 173, 174, 186, 190
Montgomery, Robert, 315
Mooney, Booth, 195
Moore, Tom, 374
Moran, Edward E., 242–243
Moretti, Vincent, 382
Morgan, Edward P., 355, 357
Morin, Relman, 289
Morrow, E. Frederic, 302–303, 305
Morse, Wayne, xvii, 54–55, 77, 79, 80,
    82, 99, 113, 132, 157, 251
Mortimer, Lee, 244
Morton, Thruston, xvii, 99, 102, 106,
    209, 223, 226, 228, 286, 362, 384
Mostel, Zero, 322
Moyers, Bill, xvii, 204, 264, 387
Moynihan, Daniel Patrick, 392
Munnell, Bill, 174
Murphy, George, 182
Murrow, Edward R., 327, 342
Muskie, Ed, 54

Nash, Phileo, 139
National Association for the
    Advancement of Colored People
    (NAACP), 50, 292, 299
National Press Club, 31, 250, 358
NBC, 163–164, 307–308, 335, 340, 355,
    361, 400–401
Nebraska, 77, 98, 111
Nelson, Gaylord, 91
Nestigen, Ivan, 79
Neville, Mike, 7–9
Nevins, Allen, 139
New Deal, 21, 36, 56, 58, 123, 197, 336
New Hampshire, 77, 81–82, 95, 96, 392
New Jersey, 81, 111
New York, 68, 81
Nidecker, John, 222
Niven, Paul, 355
Nixon, Arthur, 35
Nixon, Clara, 221
Nixon, Edward, 221, 400
Nixon, F. Donald, xvii, 221, 383, 400, 409
Nixon, Francis Anthony, 34, 45
Nixon, Gay Lynne, 221
Nixon, Hannah Milhous, 34, 221, 345,
    397, 400
Nixon, Harold, 35
Nixon, Julie, 221, 345, 389, 400, 408
Nixon, Patricia Ryan, xvii, 35–36, 42,
    51, 221, 345, 377, 386, 389, 396,
    400, 405–406
Nixon, Richard Milhous, xvii, 38
    and African Americans, 299–306
    Alaska, 382
    anti-communism, 37–39
    California congressional race (1946),
        36–37
    California governor's race, 412
    and Whitaker Chambers, 97–98
    "Checkers" speech, 41–43, 315
    childhood and education, 34–35
    Cuba, 367–380
    in Dallas on November 22, 1963, 413
    debating skills, 310
    Democratic National Convention,
        184
    and Dwight Eisenhower, 44, 96–97
    and election of 1960, 268–276,
        279–281, 389, 391–393,
        396–398, 400, 405, 407–410
    and Arnold Hutschnecker, 383
    and JFK, 45–46, 49–50, 209
    and Joseph Patrick Kennedy Sr., 90
    and LBJ, 31, 262, 264
    and media, 280–281
    political style, 50–52
    in polls, 48–49, 84, 157, 342–353
    presidency, 416–417
    presidential aspirations, 47–49
    primary campaign, 82, 95–96, 98–99
    religious issue, 253–255
    and Republican National
        Convention, 213–232
    and Nelson Rockefeller, 71–74, 76,
        95–96, 99–108
    and Eleanor Roosevelt, 251
    Senate race (1950), 38
    Alan Shivers's endorsement, 263
    Soviet Union, 278–279
    telethon, 389–390
    television debates, 307–367, 374–380
    Texas, 201
    Harry S. Truman on, 285–287
    vice-presidential campaign, 39–43
    in World War II, 36
Nixon, Trisha, 42, 345, 389, 400
Norton, Howard, 125
Novak, Robert, 25, 158, 191, 219, 261,
    269, 270
Novins, Stuart, 335

O'Brien, Lawrence F., xviii, 64, 79, 109–112, 116, 123, 125, 129–130, 142, 180, 186, 198, 257, 290, 330, 333–334, 388, 411, 413, 416
O'Connell, Daniel P., 81, 159
O'Daniel, W. Lee, 22, 23, 25
Odets, Clifford, 178
O'Donnell, Kenneth P., xviii, 27, 64, 79, 80, 109–110, 129, 159, 183, 202, 203, 211, 285, 330, 347, 383, 402, 411, 413
Ohio, 77, 78, 95, 98, 113
O'Meara, Robert W., 195
O'Neal, Patrick, 323
O'Neill, Thomas P., xviii, 8, 15, 16, 38, 63, 64, 124–125, 159–160, 195, 196, 273, 293, 394
Oregon, 77, 95
Oswald, Lee Harvey, 414
Otten, Al, 128, 191

Parker, Robert, 294
Parker, Tom, 241, 244
Parmet, Herbert, 150, 205, 373
Parr, George B., 26
Patman, Wright, 195
Patterson, John M., 186, 292, 300, 301, 347
Peale, Norman Vincent, xviii, 251–254, 407
Pearson, Drew, 15, 148, 383
Pegler, Westbrook, 284
Pell, Claiborne, 115
Pell, Nuala, 115
Pennsylvania, 77, 78, 98, 111–112, 172–173
Percy, Charles, 68, 102, 213, 216
Perot, Ross, 406
Persico, Joseph, 105
Peters, Charles, 114, 120
Peterson, P. Kenneth, 402
Pierpont, Robert, 51
Pietrowski, Jarri, 396–397
Pius IX, Pope, 257
Poland, 88
Poling, Clark V., 250
Poling, Daniel A., 249–251, 253
Potter, Philip, 281, 315
Poulson, Norris, 183
poverty, 29, 118–119, 414
Powell, Adam Clayton, Jr., 294, 303

Powell, Dick, 272
Powell, Wesley, 82
Powers, David F., xviii, 15, 80, 200, 246, 283, 328, 406, 411
Powers, Francis Gary, 101, 279
Prendergast, Mike, 81
Presley, Elvis, 241, 244
Price, Vincent, 178, 233, 235
Proxmire, William, 54
Purdom, Edmund, 148

Quemoy Island, 341, 357, 361, 363–364, 369, 370, 372, 374

Rains, Claude, 366
Raskob, John Jacob, 233
Rat Pack, 126–127, 234–235, 238, 241, 243
Rauh, Joseph L., 15–16, 60, 93, 124, 131, 139, 190–191, 207–209
Rayburn, Sam, xviii, 14, 20–21, 23, 26, 32, 160–161, 166, 170–171, 185, 195–202, 204, 205, 234, 255, 257, 263, 267
Reagan, Nancy, 271
Reagan, Ronald Wilson, 48, 271–272
Rebozo, Bebe, 400
Reece, B. Carroll, 228
Reedy, George, xviii, 28, 32, 260–262
Reinsch, J. Leonard, 313, 314, 332, 344
religion, 89–90, 93, 115–116, 247, 265. See also anti-Catholicism; Catholicism
Remick, Lee, 178
Republican Party, 75, 95, 98, 99, 101, 107, 221–232
Reston, James, 137, 139, 216, 280, 342, 359, 364, 377–379
Reuther, Walter P., xviii, 14, 15, 110, 124, 141, 192, 203, 208–209, 270, 287
Rhee, Syngman, 102
Ribbentrop, Joachim von, 146
Ribicoff, Abe, 180, 285, 388
Rickey, Branch, 299, 305
Ridder, Walter, 147
Roberts, Chuck, 289
Robinson, Bill, 209
Robinson, Claude, 364
Robinson, Edward G., 235
Robinson, Jack Roosevelt, xviii, 299–302
Robinson, Rachel, 305

Rockefeller, John Davison, 66–67
Rockefeller, John Davison, Jr., 67
Rockefeller, Mary Todhunter Clark, 71, 103
Rockefeller, Nelson Aldrich, xix, 47, 53, 66–77, 95–96, 98, 99, 101, 102, 108, 213–218, 223, 224, 227, 230, 269, 270, 317, 364, 407, 416
Rogers, Bill, 327
Rogers, Edward A., 42, 275, 315–316, 327–332, 340, 351–352
Rogers, William P., 102, 305
Rojas, Norma Rae, 390
Rojas, Victor, 390
Roman Catholicism, 89–90, 93, 109–111, 115–116, 128, 159, 174, 245–258. *See also* Anti-Catholicism
Rooney, Art, 159–160
Roosevelt, Eleanor, xix, 17–18, 31, 59, 121, 140–141, 159, 165, 174–175, 179, 186, 207, 250–252, 282–284, 353, 378, 395
Roosevelt, Franklin Delano, 21, 70–71, 121, 165, 209, 233, 270, 336, 339, 358, 414
Roosevelt, Franklin Delano, Jr., xix, 116, 121–124, 140–141
Roosevelt, James, 233
Roosevelt, John, 225, 282, 384
Roosevelt, Sara Delano, 282
Roosevelt, Theodore, 18, 50
Roper poll, 391
Rose, Alex, 110, 203
Roselli, Johnny, 153
Rosellini, Albert D., 188
Rostenkowski, Dan, 172–173
Rostow, Walt Whitman, 31
Rovere, Richard, 167
Rowan, Carl, 280, 305
Rowan, Roy, 390
Rowe, James H., Jr., 21
Rowe, James M., xix, 31, 57, 60, 110, 127, 204–206, 261–263
Rusher, William A., 45
Rusk, Dean, 68
Russell, Bob, 297
Russell, Richard B., 26–27, 30, 260, 264, 293, 294, 387
Russo, Joseph, 8, 9
Ryan, Bill, 344
Ryan, Cornelius, 398

Ryan, Robert, 233
Ryan, Thelma Catherine "Pat." *See* Nixon, Patricia Ryan

Safire, William, 273, 280
Sahl, Mort, 56, 171, 235
St. John, Adela Rogers, 327
Salinger, Herbert, 181
Salinger, Pierre, xix, 87, 128, 148, 168, 181, 254, 255, 261, 262, 290, 308, 314, 328, 330, 333, 367, 372, 385, 388, 406, 409, 411
Saltonstall, Leverett, 402
Sanicola, Hank, 237
Sargent, Maria, 325
Sargent, Robert, 325
Sargent, Timothy, 325
Sarnoff, Robert W., 68, 307–309, 312, 366
Schary, Dore, 14, 178, 186
Schiff, Dorothy, 72
Schlesinger, Arthur M., Jr., xix, 31, 64, 108, 122, 135, 139, 140, 142, 143, 177, 178, 184, 190, 198, 200, 218, 266, 284, 298, 322, 345, 360, 369, 372–373, 379, 393, 411
Schlesinger, Marian, 345
Schultz, Charles M., 89
Scott, Hugh, 102, 226, 416
Screen Actors Guild, 271
Scribner, Fred, Jr., 313
Seaton, Fred A., 102, 225, 226, 386
Seib, Charles, 150
Selzer, Louis, 354
Sevano, Nick, 241
Sevareid, Eric, 134
Shaw, Mark, 323–324
Shepley, Jim, 275, 327
Sheppard, Morris, 22
Sherwood, Jack, 397
Shivers, Alan, 263
Shriver, Eunice Kennedy, xix, 11, 85, 93, 155, 245, 292, 325, 401, 402
Shriver, R. Sargent, xx, 11, 86, 91, 92, 113, 186, 187, 195, 200, 262, 295–296, 325, 411, 416
Sidey, Hugh, 176, 182, 261
Sinatra, Frank, xx, 126, 127, 151–154, 182, 234–244, 383
Singiser, Frank, 374
Singleton, John, 266–267

Sirhan, Sirhan B., 415
Slovik, Eddie, 238
Smathers, George, 9, 46, 158, 186, 188, 196, 265
Smith, Alfred E., 233, 252, 290
Smith, Gerald L. K., 270
Smith, Howard K., 328, 330, 335–336, 342
Smith, Jean Kennedy, 155, 175
Smith, Merriman, 96
Smith, Stephen E., xx, 88–89, 125, 130
Snyder, Howard, 386
Social Security, 282, 336
Sorensen, Theodore C., xx, 12, 14, 15, 63, 118, 142, 164, 177, 231, 249, 254–256, 321, 322, 330, 336, 360, 365, 368, 372, 379, 409, 411
Soviet Union, 134–135, 364
Spalding, Charles F., 9–10, 13, 85, 125, 146, 208, 245–246, 322
Spellman, Francis Cardinal, 245, 253
Stanton, Frank, 266, 328, 330–332, 344
Starr, Blaze, 326
Stassen, Harold, 44–45, 48, 72, 102, 106, 308, 378
Stennis, John, 30, 204
Sterling, Jan, 178, 233, 235
Stevenson, Adlai E., xx, 29, 42, 45, 50–51, 53, 55, 57, 63, 73, 78, 80, 81, 83–85, 90, 91, 99, 110, 111, 113, 120, 128, 131–144, 157, 158, 160, 161, 165, 171, 173, 174, 177–180, 183, 185–186, 188, 191, 196, 206, 207, 209, 211, 224, 233, 239, 252, 253, 279, 283, 284, 291, 295, 378, 395, 411, 413
Stevenson, Coke, 26
Stewart, George D., 297
Stewart, James, 271
Stratton, William G., 221, 226–228, 402
Sullivan, Barry, 235
Summerfield, Arthur, 225
Suzuki, Pat, 324
Swanson, Gloria, 145, 182
Swisher, Mrs. Fred, 393
Sylvester, Arthur, 281
Symington, James, 57, 112, 187, 192
Symington, Stuart, Jr., 57, 112, 192
Symington, William Stuart, III, xx, 54–57, 73, 77, 78, 80–84, 99, 105, 110, 111, 120, 124, 128, 132, 138, 149, 157, 158, 160, 161, 164–166, 171–173, 188, 190–193, 197, 199, 203, 206, 211, 294

Taft, Robert, 11, 27, 38, 39, 98, 227, 228, 269, 270, 278
Taiwan, 357
Talbott, Harold, 61–62
Talmadge, Herman, 264
Tandy, Jessica, 233
Tawes, J. Millard, 157
Taylor, Elizabeth, 130
Taylor, T. J., 267
Teamsters union, 15, 55, 62, 123, 391
television, 118–119, 241, 261, 313, 389–390
Texas, 21, 22, 25–26, 168, 175–176, 197
Thalberg, Irving, 233
Thomas, Evan, 70
Thompson, Claude, 361
Thornberry, Homer, 200, 260
Thurmond, Strom, 30
Tibet, 364
Tierney, Gene, 146
Tierney, Mary, 346
Tillotson, Neil, 392
Tkach, Walter, 317
Todd, Malcolm C., 318, 351–352
Toledano, Ralph de, 46, 98, 273, 302, 312, 332, 350, 407
Tower, John, 402
Trautman, Robert B., 181–182
Travell, Janet T., xx, 13, 169, 384
Trujillo, Rafael, 121
Truman, Harry S., xxi, 16, 27, 51, 56, 57, 67, 78, 112, 129, 133–135, 149, 160, 161, 163–166, 173, 206, 207, 211, 230, 234, 284–287, 294, 337, 339, 358, 361–362, 395
Trumbo, Dalton, 239
Tuck, Dick, 347
Tugwell, Rexford, 71
Turnure, Pamela, 149
Tydings, Joseph, 64

U-2 spy plane incident, 138, 227, 279, 361
Udall, Stewart, 162
unions. See Labor
United Auto Workers (UAW), 14–16, 124, 190, 208–209, 287

United Brotherhood of Carpenters and Joiners, 320–321, 326
United Mine Workers (UMW), 124, 129
United Nations, 227, 350, 367–368, 375, 411

Valenti, Jack, 171, 176, 260, 387
Vandiver, Ernest, 293, 297, 408
Van Meter, Jonathan, 152
Vanocur, Sander, 281, 335, 340–341, 345
Vatican, 247
Vidal, Gore, 141, 167, 282, 402
Viereck, Peter, 249
Vietnam War, 411, 414–416
Vinson, Carl, 21, 22, 26
Von Fremd, Charles, 362
Voorhis, Jerry, 36–37, 310, 350

Wagner, Robert, 289
Wallace, George, 292
Wallace, Henry, 71
Wallace, Mike, 186
Walters, Ed, 153
Walton, Bill, 86, 282
Ward, Daniel, 381
Warner, Harry, 233, 276
Warner, Jack, 233
Warner Bros., 271
Warren, Charles, 335
Warren, Earl, 39, 78, 98, 292, 412
Washburn, A. H., 254
Washington, George, 165
Washington State, 160
Wayne, John, 239, 241–243, 271, 272
Weaver, Sylvester, 71
Welch, Robert, 270
Welk, Lawrence, 390

Wells, Jim, 26
West Virginia, 77, 109–132
Wham, James B., 229
White, Theodore H., 46, 74, 170, 173, 178, 216–217, 274, 276, 277, 288, 364, 377, 388
White, William S., 56
Whitman, Ann, 46, 101, 105–106
Wicker, Tom, 342, 349, 373
Wiener, Mickey, 148
Wilkins, J. Ernest, 304
Wilkins, Roy, 292
Williams, G. Mennen, 53, 55, 80, 192, 207–209
Williams, Nancy, 207
Williams, Tennessee, 130
Willis, Monk, 267
Willkie, Wendell, Jr., 225–226
Wills, Gary, 411
Wilson, Bill, 314–315, 330, 333, 338, 340
Wilson, Woodrow, 50, 165, 339, 358
Winchell, Walter, 145, 146, 183, 234, 240, 243, 383
Winters, Shelley, 235
Wisconsin, 77, 79–80, 82–94, 98
Wofford, Harris, xxi, 292, 295, 296, 298, 411
Woods, Rose Mary, 275, 281, 345
Wyckoff, Gene, 277–278, 385
Wyoming, 187–188

Yarnell, Harry E., 364
Young, Linn B., 392

Zablocki, Clement J., 88
Zukor, Adolph, 233

About the Author

DAVID PIETRUSZA is the author of *1920: The Year of the Six Presidents* (named one of the Best Books of 2007 by Kirkus Reviews); *Rothstein: The Life, Times and Murder of the Criminal Genius Who Fixed the 1919 World Series* (a nominee for an Edgar Award); *Teddy Ballgame: My Life in Pictures* (with Ted Williams); and *Judge and Jury: The Life and Times of Judge Kenesaw Mountain Landis* (winner of the Casey Award). His body of historical work has garnered media attention from such outlets as the *New York Times, Newsweek, US News & World Reports,* the *Washington Post,* N   P   R   , C-SPAN, the Fox News Channel, Bloomberg Radio, the *New York Daily News, New York Post, Jerusalem Post, New York Law Journal, New York Sun, Denver Post, Weekly Standard, Washington Times, Seattle Times, Raleigh News & Observer,* and *Tucson Sun.* He lives in upstate New York.